THE CANADIAN ROCKIES
TRAIL GUIDE

Seventh Edition—Revised

"We were not pioneers ourselves, but we journeyed over old trails that were new to us, and with hearts open. Who shall distinguish?"
J. Monroe Thorington,
The Glittering Mountains of Canada

THE CANADIAN ROCKIES
TRAIL GUIDE

Seventh Edition—Revised

A hiker's guide to Banff, Jasper,
Yoho, Kootenay, Waterton Lakes,
Mount Robson, Mount Assiniboine,
Peter Lougheed, Elk Lakes and
Akamina-Kishinena Parks

Brian Patton & Bart Robinson

Summerthought Ltd.

Banff, Alberta

Copyright © Brian Patton and Bart Robinson
1971, 1978, 1986, 1990, 1992, 1994, 2000

Seventh edition 2000
Third printing with revisions 2005
ISBN 0-919934-90-0

Published by:
Summerthought Ltd.
P.O. Box 1420
Banff, Alberta T1L 1B3
Canada

Design: Brian Patton
Cover design: Johanna Van Waarden, Rhonda Allen
Text composition: Linda Petras
Map composition: Dave Good, homefyre
All photographs by the authors unless otherwise credited.
Printed and bound in Canada by Friesens Printers.

Cover: Opabin Plateau, Yoho National Park. Photo by Brian Patton.

Contents

YOHO NATIONAL PARK   266

KOOTENAY NATIONAL PARK   318

TRAIL GUIDE MAP KEY

🏕 Backcountry Campground

🏕 Roadside Campground

🏠 Lodge

P Parking

? Information

V Viewpoint

, Trail

⋯ Route

(35) Trail Reference Number

Scale Conversion:

DISTANCE

```
0  1  2  3  4  5  6  7  8  9  10  11  12  13  14  15  16  17  18  19  20 KILOMETRES
0     1     2     3     4     5     6     7     8     9     10    11    12  MILES
```

1 kilometre = 0.62 mile   1 metre = 3.28 feet
1 mile   = 1.61 kilometres   1 foot = .3048 metre

ELEVATION

```
3800 ┐
     ├ 12000
3600 ┤
     ├ 11500
3400 ┤
     ├ 11000
3200 ┤
     ├ 10500
3000 ┤
     ├ 10000
     ├ 9500
2800 ┤
     ├ 9000
2600 ┤
     ├ 8500
2400 ┤
     ├ 8000
2200 ┤
     ├ 7500
2000 ┤
     ├ 7000
     ├ 6500
1800 ┤
     ├ 6000
1600 ┤
     ├ 5500
     ├ 5000
1400 ┤
     ├ 4500
1200 ┤
     ├ 4000
     ├ 3500
1000 ┤
     ├ 3000
800 ┘
METRES   FEET
```

Preface

It was a different world when we set out to write *The Canadian Rockies Trail Guide* in 1970. Annual park visitation was half of what it is today. Mountain bikes, Gore-Tex, GPS location devices, pepper spray, and water purification pumps were unknown. Backcountry campgrounds were mere suggestions (there were no backcountry permits or fees), and generally we camped where we pleased. And there were no trail guidebooks.

The hikers you encountered on backcountry trails in the 1970s were usually from Canada (primarily Alberta) and the United States. Today you meet people from all over the world on day trips, and when you travel more than 10 kms into the backcountry, you are far more likely to encounter someone from Europe than Canada.

We have worked to keep the trail guide up-to-date over the past 30 years with numerous revisions and two major expansions. However, this 7th edition marks the first time we have reconsidered the entire book in light of evolving patterns of backcountry use and policies, as well as our own repeated experience on many of the trails. Every trail has been totally reconsidered and rewritten.

In recent years there has been an increased interest in shorter, less ambitious trips. While we always provided brief descriptions for nature trails and half-day hikes, in this edition we highlight the most rewarding of these shorter trips with more complete descriptions and photographs.

While there are more day hikers today than ever before, the popularity of backpacking has never fully recovered to its peak in the late 1970s. Nonetheless, we felt that many of these wilderness treks deserved more complete descriptions and better photographic coverage than we'd given them in the past.

Unlike other parks, Banff National Park has never actively encouraged multi-day backpacking within its borders, even though there are a number of exceptional possibilities. Rather than simply describe individual trail segments in Banff's backcountry, as in past editions, we have highlighted some of the best routes and circuits that can be completed by linking these trails together.

Full trail coverage for Mount Assiniboine and Mount Robson Provincial Parks was added to the third edition of the book in 1985, but we have always wanted to include all the provincial parks bordering the national parks. With the inclusion of Peter Lougheed, Elk Lakes and Akamina-Kishinena in this edition, we have neared that goal.

All of this has resulted in the most ambitious revision ever for *The Canadian Rockies Trail Guide*. The book has been expanded by nearly 90 pages. Forty new maps have been created to replace the 25 maps in the previous edition. Photographic coverage has been increased to 156 images from 107, including many new photographs taken by the authors or provided by contributors.

We have also attempted to make the guide more "user friendly," particularly for visitors who are not familiar with the area. To that end we have numbered the 233 core trails described in the book and placed these numbers on the maps. By locating maps at or near the beginning of each regional section, hikers should find it a lot easier to find specific hikes and backpacking routes.

In preparing this major revision, we have measured all new trails and remeasured many old ones to improve the accuracy of trail distance outlines and descriptions. We have been aided in this task by some of the new technology that has emerged in the past 30 years, such as digital odometres, altimetres and, occasionally, GPS units.

All of this effort has been expended to achieve the original goal we set for ourselves three decades ago—to produce a guide to all major trails in the mountain parks and expose park visitors and residents to the enormous variety of hiking opportunities and possibilities that are available in the Canadian Rockies. We still believe, as we did then, that hiking beyond the highways is the best way to appreciate the landscape and natural environment protected within this exceptional collection of national and provincial parks.

Acknowledgements

Attempting to convey accurate information for so many trails spread over such a wide geographical area is a task that is well beyond the ability of two authors. In producing this expanded edition of *The Canadian Rockies Trail Guide,* we have relied on the experience and knowledge of parks' personnel and fellow hikers, both friends and strangers, to supplement our own fieldwork.

We are especially indebted to the following park information staff and personnel, wardens and rangers who managed to take time from their ever-increasing work commitments to read through our manuscript or provide information for this edition: Andre Dmytriev, Gordon Burles, Don Mickle, Ian Syme, Ian Pengelly (Banff); Jenny Klafki, Kathryn Cameron, Ed Robert, John Niddrie (Lake Louise–Yoho); Larry Halverson, Gerry Israelson (Kootenay); Wendy Niven, Brian and Vicki Wallace (Jasper); Greg Redies, Wayne Van Velzen (Robson); Alex Green (Elk Lakes, Akamina-Kishinena, Mount Assiniboine); James Cieslak (Peter Lougheed).

We owe a special debt of gratitude to Don Beers, dean of Canadian Rockies' hikers, who graciously provided information and distances from his extensive fieldwork to supplement and update our descriptions. And the detailed field notes donated by veteran backpacker Mike McReynolds over the years continue to serve us well in this edition.

We are continually receiving feedback from hikers who have used our guide. We offer thanks to the many who have contributed information for this edition, with special appreciation for the contributions of Phil Lister, a faithful correspondent for many years, and Christopher Chapman and Johanne Béland.

This is the first edition where the authors have supplemented their own photography with that of outside contributors. We thank Don Beers, Mike McReynolds, Rick McDonald, Jim Thorsell and Cyndi Smith for providing these images.

The process of getting all of these revisions to the printed page was far more arduous than all the fieldwork. (Don't let them fool you, going desktop is not easier than cut-and-paste!) Without Linda Petras (desktop composition) and Dave Good (maps), this book never would have seen the light of day.

Johanna Van Waarden took on the responsibility of designing a new cover when it was the furthest thing from the authors' minds. Mike Kerr was always available as unpaid-consultant-at-large whenever we needed feedback. And Rhonda Allen went along for the complete two-year journey that this revision required, hiking in front of a man with a trail wheel, providing continual feedback and suggestions, proofreading, and initiating the cover design. Our thanks to you all.

And these are only the people involved with this edition. Looking back over 30 years, we remember dozens of individuals who provided support for this book. We remember them all fondly, though we only have room to mention four special people who made the original book and subsequent editions possible: Jim Thorsell, Louise Mayer, Peter Steiner and the late Jon Whyte.

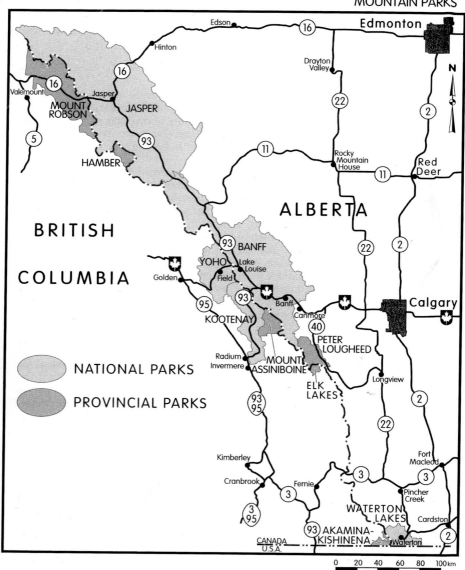

N

NATIONAL PARKS

PROVINCIAL PARKS

0   20   40   60   80   100 km

Introduction

In 1885, the Dominion of Canada created a 26 square km reserve near Banff, Northwest Territories, to protect the Sulphur Mountain Cave and Basin hot springs from commercialization. Two years later the reserve was expanded to 673 square km and named Rocky Mountains National Park—the second national park in North America following the creation of Yellowstone in 1872. The park, which was subsequently expanded and renamed Banff, was the beginning of a system of national and provincial parks that now protects more than 30,000 square km of mountain landscape in the southern half of the Canadian Rockies.

The creation of recreational trails for hikers and horseback riders was a priority for Banff's first park superintendent. The Canadian Pacific Railway also played an early and important role in the development of hiking trails, particularly in Banff and Yoho National Parks. Other trails were blazed by outfitters, and still others were built by park wardens and trail crews for patrol and fire protection purposes. When provincial parks were established throughout the 20th century, the construction and maintenance of hiking trails was always the first priority.

Today a trail system totalling more than 3,000 km threads its way through the valleys and passes and by the lakes and glaciers of one of the world's most spectacular mountain ranges.

This book is an invitation to park visitors to experience one of North America's finest hiking areas. It has been designed as a comprehensive guide to the trails of Banff, Jasper, Yoho, Kootenay and Waterton Lakes National Parks, and Mount Robson, Mount Assiniboine, Peter Lougheed, Elk Lakes and Akamina-Kishinena Provincial Parks. We have endeavoured to describe every trail that could conceivably be of interest to hikers, ranging from short walks of an hour or less to two week-long wilderness treks.

Hiking has always been considered an appropriate and effective means of appreciating the natural heritage preserved within our parks. We have always believed that anyone who walks these mountain trails will come away with a better appreciation of the importance of parks and why we should continue to preserve them "unimpaired for the enjoyment of future generations."

Weather, climate and hiking season

Despite the northerly latitude of the range, the Canadian Rockies experience climate and weather patterns that compare closely with mountain ranges hundreds of kilometres to the south. Because the elevation of the Rocky Mountains increases progressively from north to south, mean temperature and annual precipitation in Banff and Jasper are very similar to those of West Yellowstone, Montana, and Leadville, Colorado.

The chart on page 2 displays average daily maximum and minimum temperatures, precipitation averages, and the average number of days per month with measurable precipitation recorded at various recording stations in the mountain parks during the hiking season.

The mountain snowpack usually begins to disappear as temperatures moderate in April. By mid-May hiking is possible on a handful of low elevation trails in the major valleys and on south-facing slopes in the Front Ranges. By the first of July most trails below treeline are open, but many are still wet and muddy. Above treeline trails open gradually from early July to early August, depending on slope exposure, snowpack and weather.

Climate averages

	May	June	July	Aug.	Sept.	Oct.
Banff 1397 m / 4,580 ft						
Maximum temp °C	14.2°	18.7°	22.1°	21.6°	16.1°	10.1°
Minimum temp °C	1.5°	5.4°	7.4°	6.8°	2.7°	-1.1°
Precipitation /mm	57.5	60.0	51.2	51.3	43.8	30.3
Days with precip.	13	14	13	13	12	9
Lake Louise 1524 m / 5,000 ft						
Maximum temp °C	12.8°	17.2°	20.4°	20.1°	14.3°	7.9°
Minimum temp °C	-1.7°	2.1°	3.6°	3.1°	-0.8°	-5.3°
Precipitation /mm	43.0	54.6	61.3	54.0	45.3	38.9
Days with precip.	11	15	14	14	11	9
Jasper 1061 m / 3,480 ft						
Maximum temp °C	15.4°	19.5°	22.2°	21.7°	16.2°	10.3°
Minimum temp °C	2.0°	6.0°	8.0°	7.4°	3.2°	-0.9°
Precipitation /mm	28.6	49.9	56.2	50.6	37.0	30.9
Days with precip.	10	13	13	13	11	10
Icefield Centre 1981 m / 6,500 ft						
Maximum temp °C	9.1°	13.0°	15.1°	15.2°	9.8°	4.6°
Minimum temp °C	-2.7°	1.1°	3.0°	3.0°	-1.1°	-5.7°
Precipitation /mm	40.1	70.4	66.1	55.0	63.5	70.7
Days with precip.	10	15	15	14	14	12
Waterton 1281 m / 4,200 ft						
Maximum temp °C	14.5°	19.0°	23.1°	22.2°	17.6°	11.9°
Minimum temp °C	2.6°	5.9°	7.8°	6.9°	3.9°	0.9°
Precipitation /mm	85.3	90.0	52.4	61.4	70.7	56.0
Days with precip.	11	12	9	9	10	9

Mid-July to mid-August is considered peak hiking season. During this period we experience the warmest weeks of summer, there is usually less rainfall than June and early July, most trails are snowfree, and high country wildflowers are in bloom. Of course, this is also when trails are most heavily used and insect pests are flourishing.

High country temperatures start to fall in mid-August, and early September usually sees the first snow falling in the high country. However, these early storms are usually short-lived, and the latter weeks of September and early October are often blessed by beautiful Indian Summer weather. (Most locals consider this the best hiking season.) However, weather changes quickly and dramatically at this time of year, so autumn backpackers should be prepared for surprise storms and the possibility of some cold, snowy hiking.

Topographic maps

While the maps in this book provide total or partial coverage for most of the trails described, they are only designed to give you a general idea of trail location, course and surrounding topography. These maps are adequate for short walks and most day hikes, but it's always nice to have a more detailed map along to identify natural features and to help dispel confusion. A good topographic map also provides an overview of trail systems, which allows you to customize your itinerary. And these maps are a necessity when heading into more remote regions.

Canadian Government Maps. All areas in the mountain parks are covered by National Topographic System (NTS) 1:50,000 scale maps (approximately 2 cm = 1 km). These sheets provide a high degree of detail and are extremely useful for both navigation and the identification of natural features.

The most recent of these government produced maps (released in 1996) are much improved over earlier editions. They now show most of the trails, though not always with a high degree of accuracy. Elevations are metric on most sheets, usually with a contour interval of 40 m (occasionally 20 m at lower elevations). Most of the NTS maps covering the mountain parks are available in TYVEK™, which is water and tear resistant.

Unfortunately, it takes over 40 of these maps to cover the mountain parks, and even shorter trails can sometimes run over two or three sheets. The government does produce single sheet 1:50,000 scale maps covering Waterton Lakes National Park and Yoho National Park. These maps provide the same topographical detail available on NTS maps and better detail for trails and campgrounds; anyone hiking in Waterton or Yoho would be better off with these maps than the standard NTS 1:50,000 sheets.

The federal government also publishes 1:200,000 topographic maps for the four contiguous mountain parks, which should be adequate for those who can get by with less detail. There are two maps in this series—one sheet covering Banff, Kootenay, Yoho National Parks and another for Jasper National Park. These maps show most of the trails, display topography with a 200 m contour interval, and provide reasonably good coverage of adjacent provincial park and forest areas.

Gem Trek Maps. A number of privately produced topographic maps covering sections of the mountain parks have been published in recent years, but the most comprehensive and up-to-date series is produced by Gem Trek Publishing of Cochrane, Alberta. (Parks Canada has selected these maps for trailhead kiosks.) While the Gem Trek series does not currently provide coverage for Waterton Lakes National Park or the more remote areas of Banff and Jasper National Parks, it does cover most of the popular hiking areas in our book.

The scale of these recreational topo maps varies from 1:35,000 to 1:100,000, and contour intervals range from 25 m to 50 m. These maps are generally more accurate than government maps for locations of trails, backcountry campsites, lodges, huts and other cultural features, they provide point-to-point distances, and they are up-dated and corrected with each printing. The current series is produced on waterproof, tear-resistant paper and displays topography with both contour lines and 3-D relief imagery.

Sources for government and Gem Trek maps are listed in *Sources-Maps and books*.

Bears, bugs and other hazards

Compared to many of the world's wild regions, this is a relatively benign area when it comes to dangerous beasts and other natural hazards. Yet there are a few creatures, both great and extremely small, worthy of discussion.

Bears. Does anyone go hiking in the Rockies without imagining a run-in with a bear? If so, we have yet to meet them. In fact, we are encountering an increasing number of folks who won't hike here at all because of their irrational fear of bears. It seems that bear paranoia is at an all-time high.

Yes, the mountain parks are home to a modest population of black and grizzly bears. And, yes, most every year at least one person comes to grief in a bear encounter somewhere in the Rockies, usually with grizzlies and more rarely with black bears. But when you consider the tens of thousands of people who hike the trails each summer, these incidents are extremely rare. (Driving to the trailhead is far more hazardous.)

Yet it is always a good idea to be prepared for an unexpected bear encounter and, even more importantly, to follow a few basic rules to avoid the encounter in the first place:

- Check trail reports and posted warnings at park visitor centres for a listing of trails where bears have been sighted. If a bear is active on the trail you were planning to hike, you may want to go elsewhere. If you do hike the trail, be extra vigilant and make noise where visibility is poor.

- Watch for bear sign, such as fresh droppings, diggings or tracks. If you come across an animal carcass, leave the area immediately.

- Always stay alert. You don't want to come upon a bear suddenly at close range. You should continually scan your surroundings, and peruse the slopes and valley ahead before descending from a pass or ridge.

- Make noise in areas where bears have been seen or any prime bear habitat where visibility is limited. The occasional loud shout or whistle will alert bears to your presence. Talking loudly or singing can also be effective. Most bear bells are not loud enough to warn bears at a safe distance—unless it's a Swiss cow bell!

- Groups of three or more hikers have far less chance of being charged or attacked. Nearly all serious attacks in the Rockies have occurred when a single individual encountered a bear at close range; attacks on two hikers are less common and usually involve mother grizzlies with cubs.

- Never leave garbage or food around your camp. Seal all food and garbage and hang it from the bear poles provided at most campsites. Where bear poles are not provided, pack along 20 m of nylon cord and hang food from a strong tree well away from your campsite. (Food should be suspended at least 4 m above the ground and 1 m from the tree trunk.)

- Avoid cooking in your tent (food smells linger). Cook away from your campsite, wash cooking utensils immediately and dispose of dishwater well away from your campsite.

- If you do see a bear, stop immediately and retreat slowly from the area.

It is beyond the scope of this book to get into all the variables that must be considered during an encounter with an aggressive bear or a bear attack. The national and provincial parks publish excellent brochures covering all aspects of avoidance, etiquette and what to do in an attack situation. Pick up one of these free pamphlets at a park visitor centre and read it thoroughly.

Other mammals. Far more people are charged and injured by elk each year than by bears. Aggressive elk are much more common in park townsites and on nearby trails than elsewhere in the parks since these "urbanized" animals have lost their fear of humans. Never approach elk at any time of year, but give females with young a very wide berth during the calving season (late May and early June), and the same with bulls during the mating season (late August to early October).

There are no other mammals that pose a significant threat to backcountry travellers. While animals such as cougar and wolverine have fierce reputations, they are usually very shy around humans and very rarely seen.

Of course, there are records of nearly every species having charged or chomped tourists at one time or another. (These include an irate mother spruce grouse that permanently scarred one of the authors.) The golden rule around all wildlife: always give animals room and never harass or feed them.

Insect pests. Mosquitoes are generally less of a problem in the southern Canadian Rockies than they are in the mountains and wetlands farther north. However, some summers are worse than others and certain areas are renowned for their bloodsucking hordes. Hikers do not need headnets or bug jackets, but repellent should be carried throughout the hiking season until early September.

Horseflies are another common nuisance during midsummer. Insect repellent has no effect on these large biting flies. While a heavy shirt and pants will protect you, horseflies are most active on warm, sunny days, when you are inclined to wear only shorts and a t-shirt. At least they're slow to bite, so you can club 90 percent of them before they take their pound of flesh.

Wood ticks. Second to bears, visitors worry about wood ticks—small, flat-bodied arachnids (related to spiders) that require a meal of mammal blood as part of their reproductive cycle. Ticks are abundant in dry grassy areas of the Rockies in the spring (early May through late June), and at elevations ranging from the lowest valley bottoms to 2130 m (7,000 ft). They cling to low-lying shrubs and grasses, waiting for a potential meal to pass by. Once on a mammal, they can spend three hours or more exploring before burying their heads in its flesh, so hikers have a good chance of discovering and removing the beasts before the feast begins.

Although ticks in the Canadian Rockies have been free of Rocky Mountain Spotted Fever and Lyme disease (so far), they can cause a potentially fatal tick paralysis if they burrow at the base of the skull. The best precaution is to wear long pants tucked into socks or gaiters and to avoid lounging about on grassy slopes. Always check your clothing and body carefully following a spring hike (ticks are partial to heads, armpits and crotches).

When a tick is discovered, a simple touch or gentle tug often dislodges it. If it has already burrowed into the skin, do not try to burn it with a match or coat it with some noxious liquid, like gasoline or nail polish. Instead, grasp its head as close to the skin as possible with tweezers and pull slowly. If you can't remove it, or mouthparts remain in the skin, see a doctor.

Giardia. Another addition to the list of hiker miseries is the protozoan *Giardia lamblia,* a waterborne parasite that can cause severe and prolonged gastrointestinal distress. *Giardia* is carried by many species of animals, but the human infective strain is most frequently found in beaver, domestic dogs and, of course, humans. The parasite finds its way into mountain streams and rivers through the feces of these animals, but beaver are the animals best equipped to perpetuate the parasite in wilderness water systems.

Many local hikers are willing to take their chances in the upper portions of watersheds, particularly above treeline or where they feel secure there is no beaver activity or human sources of infestation. But the only way to be totally safe is to boil your drinking water for at least 3 minutes or use a portable water filter.

Stream crossings. The only other hazard worth noting is unbridged stream crossings, which occur on some remote backcountry trails. While the creeks and rivers of the Canadian Rockies are relatively tame compared to the thundering torrents of the Interior and Coast Ranges, they can still be dangerous at certain times of the year.

As a general rule, rivers run highest in June and July. In the Front Ranges streams are usually highest during rainy periods when runoff sluices down into drainages from bare limestone peaks; stream levels in these eastern ranges usually drop dramatically once the rain stops. In the heavily glaciated Main Ranges, the highest runoff usually occurs during warm spells in July and August when glaciers are in full melt; these rivers are easier to cross in the morning after the flow has subsided with the cool of the night.

Any trail involving a major ford should only be attempted by river-wise backpackers. If the current is strong and water threatens to rise above your crotch, you should abandon the crossing altogether. Either look for a better place to cross, wait for water levels to subside or, if that is unlikely, retreat the way you came and live to ford another day.

Backcountry information

We recommend that all hikers stop by a park visitor centre before embarking on any serious hiking in the mountain parks. These centres provide current weather forecasts, reports on trail conditions and closures, and warnings concerning bear activity. They also dispense free park visitor guides, day hiking and backcountry camping brochures, and a variety of pamphlets relating to bear safety, mountain biking, fishing, etc.

While you can obtain information from park visitor centres in person, you can also obtain specific information by mail, phone, fax or e-mail. Parks websites are also becoming an increasingly effective way of obtaining information in advance of your trip. (See *Sources-Park information.*)

Visitor centres are located in all five national parks (see park introductions for locations). Of the provincial parks included in this guidebook, only Peter Lougheed in Alberta and Mount Robson in British Columbia have visitor centres. (The Mount Robson Visitor Centre only operates May to September 30.)

Park rangers are stationed in core areas of British Columbia's Mount Assiniboine, Elk Lakes and Akamina-Kishinena Provincial Parks during the summer. Information can also be obtained through the Kootenay District Office in Wasa, B.C. and on the B.C. government website (See *Sources-Park information.*)

Camping

Due to the growth in backcountry use, most parks require that backcountry visitors stay in designated campgrounds. With only a few exceptions, these campgrounds have quotas on the number of people who can overnight there. All parks on a camping permit system require that backpackers indicate the campgrounds where they will be overnighting and the dates of occupation.

Banff and Yoho are the only national parks where random camping is permitted, but only in specific areas where visitation is low. In selecting a campsite in a random camping zone, you must be 5 km from a trailhead, at least 50 m off the trail, and 70 m from the nearest stream or lake.

Campfires are only permitted at certain campgrounds, and only where metal fireboxes and firewood are provided.

Park visitor centres are your primary outlet for camping permits and information about backcountry campgrounds.

National parks. Parks Canada requires anyone overnighting in the backcountry to purchase a Wilderness Pass. These passes were instituted in 1994 to recover some of the costs of maintaining trails, backcountry facilities and warden patrols.

In obtaining a Wilderness Pass, you must indicate which campgrounds you will be staying at on specific nights during your trip.

As of summer 2000, a Wilderness Pass costs $6 per person/per night; the maximum charge for any single trip is $30 per person. An annual pass costs $42 per person and allows for an unlimited number of nights in the backcountry.

National Park campsites can be reserved up to 3 months in advance of your trip, and a $10 fee is charged for this service. Subsequent modifications of a reservation costs an additional $10.

In Banff National Park a $5 per night fee is charged to stay at the Bryant Creek or Egypt Lake Shelters.

Provincial parks. Most provincial parks have instituted camping fees on a per person/per night basis. Camping permits are required for all backcountry campgrounds in Alberta's Peter Lougheed Park and for sites on the Berg Lake trail in B.C.'s Mount Robson Park. These permits are obtained in person at park visitor centres or in advance through special reservation phone lines.

Camping fees are collected on site at Lake Magog Campground and the Naiset Cabins in Mount Assiniboine Park, at Akamina Creek Campground in Akamina-Kishinena Park, and at Lower Elk Lake and Petain Creek Campgrounds in Elk Lakes Park. (See park chapter introductions for procedures and current fees.)

Voluntary safety registration

Anyone concerned about their safety on their backcountry trip can voluntarily register at Parks Canada visitor centres or warden offices. If you do not return on the date and time indicated, a search will be initiated.

While this registration is designed for individuals or groups involved in off-trail risk activities, solo backpackers journeying into remote areas can also register. While there is no charge for this service, you must report back in at a park visitor centre or warden office immediately upon your return.

Regardless of whether you use this service or not, it is always best to leave a detailed copy of your itinerary with a responsible person.

Using this book

This guidebook is designed to be comprehensive, describing all trails of any significance within the mountain parks of the Canadian Rockies.

Trails are presented by regions within each park, usually oriented to the roads that provide access to the trailheads or to a central area serving as a core for several hikes. These regional sections include a map showing trails and their reference numbers.

Walks, short hikes and a few secondary routes are presented without trail summaries or distance outlines. Half-day trips, day trips and backpacks are presented with a trail summary, distance outline, descriptive text and, in many cases, a photo.

Trail summary. Beneath each trail heading is its distance in both kilometres (km) and miles (mi). Whenever a hike runs out and back on the same trail, distances are one-way. But for loop trips (circuits) and long distance trails ending at a different trailhead than point of origin, total distance is provided.

The general round trip duration of the hike is indicated as a half-day trip (usually up to 3 hours), day trip, or backpack.

Hiking time is the one-way number of hours or days it will take to reach your objective. (In the case of loop trips and long distance trails to another trailhead, total time is presented.) The times are estimated for a strong, steady pace with few breaks along the way. Strong hikers may "beat" listed times, while slower walkers and those who make frequent stops will take longer.

Elevation gain is the total ascent, in metres (m) and feet (ft), over the one-way course of the trail; if there is a significant loss of elevation, it is also noted. On longer trails with lots of ups-and-downs, maximum and minimum elevations are provided instead of elevation gain.

Maximum elevation is the highest point reached on the hike, often at the trail's destination.

Map references are provided for NTS 1:50,000 topo maps and national park topo maps for Waterton and Yoho National Parks. Gem Trek map references are also included when a trail is covered by a map in that series with a scale of 1:70,000 or better.

Distance outlines. Trail distance outlines give you a brief, point-to-point summary of the route in kilometres. All basic directions are presented in the outline. These reference points along the route, including both natural and man-made features, can be used to calculate how far you've hiked and how far you have to go. The outlines also contain important access directions for reaching the trailhead.

The authors have pushed trail wheels with odometres over most of these trails to obtain accurate distances. We have also used some distances from parks trail inventories and trustworthy outside contributors. When we have been forced to estimate distances, this is indicated by a footnote.

Trail distances in this guide seldom agree exactly with those on parks trail signs or other resources (like Gem Trek maps), but these discrepancies are usually minor.

Text description. The text is written to describe the trail's scenic rewards, to provide a running description of the trail, and to interpret natural features and historical points-of-interest along the way. Where applicable, optional routes and extensions are provided at the end of the main trail description.

Photos. With the exception of a few shots provided by friends and outside contributors, all photographs were taken by the authors. They have been selected to illustrate the scenic highlights of the hike.

Maps. Maps in this book provide only a general overview of trails and their location. Specific trails can be found by referring to trail numbers on the maps. (Some trails described in this book are not covered by these maps, and a notation to this effect is made at the bottom of the trail outline.)

On most of these maps land above 2300 m is shaded to give a general impression of topography, particularly major mountains and passes. Where regional elevations are lower, shading shows land above 2000 m. (See key at bottom of maps.)

Some final words

- Plan ahead. Choose trips you are in shape to handle. Allow time for unexpected weather and other events that might alter your schedule.

- Stay on the trail, even if it means muddy boots. Leaving the trail creates parallel tracks and widens existing trails. Shortcutting switchbacks causes erosion.

- Leave rocks, flowers, antlers and other natural objects undisturbed. Never pick wildflowers or other plants.

- Never feed, disturb or harass wildlife. It is illegal, harmful to the animal's health, and alters their natural behavior.

- Pack out all garbage. Carry plastic bags and, whenever possible, pack out litter that other, less considerate hikers have left behind. Do not throw garbage into privies.

- Where facilities are not provided, your toilet duties should be carried out well away from trails, campsites, and at least 50 m from lakes and streams. Dig a small pit (15 cm maximum) and restore the ground as closely as possible to its original state. Pack out toilet paper or burn it if fire danger is low.

- All dogs on parks trails must be kept on a leash. If your dog is not well trained or is difficult to control, be considerate of other hikers and leave it at home. Also, be aware that dogs have incited grizzly attacks.

- Even where campfires are permitted in the backcountry, it is preferable to use lightweight gas stoves for cooking. If you do have a campfire at a site where fires are permitted, it should only be set in metal fireboxes utilizing firewood provided at the site or, where permitted, dead wood lying on the ground. Keep all fires small and make sure they are totally extinguished before you depart.

- Keep food, soap, toothpaste, and detergent out of lakes and streams. Dispose of wash water on well-drained soil well away from the nearest surface water. Even biodegradable soaps are pollutants.

- Be considerate of fellow hikers when sharing a campsite or backcountry shelter. Be considerate as well of horseback riders: move well off the trail (preferably downslope), remain still and be prepared to comply with the guide's requests.

- Cyclists should avoid surprising hikers, horses and wildlife. Be particularly careful on blind corners and rises. Be prepared to dismount if you encounter hikers or horseback parties on narrow, rough trails.

Banff National Park

With an area of 6,641 sq km, Banff is second in size to Jasper among the mountain parks. It is bordered by Yoho and Kootenay National Parks to the west, Jasper National Park to the north, and Mount Assiniboine, Height of the Rockies, and Peter Lougheed Provincial Parks on the south.

Banff contains more than 1500 km of trail, more than any other mountain park. Since many of these trails are near the park's world renowned tourist centres, they are also among the most heavily travelled in the Rockies.

The park is noted for its day hiking, and the trails leading into the spectacular peaks and glaciers of the Bow Range surrounding Lake Louise and nearby Moraine Lake are by far the most popular. The town of Banff and nearby Lake Minnewanka is another hiking centre, with trips ranging from short walks near the town to day trips into the hanging valleys and passes of the Front Ranges.

Many excellent hikes originate in the Bow Valley between Banff and Lake Louise, utilizing trailheads on the Trans-Canada Highway, the Bow Valley Parkway and Highway 93. The Sunshine Meadows area is off the beaten track 20 km southwest of Banff, but an exceptional alpine region that is near-and-dear to day hikers. And Canada's highest road, the Icefields Parkway, provides access to a variety of trails leading through some of the park's most dramatic scenery north of Lake Louise.

The park's two most popular backpacking destinations are the Skoki Valley east of Lake Louise and Egypt Lakes west of Banff. You can backpack to these areas in a single day, then spend a day or two exploring from your campsite.

Serious backpackers focus on the longer Sawback and Bow Valley Highline Trails running along the ranges to the east and west of the Bow Valley, or the Upper Spray and Bryant Creek Valleys at the south end of the park. More adventurous souls roam the park's eastern wilderness for the ultimate in challenge and solitude.

Information and services. Park Visitor Centres are located in downtown Banff (224 Banff Avenue) and beside the Samson Mall in Lake Louise village. They provide a full range of information on the park and are an important stop for anyone planning to hike in the park. They also dispense Wilderness Passes, which are required for overnighting in the backcountry.

Roadside campgrounds are scattered throughout the park. Full service sites are available at Tunnel Mountain and Lake Louise, and showers are provided at Tunnel Mountain, Two Jack Lakeside, Johnston Canyon and Lake Louise.

Gas, groceries, restaurants and accommodation are available in the town of Banff, Lake Louise village and, in a limited fashion, at Johnston Canyon, Castle Junction and Saskatchewan River Crossing. Banff offers all the services of a major resort town, including outdoor recreation specialty shops. Canmore, just outside the park's east gate, is slightly larger and provides similar services.

Access: Banff is 130 km west of Calgary via the Trans-Canada Highway—the main east-west artery through Banff Park. The Icefields Parkway runs north 230 km from Lake Louise to Jasper. Highway 93 runs southwest from the Trans-Canada Highway to Kootenay National Park and southeastern B.C. The David Thompson Highway (Hwy 11) connects Red Deer, Alberta, with the Icefields Parkway at Saskatchewan River Crossing in the northern section of the park.

The nearest commercially serviced airport is Calgary International, and numerous airporter buses and shuttles run between the airport and Banff every day. Greyhound buses also run east and west through the park on the Trans-Canada Highway several times a day, with scheduled stops at Banff, Lake Louise and Canmore.

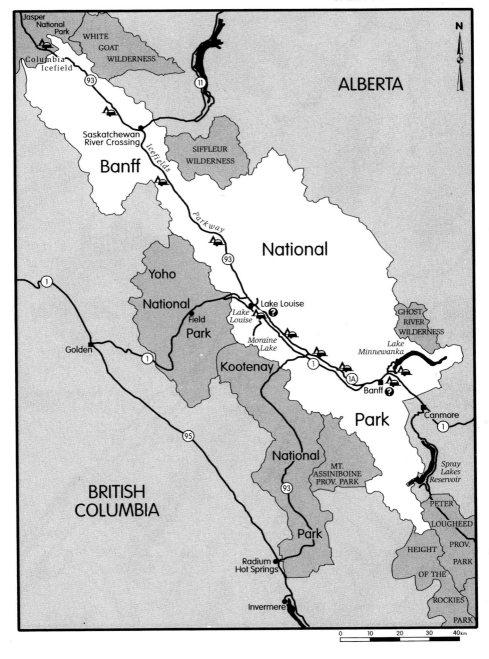

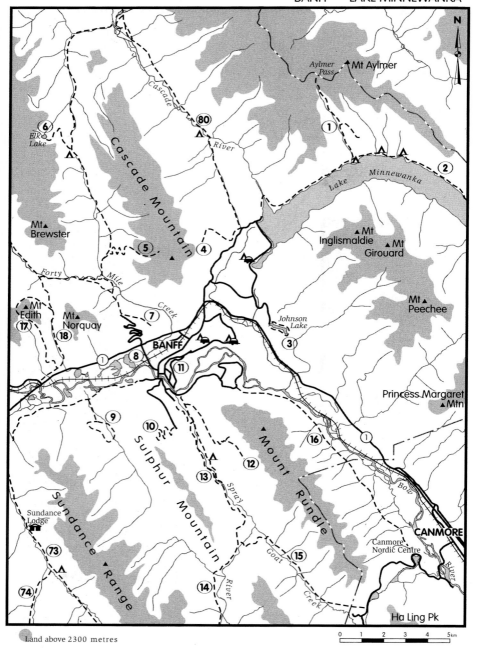

Land above 2300 metres

0 1 2 3 4 5km

Mountain sheep at Aylmer Lookout

1 Aylmer Lookout and Pass

Minnewanka Parking Area to Aylmer Lookout—11.8 km (7.3 mi)
Minnewanka Parking Area to Aylmer Pass—13.5 km (8.4 mi)

Day trip or backpack

Allow 4 to 5 hours to lookout

Elevation gain: 575 m (1,890 ft)

Maximum elevation: 2055 m (6,750 ft)

Maps: Canmore 82 O/3
     Lake Minnewanka 82 0/6

Access: From the Trans-Canada Highway at the Banff East Exit interchange, follow the Lake Minnewanka Road 5.5 km (3.5 mi) to the parking area at the lake. Walk to the access gate leading to the tour boat concession.

0.0—Access gate (1480 m).

    —Paved road through picnic area.

0.6—Trail sign at end of picnic area.

1.4—Stewart Canyon bridge.

1.6—Junction. Stewart Canyon left. Aylmer Pass ahead.

3.0—Lake viewpoint (1525 m).

    —Trail descends to lakeshore.

7.8—Aylmer Pass Junction (1490 m). Campground (Lm8) right 100 m. *Lake Minnewanka* trail ahead. Aylmer Lookout and Pass left.

    —Steep uphill.

10.1—Junction: Aylmer Lookout right (1.7 km). Aylmer Pass ahead.

    —Steep, steady climb toward pass.

13.5—Aylmer Pass (2285 m).

When Sir George Simpson, Governor of the Hudson's Bay Company, made the first recorded visit to Lake Minnewanka in August, 1841, he marvelled at the beauty of the lake and exclaimed that "the surrounding mountains were very grand, of every varied form...their craggy summits resembling battlements among which dizzy heights the goat and sheep delight to bound." Hikers who journey to Aylmer Lookout and Pass can retrace part of Sir George's route and visit those dizzy heights where many sheep (and wood ticks) delight to bound.

Strong hikers can reach Aylmer Lookout and return in a day, though many bound for both the lookout site and the pass prefer to camp at Aylmer Pass Junction Campground (Lm8) and day hike from there.

Though the first 7.8 km of the journey follows Lake Minnewanka's north shore over gentle, undemanding trail, you should be ready for the ordeal beyond. Forking uphill, away from the tranquillity of the lake, the trail to the pass and the old Aylmer fire lookout site is strenuous indeed.

Stock up on water at the stream near the Lake Minnewanka trail junction in preparation for gaining nearly 600 vertical metres over the next 2 km. The next water is at least an hour beyond this stream, and the south-facing slope, which is usually snowfree in early June, is also one of the hot spots in the Rockies on sunny days.

Most day hikers opt for the shorter trip to the fire lookout site, which is situated on the end of an open ridge below the summit of Mount Aylmer. As you labour up the steep draw leading toward Aylmer Pass, watch for the lookout trail branching right 2.3 km beyond the Minnewanka junction.

The trail to the lookout continues steeply upwards, angling southeast towards

Aylmer Pass

the crest of the ridge. Along the way it passes through a prescribed burn that was set on this slope in 1990.

From this 2040 m-viewpoint nearly all of Lake Minnewanka can be seen. The water, over 500 m below, is of the deepest blue, and boats look like tiny water insects skimming to-and-fro.

Across the lake stand the twin summits of Mount Inglismaldie (2965 m) and Mount Girouard (2995 m), displaying massive cliffs of Mississippian and Devonian age limestone. Looming above the ridge, less than 3 km to the north, is Mount Aylmer (3162 m)—the highest peak in the Banff-Lake Minnewanka area. The Mount Rundle massif and the Bow Valley near Banff can be seen to the southwest.

Though the lookout tower and cabin are long gone, the open ridge is often visited by herds of mountain sheep who, perhaps, have some ancestral memory of the days when fire lookouts used to live here and put out salt blocks. Another form of wildlife found here in abundance in the spring is the wood tick (check your body and clothes carefully upon returning from this trip).

Aylmer Pass. From the fire lookout trail junction at km 10.1, the left fork continues its steady climb to the park boundary and the open alpine meadows of Aylmer Pass. The pass lies well above the last forest cover and is free of snow considerably later than the lookout ridge.

From the crest of the pass, views open into the highly folded and faulted mountains of the Palliser Range. Directly above the pass to the east is the summit of Mount Aylmer, a gruelling but straight-forward scramble for hikers with good boots. Like the Aylmer Lookout area, the slopes above the pass are prime mountain sheep habitat.

Backpackers with a few days to spare can continue over the pass to explore the Ghost River Wilderness Area. Good trail continues down the north side of the pass to Spectral Creek, but the descent to Ghost River and beyond is strictly for explorers who are willing to make numerous fords of Spectral Creek and the Ghost, or else bushwhack along their banks.

2 Lake Minnewanka

Minnewanka Parking Area to Devil's Gap—29.5 km (18.3 mi)

Backpack

Allow 8 to 10 hours to Ghost Lakes

Elevation gain: 45 m (150 ft)

Maximum elevation: 1525 m (5,000 ft)

Maps: Lake Minnewanka 82 0/6

Access: From the Trans-Canada Highway at the Banff East Exit interchange, follow the Lake Minnewanka Road 5.5 km (3.5 mi) to the parking area at the lake. Walk to the access gate leading to the tour boat concession and picnic area.

0.0—Access gate (1480 m).

—Paved road through picnic area.

0.6—Trail sign at east end of picnic area.

1.4—Stewart Canyon bridge.

1.6—Junction. Stewart Canyon left. Lake Minnewanka straight ahead.

3.0—Lake Minnewanka viewpoint (1525 m).

—Trail descends and rolls along just above lakeshore.

7.8—Aylmer Pass Junction and Campground (Lm8). *Aylmer Pass* left.

9.3—Aylmer Canyon Campground (Lm9).

11.1—Mt Inglismaldie Campground (Lm11).

18.8—Mt Costigan Campground (Lm20).

20.6—Narrows Campground (Lm22).

22.8—East end of Lake Minnewanka.

23.8—First Ghost Lake.

25.6—Shallow ford between 1st and 2nd Ghost Lake.

25.7—Junction. Minnewanka south shore, Ghost Lake Campground (Lm31) right. Devil's Gap left.

29.5—Devils Gap (1510 m). Park boundary.

The trail along the north shore of Banff's largest lake is attractive to early and late season backpackers since its low elevation and location in the Front Ranges usually provides dry, snow-free hiking from May until mid-autumn. Mountain bikes are also permitted along the entire length of the trail.

From the boat dock and picnic area at the west end of Lake Minnewanka, the trail crosses Stewart Canyon, climbs over a low, forested ridge, then rolls along the north shore for the next 20 km with little gain or loss of elevation.

There are many fine campgrounds along the trail, and pleasant gravel beaches scattered with driftwood provide numerous opportunities to stop and relax. The most popular site is Aylmer Pass Junction Campground, where backpackers often camp and then day trip to Aylmer Lookout or Pass. (See *Aylmer Pass.*)

Burned forest along much of the route dates to 1988 and 1990 when Parks Canada set prescribed burns to restore the valley's centuries old fire regime.

Approaching the lake's east end, the landscape becomes noticeably drier and the vegetation more typically montane. Limber pine is scattered among the stands of lodgepole pine, and western wood lilies, brown-eyed Susan, wild blue flax, harebells and other dry-land wildflowers cover the open hillsides and meadows in early summer.

Past the east end of Lake Minnewanka, the trail skirts the shore of the first Ghost Lake to a channel connecting it with the second Ghost Lake. Cross to the opposite side (an easy ford), where you can either wander eastward into the Devil's Gap or turn right and follow a 9 km trail running back to the south shore of Lake Minnewanka. (The extension of the south shore trail over Carrot Creek Summit has been closed as part of a special protection zone around the Fairholme Range.)

Mounts Norquay, Louis and Fifi from Johnson Lake

3 Johnson Lake

Johnson Lake Circuit—3.5 km (2.2 mi)

Due to its low elevation, the trail around Johnson Lake is a fine walk in the early season (the trail is often snowfree by late April). There is a lot of variety in the montane forest of the lower Bow Valley, and this short trail samples much of it, as well as a couple of marshy areas where waterfowl and muskrat are sometimes seen. By hiking around the lake counterclockwise, you will enjoy continuous views of Cascade Mountain on the return along the sparsely forested north shore.

From the picnic area parking lot, walk downhill and across a small earth-fill dam and bridge. Beyond the bridge the trail angles uphill briefly beneath a powerline, then branches left into the forest where it rolls along through a dense forest of pine and spruce above the lake's south shore. In May, the forest floor is alive with the blooms of purple calypso orchids.

At the far end of the lake, the trail crosses an earthen dike, where you get your first good views down the length of this peaceful lake to Cascade Mountain.

Returning along the north shore, there are grassy slopes and an open forest of Douglas fir and low growing junipers. The trail returns to the picnic area after a short detour around a marshy bay created by a small tributary stream.

Access: Follow the Lake Minnewanka Road from the Trans-Canada Highway 1.0 km (0.6 mi) to the Lake Minnewanka-Johnson Lake road split. Turn right and continue 3.7 km (2.3 mi) to where the Johnson Lake road branches right. The Johnson Lake parking lot and picnic area are reached in 2.3 km. *Maps: Canmore 82 O/3; Banff Up-Close (Gem Trek.).*

4 C Level Cirque

Half-day trip

Allow 1.5 hours one way

Elevation gain: 455 m (1,500 ft)

Maximum elevation: 1920 m (6,300 ft)

Maps: Banff 82 O/4
        Banff Up-Close (Gem Trek)

Access: From the Trans-Canada Highway at the Banff East Exit interchange, follow the Lake Minnewanka Road 3.5 km (2 mi) to the Upper Bankhead Picnic Area. The trail begins at the far (west) end of the picnic area parking lot.

0.0—Upper Bankhead Picnic Area (1465 m).

—Steady uphill through forest.

1.1—Old mine buildings.

1.3—Lake Minnewanka viewpoint.

1.8—Mine shaft vent holes.

—Steady climb through forest.

3.9—C Level Cirque (1920 m).

The C Level Cirque trail is one of the more attractive hikes in the Banff-Lake Minnewanka vicinity. In less than 4 km it climbs past artifacts of the long-defunct Bankhead coal operation and a panoramic viewpoint for Lake Minnewanka to a high, rockbound pocket beneath the sheer east face of Cascade Mountain.

The trail begins its ascent through a pleasantly varied forest of lodgepole pine, aspen and spruce, where calypso orchids, blue clematis and many colourful violets bloom in early summer.

Within a half-hour you reach two skeletal buildings, the remnants of an anthracite coal operation that flourished in the area from 1904 to 1922. A town of nearly 1,000 inhabitants called Bankhead was spread across the valley where the trail begins, and these old buildings were a part of the "C Level" operation—the highest coal seams worked within the eastern slope of Cascade Mountain.

From a coal tailing pile 100 m beyond the buildings there is an excellent view out to Lake Minnewanka. As the trail climbs above the buildings and viewpoint, it passes by several fenced holes, which were once air vents for the mine shafts below.

The rest of the hike is a steady climb through forest until, 200 m before reaching the cirque, views open down the Bow Valley to Mount Rundle, the Three Sisters and other mountains beyond the town of Canmore.

Cirque is a French word you will not likely find in your English dictionary—a term used by geologists to describe a semicircular, bowl-shaped depression created by an alpine glacier. C Level Cirque is a miniature example of the phenomenon. Though the glacier that produced the basin has long since disappeared, snow often lingers in the basin into midsummer. As it retreats, a carpet of yellow glacier lilies spreads across the damp, subalpine soil near its entrance. A

Lake Minnewanka from C-Level Cirque trail

tiny pond below the trail provides water throughout the summer, fed by the extensive snowfield on the talus slopes above.

From the rockslide at the edge of the cirque, a faint trail continues up to the right along a sparsely forested ridge to an even higher vantage point above the basin. However, most hikers prefer to "boot ski" the snowfield beneath Cascade's cliffs or simply relax on a convenient rock to watch the antics of the local inhabitants—hoary marmots, pikas and golden-mantled ground squirrels.

Another local resident in spring is the wood tick, so no lounging in the grass! And be sure to check your body and clothes carefully following early season outings.

5 Cascade Amphitheatre

Mount Norquay Lodge to Cascade Amphitheatre—6.6 km (4.1 mi)

Day trip

Allow 2 to 3 hours one way

Elevation loss: 150 m (490 ft)
        gain: 640 m (2,100 ft)

Maximum elevation: 2195 m (7,200 ft)

Maps: Banff 82 O/4
      Banff Up-Close (Gem Trek)

Access: From the Trans-Canada Higway at the Banff West Exit, follow the Mount Norquay Road north from the Trans-Canada Highway 6.0 km (3.5 mi) to the Mount Norquay Ski Area. Park at the trail kiosk sign located at the entrance to the first parking area on the left. Walk 200 m through the parking lot opposite the kiosk (right) leading to the ski area's lodge complex.

0.0—Mount Norquay Lodge (1705 m).

  —Walk through lodge complex and down-valley on ski area service road.

0.8—Junction. Forty Mile Creek trail (*Sawback Trail*) left. Cascade Amphitheatre ahead.

  —Trail descends into forest.

2.9—Junction. Lower Forty Mile Creek trail left. Cascade Amphitheatre right.

3.1—Forty Mile Creek bridge (1555 m).

  —Steady uphill.

4.3—Junction. *Elk Lake* ahead. Cascade Amphitheatre right.

  —Steady switchbacking climb.

6.6—Cascade Amphitheatre.

  —Gradual uphill.

7.7—Amphitheatre headwall (2195 m).

One of the longer and more strenuous day trips near Banff leads up the western flank of Cascade Mountain to a large natural amphitheatre at just over 2100 m. This hanging valley, enclosed by the limestone cliffs of the mountain's summit ridges, features lush subalpine wildflower meadows and immense rockslides inhabited by marmots and pikas.

The hike begins at the ski area's lodge complex at the far end of the main parking area. Continue through the lodge plaza and down-valley on a service road.

The first kilometre can be a bit confusing as you work your way past the base stations of a number of ski lifts, but stay on the valley bottom and watch for trail markers. At 0.8 km, in the middle of the last ski run, the trail branches right from the Forty Mile Creek trail, skirts behind the last lift terminal, and drops into forest on a broad path.

At km 2.9 the trail reaches Forty Mile Creek, turns right and crosses the creek 200 m beyond on a substantial bridge. This is a good place to fill your water bottles as the rest of the hike is steady uphill and bone dry.

Just beyond the bridge, the forest opens to a view of the sheer 390 m face of Mount Louis rising to the west. This vertical wall of Palliser limestone is one of the more popular and demanding climbs in the Rockies. The rugged summit of Mount Edith, another popular climb, can be seen south of Louis and behind Mount Norquay.

The last trail fork on the trip appears 1.2 km beyond the Forty Mile Creek bridge, where the Amphitheatre trail branches uphill to the right from the Elk Summit trail. A relentless series of switchbacks transport you upwards through a dense forest of spruce and lodgepole pine for 2.3 km to the cool, subalpine forest at the mouth of the Amphitheatre.

From the Amphitheatre entrance, the

Cascade Amphitheatre

trail extends for just over a kilometre to a headwall created by the mountain's main summit ridge. The moist meadows along the way are carpeted with wildflowers throughout much of the summer, beginning with white-flowered western anemone and nodding yellow glacier lilies along the edges of receding snow banks in late June.

Two small sink lakes also appear in the meadows with the spring snow melt, but these usually disappear by early July.

Rockslides enclosing the upper end of the cirque are home to hoary marmots and pikas as well as the occasional white-tailed ptarmigan.

While the ascent of Cascade Mountain from the Amphitheatre is not particularly difficult, the route is tricky and can be dangerous at certain times of the year. If you want to go for the summit, pick-up a copy of *A Climber's Guide to Cascade Mountain* at the Park Visitor Centre in Banff.

6 Elk Lake

Mount Norquay Lodge to Elk Lake — 13.5 km (8.4 mi)

Day trip or backpack

Allow 4 to 5 hours one way

Elevation loss: 150 m (490 ft)
gain: 610 m (2,000 ft)

Maximum elevation: 2165 m (7,100 ft)

Maps: Banff 82 O/4
Castle Mountain 82 O/5

Access: Follow the Mount Norquay Road north from the Trans-Canada Highway 6.0 km (3.5 mi) to the Mount Norquay Ski Area. Park at the trail kiosk sign located at the entrance to the first parking area to the left. Walk 200 m through the parking lot opposite the kiosk (right) leading to the ski area's lodge complex.

0.0—Mt Norquay Lodge (1705 m).

—Trail runs downhill across ski runs and past ski lift terminals.

0.8—Junction. Forty Mile Creek trail (*Sawback Trail*) left. Elk Lake ahead.

—Trail descends through forest.

2.9—Junction. Lower Forty Mile Creek trail left. Elk Lake right.

3.1—Forty Mile Creek bridge (1555 m).

—Steady uphill.

4.3—Junction. *Cascade Amphitheatre* right. Elk Lake ahead.

—Gradual uphill through forest.

6.8—Trail enters subalpine meadows.

11.5—Elk Summit and Junction (2055 m). Elk Lake Summit Campground (Ek13). Cascade Valley and Stony Creek ahead (9.5 km). Elk Lake left.

—Steady uphill through forest followed by a short descent to lake.

13.5—Elk Lake (2120 m).

Mount Brewster, visible from Banff between Mount Norquay and Cascade Mountain, is the southern end of a 20 km-long massif that runs due north into the eastern wilderness of Banff Park. Along the eastern face of this unbroken chain of peaks are numerous amphitheatres, some containing small lakes. Almost a third of the way down the range is Elk Lake, the largest and most scenic of these tarns.

Elk Lake can be visited as a long day hike or an easy overnight trip, and the trail continuing north from Elk Summit to the Cascade River is a key route for backpacking trips into Banff's Front Ranges.

The first 4.3 km of trail follows the same route as the Cascade Amphitheatre hike, cutting down through the Mount Norquay ski area, across Forty Mile Creek, and up the western flank of Cascade Mountain. At the Cascade Amphitheatre junction, it stays to the left and continues northward through a forest of lodgepole pine, Engelmann spruce and alpine fir. The path is wide and well-defined throughout.

Two hours or so into the hike, you enter an extensive subalpine meadow, characterized by few trees, low willows, dwarf birch, shrubby cinquefoil, and a profusion of wildflowers. The vale is dominated by Mount Brewster (2859 m) and its subsidiary peaks to the west. (The mountain is named for John Brewster, an early Banff settler who opened the town's first dairy in 1887.)

The trail continues through this open forest for the next 5 km—a beautiful stretch where an occasional over-the-shoulder glance reveals a long, unobstructed view down-valley to Mount Norquay, Sulphur Mountain, and a section of the Sundance Range.

You eventually reach Elk Summit and its campground at km 11.5. Just beyond the campground the trail to Elk Lake

Elk Lake and Mount Brewster

branches left from the main trail over the summit. It gradually ascends a forested ridge for just over 1.0 km before dropping into the amphitheatre containing Elk Lake. The high point on the ridge (2165 m) offers an excellent, unobstructed view back down the length of the approach valley to Mount Norquay and points south.

Elk Lake lies beneath a 500 m wall of limestone, and since it is located very near treeline, its environment differs markedly from the lush meadows along the approach from Forty Mile Creek. The forest above the lake is predominantly alpine larch, and the boggy meadows leading to its shores support a number of wildflowers typical of saturated tundra regions, such as globeflower, marsh marigold, elephant-head and mountain laurel. The nearby rockslides are inhabited by hoary marmots and pikas.

Since there is no campsite at the lake, backpackers should set camp at the Elk Lake Summit Campground. In addition to Elk Lake, the ridges and slopes of Cascade Mountain to the east are gentle and open, offering numerous opportunities for day trips from the campground.

Cascade Valley. Backpackers bound for the remote Front Ranges of the park can follow the trail north from Elk Summit to reach the Cascade Valley near the mouth of Stony Creek—a distance from Elk Summit of 9.5 km.

The trail descends 475 vertical metres through a narrow, forested valley from Elk Summit. It follows a well-defined if sometimes muddy track then, when it reaches the Cascade Valley, crosses bridges over the Cascade River and Stony Creek just before reaching the broad trail running along the Cascade River. (See *Cascade Fire Trail*.)

7 Stoney Squaw

Mt Norquay Ski Area to Stoney Squaw Summit — 2.1 km (1.3 mi)

Like Tunnel Mountain, across the valley, Stoney Squaw is not really a mountain, just an 1884-m promontory extending east from the slopes of Mount Norquay. It is one of the highest, easily reached viewpoints above Banff, and though there are a lot of trees to contend with, a few openings provide "windows" to the town and the Bow Valley far below.

This moderately graded but steady uphill trail is enclosed in a dense forest of lodgepole pine and spruce most of the way, but within 200 m of the top you begin to catch glimpses of the Banff environs. The Bow Valley and the town of Banff lie immediately below, and Tunnel Mountain, Mount Rundle, and Sulphur Mountain are all visible beyond.

At the summit, nearby Cascade Mountain rises to the north and the Bow Valley stretches away to the southeast.

You can make a loop back to the trailhead by descending northwest from the summit on a faint path that soon turns into good trail. This track descends through a dense, mossy forest on the cool north side of Stoney Squaw.

When you reach the top of a ski run, walk down the slope to the ski area access road, turn left and follow the road to the ski lodge complex and the main parking lot.

Access: From the Trans-Canada Highway at the Banff West Exit, follow the Mount Norquay Road north, climbing 6 km (3.5 mi) to the Mount Norquay Ski Area. Turn right at the main parking lot and watch for the trail sign just inside the entrance to the right. *Maps: Banff 82 O/4; Banff Up-Close (Gem Trek).*

8 Fenland Trail

Fenland Circuit — 2.1 km (1.3 mi)

This flat, easy loop trail near downtown Banff leads you through forest at the eastern edge of the Vermilion Lakes marshland. The trail runs beside the peaceful waters of Echo and Forty Mile Creeks and through a spruce forest carpeted with bunchberry and a green cloud of horsetails. With the exception of periods following heavy snowfalls, it can be hiked year round.

Follow the trail from the rear of the Forty Mile Picnic Area, cross a bridge over the creek, and continue 100 m to a trail split. You can either turn left or right at this point, since the trail makes an elongated loop through the forest and returns to this junction in just under 2 km.

The trail can also be used as access to the Vermilion Lakes Road, where you can extend your walk another 4 km along one of the best wetland environments in the Bow Valley (watch for a branch trail part way around the loop that immediately crosses a bridge to the road).

Female elk have used the Fenland area as a calving ground for a number of years, and the trail is usually closed from late May through early June when these protective new mothers can be very aggressive.

Access: Follow the Mount Norquay Road from downtown Banff, cross the railway tracks, and continue 0.3 km to the Forty Mile Picnic Area. Walking from town, access the loop via a short connector trail, which branches left into the forest as soon as you cross the tracks. *Maps: Banff 82 O/4 (trail not shown); Banff Up-Close (Gem Trek).*

9 Sundance Canyon

Cave and Basin to Sundance Canyon — 4.3 km (2.7 mi)

Half-day trip

Allow 1.5 hours

Elevation gain: 145 m (470 ft)

Maximum elevation: 1545 m (5,070 ft)

Maps: Banff 82 O/4
      Banff Up-Close (Gem Trek)

Access: From the intersection at the south end of the Bow River bridge in Banff, follow Cave Avenue 1.2 km to the parking area for the Cave and Basin Centennial Centre. A paved walkway leads to the Cave and Basin complex and continues 200 m beyond to the trailhead kiosk.

0.0—Trail head kiosk (1400 m).

—Gradual descent on broad paved trail through forest.

0.7—Junction. Cave and Basin Marsh Trail right; Sundance Canyon ahead.

—Flat walking beside Bow River.

1.8—Trail leaves open valley and climbs into forest.

2.2—Junction. Sulphur Mtn summit left; Brewster Creek (2.9 km) and Sunshine Road (4.6 km) right; Sundance Canyon ahead.

3.3—Sundance Canyon Picnic Area. End of paved trail and bike access.

—Foot trail climbs into Sundance Canyon, moderate to steep grades.

4.3—Top of Sundance Canyon (1545 m). Trail loops back through forest to picnic area.

Throughout most of its long history, the short 2-km loop trail leading through Sundance Canyon was accessible by road from the town of Banff. In the mid-1980s, the road beyond the Cave and Basin was converted to a paved walking and cycling path, which made the trip longer but more scenically varied. Many people bike to the canyon on the broad, paved trail, but the first half of the trip is an open and pleasant route for walkers as well.

From the Cave and Basin, the trail descends gradually through forest to the Bow River. For the next 1.5 km it follows along the river and its side channels with views of the rugged peaks to the north, including the sharp spire of Mount Edith. The final stretch to the canyon climbs gradually through forest.

Pavement and bike access end at the Sundance Canyon picnic area, where a foot trail climbs into this pleasant little canyon and then loops back through forest to the picnic area.

Marsh Trail. The 1.6-km trail around the north side of the Cave and Basin marsh is an interesting way to return from Sundance Canyon.

Follow the trail that branches right from the Sundance trail at km 0.7 (where the paved trail first meets the river). It runs downstream along the banks of the Bow River to the marsh, skirts the edge of this wetland, then turns right at a junction and crosses an earthen dike to return to the Cave and Basin parking lot.

Healy Creek. This roadbed branches right from the Sundance Canyon trail at 2.2 km and rolls through forest along the south side of the Bow Valley to Brewster Creek junction (2.9 km) and the Sunshine Road (4.6 km). The smooth, broad track is of more interest to mountain bikers than hikers. (See also *Brewster Creek*.)

10 Sulphur Mountain

Upper Hot Springs to Summit Gondola Terminal—5.5 km (3.4 mi)

Half-day trip

Allow 2 hours one way

Elevation gain: 700 m (2,300 ft)

Maximum elevation: 2281 m (7,486 ft)

Maps: Banff 82 O/4
      Banff Up-Close (Gem Trek)

Access: Follow Sulphur Mountain Drive from downtown Banff 3.5 km to its termination at the Sulphur Mountain Gondola Lift and Upper Hot Springs parking lots. Park in the Upper Hot Springs lot and walk back to the trailhead just above the entrance to the parking area.

0.0—Upper Hot Springs (1580 m).

—Follow broad trail uphill through forest. Steady ascent via long switchbacks.

2.4—Trail passes within 200 m of waterfall.

2.7—Old trail shelter site (1890 m).

—Steady switchbacks continue, passing back and forth beneath gondola line.

5.5—Sulphur Mountain Gondola summit tea-house (2281 m).

For those who disdain using a gondola lift to reach a mountaintop, the 5.5-km trail from the Upper Hot Springs is the preferred route to the summit ridge of Sulphur Mountain. While the trail gains 655 m from bottom to top, 28 switchbacks keep the grade reasonable and ease the strain of the ascent. And once you get to the top, you can partake of one of the few perks in the Rockies—a free ride down on the gondola!

The track is wide and uphill grades are moderate as the trail climbs into the forest and begins a somewhat tedious switchbacking ascent of the mountain. Views do open briefly as the trail passes just north of a waterfall on the mountain's east slope.

At km 2.7, a short side trail branches right at a left-turn switchback and leads to the site of an old trail shelter (removed in 2002). Prior to the completion of the gondola lift in 1959, a tractor and wagon transported visitors up the trail to this point. This is the halfway point on the hike.

The grade steepens as the trail nears the summit and begins switchbacking back and forth beneath the gondola line. A few scattered alpine larch in the dense forest herald the summit ridge and the upper gondola terminal with its restaurant and much-needed refreshment kiosk.

From the gondola terminal, you can hike a boardwalk trail north along the summit ridge for 0.4 km to a stone weather observatory on Sanson Peak. (The 2337-m peak is named for park meteorologist Norman Sanson, who hiked up the mountain over 1,000 times from 1903 until his retirement in 1931 to take readings at the observatory.)

Another trail runs south along the ridge for 0.8 km to steeply tilted limestone slabs and views of the Sundance Range and Valley.

Hikers who walked up the trail can ride the lift down for free.

Banff and the Bow Valley from Tunnel Mountain summit

11 Tunnel Mountain

St. Julien Road to Tunnel Mountain summit — 2.3 km (1.4 mi)

The Tunnel Mountain hike is short, easy and readily accessible from downtown Banff. The summit, 300 m above the town, offers excellent views of the Banff environs, the north ridge of Mount Rundle, and a 30 km stretch of the Bow Valley. The trail is one of the oldest in the park and a popular outing for Banff residents.

After climbing 0.4 km from the St. Julien Road trailhead, the trail crosses Tunnel Mountain Road at a viewpoint-parking area (an optional starting point if you want to shorten the hike).

Above the road a series of sweeping switchbacks make a gradual ascent through a thick forest of lodgepole pine and Douglas fir. There are occasional glimpses of the town and valley culminating at a good viewpoint beside a series of limestone slabs near the summit ridge.

On the summit ridge, the trail doubles back and runs above the mountain's sheer east-facing cliffs. Views along the ridge extend over the Banff Springs Golf Course and down-valley to the park's eastern boundary. (Stay well back from these dangerous cliff-edge viewpoints.)

The trail ends on the sparsely forested 1690-m summit, which was once the site of a fire lookout tower. Limestone outcrops just west of the summit provide the best views of Banff, the Vermilion Lakes and Massive Range.

Access: Drive or walk from downtown Banff on Wolf St. to St. Julien Road. Follow St. Julien 0.3 km to the trailhead parking area. To shorten the hike by 0.4 km, drive to the viewpoint-parking area on the Tunnel Mountain Road above the Banff Centre. *Map: Banff 82 O/4 (trail not shown); Banff Up-Close (Gem Trek).*

12 Mount Rundle

Banff Springs Golf Course to Trail's End—4.7 km (2.9 mi)

Half-day or day trip

Allow 1.5 to 2 hours to trail's end

Elevation gain: 470 m (1,550 ft)

Maximum elevation: 1830 m (6,000 ft)

Maps: Banff 82 O/4
       Banff Up-Close (Gem Trek)

Access: From downtown Banff, cross the Bow River bridge and turn left onto Spray Avenue. Continue on Spray Avenue 0.8 km to Bow Falls Ave. Turn left and follow it downhill to the Bow Falls parking area. Continue around the parking area and across the Spray River bridge on the Banff Springs Golf Course Road. Park in a small parking area on the right 150 m past the bridge and walk along the road another 200 m to where a trail branches right ("hiker" symbol sign).

0.0—Golf course road trailhead (1360 m).

    —Trail skirts behind golf course's 1st hole.

0.3—Junction. Stay left.

1.0—Junction. Mt Rundle trail branches left from the Spray River east side trail.

    —Trail climbs and switchbacks through pine forest.

3.9—Junction. Trail to 1st peak of Mt Rundle branches uphill to left. Mt. Rundle trail ahead.

4.7—Trail's end (1830 m). Route to main peak of Mt Rundle continues across major gully.

The trail up the southwest slope of Mount Rundle is steep and mostly enclosed by forest. While it does offer occasional views of the Spray Valley and the town of Banff, its primary function is as an approach route to the mountain's 2949 m summit—the most popular climb in Banff Park.

The first 1.0 km follows along the east arm of the *Spray River Circuit*. The trail strikes off from the golf course access road just beyond the first hole, skirts behind the green and branches left on a broad track leading up into the forest. This old access road climbs well above the Spray River on its ascent along the east side of the valley.

Just 0.7 km beyond the golf course, the Mount Rundle trail branches left from the Spray River trail and begins its steady climb up the mountain's southwest slope. You are enclosed by forest for 2.4 km, where the trail finally switchbacks onto open slopes and there are good views of Banff and the Spray Valley.

At km 3.9, a faint track leading toward Mount Rundle's first peak cuts uphill to the left. The main trail contours along the slope for another 0.8 km and ends at a large gully. Looking up this gully, you can see the limestone slabs and talus slopes leading to the top of the mountain.

The climb to the summit can be made by fit scramblers, but the peak lies a gruelling 1120 m above. The correct route follows across the gully and up the ridge on the opposite side (ascending the gully itself leads to serious problems). Anyone continuing beyond the end of the trail should pick up a copy of the pamphlet *A Climber's Guide to Mount Rundle* at the Park Visitor Centre in Banff.

The trail and the mountain slopes beyond are bone dry, so be sure to carry water on the hike or the climb.

13 Spray River Circuit

Spray River Circuit—12.4 km (7.7 mi)

Half-day trip

Allow 3 to 4 hours round trip

Elevation gain: 75 m (250 ft)

Maximum elevation: 1435 m (4,700 ft)

Maps: Banff 82 O/4
      Banff Up-Close (Gem Trek)

Access: From downtown Banff, cross the Bow River bridge and turn left onto Spray Avenue. Continue on Spray Avenue 0.8 km to Bow Falls Ave. Turn left and follow it downhill to the Bow Falls parking area. Continue around the parking area and across the Spray River bridge on the Banff Springs Golf Course Road. Park in a small parking area on the right 150 m past the bridge and walk along the road another 200 m to where a trail branches right ("hiker" symbol sign).

0.0—Golf course road trailhead (1360 m).

—Trail skirts behind golf course's 1st hole.

0.2—Junction. Spray River Circuit trail split. Stay right.

0.4—Spray River.

—Follow trail upstream.

1.2—Spray River footbridge.

1.4—Junction with *Spray River* trail at km 0.7. Turn left.

6.4—Junction and picnic area (1435 m). *Spray River* and *Goat Creek* ahead. Spray River Circuit east side left.

6.5—Spray River footbridge.

7.3—Mt Rundle Campground (Sp6).

11.0—Banff Springs Hotel viewpoint.

11.5—Junction. *Mt Rundle* trail right. Continue ahead.

12.2—Junction. Spray River Circuit trail split. Turn right.

12.4—Golf course road trailhead (1360 m).

This popular loop trip runs up one side of the Spray River and back down the other from the Banff Springs Golf Course. Though it follows abandoned park fire roads most of the way, it is a pleasant outing—a favourite trip for cyclists in summer and cross-country skiers in winter.

Start the trip at the "hiker" sign beside the first hole on the Banff Springs Golf Course. Follow the broad, dirt track skirting through the forest behind the green and fairway for 200 m to a signed junction. From this point you can hike the circuit clockwise by turning left or, our preference, counterclockwise by keeping right. Either way, you will return to this junction at the completion of the circuit.

By staying right, you climb over a forested rise to the Spray River, then follow the trail leading upstream. At km 1.2 you reach a footbridge beside an old limestone quarry (the "Rundle Rock" used to construct the Banff Springs Hotel). Cross the bridge, where there is a view back to the hotel, and follow the trail up through the forest to the *Spray River* trail.

Turn left and follow the broad track of this abandoned fire road upvalley for the next 5 km. Views are limited, but the river is a constant companion as you near the south end of the circuit.

At km 6.4, you arrive at a junction and picnic area on open flats beside the river. Turn left and cross the footbridge to return down the east side of the valley.

The trail is a bit more pleasant and varied along the east side, rolling through forest, passing a campground and climbing gradually to an open benchland overlooking the river and the Banff Springs Hotel, which rises from the forest like a medieval castle. From this viewpoint, a short, gradual descent brings you back to the 0.2-km trail junction beside the golf course fairway.

14 Spray River

Banff Springs Hotel trailhead to Spray Lakes Reservoir—38.8 km (24.1 mi)

Backpack

Allow 2 to 3 days one way

Elevation gain: 335 m (1,100 ft)

Maximum elevation: 1735 m (5,700 ft)

Maps: Banff 82 O/4
      Canmore 82 O/3
      Spray Lakes Reservoir 82 J/14

Access: From downtown Banff, cross the Bow River bridge and turn left onto Spray Avenue. Stay left at the next intersection and continue on Spray Avenue 1.0 km to the Banff Springs Hotel. Continue around the hotel traffic circle and beneath the skywalk. Stay right after you pass the hotel parking deck to reach road's end at the Spray River trail parking area in another 300 m.

0.0—Spray River trailhead kiosk (1400 m).

0.7—Junction. Trail from golf course intersects from left.

5.7—Junction. Spray River east side trail intersects from left. (See *Spray River Circuit*.)

9.8—Junction. *Goat Creek* trail left. Spray River ahead.

—Follow trail upstream.

10.2—Spray Warden Cabin (100 m to left).

15.1—Rink's Camp Campground (Sp16).

22.7—Eau Claire Campground (Sp23). Spray River Warden Cabin.

23.2—Spray River bridge.

33.7—Mt Fortune Campground (Sp35).

35.6—Fortune Warden Cabin.

37.2—Park boundary.

38.8—Spray Lakes West Road Junction (1705 m). Spray Lakes West Road access gate and Spray Lakes West Campground left 11 km. Trail Centre (*Bryant Creek* trail) right 5.5 km.

The Spray River trail begins near the Banff Springs Hotel and follows the wide track of an abandoned fire road south along the course of the Spray River to the Spray Lakes Reservoir just beyond the park boundary. There it intersects with a trail along the west side of the reservoir, which in turn connects to Bryant Creek and other trails in the south end of Banff Park.

Since the trail is a long and somewhat mundane way to reach the south end of the park, it sees limited use by backpackers. However, it does traverse a peaceful, wilderness valley with frequent riverside views and is appointed with some very fine campgrounds.

From the parking area behind the Banff Springs Hotel, the trail runs south along the west side of the Spray Valley and passes junctions with the Spray River east side and Goat Creek trails. (See *Spray River Circuit* and *Goat Creek*.) This lower section is a popular mountain bike route, so don't expect too much solitude.

The trail is less travelled beyond Goat Creek, where it immediately turns southwest and cuts between Sulphur Mountain and the Goat Range. After traversing this gap, it takes a southeasterly tack once again until it crosses the park boundary and reaches Spray Lakes Reservoir.

At the reservoir it intersects the abandoned west side road. You can turn right and follow this road 5.5 km to the Bryant Creek and Upper Spray River trails (see *Bryant Creek* and *Upper Spray River-Palliser Pass*).

Travel restrictions: As of this writing (2000), the trail is closed between Goat Creek junction (km 9.8) and the park boundary. This closure has been ordered to reduce disturbance to grizzly bears in the upper valley. Check the park website or at a visitor centre for any changes in this policy.

15 Goat Creek

Spray Lakes Road to Spray River Junction—9.3 km (5.8 mi)
Spray Lakes Road to Banff Springs Golf Course—19.4 km (12.1 mi)

Day trip

Allow 5 hours

Elevation loss: 300 m (985 ft)

Maximum elevation: 1660 m (5,450 ft)

Maps: Canmore 82 O/3
      Banff 82 O/4

Access: The trailhead is located on the Spray Lakes Road 9 km (5 mi) from downtown Canmore. Follow the Spray Lakes Road west from Canmore to Whiteman's Gap (steep gravel road after passing the Canmore Nordic Centre). The road skirts a lake in the gap and descends a hill to the trailhead parking area on the right.

0.0—Goat Creek parking area (1660 m).

1.0—Park boundary.

—Gradual descent near creek.

7.2—Goat Creek footbridge.

9.0—Spray River footbridge.

9.3—Junction with *Spray River* trail at km 9.8. Turn right.

—Follow downstream on roadbed.

13.4—Junction. Straight ahead to *Spray River* trailhead (5.7 km) and Banff Springs Hotel. Keep right for Spray River east side trail and golf course.

13.5—Spray River footbridge.

14.3—Mt Rundle Campground (Sp6).

18.0—Banff Springs Hotel viewpoint.

18.5—Junction. Mt Rundle trail right. Golf course ahead.

19.4—Golf course road (1360 m).

The Goat Creek trail connects the Spray River trail to the Spray Lakes Road just beyond the park boundary in Kananaskis Country. However, it is usually travelled from south to north as a day trip from the Spray Lakes Road to Banff. Since it loses elevation gradually but steadily (300 m over 19.4 km), the trip is very popular with cyclists in summer and skiers in winter. It is also a pleasant hike along the rushing waters of Goat Creek and the Spray River.

From the Spray Lake Road parking area, you can look down the long corridor you will be travelling to Banff, contained by Mount Rundle on the right and Goat and Sulphur Mountains on the left. Soon after passing the park boundary, the trail comes abreast of Goat Creek and follows near that stream for the next 5 km.

Footbridges span Goat Creek at km 7.2 and the Spray River at km 9.0. These bridges appear suddenly at the bottom of short, moderately steep grades, so cyclists and skiers should control their speed as they near these crossings.

Turn right when you reach the Spray River trail and follow the broad track of this old fire road downstream along the west side of the Spray.

When you reach a trail split on an open flat beside the river at km 13.4, you have a choice: stay on the left side of the river and continue to the Spray River trailhead behind the Banff Springs Hotel (see *Spray River*); or take the right-hand branch, which immediately crosses a bridge to the east side of the river, and follow down-valley to a trailhead on the Banff Springs Golf Course road (see *Spray River Circuit*). We prefer the latter option, though it is marginally longer.

Unless you are a cyclist making a circuit around Mount Rundle, you will want to arrange transportation between the two distant trailheads.

16 Rundle Riverside

Banff Springs Golf Course Road to Canmore Nordic Centre—14.6 km (9.1 mi)

Day trip

Allow 3.5 hours hiking

Elevation gain: 135 m (450 ft)

Maximum elevation: 1490 m (4,880 ft)

Maps: Banff 82 O/4
Canmore 82 O/3

Access: Drive to Bow Falls below the Banff Springs Hotel. Continue past the falls parking area and across the Spray River bridge onto the golf course loop road. Continue along this road 4.4 km, keeping right at a road split, to the small, trailhead parking area on the right side of the road.

The south end of the trail is at the Canmore Nordic Centre, 4 km from downtown Canmore on the Spray Lakes Road. Follow the "Banff Trail" from the Nordic Centre.

0.0—Golf course road (1355 m).

0.8—Trail comes abreast of Bow River.

—Gentle, rolling trail through forest near river.

2.7—Rock outwash.

4.9—Trail angles away from river.

5.7—Rock outwash.

7.5—Rock-mud outwash.

7.8—Trail begins moderate climb through rooty forest.

8.4—Park boundary.

—Steady uphill on wide gravel trail.

8.8—Trail enters Nordic Centre trail network.

—Follow gravel trail ("Banff Trail").

11.9—Trail summit (1490 m).

—Steady downhill.

14.6—Canmore Nordic Centre (1435 m). Day lodge and parking area.

The Rundle Riverside trail reaches the Bow River in less than 15 minutes—a peaceful spot with a nice view of the Fairholme Range. Past this idyllic spot, the trail has little attraction for hikers beyond a few more riverside viewpoints. However, it is the most direct route between Banff and Canmore and a popular biking trail.

The trail runs from the end of the Banff Springs Golf Course loop road to the Canmore Nordic Centre beyond the park boundary. It is rough, forest-enclosed, and sometimes very rocky (it crosses three major outwashes).

You reach the Bow River at km 0.8 and stay close to its true right bank for the next 4 km. There are numerous opportunities to stop and relax beside the river, and the sheer buttresses of Mount Rundle, visible through the trees, are constant companions on the journey.

The last access to the river is at km 4.9, where the trail angles off to the right and starts climbing to the park boundary.

After crossing the boundary at km 8.4, the trail becomes a wide gravel track that rises steeply into the midst of the Nordic Centre ski trail network. This smooth roadbed leads you through the maze of trails (follow signs indicating "Banff Trail" and "Stadium" at trail intersections).

The highest elevation on the trip, 180 m above the Bow Valley, is reached in the middle of a large, grassy clearing (an old strip mine scar from the dying days of the Canmore coal industry in the 1970s). If you are on a bike, this lofty viewpoint is followed by a quick downhill run to the Nordic Centre lodge and stadium, where the 1988 Winter Olympic Nordic events were staged.

Some cyclists return to Banff on the Trans-Canada Highway or via the Goat Creek trail. One-way hikers and cyclists will need to arrange transportation between the two trailheads.

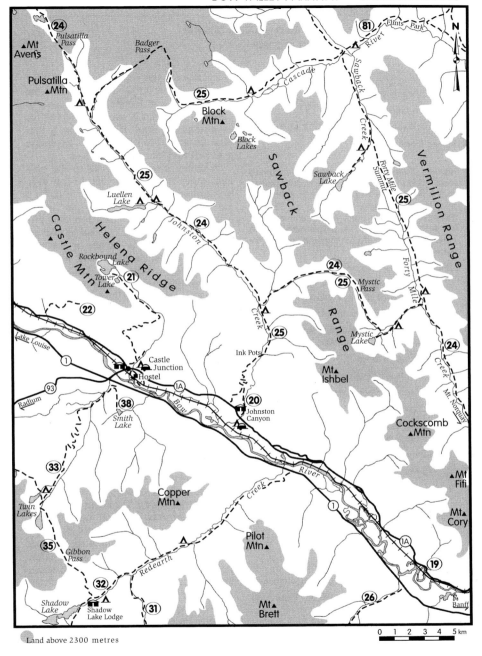

Land above 2300 metres

0 1 2 3 4 5 km

17 Cory Pass—Mount Edith Circuit

Fireside Picnic Area to Cory Pass—5.8 km (3.6 mi)
Mount Edith Circuit—13.0 km (8.1 mi)

Day trip

Allow 3 hours to Cory Pass

Elevation gain: 915 m (3,000 ft)

Maximum elevation: 2350 m (7,700 ft)

Maps: Banff 82 O/4

Access: Follow the Trans-Canada Highway west 5.5 km from Banff's west exit interchange to the Bow Valley Parkway exit. Continue on Bow Valley Parkway 0.5 km to the Fireside Picnic Area access road. Follow the road 1.0 km to the picnic area. A bridge spanning the creek to the picnic area is the starting point for the trail.

0.0—Fireside Picnic Area (1435 m).

—Trail angles away from the rear of the picnic area on an old roadbed.

0.2—Trail cuts left into forest from roadbed.

1.1—Junction. Edith Pass trail straight ahead, Cory Pass uphill to left.

—Stiff uphill climb.

1.7—Cory Knoll viewpoint.

—Extremely steep uphill.

2.4—Crest of narrow forested ridge.

—Trail follows ridge crest then climbs steeply across open slope to pass.

5.8—Cory Pass (2350 m).

—Steep, rocky descent to Gargoyle Valley.

6.8—Exit Gargoyle Valley. Keep right up steep talus slope.

7.1—Trail contours southeast on slopes above Edith Pass.

8.2—Trail descends avalanche slope.

9.0—Junction with Edith Pass trail.

—Steady descent through heavy forest.

11.9—Junction. Cory Pass-Edith Pass trail junction.

13.0—Fireside Picnic Area (1435 m).

Cory Pass is the most spectacular hike near Banff. The 2300-m defile frames the monolithic south face of Mount Louis to create a view that is usually reserved for mountaineers. And after gaining a vertical kilometre in elevation to get there, you will feel like a mountaineer.

Whether you simply hike to the pass and return or complete the 13-km loop trip around Mount Edith, you are in for a good workout. (Caution: do not underestimate the physical exertion that this hike requires. The trail is also hazardous when the ground is frozen or there is snow and ice on sections of the route.)

From the Fireside Picnic Area the trail runs through coniferous forest and pleasant aspen groves to a junction at km 1.1. (If you complete the Mount Edith Circuit, you will return to this junction ...someday!) The trail to Cory Pass cuts uphill to the left at this split and begins a heart-pounding climb on an open, south-facing slope. After a brief respite on a grassy knoll overlooking the Bow Valley, it continues its relentless ascent for another 1.3 km to a forested ridge and the first views of your objective—the lofty notch of Cory Pass.

You climb along this rocky, sparsely forested ridge for another kilometre or so to the top of a small cliff band, which requires that you down-climb through an obvious but steep break in the rock. (Nothing serious, but you will have to use your hands to steady yourself.)

The trail picks up again at the base of this cliff and, a few moments later, emerges from the trees and ascends across a long open slope to the pass (take care if snow is lingering in the steep gullies traversed by the trail).

Cory Pass is often a very cold and windy place. Sandwiched between the cliffs of Mounts Edith (2555 m) to the east and Cory (2800 m) to the west, this high, rockbound gap might more appro-

Mount Louis from Cory Pass

Mount Louis from the Edith Pass high route

priately be considered a col—a French term for a high gap between two peaks. However, the views are worth any discomforts of trail or pass, highlighted by the towering slabs of grey limestone that form the 500-m face of Mount Louis. This forbidding, unapproachable mountain has been a popular objective for rock climbers ever since it was first ascended by the Austrian guide Conrad Kain and A.H. MacCarthy in 1916.

Mount Edith Circuit. Instead of going back the way you came (a knee-jarring experience), you can descend the north side of the pass and make a loop around Mount Edith via the Edith Pass high trail.

Barring lingering snow in early summer, a vague trail is followed down the steep talus slope beyond the pass and into the Gargoyle Valley, which receives its name from the rock pinnacles just north of the summit. After a quick loss of elevation, a rocky but defined track traverses to the right beneath Mount Edith's cliffs and just above the floor of the valley—an incredible, rock-filled sanctuary dominated by Mount Louis's imposing south face.

The rocky trail leads you through the mouth of the Gargoyle Valley to an open rockslide, where you are greeted by a view of the broad Forty Mile Valley. This is a spot where hikers sometimes lose the trail, so watch for the long scree slope leading up to the right. A faint trail climbs directly up this rocky slope for approximately 300 m. Near the top, watch for a trail running left off the scree and into stunted trees.

The route continues as a high traverse across lightly forested slopes beneath Mount Edith's cliffs, where there are impressive views back to Mount Louis and down to the summit of Edith Pass.

The trail eventually plunges down the mountainside on an avalanche slope, re-enters the forest, and intersects the main Edith Pass trail 0.6 km south of its summit.

The loop is completed by following a lively little stream down through mossy-floored forest and back to the 1.1-km junction with the Cory Pass trail. Total distance for the loop is 13 km, and taking into account the steep climbs and descents, it makes for a very strenuous day.

18 Edith Pass

Fireside Picnic Area to Edith Pass — 4.6 km (2.9 mi)

Hikers who aren't up to the arduous Cory Pass-Mount Edith Circuit sometimes hike to Edith Pass instead. The trail is a lot shorter and not nearly as steep. However, it is forest-enclosed all the way, and views from the pass are limited to a few glimpses of Mount Louis through the trees. Or you can branch off onto the Mount Edith Circuit just below the pass—a longer, more demanding option that climbs steeply to open slopes above the pass and better views, particularly for Mount Louis.

Whichever you choose, begin at the Fireside Picnic Area and stay right when you reach the Cory Pass junction at 1.1 km. Just beyond this junction, the trail begins its steady climb through a cool, mossy, stream-fed forest to a trail split at km 4.0. Here you can turn left onto the Mount Edith Circuit, attaining the high trail viewpoint in 1.9 km, or continue right 0.6 km to Edith Pass.

The low trail over Edith Pass continues north, descending in 2.3 km to an intersection with the Forty Mile Creek trail at km 6.0 (see *Sawback Trail*).

Access: Same as *Cory Pass—Mount Edith Circuit*.

19 Muleshoe

Muleshoe Picnic Area to Muleshoe Meadows — 0.9 km (0.6 mi)

This short trail gains 255 heart-pounding metres up the steep, southwest slope of Mount Cory. At the top you discover lush montane meadows and expansive views of the Bow Valley stretching up-valley to Castle Mountain and Mount Temple near Lake Louise.

Starting from the trail sign opposite Muleshoe Picnic Area, a narrow path climbs briefly through a stand of aspen before entering a fire-blackened Douglas fir forest. This fire was set by park wardens in May 1993 in their on-going efforts to restore the montane forest fire regime to this section of the valley.

After traversing steeply to the right across the slope, the trail turns straight uphill and becomes extremely steep.

You finally struggle out of partially burned forest and into a meadow, angling left to the edge of a large gully filled with burned trees. The trail levels out briefly here, where you have the best viewpoint for the valley.

The trail receives its name from the horseshoe-shaped lake beside the picnic area below. The small lake was once a channel of the Bow River, but was isolated from the main flow by railway construction.

A steep but well defined track continues upwards along the gully and into subalpine forest, climbing another 2 km to a 2200-m promontory on the west ridge of Mount Cory. This extension is not worthwhile since it stays mainly in the forest and views are limited.

While the Muleshoe trail makes an ideal spring hike, the slope is infested with wood ticks early in the season. Be sure to check yourself over carefully after the hike.

Access: Follow the Bow Valley Parkway west from its eastern intersection with the Trans-Canada Highway 5.5 km (3.4 mi) to the Muleshoe Picnic Area. *Maps: Banff 82 O/4 (trail not shown).*

20 Johnston Canyon—Ink Pots

Johnston Canyon Resort to Upper Falls—2.7 km (1.7 mi)
Johnston Canyon Resort to Ink Pots—5.8 km (3.6 mi)

Half-day trip

Allow 45 minutes to Upper Falls

Elevation gain: 215 m (700 ft)

Maximum elevation: 1645 m (5,400 ft)

Maps: Banff 82 O/4
      Castle Mountain 82 O/5

Access: Follow the Bow Valley Parkway west from its eastern interchange with the Trans-Canada Highway 17.5 km (11 mi) to Johnston Canyon. The parking area is on the east side of Johnston Creek. From the rear of the parking area, follow the trail leading across a footbridge to the lodge and trailhead on the west side of the creek.

0.0—Johnston Canyon Lodge (1430 m).

1.1—Lower Falls.

2.7—Upper Falls (1565 m).

3.2—Junction. Intersection with Johnston Creek trail at km 2.7 (see *Sawback Range Circuit*). Keep right for Ink Pots.

5.3—Trail narrows.

—Gradual descent to Johnston Creek meadows.

5.8—Ink Pots (1645 m).

The trail to the waterfalls of Johnston Canyon has to be the busiest in the Canadian Rockies. Nearly every day throughout the summer, hundreds of hikers follow its canyon-clinging catwalks and cliff-mounting staircases to the gorge's Lower and Upper Falls. While the canyon and its unique trail are certainly worthy of a visit, you'll have to do the hike in the evening or very early in the morning to avoid the hordes.

The trail begins immediately behind Johnston Canyon Lodge. After a short climb through the forest, it descends and stays close to Johnston Creek all the way to Lower Falls. Along the way you pass over sturdy iron catwalks attached beneath overhanging canyon walls, where the turbulent waters of the creek flow beneath your feet.

Lower Falls is reached at km 1.1. A bridge across the creek serves as a viewpoint for the thundering cataract, and a short tunnel through the canyon bedrock allows passage to an even more intimate vantage point (albeit a wet one).

Back on the main trail, you continue up the canyon via more catwalks and broad, well graded trail. There are many viewpoints overlooking the canyon and a small waterfall.

Throughout the journey, scan the creek and its banks for dippers. Also known as water ouzels, these solitary, slate-grey birds are often seen bouncing up and down on streamside rocks.

At the 30-m Upper Falls, there are two viewpoints: the bottom of the falls is reached by a side-trail and catwalk leading to a viewing platform; a short steep climb on the main trail takes you to the top of the falls and another viewing platform, which hangs out over the gorge above the waterfall.

While the rock slabs near the brink of the falls are fenced, people still clamber through to be near the creek. Be fore-

Johnston Canyon

warned: if you slip into the stream, you will be swept over the falls and you will not survive! (Accidents have claimed a number of people all along the Johnston Canyon trail over the years, so always stay on the trail and keep young children under control.)

Ink Pots. A small percentage of those who hike to the Upper Falls continue another 3 km to the Ink Pots—seven cold mineral springs bubbling to the surface in the open meadows beside Johnston

Creek. Above Upper Falls, the trail climbs out of the canyon to join the trail from Moose Meadows. In just over 2 km, it descends to the meadows and the springs, located on the right side of the trail not far from the creek.

While these springs are unique (they have a constant temperature of 4 degrees C. and their basins are composed of quicksand), many hikers find the extended journey above the canyon a bit of a disappointment. Hopefully open views of the Johnston Creek valley from the site offer some consolation.

21 Rockbound Lake

Bow Valley Parkway to Rockbound Lake—8.4 km (5.2 mi)

Day trip

Allow 2.5 to 3 hours one way

Elevation gain: 760 m (2,500 ft)

Maximum elevation: 2210 m (7,250 ft)

Maps: Castle Mountain 82 O/5

Access: Follow the Bow Valley Parkway (Hwy 1A) to Castle Junction 30 km (18.5 mi) west of the town of Banff. The paved parking area for the trail is beside a warden residence on the north side of the Parkway 200 m east of the intersection and Castle Mountain Village lodge.

0.0—Parking area (1450 m).

—Follow old roadbed track.

0.3—Junction. Silverton Falls right 0.6 km; Rockbound Lake ahead.

—Gradual to moderate uphill grades.

5.0—Old roadbed narrows to single track.

5.3—Boggy and wet conditions during early season and rainy periods.

7.7—Tower Lake (2120 m).

—Trail skirts to right of lake and switch-backs up headwall.

8.4—Rockbound Lake (2210 m).

A rigorous outing to a high valley hidden behind the ramparts of Castle Mountain and two distinctly different lakes: one a placid, green mirror fringed by open subalpine forest and lush wildflower meadows; the other a cold, grey sheet contained by steep talus slopes and massive, tumbled boulder-fields. Both lakes are overshadowed by the impressive Eisenhower Peak tower and the limestone cliffs of Castle Mountain.

The trail starts on an old access road, which provides little scenic interest as it climbs gradually along the southern flank of Castle Mountain for the first 2.4 km. Eventually it gains sufficient elevation to provide glimpses of the Bow Valley and the mountains across the Bow Valley to the west. Prominent are pyramid-shaped Copper Mountain and, to the south, Pilot Mountain, which served as a landmark to CPR surveyors charting the line of the railway down the valley in 1881. The trail, still following the old roadbed, continues its traverse around the end of Castle Mountain and finally enters the high valley running northwest between its ramparts and Helena Ridge.

At 5.3 km the trail narrows to a single track and, just a bit farther on, views open to the Eisenhower Tower on Castle Mountain, a 2752-m limestone pinnacle rising in front of the main body of the mountain. The trail beyond this point can be rather messy, particularly early in the season when the entire area is soggy from the melting snow.

An extensive meadow leads to Tower Lake, a small body of water set within a semicircle of rock. This appears to be the end of the journey, but the trail continues to the right of the lake and climbs steeply up the headwall beyond.

At the top of the cliff you catch your first view of Rockbound Lake and immediately appreciate the aptness of the name. It is totally enclosed by rock.

Rockbound Lake

Cathedral Formation limestone contains the bed of the lake, while limestones of the Stephen and Eldon Formations create the high walls of the cirque. The lake lies precisely in the centre of a major downfold in the strata—the Castle Mountain Syncline, which starts near here and runs all the way to Mount Kerkeslin in Jasper Park, some 260 km to the northwest.

From the scattered forest of Engelmann spruce, alpine fir and larch at the top of the headwall, you can spend a full day exploring the Rockbound basin: huge boulders beyond the southern shore provide a playground for novice rock climbers; the slopes of Helena Ridge to the east are easily ascended for a better perspective of the amphitheatre; and experienced rock scramblers can ascend the main peak of Castle Mountain from the slopes beyond the lake's north shore (see Alan Kane's *Scrambles in the Canadian Rockies*).

Silverton Falls—0.9 km. A 50-m staircase-style waterfall hidden in the forest just off the Rockbound Lake trail near Castle Junction. Though this impressive waterfall is less than a kilometre from the Bow Valley Parkway, it is a natural feature few people know about or visit. The creek and falls are named for the nearby mining town of Silver City (Silverton was a name proposed for the town), which boomed briefly in 1883-84 then disappeared.

The short hike starts on the Rockbound Lake trail and branches right from that route at 0.3 km. Another 0.6 km through dense forest brings you to a viewpoint near the top of the falls. Total elevation gain for the trip is only 90 m.

22 Castle Lookout

Bow Valley Parkway to Castle Lookout—3.8 km (2.4 mi)

Half-day trip

Allow 1.5 to 2 hours one way

Elevation gain: 550 m (1,800 ft)

Maximum elevation: 2010 m (6,600 ft)

Maps: Castle Mountain 82 O/5

Access: Follow the Bow Valley Parkway 5 km (3 mi) west from Castle Junction to the paved, trail head parking area—set back in the forest on the north side of the highway. The trail begins at the upper end of the parking area.

0.0—Parking area (1460 m).

— Steady moderate to steep uphill on old roadbed.

1.5—Old cabin.

2.2—Broad trail narrows to single track.

— Moderate to steep uphill via switch-backs.

3.8—Castle Lookout (2010 m).

This short, steep trail up the slopes of Castle Mountain leads to the site of the old Mount Eisenhower fire lookout and an excellent panorama of the Bow Valley stretching from the grey limestone peaks near Banff to the glacier-capped summits near Lake Louise. Since it climbs along a slope with a southwesterly exposure, it is one of the earliest trails at this elevation to be free of snow in the spring (early to mid-May) and one of the latest to remain snowfree in autumn.

From the parking area, follow a steep, wide pathway upward through forest of lodgepole pine, spruce and occasional Douglas fir. The dense forest allows only a few glimpses of the Bow Valley over the first 2 km, but an old dilapidated cabin offers a stop of interest at 1.4 km (the collapsing structure possibly dates to the short-lived mining boom in this part of the valley circa 1884).

The broad trail eventually reverts to single-track 0.7 km beyond the cabin and traverses out onto the steep, sparsely forested slopes overlooking the Bow Valley. In early summer this open forest produces a colourful array of wild-flowers, including Indian paintbrush, columbine, and heart-leaved arnica.

As you gain elevation, views up and down the Bow Valley improve. Finally the trail twists up through a cliff band, enters a stand of whitebark pine, and contours to the right above the precipice for 100 m to the old lookout site.

All that remains at the site is the foundation of the lookout cabin, which was constructed by labourers from the park's conscientious objector camps in the autumn of 1942. It was abandoned by Parks Canada in the mid-1970s and accidently burned by visiting hikers in 1983.

Check yourself over closely for wood ticks after any early season trip to the lookout.

Jim Thorsell photo

Bow Valley from Castle Lookout

23 Baker Creek

Baker Creek Picnic Area to Baker Creek Crossing—5.6 km (3.5 mi)

Though the Baker Creek trail once served as an optional access-exit route for the Sawback Trail, it was always a long, muddy, uninspiring trip with vague and confusing intersecting paths in its lower section. Parks Canada has spared hikers a lot of misery by "decommissioning" the trail beyond the creek's first crossing for environmental reasons.

The first 5.6 km remains open for cross-country skiing in winter and a place to get mud on your boots with little scenic reward in summer. (The trail's upper section, north of Wildflower Creek, is still accessible to *Sawback Trail* backpackers.)

Just 100 m beyond the picnic area parking lot, the trail crosses a bridge to the west side of Baker Creek. After backtracking downstream briefly to join the old west-side trail, it runs off to the

north on a gradual, steady ascent through lodgepole pine forest. The trail follows well to the west of the creek, so there is little inspiration along the way beyond a brief glimpse of the creek from the edge of a gorge.

The trail splits right from the winter ski trail near 4 km and descends to willow meadows along the creek. Here views open to the valley and the long ridge of Protection Mountain to the east. Trail's end arrives where a bridge once crossed to the east side of Baker Creek.

Access: Follow the Bow Valley Parkway to the Baker Creek Picnic Area, 12 km (7.5 mi) east of the Parkway's western terminus at the Lake Louise Trans-Canada Highway interchange or 14.5 km (9.0 mi) west of the Castle Junction intersection. The trail begins at the rear of the picnic area. *Maps: Lake Louise 82 N/8.*

24 Sawback Trail

Mount Norquay Ski Area to Lake Louise Ski Area—74.0 km (46.0 mi)

Backpack

Allow 4 to 6 days

Maximum elevation: 2345 m (7,700 ft)

Minimum elevation: 1615 m (5,300 ft)

Maps: Banff 82 O/4
      Castle Mountain 82 O/5
      Lake Louise 82 N/8

Access: Travelling from south to north, start at the Mount Norquay ski area (see Cascade Amphitheatre or Elk Lake access descriptions). Travelling from north to south, start from the Fish Creek parking area at the Lake Louise ski area (see Boulder Pass-Skoki Valley access description).

0.0—Mount Norquay Lodge (1705 m).

0.8—Junction. *Cascade Amphitheatre* and *Elk Lake* right. Sawback Trail left.

4.0—Forty Mile Creek bridge (1615 m).

6.0—Junction. Edith Pass left 2.3 km. Sawback Trail ahead.

8.2—Mt Cockscomb Campground (Fm10).

15.9—Junction (1845 m). Mystic Junction Campground (0.3 km) and Forty Mile Summit ahead. Sawback Trail left.

16.0—Mystic Warden Cabin.

18.6—Mystic Valley Campground (Ml22).

19.1—Junction. Mystic Lake left 0.5 km; Sawback Trail and Mystic Pass ahead.

22.7—Mystic Pass (2285 m).

29.3—Junction (1680 m). Larry's Camp Campground (Jo9), Johnston Canyon and Moose Meadows left. Sawback Trail right.

33.0—Johnston Creek Warden Cabin.

37.9—Johnston Creek bridge to west bank.

38.0—Junction. Johnston Creek Campground (Jo18). Luellen Lake and Campground (Jo19) left 1.0 km. Sawback Trail ahead.

39.4—Johnston Creek ford to east bank.

43.3—Junction (2025 m). Badger Pass and *Sawback Range Circuit* right. Sawback Trail ahead.

The Sawback Trail is a name we coined for an extended backpack running from Banff to Lake Louise. The route travels through the jagged limestone peaks of the Sawback Range and over three 2300-m passes—Mystic, Pulsatilla and Boulder. Along the way it utilizes trails in the Forty Mile Creek valley and the upper reaches of Johnston and Baker Creeks. It is an exceptional wilderness trip that usually takes four to six days to complete and is one of the more popular long distance backpacks in Banff Park.

Mount Norquay Ski Area to Johnston Creek Junction—29.3 km. We prefer to start this trip from the Banff end since there is a steady improvement in scenery travelling toward Lake Louise. Departing from the Mount Norquay ski area, the first portion of the trip makes a gradual descent around the heavily forested northern flank of Mount Norquay to Forty Mile Creek.

After crossing Forty Mile Creek at 4.0 km, the trail proceeds upstream along its eastern side, with sporadic views of Mount Brewster to the east and Mount Louis ahead. (Since this trail is used for commercial horse trips, expect muddy conditions and rough track as far as Mystic Lake.)

A junction at km 15.9 marks the point where you cross back to the west side of Forty Mile Creek and begin the climb toward Mystic Pass. (The trail is plagued by rocks and roots beyond the Mystic Warden Cabin.) At km 18.6, it crosses the creek below a large avalanche path and passes the Mystic Valley Campground. In a few minutes you reach the junction for the 0.5-km side-trail to Mystic Lake—a serene body of water contained by the massive cliffs of Mount Ishbel.

Though the origin of the lake's name is somewhat obscure, it likely dates back to around 1891 when the Stoney Indian

Pulsatilla Lake and the Wildflower Creek valley from Pulsatilla Pass

43.8—Badger Pass Jct. Campground (Jo29).

47.2—Pulsatilla Pass (2345 m).

48.3—Pulsatilla Lake.

53.6—Junction (1830 m). Wildflower Creek Campground (Ba15). Sawback Trail right.

58.9—Junction. Red Deer Lakes ahead. Sawback Trail left.

59.6—Baker Lake and Campground (Sk11).

62.1—Junction (1680 m). Intersection with *Boulder Pass-Skoki Valley trail* at km 10.5. Deception Pass-Skoki Valley to right. Continue ahead.

65.4—Boulder Pass (2345 m).

66.9—Junction. Halfway Hut. Hidden Lake Campground (Sk5) and Hidden Lake to right. Continue ahead.

70.1—Temple Lodge. Ski area service road.

74.0—Fish Creek Parking Area (1690 m).

William Twin guided 11 year old Bill Brewster and his nine year old brother Jim to the lake. The Banff boys, who would later create an outfitting and tourist transportation empire, are reputed to be the first white folks to visit the lake.

Mystic Pass is a 3.6 km climb from Mystic Lake junction. The trail over this 2285 m summit runs through beautiful alpine meadows flanked by outcrops and sweeping layers of Devonian limestone.

East of the pass, the trail drops through the heart of the Sawback Range, traversing some spectacular rockslides and avalanche paths and passing delicate waterfalls. At km 29.3 it emerges into the Johnston Creek valley at an intersection with the trail running upvalley from Johnston Canyon and Moose Meadows. (See *Johnston Canyon-Ink Pots* and *Sawback Range Circuit*.)

Johnston Creek Junction to Baker Creek Junction—24.3 km. From the junction, turn right and begin a gradual, mostly forested ascent along the east side of Johnston Creek. At 37.9 km the hiker's trail branches left and crosses the creek to Johnston Creek Campground and the

Luellen Lake trail junction. This side trail reaches Luellen Lake and Campground in 1.0 km. Since the lake is a must-see feature, these campgrounds should be considered as potential overnight stops.

Luellen is a long, narrow lake contained by the cliffs of Helena Ridge and a forest of Engelmann spruce and alpine fir. Whether viewed beneath evening shadow or the first rays of morning sun, it is a remarkably peaceful body of water. While the lake hasn't been stocked for many years, it still provides trout fishermen and a resident osprey family with sporadic success.

Continuing beyond Luellen Lake junction, the trail soon crosses back to the east side of Johnston Creek, where it enters open willow meadows with views of the jagged summits of the Sawback Range to the east.

Badger Pass junction is reached at km 43.3. A campsite 500 m beyond the junction is a good base for a side trip to 2545 m Badger Pass, one of the highest trail-accessible passes in the Canadian Rockies. The pass, which is reached following a steady 5 km climb, serves as a gateway to the remote headwaters of the Cascade River (see *Sawback Range Circuit*).

Just 1.4 km beyond Badger Pass Junction the trail swings across the creek one last time (easy ford) and begins its ascent to Pulsatilla Pass. Unless you want to explore the large alpine cirque just east of the pass, ignore the trail leading in that direction. Instead, stay left beneath the glacier-draped cliffs of Pulsatilla Mountain and follow the trail that climbs to the obvious low notch.

The view beyond the 2345-m summit is one of the classic wilderness scenes in the Rockies—the sparkling waters of Pulsatilla Lake perfectly framed between mountain chains marching away to the north. Pulsatilla is an old genus designation for western anemone, just one of a myriad of wildflowers that spread over the alpine meadow headwaters of the appropriately named Wildflower Creek in mid-summer.

The trail descends northward from the pass, skirts the shores of Pulsatilla Lake, then drops sharply down the narrow Wildflower Creek valley to Baker Creek and the Wildflower Creek Campground. (A rough trail down Baker Creek once provided an optional exit to the Bow Valley Parkway at this point, but it is no longer maintained and using it is discouraged to minimize disturbance to wildlife that range in the valley.)

Baker Creek Junction to Fish Creek Parking Area—20.4 km. Boulder Pass is the last pass on your journey. While it is a gem, you will suffer a bit over the next 5 km to attain this sublime summit.

After crossing Wildflower Creek at its confluence with Baker Creek (hopefully there is a log bridge so you can avoid the wade), climb through forest and across avalanche paths on rough trail along the east side of the creek. After 2 km, the trail descends into a boggy meadow, where it becomes indistinct and difficult to follow. At the north end of the meadow, cross a side-stream and rocky outwash, followed by a short steep climb over rough, rocky and often muddy trail.

You finally emerge into pleasant subalpine meadows and cross to the west side of the creek. At km 58.9, turn left at a junction onto the trail leading west to Baker Lake.

From Baker Lake Campground, the trail travels along the lake's north shore and then climbs to Ptarmigan Valley and an intersection with the Boulder Pass-Skoki Valley trail just below Deception Pass.

You are on a popular trail now and traversing one of the finest summits in the Rockies. The trail rolls along above Ptarmigan Lake, with little gain or loss of elevation, to the crest of Boulder Pass, where views stretch west beyond the Bow Valley to Mount Temple and the Valley of the Ten Peaks region.

From Boulder Pass, you complete your trip by following the *Boulder Pass-Skoki Valley* trail down Corral Creek to the Lake Louise ski area and Fish Creek trailhead.

25 Sawback Range Circuit

Badger Pass-Flint's Park-Mystic Pass Circuit—72.5 km (45.0 mi)

Backpack

Allow 4 to 6 days

Maximum elevation: 2545 m (8,350 ft)

Minimum elevation: 1430 m (4,700 ft)

Maps: Castle Mountain 82 O/5

Access: Follow the Bow Valley Parkway to the Moose Meadows parking area, located on the north side of the highway 2.3 km (1.4 mi) west of Johnston Canyon and 4 km (2.5 mi) east of Castle Junction. The parking area is situated 100 m off the Parkway.

0.0—Moose Meadows (1430 m).

2.7—Junction. *Johnston Canyon* trail intersects from right.

5.3—Ink Pots.

5.6—Johnston Creek bridge to east bank.

7.4—Junction and bridge (1680 m). Larry's Camp Campground (Jo9). Mystic Pass right. Sawback Range Circuit ahead.

11.1—Johnston Creek Warden Cabin.

16.0—Johnston Creek bridge to west bank.

16.1—Junction and Johnston Creek Campground (Jo18). Luellen Lake and Campground (Jo19) left 1.0 km. Sawback Range Circuit ahead.

17.5—Johnston Creek ford to east bank.

21.4—Junction (2025 m). Badger Pass Junction Campground (Jo29) 0.5 km and Pulsatilla Pass 3.9 km ahead. Sawback Range Circuit right.

26.4—Badger Pass (2545 m).

33.4—Block Lakes Junction Campground (Cr37).

38.9—Junction and Flint's Park Warden Cabin (1830 m). Flint's Park and Cascade Trail ahead. Sawback Range Circuit right.

39.0—Cascade River bridge.

43.7—Junction. Sawback Lake Campground (Fm29) 1.4 km and Sawback Lake 2.2 km to right. Sawback Range Circuit ahead.

45.7—Forty Mile Summit (2150 m).

The Sawback Trail connecting Banff and Lake Louise is a popular long-distance backpacking route, however, you can sample some of the region's best scenery by making a loop trip through the heart of the range via Johnston Creek, Badger Pass, Flint's Park, Forty Mile Summit and Mystic Pass.

The Sawback Range Circuit passes through some of the highest and wildest country in the Front Ranges, covers the same distance as the Sawback Trail, and conveniently brings you back to where you started.

Some cautionary notes: sections of trail on the east side of the Sawback Range are utilized by a commercial horse operation, so expect the mud and muck of a heavily-used horse trail; much of this circuit travels through prime grizzly bear habitat, particularly between Badger Pass and Forty Mile Summit, so follow all the rules for safe travel in bear country; and a major snow cornice on the eastern lip of Badger Pass may cause difficulties early in the season.

Moose Meadows to Badger Pass Junction—21.4 km. The Sawback Range Circuit starts and ends at the Moose Meadows parking area on the Bow Valley Parkway—the trailhead for most trips into the Johnston Creek valley. From the parking area, you climb through forest and, soon after passing the intersection with the Johnston Canyon trail, emerge into open willow-dwarf birch meadows at the Ink Pots. After crossing to the true left side of Johnston Creek just beyond the cold mineral springs, the trail remains near the creek and makes a gradual, straightforward ascent of the valley.

At just over 7 km you pass Larry's Camp Campground and, a few moments later, arrive at a bridged side stream and the junction for Mystic Pass. This junction is the trail split for your round-trip

Mystic Pass

51.4—Juntion (1860 m). Mystic Junction Campground (Fm19). Forty Mile Creek ahead. Sawback Range Circuit right.

54.4—Mystic Valley Campground (Ml22).

54.9—Junction. Mystic Lake left (0.5 km). Mystic Pass ahead.

58.5—Mystic Pass (2285 m).

65.1—Johnston Creek junction (1680 m). Larry's Camp Campground (Jo9). Moose Meadows trailhead left.

72.5—Moose Meadows (1430 m).

circuit through the Sawback Range. Here you must decide whether to follow the loop in a counter-clockwise direction by heading toward Mystic Pass or clockwise by continuing along Johnston Creek. Our preference is clockwise (as described here), since the approaches to both Badger and Mystic Passes are more gradual.

As you continue up Johnston Creek, you are following the central section of the Sawback Trail, reaching the Luellen Lake Junction at km 16.1 and Badger Pass junction at km 21.4 (see *Sawback Trail,* km 29.3 to km 43.3).

If you arrive at Badger Pass junction early in the afternoon, consider pitching camp in the campground 0.5 km north of the junction. From there you can side-trip north along the Sawback Trail 3.4 km to the alpine meadows of Pulsatilla Pass—a magnificent viewpoint overlooking Pulsatilla Lake and the upper reaches of the Wildflower Valley.

Badger Pass Junction to Flint's Park—17.5 km. At Badger Pass junction you leave the Sawback Trail, turning northeast to begin the steady ascent to Badger Pass—one of the highest trail-accessible points in Banff Park. The climb to the pass is moderate to steep, and you cross the creek draining its western slope twice as you climb through forest-fringed meadows. Once you emerge above the last trees, the trail is faint to non-existent through rocky, alpine meadows and along talus slopes, but the route to the pass is always obvious ahead.

Badger Pass (2545 m) is about as wild and remote a place as you could imagine. The summit is surrounded by a sea of peaks typical of the Front Ranges, composed of steeply tilted layers of limestone and shale; Bonnet Peak (3234 m), one of the highest mountains in the Sawback Range, rises immediately to the north. On warm, sunny days the pass is a wonderful place to relax and enjoy the high point on your journey, but if the weather is poor, you won't want to linger on this exposed summit.

Continuing eastward, you may have to circumnavigate a snow cornice before beginning the descent to the headwaters of the Cascade River (the big drift often lingers into late July). It is a dramatic drop over steep, broken rock and through a boulder-filled basin, where you will likely lose the track. (Persevere through the rocks until you pick up the trail again.)

Approximately 7 km beyond the pass, you arrive at Block Lakes Junction Campground, situated on the flats where two tributary streams flow into the Cascade from Bonnet Peak to the north and Block Mountain to the south. The spur trail to Block Lakes crosses the river at this point, but this side trip should only be attempted by experienced rock climbers since a major cliff guards the final approach to the lakes.

The trail continues eastward along the north side of the Cascade River, rolling through forest and along willow flats on the wide track of an old fire road. At km 38.9, you reach the Flint's Park Warden Cabin and a junction. While the main valley trail continues eastward for 8 km to intersect the Cascade Fire Trail (see *Flints Park*), you turn south at this junction, immediately cross a bridge over the Cascade River and begin the ascent of Sawback Creek.

Flint's Park to Mystic Junction—12.5 km. The route up Sawback Creek follows a much-used horse trail, so expect mud and sloppy hiking until you reach Forty Mile Summit. A welcome break, and the major attraction on this leg of the journey, is Sawback Lake—a 2.2 km side-trip that should be included in your itinerary. The lake, set beneath the eastern wall of the Sawback Range, has been popular with fishermen since the early years of the 20th century. A campground 0.8 km before you reach the lake is worth considering as a spot to overnight.

Continuing to Forty Mile Summit from Sawback Lake junction, you have a good viewpoint back to Sawback Lake as you crest the pass. At 2150 m, Forty Mile Summit is still below treeline, but you do pass through a long meadow bordered with alpine larch. Watch for the hiker's trail, which splits left from the horse trail on the pass and leads down along Forty Mile Creek to Mystic Lake junction on a less-trammeled track.

Mystic Junction to Moose Meadows— 21.1 km. At Mystic Lake Junction Campground, the hiker trail rejoins the horse trail and crosses to the west side of Forty Mile Creek. You are joined by a cut-off trail from lower Forty Mile Creek in less than a kilometre. Now you are headed west on the last leg of the circuit, which follows the same route as the Sawback Trail past Mystic Lake, over Mystic Pass and down the west side of the Sawback Range to the 7.4 km junction near Larry's Camp Campground in the Johnston Creek valley. (see *Sawback Trail*, km 15.9 to km 29.3.)

26 Bourgeau Lake

Trans-Canada Hwy to Bourgeau Lake—7.5 km (4.6 mi)
Trans-Canada Hwy to Harvey Pass—9.7 km (6.0 mi)

Day trip

Allow 2.5 to 3 hours to lake

Elevation gain: 725 m (2,380 ft)

Maximum elevation: 2160 m (7,100 ft)

Maps: Banff 82 O/4

Access: Follow the Trans-Canada Highway to the Bourgeau Lake trailhead parking area, 2.8 km (1.7 mi) west of the Sunshine Village interchange. The parking area is set back in the forest on the southwest side of the twinned highway. (A cross-over road provides access from westbound lanes.)

0.0—Bourgeau Lake parking area (1435 m).

—Steady uphill via switchbacks, moderate.

1.6—Switchbacks end, trail climbs up southeast side of valley.

3.7—Tributary stream bridge.

5.5—Wolverine Creek bridge. Cascades.

—Steep switchbacks.

6.8—Trail levels out into meadows.

7.5—Bourgeau Lake (2160 m).

—Trail veers away from northwest side of lake and climbs steeply to obvious notch due west.

8.8—Small unnamed lake in alpine bowl.

—Veer left and climb to pass.

9.7—Harvey Pass and Lake (2454 m).

Set within an amphitheatre carved from the limestone walls of the Massive Range, Bourgeau Lake exhibits a variety of subalpine and alpine scenery, flowers and wildlife. Its waters are bordered by alpine fir and larch stands, meadows and barren talus slopes, where ptarmigan, marmots and pikas pursue their daily chores. In spring, avalanches thunder down over Mount Bourgeau's cliffs and goats stroll placidly along the slopes of Mount Brett to the north. These attractions, coupled with some spectacular scenery on Harvey Pass above the lake, make this an outstanding full day's outing.

Striking off from a parking area beside the Trans-Canada Highway, the trail quickly buries itself in a forest of lodgepole pine and spruce, then slowly gains elevation along the southeast side of the Wolverine Creek valley. At km 2.4 views open back to the Bow Valley and the sharp, serrated peaks of the Sawback Range. The broad summit of Mount Brett (2984 m), the highest mountain in the Massive Range, dominates the scene ahead.

At km 5.5 the trail crosses Wolverine Creek, where the stream descends from the Bourgeau Lake cirque in a series of cascades. The log bridge at the foot of the waterfall is a good spot for rest and refreshment before tackling the steep switchbacks that complete the climb to a long, stream-side meadow leading to the lake.

The amphitheatre containing the lake is carved into the northwest side of Mount Bourgeau (2930 m). Like other peaks in the range, its cliffs are formed by Devonian and Mississippian limestones and shales—formations bearing fossils of brachiopods, corals, and other examples of early ocean life. Dr. James Hector named the mountain for the French botanist Eugene Bourgeau, his

Bourgeau Lake

comrade-in-exploration with the Palliser Expedition during the summer of 1858.

Snowbanks often linger in the meadows bordering the lake until mid-July, their meltwaters feeding a wide variety of subalpine wildflowers. White-tailed ptarmigan are often seen along the lake's outlet stream or in the nearby talus slopes, their mottled summer plumage making them all but invisible among the piles of broken rock. Pikas, golden-mantled ground squirrels and chipmunks scurry back and forth through the boulders, closely watching passing hikers for a possible handout.

Harvey Pass. You can explore above the lake to an alpine basin and pass, which lies 2.2 km beyond and 310 vertical metres higher up. A path follows above the forested north shore of Bourgeau Lake then climbs steeply toward the obvious notch where a stream drops from between Mounts Bourgeau and Brett. After some strenuous climbing, the track skirts a small, rockbound lake and emerges into an open alpine bowl complete with small ponds.

While this lofty cirque is quite pleasant, you will want to continue climbing south to the obvious pass at the foot of Mount Bourgeau's long summit ridge. In less than 15 minutes you crest Harvey Pass (2470 m) and are greeted with an exceptional view south to the towering pyramid of Mount Assiniboine. Harvey Lake is a small tarn cradled on the summit and, like the pass, is named for Ralph Harvey, who was a manager in Banff's Brewster Transport Co. and involved in the development of skiing at nearby Sunshine Village.

If you are a very stong hiker and got an early start, you can cap your day's outing by climbing the long ridge to the summit of Mount Bourgeau—one of the most easily ascended 2900 m-plus peaks in the Rockies.

Sunshine Meadows

The Sunshine Meadows region is unique in the Canadian Rockies. Unlike most of the Great Divide, which is composed of heavily glaciated peaks and towering limestone and quartzite walls, the 15-km stretch of the divide between Citadel Pass and the Monarch Ramparts is a mixture of rolling subalpine and alpine meadowland. Moist Pacific weather systems flowing in from the west deposit copious amounts of precipitation here, and the result is a vast, rolling rock garden with an incredible variety of wildflowers, some of which appear nowhere else in the range.

In the centre of this exceptional landscape is the Sunshine Village ski area. For fifty years the resort operated only in winter, but in 1984 management began promoting the summer season as well. With improved access provided by a 5 km-long gondola, visitation to the area quickly grew from a few hundred hikers per season to many thousands. This increased use threatened the fragile meadows, so Parks Canada and the resort worked together widening and resurfacing most of the trails in the core area and constructing wooden platforms at popular viewpoints. Then, in 1991, the resort decided the summer operation was not viable and discontinued the gondola service.

Today, the trails radiating from Sunshine Village can be reached by walking or biking up the 6.5-km access road (bicycles are allowed as far as the lodge, but the road is steep); or by making a reservation on the shuttle buses that run between the Bourgeau Parking Lot at the gondola base station and the upper lodge complex (bus service operates from early July to mid-September). The day lodge at the top serves light meals and refreshments and is a welcome refuge during foul weather. Guided interpretive hikes are also available.

While the bus service makes day hiking the Sunshine trails more feasible, there are some drawbacks: the cost per adult as of this writing (2002) is $18 for the round-trip (no one-way fare), and the last bus down from the lodge departs at 5 p.m., which doesn't leave a lot of time to complete longer trips.

All trails in the following Sunshine Meadows section are described for the majority of hikers who use the shuttle bus and start from Sunshine Village (the upper ski lodge complex).

You also have the option of camping in the meadows. Backpackers can hike or bus up the access road then follow the Citadel Pass trail another 5.8 km to Howard Douglas Lake Campground—the only campsite in the Sunshine Meadows. From this base camp, you can make easy day trips to Citadel Pass, Rock Isle Lake and other points of interest.

Access: Follow the Trans-Canada Highway to the Sunshine Village interchange, 9 km (5.5 mi) west of the town of Banff. Continue on the Sunshine Road for another 9 km to the Bourgeau Parking Lot at the gondola base station. The access road to Sunshine Village starts at a gate to the left of the gondola base station; the Healy Pass trail begins from the parking area to the right and behind the base station.

Shuttle buses to Sunshine Village depart from the gondola base station throughout the late morning and early afternoon. Return trips to the parking area run throughout the afternoon until 5 p.m. There is also direct service from downtown Banff at additional cost. Reservations for shuttle services should be made in advance by calling White Mountain Adventures (see *Sources-Transportation* for contact information).

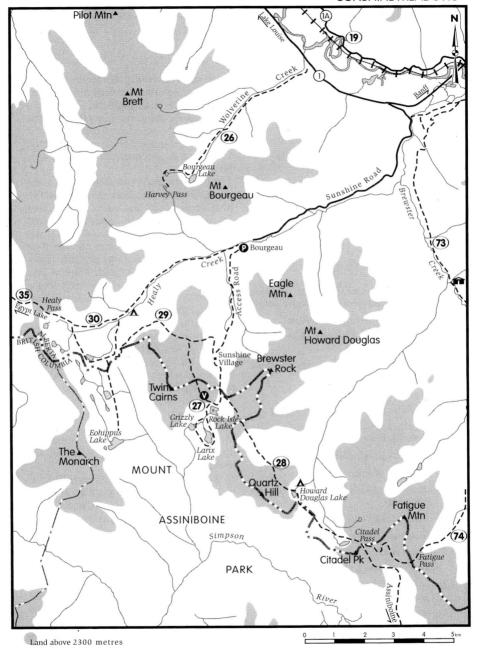

Land above 2300 metres

27 Rock Isle, Grizzly and Larix Lakes

Sunshine Village to Rock Isle Lake outlet—2.5 km (1.6 mi)
Sunshine Village to Larix Lake—4.2 km (2.6 mi)

Half-day trip

Allow 1 to 1.5 hours to Larix Lake

Elevation gain: 105 m (350 ft)
  loss: 80 m (260 ft)

Maximum elevation: 2305 m (7,560 ft)

Maps: Banff 82 O/4

Access: Travel to Sunshine Village as described in the Sunshine Meadows area introduction. From the log building (Nature Centre) in the core of the lodge complex, follow a gravel road leading uphill to the southeast.

0.0—Sunshine Village (2200 m).

—Gravel road leading uphill from Nature Centre.

0.2—Avalanche Control Cabin. Trail branches left from road immediately above cabin.

—Steady uphill through meadows.

1.2—Great Divide (2305 m). Alberta-B.C. boundary.

1.3—Junction. *Citadel Pass* trail left; Rock Isle Lake ahead.

1.8—Rock Isle Lake viewpoint.

—Trail continues around lake to right.

2.1—Junction. Twin Cairns-Meadow Park right; Rock Isle Lake outlet left.

2.5—Rock Isle Lake outlet. Viewpoint.

—Moderate downhill.

3.0—Junction. Grizzly-Larix Loop begins. Keep right.

3.5—Grizzly Lake (2225 m).

4.1—Simpson Valley viewpoint.

4.2—Larix Lake.

—Trail continues around lakeshore.

5.5—Junction. Grizzly-Larix Lakes Loop ends. Return to Rock Isle Lake.

In the early morning, the waters of Rock Isle Lake are often a mirror reflecting its rocky island and shoreline. There is a peacefulness and natural symmetry in the scene, which includes distant peaks in British Columbia, that has attracted artists and photographers for many decades.

While the trip to the Rock Isle Lake viewpoint and back can be completed in little more than an hour, most hikers extend their outing by continuing around the lake and descending to Grizzly and Larix Lakes. Others return to Sunshine Village in high style on the lofty Twin Cairns-Meadow Park trail. And, if you complete all of the options, including a side-trip to Standish Ridge viewpoint, you will have covered a total round trip distance of only 11.7 km.

Following a broad gravel trail from the centre of Sunshine Village, you make a steady but brief climb to the Great Divide, passing through the last scattered stands alpine fir into a treeless alpine landscape. On the 2300-m summit, views stretch south across the vast Sunshine Meadows to the distant pyramid of Mount Assiniboine (a scene somewhat diminished by the presence of ski lift towers).

West of the divide, you enter British Columbia and Mount Assiniboine Provincial Park, passing the Citadel Pass junction and descending to the Rock Isle Lake overlook. Beyond this classic viewpoint, the trail narrows and skirts around the shoreline to the right. After passing the junction for the Twin Cairns-Meadow Park trail, it climbs over a low, rocky hill to where the lake's outlet stream plunges down steep limestone slabs. From this wonderful natural waterslide, you see Larix and Grizzly Lakes below and, across the Simpson Valley, the distant peaks of Kootenay Park.

Rock Isle Lake

Grizzly-Larix Lakes Loop. Continuing beyond Rock Isle Lake, the trail drops into alpine larch and fir and incredibly lush wildflower meadows. Soon the trail splits to begin a 2.5-km loop around Grizzly and Larix Lakes. Keep right and descend to Grizzly Lake in 0.5 km. From the lake's inlet bridge, the trail turns left and contours the lip of the basin to a fine viewpoint for the Simpson Valley.

Larix, the largest of the two lakes, is just beyond the viewpoint. The lake lies between meadow and larch forest (the Latin botanical name for alpine larch is *Larix lyallii*, hence the lake's name.) You follow the shoreline for nearly a kilometre before climbing back to the loop split and returning to Rock Isle Lake.

Twin Cairns-Meadow Park. Even if you only go as far as Rock Isle Lake, consider returning to Sunshine Village on the high trail looping around the west side of Standish Ridge. The trail branches from the Rock Isle Lake trail at the lake's northwest corner and climbs 0.5 km through thinning forest to the Standish Ridge viewpoint junction.

Though the 0.5-km side-trip to the top of Standish Ridge will add some distance and climbing to your journey, the viewing platform near the top of this 2420-m promontory boasts an outstanding panorama of the Sunshine Meadows region. Wildflowers on this slope are exceptional throughout late July and early August, and we have often seen ptarmigan with chicks along this trail.

Back on the main trail, you immediately enter the alpine valley between Standish Ridge and Twin Cairns. The trail runs through this mostly flat, open meadow for nearly 2 km to a junction with the Simpson Pass trail. From this intersection you can make a short (300 m) side-trip left to the summit of Wawa Ridge for even more high-level views of the Sunshine Meadows and Mount Assiniboine. Then return to the junction and descend to Sunshine Village in 1.6 km.

28 Quartz Hill—Citadel Pass

Sunshine Village to Quartz Hill—5.2 km (3.2 mi)
Sunshine Village to Citadel Pass—9.3 km (5.8 mi)

Day trip or backpack

Allow 2.5 to 3 hours one way

Elevation gain: 195 m (640 ft)
          loss: 115 m (375 ft)

Maximum elevation: 2395 m (7,850 ft)

Maps: Banff 82 O/4

Access: Travel to Sunshine Village as described in the Sunshine Meadows area introduction. From the log building (Nature Centre) in the core of the lodge complex, follow a gravel road leading uphill to the southeast.

0.0—Sunshine Village (2200 m).

    —Gravel road leading uphill from Nature Centre.

0.2—Avalanche Control Cabin. Trail branches left from road above cabin.

    —Steady uphill through meadows.

1.2—Great Divide (2305 m). Alberta-B.C. boundary.

1.3—Junction. Rock Isle Lake ahead 0.5 km; Citadel Pass left.

    —Flat followed by gradual descent across open meadows.

4.7—Trail begins climb over east ridge of Quartz Hill.

5.2—Quartz Hill east ridge (2395 m).

    —Steep descent.

5.8—Howard Douglas Lake and Campground (Su8).

    —Gradual climb through meadows.

9.3—Citadel Pass (2360 m). Junction. Fatigue Pass left 2.5 km; Mt Assiniboine ahead 18.2 km. (See Mt Assiniboine via Citadel Pass.)

Citadel Pass is one of the most scenic trips from Sunshine Village. Rolling up and down through the heart of the Sunshine Meadows, the trail is seldom more than a few hundred metres from the crest of the Great Divide. Highlights include wildflower meadows, which are justifiably renowned as some of the finest in the Rockies, and frequent vistas of the rugged peaks of British Columbia to the south and west.

If you use the shuttle bus to and from Sunshine Village, it is a real whirlwind trip to reach Citadel Pass and then get back to catch the last bus down in the afternoon. Most hikers only go as far as Quartz Ridge, the highest point on the trail and a good viewpoint for the southern reaches of the meadows. If you do decide to continue to the pass, you may have to walk down the access road in the evening, which makes for a long 25-km day. Another option is to camp at Howard Douglas Lake, which allows for a more leisurely day trip to both Citadel and Fatigue Passes.

The trail starts from the centre of Sunshine Village and follows the same route as the Rock Isle Lake hike for the first 1.3 km. Just beyond the 2305-m summit on the Alberta-B.C. boundary, the Citadel trail branches left from the Rock Isle route (Rock Isle Lake viewpoint is only 0.5 km beyond the junction and a worthwhile side-trip).

From the junction you cross a vast alpine meadow for more than 1.0 km before invisibly re-entering Alberta and gradually descending into scattered forest. The trail flattens out briefly across a meadow then ascends steeply through stands of alpine fir and larch to the summit of Quartz Hill's east ridge.

This high vantage point is a good destination for those lacking time or energy to continue farther. Howard Douglas Lake lies below the ridge to the

Mount Assiniboine from Quartz Ridge

southeast, and a long line of meadows and scattered forest stretches away beyond the lake to Citadel Pass, cradled between Citadel Peak and Fatigue Mountain.

Quartz Hill, which rises immediately above the ridge to the southwest, was described by boundary surveyor A.O. Wheeler in 1913 as "a prominent hill, with a crest of broken blocks of quartz, falling very steeply on the south west side to form the valley of the Simpson River." It is one of several rocky promontories rising from the Sunshine Meadows.

Continuing beyond the summit, the trail drops sharply to the shores of Howard Douglas Lake. The campground near its outlet is quite scenic and, with the exception of the mosquitoes that often plague the site, a good base for exploring the surrounding meadows and ridges.

Another small lake, Citadel, lies off to the right of the trail less than 2 km beyond Howard Douglas, its basin set beneath a gap in the Great Divide that serves as a window to Mount Assiniboine. This is one of the best views of this famous 3618-m "horn" peak from the Sunshine Meadows trail system. Though its summit seems to loom near, it is over 15 km away.

Citadel Pass offers several options if you have the time and a yen for exploration. One of the most interesting is the climb to Fatigue Pass—a 2395-m crest to the southeast, which can be reached in an hour or less. A trail runs to this high summit, but the junction on Citadel Pass is vague, so scan the slopes above for the obvious track leading across the scree to the pass. (See also *Fatigue Creek*.)

The main trail continues over Citadel Pass and back into British Columbia's Mount Assiniboine Provincial Park. This is one of the popular access routes to Lake Magog at the base of Mount Assiniboine, and at this point you are one-third of the way there. (See *Mount Assiniboine via Citadel Pass*, Mount Assiniboine Park chapter.)

29 Simpson Pass—Healy Meadows

Sunshine Village to Healy Meadows Junction—7.6 km (4.7 mi)
Healy Meadows Junction to Bourgeau Parking Lot—7.7 km (4.8 mi)

Day trip

Allow 2 hours to Healy Meadows

Elevation gain: 160 m (525 ft)

Maximum elevation: 2360 m (7,750 ft)

Maps: Banff 82 O/4

Access: Travel to Sunshine Village as described in the Sunshine Meadows area introduction. Walk downhill from the day lodge to the trail head, located to the left at the base of the Wawa Ridge ski lift.

0.0—Sunshine Village (2200 m).

—Steady uphill along open ski run.

1.6—Junction. Twin Cairns-Meadow Park trail left. Simpson Pass ahead.

1.9—Wawa Ridge summit (2360 m).

—Gradual descent.

5.6—Simpson Pass (2135 m).

—Steep uphill.

6.0—Junction. Eohippus Lake left 3.2 km. Healy Meadows ahead.

—Trail levels out into Healy Meadows.

7.6—Junction. Intersection with *Healy Pass-Egypt Lake* trail. Healy Pass left 1.5 km; Bourgeau Parking Area right 7.7 km.

While Simpson Pass and the Healy Meadows can be reached by ascending Healy Creek from the Bourgeau Parking Area, the shortest, easiest and most scenic approach is from Sunshine Village via Wawa Ridge. It is a route that can be used by day hikers looking for a scenically varied trip from Sunshine Village or as a highline option by backpackers bound for Healy Pass and Egypt Lake (see *Bow Valley Highline Trail*).

Ascending the most northerly ski run on Wawa Ridge, the first 1.9 km climbs directly through the upper fringes of subalpine forest to the treeless summit of the ridge—the route's highest elevation and best viewpoint. The panorama includes the Citadel Pass region and Mount Assiniboine to the southeast, and the massive pyramid of The Monarch to the southwest. Small ponds fringed with cotton grass dot the meadows and, like many open areas in the Sunshine region, the ridge is a wildflower-lover's dream.

Beyond Wawa Ridge the trail descends back into stands of alpine fir and larch. After following beneath a low escarpment for nearly 2 km, it drops down to a small meadow on the summit of Simpson Pass. Here a trail from Healy Creek intersects from the right—an optional route of descent to the Bourgeau Parking Lot. On the B.C. side of the pass, a vague trail quickly disappears into overgrown meadow and forest.

The pass was crossed by Sir George Simpson, governor of the Hudson's Bay Company, in the summer of 1841. It was a disappointment as an improved route for the company's fur brigades bound for the Oregon territory, but Sir George did linger long enough to allow his guide to carve their initials and the date in a tree. The artifact was discovered and salvaged by local outfitter Jim Brewster in 1904 and now resides at the Park Museum in Banff.

The Monarch from Healy Meadows

On the opposite side of the Simpson Pass meadow, the trail begins its climb to the Healy Meadows. Just before reaching the meadows, 0.4 km beyond the pass, a trail branches left to Eohippus Lake—an interesting 3.2 km side-trip for strong hikers who have time and energy to spare.

Just beyond the Eohippus junction, you reach the southeastern edge of the Healy Meadows beside a small lake. This lake was once the hideout of legendary outfitter and park warden Bill Peyto, and the remains of his cabin lie hidden in the forest beyond the lake's north shore. (If you find it, please leave this important historic site undisturbed!)

The trail continues for another kilometre through lake-studded meadows beneath the long ridge of the Monarch Ramparts. If you hike here from mid-July to mid-August, you will be greeted by one of the most luxuriant wildflower gardens in the Rockies—a vast snowbed community filled with the blooms of western anemone, Indian paintbrush, valerian, fleabane, ragwort, globe flower, marsh marigold and many, many more.

At km 7.6 you reach an intersection with the Healy Pass trail. While you can turn around here and hustle back to Sunshine to catch the last shuttle back to the Bourgeau Parking Lot, we prefer to walk back to the parking area on the Healy Pass trail (it is the same distance and all downhill). But first, we usually take the 1.5-km side-trip up to Healy Pass (2330 m), where we enjoy more wildflowers and a panoramic overview of the Egypt Lake region.

Healy Meadows-Simpson Pass Circuit. If you don't want to bus to Sunshine Village, you can follow the Healy Pass trail from the Bourgeau Parking Lot to access the Healy Meadows and Simpson Pass. (See *Healy Pass-Egypt Lake.*)

30 Healy Pass—Egypt Lake

Bourgeau Parking Lot to Healy Pass—9.2 km (5.7 mi)
Bourgeau Parking Lot to Egypt Lake Campground—12.4 km (7.7 mi)

Day trip or backpack

Allow 2.5 to 3 hours to Healy Pass
    3 to 4 hours to Egypt Lake

Elevation gain: 655 m (2,150 ft)
    loss: 335 m (1,100 ft)

Maximum elevation: 2330 m (7,650 ft)

Maps: Banff 82 O/4

Access: Follow the Trans-Canada Highway to
the Sunshine Village interchange, 9 km (5.5 mi)
west of the town of Banff. Continue on the
Sunshine Road for another 9 km to the Bourgeau Parking Lot at the gondola base station.
The Healy Pass trail begins from the parking
area behind the base station to the right.

0.0—Bourgeau Parking Lot (1675 m).

   —Follow broad cat-track uphill.

0.8—Junction. Sunshine Village ahead; Healy
     Pass right.

3.1—Healy Creek bridge.

5.2—Old cabin foundation.

5.5—Healy Creek Campground (E5).

5.9—Junction. Simpson Pass left 1.3 km;
     Healy Pass ahead.

   —Trail begins to climb.

7.7—Healy Meadows Junction. Simpson
     Pass left 2.0 km; Healy Pass ahead.

   —Steady climb through meadows with
     alpine larch.

9.2—Healy Pass (2330 m).

   —Steady downhill.

12.1—Junction. Egypt Lake Warden Cabin
      right 50 m. Keep left.

12.2—Junction. Natalko Lake left 4.2 km;
      campground and shelter ahead across
      bridge and meadow.

12.4—Egypt Lake Campground (E13) and
      Shelter (1995 m). Intersection with
      Pharaoh Creek trail.

Healy Pass and the vast wildflower
meadows leading to its summit are a
popular destination for hikers who are up
for a very full day of wandering and
exploration. Though the pass is not exceptionally high, views are as rewarding
as any in the park—a panorama of nearly
every peak along a 70-km stretch of the
Great Divide from Mount Assiniboine to
Storm Mountain. The trail is also the
favourite access route to Banff's most
popular backcountry campground at
Egypt Lake.

Climbing from the Bourgeau Parking
Lot at the base of the Sunshine gondola,
the trail follows a wide, bulldozed track
for nearly a kilometre before cutting off
onto a more aesthetic forest path.
Gradually, but steadily, the trail ascends
the Healy Creek valley, rising from a
dense canopy of Engelmann spruce and
alpine fir to vast subalpine meadows
where wildflowers bloom in lush
profusion from mid-July to late August.

The climb finally culminates among
the last scattered alpine larch on Healy
Pass. Since there are no nearby mountains blocking the view, this 2330-m pass
at the north end of the Monarch Ramparts ridge offers an excellent overview of
the surrounding landscape.

The block of peaks beyond the ridge to
the northeast is the Massive Range, dominated by Mount Brett on the left and
Mount Bourgeau to the right. Nearly 30
km away to the southeast, rising high
above all its neighbouring peaks, is the
3618-m "horn" of Mount Assiniboine—
the highest mountain in the Canadian
Rockies south of the Columbia Icefield.
Less than 6 km away, at the south end of
the Monarch Ramparts, is the massive
pyramid called The Monarch. And due
west of the pass, stacked beneath the
Pharaoh Peaks, lie Egypt and Scarab
Lakes.

The Monarch and Healy Meadows from near Healy Pass

Egypt Lakes. Most backpackers travel to the Egypt Lakes area by way of Healy Pass since it is both the shortest and most scenic approach. Continuing northwest over the summit of the pass, the trail drops rapidly through the forest to Pharaoh Creek in just over 3 km. Just 50 m past a right-hand spur trail to the Egypt Lake Warden Cabin, you reach the creek-side Natalko Lake trail junction and a bridge. Cross the bridge to the campground and shelter on the rise ahead.

Since all major trails for the area radiate out from the campground, it is ideally situated as a base camp for short half-day trips. (See *Egypt Lakes* introduction.)

Healy Meadows-Simpson Pass Circuit. On the way up Healy Creek you pass two side trails branching south to Simpson Pass, at km 5.9 and km 7.7. These trails provide the option of a short but scenic detour on your return from Healy Pass.

By following the higher of the two trails, you cross an extensive meadow, pass near several small lakes and descend to the summit of Simpson Pass in just 2.0 km. Take the trail branching left down the north side of the pass to rejoin the Healy Creek trail at the 5.9 km junction. This option adds only 1.5 km to the trip back from Healy Pass. (See also *Simpson Pass-Healy Meadows*.)

31 Egypt Lake via Pharaoh Creek

Trans-Canada Highway to Egypt Lake Campground—19.2 km (11.9 mi)

Backpack

Allow 5 to 6 hours one way

Elevation gain: 595 m (1,950 ft)

Maximum elevation: 1995 m (6,550 ft)

Maps: Banff 82 O/4

Access: Follow the Trans-Canada Highway to the Redearth Creek parking area, located on the south side of the highway 20 km (12.5 mi) west of Banff or 10.5 km (6.5 mi) east of Castle Junction. (A cross-over road provides access from westbound lanes.) The trail begins at a step-up gate through the wildlife control fence at the rear of the parking area.

0.0—Redearth Creek parking area (1400 m).

— Broad gravel trail through forest.

0.4—Trail joins old access road.

6.9—Redearth Creek bridge. Lost Horse Creek Campground (Re6).

10.5—Junction. Shadow Lake right 3.5 km; Pharaoh Creek ahead.

10.7—Redearth Creek Warden Cabin.

— Trail makes gradual ascent of Pharaoh Valley with bridge crossings of creek.

14.7—Pharaoh Creek Campground (Re16).

18.7—Junction. Pharaoh Lake right; Egypt Lake ahead.

19.2—Egypt Lake Campground (E13) and Shelter (1995 m). Intersection with the Bow Valley Highline and Healy Pass trails.

Hiking to the Egypt Lakes area by way of Redearth and Pharaoh Creeks is longer and not nearly as scenic as the popular approach over Healy Pass. However, this valley-bottom route is usually snow-free a week or two earlier in the season than the pass. The trail is sometimes used as an exit from Egypt Lakes (downhill all the way!) by those who arrange transportation between the Redearth Creek and Healy Pass trailheads. It also serves as the first (or last) leg of the Egypt Lakes-Shadow Lake circuit trip (see below).

Starting from the Redearth Creek trailhead on the Trans-Canada Highway, the route follows up the Redearth Valley at an easy grade to the Pharaoh Creek junction at km 10.5 (see *Redearth Creek-Shadow Lake*). From the junction, you pass the Redearth Warden Cabin and immediately enter the Pharaoh Creek valley. Continue to gain elevation gradually, crossing and recrossing the creek several times before reaching the Pharaoh Creek Campground. Over the last few kilometres to Egypt Lake Campground, there are open meadows with views of the Pharaoh Peaks.

Egypt Lakes-Whistling Pass-Shadow Lake Circuit. This loop trip allows you to sample some of the best scenery on the Bow Valley Highline Trail without the hassle of arranging transportation between distant trailheads. The clockwise approach follows the Pharaoh Creek route to Egypt Lakes, the Bow Valley Highline over Whistling Pass to Shadow Lake, and Redearth Creek back to your starting point. (There are no particular disadvantages to doing the circuit counter-clockwise.) This three to four day trip covers a total distance of 46 km. (See also *Bow Valley Highline Trail* and *Redearth Creek-Shadow Lake*.)

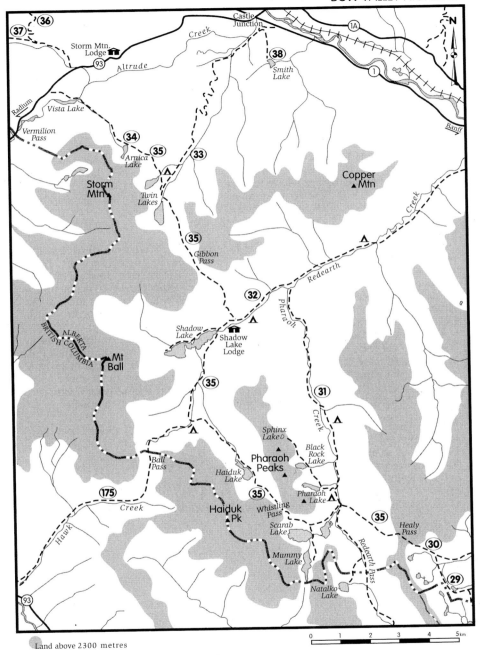

Land above 2300 metres

Egypt Lakes

"After thirty years of exploration, surveys and mapping of the main ranges of the Canadian Rockies, the writer can safely say that outstanding among them for scenic charm and interest may be classed the group of peaks, lakes and alpine meadows of the Egypt Lake area...."

—A.O. Wheeler, 1939

Pretty strong words coming from the founder of the Alpine Club of Canada and the man who surveyed the Great Divide. With that sort of endorsement, it is little wonder the Egypt Lakes area is the most popular backpacking destination in Banff Park.

The area is located near the continental divide just 25 km west of the town of Banff. Though there is only one Egypt Lake, the names of other nearby lakes—Scarab, Mummy, Pharaoh and Sphinx—have resulted in the term Egypt Lakes being applied to the area. In fact, A.O. Wheeler was responsible for naming all of the lakes when he surveyed this section of the Alberta-British Columbia boundary in 1913; the two pyramid-shaped Pharaoh Peaks overlooking the lakes had already been named, so he decided to stick with the Egyptian theme.

The Egypt Lake Campground, situated in a meadow 0.8 km from Egypt Lake, is the only site in the core area and the primary destination for most backpackers. There is also a shelter cabin that snugly accommodates 18 overnight guests; opened in 1969, it is one of only two such shelters ever constructed by Parks Canada in the mountain parks. The campground is perfectly situated as a base for half-day trips to all of the aforementioned lakes and Natalko (Talc) Lake, just over the divide in British Columbia. (All of these hikes are described on the following pages.)

This is all very nice, but the campground is one of the most popular destinations in Banff National Park, and the shelter is a rather grim, claustrophobic place when it is at capacity. Because of this popularity, it is one of only a few campgrounds in the park where the site quota is often filled. To insure a campsite or space in the shelter, you can reserve up to 3 months before your trip by contacting the Banff Visitor Centre (see *Sources-Park information*). There is an additional fee for staying at the shelter.

Access: There are three possible routes to the Egypt Lakes: the shortest and most scenic approach is the 12.4-km trail running over Healy Pass from the Bourgeau Parking Lot at end of the Sunshine Road (see *Healy Pass-Egypt Lakes*); a route following Redearth and Pharaoh Creeks is longer (19.4 km) and travels along valley bottoms, but there is less elevation gain and the ascent is gradual (see *Egypt Lake via Pharaoh Creek*); and backpackers hiking the Bow Valley Highline Trail from north to south, descend into the area from Whistling Pass (see *Bow Valley Highline Trail*).

Egypt Lake and "Sugarloaf Mountain"

Egypt Lakes Area Hikes

All of the following hikes are described from the Egypt Lake Campground.

Egypt Lake—0.8 km. The lowest of the Egypt Lakes at 2025 m, the area's namesake is a placid, green body of water bordered by forest and backed by a low, cone-shaped peak unofficially called Sugarloaf Mountain. Egypt Lake is usually the first place campers visit, often as an after-dinner stroll, following the long day's backpack to Egypt Lake Campground.

This short, flat walk begins on the Whistling Pass trail, which runs southwest from the campground. Follow the trail through the forest for 0.5 km to where the 0.3-km side-trail to Egypt Lake branches left.

Whistling Pass—3.3 km. No trip to Egypt Lakes is complete without visiting the Whistling Valley—a 2300-m pass providing far-reaching views along the eastern escarpment of the Great Divide. Along the way, you will most certainly want to include the 1.4-km side-trip to Scarab and Mummy Lakes—two *pater noster* tarns cradled in glacier-carved basins just above Egypt Lake. The round trip to Whistling Pass, including Scarab and Mummy, is 9.4 km, and can easily be completed in a half-day from the campground.

Follow the trail running southwest from the campground. After passing the Egypt Lake junction at 0.5 km, the trail switchbacks steeply upward through forest and over rockslides before descending into a larch-fringed meadow. In the middle of this meadow, at km 1.9, the trail to Scarab and Mummy Lakes branches left from the Whistling Valley trail.

Beyond Scarab-Mummy junction, the main trail continues upwards and bends northwest into the pass—a narrow rocky gap sandwiched between Haiduk Peak and the Pharaoh Peaks. Views north extend over Haiduk Lake and Valley to glacier-crowned Mount Ball (3312 m),

while Scarab Lake sparkles back to the south. And if they haven't become jaded by the continual passage of hikers, you will hear the long, shrill whistle of the resident hoary marmots, which gives the pass its name.

If you are backpacking through the Egypt Lakes region on the Bow Valley Highline route, Whistling Pass will be part of your itinerary. (See *Bow Valley Highline Trail*.)

Scarab-Mummy Lakes Option. From the 1.9-km junction on the Whistling Pass hike, the Scarab-Mummy Lakes branch descends through scattered stands of alpine larch and wildflower meadows for 0.6 km to the shore of Scarab Lake. The lake is bordered by subalpine forest and backed by scree slopes and cliffs, and its outlet stream makes a spectacular leap over a 100 m cliff to Egypt Lake below.

Continue to Mummy Lake by crossing at Scarab's outlet and scrambling up a short, steep track to a trail split beneath a cliff. The right branch ascends a 10-m escarpment to a meadow overlooking the lake's north end; the left branch takes a longer but somewhat easier route to the lake's east shore.

Mummy's setting is as high and wild as any lake in the Rockies—surrounded by alpine meadow, talus, cliffs and, at its far end, a gap in the Great Divide that serves as a window to distant mountains in British Columbia.

Pharaoh-Black Rock Lakes—2.4 km. This trail climbs to a pair of cirque lakes nestled beneath the eastern escarpment of the Pharaoh Peaks. It is one of the shortest trips from Egypt Lake Campground, but you gain 240 m of elevation in less than 2 km if you go all the way to Black Rock Lake.

Follow the Pharaoh Creek trail 0.5 km downstream from the campground to the Pharaoh Lake trail junction. The trail branches left and immediately begins a

Haiduk Lake and Valley from Whistling Pass

steep 0.8-km climb to Pharaoh Lake. While the lake's east end is densely forested with fir and larch, the cliffs of the south Pharaoh Peak create a dramatic backdrop.

Black Rock Lake lies 1.1 km beyond Pharaoh Lake via a rocky and rooty trail that climbs steeply through stands of alpine larch. It is appropriately named for the sharp, shadowy cliff of the north Pharaoh Peak, which looms above its southwest shore.

Natalko Lake—4.4 km. Situated just across the Great Divide in Kootenay National Park, Natalko Lake lies at 2180 m in a rocky bowl fringed by stands of alpine larch.

From the junction below the campground, follow the trail running due south to Redearth Pass. At a point 2.3 km from the junction, and just 0.5 km short of the park boundary on this brushy and unremarkable pass, the Natalko trail branches right. The lake is a stiff 1.9 km climb from this intersection.

Though shown on topo maps as Talc Lake, we prefer the original name, which commemorates one of the most unlikely wilderness enterprises in the Rockies. In 1917, park warden Bill Peyto filed a claim on the talc deposits at the lake. In the late 1920s, the National Talc Company (hence Natalko) took over the claim. The company built a wagon road to haul the talc down Pharaoh Creek to the CPR line—a distance of over 20 km! The claim was worked sporadically, but without any substantial production, into the 1940s. Scattered remnants of the operation and two cabins are near the lakeshore.

Experienced scramblers with a topo map can traverse the high col northwest of Natalko to Mummy Lake. This option allows you to loop back to Egypt Lake Campground via Mummy and Scarab Lakes and the Whistling Pass trail, but it can only be completed by strong, well-shod hikers who are good route-finders. Total distance for the loop is approximately 9 km.

32 Redearth Creek—Shadow Lake

Trans-Canada Highway to Shadow Lake—14.0 km (8.7 mi)

Day trip or backpack

Allow 3.5 to 4.5 hours one way

Elevation gain: 440 m (1,450 ft)

Maximum elevation: 1840 m (6,050 ft)

Maps: Banff 82 O/4

Access: Follow the Trans-Canada Highway to the Redearth Creek parking area, located on the south side of the highway 20 km (12.5 mi) west of Banff or 10.5 km (6.5 mi) east of Castle Junction. (A cross-over road provides access from westbound lanes.) The trail begins at a step-up gate through the wildlife control fence at the rear of the parking area.

0.0—Redearth Creek parking area (1400 m).

—Broad gravel trail through forest.

0.4—Trail joins old access road.

6.9—Redearth Creek bridge. Lost Horse Creek Campground (Re6).

10.5—Junction. Pharaoh Creek ahead; Shadow Lake right.

—Moderate uphill on single-track trail.

12.7—Shadow Lake Campground (Re14).

12.9—Shadow Lake Lodge.

13.0—Junction. Gibbon Pass right 3.1 km; Shadow Lake ahead.

14.0—Shadow Lake (1840 m). Outlet bridge.

—Trail continues along Haiduk Creek to Ball Pass (7.0 km), Haiduk Lake (7.5 km) and Whistling Pass (9.7 km).

Situated beneath the massive cliffs of Mount Ball, Shadow Lake is one of the more impressive lakes along the Great Divide. Many people hike to the lake and back in a day. Or you can bike-and-hike, since mountain bikes are permitted as far as Pharaoh Creek junction. Others prefer to overnight at Shadow Lake Lodge or the nearby campground and then day trip to several scenic backcountry locales, including Ball Pass, Haiduk Lake or Gibbon Pass.

The first three-quarters of the trip follow the broad track of the old talc mining road constructed up Redearth and Pharaoh Creeks in the late 1920s. The hiking is somewhat tedious, but the climb is gradual and it is easy to make good time.

At 10.5 km the Shadow Lake trail branches right from the road and climbs into the forest. (Mountain bikes are not permitted beyond this junction, and a rack is provided for lock-up.) From the junction it is only 2.2 km to Shadow Lake Campground and another 0.2 km to the lodge.

The trail to Shadow Lake continues upvalley beyond the lodge. It reaches the lake's eastern end at a footbridge spanning the outlet stream.

Shadow Lake is large compared with most subalpine lakes, stretching for over 2 km to the base of Mount Ball (3312 m). Carved from Cambrian limestone and quartzite formations and draped with glaciers, the mountain provides a photogenic backdrop for the lake.

The trail continues around the lake's south shore for a kilometre before breaking away up Haiduk Creek, bound for such destinations as Ball Pass, Haiduk Lake and Whistling Valley. (See trail descriptions on following pages.)

Mule deer at Shadow Lake's outlet and Mount Ball

Shadow Lake Area Hikes

Day trips in and around Shadow Lake originate at Shadow Lake Lodge or Campground. As of this writing, there are only 5 tent sites at the campground, so you should consider making reservations with Parks Canada if you plan to stay there.

The core of the Shadow Lake Lodge complex is the restored CPR rest cabin, which was built on the site in 1929-30. The cabin was used sporadically until the 1990s, when the Bud Brewster family of Banff, who held the lease, redeveloped the site into a backcountry cabin camp.

Today there are a dozen log guest cabins scattered along the margin of the meadow, a kitchen-dining room cabin, and the original CPR cabin, which serves as a guest lounge. In addition to overnight accommodation throughout the summer, the lodge offers afternoon tea and refreshments for guests and visiting hikers. (For contact information, see *Sources-Backcountry lodges.*)

Following are half-day and day trips from the campground and lodge.

Gibbon Pass—3.1 km. Gibbon Pass is the best short hike from Shadow Lake. The 2300-m summit is carpeted with wildflowers in summer and bordered by extensive stands of golden larch in mid-September. The pass is also an exceptional viewpoint for a long stretch of the Great Divide extending from the peaks near Lake Louise south to Mount Assiniboine.

The trail branches north from the Shadow Lake trail at 13 km, a few metres beyond the lodge junction. It climbs steeply through subalpine forest and soon emerges into alpine meadows on the pass.

You can continue over the pass to Twin Lakes, reaching Lower Twin Lake at km 6.0. While the hike to Twin Lakes is still a reasonable day trip from Shadow Lake, you will have to climb over Gibbon Pass again on the return.

If you have arranged transportation, you can exit from the Shadow Lake environs via Gibbon Pass and Twin Lakes. From Twin Lakes you can either continue over Arnica Summit to Highway 93 via the *Arnica Lake-Twin Lakes* trail, or descend to Castle Junction on the *Twin Lakes* trail. (See also *Bow Valley Highline Trail.*)

Ball Pass—8.1 km. Ball Pass is a rocky 2210-m gap on the crest of the Great Divide between Mount Ball and Haiduk Peak. While it can be reached in a long day from Highway 93 in Kootenay Park, the trail from Shadow Lake is shorter and not nearly as steep.

After hiking to Shadow Lake's outlet bridge, follow the trail continuing around the south shore and then along Haiduk Creek to Ball Pass Junction and Campground—a distance of 4.3 km from the outlet. Stay right at this junction and climb to the pass in another 2.7 km of steady uphill slogging.

The pass lies atop the Great Divide and is a passageway through the Ball Range just south of Mount Ball. The northern edge of the pass is filled with rockslides, but the remainder of the summit is composed of small meadows and stands of alpine fir and larch. A close-up view of Mount Ball's glacier-topped summit (3311 m) is the scenic highlight of the trip.

From the pass the trail continues down the Hawk Creek valley another 9.7 km to Highway 93 in Kootenay Park. (See *Hawk Creek-Ball Pass,* Kootenay Park chapter.)

Haiduk Lake—8.1 km. The rugged buttress of Haiduk Peak provides a dramatic backdrop for this peaceful lake at the foot of Whistling Pass. The hike to the lake and back is one of the longer trips from Shadow Lake, and even longer if you decide to extend the trip to or beyond Whistling Pass.

Follow the Haiduk Creek trail south from the Shadow Lake outlet for 4.3 km

Gibbon Pass

to Ball Pass Junction and Campground. Turn left and continue south for another 2.7 km, climbing steeply at first, then gradually through subalpine forest. You reach Haiduk Lake just after crossing to the east side of the creek.

Boundary surveyor A.O. Wheeler named the lake in 1913 "from a Polish word meaning 'lively, vigorous,' and when first seen with the sun, like diamonds, sparkling on its wind-blown ripples the name seemed to apply." (However, some Polish-speaking people dispute the meaning of the word.)

The trail travels briefly along the lake's east shore then makes a steep ascent in less than 2 km to the summit of Whistling Pass.

Strong hikers can make a long day trip from Shadow Lake and return by continuing over Whistling Pass to Egypt Lake and then returning to Shadow via the Pharaoh Creek and Shadow Lake trails. Total distance for the loop is 25 km. (See also *Bow Valley Highline Trail* and *Pharaoh Creek*.)

Shadow Lakeshore—3.0 km. This short hike follows rough and sometimes indistinct trail to the west end of Shadow Lake.

Follow the Shadow Lake trail to the lake from the campground or lodge. The unmarked lakeshore trail branches right from the Shadow Lake trail just before the lake's outlet bridge.

Rough trail rolls up and down through heavy forest above the north shore for 1.9 km before descending to a point near the shoreline. From there you can explore along the lake to its west end beneath the cliffs of Mount Ball.

The Ball Glacier and its ice caves were once an attractive if somewhat rigorous extension to this hike. However, one of the ice caves has collapsed and a major avalanche in 1999 covered much of the approach route with deadfall. The trip is hardly worth the effort.

Dedicated bushwhackers and scramblers can still make the very difficult journey by following up the obvious draw to the northwest for 2.7 km.

33 Twin Lakes

Altrude Creek Parking Area to Lower Twin Lake—8.1 km (5.0 mi)

Day trip or backpack

Allow 2 to 3 hours one way

Elevation gain: 605 m (2,000 ft)

Maximum elevation: 2055 m (6,750 ft)

Maps: Castle Mountain 82 O/5
      Banff 82 O/4

Access: Follow the Trans Canada Highway to the Castle Junction interchange, 30 km (18.5 mi) west of Banff and 26 km (16 mi) east of Lake Louise junction. Exit westbound to Radium on Highway 93 and watch for an access road just west of the Trans-Canada overpass branching south through the animal control fence. Follow this gravel road down into the forest 0.4 km to a parking area beside Altrude Creek and the trail head kiosk.

0.0—Altrude Creek parking area (1450 m).

—Cross bridge. Stay right at junction on old access road.

0.2—Junction. *Smith Lake* left 1.5 km. Twin Lakes ahead.

0.5—Roadbed narrows to single track.

0.8—Altrude Creek bridge.

2.4—Uphill grade steepens.

4.0—Grade moderates.

—Rocky, rooty trail with boggy sections.

6.3—Trail enters meadow.

—Track often faint following along stream.

7.9—Junction. Intersection with *Bow Valley Highline Trail*. Gibbon Pass left 2.9 km. Upper Twin Lake and Twin Lakes Campground (Tw7) right 0.8 km. Lower Twin Lake ahead.

8.1—Lower Twin Lake (2055 m).

"The Twin Lakes lie at the base of the scarped and nearly vertical front of the watershed range, which rises above them in stupendous cliffs, in the rifts and hollows of which, snow remains throughout the year."

Geologist George M. Dawson penned this apt description following a visit to the lakes on August 5, 1884.

Two trails of near equal length access Twin Lakes: our favourite, and the most scenic, runs from Highway 93 via Arnica Lake, but a lot of elevation is lost and gained en route (see *Arnica Lake-Twin Lakes*); the trail from Altrude Creek is scenery-poor, but there is less elevation gain and its all downhill on the return.

From Altrude Creek the trail climbs through uninspiring forest most of the way. At km 6.3 it emerges into meadows with views to Dawson's "stupendous cliffs." In these meadows the track becomes boggy and indistinct as it follows near the stream from Lower Twin Lake.

Just 0.2 km from Lower Twin you reach a junction: Upper Twin Lake and Campground are to the right; the Gibbon Pass trail crosses the outlet stream to the left; 200 m ahead is Lower Twin Lake—a wonderful foreground to the cliffs of Storm Mountain beyond.

You will also want to pay a visit to Upper Twin Lake—located in a near identical setting to Lower Twin. A pleasant campground is located just south of the lake's outlet meadow. Beyond Upper Twin Lake the trail continues north over Arnica Summit to Arnica Lake.

Gibbon Pass. Our favourite half-day hike from the campground—a 2.9-km climb from the junction below Lower Twin to stands of alpine larch, wildflower meadows and distant views. (See also *Bow Valley Highline Trail*.)

Lower Twin Lake

34 Arnica Lake—Twin Lakes

Vista Lake Viewpoint to Arnica Lake—5.0 km (3.1 mi)
Vista Lake Viewpoint to Upper Twin Lake—7.2 km (4.5 mi)

Half-day to day trip

Allow 1.5 to 2 hours to Arnica Lake

Elevation gain: 580 m (1,900 ft)
         loss: 120 m (400 ft)

Maximum elevation: 2150 m (7,050 ft)

Maps: Mount Goodsir 82 N/1
      Banff 82 O/4

Access: Follow the Banff-Radium Highway to the Vista Lake viewpoint, 8 km (5 mi) west of Castle Junction and 2 km (1.2 mi) east of the Banff-Kootenay Park boundary at Vermilion Pass. The viewpoint is a broad, paved pull-off on the south side of the highway overlooking Vista Lake and the Altrude Creek valley.

0.0—Vista Lake viewpoint (1450 m).

—Steady downhill through old burn.

1.4—Vista Lake outlet (1570 m).

—Steady uphill moderate to steep.

4.0—Trail enters subalpine forest.

4.2—Small pond.

—Steady climb.

4.6—Trail levels off.

5.0—Arnica Lake (2150 m).

5.8—Arnica Summit (2285 m).

—Steady downhill.

7.2—Upper Twin Lake (2090 m). Twin Lakes Campground (Tw7).

8.0—Junction. Twin Lakes trail from Altrude Creek left. Gibbon Pass ahead. Lower Twin Lake right.

8.2—Lower Twin Lake (2055 m).

Though the distance to Arnica Lake is not great, the hike is somewhat arduous—you start out by losing over 100 m of elevation, then gain nearly 600 m over the last 3.6 km. Yet, despite all its ups-and-downs, the hike to this tarn nestled against the imposing east face of Storm Mountain is one of the most popular along the Bow Valley Highline route. You can also make a full day trip—and a four-lake grand slam—by continuing on to Twin Lakes.

Starting at Vista Lake viewpoint on the Highway 93, the trail descends steadily through the silver spars of trees killed by a forest fire that swept Vermilion Pass in early July 1968. It soon reaches its lowest elevation beside Vista Lake, a peaceful green body of water that is a pleasant destination for less energetic hikers. You will want to spend some time here relaxing and enjoying the scene before tackling the steep climb ahead.

From the lake's outlet bridge, the trail climbs eastward across the lower slopes of Storm Mountain. Views along this stretch were quite open immediately following the '68 burn, but a dense cover of lodgepole pine, which seeded after the fire, is beginning to enclose the trail once more.

At km 4.0 you leave the burn and enter a mature subalpine forest, and not long after passing a small pond you reach the shores of Arnica Lake.

The lake is backed against the sheer cliffs of Storm Mountain and enclosed on three sides by a typical upper subalpine forest of Engelmann spruce and alpine fir with a scattering of larch. Its name comes from the yellow-flowered arnica, which blooms in this cool, moist forest during early summer.

From the lake's outlet the trail climbs for another 0.8 km to the summit of a forested ridge extending northeastward from Storm Mountain. By leaving the

Arnica Lake

trail and climbing along the ridge to the southwest, you are rewarded with extensive views north and south along the Bow Valley.

Twin Lakes. The trail continues over Arnica Summit to Twin Lakes, reaching Upper Twin and the campground after a steady 1.4-km descent. We prefer this approach to Twin Lakes over the more direct route from lower Altrude Creek because it is more open and scenic, and the distance is virtually the same. However, we often arrange transportation between the two trailheads and hike down to the Altrude Creek trailhead at Castle Junction on the way out, thereby avoiding all the ups-and-downs of returning via Arnica and Vista Lakes. (See also *Twin Lakes* and *Bow Valley Highline Trail*.)

35 Bow Valley Highline Trail

Sunshine Village to Highway 93—40.3 km (25.0 mi)

Backpack

Allow 3 to 4 days

Maximum elevation: 2360 m (7,750 ft)

Minimum elevation: 1570 m (5,150 ft)

Maps: Banff 82 O/4
      Mount Goodsir 82 N/1

Access: To reach the southern end of the Highline Trail, travel to Sunshine Village as described in the Sunshine Meadows area introduction. Start from the Simpson Pass-Healy Meadows trail head, below the day lodge at the base of the Wawa Ridge ski lift.

To reach the northern end, follow the Banff-Radium Highway to the Vista Lake viewpoint, 8 km (5 mi) west of Castle Junction and 2 km (1.2 mi) east of the Banff-Kootenay Park boundary at Vermilion Pass (see *Arnica Lake-Twin Lakes* trail description).

0.0—Sunshine Village (2200 m).

1.6—Twin Cairns-Meadow Park Junction.

1.9—Wawa Ridge summit (2360 m).

5.6—Simpson Pass (2135 m) and Junction.

6.0—Eohippus Lake Junction.

7.6—Healy Meadows Junction.

9.1—Healy Pass (2330 m).

12.3—Eygpt Lake Campground (E13) and Shelter (1995 m). Pharaoh Creek Junction.

12.8—Egypt Lake Junction.

14.2—Scarab-Mummy Lakes Junction.

15.6—Whistling Pass (2300 m).

17.8—Haiduk Lake.

21.0—Ball Pass Junction and Campground (Re21).

25.3—Shadow Lake.

26.3—Shadow Lake Lodge Junction (1820 m).

29.4—Gibbon Pass (2300 m).

32.3—Lower Twin Lake Junction (2055 m).

33.1—Upper Twin Lake and Twin Lakes Campground (Tw7).

The dream of a highline trail running along the southwest side of the Bow Valley from Banff to Lake Louise was hatched in August 1915, when Banff outfitter Jim Brewster, parks commissioner J.B. Harkin and two CPR officials rode north along the proposed route from the Sunshine Meadows. As reported in the Banff Crag and Canyon "the officials were more than delighted with the magnificent views of mountains, lakes and watersheds the section of the country traversed afforded, and firmly convinced of the desirability of such a trail being constructed...."

The CPR promoted and expanded the idea over the next 25 years and, in 1929-30, built "rest house" cabins for hikers and horseback riders at Sunshine and Shadow Lake. In 1929, the Trail Riders of the Canadian Rockies rode the southern half of "the long-wished-for High Line Trail from Banff to Lake Louise" for the first time. Ten years later the Trail Riders blazed the northern half of the route to Moraine Lake.

Though it is not officially designated as the Highline Trail today, the historic name seems appropriate. While the northern section is not well-defined or frequently hiked, the 40-km stretch from Sunshine Village to Highway 93 is a much travelled route linking the popular hiking destinations of Egypt Lakes, Shadow Lake and Twin Lakes. This attractive three to four day trip passes beneath the eastern escarpment of the Great Divide, over four 2300 m summits, near a dozen high lakes, and through vast wildflower meadows and stands of alpine larch.

The hike's only drawback is the popularity of the areas it passes through. There are only four campgrounds en route and campsite quotas are often filled (consider making advance reservations). However, it is possible to complete the trip without a tent by overnighting at

Egypt Lakes from Healy Pass on the Bow Valley Highline Trail

Haiduk Lake and Peak

34.5—Arnica Summit (2285 m).

35.3—Arnica Lake.

38.9—Vista Lake (1570 m).

40.3—Vista Lake Viewpoint on Highway 93 (1690 m).

Parks Canada's Egypt Lake Shelter and the commercially operated Shadow Lake Lodge (two opposite extremes in back-country accommodation!).

The southern section of the Highline Trail follows several trails described in more detail over the preceding pages of this section, starting from the south end on the *Simpson Pass-Healy Meadows* trail and finishing up on the *Arnica Lake-Twin Lakes* trail. Though we describe this trip from south to north, the direction it was travelled by the Trail Riders in 1929 and 1939, there is no disadvantage to hiking it in the opposite direction. (See also *Bow Valley Highline Trail—North.*)

Sunshine Village to Egypt Lake—12.3 km. The first 7.6 km of the Highline route follows the *Simpson Pass-Healy Meadows* trail to an intersection with the *Healy Pass-Egypt Lake* trail. (You can also hike the *Healy Pass-Egypt Lake* trail to this junction, but you will miss one of the 2300-m summits.)

At that junction, you turn left and continue over Healy Pass and down to

Egypt Lake Campground. Highlights of the trip are views from the summits of Wawa Ridge and Healy Pass and the wildflowers of Healy Meadows.

Backpackers usually travel from Sunshine Village or Bourgeau Parking Area to Egypt Lake Campground on the first day, and often spend a day there partaking of one or two of the area's excellent half-day hikes. (See descriptions for *Simpson Pass-Healy Meadows*, *Healy Pass-Egypt Lake* and *Egypt Lakes Hikes*.)

Egypt Lake to Shadow Lake—14.1 km. From Egypt Lake Campground, the trail climbs steeply through forest and across rockslides to the intersection with the Scarab and Mummy Lakes trail—a short, worthwhile detour to a pair of very scenic lakes (see *Egypt Lakes Hikes*).

Beyond the junction, you climb into the open meadows and rockslides of Whistling Valley and over 2300-m Whistling Pass. The valley was named for the resident hoary marmots, who provide ample warning of approaching hikers with a long, shrill whistle. The vale is also home to a healthy population of pikas, which can be seen darting over the rockslides near the trail.

As you near Whistling Pass there are views back to Scarab Lake and, when you crest the summit, an even more expansive vista north to Haiduk Lake and the escarpment of the Ball Range stretching to Mount Ball and Storm Mountain.

The trail drops rapidly from the pass to the shores of Haiduk Lake. After passing along the east shore of this sparkling lake with its Haiduk Peak backdrop, it crosses to the true left side of Haiduk Creek just below the outlet. The trail makes a gradual descent of the valley through scattered forest and then drops steeply to Ball Pass Junction and Campground.

Ball Pass is a worthwhile 2.7-km side-trip from this intersection, particularly if you camp here. (See Ball Pass description, *Shadow Lake Hikes*.)

The final 4.3 km to Shadow Lake is a rather humdrum stroll through forest and willow meadow; Shadow Lake Lodge and Campground lie just over a kilometre beyond the lake's outlet bridge. (For more details, see *Redearth Creek-Shadow Lake*.)

Shadow Lake to Highway 93—14.0 km. The Highline Trail route continues north from a junction just a few metres west of Shadow Lake Lodge. The trail climbs steeply through subalpine forest of spruce and fir and into meadows scattered with alpine larch on the summit of Gibbon Pass—3.1 km from the junction.

Since there are no nearby peaks blocking views to the north and southeast, the vista from the pass is quite remarkable. The most notable landmark is Mount Assiniboine (3618 m), which rises high above its neighbouring peaks 40 km to the southeast.

A cairn with a bronze plaque on the summit commemorates its naming for John Murray Gibbon, an author and CPR publicist who helped establish the Trail Riders of the Canadian Rockies in 1924 and Sky Line Hikers in 1933. Gibbon, who was a promoter of the Highline Trail and other long-distance trails in the Rockies, rode over this pass with the Trail Riders in 1929 and accompanied the crew that blazed the northern section of the trail in 1938.

While the trail over the pass is indistinct in places, you should have no trouble finding it again as you descend the northern slope. Just before re-entering dense forest there are views to your next objective—Lower Twin Lake.

You intersect the Twin Lakes trail 2.9 km from Gibbon Pass, just 0.2 km below the lower lake. After visiting the lake, return to the junction and climb to nearby Upper Twin Lake and Twin Lakes Campground—the last campground on the Highline route.

The final 7.2 km of the Highline Trail crosses Arnica Summit to Arnica Lake, plunges down to Vista Lake, and then makes one last brief climb to Highway 93. (See *Arnica Lake-Twin Lakes*.)

36 Bow Valley Highline Trail—North

Banff-Radium Highway to Moraine Lake—23.2 km (14.4 mi)
Banff-Radium Highway to Lake Louise—44.3 km (27.5 mi)

Day trip or backpack

Allow 7 to 9 hours to Moraine Lake

Elevation gain: 650 m (2,150 ft)
loss: 485 m (1,600 ft)

Maximum elevation: 2180 m (7,150 ft)

Maps: Lake Louise & Yoho (Gem Trek)

Access: Northbound hikers begin at the Boom Creek Picnic Area on the Banff-Radium Highway, 7 km (4.5 mi) west of Castle Junction (see *Boom Lake*). Southbound travellers start on the *Consolation Lakes* trail at Moraine Lake.

0.0—Boom Creek Picnic Area (1720 m).

2.3—Junction. *Boom Lake* trail ahead 2.8 km; Highline Trail right.

—Steep uphill over tight switchbacks.

3.9—Forested ridgetop (2180 m).

—Trail descends then contours northwest. Track disappears in meadow sections.

8.2—Junction. O'Brien Lake left 0.5 km. Taylor Lake and Highline ahead.

9.8—Taylor Creek crossing. Intersection with *Taylor Lake* trail. Turn left.

10.1—Taylor Lake (2300 m).

10.2—Taylor Lake Campground (Ta6).

—Steady climb through forest.

10.6—Panorama Meadows. Trail disappears.

11.7—Trail reappears on right side of meadow.

11.9—Old prospector cabins.

—Track vague to non-existent across meadow.

16.6—Trail descends and bends west.

—Rough, wet track.

21.2—Large meadow and pond.

21.6—Babel Creek bridge. Intersection with *Consolation Lakes* trail. Moraine Lake right.

23.2—Moraine Lake Picnic Area (1885 m).

Though not as scenic as its southern section, the northern extension of the Bow Valley Highline Trail does offer occasional views out over the Bow Valley, passes by O'Brien and Taylor Lakes, and traverses numerous wildflower meadows bordered by alpine larch.

Unfortunately the trail has received little attention or maintenance since 1938, when it was first blazed by Banff outfitter Claude Brewster and his crew in preparation for the Trail Riders' annual ride the following summer. Expect the worst and plan on rough, boggy trail coupled with long periods of tedious route-finding. (This trip is reserved for experienced route-finders armed with a topo map.)

While this route is sometimes referred to as the Panorama Ridge trail, the section from Boom Creek to Taylor Lake is well south of the ridge. A steep but well defined track leads up from the Boom Lake trail to the forested summit of a ridge extending southeast from Mount Bell.

As the trail descends beyond the ridge problems develop quickly. In several meadows the track disappears entirely, and you must search around on the opposite side of each meadow for its reappearance. (We followed fresh flagging when we did this trip a long time ago, but though you may be lucky enough to find ribbons, markers or cairns, don't expect many visual aids other than tree blazes.)

In the midst of dense forest at km 8.2 you reach the short side-trail to O'Brien Lake. From this point a rough but defined track leads you the rest of the way to Taylor Lake. Taylor Lake makes an excellent lunch stop for day hikers, and there is a campsite at the east end for backpackers. (See *Taylor Lake*.)

The trail continues from the rear of the

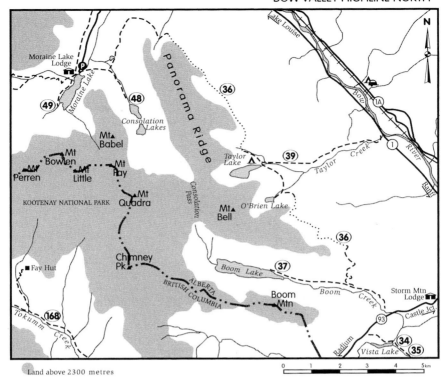

Land above 2300 metres

0   1   2   3   4   5km

campground and climbs to the Panorama Meadows in 0.5 km. This is a remarkable area in mid-September when the larch stands have turned to gold, but during the summer the track disappears in the lush meadows. (By continuing along the right side of the meadow for just over a kilometre, you should rediscover the trail exiting to the right into the forest.)

Two old prospector cabins, which date to the days of Silver City (circa 1883), are passed soon after you leave the meadow, followed by more meadows and route-finding headaches. (Nice views over the valley, though.)

The route stays high along the northeast slope of Panorama Ridge for the next 4 km. This is the most difficult section on the entire trip, and you can only persevere while looking for markers, cairns or other signs of human passage along the edges of meadows and

through sections of forest. When the track begins its descent beyond the meadows, you're home free.

Though it is rough, rooty and often boggy, the trail becomes more defined as it quickly loses elevation and bends around the north end of Panorama Ridge. After skirting a shallow pond set in a large, marshy meadow, you reach the much-travelled Consolation Lakes trail. Turn right to reach Moraine Lake in another 1.6 km.

You can complete the trip to Lake Louise by hiking the final 22 km via Sentinel Pass, Paradise Valley, Sheol Valley and Saddleback. However, since there is some doubt about the future of the Paradise Valley Campground, you may have to day hike it. (See *Larch Valley-Sentinel Pass, Paradise Valley,* and *Saddleback-Fairview Mountain.*)

37 Boom Lake

Banff-Radium Highway to Boom Lake—5.1 km (3.2 mi)

Half-day trip

Allow 1.5 hours one way

Elevation gain: 175 m (575 ft)

Maximum elevation: 1895 m (6,210 ft)

Maps: Mount Goodsir 82 N/1
 Lake Louise 82 N/8
 Lake Louise & Yoho (Gem Trek)

Access: Follow the Banff-Radium Highway (Hwy 93) to the Boom Creek Picnic Area, located on the north side of the highway 7 km (4.5 mi) west of Castle Junction. The trail begins from the bridge at the rear of the picnic area.

0.0—Boom Creek Picnic Area (1720 m).

—Steady gradual to moderate uphill on broad track.

2.3—Junction. Bow Valley Highline Trail and Taylor Lake right. Boom Lake ahead.

5.0—Trail narrows to footpath.

5.1—Boom Lake (1895 m).

The Boom Lake trail is an easy 5-km walk to a beautifully formed lake contained by a massive 600-m limestone wall and glacier-mantled peaks. The trail is often snowfree (but still wet) in early June, which makes it a popular early season outing. It is also fun to visit the lake in late spring and early summer when the snowpack on Boom Mountain is breaking up and where, on a sunny day, you can see numerous avalanches cascading down the mountain's north face.

For most of its length the trail is a wide, bulldozed track that climbs at a moderate grade well above the creek. In the spring many small streams make the trail a bit sloppy, but the runoff redeems itself by offering numerous chances for refreshment and a well-watered forest with lush undergrowth.

Just before the trail reaches the lake it narrows to a traditional footpath, and 100 m beyond it ends abruptly at a rockslide that has tumbled down from the slope to the north into the eastern end of the lake. A bit of rock-hopping will get you to the water's edge.

The broad north face of Boom Mountain soars above the lake's south shore, and the glaciated spires of Mount Quadra (3173 m) and Bident Mountain (3084 m) rise beyond its far end.

The Alpine Club of Canada held its annual camp at nearby Vermilion Pass in 1912, and later documented how Boom Lake received its name:

"Boom Lake is so called from the fact that near its eastern extremity an old moraine, at one time the bounding wall of the lake, now just touches the surface which has overflowed it. It spans the lake in a crescent, some distance from the eastern end, and intercepts the drift wood floating down the lake. The appearance created is that of a lumber boom, and hence the name."

Boom Lake

38 Smith Lake

Altrude Creek Parking Area to Smith Lake—1.8 km (1.1 mi)

This peaceful little lake hidden in the forest on the south slope of the Bow Valley is not well known nor frequently visited. Despite the lake's relatively low elevation (1600 m), the trail to it climbs steadily and gains 150 m over the course of the journey. Views from its shores are limited to glimpses of Copper and Castle Mountains.

From the Altrude Creek trailhead cross the bridge spanning the creek and, from a junction 50 m beyond, follow the Twin Lakes trail to the right. The Smith Lake trail branches left in another 100 m.

Though you mainly travel through valley-bottom forest for the remainder of the journey, there are occasional meadows where a wide variety of wildflowers bloom in mid-July.

At 1.7 km the trail crests a forested rise where you get your first view of the lake,

then descends steeply for 100 m to its shore.

The lake was named for Joe Smith, Banff Park's most famous hermit. Smith was the lone resident of the nearby ghost town of Silver City from around 1884 until 1937. He did a lot of prospecting and trapping in the area over the years and undoubtedly visited this lake many times.

Access: Follow the Trans Canada Highway to the Castle Junction interchange, 30 km (18.5 mi) west of Banff. Exit westbound to Radium on Highway 93 and watch for an access road immediately west of the Trans-Canada overpass bridge, which branches south through the animal control fence. Follow this gravel road 0.4 km to a parking area beside Altrude Creek and the trailhead kiosk. *Maps: Castle Mountain 82 O/5.*

39 Taylor Lake

Trans-Canada Highway to Taylor Lake—6.3 km (3.9 mi)

Day trip

Allow 1.5 to 2 hours one way

Elevation gain: 585 m (1,920 ft)

Maximum elevation: 2065 m (6,780 ft)

Maps: Lake Louise 82 N/8
　　　Lake Louise & Yoho (Gem Trek)

Access: Follow the Trans-Canada Highway to Taylor Creek Picnic Area, located on the southwest side of the highway 8 km (5 mi) west of Castle Junction or 17 km (10.5 mi) east of Lake Louise Junction. The trail begins across the bridge at the rear of the parking area.

0.0—Taylor Creek Picnic Area (1480 m).

　—Gradual to moderate uphill on broad track.

1.0—Taylor Creek bridge.

　—Steady uphill.

5.8—Taylor Creek bridge.

6.1—Junction. Intersection with *Bow Valley Highline Trail-North.* O'Brien Lake left 2.1 km. Taylor Lake ahead.

6.3—Taylor Lake (2065 m).

6.4—Taylor Lake Campground (Ta6). Highline Trail to Panorama Ridge Meadows branches uphill from rear of campground.

Taylor Lake is one of the most accessible of several hanging valley lakes along the southwest side of the Bow Valley between Banff and Lake Louise. It is every bit as scenic as its sister lakes and offers the added bonus of two attractive side-trips from its shores.

The trip to the lake is straightforward and not particularly inspiring, travelling over an old cat-track that switchbacks steadily up the side of the valley through a closed forest of lodgepole pine and spruce.

The goal is well worth the drudgery of the climb, however, as the trail suddenly emerges into meadow near the lake's outlet—a moist area carpeted with western anemone, marsh marigold, buttercups, and mountain laurel through much of the summer. Fringing the meadow and much of the lakeshore is a typical upper subalpine zone forest of alpine fir and Engelmann spruce dotted with the pale green foliage of alpine larch.

The north face of Mount Bell rises abruptly from the south shore of the lake, forming a 750-m wall. The low notch of Taylor Pass to the west separates Mount Bell from Panorama Ridge and serves as a rock scrambler's route to the Consolation Valley and Moraine Lake.

A small, five-site campground lies within the forest margin at the east end of the lake—an easy destination for anyone who wants to spend a night out without travelling a great distance. It is also a welcome stop for more energetic souls beating their way along the rough northern section of Bow Valley Highline Trail (see *Bow Valley Highline Trail-North.*)

Taylor Lake

O'Brien Lake. This lake is located in a smaller cirque 2.1 km to the south. With a more lavish display of wildflowers along its shore and more alpine larch in the surrounding forest, it can be even more charming than Taylor.

To reach the lake cross Taylor Creek at the trail sign 0.2 km below Taylor Lake. Follow the rocky but well travelled track that drops below the Mount Bell cliffs and then climbs steeply to the level of the O'Brien cirque. Watch for a sign indicating the junction where the O'Brien trail branches to the right. The 0.5-km side-trail all but disappears in the boggy meadows, but by staying along the left side of the lake's outlet stream you soon reach your destination.

Panorama Meadows. By following the Panorama Ridge-Highline Trail north from the rear of the Taylor Lake Campground for 0.5 km (a steep, steady climb), you can visit one of the great wildflower meadows and larch forests in the Rockies. The snow-streaked cliffs of Panorama Ridge serve as a backdrop to this long, gently rising meadow, which in summer is quite verdant and filled with the tall showy blooms associated with snowbed communities. In mid-September the surrounding forest is awash with gold as the larch trees reach their autumn colour peak.

The meadow and scattered larch forest extend uphill for well over a kilometre. While the trail disappears at the lower end of the meadow, you can wander and explore uphill for an hour or more and, by following along the meadow's outlet stream, discover three small lakes at the head of the basin.

For travel south from O'Brien Lake junction or north from Panorama Meadows, see the *Bow Valley Highline Trail-North* trail description.

Lake Louise—Moraine Lake

There are few hiking areas that can rival the Lake Louise-Moraine Lake region. Compressed within 100 sq km are seven major hikes and a variety of options—over 70 km of trail traversing some of the most rugged alpine scenery on the continent.

Lake Louise was the birthplace of recreational hiking in the Canadian Rockies. After the completion of the Canadian Pacific Railway in 1885, tourists began making their way to the area. The CPR built a small chalet on the shore of Lake Louise in 1890, and manager Willoughby Astley immediately began clearing trails to scenic points above the lake. One of these early trails was to Lake Agnes—named in honour of Lady Susan Agnes Macdonald, wife of Canada's Prime Minister Sir John A. Macdonald, who hiked to the lake in 1890.

In 1893, a pair of young adventurers from the eastern United States, Walter Wilcox and Samuel Allen, began a systematic exploration of the region. The following summer, accompanied by three Yale University classmates, they discovered and explored Paradise Valley, Sentinel Pass and the upper end of the Valley of the Ten Peaks, and made the first ascent of Mount Temple. In 1899, Wilcox and a companion made the first recorded visit to Moraine Lake and nearby Consolation Valley.

Wilcox and Allen named many local features, and their explorations led to further trail construction by the CPR. As these trails became popular, the CPR built teahouses and shelters at strategic locations. In fact, hotel staff maintained much of the trail system through the mid-20th century.

Today these trails are the most heavily used in the Canadian Rockies, and on sunny midsummer days there is a continuous stream of humanity on the most popular routes. Still, these trips are some of the most spectacular in the Rockies, and in autumn, when the crowds have thinned, they are exceptionally rewarding.

The most popular trails from Lake Louise are Lake Agnes, Plain of Six Glaciers and Saddleback, all starting from the lakeshore near the Chateau. Moraine Lake lies at the entrance to the Valley of the Ten Peaks and is the departure point for hikes to Consolation Lakes, Larch Valley-Sentinel Pass, and Eiffel Lake-Wenkchemna Pass. Between Louise and Moraine is Paradise Valley with its circuit trail to Lake Annette and the Giant Steps.

Note: Paradise Valley and Moraine Lake trails have been subject to restrictions for several seasons due to bear activity. Check with the Lake Louise Visitor Centre or the park website for current access requirements. (See *Sources-Parks information.*)

Access: From the Trans-Canada Highway interchange, the road to Lake Louise and Moraine Lake immediately passes through Lake Louise Village. A small shopping mall and the Park Visitor Centre are in the village core, and service stations, restaurants, hotels and a hostel are nearby. Lake Louise Campground is just over 1.0 km from the village centre.

Lake Louise Drive climbs west from the village for 5.5 km to Lake Louise, where parking is available in one of several large lots just south of the Chateau.

The Moraine Lake Road branches south from Lake Louise Drive 3 km from the village and rolls along the west side of the Bow Valley for 12 km to a parking area at the end of Moraine Lake. The Paradise Valley trail begins at a parking area on the right side of the Moraine Lake Road at km 2.5.

Parking lots at Lake Louise and Moraine Lake often overflow during peak season. To alleviate some of the congestion, Parks Canada operates a bus service from Lake Louise Campground and Village to Lake Louise and Moraine Lake for those staying at the campground or in village accommodation. The service operates from late June to Labour Day. Contact the Lake Louise Visitor Centre or campground for details.

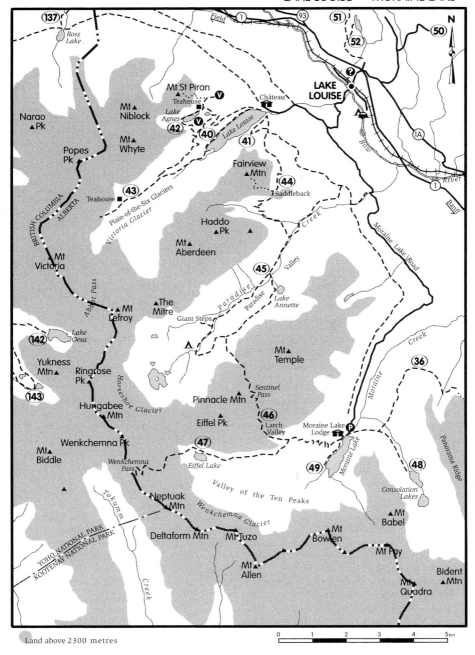

Lakeshore Trail

40 Lakeshore Trail

Chateau Lake Louise to Lake Louise west end—1.9 km (1.2 mi)

Believe it or not, we have actually walked to the west end of Lake Louise and back on the very popular lakeshore trail and not met another soul. (Admittedly it was early in the season and very late afternoon.) Yet, there are worse ways to spend an hour than strolling along this broad, flat trail with its ever-changing views of great peaks.

The walk starts from the trail sign just west of the Chateau and follows along the north shoreline to where the silt-laden waters from the Victoria Glacier feed into the lake. Away from the crowds and confusion surrounding the hotel, you can better appreciate the description by British mountaineer James Outram shortly after the turn of the 20th century: "At every season, every hour, it is wonderful.... As a gem of composition and of colouring it is perhaps unrivalled anywhere."

At the far end of the lake the trail climbs over a low rise and traverses beneath quartzite cliffs, which are often decorated by the colourful ropes of Lycra-clad rock climbers. And if you sit down to have a snack, you'll undoubtedly be greeted by other "head-of-the-lake" inhabitants, including golden-mantled ground squirrels, least chipmunks, Clark's nutcrackers and grey jays.

Back across the lake, the Chateau floats like the Titanic on the distant shore with the ski-run laced slopes of Whitehorn Mountain rising beyond. Its enough to make a person want to keep on hiking. (See *Plain of the Six Glaciers.*)

Access: Follow the paved shoreline trail in front of Chateau Lake Louise north 200 m to a junction with the Lake Agnes trail. Stay left and continue west along the lake's north shoreline. *Maps: Lake Louise 82 N/8; Lake Louise & Yoho (Gem Trek).*

Chateau Lake Louise from Fairview Lookout

41 Fairview Lookout

Lake Louise to Fairview Lookout—1.0 km (0.6 mi)

This short, moderately steep hike from the lakeshore near the Chateau Lake Louise takes you through the cool Engelmann spruce-alpine fir forest above the lake and provides a pleasant escape from the busyness of the lakeshore. The view of the Chateau and the east end of the lake from the wooden observation platform at the top is partially obscured by trees and, as advertised, only fair.

From the shoreline viewpoint near the boathouse, follow the Saddleback trail. At 0.3 km branch right onto the Fairview trail. The last 0.7 km follows a broad, smooth track, climbing steadily through mossy forest to the viewing platform, 140 m above lake level.

You can return the way you came or continue west down a steep, rocky track that descends sharply through forest and across a rockslide to the south shore of the lake. Walking back to the boathouse along the shore there are nice open views of the Chateau and canoes paddling about on the lake, though the trail is rough, wet and rooty. Round trip distance for the circuit is 2.3 km.

Access: From the paved shoreline trail in front of Chateau Lake Louise, walk to the viewpoint and trail sign on the south side of the lake's outlet stream near the boathouse. *Maps: Lake Louise 82 N/8; Lake Louise & Yoho (Gem Trek).*

42 Lake Agnes and the Beehives

Lake Louise to Lake Agnes—3.5 km (2.2 mi)
Lake Louise to Big Beehive—5.1 km (3.2 mi)

Half-day to day trip

Allow 1 to 1.5 hours to Lake Agnes

Elevation gain: 400 m (1,300 ft)

Maximum elevation: 2135 m (7,000 ft)

Maps: Lake Louise 82 N/8
 Lake Louise & Yoho (Gem Trek)

Access: From the public parking lots southeast of the Chateau Lake Louise, walk to the paved shoreline trail in front of the hotel. Continue on the shoreline trail100 m beyond the hotel to the Lake Agnes-Plain of Six Glaciers junction and trail sign.

0.0—Lake Agnes-Plain of Six Glaciers Junction (1735 m)

 —Steady uphill on broad track.

1.7—Switchback. View to Lake Louise.

2.5—Junction. Intersection with horse trail.

2.7—Mirror Lake (2025 m). Junction. Lake Agnes highline trail and Plain of Six Glaciers left. Lake Agnes right.

 —Steady climb via switchbacks.

3.2—Junction. Little Beehive right (1.2 km); Lake Agnes ahead.

3.5—Lake Agnes and Teahouse (2135 m).

3.6—Junction. Little Beehive (0.9 km) and Mt St. Piran (2.5 km) uphill to right. Lake Agnes shoreline and Big Beehive ahead.

4.3—Lake Agnes west end.

 —Steep switchbacking ascent.

4.8—Big Beehive summit ridge. Junction. Plain of Six Glaciers highline route ahead; Big Beehive Lookout left.

5.1—Big Beehive Lookout (2255 m).

Lake Agnes is hidden in a hanging valley high above Lake Louise. It has been one of the Rockies' most popular hikes ever since Lady Susan Agnes Macdonald, wife of Prime Minister Sir John A. Macdonald, hitched up her skirts and scrambled to its shores in 1890. In addition to its own charms, which include a teahouse, the lake and the nearby Beehives provide breathtaking views of Lake Louise and a broad stretch of the Bow Valley.

The first half hour from the shore of Lake Louise follows a broad, moderately graded trail through dense subalpine forest. At 1.7 km the first switchback marks a break in the trees where you have a clear view down to the pale turquoise waters of Lake Louise.

Another kilometre of forest-enclosed climbing brings you to Mirror Lake—a tiny sink lake that takes its name from its round looking-glass appearance. The dark, layered cliffs of the Big Beehive loom above, and, in the gap to the right, the roof of the Lake Agnes Teahouse is barely visible.

By taking the Plain of Six Glaciers highline trail to the left at the Mirror Lake junction, you can make a direct ascent to Lake Agnes via a steep trail that angles across rockslides beneath the Big Beehive. (This short cut branches right from the highline trail 150 m beyond this junction.) But if this steep trail is wet, icy or snowy, avoid it and follow the traditional route that branches right at Mirror Lake (it is only 0.2 km longer).

Regardless of which option you choose, the journey to Lake Agnes is completed on one of two steep, wooden staircases, which surmount a cliff band beside the waterfall created by the lake's outlet stream.

Arriving at the narrow opening where Lake Agnes tumbles from its basin, the entire length of the lake suddenly

Lake Agnes

appears, stretching westward to a jagged backdrop created by Mounts Whyte (2983 m) and Niblock (2976 m). The teahouse sits atop the cliff on the north side of the outlet stream, just a few metres from the lake.

The original Lake Agnes Teahouse was constructed shortly after the turn of the century. The present-day version was built in 1981. It serves refreshments and light snacks from mid-June to early October and is one of the big attractions for many who do this hike. While its covered porch is a relaxing place to sit and admire the view, it is usually a very busy place. (We like to stop there shortly after it opens at 10 am or just before 6 pm closing to avoid the crowds.)

The area surrounding Lake Agnes abounds with wildlife of the upper subalpine forest, especially those species who like to be where people are eating. Least chipmunks, golden-mantled ground squirrels, Clark's nutcrackers and grey jays congregate around the teahouse porch and beg for food. (Don't feed them! They do well enough from the crumbs they find on the ground.) The hoary marmots and pikas, who whistle and cheep from the rocky slopes above the lakeshore, are somewhat less corrupted by humanity.

Many hikers end their day with a stroll along the shore of Lake Agnes to its boulder-strewn western end. But there are options for more energetic souls, including side-trips to the summits of the Little Beehive and Big Beehive. You can also complete a full day circuit by crossing over the Big Beehive to the Plain of the Six Glaciers.

Lake Agnes to Little Beehive—0.9 km.
The Little Beehive is the most popular short hike beyond Lake Agnes. Though not as high as the nearby Big Beehive, it provides better views of both Lake Louise and the Bow Valley, and you won't work as hard to get there.

The trail branches uphill from the Lake Agnes shoreline trail 50 m beyond the teahouse. It climbs steadily to the northeast through alpine fir and larch forest and across avalanche slopes. Along the way there are a number of rocky viewpoints on the right overlooking Lake Louise, the hanging valley containing Lake Agnes, and Mount Aberdeen and the glacier-crowned peaks of Mounts Lefroy and Victoria. Stands of larch become thicker as you climb, making this a very rewarding trip in the last two weeks of September when their needles turn to gold.

The trail ends at the 2225 m Little Beehive summit and the foundation of the old fire lookout cabin. Views are quite impressive, including a panorama of the Bow Valley that stretches from the mountains near its headwaters to the peaks surrounding Banff to the south. Across the way the Pipestone Valley stretches north into some of the wildest country in Banff Park. (You will want to bring a map to appreciate all the landmarks visible from this vantage point.)

Lake Agnes to Mt. St. Piran—2.5 km.
The 2650 m summit of Mount St. Piran is one the best viewpoints overlooking the Lake Louise environs and the Bow Valley (second only to nearby Fairview Mountain). For strong hikers who would escape the crowds on the more popular routes, and who don't mind a good stiff climb, this side-trip from the Little Beehive trail is an excellent option.

Follow the Little Beehive trail from Lake Agnes for 0.5 km to where the St. Piran trail branches uphill to the left (marked by a pole with no sign in 1999). A narrow but obvious footpath climbs steeply through stands of larch and then switchbacks up steep, open slopes to the summit. The track disappears on the summit ridge, but the route is obvious— UP!

While views from the summit to Lake Louise are obscured, you can look down upon Lake Agnes to the south and tiny Minewakun Lake in the forested valley to the north. This lofty viewpoint also provides an exceptional perspective of nearby peaks and distant landscapes.

Lake Louise from the Little Beehive trail

Lake Agnes to Big Beehive—1.6 km.
Another popular trip beyond the Lake
Agnes Teahouse is the hike to the 2255 m
summit of the Big Beehive.

The trail to the Big Beehive continues
around the far end of the lake and climbs
a steep series of switchbacks to a
junction on the Beehive summit ridge.
Traverse eastward along the rocky,
lightly forested ridge to a gazebo-style
shelter on the northeast edge of the
promontory.

Though somewhat obscured by trees,
there are views over the Bow Valley and
down to Lake Louise, over 500 m below.
(Do not attempt to shortcut down from
the gazebo viewpoint in any direction;
there are dangerous cliffs on all sides.
Return back along the ridge the way you
came.)

**Lake Agnes-Plain of the Six Glaciers
Circuit—14.5 km.** Hikers looking for a
full day's outing can include the Plain of
the Six Glaciers in their itinerary after
visiting Lake Agnes and the Big Beehive.

Cross the Big Beehive's summit ridge
at the viewpoint trail junction and follow
a steep trail down the south side. In just
over a kilometre you reach an
intersection with the highline trail running upvalley from Mirror Lake. Turn
right and follow this trail as it descends
across the lower slopes of Devil's Thumb
to an intersection with the Plain of the
Six Glaciers trail.

Continue upvalley toward the imposing, glacier-topped summits of Mounts
Lefroy and Victoria for another 1.4 km to
the Plain of the Six Glaciers Teahouse.
After visiting the teahouse and, perhaps,
the Abbot Pass viewpoint farther
upvalley, you return to Lake Louise on
the *Plain of the Six Glaciers* trail.

43 Plain of the Six Glaciers

Lake Louise to Plain of the Six Glaciers Teahouse—5.5 km (3.4 mi)

Half-day to day trip

Allow 1.5 hours one way

Elevation gain: 340 m (1,115 ft)

Maximum elevation: 2070 m (6,800 ft)

Maps: Lake Louise 82 N/8
      Lake Louise & Yoho (Gem Trek)

Access: From the public parking lots southeast of Lake Louise, walk to the paved shoreline trail in front of the Chateau Lake Louise. Continue on the shoreline trail 100 m beyond the hotel to the Lake Agnes-Plain of Six Glaciers junction and trail sign.

0.0—Lake Agnes-Plain of Six Glaciers Junction (1730 m).

— Follow lakeshore trail.

1.9—West end of Lake Louise.

2.4—Steady climb begins.

3.3—Junction. Big Beehive shortcut right.

—Steady, moderate climb along avalanche paths.

4.1—Junction. Highline route to Mirror Lake-Big Beehive intersects from right.

—Grade steepens through glacial moraines and along valley slope.

5.5—Plain of Six Glaciers Teahouse (2070 m).

—Gradual to moderate climb from meadow and along ridge of lateral moraine.

6.8—Talus slope. Abbot Pass viewpoint (2195 m).

The Plain of the Six Glaciers trail transports you into the heart of the Canadian Rockies' most famous postcard view and sets you down beneath the glacier-capped summits of Mounts Victoria and Lefroy. And if scenery isn't enough, you can stop for a spot of tea on the sheltered verandah of one of the Rockies' oldest backcountry teahouses. However, don't expect much solitude on one of Banff's most popular trails.

Starting from the trail sign 100 m northwest of the Chateau, follow the busy lakeshore trail to the far end of Lake Louise. Beyond the lake's silty inlet, the crowds thin as the trail climbs steadily through subalpine forest and across the occasional avalanche path. Eventually it emerges into a landscape scoured by the the Victoria Glacier, where views open to Mounts Victoria and Lefroy.

After passing the intersection with the highline trail from Mirror Lake and the Big Beehive, you ascend along the edge of old glacial moraines. A final series of steep switchbacks lead to a meadow bordered by alpine fir and larch, where the teahouse suddenly appears.

The Plain of the Six Glaciers Teahouse was constructed by the CPR in the mid-1920s. Refreshments and light snacks are served throughout the summer season, and its open-air verandah is an ideal vantage point for the frequent avalanches thundering off Mounts Lefroy and Victoria in the early summer.

If the teahouse is overflowing with visitors, as it often is, you can relax in the meadow below the teahouse and scan the nearby boulder-field for hoary marmots and pikas.

The trail continues upvalley beyond the teahouse for another 1.3 km. Along the way it traverses the crest of a lateral moraine—a steep ridge of debris formed during the last advance of the Victoria Glacier, which reached its zenith during the mid-1800s. Today it provides an

Mount Victoria from the Plain of the Six Glaciers trail

excellent viewpoint for the rock and boulder-covered ice of the Victoria Glacier below.

Beyond the moraine, the trail fizzles out on a steep talus slope. While this slope is a rather precarious resting spot, it is the best viewpoint for 2922 m Abbot Pass between the towering summits of Mount Victoria (3464 m) and Mount Lefroy (3441 m). You can see the Abbot Pass Hut on the summit skyline—a substantial stone structure constructed by CPR Swiss guides in 1922 as an overnight shelter for mountaineers. Today it is operated by the Alpine Club of Canada and is Canada's highest National Historic Site.

The pass is named for the American alpinist Philip Stanley Abbot, who fell to his death while attempting the first ascent of Mount Lefroy in 1896—the first mountaineering fatality in North America. The steep, ice-filled couloir rising from the Victoria Glacier to the pass is known as "The Death Trap", so-named by early mountaineers because avalanches frequently fall into it from the cliffs above. (Don't even dream of

heading in that direction unless you are an experienced, well-equipped mountaineer and have checked with Parks Canada about current route conditions.)

Lake Agnes-Plain of Six Circuit—14.5 km. Strong hikers looking for a full day's outing can return to Lake Louise via the Big Beehive and Lake Agnes. From the trail junction 1.4 km below the teahouse, follow the highline route toward Mirror Lake for 2 km, branch left on the Big Beehive trail and cross over its summit ridge to Lake Agnes. This option adds approximately 4 km to the normal 11.0 km round trip to the Plain of Six Teahouse and includes a very strenuous climb over the Big Beehive (2255 m).

This classic loop allows you to visit the two most famous destinations above Lake Louise in one day. However, we prefer to go to Lake Agnes first and then cross the Big Beehive to Plain of Six Glaciers, since this approach seems somewhat less arduous and the views more rewarding. (See *Lake Agnes and the Beehives*.)

44 Saddleback—Fairview Mountain

Lake Louise to Saddleback—3.7 km (2.3 mi)

Half-day to day trip

Allow 1 to 2 hours to Saddleback

Elevation gain: 600 m (1,970 ft)

Maximum elevation: 2330 m (7,650 ft)

Maps: Lake Louise 82 N/8
Lake Louise & Yoho (Gem Trek)

Access: From the public parking lots southeast of Lake Louise, walk to the lake's outlet stream. Continue up along the south side of the stream to the trailhead, located on the forest margin to the left just short of the boathouse.

0.0—Trail sign (1730 m).

—Follow broad trail up through dense subalpine forest.

0.3—Junction. Fairview Lookout right 0.7 km.

0.4—Junction. Moraine Lake-Paradise Valley left. Saddleback right.

1.1—Avalanche path.

—Steady moderate to steep uphill.

2.7—Trail climbs through stands of alpine larch.

3.7—Saddleback Summit (2330 m). Fairview Mtn right 1.3 km. Sheol Valley ahead.

To see Mount Temple in its noblest grandeur I would take you to the Saddleback. This is a broad green alp, nearly 2000 feet above Lake Louise, a very favourite hour's ascent by trail, between Mount Fairview and the projecting 'horn' of the Saddle Peak. Crossing the plateau to the tree-fringed brink of the abyss beyond, our gaze is carried straight across the chasm, 1500 feet in depth, to the huge peak.

This description of Saddleback published by British mountaineer James Outram in 1905 sums up the glories of this short, strenuous hike from Lake Louise. The trail is also one of the best places to view golden-needled alpine larch in late September, and it is the approach to a spectacular viewpoint atop Fairview Mountain.

In its early stages the trail climbs steadily through the forest. At the end of the first kilometre it crosses a major avalanche path on Fairview's northeast slopes, where you have a clear view back to the Chateau and distant Mount Hector. Farther along, the trail angles up to the southwest and begins the final steep, switchbacking ascent to the pass.

Views improve just below the summit, stretching down the length of the Bow Valley to the mountains near Banff. You also pass through a stand of unusually large, and probably very old, alpine larch (core samples from similar trees in nearby Larch Valley reveal ages of more than 400 years).

Saddleback is a pleasant upland meadow where buttercups, western anemone, alpine speedwell and many other wildflowers bloom in early summer. And as Outram noted, the towering north wall of Mount Temple (3544 m) dominates the view south of the pass.

The best view of Temple, looming over tiny Lake Annette and Paradise Valley, is obtained by descending southeast

Mount Victoria from Fairview Mountain summit

approximately 200 m along the summit ridge. Follow a faint path through scrub alpine fir to an open promontory overlooking Sheol Valley—a classic alpine viewpoint that has even been exploited by Hollywood (John Barrymore gripped his leading lady Camilla Horn in a passionate embrace here during the filming of *Eternal Love* in August, 1928).

From Saddleback summit, you can scramble to Saddle Peak for even better views of Mount Temple and Paradise Valley. But many hikers are willing to expend more effort to reach the grandiose views atop Fairview Mountain.

Fairview Mountain—1.3 km. With the glacier-crowned summits of Mount Victoria, Mount Temple and Sheol Mountain close by, and the turquoise waters of Lake Louise a vertical kilometre below, the 2745 m summit of Fairview Mountain offers a true alpine experience. The peak is arguably the highest trail-accessible point in the mountain parks, though the 1.3 km track scratched up its rocky slope many decades ago has largely disappeared.

Follow faint trail northwest from Saddleback summit to begin the ascent. Continue upwards on often vague, switchbacking track, or simply scramble over loose rock towards the obvious summit. (You may have to skirt snowbanks early in the season.)

Sheol Valley Option. You can extend your journey by continuing over Saddleback and down through the Sheol Valley. You pass through several lush meadows on the descent and reach the Paradise Valley trail 4.1 km beyond Saddleback.

From the Paradise Valley trail intersection return to the Saddleback trailhead by following the Paradise trail downvalley, and then the Moraine Lake trail back around Saddle Peak. Total distance for the loop trip is 15 km.

45 Paradise Valley

Moraine Lake Road to Lake Annette—5.7 km (3.5 mi)
Paradise Valley Circuit—18.1 km (11.2 mi)

Half-day to day trip

Allow 1.5 to 2 hours to Lake Annette

5 hours for Paradise Valley Circuit

Elevation gain: 385 m (1,250 ft)

Maximum elevation: 2105 m (6,900 ft)

Maps: Lake Louise 82 N/8
  Lake Louise & Yoho (Gem Trek)

Access: Follow Lake Louise Drive from the village of Lake Louise 3 km (1.9 mi) to the junction with the Moraine Lake Road. Follow Moraine Lake Road 2.5 km (1.5 mi) to the Paradise Valley parking area, located in the forest on the right side of the road.

0.0—Paradise Valley parking area (1720 m).

1.1—Junction. Moraine Lake left; Paradise Valley right.

1.3—Junction. Lake Louise ahead 4.0 km; Paradise Valley left.

4.2—Junction. Saddleback right 4.2 km.

5.1—Junction. Paradise Valley Circuit split. Giant Steps ahead 3.7 km. Lake Annette left.

—Trail crosses Paradise Creek bridge and climbs through forest.

5.7—Lake Annette (1965 m).

—Trail climbs southwest from lakeshore.

6.5—Paradise Valley highline trail summit (2105 m).

8.8—Junction. Sentinel Pass left 2.3 km.

9.4—Horseshoe Meadows Junction (2090 m). Paradise Valley Campground (Pa8) left 0.3 km. Giant Steps ahead.

9.6—Junction. Giant Steps left 0.9 km. Paradise Circuit ahead.

9.9—Junction. Giant Steps left 0.6 km. Paradise Circuit ahead.

13.0—Lake Annette Junction. Paradise Valley Circuit split.

18.1—Paradise Valley parking area (1720 m).

When Walter Wilcox and his companions climbed to the summit of Mitre Pass from Lake Louise in 1894, they looked into "a valley of surpassing beauty, wide and beautiful, with alternating open meadows and rich forests." They named it Paradise Valley.

Today the valley is accessible by trail from the Moraine Lake Road. At a point just over halfway up the valley, the trail splits to create a circuit that visits all the major features in its upper reaches— Lake Annette, the Horseshoe Meadows and the Giant Steps. Completing the entire valley circuit takes a full day, or you can simply make a half-day trip to Lake Annette and back.

The first 3 km are uneventful and forest enclosed, but at the first bridge over Paradise Creek views open to Mount Temple and the valley headwall. In another 1.0 km you cross back to the true left side of the creek and pass the Sheol Valley-Saddleback junction.

The trail split for the upper valley loop is at km 5.1. While the Giant Steps lie 3.7 km upvalley on the low trail, most hikers will want to turn left, cross Paradise Creek and climb directly to Lake Annette. (If you are completing the valley circuit, the highline trail beyond Lake Annette allows better views of the valley's glaciated headwall than the lower Giant Steps approach.)

The British mountaineer James Outram called Lake Annette "a tiny bit of sky dropped from the heavens and almost lost in the depths of the sombre firs." Its immediate surroundings are typical of many subalpine lakes, but its backdrop— the ice-capped 1200 m north face of Mount Temple—is extraordinary. This wall is one of the most difficult ascents in North America and was unclimbed until 1966. If you see one of the massive avalanches that sweep the face, you will understand why.

Paradise Valley

Paradise Valley Circuit. The trail to the head of the valley continues southwest from Lake Annette, climbing along the base of Mount Temple. In just over a kilometre, you reach the circuit's highest elevation atop a major rockslide. There are good views ahead to the valley's headwall, formed by Hungabee Mountain and Ringrose Peak, and the Horseshoe Glacier sprawled across its base. Meanwhile, hoary marmots and pikas ignore the scenery as they go about their affairs in the surrounding boulders.

After passing Sentinel Pass junction, the trail descends to the lush Horseshoe Meadows, where it makes two bridged stream crossings in rapid succession and turns back down-valley.

If you plan on overnighting in Paradise Valley, the only campground lies in the scattered trees at the meadow's northwest corner (a site that is often booked to capacity). The campground is a good base for explorations to the Horseshoe Glacier environs or Wastach Pass.

The Giant Steps—a pretty series of waterfalls on the north fork of Paradise Creek—are just off the trail to the left on the way back down-valley. Watch for an unmarked trail branching left to the top of the this waterfall staircase 200 m beyond the campground junction. At the bottom of the falls, a rough, boggy track continues down-valley to rejoin the Paradise Valley trail. (If you come up the valley trail, the lower trail to the falls is more obvious, marked by a signed junction.)

While Giant Steps is a nice name for this photogenic cascade, we prefer the more colourful "Giant's Staircase", which was used by the Alpine Club of Canada when it held its camp here in 1907.

You complete the upper valley circuit by walking down-valley for another 3 km to the circuit trail split at the Lake Annette junction.

Sentinel Pass Option. The traverse over Sentinel Pass from Moraine Lake to the Paradise Valley trailhead is a popular trip for those who can arrange transportation between the two trailheads. (See *Larch Valley-Sentinel Pass* description.)

46 Larch Valley—Sentinel Pass

Moraine Lake to Larch Valley—2.4 km (1.5 mi)
Moraine Lake to Sentinel Pass—5.8 km (3.5 mi)

Half-day to day trip

Allow 2 hours to Sentinel Pass

Elevation gain: 724 m (2,376 ft)

Maximum elevation: 2611 m (8,566 ft)

Maps: Lake Louise 82 N/8
      Lake Louise & Yoho (Gem Trek)

Access: Follow Lake Louise Drive from the village of Lake Louise 3 km (1.9 mi) to the junction with the Moraine Lake Road. Continue on the Moraine Lake Road 12.5 km (7.5 mi) to the parking area at Moraine Lake. Walk to the lakeshore and continue past the lodge to the trail sign.

0.0—Trail sign (1887 m). Larch Valley trail branches up to the right from the shoreline trail.

1.1—Switchbacks begin.

  —Steady uphill climb.

2.4—Junction. Eiffel Lake-Wenkchemna Pass ahead. Larch Valley-Sentinel Pass right.

  —Trail climbs into Larch Valley meadows.

4.5—Upper Minnestimma Lake.

4.7—Switchbacks begin up steep talus slope.

5.8—Sentinel Pass (2611 m).

  —Very steep descent through boulders and talus to Paradise Valley.

8.1—Junction (2100 m). Intersection with *Paradise Valley* trail at km 8.8.

Larch Valley is one of the most heavily visited trail destinations in the mountain parks. And no wonder. This meadowland above Moraine Lake, with its dense stands of alpine larch and panoramic overview of the Ten Peaks, is exquisite. And above the valley, amid stark pinnacles of rock, is Sentinel Pass—the highest point reached by a major trail in the mountain national parks.

From Moraine Lake the trail climbs through a forest of Engelmann spruce and alpine fir, following a steadily ascending series of switchbacks much of the way. At km 2.4 the trail branches right from the Eiffel Lake trail and immediately enters the lower meadows of Larch Valley.

This high valley is the main focus for most hikers who walk the trail, and in late September, when alpine larch needles have turned to gold, it is the most visited area in the Rockies. In midsummer, however, the larch needles are a pale green and the meadows are carpeted with wildflowers.

The trail continues to climb through larch and meadows, and by the time it emerges above the last trees, there are fine views back to the rugged Ten Peaks, the ice-capped summit of Mount Fay (3235 m) being the most prominent and striking. The small lakes that dot the upper meadows of the valley were named Minnestimma, an Indian word meaning "sleeping water," by the pioneer alpinist Samuel Allen.

Ahead, between the rugged walls of Pinnacle Mountain on the left and Mount Temple on the right, is the 2611 m summit of Sentinel Pass. After passing the uppermost Minnestimma Lake, the trail begins a switchbacking climb of the steep, open slope leading to the pass—a vertical rise of nearly 200 m that weeds out many Larch Valley hikers.

The rock formations surrounding

Mount Fay from Larch Valley's Minnestimma Lakes

Sentinel Pass lie nearly horizontal, and erosion of these layers has created the weird spires immediately north of the summit. The pass receives its name from these towers, the tallest of which is called the Grand Sentinel.

The pass was first ascended in 1894 by Samuel Allen and Yandell Henderson, members of a group of American mountain climbers exploring the Lake Louise region. A few days later they returned to the pass with their companions and climbed 3544 m Mount Temple, which was the first ascent in Canada above 11,000 feet.

Paradise Valley Option. Strong hikers who have arranged transportation between trailheads at Moraine Lake and Paradise Valley, can continue north over Sentinel Pass and descend into Paradise Valley.

The trail down the north slope of the pass is extremely steep for more than a kilometre, switching back and forth through a field of boulders where good footwear and balance are necessary. (Route-finding is difficult on this precipitous descent, and trail-obscuring snowfields often linger into late summer near the bottom of the slope. The trail should be avoided entirely when the boulders near the pass are snow or ice-covered.)

It is 2.3 km from Sentinel Pass to the junction with the Paradise Valley trail, and a vertical descent of 500 m. (Ascending the pass from the Paradise Valley side is a brutal grunt.)

At the Paradise Valley trail junction, you can turn right to Lake Annette or left to the head of the valley and the Giant Steps. Both trails rejoin lower in the valley and follow Paradise Creek to the Moraine Lake Road. Total distance from Moraine Lake to the Paradise Valley trailhead via the Lake Annette high route is 16.9 km. (See also *Paradise Valley*.)

47 Eiffel Lake—Wenkchemna Pass

Moraine Lake to Eiffel Lake—5.6 km (3.5 mi)
Moraine Lake to Wenkchemna Pass—9.7 km (6.0 mi)

Half-day to day trip

Allow 1.5 to 2 hours to Eiffel Lake

3 hours to Wenkchemna Pass

Elevation gain: 733 m (2,405 ft)

Maximum elevation: 2620 m (8,595 ft)

Maps: Lake Louise 82 N/8
      Lake Louise & Yoho (Gem Trek)

Access: Follow Lake Louise Drive from the village of Lake Louise 3 km (1.9 mi) to the junction with the Moraine Lake Road. Continue on the Moraine Lake Road 12.5 km (7.5 mi) to the parking area at Moraine Lake. Walk to the lakeshore and continue past the lodge to the trail sign.

0.0—Trail sign (1887 m). Larch Valley-Eiffel Lake trail branches right from the shoreline trail.

1.1—Switchbacks begin.

—Steady uphill climb.

2.4—Junction. Larch Valley-Sentinel Pass right. Eiffel Lake-Wenkchemna Pass ahead.

—Trail levels out, contouring across open slopes.

5.6—Eiffel Lake (2255 m). Trail traverses talus slope above lake.

—Moderate but steady uphill over alpine meadows and talus slopes.

9.7—Wenkchemna Pass (2600 m).

Following their explorations to Wenkchemna Pass and the upper end of the Valley of the Ten Peaks in 1894, Walter Wilcox and his companions were so overwhelmed by the stark, boulder-filled landscape they named it Desolation Valley. In its deepest and most desolate heart lies Eiffel Lake.

The Eiffel Lake trail follows the same course as the Larch Valley trail for the first 2.4 km, switchbacking upward through closed forest from the north end of Moraine Lake. Splitting near the lower edge of Larch Valley, the Eiffel Lake trail continues along the north side of the Valley of the Ten Peaks. It soon emerges onto open slopes where all of the ten summits are revealed across the valley as well as the brilliant blue waters of Moraine Lake far below.

As the trail continues through flower-filled meadows the Wenkchemna Glacier is barely discernible in the valley below. Heavy rockfall from the cliffs above the glacier has completely covered most of its surface, shielding the ice from the sun's rays and accounting in part for the glacier's relatively small recession over the past century.

At km 5.6 the trail passes across a steep scree slope above Eiffel Lake. Reflecting upon one of his first visits to the lake, Walter Wilcox wrote: "It would be difficult to find another lake of small size in a wilder setting, the shores being of great angular stones, perfectly in harmony with the wild range of mountains beyond. Except in one place where a green and inviting slope comes down to the water, this rough ground is utterly unsuitable for vegetation and nearly devoid of trees."

Eiffel's rugged surroundings were created by a massive rockslide that broke away from Neptuak Mountain in the distant past and spread rock debris across the valley. In fact, the lake undoubtedly

Eiffel Lake and the Valley of the Ten Peaks

formed after the slide, which created a natural dam for water flowing from the snowfields at the head of the valley.

Immediately above the lake to the north is Eiffel Peak (3085 m), named for a rock pinnacle near its summit that resembles the famous Parisian tower. Looking at the peak from this angle, you can see the striking contrast between the grey limestone composing its summit and the orange-red quartzite of the lower cliffs.

If you don't want to labour down over 200 m of broken rock to reach Eiffel Lake, you can enjoy an overview of both lake and the Ten Peaks by continuing west along the trail to a sheltering grove of larch trees—Wilcox's "green and inviting slope."

Wenkchemna Pass. You can hike beyond Eiffel Lake for another 4 km to one of the highest trail accessible points in the mountain national parks and an outstanding viewpoint for the Valley of the Ten Peaks.

The trail continues due west across rolling alpine meadows, then climbs over moraine and along the rocky south ridge of Wenkchemna Peak before descending to the windswept gap between Wenkchemna Peak and Neptuak Mountain. (Sections of the trail may be obscured by snowfields before late July.)

Standing on the crest of the Great Divide, you overlook the entire length of the Valley of the Ten Peaks. On the west side of the divide is the rocky Eagle's Eyrie region of Yoho Park and, further south, the forested headwaters of Tokumm Creek in Kootenay Park.

The elevation of Wenkchemna Pass is listed on most maps as being 2600 m, or 11 m lower than nearby Sentinel Pass. Yet you lose at least 20 m as you descend to its summit. So, who knows, this may qualify as the highest maintained trail in the mountain national parks.

48 Consolation Lakes

Moraine Lake to Lower Consolation Lake—2.9 km (1.8 mi)

Half-day trip

Allow 45 minutes one way

Elevation gain: 65 m (215 ft)

Maximum elevation: 1950 m (6,400 ft)

Maps: Lake Louise 82 N/8
       Lake Louise & Yoho (Gem Trek)

Access: Follow Lake Louise Drive from the village of Lake Louise 3 km (1.9 mi) to the junction with the Moraine Lake Road. Continue on the Moraine Lake Road 12.5 km (7.5 mi) to the parking area at Moraine Lake. Walk down through the picnic area to the bridge over Moraine Creek, just below the lake outlet.

0.0—Trail sign and bridge (1887 m).

—Trail climbs around rockslide.

0.1—Junction. Spur trail to top of Rockpile left 0.3 km.

—Gradual climb into forest.

1.6—Junction. Panorama Ridge left.

2.3—Open meadow.

2.9—Lower Consolation Lake (1950 m).

The hike to Lower Consolation Lake is the shortest of the popular hikes beyond Moraine Lake, but the rugged scenery is as rewarding as that found on many longer journeys.

After departing the Moraine Lake Picnic Area, the trail passes over a substantial rockslide, which is the natural dam that created Moraine Lake. A short trail branches to the top of the "Rockpile", where you are greeted by the classic view of Moraine Lake and the Valley of the Ten Peaks.

Beyond the rockslide, the trail enters a forest of spruce and fir and climbs gradually along the west side of Babel Creek. Just over halfway to the lake you pass the Panorama Ridge trail junction (see *Bow Valley Highline-North*), and a short distance beyond the trail levels out along a meadow. The track in this section is often quite muddy.

A large rockslide blocks direct access to the north end of Lower Consolation Lake, but you can scramble onto one of the many large boulders in the slide for a relaxed view of the lake and the glacier-capped summits of Bident and Quadra beyond. Mount Temple commands the view back down-valley to the north—at 3544 m, the third highest mountain in Banff Park and the highest in the Lake Louise-Moraine Lake vicinity.

Upper Consolation Lake. If you want to spend a little more time in the area and are well shod, you can visit Upper Consolation Lake. Cross Babel Creek below Lower Consolation Lake on rickety log booms, then follow a rough, muddy track along the lake's eastern shore. At the far end, climb over a ridge of rock debris separating the two lakes.

Bident Mountain and Mount Quadra from Lower Consolation Lake

49 Moraine Lakeshore

Moraine Lake Lodge to Moraine Lake inlet—1.2 km (0.7 mi)

In 1899, Walter Wilcox and Ross Peacock set out to explore the lower reaches of "Desolation Valley", which Wilcox had surveyed from the summit of Mount Temple five years earlier. After a hard bushwhack into the valley, Wilcox came to a "massive pile of stones" blocking the way ahead. He climbed to the top and, behold, "there lay before me one of the most beautiful lakes that I have ever seen."

Today, thousands climb to Wilcox's viewpoint to photograph the classic view of the lake. However, the trail down its west shoreline, away from the crowds milling about the parking lot, lodge and viewpoint, allows for peaceful appreciation of what many visitors feel is one of the most beautiful lakes they've ever seen.

From the trail sign just beyond Moraine Lake Lodge, continue on the lakeside trail. The trail remains flat and close to the shoreline all the way to the lake's inlet at its southwest end. Along the way, you have continuous views across the lake to the rugged summits of the first five of the Ten Peaks rising from its eastern shore. Most impressive is Peak #1, Mount Fay, with its prominent summit glacier.

Access: Follow Lake Louise Drive from the village of Lake Louise 3 km (1.9 mi) to the junction with the Moraine Lake Road. Continue on the Moraine Lake Road 12.5 km (7.5 mi) to the parking area at Moraine Lake. Walk to the lakeshore and continue past the lodge along the lake. *Maps: Lake Louise 82 N/8; Lake Louise & Yoho (Gem Trek).*

Boulder Pass and Skoki

Hidden behind the Lake Louise ski area are the high valleys, passes and lakes of the Slate Range—an area of over 200 sq km that is one of the exceptional hiking areas in the Canadian Rockies.

Despite the area's proximity to Lake Louise, it was not visited or explored to any extent before the first decade of the 20th century. After A.O. Wheeler conducted the first topographical survey of the region in 1906, pioneer mountain adventurers, like Walter Wilcox and Mary Schäffer, began to visit the range and explore its many wonderful features.

James Foster Porter, a mountaineer from Winnetka, Illinois, visited the region in 1911 and named many of the natural features, including the Skoki Valley. "Skokie", as he spelled it, is a Potawatomi (Ojibwa) word meaning "swamp", which probably refers to the well-watered Merlin Meadows. (Porter would use the name again many years later when the Chicago suburb of Skokie was being created.)

Skoki Lodge was built in the valley by a group of Banff ski enthusiasts in 1930. It began operation as one of the first backcountry ski lodges in the Canadian Rockies in 1931 and was enlarged to its present dimensions in 1936. Designated a National Historic Site in 1992, it continues to serve hikers and skiers.

The main access route, the *Boulder Pass-Skoki Valley* trail, starts at the base of Whitehorn mountain, not far from the Lake Louise ski area's parking area and day lodge. The trail runs up the Corral Creek valley from the Fish Creek Parking Area to Boulder Pass, through the Ptarmigan Valley, across Deception Pass, and down into the Skoki Valley.

While this is the most popular route, there are many side trails and countless options for both day hikers and backpackers. You should have 1:50,000 scale maps with you on any trip to this region; study them before you depart so you understand all the possibilities and can customize the outing to fit your party's tastes and abilities.

The trail is also an access point for more serious wilderness adventures, including trips into the remote Red Deer Valley and along the Sawback Trail between Lake Louise and Banff. (See *Sawback Trail*.)

Boulder Pass–Ptarmigan Valley. A lofty treeline-alpine region that is noted for its high lakes surrounded by lush wildflower meadows. In essence it encompasses the area south and east of Deception Pass on the *Boulder Pass-Skoki Valley* trail, and much of it can be accessed by strong hikers in a long day. But since there are a number side-trips, to places like Hidden Lake, Redoubt Lake and Baker Lake, you may prefer to backpack to the Hidden Lake Junction or Baker Lake Campgrounds and explore in a more leisurely manner.

Skoki Valley. Deception Pass (2475 m) is the highest point on the *Boulder Pass-Skoki Valley* trail. Everything north of the pass is considered part of the Skoki Valley area.

Skoki Lodge is in the heart of the valley. The rustic lodge with outlying cabins provides accommodation and meals for guests throughout the summer and winter months. It also serves afternoon tea to drop-in visitors. (See *Sources-Backcountry lodges*.)

Strong hikers can visit the Skoki Valley in a long day, but most visitors overnight at Skoki Lodge or the Merlin Meadows Campground just below the lodge. Merlin Lake is the best day hike from Skoki Lodge and the campground.

Note: Skoki Valley has been identified as important range for female grizzly bears. To reduce disturbance of these animals, Parks Canada requests hikers to stay on designated trails and limit travel to daylight hours.

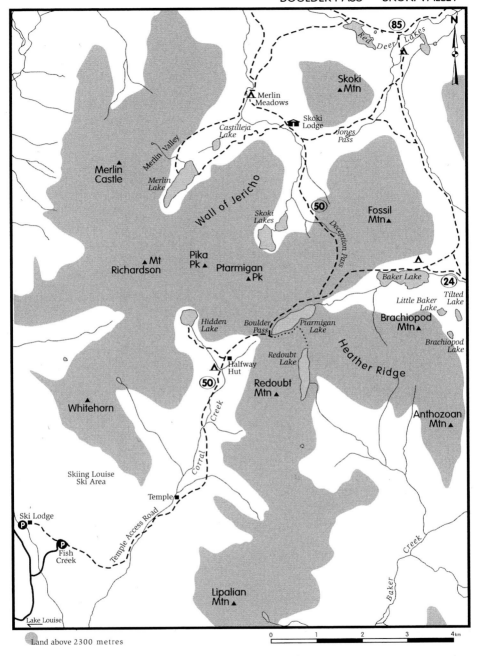

Land above 2300 metres

0   1   2   3   4 km

50 Boulder Pass—Skoki Valley

Fish Creek Parking Lot to Boulder Pass—8.6 km (5.3 mi)
Fish Creek Parking Lot to Skoki Lodge—14.4 km (8.9 mi)

Day trip or backpack

Allow 2 to 3 hours to Boulder Pass
    3.5 to 5 hours to Skoki Valley

Elevation gain: 785 m (2,575 ft)

Maximum elevation: 2475 m (8,120 ft)

Maps: Lake Louise 82 N/8
      Hector Lake 82 N/9
      Lake Louise & Yoho (Gem Trek)

Access: From the Trans-Canada Highway interchange at Lake Louise, follow Whitehorn Road uphill toward the Lake Louise ski area. At 1.7 km turn right onto the gravel Fish Creek Road and follow it 1.0 km to the Fish Creek Parking Area.

0.0—Fish Creek Parking Area (1690 m).

—Follow Temple access road.

3.9—Temple Lodge and ski lifts (2010 m).

—Trail climbs across ski slope for 200 m and enters forest.

6.3—Corral Creek meadow.

7.1—Junction. Left 0.1 km to Hidden Lake Campground (Sk5) and Hidden Lake (1.3 km). Halfway Hut right 100 m. Boulder Pass ahead.

—Steady uphill.

8.6—Boulder Pass (2345 m). Ptarmigan Lake (west end).

10.5—Junction. Baker Lake ahead 1.3 km. Deception Pass and Skoki Valley left.

—Steep uphill over open terrain.

11.0—Deception Pass (2474 m).

—Steady downhill.

13.9—Junction. Red Deer Lakes Campground right 4.6 km. Skoki Lodge ahead.

14.4—Skoki Lodge (2165 m).

15.6—Merlin Meadows Campground (Sk18).

This is the main access trail running to Skoki Valley in the heart of the Slate Range. Boulder Pass-Ptarmigan Valley is a spectacular destination for day hikers, highlighted by Ptarmigan Lake, wildflower meadows, rugged mountains and views to the distant peaks of Lake Louise. Backpackers usually travel on over Deception Pass to Skoki Valley, where they use Skoki Lodge or the Merlin Meadows Campground as base camps for half-day to day long trips to nearby points of interest.

The trail begins at the Fish Creek Parking Area, located at the bottom of the 4 km-long service road to the Temple day lodge and ski lifts. The hike up the gravel access road will not bring joy to your heart, but it is the fastest way to the sublime landscape beyond. (Mountain bikes are currently permitted to the end of the road, and lodge guests are transported to the end of the road by van to begin the hike.)

Once past the ski lifts at Temple, the road reverts to trail, which climbs steeply across a ski run and into a pleasant subalpine forest of spruce and fir with a scattering of alpine larch. The trail is wide and easily graded, but since it is used for commercial horse trips and pack trains supplying the lodge, it is often quite muddy.

You enter a long meadow 2.4 km beyond Temple, where there are views ahead to Boulder Pass and the rugged summits of Mount Richardson, Pika Peak and Ptarmigan Peak—the mountains that form the core of the Slate Range. Back to the southwest, 15 km away, glacier-topped Mount Temple (3544 m) dominates the skyline.The meadow is filled with a wide variety of colourful wildflowers in mid-summer, and slate-coloured dippers are often seen flying from rock to rock along nearby Corral Creek.

Redoubt Mountain and Ptarmigan Valley from Deception Pass

At km 7.1 you reach the junction for the 1.3 km trail running north to Hidden Lake Junction Campground and Hidden Lake. Halfway Hut sits on a low bluff just south of the junction. The log cabin received its name during the early days of skiing when it served as an overnight stop for skiers—halfway between the Lake Louise railway station and Skoki Lodge. Today it is a day use-only shelter for hikers.

Beyond Hidden Lake junction, the trail climbs through scattered forest to the summit of Boulder Pass and the west end of Ptarmigan Lake. At an elevation of 2345 m, this unique, lake-filled pass is at the upper limits of tree growth. There are open views down the lake to the distant peaks of Mount Douglas and Mount St. Bride, and the surrounding meadows and rockslides are well-populated with hoary marmots, pikas and white-tailed ptarmigan.

The trail continues along the slopes above the north shore of Ptarmigan Lake. Near the east end of the lake, at Baker Lake junction, it branches left and climbs to the summit of Deception Pass.

This rocky, alpine pass was named by Skoki ski pioneer Cyril Paris because he always thought its summit was closer than it really was when he was crossing it. From this lofty 2475 m vantage point, there is an all-encompassing view over the Ptarmigan Valley to Redoubt Mountain and through Boulder Pass to the distant mountains near Lake Louise. The pass is the best viewpoint on the trail and usually the farthest point reached by day hikers.

From Deception Pass the trail drops steadily northward towards the Skoki Valley. Views to the west include Ptarmigan Peak and the turquoise Skoki Lakes—Myosotis and Zigadenus (genus names for the forget-me-not and camas lily). After descending over rocky slopes and alpine meadows, the trail passes through scattered alpine larch and re-enters the forest.

You reach Skoki Lodge 3.4 km beyond the pass, and Merlin Meadows Campground (Sk18) is just over a kilometre below the lodge.

Boulder Pass Area Hikes

Strong day hikers can include a short side-trip to one of three high lakes just off the Boulder Pass trail. Any of these diversions add no more than 2.6 km to your day's total. If you stay at Hidden Lake Junction or Baker Lake Campgrounds, you can visit any of these destinations on an easy half-day trip from your campsite.

Hidden Lake—1.3 km. This diminutive lake is embraced by the walls of Mount Richardson, Pika Peak and Ptarmigan Peak and surrounded by some of the finest wildflower meadows in Banff Park. The lake is reached by a short trail running north from the Boulder Pass trail at km 7.1 (100 m north of Halfway Hut).

From the junction, you immediately pass the Hidden Lake Junction Campground and begin a steady climb up a shallow vale leading to the lake. The forest thins out during the ascent, giving way to stands of alpine larch and, finally, to lush, treeless meadows surrounding the lake.

Redoubt Lake—1.1 km. This high lake is hidden above Ptarmigan Lake beneath the east-facing cliffs of Redoubt Mountain. The short side-trip begins at the west end of Ptarmigan Lake on the summit of Boulder Pass.

The trail to Redoubt Lake is not well-defined, but with a little perseverance you should reach the lake in 20 minutes or so from Boulder Pass. Follow close along the south shore of Ptarmigan Lake for 0.8 km, skirting (and sometimes clambering through) a major boulder field. Then cut straight up over open slopes to the obvious gap between Redoubt Mountain and Heather Ridge.

Once you reach the lake, continue down along the east side to its outlet, where you have a fine overview of larch forest, lush meadows and the Baker Creek valley to the southeast.

Baker Lake—1.1 km. Baker Lake lies in marshy meadows just east of and 120 m below the Ptarmigan Valley. Though it is only a short side-trip off the Boulder Pass-Skoki Valley trail, it is often visited as an overnight destination rather than an extension to the Boulder Pass day hike.

The trail to Baker Lake branches right from the Boulder Pass-Skoki trail at km 10.5. From this junction, on the open slopes beneath Deception Pass, it descends at a gradual to moderate grade to the lakeshore. Continue east along the north shoreline for just over a kilometre to reach Baker Lake Campground near the lake's outlet.

Anyone camping at Baker Lake should be extra fastidious in storing food. Not only are you in prime grizzly country, but the campground has a past history of camp-robbing wolverines.

Fossil Mountain Circuit—12.3 km. While most visitors to Skoki Valley camp there or stay at the lodge, others like to overnight in the high country at Baker Lake. However, it is still possible to sample the best of Skoki on a full day circuit around Fossil Mountain from Baker Lake Campground, including a side-trip to Merlin Lake.

Stay left at a junction just east of Baker Lake Campground and descend northeast gradually for 2 km to the open meadows of Cotton Grass Pass. The trail continues north through the pass for another kilometre, passing beneath the eastern slopes of Fossil Mountain to a junction where the trail to the Skoki Valley branches left (main trail continues north for another 2 km to Red Deer Lakes).

The Skoki branch bends west and runs between Fossil and Skoki Mountains for 3 km to intersect the Boulder Pass-Skoki Valley trail at km 13.9—500 m south of Skoki Lodge. You complete the loop by returning to Baker Lake via Deception Pass. (See *Boulder Pass-Skoki Valley*.)

Hidden Lake

BANFF NATIONAL PARK   111

Skoki Valley Area Hikes

Skoki Lodge and Merlin Meadows Campground serve as base camps for a handful of half-day and full day trips in the Skoki Valley and to points of interest in adjacent valleys. Following are three of the more popular routes that utilize designated trails (* indicates distance approximate).

Skoki Lodge to Merlin Lake–3.1 km. Set between the colourfully named Wall of Jericho and Merlin's Castle, Merlin Lake is one of the little known gems of the Rockies. However, it is well-known to anyone staying in the Skoki Valley and is the most popular hike from Skoki Lodge and Merlin Meadows Campground.

The high trail to the lake starts at the footbridge in front of Skoki Lodge. The trail was designed and partially constructed in the 1940s by mountaineer and master trail-builder Lawrence Grassi. Like other Grassi trails, it takes you through high boulder-fields, in this case along the Wall of Jericho, and allows you to traverse this tumbled slide with relative ease.

Emerging from the boulders, the trail skirts above Castilleja Lake and, following cairns and more recently constructed sections of trail, climbs to the cliff immediately below the Merlin Lake cirque. To ascend the cliff, pick the line of least resistance via the scree gully on the left side—a steep scramble over loose rock. From the top of the cliff, you descend through meadow and stunted trees to the lakeshore.

Massive Mount Richardson provides the backdrop for the lake, while Merlin's Castle contains its western shores. James Porter named the latter peak in 1911 for a "picturesque cluster of tower-like rocks" near the summit, which reminded him of a castle Merlin the Magician might have inhabited.

Merlin Meadows Campground to Merlin Lake—2.6 km*. You can also reach Merlin Lake via a horse trail along the northwest side of Merlin Valley. While this is a shorter and more direct route from Merlin Meadows Campground, escaping the meadows is a bit messy.

Cross Skoki Creek just below the campground (look for a makeshift log bridge), then follow indistinct trail upstream. Watch for a defined track branching right from the meadows.

This trail switchbacks up along the northwest side of the valley toward the Merlin cirque. In circumnavigating the cliff beneath the lake, it climbs above the cirque, then drops through scrub forest to the lake's north shore. (We prefer to hike to the lake via Grassi's highline route and return on the horse trail.)

Skoki Lodge to Natural Bridge–9.5 km*. The Red Deer Lakes and Campground can be reached over good trail branching east from the Boulder Pass-Skoki Valley trail near Skoki Lodge. The three Red Deer Lakes lie in low marshy terrain with willow meadows, and trails between the campground and lakes are many and muddy.

The most compelling reason to hike this trail is to continue down the Red Deer River to Natural Bridge—an impressive cataract that thunders through a hole in limestone bedrock. However, the hike is a rather long, messy adventure that requires two leg-chilling fords.

From the junction 0.5 km south of Skoki Lodge, follow the trail running due east between Skoki and Fossil Mountains—a gap known locally as Jones Pass. As the trail emerges from the pass and bends north around Skoki Mountain, trails from Baker Lake and Cotton Grass Pass intersect from the right (stay left at all intersections).

Merlin Lake and Mount Richardson

At the Red Deer Lakes Campground junction, you can stay left and make a short side-trip to Upper Red Deer Lake—the largest and most scenic of the three Red Deer Lakes.

To continue down the Red Deer Valley to Natural Bridge, follow the trail leading to Red Deer Lakes Campground. Continue on the hiker's trail leading east from the campground. This alternative to the horse trail runs 0.3 km to a bridge across the headwaters stream that forms the Red Deer River. On the opposite side you intersect the Red Deer River trail 200 m west of Cyclone Warden Cabin.

Turn right and continue down-valley along the north side of the Red Deer 2.3 km to the Natural Bridge junction. Follow the Natural Bridge trail right to a ford of the Red Deer (usually calf deep).

The trail continues south up a narrow side-valley between Oyster Peak and Mount Douglas for 2 km to Natural Bridge, but before you reach the falls, you must make yet another soaking ford of the valley's main stream.

Little Pipestone Creek. The trails running down Little Pipestone Creek to the Pipestone River are tempting for many who are staying in the Skoki Valley or at Red Deer Lakes Campground. However, both routes consist of multiple tracks that are brushy, vague, muddy and cut-up by horse traffic, and the route down Skoki Creek from Merlin Meadows requires a ford of Little Pipestone Creek. And if that isn't enough, views are limited until you reach the Pipestone River.

We can only recommend these trails to curious explorers or backpackers bound for Molar Pass or the upper Pipestone River valley (see *Pipestone River* and *Molar Pass*).

51 Pipestone River

Pipestone Parking Area to Pipestone Pass—36.2 km (22.5 mi)*

Backpack

Allow 2 to 3 days to Pipestone Pass

Elevation gain: 894 m (2,933 ft)

Maximum elevation: 2449 m (8,036 ft)

Maps: Lake Louise 82 N/8
  Hector Lake 82 N/9
  Lake Louise & Yoho (Gem Trek)

Access: Follow the Trans-Canada Highway west 1.1 km from the Lake Louise exit overpass to Slate Avenue (intersection marked by "Pipestone" trail sign). Follow this paved access road uphill and to the left 0.2 km to another intersection. Follow "Pipestone" trail sign to right 100 m to the trailhead parking area beside a horse corral.

0.0—Trail kiosk-access gate (1555 m).

0.9—Junction. Mud Lake right 0.8 km.

3.0—Trail comes abreast of Pipestone River.

7.0—End of bicycle access.

14.5—Pipestone River ford. Major crossing to west bank.

17.5—Little Pipestone River ford.

18.0—Little Pipestone Warden Cabin and junction (1850 m). Red Deer Lakes and Skoki Valley right. Pipestone River trail fords river to west bank.

18.1—Junction. Molar Pass left. Pipestone Pass right.

27.0—Singing Meadows (old campsite). Pipestone River ford to east bank.

28.0—Junction. Fish Lakes-North Molar Pass left. Pipestone Pass ahead.

36.2—Pipestone Pass (2449 m). Trail continues north down Siffleur River. See also *North Molar-Pipestone-Dolomite Circuit*.

* Distances approximate

(Trail not fully shown on maps in this book.)

The Pipestone River trail is broad, well-graded and a popular bike route for the first 7 km. Beyond that point it is a rather grim, uninspiring journey over heavily-used horse trail. A serious ford of the Pipestone makes all of this tedium seem rather silly. There are better ways to reach the upper Pipestone Valley (see *North Molar-Dolomite Circuit*). But if you must persevere, here are the details:

From the Bow Valley, the trail climbs quickly past Mud Lake junction and onto a forested plateau. The broad, solid track flattens out and soon comes abreast of the Pipestone River. At the 7 km mark bike access ends and so does the good trail. A rough, muddy horse trail leads onward along the west side of the river.

At approximately 14.5 km, the track swings across the Pipestone's multi-channels to the east bank. While this ford has been navigated by hikers, it can be hazardous during high runoff.

Further upstream there are fords across Little Pipestone Creek and, at Little Pipestone Warden Cabin, back across the Pipestone to its west bank (usually mid-calf to thigh deep over slippery rocks). Two trails intersect at this crossing: the Little Pipestone trail from Skoki on the east side and the Molar Creek trail on the west.

The remainder of the trip to Pipestone Pass is relatively open and scenic. You enter Singing Meadows around 24 km and, at the north end of the meadows, pass an old campsite to a relatively easy ford to the east side of the river. After passing the Fish Lakes junction, the trail climbs to open subalpine forest and wildflower meadows.

The final 2 km to the pass is steep, rocky and windswept. The high route from Fish Lakes intersects from the left near the summit. (See *North Molar-Pipestone-Dolomite Circuit*.)

52 Mud Lake

Pipestone Parking Lot to Mud Lake—1.7 km (1.1 mi)

For anyone in search of an escape from the bustling village of Lake Louise, Mud Lake is a pleasant if not overly spectacular destination. The lake is just over 500 m in length and encircled by a dense forest of lodgepole pine, but the lakeshore is open enough to allow views to Whitehorn and Lipalian Mountains.

The short hike begins from the Pipestone trailhead on the opposite side of the Trans-Canada Highway from Lake Louise Village. Beyond the trailhead kiosk and access gate, you follow a gravel service road that climbs gradually into dense pine forest. At 0.4 km, the Mud Lake and Pipestone River trails branch left from the road. In another 0.5 km, the Mud Lake trail forks uphill to the right from the broad Pipestone track. From this final junction, it is an easy 0.8 km ascent to the lakeshore.

Access: Follow the Trans-Canada Highway west 1.1 km from the Lake Louise exit overpass to Slate Avenue (intersection also marked by "Pipestone" trail sign). Follow this paved residential access road uphill and to the left 0.2 km to another intersection. Follow "Pipestone" trail sign to right and continue another 100 m to the trailhead parking area beside a horse corral. *Maps: Lake Louise 82 N/8; Lake Louise & Yoho (Gem Trek).*

Icefields Parkway

The 230-km Icefields Parkway between Lake Louise and Jasper is undeniably one of Canada's most scenic highways. More importantly for hikers, the road's southern section, running through the northern part of Banff Park and into southern Jasper Park, is the highest stretch of road in Canada.

Many of the hikes originating from the Parkway, particularly in the vicinity of Bow Summit (2069 m/6,787 ft) and Sunwapta Pass (2035 m/6,675 ft), allow you to reach the alpine a lot quicker than elsewhere in the mountain parks. On the Banff Park section of the Parkway there are three trails that reach treeline in less than 5 km—Helen Lake, Bow Summit Lookout and Parker Ridge.

There are also a number of low elevation trails in the North Saskatchewan Valley near Saskatchewan River Crossing—Mistaya Canyon, Howse River Flats, Warden Lake and Glacier Lake—which are usually snowfree by early June. And trails running over North Molar and Dolomite Passes are the most direct routes to the park's remote northeast wilderness.

BANFF ICEFIELDS PARKWAY — SOUTH

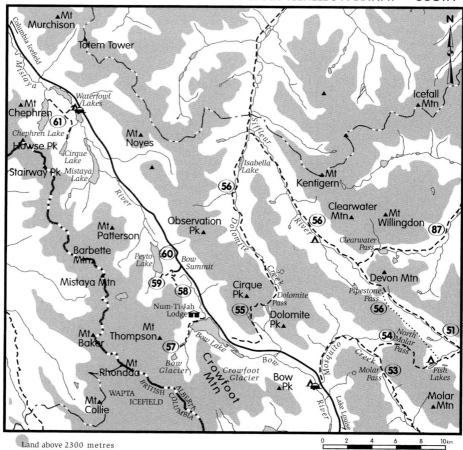

Land above 2300 metres

0 2 4 6 8 10km

Helen Lake

53 Molar Pass

Icefields Parkway to Molar Pass—10.5 km (6.5 mi)

Day trip or backpack

Allow 3 hours one way

Elevation gain: 510 m (1,675 ft)

Maximum elevation: 2340 m (7,675 ft)

Maps: Hector Lake 82 N/9

Access: Follow the Icefields Parkway north from the Trans-Canada Highway 24 km (15 mi) to the Mosquito Creek Campground. The trail is across the highway from the campground entrance at the northeast corner of the Mosquito Creek bridge. (A parking area is located on west side of road beside the entrance to the Mosquito Creek Hostel).

0.0—Trailhead kiosk (1830 m).

— Short, steep climb followed by gradual uphill on rooty, rocky trail.

3.3—Side stream (bridged).

3.5—Side stream (bridged).

4.1—Major side stream (bridged).

5.0—Mosquito Creek Campground (Mo5). Bridge to south side of Mosquito Creek 150 m past campground.

6.8—Bridge to north side of Mosquito Creek.

7.4—Junction. *North Molar Pass—Fish Lakes* trail left. Molar Pass right.

— Steady climb toward pass.

10.2—Trail crests Molar Pass meadows.

10.5—Molar Pass summit (2340 m).

When you hike the trail up Mosquito Creek, you have a choice of two high routes near the headwaters—Molar Pass or North Molar Pass. While both possess expansive views and some of the finest wildflower meadows in Banff Park, most day hikers find Molar Pass a more reasonable goal. Beyond Molar Pass, the trail continues down the Molar Creek valley, providing backpackers with an optional, if somewhat lacklustre and muddy, route to the Pipestone Valley.

Through its first 7 km, the trail rises gradually along open willow flats and subalpine forest near Mosquito Creek. The track is rocky and rooty most of the way, and there are numerous wet sections that can be particularly messy during wet summers or when a horse party has preceded you.

Three small tributary streams (all bridged) are crossed in the first 4 km. At km 5.0 you pass Mosquito Creek Campground—a good base for a more leisurely day trip to either Molar or North Molar Pass.

Beyond the campground you immediately cross Mosquito Creek and then recross it 1.8 km farther along. At km 7.4, you reach the junction where the North Molar Pass route branches left from the Molar Pass trail. The Molar trail is a bit indistinct over the next kilometre, but horse tracks and churned-up meadow span the brief gaps.

As the forest opens up, you get your first views of Molar Pass ahead. There are also numerous lush meadows sporting showy wildflowers, such as western anemone, globe flower, marsh marigold, purple fleabane, valerian, and ragwort.

Over the last 2 km the trail climbs out of the trees and ascends across the valley's steep headwall to the crest of the pass. Another 300 m of nearly flat, alpine meadow brings you to the true summit.

The Molar Pass meadows are just as impressive as those beneath nearby

Molar Pass

North Molar Pass, though the flowers are smaller, ground-hugging alpine varieties. The pass also offers an excellent view of twin-peaked Molar Mountain (3022 m), rising above the meadows to the southeast. Farther off in that direction, across the Pipestone Valley, are the rugged peaks of the Slate Range, which contain the Skoki region. The glacier-crested summits of the Mount Hector massif rise immediately above the pass to the west and south.

Molar Pass is so extensive, it invites exploration and aimless wandering. Another option is to visit Mosquito Lake and the meadows beneath North Molar Pass on your way back by hiking up that branch trail for 3 km; or you can traverse due north across open meadows to intersect with the North Molar trail near tiny Mosquito Lake. However, either of these options makes for a rather strenuous day trip. Visiting both passes in one day is far more reasonable from the Mosquito Creek Campground. (See also *North Molar Pass-Fish Lakes*.)

Molar Creek. The Molar Creek trail runs southeast from the summit of Molar Pass for another 14 km to the Pipestone River trail. From that junction you can either ford the Pipestone and ascend Little Pipestone Creek to Skoki Valley or turn left toward Pipestone Pass and Fish Lakes. The trail also serves as an optional last leg for the Clearwater-Red Deer Circuit (see *Clearwater River*).

Be forewarned, however, that the trail down Molar Creek is rough, very wet, and has been a disappointment to most people who have hiked it.

'r Pass—Fish Lakes

Molar Pass—11.9 km (7.4 mi)

'es Campground—15.2 km (9.5 mi)

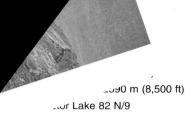

_ _90 m (8,500 ft)

_ _or Lake 82 N/9

Access: Follow the Icefields Parkway north from the Trans-Canada Highway 24 km (15 mi) to the Mosquito Creek Campground. The trail is across the highway from the campground entrance (parking available on west side of road beside the entrance to Mosquito Creek Hostel).

0.0—Trailhead kiosk (1830 m).

—Short, steep climb followed by gradual uphill on rooty, rocky trail.

3.3—Side stream (bridged).

3.5—Side stream (bridged).

4.1—Major side stream (bridged).

5.0—Mosquito Creek Campground (Mo5). Bridge to south side of Mosquito Creek 150 m past campground.

6.8—Bridge to north side of Mosquito Creek.

7.4—Junction. *Molar Pass* right 3.1 km. North Molar Pass left.

—Trail climbs above trees and levels out into alpine meadows.

9.2—Mosquito Lake.

10.9—Steep climb to North Molar Pass begins.

11.9—North Molar Pass (2590 m).

—Short steep descent levelling out into alpine meadow.

15.2—Fish Lakes Campground (Mo18) and Upper Fish Lake (2225 m).

15.4—Junction. Fish Lakes Warden Cabin and Pipestone Pass highline route left. Lower Fish Lake ahead.

16.1—Lower Fish Lake.

The trail running up Mosquito Creek from the Icefields Parkway leads to one of the most extensive alpine meadows in Banff Park. While it is possible to day hike to the best of this meadow, or even lofty North Molar Pass, most folks prefer to backpack over North Molar to Fish Lakes Campground. From there they can spend days exploring the lakes and meadows above the Pipestone Valley. In addition, the trail provides the easiest and most direct route to the Pipestone Pass—Clearwater Pass environs.

The first 7.4 km of the trail follows the same route as Molar Pass (see *Molar Pass*). At a junction near the Mosquito Creek headwaters, the North Molar trail branches east and climbs through verdant subalpine meadows—an exceptional wildflower garden dominated by the showy purple blooms of fleabane during late July and early August.

Sharp fingers of rock and steep talus slopes form a huge amphitheatre that encloses the treeless upper meadows. To the west the glacier-clad ramparts of Mount Hector create a rugged backdrop for tiny Mosquito Lake.

Near the 11 km mark, the rolling meadows are left behind and the stiff climb to North Molar Pass commences. Near the pass views extend westward to the mountains of the Bow Valley.

At 2590 m, this rockbound notch is the third highest trail-accessible pass in Banff Park. Winds whistle through the gap throughout the year, and these prevailing westerlies form a snowdrift on the east side of the summit, which can be a bit of an obstacle before late July.

The drop to Upper Fish Lake from the pass is rapid and steep, passing through an alpine landscape constricted by vertical walls and rockslide debris. The lake is seen from above long before it is reached, cradled in a pretty basin overlooking the Pipestone Valley. Just over 3

Upper Fish Lake

km below the pass, the trail finally reaches the open shoreline and campground—a peaceful spot but for the occasional cascade of rock falling from cliffs on the opposite shore.

The campground is an excellent base for wandering and exploration. It is just under a kilometre to Lower Fish Lake—a much smaller body of water bordered by one of the most northerly stands of alpine larch in North America. By contouring south along the slope of Molar Mountain from the lower lake, you can reach another small lake after approximately 2 km of trail-less hiking.

Pipestone Pass. One of the most popular destinations beyond Fish Lakes is the Pipestone Pass region. The pass can be reached as a day trip from the campground or by extending your backpack to the north. (See *North Molar-Pipestone-Dolomite Circuit.*)

While it is possible to descend directly from Lower Fish Lake to the Pipestone River trail via a rough, steep 2 km trail, most people prefer a more direct approach to Pipestone Pass via a highline route that contours around to the northwest from Upper Fish Lake. This trail stays at or above treeline throughout its 9 km journey to the pass. At last report, the trail is reasonably well defined with occasional marshy sections, but where the track is indistinct, the route to the pass is quite obvious in this open country.

The trail branches north near the Upper Fish Lake outlet and runs to the nearby warden cabin. On the opposite side of a small stream flowing behind the cabin, pick up the trail again as it begins its contour around to the northwest.

Just over 2 km from the warden cabin the trail passes below Moose Lake (unnamed on the topo map) and, 2.5 km farther along, skirts another small unnamed lake. The route continues high to the northwest along open slopes and meadows, intersecting with the Pipestone River trail on the 2449 m summit of the pass.

55 Helen Lake—Dolomite Pass

Icefields Parkway to Helen Lake—6.0 km (3.7 mi)

Icefields Parkway to Dolomite Pass—8.9 km (5.0 mi)

Half-day to day trip

Allow 1.5 to 2 hours to Helen Lake

Elevation gain: 550 m (1,800 ft)

Maximum elevation: 2500 m (8,200 ft)

Maps: Hector Lake 82 N/9
      Bow Lake-Sask Crossing (GemTrek)

Access: Follow the Icefields Parkway north from the Trans-Canada Highway 33 km (20.5 mi) to the Crowfoot Glacier Viewpoint. The road to the Helen Lake trail parking area is on the opposite side of the highway from the viewpoint.

0.0—Helen Lake parking area (1950 m).

   —Moderate to steep climb through subalpine forest.

2.4—Avalanche slope with open views.

2.9—Open views for remainder of hike.

3.4—Trail turns north at end of ridge.

   —Grade moderates, trail contours into Helen Lake cirque.

4.5—Rockslide.

5.0—Helen Creek crossing.

6.0—Helen Lake (2405 m).

   —Steep switchbacking ascent.

6.9—Helen Lake Summit (2500 m).

   —Steep descent.

8.1—Katherine Lake (2375 m).

8.9—Dolomite Pass (2395 m). Trail continues down Dolomite Creek (see *North Molar-Pipestone-Dolomite Circuit*).

Wildflower meadows, lofty lakes and castellate peaks provide a constant change of scene that will draw you onward to a remarkable panorama of a vast, alpine landscape. The Helen Lake meadows are also home to an amazing number of hoary marmots, who seem to have nothing better to do than sit in the sun and count passing hikers. However, when the weather is deteriorating in the Bow Valley, it is absolutely vile on these exposed highlands.

The trail climbs steadily through forest along the west-facing slopes of the Bow Valley for the first 3 km, then emerges onto steep mountainside meadows. Views open across the valley to Crowfoot Mountain and Glacier, and the sharp summit of Mount Hector (3394 m) down valley to the southeast.

The trail reaches the south end of a long ridge at km 3.4, where a scattering of whitebark pine indicate that you are nearing treeline. Here it switches around 180 degrees and contours into the amphitheatre containing Helen Lake.

After another kilometre of gradual ascent through lightly forested meadows, you drop beneath the toe of a relatively recent rockslide. The pile of tumbled boulders is surrounded by a lush snow-bed plant community filled with the colourful blooms of purple fleabane, paintbrush, ragwort and valerian. Beyond the slide the trail climbs above the last trees and remains above treeline to Dolomite Pass and beyond.

Helen Lake is bordered by open alpine meadows and scree slopes beneath the summit of Cirque Peak. It is a great place to kick-back and enjoy the scene, which is animated by the antics of the resident hoary marmots and, occasionally, by the over-flight of a golden eagle.

Helen Lake would be an above average destination on most hikes, but you shouldn't end your day there. Gather

Katherine Lake and Dolomite Pass from Helen Lake Summit

your strength and continue for at least another 0.9 km up a steep series of switchbacks to the rocky ridge extending south from Cirque Peak.

The 2500-m summit is the highest point on the trail, and it provides an outstanding overview of Katherine Lake and Dolomite Pass to the east and Helen Lake and its meadows back to the southwest. By leaving the trail and hiking to the southeast end of this ridge, you gain another 50 m of elevation and unobstructed views south along the Great Divide.

For most day hikers the ridge is a good spot to turn for home. Stronger hikers, who don't mind climbing back over this ridge at the end of the day, can descend to Katherine Lake and Dolomite Pass.

The trail drops nearly 100 m to the north end of Katherine Lake, which stretches beneath the castellate cliffs of Dolomite Peak. An opening beyond the south end of the lake serves as a window to the southern half of Banff Park, and on

a clear day the sharp horn of Mount Assiniboine can be seen 100 km away.

Though the trail is not well-defined beyond Katherine Lake, it is an easy climb over spongy alpine meadows to a small lake on the crest of Dolomite Pass.

Katherine and Helen Lakes were both named for the daughters of the Rev. Harry P. Nichols, who was with a party of wayward mountaineers who stumbled across the pass in July 1898. Dolomite Peak received its name because it reminded the alpinists of the European Dolomites.

Dolomite Creek–Isabella Lake. Backpackers can continue over Dolomite Pass and down Dolomite Creek to Isabella Lake, 13.4 km north of the pass. The trail is rugged and reserved for experienced hikers who don't mind fording swift-flowing streams. (See *North Molar-Pipestone-Dolomite Circuit.*)

56 North Molar-Pipestone-Dolomite Circuit

Mosquito Creek to Crowfoot Glacier Viewpoint—68.9 km (42.8 mi) *

Backpack

Allow 4 to 5 days

Maximum elevation: 2590 m (8,500 ft)

Minimum elevation: 1830 m (6,000 ft)

Maps: Hector Lake 82 N/9
      Siffleur River 82 N/16

Access: Southern access to the circuit is from the Icefields Parkway opposite the Mosquito Creek Campground (see *North Molar Pass-Fish Lakes*). Northern access is from the Helen Lake parking area opposite the Crowfoot Glacier viewpoint (see *Helen Lake-Dolomite Pass*).

0.0—Mosquito Creek trailhead (1830 m).

5.0—Mosquito Creek Campground (Mo5).

7.4—Junction. *Molar Pass* ahead 3.1 km. North Molar Pass left.

9.2—Mosquito Lake.

11.9—North Molar Pass (2590 m).

15.2—Upper Fish Lake (2225 m). Fish Lakes Campground (Mo18).

15.4—Junction. Lower Fish Lake ahead. Pipestone Pass left.

18.0—Moose Lake.

24.0—Pipestone Pass (2449 m). Intersection with the *Pipestone River* trail.

27.0—Junction. Clearwater Pass right 1.0 km.

34.3—Abandoned warden cabin.

36.2—Siffleur Campground (Sf).

39.4—Siffleur River ford.

43.2—Dolomite Creek ford.

43.3—Junction (1800 m). Park boundary right 1.5 km. Dolomite Pass left.

43.7—Abandoned warden cabin.

46.6—Isabella Lake (1830 m). Primitive campsite.

51.9—Dolomite Creek ford.

55.2—Dolomite Creek ford.

56.5—Waterfall.

60.0—Dolomite Pass (2395 m).

62.0—Helen Lake Summit (2500 m).

62.9—Helen Lake.

68.9—Helen Lake trailhead. (1950 m).

*distance approximate

This four to five day backpack crosses three high passes and traverses one of Banff Park's prime wilderness regions—the domain of grizzly bears and the park's only resident herd of mountain caribou. Approximately 32 km of the circuit is at or above treeline. It is an exceptional trip, but you should be comfortable fording swift streams—there are three crossings of Dolomite Creek that can be tricky when water levels are high.

We prefer to start this circuit from the North Molar Pass trailhead at Mosquito Creek and hike it in a counter-clockwise direction. By travelling in this direction it is easier to follow the high traverse from Fish Lakes to Pipestone Pass than visa versa, and you save most of the fords until the latter part of the trip.

Since the circuit doesn't make a complete loop, you must arrange transportation or plan on hitchhiking between the Mosquito Creek and Helen Lake trailheads.

Mosquito Creek trailhead to Pipestone Pass—24.0 km. The first leg of the journey follows the trail up Mosquito Creek and over North Molar Pass to Fish Lakes—the usual first night destination. From Fish Lakes Campground, you follow the highline route northwest past Moose Lake and another small, unnamed lake to the summit of Pipestone Pass. (See *North Molar Pass-Fish Lakes*.)

From Pipestone Pass views open to the northwest, carrying the eye down the Siffleur Valley nearly as far as the Kootenay Plains. This is a very exposed viewpoint, a long way from the nearest trees, and a grim place in a storm.

Pipestone Pass to Isabella Lake—22.6 km. North of the pass the trail continues into the Siffleur Valley. Approximately 3 km beyond the pass the trail to Clearwater Pass branches right. The junction is not obvious and the track to the pass is

Upper Pipestone Valley from Pipestone Pass

poorly defined, but the route is straight-forward across meadows and rocky open terrain. If the weather is reasonable, you should consider a side-trip to the pass (1.0 km) and the Devon Lakes (2.6 km).

Beyond Clearwater junction the trail descends a glacial staircase and drops into heavy forest, where conditions are often boggy. Lower down it enters willow meadows and passes the Siffleur Campground.

Approximately 15 km north of Pipe-stone Pass, the trail fords the Siffleur to its west bank (usually knee-deep and straightforward). Nearly 4 km farther along, after crossing a low, forested ridge, there is yet another ford—a more difficult wade of Dolomite Creek that can be treacherous during high water. On the opposite, the Dolomite Creek trail intersects from the south. Turn left and begin the long ascent of Dolomite Creek to Dolomite Pass.

After passing an abandoned warden cabin, you reach the south end of Isabella Lake and a primitive campsite in just under 3 km. While random camping is allowed in the Dolomite Valley, this is as good a spot to overnight as any.

Isabella Lake to Helen Lake trail-head—22.3 km. Continuing upvalley from Isabella Lake, you immediately encounter erratic track along multi-channeled mudflats (follow the forest margin on the west side and watch for the trail's reappearance). Less than 2 km beyond these flats, you make a knee to thigh-deep crossing to the east side of Dolomite Creek. After a series of switchbacks and a mudslide traverse, you recross to the west side of the creek—another swift, moderately difficult ford during periods of high runoff.

The last 5 km to Dolomite Pass climbs steeply beside a waterfall and across a rockslide before emerging into the stark treeless landscape at the creek's head-waters. The trail is faint below Dolomite Pass, but the route to its summit is obvious—veering up to the right across open, rolling alpine meadow.

From Dolomite Pass, the final 8.9 km climbs over a 2500-m ridge to Helen Lake and descends to the Helen Lake trailhead on the Icefields Parkway. (See *Helen Lake-Dolomite Pass.*)

57 Bow Glacier Falls

Bow Lake Parking Area to Bow Glacier Falls—4.7 km (2.9 mi)

Half-day trip

Allow 1.5 hours one way

Elevation gain: 95 m (310 ft)

Maximum elevation: 2055 m (6,740 ft)

Maps: Hector Lake 82 N/9
      Bow Lake-Sask Crossing (GemTrek)

Access: Follow the Icefields Parkway north from the Trans-Canada Highway 36 km (22.5 mi) to the Num-Ti-Jah Lodge access road at Bow Lake. Follow the gravel lodge road 0.4 km to the trailhead parking area, located on the left side of the road opposite public washrooms.

0.0—Trailhead kiosk (1960 m).

—Trail follows Bow Lake shoreline.

0.3—Lodge parking area.

—Trail angles across willow flats to lake's north shore.

1.9—Bow Lake inlet.

—Trail follows along stream.

2.7—Broad gravel flats.

3.4—Bottom of canyon.

—Steep uphill along canyon for 200 m.

3.6—Bow Glacier basin viewpoint.

—Trail descends and crosses basin to falls.

4.7—Bow Glacier Falls (2055 m).

The Bow Glacier basin has been a popular half-day side trip for travellers ever since the tourist-explorer Walter Wilcox visited it in 1896. The glacier, which filled much of the basin in Wilcox's day, has retreated above the headwall, leaving a 120-m waterfall as the only hint of the icefield hidden above.

A broad pathway skirts along Bow Lake from the trailhead parking area, passes behind the historic Num-Ti-Jah Lodge, and crosses willow flats to the lake's northern shoreline. A more modest track, often muddy and sometimes flooded in spots, follows along the lake for more than a kilometre to the alluvial flats at its inlet. Views over the first 2 km include Crowfoot Mountain across the lake and the leaning spire of Mount St. Nicholas rising from the white expanse of the Wapta Glacier on the skyline ahead.

The route beyond the lake is mainly flat, with an occasional brief climb, and follows near the silty, glacier-fed steam draining the basin. At 3.4 km you reach a narrow gorge and make a short, steep climb along its rim (this section is hazardous when wet, icy or snowcovered). As described by Wilcox: "Where the canyon is deepest an immense block of limestone about twenty-five feet long has fallen down, and with either end resting on the canyon walls, it affords a natural bridge over the gloomy chasm."

Fortunately, the trail does not cross the hazardous natural bridge, but continues up along the gorge to the sparsely forested crest of a terminal moraine. From this viewpoint the glacier basin lies beneath you, and Bow Glacier Falls pours off the headwall beyond.

The trail continues another kilometre across the rocky basin to the base of the falls, which is fed by a small meltwater lake near the toe of the Bow Glacier. The waterfall is most impressive during the warmest days of summer.

Bow Glacier Falls

58 Bow Summit Lookout

Bow Summit Parking Area to Bow Summit Lookout—3.1 km (1.9 mi)

Half-day trip

Allow 1 hour one way

Elevation gain: 230 m (760 ft)

Maximum elevation: 2315 m (7,600 ft)

Maps: Blaeberry River 82 N/10
    Bow Lake-Sask Crossing (GemTrek)

Access: Follow the Icefields Parkway to Bow Summit, 41 km (25.5 mi) north of its junction with the Trans-Canada Highway. Follow the viewpoint access road branching west from the Parkway 0.5 km (0.3 mi) and turn right at the road split into the Bow Summit parking area. (The road leading to the upper parking area is reserved for tour buses and the handicapped.)

0.0—Bow Summit Parking Area (2085 m).

—Steady uphill on paved trail.

0.6—Peyto Lake Viewpoint (2120 m).

—Follow paved trail branching uphill to right.

0.7—Junction. Follow middle trail angling uphill to left from interpretive sign.

0.9—Junction (unsigned). Paved nature trail turns right. Follow old road track ahead.

—Steady uphill on roadbed.

2.4—Descent into basin.

2.6—Stream crossing.

—Steep climb.

3.1—Bow Summit Lookout (2315 m).

The paved trail leading to Peyto Lake viewpoint is the most popular short walk along the Icefields Parkway. However, after you visit this teeming overlook, leave the crowds behind and continue upwards to the Bow Summit fire lookout site. There you will find peace, sublime alpine meadows and a lofty viewpoint for the Bow Summit environs.

From the Bow Summit parking area, follow the paved nature trail uphill to the viewing platform overlooking Peyto Lake. Take the obligatory photo, then escape on the right-hand of two paved trails leading uphill.

In 100 m you arrive at a three-way junction at an interpretive sign. Continue on the middle branch angling uphill to the left of the sign—an arm of the upper Bow Summit loop nature trail. In a few minutes the paved nature trail turns right, but you will continue straight ahead on the old fire lookout service road.

The road soon switchbacks over a rise with views back to Peyto Lake. Just in case you think you are entering little known territory at this point, be aware that this thinly forested knoll was where Hollywood movie stars Alan Ladd and Jay Silverheels (aka Tonto) galloped on horseback during filming of the motion picture *Saskatchewan* in 1953.

From the rise, the trail turns southeast and climbs steadily along the mountain slope. Views out across Bow Summit continue to improve throughout the ascent. As you climb, you enter the krummholtz zone—an area where stunted islands of alpine fir dwindle into treeless alpine meadow.

Wildflowers bloom in profusion throughout this section in July and August, dominated by white-flowered valerian and white, pink and magenta varieties of Indian paintbrush. Higher up the lush growth is replaced by fields of ground-hugging white mountain avens, and white and pink mountain heather.

Mistaya Valley from Bow Summit Lookout

At km 2.4 the trail drops into a draw and crosses a small stream beneath a huge rockslide. We call this Marmot Basin, since we have often encountered curious hoary marmots bounding along the stream and sunning themselves on the nearby boulders. The stream is bordered with moisture-loving flowers, including yellow ragwort and red-stemmed saxifrage.

The roadbed climbs steeply beside a great mound of rock rubble over the final 0.5 km to the alpine knoll where the Bow Summit lookout cabin once stood. (Until it was removed in the 1970s, it was the highest fire lookout in Banff Park.)

From the lookout site you have open views of the Icefields Parkway crossing Bow Summit and the entire Mistaya Valley, including Waterfowl Lakes, to the north. By following a steep footpath for another 200 m beyond the knoll, you reach the best viewpoint for Bow Lake and the glaciated peaks to the south.

The mountain rising directly above you is Mount Jimmy Simpson, named for the pioneer guide and outfitter who began the development of Num-Ti-Jah Lodge on the shores of Bow Lake in 1922. He lived there until his death in 1972 at age 95.

59 Peyto Lake South

Bow Summit Parking Lot to Peyto Lake—2.8 km (1.7 mi)

Though many travellers admire the turquoise waters of Peyto Lake from the viewpoint at Bow Summit, few ever walk to its shore. And that, for most, is fortunate, since the 2.4 km trail connecting the viewpoint to the lakeshore drops 275 m—a formidable hole that might prove the undoing of many idle tourists.

Two trails lead to Peyto's shores. The trail descending from the viewpoint, while being the most strenuous, is probably the most interesting since it allows hikers to explore the vast alluvial fan at the lake's south end or continue on towards Peyto Glacier.

After hiking from the Bow Summit parking area to the Peyto Lake viewing platform, follow the right of two paved trails leading uphill. Just 40 m above the viewpoint, beyond the end of the guard rail, the unmarked trail to the lake plunges into the forest.

After switchbacking madly downward through dense forest for 2 km, the trail emerges onto the alluvial flats southeast of Peyto Lake's inlet. From here you can roam across the flats to the lakeshore or head off in the direction of Peyto Glacier to the south.

Access: Follow the Icefields Parkway to Bow Summit, 41 km (25.5 mi) north of its junction with the Trans-Canada Highway. Follow the viewpoint access road branching west from the Parkway 0.5 km (0.3 mi) and turn right at the road split into the Bow Summit parking area. (The road leading to the upper parking area is reserved for tour buses and the handicapped.) *Map: Blaeberry River 82 N/10; Bow Lake-Saskatchewan Crossing (Gem Trek).*

60 Peyto Lake East

Icefields Parkway to Peyto Lake—1.4 km (0.9 mi)

A short, seldom travelled trail descends through dense forest to a shallow bay on the east shore of Peyto Lake. There are good views south from this shoreline to the Peyto Glacier and surrounding peaks, and across the lake to Caldron Peak and Mount Patterson.

From the parking area, follow a steep path downhill 100 m to the old Banff-Jasper Highway roadbed. Turn left and continue on a gradual descent of the old road for 0.3 km to where an unsigned footpath branches left into dense spruce-pine forest.

Another 1.0 km of rooty, occasionally muddy, mostly downhill trail brings you to the lakeshore. Elevation loss from the parking area is 85 m.

If you arrive on the shores of Peyto Lake early in the season, you will likely be pinned against the shore by high water levels. However, later in the season, when lake levels are lower, it is possible to walk south along a pleasant gravel beach for 400 m or more.

While you lounge upon the beach, you may commune with the spirit of pioneer guide and outfitter Bill Peyto, the lake's reclusive namesake. Legend says when Peyto guided clients here at the turn of the 20th century, he would leave the "dudes" in camp on Bow Summit and hike to the lake to spend the night away from the campfire chatter.

Access: Follow the Icefields Parkway north 2.4 km (1.5 mi) from Bow Summit and watch for the trailhead parking area on the west side of the highway. The unsigned trail departs from the north edge of the parking area. *Map: Blaeberry River 82 N/10; Bow Lake-Saskatchewan Crossing (Gem Trek).*

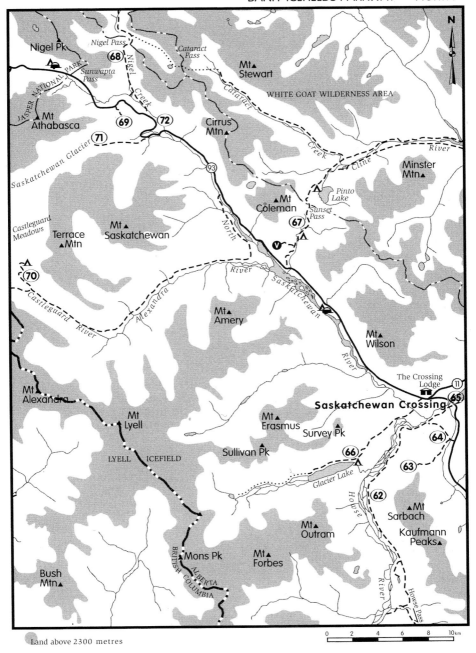

N

Nigel Pk

Nigel Pass

68

Cataract Pass

Mt Stewart

WHITE GOAT WILDERNESS AREA

JASPER NATIONAL PARK

Sunwapta Pass

Nigel Creek

Cataract Creek

Cline River

Mt Athabasca

69

72

Cirrus Mtn

Minster Mtn

Saskatchewan Glacier

71

93

Mt Coleman

Pinto Lake

Sunset Pass

67

Castleguard Meadows

Terrace Mtn

Mt Saskatchewan

V

North Saskatchewan River

70

Castleguard River

Alexandra

Mt Amery

Mt Wilson

Mt Alexandra

Mt Lyell

Mt Erasmus

Survey Pk

The Crossing Lodge

11

65

Saskatchewan Crossing

64

LYELL ICEFIELD

Sullivan Pk

66

Glacier Lake

63

62

Mt Sarbach

Kaufmann Peaks

Mons Pk

Mt Outram

Howse River

BRITISH COLUMBIA
ALBERTA

Mt Forbes

Bush Mtn

Howse Pass

0   2   4   6   8   10 km

Land above 2300 metres

61 Chephren Lake—Cirque Lake

Waterfowl Lakes Campground to Chephren Lake—3.5 km (2.2 mi)
Waterfowl Lakes Campground to Cirque Lake—4.2 km (2.6 mi)

Half-day or day trip

Allow 1 to 1.5 hours to Chephren Lake

Elevation gain: 105 m (345 ft)
loss: 42 m (140 ft)

Maximum elevation: 1755 m (5,750 ft)

Maps: Mistaya Lake 82 N/15
Bow Lake-Sask Crossing (GemTrek)

Access: Follow the Icefields Parkway to Waterfowl Lakes Campground, 58 km (36 mi) north of the Trans-Canada Highway or 19 km (12 mi) south of the David Thompson Highway junction at Saskatchewan River Crossing. Follow the campground access road 100 m to a split. Bypass the entrance kiosk and continue ahead on a service road 200 m to a parking area on the left. The trail starts across the road and skirts the south boundary of the campground for 0.4 km to the trailhead kiosk at the Mistaya River bridge. (Registered campers can follow a trail along the Mistaya River at the west edge of the campground to the trailhead.)

0.0—Mistaya River bridge (1650 m).

—Moderate uphill through subalpine forest.

1.3—Junction. Cirque Lake left 2.9 km. Chephren Lake right.

—Flat through forest with muddy sections.

1.6—Meadow to left of trail (1755 m). View of Howse Peak.

3.5—Chephren Lake (1713 m).

While you can admire the rugged mountains on the west side of the Mistaya Valley from roadside pull-outs at Lower Waterfowl Lake, they are best appreciated from the shores of Chephren or Cirque Lakes, which are nestled beneath the escarpment. Either lake can be visited in a half-day from Waterfowl Lakes Campground, or you can hike to both in a day.

The hike begins at the Mistaya River footbridge at the rear of Waterfowl Lakes Campground. (If you are not registered at the campground, use the 0.4 km trail from the campground service road to reach the bridge.)

After crossing the Mistaya bridge, you climb quickly through forest to a trail junction at km 1.3. Chephren Lake, the most popular destination, is to the right, Cirque Lake to the left. There is little gain or loss of elevation from the junction to Chephren Lake, but the trail is often a muddy mess. Views en route are limited to a brief glimpse of Howse Peak at a trailside meadow.

Two great peaks rise above Chephren Lake: the imposing, glaciated mountain to the south is Howse Peak, site of frequent avalanches in spring and early summer; Mount Chephren (pronounced kefren) forms the west shore and is named for the second of the three great pyramids of Egypt.

Cirque Lake. Because it is a bit smaller and the approach a bit longer and steeper, Cirque Lake is less frequently visited than Chephren.

From the 1.3 km junction, the trail soon reaches Cirque's outlet stream, then climbs beside it through heavy subalpine forest to the lake. Midway, Stairway and Aries Peaks create the 800 m wall rising beyond its far shore.

If you visit both lakes on your trip, the total round trip distance is 12.8 km.

Chephren Lake and Howse Peak

62 Howse Pass

Icefields Parkway to Howse River Flats—4.5 km (2.8 mi)
Icefields Parkway to Howse Pass—26.8 km (16.7 mi)

Day hike or backpack

Allow 2 days to Howse Pass

Elevation loss: 85 m (280 ft)
       gain: 150 m (500 ft)

Maximum elevation: 1585 m (5,200 ft)

Maps: Mistaya Lake 82 N/15
     Bow Lake-Sask Crossing (GemTrek)

Access: Follow the Icefields Parkway to the Mistaya Canyon parking area, located on the west side of the highway 31 km (19 mi) north of Bow Summit and 3 km (2 mi) south of Saskatchewan River Crossing Warden Station.

0.0—Mistaya Canyon parking area (1520 m).

0.5—Mistaya Canyon bridge (1485 m).

0.7—Junction. Sarbach Lookout left. Howse River ahead.

—Gradual descent through forest.

4.3—Junction. Horse trail to Icefields Parkway right. Howse Pass left.

4.5—Howse River flats (1435 m).

—Trail rolls through sandy, sparsely forested hills.

6.2—Trail re-enters forest.

15.5—Trail emerges briefly on river flats.

—Gradual climb through dense forest.

24.0—Junction. Howse Warden Cabin right. Howse Pass ahead (ford stream).

—Trail climbs above Conway Creek.

26.5—Stream crossing (ankle-deep).

26.8—Howse Pass (1527 m). Historic plaque, Alberta-B.C. boundary marker.

31.7—Lambe Creek bridge.

34.8—Tributary stream (log bridge).

39.2—Cairnes Creek (single log bridge).

39.5—Parking area in clearcut.

Howse Pass was the first fur trade route across the Great Divide, and the valley leading to it is nearly as wild today as it was when David Thompson passed this way in 1807. Despite its historical significance, the trek up this broad, mostly forested valley is tedious and often difficult—strictly for experienced wilderness travellers who are good route-finders.

However, if you aren't up for slogging to the pass, you can day trip to the pleasant, open flats near the confluence of the Howse and North Saskatchewan Rivers. This section is snowfree early in the season, and the grassy montane riverside is awash with the colourful blooms of montane wildflowers in early summer.

Howse River Flats. The first 15 minutes of the journey follows the trail to Mistaya Canyon. After crossing the canyon, the trail immediately passes the Sarbach Lookout junction and makes a gradual descent through heavy forest to the Howse River.

Immediately after emerging from the forest, the horse trail from Saskatchewan River Crossing Warden Station intersects from the right. For the next 2 km travel is flat and undemanding along sandy hills and meadows with open views across the Howse River to massive Mount Wilson.

The flats are the furthest point David Thompson and his men reached by canoe in June 1807. They camped here and waited for the snow to melt on Howse Pass for two weeks. Other than a black bear that stuck its head into their tent, and got shot for its efforts, they found little game and were forced to live on meagre rations.

Howse Pass. The trail re-enters forest at km 6.2—the furthest point that day hikers will want to travel. Backpackers bound for Howse Pass continue in the

Conway Creek near its confluence with Howse River

trees for the rest of the journey, except for a brief re-emergence at 15.5 km. Whenever the trail runs close to the river, the track is often flooded early in the season and during warm weather. Look for alternate trails in the forest to detour these problem stretches.

Beyond km 15.5, the trail re-enters dense forest and climbs away from the river. The track is rough, rooty and depressing.

At 24.0 km you descend to a junction. The trail to the right descends Conway Creek and fords it (knee to thigh-deep) to open alluvial flats near the Howse River Warden Cabin (1.3 km) and the confluence of Conway, Freshfield and Forbes Creeks—the true headwaters of the Howse River. With excellent views to the surrounding peaks, the flats are one of the best places to camp in the valley.

The trail to the pass continues ahead at the junction and immediately crosses a tributary stream 100 m above its confluence with Conway Creek. It then climbs through forest above Conway Creek canyon and onwards to the summit of Howse Pass.

While more open than much of the upper valley, views from the pass are unexceptional. A historic plaque and an old interprovincial boundary marker are the only indication that you are atop the Great Divide.

Good trail continues across the pass and onto the headwaters of British Columbia's Blaeberry River. The track passes through meadows and beside small pools before descending to an aluminum bridge over Lambe Creek, just below a small waterfall.

The trail stays close to the Blaeberry, travelling through heavy forest for the remainder of the journey. (A tributary stream and Cairnes Creek were both spanned by single-log bridges when we last passed that way.)

After crossing Cairnes Creek, you scramble up through an old clearcut for 300 m to the parking area just off the Blaeberry Forestry Road. This trailhead is 55 km north of the Trans-Canada Highway via the forestry road and just before the road's final crossing of the Blaeberry River below Doubt Hill.

63 Sarbach Lookout

Icefields Parkway to Sarbach Lookout Site—5.2 km (3.2 mi)

Half-day or day trip

Allow 1.5 to 2 hours one way

Elevation loss: 40 m (130 ft)
           gain: 595 m (1,950 ft)

Maximum elevation: 2075 m (6,800 ft)

Maps: Mistaya Lake 82 N/15
        Bow Lake-Sask Crossing (GemTrek)

Access: Follow the Icefields Parkway to the Mistaya Canyon parking area, located on the west side of the highway 31 km (19 mi) north of Bow Summit and 5.5 km (3.5 mi) south of the David Thompson Highway junction at Saskatchewan River Crossing. The trail begins at the lower end of the parking area.

0.0—Mistaya Canyon parking area (1520 m).

0.5—Mistaya Canyon bridge (1480 m).

0.7—Junction. Howse Pass ahead; Sarbach Lookout left.

—Gradual ascent through forest.

3.1—Moderate to steep grades begin.

5.2—Sarbach Lookout site (2075 m).

The steep trail to the old Sarbach fire lookout site is hardly worth the effort— the climb is steep and steady, and views at the top are mostly obscured by trees. But if you are willing to scramble up-slope for another 45 minutes or so, there are panoramic views encompassing the confluence of three rivers and a sea of massive peaks and glaciers.

From the Icefields Parkway, the trail descends and crosses the Mistaya Canyon bridge. At a junction 200 m beyond the bridge, the Sarbach trail cuts back sharply to the left from the Howse River trail.

You soon begin a steady, steep switch-backing ascent that continues all the way to the lookout. Scattered forest limits views from the spot where Banff's only wooden fire tower and a small cabin once stood, but with a bit more effort you can obtain a scenic reward.

Old trails, constructed by a former fire lookout, continue behind the site (border-ed by rocks in their early stages). One contours to the left) across the slope and, in 200 m, reaches an avalanche path with open views across the valley to Mount Murchison.

A higher trail climbs through the forest and provides a head start for a steep scra-mble to a rocky viewpoint at the end of Mount Sarbach's north ridge. From this vantage point, 300 vertical metres above the lookout site, you see Glacier Lake and the sprawling glaciers of the Lyell Icefield to the west. The confluence of the North Saskatchewan, Howse and Mistaya Rivers is immediately below the ridge to the north. Mounts Wilson and Murchison are quite massive from this prospect, the latter rising 1900 m above the valley floor.

Mount Sarbach was named for the Swiss guide Peter Sarbach, who com-pleted the first ascent of the peak via this ridge with J. Norman Collie and G.P. Baker in 1897.

64 Mistaya Canyon

Icefields Parkway to Mistaya Canyon—0.5 km (0.3 mi)

This limestone slot canyon compares favourably with the better known canyons of Maligne in Jasper and Marble in Kootenay. Though not as heavily visited as its sister canyons, the short downhill walk is still a popular diversion for many travellers along the Icefields Parkway.

Follow an old roadbed leading gradually downhill through the forest for 10 minutes to reach the canyon. A bridge spans the canyon at its narrowest point, where you can peer down into its dark depths.

The canyon has been carved from limestone bedrock by the Mistaya River, which originates in Peyto Lake, 28 km to the southeast. The river flows through open willow meadows just upstream from the bridge, and rock slabs near the point where the river plunges into the abyss are a pleasant place to relax and enjoy the upstream view.

Avoid the temptation of looking into the canyon from anywhere except the bridge. Unfenced, canyon-rim viewpoints below the bridge are very dangerous, particularly when conditions are wet or snowy.

The trail continues beyond the canyon to Sarbach Lookout and the Howse Valley. (See *Sarbach Lookout* and *Howse Pass*.)

Access: Follow the Icefields Parkway to the Mistaya Canyon parking area—a long pull-off on the west side of the highway 31 km (19 mi) north of Bow Summit and 5.5 km (3.5 mi) south of the David Thompson Highway junction at Saskatchewan River Crossing. The trail begins at the lower end of the parking area. *Maps: Mistaya Lake 82 N/15; Bow Lake-Saskatchewan Crossing (Gem Trek).*

65 Warden Lake

Icefields Parkway to Warden Lake—2.2 km (1.4 mi)

The trail to Warden Lake is a nice evening stroll for anyone camping or lodging near Saskatchewan River Crossing. The trail is flat and totally undemanding, and the views along the North Saskatchewan River are open and wonderful. The lake itself is a peaceful body of water where waterfowl are often seen swimming in the reflection of mighty Mount Murchison. While we have not seen moose in the lake for many years, we always encounter tracks along the way.

The trail begins by skirting along the south side of the warden station and its horse corral, then traverses rocky spruce flats to come abreast of the North Saskatchewan River on an old road track.

The track continues beside the river for nearly a kilometre before breaking away to the right along a marshy meadow.

After passing a small pond at km 1.9, the road reverts to single-track trail and climbs through the forest to the lake's north shore.

A rough trail runs along the shoreline to the east end of the lake and points beyond (connecting with horse trails running east along the North Saskatchewan River to the park boundary).

Access: Follow the Icefields Parkway to the Saskatchewan River Crossing Warden Station, 2.0 km (1.2 mi) south of the Parkway's junction with the David Thompson Highway. A gravel access road across the highway from the warden station entrance serves as a parking area for the trail. The trail sign is 100 m south of the warden station on the east side of the highway. *Maps: Mistaya Lake 82 N/15; Bow Lake-Saskatchewan Crossing (Gem Trek).*

66 Glacier Lake

Icefields Parkway to Glacier Lake—8.9 km (5.5 mi)

Day trip or backpack

Allow 2.5 to 3 hours one way

Elevation gain: 210 m (700 ft)
        loss: 225 m (750 ft)

Maximum elevation: 1660 m (5,450 ft)

Maps: Mistaya Lake 82 N/15
       Bow Lake-Sask Crossing (GemTrek)

Access: Follow the Icefields Parkway to the trailhead parking area, located in an old roadside gravel pit on the west side of the highway 1.0 km (0.5 mi) north of The Crossing Resort service centre.

0.0—Trailhead parking area (1450 m).

   —Flat followed by a sharp descent to river.

1.1—North Saskatchewan River footbridge.

   —Brief steep climb followed by flat.

2.3—Howse River viewpoint (open benchland to left of trail).

   —Trail descends to Howse River flats then begins a long climb over a forested ridge.

8.9—Glacier Lake (1435 m).

9.2—Glacier Lake Campground (Gl9).

   —Rough trail follows north shore of lake.

12.6—Glacier Lake west end.

14.4—Trail becomes indistinct along meadow and braided stream channels.

In June 1807, David Thompson and a party of North West Company fur traders entered the Howse Valley on their way across the Rockies to build the first trading post on the Columbia River. While camped on the Howse River, Thompson wandered into a side valley and discovered a large lake. He marvelled that "all the Mountains in sight from the end of the Lake are seemingly of Ice." The lake was named Glacier 51 years later when Dr. James Hector, geologist with the Palliser Expedition, camped by its shores.

Today the lake can be visited over good trail. Because of its relatively low elevation, it can be hiked earlier and later in the season than many of the park's trails. Some folks hike to Glacier Lake and back in a day, while others backpack to the campsite near the lake's east end. Less energetic souls only travel as far as the bridge across the North Saskatchewan River canyon (1.1 km) or the benchland overlooking the Howse Valley (2.3 km).

The trail to Glacier Lake begins on an old roadbed running southwest through a forest of lodgepole pine—regrowth following one of Banff Park's last big forest fires, the Survey Peak burn of 1940. As you near the end of the first kilometre, the trail plunges down to the North Saskatchewan River, which is crossed on a deluxe footbridge where the river funnels through a short canyon.

After climbing from the gorge, there is more flat walking through pine trees for another kilometre to where the trail skirts the end of an open, grassy bluff—an outstanding viewpoint for the valley leading to historic Howse Pass.

Dropping from the bench, the trail passes close to a bend in the Howse River then cuts inland from the braided flats to begin the long, forest-enclosed climb over a ridge to Glacier Lake. The high point of hike, approximately 1660 m, is

Division Mountain and Southeast Lyell Glacier from Glacier Lake

reached around 7 km. From there the trail plunges down to the east end of the lake.

Glacier Lake is 3 km in length and nearly 1 km wide—one of the largest backcountry lakes in Banff Park. A campground not far from the lake's outlet is a good base for explorations along the north shore and to the Southeast Lyell Glacier beyond.

Lakeshore-Southeast Lyell Glacier. A rough trail continues along the lake's north shore from the campground 3.4 km to the brushy Glacier River flats at the west end of the lake. The river is the lake's major tributary, and you can follow along the north side of its braided channels for another 5 km to terminal moraines beneath the Southeast Lyell Glacier.

The trail is indistinct along the meanders and shifting gravels of the alluvial plain, and you are forced to do a bit of bushwhacking where river channels force you into the willows. However, the route stays to the right of the river and is obvious.

Scramble to the top of the steep moraines at the end of the valley for a fantastic view of the Southeast Lyell Glacier icefall and a small meltwater lake.

67 Sunset Pass

Icefields Parkway to Sunset Lookout—4.5 km (2.8 mi)
Icefields Parkway to Sunset Pass Viewpoint—8.2 km (5.1 mi)
Icefields Parkway to Pinto Lake—13.7 km (8.5 mi)

Day trip or backpack

Allow 2.5 to 3 hours Sunset Pass

Elevation gain: 725 m (2,380 ft)

Maximum elevation: 2165 m (7,100 ft)

Maps: Cline River 83 C/2
　　　Bow Lake-Sask Crossing (GemTrek)

Access: Follow the Icefields Parkway to the trailhead parking area, located on the east side of the highway 16.5 km (10.5 mi) north of The Crossing resort and service centre.

0.0—Trailhead parking area (1440 m).

　—Moderate uphill grade.

0.6—Grade becomes steep.

1.0—Norman Creek gorge viewpoint.

　—Steady uphill via switchbacks.

2.9—Junction. Sunset Lookout site left 1.6 km. Sunset Pass ahead.

4.0—Trail levels out into extensive meadow.

4.4—Norman Lake Campground (No5).

　—Flat to rolling through open meadow.

6.7—Trail climbs moderate to steep through open forest.

8.2—Sunset Pass (2165 m). Park boundary.

8.7—Pinto Lake Viewpoint.

　—Steep descent.

13.7—Pinto Lake Campsite (1750 m).

The Sunset Pass trail travels through extensive meadows beneath the cliffs of Mount Coleman to an exceptional viewpoint overlooking Pinto Lake, the remote Cline River valley, and the sea of peaks comprising Alberta's White Goat Wilderness Area.

It is a long day to the pass viewpoint and back, so many backpack to Norman Lake or Pinto Lake Campground and explore from there. Or you can simply hike 4.5 km to the old Sunset fire lookout site for its overview of the North Saskatchewan and Alexandra River valleys.

A steep climb from the Icefields Parkway makes any itinerary an arduous one. The first 3 km rise at an excruciating grade over a trail that is forest-enclosed and dry (make sure to pack water for the first hour or so of the trip). The only scenic respite on this ascent is a brief glimpse of the Norman Creek gorge.

After you pass the Sunset Lookout junction, the grade moderates somewhat. A kilometre further along the trail levels out and drops into the Norman Creek meadows, which extend unbroken for the next 2.5 km.

Norman Lake Campground is located in a grove of large spruce trees on the eastern edge of the meadow. While it is nearly 500 m distant from the marshy lake on the meadow's western margin, it is still a very pleasant site with open views to Mount Coleman.

The trail continues flat through the meadow, but the track is often muddy and there are minor streams you must hop across. At the north end of the meadow, you climb through scattered trees to the park boundary and, 0.5 km beyond, emerge on a high open ridge.

The ridgetop viewpoint is actually higher than the true summit of Sunset Pass, which lies nearly 2 km away to the southeast. By detouring off the trail to

Pinto Lake from Sunset Pass summit

the precipitous edge of the ridge, fantastic views open down to Pinto Lake and the Cline River valley.

Most day hikers turn back at the viewpoint, but backpackers can continue to a primitive campground at the northwest corner of Pinto Lake—a steep descent of 415 m in just over 5 km.

Many place names along the trail commemorate the first recorded traverse of the pass by geologist Arthur P. Coleman in 1893. Mount Coleman was named in his honour in 1903, and Pinto Lake immortalizes one of the expedition's most troublesome packhorses.

Sunset Lookout. The trail to Sunset Lookout branches left from the Sunset Pass route at km 2.9. This side trail climbs northwest for more than a kilometre along the heavily forested slopes of Mount Coleman before descending to a fine viewpoint on the lip of a sheer limestone cliff 450 m above the Icefields Parkway and North Saskatchewan River.

The small, one room Sunset Lookout cabin was built here during the summer of 1944 and was demolished in 1977 after Parks Canada abandoned its fire lookouts. In addition to the massive summits of Mount Amery (3329 m) and Mount Saskatchewan (3342 m), the lookout commanded a view directly up the Alexandra River to the ice-covered peaks of the Great Divide over 18 km away.

There is no water on the trail to the lookout site, so remember to pack enough to quench your thirst for the duration of the trip.

68 Nigel Pass

Icefields Parkway to Nigel Pass—7.2 km (4.5 mi)

Day trip

Allow 2 hours one way

Elevation gain: 335 m (1,100 ft)

Maximum elevation: 2195 m (7,200 ft)

Maps: Columbia Icefield 83 C/3

Access: Follow the Icefields Parkway to the Nigel Pass parking area, located on the northeast side of the highway 8.5 km (5.5 mi) south of the Banff—Jasper Park boundary at Sunwapta Pass. The parking area is on a gravel side road running downhill to a barrier and the trailhead.

0.0—Trail sign (1860 m).

—Footbridge to northeast side of Nigel Creek.

2.1—Old Camp Parker.

—Ascent along east side of Nigel Creek valley.

5.1—Trail enters open meadows.

—Steady ascent to park boundary.

7.2—Nigel Summit (2195 m). Banff-Jasper Park boundary. Trail crosses Brazeau River headwaters and continues down Brazeau Valley (see *Jonas Pass–Brazeau Lake Loop* and *South Boundary Trail,* Jasper Park chapter).

Nigel Pass is one of the most rewarding day trips in the Columbia Icefield vicinity. The trail climbs moderately through scattered forest and flower-filled meadows to a point above the true pass. Atop this open, rocky ridge on the boundary of Banff and Jasper Parks, there are expansive views back to rugged, glaciated peaks near the Icefield and north into Jasper's remote Brazeau Valley.

From the lower end of the parking area, the trail immediately crosses Nigel Creek and contours across avalanche paths along the east side of the valley.

At km 2.1 the site of old Camp Parker is passed in a stand of large Engelmann spruce. This area was used as a campsite by native hunters before the arrival of the white man, and mountaineers exploring the Columbia Icefield region at the turn of the 20th century continued the tradition. The carvings on the surrounding trees record the visits of many of these early campers, though most date to the period following the opening of the Banff-Jasper Highway in 1940.

At Camp Parker the trail turns north and begins the ascent of the upper Nigel Valley. Throughout this section there are good views back to Parker Ridge and Hilda Peak—a sharp sub-peak of Mount Athabasca. Nigel Pass is seldom out-of-sight ahead.

The trail climbs more seriously over the last kilometre to the trail summit, attained on a rocky ridge where a cairn marks the boundary between Banff and Jasper Parks. (The true summit of Nigel Pass lies just over a kilometre to the northeast.) Forest cover is very sparse and stunted on this 2195-m ridge, an indication of the upper limit of tree growth in this latitude.

Back down-valley to the south, the ice-clad summit of Mount Saskatchewan (3342 m) rises beyond Parker Ridge. To the north is the wild Brazeau River valley and the maze of peaks comprising the

southern region of Jasper Park. Directly west of the pass, rising above a large cirque, is Nigel Peak (3211 m), named in 1898 by British mountaineers Hugh Stutfield and Norman Collie for their packer Nigel Vavasour.

You can discover more views by continuing north into Jasper Park another kilometre or so. A short 0.4 km descent brings you to the south fork of the Brazeau River (an easy rock-hop crossing). Continue down across a rocky slope to a large, marshy meadow where there are even better views of the Brazeau Valley and back to the north side of Nigel Pass—a fine rock wall featuring several small waterfalls.

Strong hikers will find the descent of the valley as far as Boulder Creek Campground (3.5 km beyond Nigel Pass) quite rewarding. (See *Jonas Pass-Brazeau Lake Loop,* Jasper Park chapter.)

Cataract Pass. This high pass at the headwaters of the south fork of the Brazeau River lies approximately 6 km southeast of Nigel Pass. While no defined trail leads in this direction, energetic explorers with a topo map can strike out from Nigel Summit and pick a route through the rocky, open terrain to a small lake at the foot of Cataract Pass.

Backpackers can continue over Cataract Pass to Pinto Lake. After crossing its 2485-m summit, descend to the headwaters of Cataract Creek. Trail reappears near treeline on the east side of the creek, which is followed down-valley to a junction with the Cline River trail just below Pinto Lake.

This trip is best reserved until late in the season since snowbanks often cover the very steep approaches to Cataract Pass into August. There are also fords of Cataract Creek near its confluence with the Cline River and at Huntington Creek; both may present some difficulty during periods of high runoff.

The distance from Nigel Summit to Pinto Lake is approximately 26 km. (See also *Sunset Pass.*)

69 Parker Ridge

Icefields Parkway to Saskatchewan Glacier Viewpoint—2.7 km (1.7 mi)

Half-day trip

Allow 1 hour one way

Elevation gain: 250 m (820 ft)

Maximum elevation: 2250 m (7,380 ft)

Maps: Columbia Icefield 83 C/3

Access: Follow the Icefields Parkway to the Parker Ridge parking area, located on the west side of the highway 4.0 km (2.5 mi) south of the Banff—Jasper Park boundary at Sunwapta Pass.

0.0—Trailhead parking area (2000 m).

　—Steady, switchbacking ascent through open forest.

1.1—Trail emerges onto open alpine slopes.

　—Switchbacks continue across open slopes.

2.1—Parker Ridge summit (2250 m).

　—Trail contours left across south side of ridge.

2.5—First Saskatchewan Glacier viewpoint.

2.7—Second Saskatchewan Glacier viewpoint (2235 m).

The Parker Ridge hike is a short, highly rewarding excursion into the alpine life zone. The northernmost trail in Banff Park rises quickly above the treeline and crosses a high, open ridge to a spectacular view of the Saskatchewan Glacier—the Columbia Icefield's longest outlet valley glacier. However, as one of the most scenic and well-publicized short trails in the Rockies, it is also one of the most heavily used, particularly on sunny mid-summer days.

The lower section of trail switchbacks steadily upward through scattered stands of alpine fir and open meadows created by snowslides. Wildflowers in this section are protected from the elements and nourished by abundant moisture from snowmelt. Tall, showy species, like paintbrush, valerian, purple fleabane, and fringed grass-of-Parnassus, bloom here from early July through mid-August.

Halfway up the north-facing slope, at an elevation of 2100 m, you emerge above treeline into the alpine zone—a region of tiny ground-hugging plants. In this harsh, wind-scoured environment the blooms of moss campion, white mountain avens, rock jasmine, and forget-me-nots last only a couple of weeks.

After passing above an extensive talus slope (domain of pikas), the trail makes its final switchbacking ascent to the 2250 m crest of the ridge. From this summit it veers left and makes a slight descent to the first of two viewpoints for the 9 km-long Saskatchewan Glacier.

While many hikers stop at the first viewpoint, another one 0.2 km farther along provides the most rewarding prospect of the glacier and the uppermost limits of the North Saskatchewan River valley. A rocky promontory at the viewpoint is filled with fossil coral and covered by orange foliose *(Xanthoria)* lichen.

The ridgetop is also a rich area for alpine wildlife and birds. It is frequently

Saskatchewan Glacier from Parker Ridge

visited by both mountain sheep and goat, and occasionally a grizzly bear wanders through. Rosy finches and horned larks nest here in summer, white-tailed ptarmigan are year-round residents, and golden eagles and hawks patrol the meadows around the glacier viewpoints for Columbian ground squirrels.

The Parker Ridge trail was built in the 1960s, one of the last trails to be constructed in Banff Park. Unfortunately, it was designed with a series of gradually ascending switchbacks. This encouraged people to shortcut straight downhill on their return from the summit. A number of barriers and "official" shortcuts (staircases) were constructed to discourage this slope damaging practice. Be considerate of this fragile, easily eroded environment and stay on the designated trail or staircases.

Because the trail ascends a north-facing slope, snowbanks often cover the route into early July. To help preserve the fragile meadows, Parks Canada usually keeps the area closed until the track is snowfree. You should check on the trail's status at a park visitor centre if you plan on hiking it before mid-July.

70 Castleguard Meadows

Icefields Parkway to Castleguard Meadows—35.1 km (21.8 mi)

Backpack

Allow 2 days one way

Elevation gain: 535 m (1,750 ft)

Maximum elevation: 2060 m (6,750 ft)

Maps: Cline River 83 C/2
      Columbia Icefield 83 C/3

Access: Follow the Icefields Parkway to the Alexandra River trailhead, 26 km (16 mi) north from the David Thompson Highway (Hwy 11) junction. The unmarked trailhead is below a pull-out on the west side of the highway 1.3 km (0.8 mi) north of the Coleman Picnic Area.

0.0—North Saskatchewan River bridge (1525 m).

— Flat to gently rolling on abandoned fire road.

5.8—Road bends west into Alexandra Valley.

10.9—Road comes abreast of river flats.

11.7—Road crosses river flats. Unbridged Alexandra River channel. End of bicycle access.

— Road crosses unbridged river channels. Thigh deep fords or worse.

13.5—Terrace Creek crossing. Old campsite.

20.5—Road reverts to trail, enters forest.

20.9—Castleguard Warden Cabin (1555 m).

21.4—Old campsite.

— Gradual to moderate climb up Castleguard Valley.

30.6—Major stream crossing (log bridge?).

31.9—Outram's Shower Bath Falls.

— Steep climb.

35.1—Castleguard Campground (2060 m). South edge of Castleguard Meadows.

Located on the edge of the Columbia Icefield in the remote northwest corner of Banff National Park, the Castleguard Meadows lie between Castleguard and Terrace Mountains—a pass between the headwaters of the North Saskatchewan and Castleguard Rivers. But what a pass! As Dalton Muir and Derek Ford have aptly described in their book *Castleguard,* "so many natural features compete for attention that the senses become saturated."

Like many remote trails in Banff Park, this trail is not maintained. It is long, gruelling, and plagued with deadfall. The main obstacles are hazardous crossings of the unbridged Alexandra River channels during periods of high water. We recommend hiking this trail in late summer when water levels are lower.

The trip starts on an old fire road running up the Alexandra River to the Castleguard Warden Cabin. While the road is slowly becoming overgrown, the first section is straightforward and open for mountain biking. However, at km 11.7 the road descends onto the Alexandra River flats and your troubles begin. Bridges that once spanned the wandering river channels have long since washed away. When warm weather brings high water, these crossings are dangerous.

When the river is running high, hikers abandon the road and follow along the forest margin on the north side of the river flats. The main difficulties are thrashing through mostly untracked forest and fording side streams, particularly Terrace Creek, which is tricky at high water.

The road ends near the confluence of the Alexandra and Castleguard Rivers, just a short distance before the warden cabin. Here it reverts to single-track and turns northwest up the Castleguard Valley.

Rocky and rooty trail follows the northeast side of the Castleguard for just

Mike McReynolds photo

Castleguard Meadows

over 10 km (tributary streams must be forded if log bridges are not in place).

After passing the trail branching west to Watchman Lake and Thompson Pass, you make a steep 3 km climb through the forest to a campground on the southern edge of the Castleguard Meadows. Here the trail ends and the meadows are yours to explore at your leisure.

The meadows comprise a narrow corridor running north from the campsite for 4 km to a 2250 m pass overlooking the Saskatchewan Glacier. Ascending this broad vale, you pass from well-watered, marshy meadows bordered by stands of alpine fir, through extensive alpine meadows dotted with islands of krummholz (dwarfed and stunted trees), and finally emerge onto the barren, windswept pass.

The climb through the meadows is quite gradual. The dominant feature throughout is glacier-draped Castleguard Mountain (3090 m) looming above to the west. Nearly as impressive is Terrace Mountain, which rises on the east side of the valley. Though they have long since retreated to higher levels, glaciers descended from both of these peaks,

leaving great terminal moraines along the valley margins.

The view from the summit is quite amazing. The Saskatchewan Glacier flows at your feet—the longest valley glacier descending from the Columbia Icefield. Directly across the valley, tributary glaciers tumble down the slopes of Mount Andromeda (3450 m). And, off to the west, peeking over the white expanse of the Icefield, is Mount Columbia—the highest point in Alberta at 3747 m.

Saskatchewan Glacier Route. For experienced mountain travellers who understand and are equipped for the hazards of glacier travel, the most direct route to the meadows is via the Saskatchewan Glacier. This journey entails a 7 km hike to the toe of the glacier followed by a 5 km ascent up the centre of the icy tongue to a point where you traverse across to the northern edge of the meadows.

Anyone attempting this route should inquire at the Lake Louise Visitor Centre for a report on current conditions and a route description.

71 Saskatchewan Glacier

Icefields Parkway to Saskatchewan Glacier Basin—6.0 km (3.7 mi)

During World War II, an access road was built to the Saskatchewan Glacier so U.S. Army engineers could test oversnow vehicles that would be used for Alaska Highway construction. However, the glacier has receded nearly a kilometre since then, and the road now ends far short of the ice. This old track to the glacier basin is of marginal interest, except for experienced glacier-travellers bound for the Castleguard Meadows. (See *Castleguard Meadows.*)

Cross the concrete bridge at the trailhead and turn right immediately onto a rough forest path. The path joins the old army road in 0.5 km.

The road climbs over a forested ridge and descends to the glacier's outwash plain at km 2.6. Sections of road on the flats have been washed away by the river, but rough trails through brushy spruce detour these washouts and bring you back to the roadbed.

Around km 6.0 the road ends in a hummocky moonscape of recessional moraines. The glacier is visibile far ahead, and some hikers continue beyond this point in an attempt to reach it. However, steep ice-cored moraines and treacherous footing await the foolhardy who would attempt the final scramble to its surface.

Access: Follow the Icefields Parkway to the Big Bend—a prominent highway switchback on open gravel flats 11 km (7 mi) south of the Banff-Jasper boundary at Sunwapta Pass. An old concrete bridge just below the highway 0.7 km (0.4 mi) south of Big Bend is the trailhead. A small parking area at the bridge accommodates 2 or 3 vehicles, otherwise, walk from the Big Bend pull-out. *Maps: Columbia Icefield 83 C/3.*

72 Panther Falls

Icefields Parkway to Panther Falls Viewpoint—0.5 km (0.3 mi)

Mary Schäffer and her companions came upon this waterfall in July, 1907: "As we later found a panther (or wild-cat) had followed in our footsteps for a considerable distance along this special bit of trail, we named them the Panther Falls."

The 1999 Canadian Encyclopedia lists the height of the waterfall at 183 m—the fourth highest in Canada! We've roughly measured it at less than half that— around 60 m. It is still a very impressive waterfall, mainly for the volume of water that Nigel Creek funnels over the abyss, and it is only short walk from the Icefields Parkway.

At Bridal Veil Falls viewpoint, walk downhill to the trail sign atop an earthen barrier at lower end of the lengthy pull-

off. The trail drops into the forest on the opposite side of the earthwork and, after a few switchbacks, arrives at a muddy, spray-soaked slope, which serves as the viewpoint at the base of the falls. (This slope can be hazardous, particularly for those with smooth-soled shoes.)

Do not visit the top of this falls. The smooth rocks at the lip of the abyss make it an incredibly dangerous place.

Access: Follow the Icefields Parkway to the Bridal Veil Falls viewpoint, a long pull-out located on the east side of the highway 9.0 km (5.5 mi) south of the Banff-Jasper Park boundary at Sunwapta Pass. *Maps: Columbia Icefield 83 C/3.*

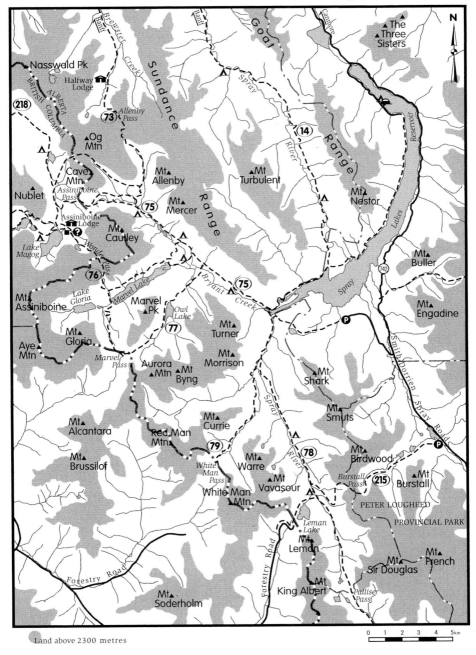

N

Nasswald Pk

BRITISH COLUMBIA
ALBERTA

218

Halfway
Lodge

Brewster Creek Banff

Sundance Range

73 Allenby Pass

Og Mtn

Cave Mtn

Nublet

Assiniboine Pass

Assiniboine Lodge

Lake Magog

75

Mt Allenby

Mt Mercer

Mt Cautley

Wonder Pass

76

Lake Gloria

Marvel Lake

Marvel Pk

Owl Lake

Banff

14

Goat Range

Spray River

Mt Turbulent

Mt Nestor

Reservoir

742

Mt Buller

75 Bryant Creek

77

Mt Turner

Mt Assiniboine

Mt Gloria

Aye Mtn

Marvel Pass

Aurora Mtn

Mt Byng

Mt Morrison

Spray Lakes

Mt Engadine

P

Mt Shark

Smith-Dorrien Spray Road

Mt Alcantara

Mt Brussilof

Red Man Mtn

Mt Currie

79

White Man Pass

78

Mt Warre

White Man Mtn

Mt Vavasour

Spray River

Mt Smuts

Mt Birdwood

Burstall Pass

215

P

Mt Burstall

PETER LOUGHEED

PROVINCIAL PARK

Forestry Road

Forestry Road

Leman Lake

Mt Leman

Mt King Albert

Mt Sir Douglas

Mt French

Palliser Pass

Mt Soderholm

The Three Sisters

Canmore

Land above 2300 metres

0 1 2 3 4 5km

73 Brewster Creek—Allenby Pass

Sunshine Road to Allenby Pass—27.0 km (16.8 mi)
Sunshine Road to Bryant Creek—32.8 km (20.4 mi)

Backpack

Allow 2 days to Allenby Pass

Elevation gain: 1020 m (3,350 ft)

Maximum elevation: 2440 m (8,000 ft)

Maps: Banff 82 O/4
    Mount Assiniboine 82 J/13

Access: Follow the Trans-Canada Highway to the Sunshine Village Road exit, 9 km (5.5 mi) west of the Banff town west exit. Follow the Sunshine Road to the trailhead parking area, located on the left side of the road 0.3 km (0.2 mi) beyond the Trans-Canada Highway overpass.

0.0—Healy Creek parking area (1420 m). Healy Creek footbridge.

0.6—Junction. *Sundance Canyon* trail and Banff ahead. Brewster Creek right.

3.3—Junction (1570 m). Intersection with Brewster Creek access road. *Sundance Canyon* trail and Banff left. Brewster Creek right.

8.7—Sundance Lodge.

10.3—Junction (1630m). Brewster Creek Campground (Bw10) and *Fatigue Creek* right. Allenby Pass ahead.

13.2—Brewster Creek bridge to west side.

23.0—Halfway Lodge (1950 m).

—Trail crosses creek south of cabin.

24.0—Steep switchback ascent to Allenby Pass begins.

27.0—Allenby Pass (2440 m).

—Moderate to steep descent south from pass.

31.7—Junction. Intersection with Og Pass trail. Right to *Og Pass* (5.5 km) and Mt Assiniboine Lodge (11.0 km). Bryant Creek trail ahead.

32.6—Junction. Og Pass shortcut right. Bryant Creek ahead.

32.8—Junction. Intersection with *Bryant Creek* hiker's trail at km 18.0.

The Brewster Creek trail has long been a major access route to the Bryant Creek area in the south part of Banff Park. It was also the original route used by skiers between Banff and Mount Assiniboine Lodge starting in 1928, and soon thereafter it became a primary route for Assiniboine-bound horse parties in the summer.

While Allenby Pass, at the head of the Brewster Valley, is a fine destination, regular horse use and a long forested approach discourage many backpackers from hiking the trail. Two lodges in the valley are operated by a commercial outfitter, and they sometimes accommodate hikers early or late in the season.

While it is possible to reach Brewster Creek directly from Banff by way of the Sundance Canyon trail and the old Healy Creek access road, the shortest approach is from the Sunshine Road.

From the Sunshine Road trailhead you immediately cross a footbridge over Healy Creek and follow the broad track of the old Healy Creek road 0.6 km to the shortcut trail branching right to Brewster Creek. (Cyclists and skiers will find a wider, smoother track and less demanding grades by continuing another 1.3 km on the Healy Creek road to where the Brewster Creek access road branches right. This option adds 2.2 km.)

The shortcut climbs steeply through dense forest on rocky, muddy horse trail to km 3.3, where it intersects the access road from Banff. This broad track rolls southward into the Brewster Creek valley and follows along the east side of the creek to Sundance Lodge.

The lodge's primary function is as an overnight destination for horse parties. Like Halfway Lodge, which lies farther upvalley, it provides accommodation for hikers when there are empty beds, usually early or late in the season (see *Sources-Backcountry lodges*).

The historic Ten Mile Cabin, built by the CPR in the 1920s, is located beside the lodge. It was one of several backcountry shelters constructed by the company along the Great Divide between Assiniboine and Lake Louise to encourage hiking and horseback recreation. For 50 years it operated as a waystation between Banff and Mount Assiniboine Lodge by lodge owner and ski pioneer Erling Strom.

Beyond Sundance Lodge the smooth access road reverts to heavily travelled horse trail, continuing upvalley through heavy forest with occasional views of the Sundance Range to the east. At km 10.3 the Fatigue Creek trail branches right to Brewster Creek Campground, the valley's only campsite.

Nearly 3 km beyond Fatigue Creek junction you cross a bridge to the west side of Brewster Creek and continue the long, uneventful ascent of the valley. A short distance before arriving at a sidestream ford, views open southeast to the Brewster Glacier—one of the valley's scenic highlights.

After sloshing across a main tributary flowing into Brewster Creek from the southwest, the trail begins to climb at a moderate but steady grade. Soon after passing Brewster Creek Warden Cabin, it bends south into a side-valley and climbs to Halfway Lodge—so-called because it was used as the halfway overnight stop for skiers and horse parties travelling between Banff and Mount Assiniboine

Just beyond the lodge, you make one final stream crossing before starting the steep climb to Allenby Pass—a vertical ascent of 450 m to this spectacular defile composed of rockslides and alpine meadows.

Beyond the pass you can descend to the Bryant Creek trail in another 5.8 km (see *Bryant Creek*). or take the Og Pass cutoff to Mount Assiniboine Provincial Park (see *Og Pass-Windy Ridge*, Mount Assinboine Park chapter).

The trail up Brewster Creek to Allenby Pass has been open to mountain bikes in recent years, but beyond Sundance Lodge it is one longest and roughest bike routes in the park. It may be subject to closure in the future to reduce impact on the valley's grizzly bears.

74 Fatigue Creek

Brewster Creek to Fatigue Pass—10.9 km (6.8 mi)
Brewster Creek to Citadel Pass—13.4 km (8.3 mi)

The Fatigue Creek trail links Brewster Creek to the Citadel Pass trail via 2395 m Fatigue Pass—a lofty alpine summit with marvelous views of the southern Sunshine Meadows. The trail is rough, wet and seldom used by hikers, but the track is maintained by regular horse trips from Sundance Lodge in the Brewster Valley.

From the 10.3-km junction on the *Brewster Creek-Allenby Pass* trail, you branch west to the valley's only campground. Immediately beyond the campground the trail crosses Brewster Creek—the first of many foot-soaking fords.

The Fatigue Creek valley is narrow, forcing the trail to swing back and forth across the creek six times in the first 5 km—all unbridged crossings. Above the last ford you climb steadily and steeply onto the alpine meadows of Fatigue Pass (2395 m).

Beyond the pass, the trail descends northwest across the rocky, open slopes of Fatigue Mountain for another 2.5 km to the crest of Citadel Pass. (See *Citadel Pass*.)

Access: To reach the north end of the trail, follow the Brewster Creek-Allenby Pass trail to the Fatigue Creek trail junction, 1.6 km south of Sundance Lodge. The south end of the trail is accessed from a junction on the crest of Citadel Pass (see *Citadel Pass*). Maps: Banff 82 O/4.

75 Bryant Creek—Assiniboine Pass

Mt Shark Parking Area to Marvel Lake Campground—13.6 km (8.5 mi)
Mt Shark Parking Area to Mount Assiniboine Lodge—25.3 km (15.7 mi)

Backpack

Allow 3.5 to 4 hours to Marvel Lake

Elevation loss: 65 m (200 ft)
gain: 460 m (1,500 ft)

Maximum elevation: 2165 m (7,100 ft)

Maps: Spray Lakes Reservoir 82 J/14
Mount Assiniboine 82 J/13

Access: Follow the Spray Lakes Road west from the town of Canmore 38 km (23.5 mi) to the Mount Shark Road junction. Follow the Mount Shark Road 5.3 km (3.3 mi) to its termination at the trailhead parking area.

0.0—Mount Shark Parking Area (1770 m).

3.7—Junction. Watridge Lake left 150 m. Bryant Creek ahead.

5.9—Spray River bridge.

6.0—Junction (1705 m). *Palliser Pass* left. Bryant Creek right.

6.6—Bryant Creek bridge.

6.7—Trail Centre Junction. Bryant Creek left.

9.6—Big Springs Campground (Br9).

12.0—Junction. *Owl Lake* trail left.

13.0—Junction. Left 0.6 km to Marvel Lake Campground (Br13) and Marvel Lake (1.6 km).

13.6—Junction. Bryant Creek Shelter left 0.2 km.

14.2—Junction. McBride's Camp Campground (Br14) right 0.2 km. *Wonder Pass* trail left.

14.3—Bryant Creek Warden Cabin.

17.3—Allenby Junction Campground (Br 17).

17.5—Junction. Assiniboine Pass horse trail left (stream crossing); hiker trail right.

18.0—Junction. Allenby Pass right. Assiniboine Pass left.

22.4—Junction. Horse trail rejoins hiker trail.

—Steady uphill switchbacks.

23.0—Assiniboine Pass (2165 m). Banff–Mt. Assiniboine Park boundary.

When many hikers think of the Bryant Creek trail, they only think of the most direct route to Mount Assiniboine. Yet, the valley's campgrounds and shelter cabin serve as base camps for a number of fine day trips. Worthwhile destinations include Assiniboine Pass, Wonder Pass, Owl Lake, Marvel Pass and Allenby Pass —all within a day hike of your camp.

Starting from the Mount Shark parking area in Alberta's Kananaskis Country recreation area, a broad, well graded trail runs due west and descends to a bridge across the Spray River. Follow the Spray River trail right 0.7 km, crossing Bryant Creek, to the Trail Centre junction.

The ascent of the Bryant Creek valley begins at Trail Centre on a broad track— a straightforward if uninspiring trek. Owl Lake junction is passed at km 12.0, and 1.0 km farther along, the trail to Marvel Lake Campground and the east end of Marvel Lake.

At km 13.6 you reach the Bryant Creek Shelter. Lying just off the trail to the left, the shelter is popular with tentless hikers. Because of this popularity, you should make reservations through the Banff Visitor Centre if you plan on staying there.

Another kilometre brings you to McBride's Campground, the Wonder Pass trail junction, and the Bryant Creek Warden Cabin. McBride's is a good centrally-located campground for backpackers who don't want to stay at the shelter.

Assiniboine Pass. The Bryant Creek trail continues upvalley beyond the warden cabin and immediately enters an extensive meadow covered with shrub willow and dwarf birch.

At km 17.3 you reach the valley's last campground, Allenby Junction. This is another good base camp, particularly for day trips to Allenby, Og and Assiniboine

Bryant Creek Warden Cabin

24.8—Junction. Og Pass, Og Lake, Citadel Pass right. Lake Magog ahead.

25.1—Junction. Lake Magog Campground ahead 1.6 km. Mt. Assiniboine Lodge, Naiset Cabins and Mt. Assiniboine Park Headquarters Cabin left.

25.3.—Mount Assiniboine Lodge (2180 m).

Passes. If you shoulder your backpack past this point, you are likely bound for Mount Assiniboine via Assiniboine Pass.

A hikers' trail branches right from the old horse trail just beyond the campground. While this trail stays on higher and drier ground on the north side of the valley, and eliminates an immediate ankle-deep crossing of Bryant Creek, it adds approximately 1.5 km to the distance to Assiniboine Pass.

The hikers' trail soon reaches the junction for Allenby Pass. Keep left and continue upvalley to the last series of switchbacks leading to Assiniboine Pass.

While the subalpine meadows of the pass would be a pleasant destination on many other trails, hikers who take the trouble of climbing to its summit are inevitably bound for Lake Magog at the foot of Mount Assiniboine, just 2.5 km beyond (see Mount Assiniboine chapter).

Marvel Lake. Ringed by heavy subalpine forest, Marvel is one of Banff Park's largest backcountry lakes and the shortest hike from the upper Bryant Creek campgrounds and shelter. The

Marvel Lake from the Wonder Pass trail

lake's main attraction is not the scenery but the fishing, and its deep waters have been known to produce large trout. (Contact Parks Canada for current fishing regulations.)

The east end of the lake can be reached via the 1.6-km trail that branches from the Bryant Creek trail at km 13.0 (only 1.0 km beyond Marvel Lake Campground). It can also be reached in 1.6 km from McBride's Campground via the *Wonder Pass* trail (see page 155).

The west end of the lake is accessed from the *Wonder Pass* and *Owl Lake-Marvel Pass* trails.

Allenby Pass. This lofty, rockbound pass is usually associated with the long, tedious backpack up Brewster Creek. However, it can be reached in a day from any of the campgrounds or the shelter in the upper Bryant Creek valley.

At the 17.5-km junction, just beyond Allenby Junction Campground, keep right on the hikers' trail leading to Assiniboine Pass. At the next junction, 500 m farther along, stay right for Allenby Pass.

The trail climbs steadily for 5.8 kms to the 2440-m summit, traversing some delightful wildflower meadows and alpine larch stands along the way. One way distance to the pass from Allenby Junction Campground is 6.5 km. (See also *Brewster Creek-Allenby Pass.*)

Bryant Creek Options. In addition to the short hike to Marvel Lake and the day trip to Allenby Pass, you can also day trip to Wonder Pass, Owl Lake and Marvel Pass, as described on the following pages.

Longer loop trips can also be completed into Mount Assiniboine Park from upper Bryant Creek campgrounds and shelter: Assiniboine Pass and Og Pass can be linked together to complete a loop around Cave Mountain—total round trip distance from Allenby Junction Campground, including a side-trip to Lake Magog, is 19.2 km; or you can make a circuit around Wonder Peak via Assiniboine Pass, Lake Magog and Wonder Pass—approximately 24 km round trip from any of the upper Bryant Creek campgrounds or the shelter.

76 Wonder Pass

McBride Campground Jct to Wonder Pass—8.9 km (5.5 mi)
McBride Campground Jct to Mount Assiniboine Lodge—12.0 km (7.5 mi)

Backpack
Allow 3 hours to Wonder Pass
Elevation gain: 550 m (1,800 ft)
Maximum elevation: 2395 m (7,850 ft)
Maps: Mount Assiniboine 82 J/13

Access: Follow the *Bryant Creek* trail to the McBride Campground Junction at 14.2 km. The Wonder Pass trail branches southwest (left) at this junction. (The trail can also be accessed by connector trails running northwest from Marvel Lake Campground and Bryant Creek Shelter.)

0.0—McBride Camp Junction (1845 m).

—Trail crosses large meadow.

0.3—Junction—Bryant Creek bridge. Bryant Creek Shelter left 0.5 km. Wonder Pass ahead.

—Trail enters forest.

1.1—Junction. Left to Marvel Lake (0.5 km) and Marvel Lake Campground (1.5 km).

2.0—Avalanche path.

—Contour across avalanche paths.

5.6—Junction. Left to *Marvel Pass* and Marvel Lake (0.5 km).

—Steady switchbacking ascent.

7.3—Enter scattered subalpine forest.

—Moderate climb through meadows.

8.9—Wonder Pass (2395 m). Intersection with *Wonder Pass* trail from Lake Magog (see Assiniboine Park chapter, page 412).

10.5—Gog Lake.

11.5—Naiset Cabins—Mt. Assiniboine Park Headquarters Cabin.

12.0—Mount Assiniboine Lodge (2180 m).

13.5—Lake Magog Campground (2165 m).

Wonder Pass is one of the most scenic day hikes from the campgrounds and shelter near the east end of Marvel Lake. In addition to providing a good overview of Marvel Lake, the pass is an outstanding viewpoint for the vast meadows above the Lake Magog district of Mount Assiniboine Park.

The pass can also be used to access the Lake Magog area of Assiniboine Park. However, the trail is a kilometre longer and much steeper than the more popular Assiniboine Pass route. Most backpackers use Assiniboine Pass on the way in and Wonder Pass on the way out.

Starting from the 14.2-km junction on the Bryant Creek trail, the Wonder Pass trail runs west across a meadow to a bridge over Bryant Creek. Trails from the Bryant Creek Shelter and Marvel Lake Campground intersect from the left at km 0.3 and 1.1, providing access to the trail from either of those sites. The latter trail also leads 0.5 km to a fine viewpoint at the east end of Marvel Lake.

The main trail continues upvalley, contouring well above the lake across the lower slopes of Wonder Peak. Numerous avalanche paths between km 2.0 and 5.3 provide views of Marvel Lake and the glaciated summits of Aye Mountain, Eon Mountain and Lunette Peak at the head of the valley.

At km 5.6 you pass a side-trail leading down to the west end of Marvel Lake (see *Owl Lake–Marvel Pass*). The junction is also a viewpoint for Lakes Gloria and Terrapin at the head of the valley.

Beyond the junction the trail makes a steep ascent to the pass—a tough climb on a hot day. However, the scenery near the summit more than compensates for the struggle.

If you are continuing into Assiniboine Park, it is a short downhill walk through meadows and larch forest to Lake Magog. (See *Wonder Pass*, page 412.)

77 Owl Lake—Marvel Pass

Bryant Creek Trail Junction to Owl Lake—3.5 km (2.2 mi)
Bryant Creek Trail Junction to Marvel Pass—9.3 km (5.8 mi)

Backcountry day hike

Allow 1 hour to Owl Lake

Elevation gain: 150 m (500 ft)

Maximum elevation: 1890 m (6,200 ft)

Maps: Mount Assiniboine 82 J/13

Access: Follow the *Bryant Creek-Assiniboine Pass* trail to the junction with the Owl Lake trail at 12.0 km.

0.0—Bryant Creek Junction (1770 m).

　—Gradual descent.

0.3—Bryant Creek bridge (200 m upstream from horse crossing).

1.9—Trail crests rise above Owl Lake basin.

3.4—Junction. South end of Owl Lake and Marvel Pass ahead. North end of Owl Lake left 100 m.

3.5—Owl Lake (1890 m).

5.0—Owl Lake south end.

5.4—Old campsite in meadow.

　—Trail climbs through forest and across avalanche paths.

9.3—Marvel Pass (2200 m).

Owl Lake is a charming blue-green body of water set in the central portion of a valley contained by Marvel Peak and Mounts Byng, Morrison and Turner. Its pleasant subalpine setting makes it a worthy destination or a scenic waypoint on an extended journey to Marvel Pass.

Owl Lake is usually visited as a day hike from one of the Bryant Creek valley campgrounds. Marvel Lake Campground and the Bryant Creek Shelter are both within 1.8 km of Owl Lake junction; McBride's Camp and Big Springs Campground are 2.4 km from the trail.

From its junction with the Bryant Creek trail at 12.0 km, the trail to Owl Lake gradually descends to the valley bottom and swift-flowing Bryant Creek (crossed on a footbridge 200 m above the horse ford). Beyond the creek it climbs moderately for a little over 1.5 km to the Owl Lake basin.

Once the basin is reached you traverse some intriguing meadows, characterized by low ridges of peculiarly jumbled rock. This section of twisted and broken terrain also provides a good opportunity to take your bearings on the surrounding country.

At km 3.4 the trail splits, the left branch descending to the north end of Owl Lake in 100 m, the right contouring above the lake's western shore to the south end in another 1.5 km. With Mount Byng and Aurora Mountain serving as a backdrop, the view from the north shore is quite scenic, particularly in early morning.

Marvel Pass. Lying 4.3 km beyond and 300 m above the southern end of Owl Lake, Marvel Pass is an interesting option for experienced hikers. Located at the apex of three high alpine valleys on the Great Divide, the pass is a wonderful destination in an area celebrated for its scenic wonders.

Mount Alcantara from Marvel Pass

The pass is sometimes visited as part of a 23-km loop trip from the campgrounds or shelter near the east end of Marvel Lake, approaching from Owl Lake and returning via the west end of Marvel Lake and the Wonder Pass trail. However, this is a demanding trip requiring some route-finding skills, and you should be armed with a 1:50,000 topo map.

From the south end of Owl Lake an obvious trail runs 0.4 km to an old campsite in a broad meadow. Watch for cairns leading out of the meadow and up along the northwest side of the Owl Creek drainage.

The remainder of the trip to the pass climbs beneath the south-facing slopes of Marvel Peak and its lush avalanche paths. This approach and the pass itself are prime grizzly habitat (bears are frequently seen here), so travel with care and make noise when visibility is limited.

A small lake on the pass provides a pleasant rest stop and viewpoint and is also a bit of a curiosity. Though its waters drain west into British Columbia, it was mapped as part of Alberta and actually lies within Banff National Park. A partially constructed log cabin sits on the lake's north shore, where a British Columbia resident started building in the 1970s believing he was on the B.C. side of the border; he was informed otherwise by park authorities.

You can complete the loop trip by continuing north down Marvel Creek. The route from the pass runs down the east side of the Marvel Creek valley to the west end of Marvel Lake, then climbs steeply to the Wonder Pass trail. However, there are some rather sketchy sections across boggy meadows and a double ford just above Marvel Lake (look for log bridges). It is a trip reserved for good route finders.

Distance from Marvel Pass to the Wonder Pass trail is 6.2 km. (See also *Wonder Pass*, page 155.)

78 Upper Spray River—Palliser Pass

Mt Shark Parking Area to Palliser Pass—26.7 km (16.6 mi)

Backpack

Allow 2 days to Palliser Pass

Elevation loss: 65 m (200 ft)
gain: 400 m (1,300 ft)

Maximum elevation: 2105 m (6,900 ft)

Maps: Spray Lakes Reservoir 82 J/14
Kananaskis Lakes 82 J/11
Canmore-Kananaskis (GemTrek)
Kananaskis Lakes (GemTrek)

Access: Follow the Spray Lakes Road west from the town of Canmore 38 km (23.5 mi) to the Mount Shark Road junction. Follow the Mount Shark Road 5.3 km (3.3 mi) to its termination at the trailhead parking area.

0.0—Mount Shark Parking Area (1770 m).

—Broad well-marked trail.

3.7—Junction. Watridge Lake left 150 m.

5.9—Spray River bridge.

6.0—Junction (1705 m). *Bryant Creek* trail right. Palliser Pass left.

9.2—Junction. Spray River bridge. *White Man Pass* trail right. Palliser Pass ahead (across bridge).

12.8—Junction. South cutoff to White Man Pass right.

15.2—Birdwood Campground (Us15).

15.8—Birdwood Creek. Palliser Warden Cabin.

19.3—Stay left on bench trail above river.

19.8—Junction. *Burstall Pass* trail left.

20.0—Junction. Burstall Campground right 0.3 km, Leman Lake (1.3 km).

24.6—Steep ascent to Palliser Pass begins.

25.9—Belgium Lake.

26.7—Palliser Pass (2105 m). Park boundary.

The upper Spray River valley forms the extreme southern end of Banff Park—a wild, scenic region contained by rugged limestone peaks and home to a wide variety of wildlife, including moose and grizzly bear.

The trail running up the valley receives only moderate use during the summer. With Palliser Pass as a primary destination, you can spend several days exploring, taking side trips to White Man Pass, Leman Lake or Burstall Pass. The latter pass also serves as an optional route of access or exit to the upper end of the valley.

The first 6 km of the hike follows the same route as the *Bryant Creek–Assiniboine Pass* trail. This section, which mostly lies within Alberta's Kananaskis Country recreation area, tends to be very busy, particularly on weekends when families are strolling to Watridge Lake and mountain bikers are out in force. But once you cross the Spray River and begin your ascent of the valley proper, things become quite peaceful.

From the Spray River bridge junction, the trail runs upvalley through a stretch of heavy forest before emerging into open willow meadow. At km 9.2 the White Man Pass trail branches west (see *White Man Pass*), and the Spray River trail crosses back to the east side of the river on a log footbridge.

At 15.2 km you pass Birdwood Campground and, 0.6 km farther along, the Palliser Warden Cabin. Beyond the cabin the trail crosses an extensive meadow, revealing mountains at the upper end of the valley, including Mount Leman. After traversing a long stretch of meadow, it angles left onto higher and drier ground along the forest margin.

The Burstall Pass trail intersects from the left at 19.8 km (a junction that was not well-marked the last time we passed that way). Just 200 m farther along the

Mount Leman from the Upper Spray Valley

trail to Burstall Campground and Leman Lake branches right across the river via a footbridge. This campground is only 0.3 km off the main trail and well situated as a base for day trips to all points of interest in the upper valley, including Palliser Pass, Burstall Pass and nearby Leman Lake.

The trail to Palliser Pass continues up-valley along the eastern side of the Spray. After sloshing across two small streams, the steep, final ascent to the pass begins.

Emerging from the forest at the top of the grade, the trail flattens out across subalpine meadows beside Belgium Lake and, less than a kilometre beyond, the summit of Palliser Pass. Back and Palliser Lakes lie beyond the pass (off-trail to the right) in British Columbia's Height of the Rockies Provincial Park, and serve as possible campsites.

Leman Lake—1.3 km. This forest-encircled lake lies between Mounts Leval and Leman just east of Spray Pass and the Alberta-B.C. boundary. It is a short hike from Burstall Campground.

From the 20.0-km junction, cross log footbridges spanning Spray River and Leman Creek. The trail passes Burstall Campground and climbs steeply through forest before making a final, quick descent to the lakeshore.

Leman is a peaceful lake that reflects its namesake mountain to the south. It is also a place where we have always seen or heard loons.

A path continues along the west shoreline for just over 1.0 km to the park boundary at Spray Pass—a forested gap with no views.

The lake and pass may seem quite remote, but a brief descent into B.C. brings you to the end of a forestry road extending up the Albert River. Don't be surprised if you encounter casual day hikers strolling in from the end of the road.

Burstall Pass—5.3 km. This 12-km trail running from the Smith-Dorrien/Spray Lakes Road in Peter Lougheed Park is often used as an optional access or exit route for Upper Spray Valley backpackers. The pass is also a rewarding day trip from Burstall Campground. (See *Burstall Pass,* Peter Lougheed Park chapter.)

79 White Man Pass

Mount Shark Parking Area to White Man Pass—16.9 km (10.5 mi)

Backpack

Allow 4 to 5 hours one way

Elevation loss: 65 m (230 ft)
      gain: 445 m (1,460 ft)

Maximum elevation: 2150 m (7,050 ft)

Maps: Spray Lakes Reservoir 82 J/14
     Canmore-Kananaskis (Gem Trek)
     Kananaskis Lakes (Gem Trek)

Access: Follow the Spray Lakes Road west from the town of Canmore 38 km (23.5 mi) to the Mount Shark Road junction. Follow the Mount Shark Road 5.3 km (3.3 mi) to its termination at the trailhead parking area.

0.0—Mount Shark Parking Area (1770 m).

3.7—Junction. Watridge Lake left 150 m.

5.9—Spray River bridge.

6.0—Junction (1705 m). *Bryant Creek* right. Upper Spray River and White Man Pass left.

9.2—Junction. *Upper Spray River–Palliser Pass* ahead (across Spray River bridge). White Man Pass right.

10.5—Currie Creek ford.

10.8—White Man Creek ford.

   —Gradual climb.

13.1—Junction. South cutoff to Palliser Pass trail left. White Man Pass right.

14.8—Begin steep ascent to pass.

16.4—Small unnamed lake.

16.9—White Man Pass (2150 m).

Whatever White Man Pass may lack in scenery, it more than compensates with a rich and colourful past. This is the pass that James Sinclair led the Red River emigrants and their livestock through on the way to the Oregon Territory in 1841. Beside a small lake just east of the pass, the halfbreed guides of Jesuit missionary Father Pierre DeSmet erected a wooden cross in his honour in 1845. Two British officers, Henry James Warre and Nigel Vavasour, crossed the pass the same year, bound for Oregon to spy on the Americans.

The trip to White Man Pass utilizes the same approach as the *Upper Spray River–Palliser Pass* hike. Starting from the Mount Shark trailhead, the trail leads 6 km to the Spray River bridge. On the opposite side of the bridge, you arrive at a junction with the trail leading up the Spray Valley, which you follow south for 3.2 kms.

The White Man Pass trail branches right from the Upper Spray-Palliser route at km 9.2. Entry into the White Man Creek valley is not without its toll—a knee-deep ford of Currie Creek 1.3 km from the Upper Spray junction followed by an ankle-deep crossing of White Man Creek 0.3 km beyond.

The remainder of the ascent to the pass is straightforward and uneventful, travelling through a mix of meadow and subalpine forest for 4 km before starting a strenuous 2 km climb to the divide.

White Man Pass is a forested summit with few views, but the tiny lake just east of the pass, where Father DeSmet's guides erected the cross, makes a fine place to rest and contemplate the pioneers who passed this way.

Latter-day explorers can continue this historic journey by venturing down the Cross River headwaters to the end of the B.C. forestry road 6 km beyond the pass.

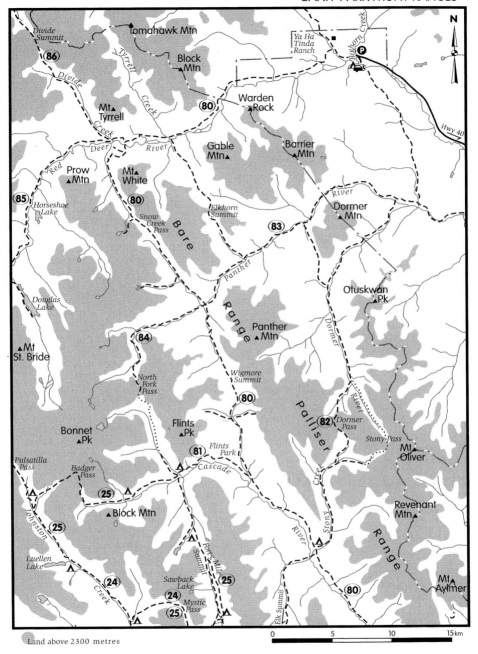

N

86

Divide
Summit

Tomahawk Mtn

Divide

Tyrrell

Creek

Block
Mtn

Ya Ha
Tinda
Ranch

P

Bighorn Creek

Hwy 40

80

Warden
Rock

Mt
Tyrrell

Deer

River

Gable
Mtn

Barrier
Mtn

Red

Creek

Prow
Mtn

Mt
White

River

Dormer
Mtn

85

Horseshoe
Lake

80

Snow
Creek
Pass

Elkhorn
Summit

83

Bare

Douglas
Lake

Panther

Range

Otuskwan
Pk

Mt
St. Bride

84

Panther
Mtn

Dormer

North
Fork
Pass

Wigmore
Summit

Palliser

Bonnet
Pk

Flints
Pk

80

River

82

Dormer
Pass

Stony Pass

Mt
Oliver

Pulsatilla
Pass

Badger
Pass

81

Flints
Park

Cascade

Stony Creek

Revenant
Mtn

25

25

Block Mtn

Range

Johnston

Luellen
Lake

Fort Mile Summit

River

25

24

Creek

Sawback
Lake

24

25

Mystic
Pass

Elk Summit

80

Mt
Aylmer

Land above 2300 metres

0   5   10   15 km

80 Cascade Fire Trail

Lake Minnewanka Road to Ya-Ha-Tinda Ranch—83.0 km (51.6 mi)

Backpack

Allow 3 to 5 days one way

Maximum elevation: 2255 m (7,400 ft)

Minimum elevation: 1465 m (4,800 ft)

Maps: Banff 82 O/4
      Castle Mountain 82 O/5
      Barrier Mountain 82 O/12

Access: Northbound hikers begin from the Upper Bankhead Picnic Area, located on the west side of the Lake Minnewanka Road 3.5 km (2.2 mi) north of the Trans-Canada Highway interchange (Banff east exit). Trail begins at the north corner of the picnic area parking lot.

Southbound hikers start at Ya-Ha-Tinda Ranch just beyond Banff Park's eastern boundary. Follow Highway 1-A east from Canmore 59 km (37 mi) to Highway 940 junction. Continue north 81 km (50 mi) on Highway 940. Turn left onto the Ya-Ha-Tinda road immediately after crossing the Red Deer River bridge. Follow this road west 23 km (14 mi) to Ya-Ha-Tinda Ranch. The Bighorn Creek bridge parking area is 2.6 km (1.6 mi) past the ranch entrance gate, opposite the Bighorn Creek Campground.

0.0—Upper Bankhead Picnic Area (1465 m).

—Follow trail across open meadow and into forest.

1.2—Junction. Trail joins roadbed. Turn left.

6.4—Cascade River bridge (1555 m). Cascade Bridge Campground (Cr6).

13.3—Junction. Stony Creek Warden Cabin left.

14.2—Junction. Stony Creek Warden Cabin rejoins from left.

14.7—Junction. *Elk Pass* trail left.

14.8—Stony Creek bridge (1645 m).

15.0—Junction. Stony Creek Campground (Cr15) and *Dormer Pass* right.

23.1—Junction. *Flint's Park* trail left.

30.1—Junction. Big Horn Lake right (4.0 km); Cuthead Lake left (4.0 km).

33.0—Wigmore Summit (2010 m).

The Cascade Fire Trail traverses the park's remote Front Ranges enclosing the Cascade and Red Deer Valleys. While there are no alpine passes on the trail, there is plenty of wild, rugged scenery, and you will experience a real sense of having escaped the madding crowds found elsewhere in the park. It is a region reserved for experienced, self-reliant wilderness travellers who are well schooled in how to travel and camp safely in prime grizzly bear habitat.

The Cascade Fire Road was completed during the late 1930s after large forest fires swept the region. Until 1984 the road was utilized by Parks Canada vehicles, but when two bridges collapsed, it was allowed to revert to foot and horse trail.

The roadbed remains one of the primary access routes into the Front Ranges and is the core for the park's eastern trail system. While the track is broad and well-graded, the removal of bridges and culverts in 1990 left a number of unbridged streams (the Cascade River, Stony Creek and the Red Deer River are the only waterways still bridged). The most formidable crossing is the Panther River, and any trips over the central section of the trail are best postponed until later in the summer when the Panther's waters have subsided.

Starting from the southern trailhead at Upper Bankhead Picnic Area, the trail ascends the Cascade Valley for 23 km before breaking away to cross Wigmore and Snow Creek Passes to the Red Deer Valley. It then follows along the north side of the Red Deer to the park's eastern boundary and the historic Ya-Ha-Tinda Ranch, where warden horses are billeted during the winter.

Few people hike the trail end-to-end, since arranging transportation between the two distant trailheads is a time-consuming enterprise. Most prefer to explore the country and side trails that

Cascade River from Cascade bridge

39.1—Junction (1875 m). Windy Warden Cabin and *Panther River* right.

39.3—Junction. Panther River headwaters and *North Fork Pass* left.

39.4—Panther River crossing (major ford). Panther Falls right (0.4 km).

42.8—Junction. Harrison Lake left (4.0 km).

46.8—Junction. Grouse Lake right (1.2 km).

49.3—Snow Creek Summit (2255 m).

49.5—Junction. Snowflake Lake left (2.0 km).

57.5—Junction. Scotch Camp Warden Station left.

58.2—Red Deer River bridge (1740 km).

58.4—Junction. *Upper Red Deer River* trail left.

62.9—Tyrell Creek crossing (ford).

69.3—Park boundary (1660 m).

81.4—Scalp Creek crossing (ford).

81.6—Ya Ha Tinda Ranch Road Junction. Turn right.

83.0—Bighorn Creek bridge and parking area (1580 m).

can be easily accessed from either the south or north trailheads.

The first 15 km beyond the southern trailhead is the most heavily used section. Since mountain bikes are permitted as far as the Stony Creek Warden Cabin, much of this visitation comes from cyclists. (The road's surface has been churned-up by commercial horse parties, so cycling is not as smooth and speedy as you might expect.) The trail's only two designated campgrounds are located on this section—a very pleasant site at the Cascade River bridge (6.4 km) and at Stony Creek (15.0 km).

Except for the occasional horse party or park warden, you are not likely to encounter many travellers between Flint's Park junction and the park's eastern boundary. Random camping is permitted on this section, which means you can camp anywhere as long as your site is at least 50 m off the trail and 70 m from the nearest water source.

You will pass by a number of recently burned slopes along the way. Most of these fires date to the 1990s and were intentionally set by the Park Warden Service to improve wildlife habitat.

Following is a brief summary of the Cascade Fire Trail, travelling from south to north:

Upper Bankhead to Flint's Park Junction—23.1 km. Starting from the southern trailhead at Upper Bankhead Picnic Area, the trail climbs over a low divide adorned by a marshy willow meadow, then descends sharply to the Cascade River bridge at km 6.4. Beyond the Cascade bridge, there is very little elevation gain for 7 km as the old road-bed follows upvalley along the Cascade River to Stony Creek.

After passing two side roads to Stony Creek Warden Station, you arrive at Stony Creek bridge. Just south of the bridge a trail branches west to Elk Summit (see *Elk Lake*); on the north side of the bridge the trail to Stony Creek Campground (0.3 km) and *Dormer Pass* strikes off to the east.

The trail continues its gradual ascent along the east side of the Cascade River from Stony Creek to Flint's Park Junction. At this intersection, the Flint's Park trail branches west to link up with trails leading over Badger Pass and Forty Mile Summit (see *Flint's Park* and *Sawback Range Circuit*).

Flint's Park Junction to Red Deer River—35.1 km. From Flint's Park Junction, the trail branches north up Cuthead Creek to Wigmore Summit. Highlights on the ascent are two 4-km side-trails, which branch east and west at 30.1 km: the westbound trail climbs to Cuthead Lake beneath the cliffs of Flints Peak; the eastbound makes a steep ascent to Bighorn Lake in a 2350-m cirque on the slopes of the Palliser Range. (While both lakes are shown on the NTS topo map, the trails are not.)

Wigmore Summit is a long pass with a small lake at its north end. North of the pass the trail descends to Panther River and the Windy Warden Cabin.

One of the earliest warden cabins in the park was constructed on this site in 1915. (This original Windy Cabin now sits on the grounds of Banff's Whyte

Museum). The present cabin was constructed in the 1950s with all the modern amenities of the day—including a furnace and a nuclear bomb shelter!

After splashing across the Panther River (quite difficult during high water), you climb to Snow Creek Summit (2255 m)—the trail's highest elevation. There are worthwhile side-trails on this section leading to cirques containing Harrison, Grouse, and Snowflake Lakes.

The trail drops steadily beyond Snow Creek Summit to the Scotch Camp Warden Cabin and the Red Deer River.

Red Deer River bridge to Bighorn Creek—24.8 km. The Red Deer Valley has been used as a route between the mountains and the Foothills for many centuries. A number of archaeological sites have been discovered in the valley, including 600 to 2800-year-old housepit depressions associated with the Salish tribes of British Columbia's Interior Plateau.

After crossing the bridged Red Deer River, the trail turns east and climbs along the southern slopes of Mount Tyrell for a kilometre or so before descending to open valley-bottom and Tyrell Creek. Following this calf-deep ford, it follows along the Red Deer for 2 km before bending northeast to exit the park and the Front Ranges between Wapiti Mountain and Warden Rock.

Throughout the descent of the valley, you will notice sections of burned forest to the north of the trail—slopes that were burned during a major prescribed fire in the autumn of 1994.

The final 12.5 km of the journey rolls into the foothill parklands comprising Parks Canada's Ya-Ha-Tinda Ranch. (Mountain bikes are permitted on this section to the park boundary.)

Just beyond a calf-deep ford of Scalp Creek, you reach the Ya-Ha-Tinda Ranch access road. While vehicles are permitted on the road, parking is not, so you will likely turn right and follow the ranch road another 1.4 km to the Bighorn Creek bridge parking area.

81 Flint's Park

Cascade Fire Trail to Flint's Park Warden Cabin—7.8 km (4.8 mi) *

Backpack

Allow 2 to 3 hours one way

Elevation gain: 85 m (280 ft)

Maximum elevation: 1820 m (5,970 ft)

Maps: Castle Mountain 82 O/5

Access: Follow the *Cascade Fire Trail* to km 23.1 to reach the trail's east end, or the *Sawback Range Circuit* to km 38.9 for the west end of the trail.

0.0—Cascade Fire Trail Junction (1735 m).

—Trail follows old road track.

0.3—Cuthead Creek bridge and junction. Cuthead Warden Cabin right. Flint's Park ahead.

—Flat to rolling trail north of Cascade River.

4.0—Junction. Shortcut trail from Cascade Fire Trail (upper Cuthead Creek) intersects from right; Flint's Park ahead.

4.5—Junction. Outfitter's camp left; Flint's Park ahead.

7.5—North Cascade River bridge. Flint's Park Campground (Cr 31).

7.7—Flint's Park Warden Cabin.

7.8—Junction (1820 m). Intersection with *Sawback Range Circuit* at km 38.9 and southern end of *North Fork Pass* trail. Forty Mile Summit left; Badger Pass ahead; North Fork Pass right.

*All distances approximate.

Flint's Park, which is situated near the confluence of Sawback Creek and the Cascade and North Cascade Rivers, has long been a popular camping area and centre of operation for horseback parties. Lying beneath the twin summits of Flints Peak, its open meadows and sparkling waters make a very pleasant base camp for backpackers as well. More importantly, it is a hub for several interesting excursions.

Though the well travelled track from the Cascade Fire Trail is relatively flat and humdrum, it is an important east-west link through Banff's Front Ranges. The route follows an old roadbed branching from the Cascade Fire Trail at km 23.1 and, at the Cuthead Creek bridge, passes the junction to the historic Cuthead Warden Cabin.

After crossing Cuthead Creek, it rolls westward through forest to the north of the Cascade River. Just past the halfway point, a well-trodden horse trail branches left to an outfitter's camp (keep ahead on the less-pounded track).

Flint's Park Campground and the North Cascade River bridge are reached at km 7.5. The important four-way trail junction, which serves as trail centre for the upper Cascade Valley, lies 300 m west of the bridge near the Flint's Park Warden Cabin.

The campground is a good base for trips to local attractions, such as Sawback Lake, North Fork Pass, and the Block Lakes (for experienced rock climbers only). It also serves as a way-point for extended trips over Forty Mile Summit or Badger Pass (see *Sawback Range Circuit*).

Expect all trails in this area to exhibit signs of heavy horse use and to be churned-up during rainy periods. And remember, you will be camping in prime grizzly country, so take extra care at your campsite and while travelling the trails.

82 Dormer Pass

Cascade Fire Trail to Dormer Pass—12.5 km (8.0 mi) *
Cascade Fire Trail to Stony Pass—14.5 km (9.0 mi) *

Backpack

Allow 4 to 6 hours to Dormer Pass

Elevation gain: 730 m (2,400 ft)

Maximum elevation: 2375 m (7,800 ft)

Maps: Castle Mountain 82 O/5
      Barrier Mountain 82 O/12

Access: Trail branches from the *Cascade Fire Trail* at km 15.0, just north of the Stony Creek bridge.

0.0—Cascade Fire Trail Junction (1630 m).

0.3—Stony Creek Campground (Cr15).

1.3—Stony Creek ford to east bank.

6.5—Stony Creek ford to west bank.

6.8—Stony Creek ford to east bank.

9.0—Junction. Stony Pass ahead (5.5 km). Dormer Pass left.

9.2—Stony Creek ford.

12.5—Dormer Pass (2375 m).

18.5—Dormer River ford to east bank.

18.6—Junction. Stony Pass trail intersects from right.

24.5—Junction (1770 m). Park boundary ahead (6.0 km). Panther River via Dormer-Panther Divide left (7.5 km).

*All distances approximate.

The trail running up Stony Creek to Dormer Pass is one of the most attractive side-trips from the Cascade Fire Trail. In addition to the 2375-m pass, which breaks through the limestone walls of the Palliser Range in spectacular fashion, there are optional trips to nearby Stony Pass or over the Dormer-Panther Divide to the Panther River.

The trail to Dormer Pass is well-defined throughout, but there are a number of unbridged streams along the way. The first of these is at 1.3 km, where the trail swings to the east side of Stony Creek—a troublesome ford during periods of high runoff. Three fords of the creek farther upvalley are less demanding.

At km 9.0 the trail to Stony Pass stays right while the Dormer Pass trail branches left. The Dormer option immediately crosses Stony Creek and makes a steep ascent to the pass.

Dormer Pass is a long, narrow corridor with an extensive alpine meadow—a wonderful area for alpine wildflowers in late July and early August. The pass is within the range of a large population of mountain sheep and frequently visited by grizzly bear. (A few years back a grizzly thwarted travel through the pass while it fed on a bighorn sheep carcass.)

Beyond the summit, the trail switchbacks down to a tributary and meadows leading to the Dormer River. Just above the Dormer Warden Cabin, you reach the river and cross to the east side. Stay on the east side for the next 6 km, passing through open meadows with fine views of the surrounding peaks.

At km 24.5 a major junction is reached. The trail ahead continues down the Dormer River to the park boundary and points east; the left branch fords the river and runs north to the Panther River via the Dormer-Panther Divide.

Dormer Meadows from Dormer Pass

Stony Pass. This 2330-m pass lies east of Dormer Pass on the opposite side of a block of unnamed limestone peaks. The pass is seldom visited, and the trail is vague to non-existent in many places. However, the few people who do go there often continue north down the Dormer River and then back to Stony Creek via Dormer Pass. Total round-trip distance for the Stony-Dormer Pass circuit from Stony Creek Campground is approximately 41 km.

To reach the pass, follow the Dormer Pass trail to the 9.0-km junction. The Stony Pass trail continues due east along the south side of Stony Creek for just over 3 km before crossing to the north side. The track often disappears through willow meadows, but the gap is quite obvious to the north as you near the creek's headwaters.

If you continue north from Stony Pass onto the Dormer River headwaters, you will again encounter willow-dwarf birch meadows and vague trail. However, if you persevere you will intersect the more obvious Dormer Pass trail approximately 8 km beyond Stony Pass.

Dormer–Panther Divide. Backpackers who continue down the Dormer River beyond the Dormer Warden Cabin are inevitably bound for the Panther River via the Dormer-Panther Divide trail. While the trip has little to recommend scenery-wise, it does take you into some very remote wilderness that is considerably more challenging than following the Cascade Fire Trail.

The 7.5-km-long Dormer–Panther Divide trail branches west from the Dormer River trail at 24.5 km. You immediately ford the Dormer River and make a steady climb north through mixed forest for nearly 4 km before cresting an unremarkable divide and then descending to the Panther River.

To return to the Cascade Fire Trail, ford the Panther to its north bank, and follow the Panther River trail back upstream. (See *Panther River*.)

83 Panther River

Cascade Fire Trail to Park Boundary—15.2 km (9.4 mi) *

Backpack

Allow 5 hours to park boundary

Elevation loss: 140 m (450 ft)

Maximum elevation: 1875 m (6,150 ft)

Maps: Barrier Mountain 82 O/12

Access: Eastbound backpackers can reach the west end of the trail by following the *Cascade Fire Trail* to the Windy Warden Cabin at km 39.1 (the trail departs from the meadow behind the cabin). Westbound travellers usually approach from the south via the Dormer-Panther Divide trail (see *Dormer Pass* trail description), intersecting with the Panther River trail at km 12.0, approximately 3 km west of the park boundary.

0.0—Windy Warden Cabin (1875 m).

1.5—Panther River ford to north bank (mid-calf to knee deep).

1.8—Panther River ford to south bank.

2.2—Panther River ford to north bank.

　—Flat to rolling trail.

5.7—Old cabin.

6.0—Junction. Elkhorn Summit and Red Deer River left (poorly marked).

8.0—Cold sulphur spring.

12.0—Junction (1770 m). Dormer-Panther Divide trail right. Panther River trail ahead.

15.0—Park boundary (1735 m).

*All distances approximate.

The Panther River is one of the least visited of the major valleys in the eastern part of Banff Park. While it does not contain the spectacular mountains and views found elsewhere in the Front Ranges, it does have a certain quiet and haunting beauty that lingers in the memory.

The Panther River trail branches east from the Cascade Fire Trail at the Windy Warden Cabin. It immediately enters a gorge, where it is forced back and forth across the river three times in the space of a kilometre (fords usually only calf-deep). Once through this defile, good trail leads down-valley along the north side of the river to the Dormer-Panther Divide trail junction.

At 5.7 km the charred remains of an old cabin are passed, and just beyond there is an excellent campsite beside a creek flowing into the Panther from the north. A trail to Elkhorn Summit and Red Deer River branches north on the east side of this stream.

The junction with the Dormer-Panther Divide trail at km 12.0 marks the end of travel down the Panther River for many hikers (most use this trail to connect back to Dormer River and Pass). The main trail, used almost exclusively by horse-back parties, continues eastward to the park boundary in 3 km and beyond to The Corners—the confluence of the Panther and Dormer Rivers.

Elkhorn Summit. This 13.5-km trail follows along the east side of the Bare Range between the Panther and Red Deer Rivers. From its junction with the Panther River trail at km 6.0, it climbs steadily to a 2200-m divide. From this summit it descends to extensive meadows and a small lake before continuing north to a difficult crossing of the Red Deer River and an unsigned junction on the Cascade Fire Trail.

84 North Fork Pass

Cascade Fire Trail to North Fork Pass—12.0 km (7.5 mi) *
Cascade Fire Trail to Flint's Park Junction—20.5 km (12.5 mi)

Backpack

Allow 4 hours to North Fork Pass

Elevation gain: 550 m (1,800 ft)

Maximum elevation: 2425 m (7,950 ft)

Maps: Barrier Mountain 82 O/12
Castle Mountain 82 O/5

Access: To reach the north end of the trail, follow the *Cascade Fire Trail* to 39.3 km, where the trail branches west less than 100 m south of the Panther River crossing. Access to the south end of the trail is from a junction at the east end of the *Flint's Park* trail, just a few metres from the Flint's Park warden cabin.

0.0—Cascade Fire Trail (1875 m).

0.4—Panther River ford to north bank (mid-calf deep).

— Flat valley-bottom trail.

5.2—Panther River ford to south bank.

— Trail climbs then swings south toward pass.

10.7—Steep climb begins.

— Trail ascends left side of bowl toward pass.

12.0—North Fork Pass (2425 m).

— Steep descent south of pass.

14.0—Grade moderates.

— Intermittent trail through deadfall.

16.3—Good trail reappears on east side of creek.

18.0—Cross to west side of creek.

— Steady, gradual downhill.

20.5—Junction (1830 m). Intersection with *The Sawback Circuit* at 38.9 km and west end of *Flint's Park* trail.

*All distances approximate.

This 2425-m divide between the headwaters of the Panther River and the Cascade River's north fork is probably one of the least hiked trail-accessible passes in Banff Park. The pass can be reached as a day trip from campsites near the Flint's Park Warden Cabin on the south or the Cascade Fire Trail near Windy Warden Cabin to the north. You can also use the pass as part of an extended backpack through Banff's Front Ranges.

Starting from its intersection with the Cascade Fire Trail (on the south side of the Panther River just 200 m from the Windy Warden Cabin), the trail runs a short distance upstream along the south side of the Panther before crossing to the north side.

Near the 5-km mark the trail recrosses to the south side, climbs over a shoulder, and then turns south into a narrow valley, where it begins its ascent to North Fork Pass. Nearly 400 m are gained over the last 5 km to the summit.

The narrow gap of North Fork Pass provides excellent views due south across Forty Mile Summit to Mounts Edith, Louis and Fifi and the peaks south of Banff. Nearby, you are circled by the steeply tilted limestone summits of the Sawback Range.

South from the pass the trail drops steeply to the North Cascade River and passes through the weathered remains of a major forest fire that swept this area in 1936. The trail promptly disappears into deadfall and is intermittent for the next 2 km. By persevering down the east side of the stream, you should come upon it again where it reappears as a well defined track.

You soon swing to the west side of the stream and complete the remainder of the descent to the Flint's Park trail junction on a broad obvious path. (See *Sawback Circuit* and *Flint's Park*.)

85 Upper Red Deer River

Cascade Fire Trail to Cyclone Warden Cabin Junction—26.7 km (16.6 mi)

Backpack

Allow 8 hours

Elevation gain: 365 m (1,200 ft)

Maximum elevation: 2105 m (6,900 ft)

Maps: Hector Lake 82 N/9
　　　Barrier Mountain 82 O/12

Access: Reach the east end of the trail by hiking the *Cascade Fire Trail* to the 58.4 km junction—200 m north of the Red Deer River bridge.

Access the west end of the trail at Cyclone Warden Cabin by hiking the Red Deer Lakes-Natural Bridge trail from Skoki Valley to Red Deer Lakes Campground. The junction with the Upper Red Deer trail is on the north side of the Red Deer River, 400 m beyond the campground.

0.0—Cascade Fire Trail Junction (1740 m).

—Follows old roadbed.

1.4—Divide Creek crossing (rock-hop or ankle-deep ford).

1.6—Junction. *Divide Creek–Peters Creek* trail right.

—Gradual to rolling ascent along north side of Red Deer Valley.

6.1—McConnell Creek ford (calf-deep).

10.4—Junction. Horseshoe (Skeleton) Lake left.

12.3—Red Deer River gorge and waterfall.

14.1—Tributary creek crossing (on logjam).

14.5—Red Deer Warden Cabin.

20.3—Junction. Douglas Lake left 3.0 km.

22.2—Drummond Creek ford (calf-deep).

24.9—Junction. Natural Bridge left 2.5 km.

26.7—Junction. Cyclone Warden Cabin. Red Deer Lakes Campground left 0.4 km. (See Red Deer Lakes-Natural Bridge, *Skoki Valley Area Hikes*.)

The Red Deer Valley is one of the great wilderness valleys in Banff Park. Most hikers only know the valley's headwaters, which is often visited on day trips from the Skoki Valley. Yet the entire valley offers fine scenery, interesting side-trips, and lots of solitude.

The lower valley is traversed by the Cascade Fire Trail and usually accessed from the Ya-Ha-Tinda Ranch just east of the park boundary. (See *Cascade Fire Trail*.) The upper valley trail branches from the Cascade trail 200 m north of the Red Deer River bridge.

The first 1.6 km follows an old roadbed, but after crossing Divide Creek and passing the *Divide Creek-Peters Creek* trail junction, it reverts to single track. Following a calf-deep ford of McConnell Creek at km 6.1, the trail traverses open meadows interspersed with sections of forest.

At 10.4 km a short side trail crosses the Red Deer to Horseshoe Lake (aka Skeleton Lake). While the lake has a reputation for good trout fishing, fording the river at this point can be difficult.

A more interesting side-trip is Douglas Lake, which branches left at a signed junction on riverside flats at km 20.3. After wading the Red Deer's braided channels, continue to the north end of the lake in 3 km. There is no trail beyond this large, scenic lake, but you can camp here and then explore south to the head of the Valley of Hidden Lakes.

After another calf-deep ford at Drummond Creek (good views northwest to Drummond Glacier), you pass the trail to Natural Bridge and reach the Cyclone Warden Cabin. At the junction just beyond the cabin, most hikers turn south to the Red Deer Lakes Campground en route to the Skoki Valley (see Red Deer Lakes-Natural Bridge, *Skoki Valley Area Hikes*).

86 Divide Creek—Peters Creek

Red Deer River to Clearwater River—25.7 km (16.0 mi)

Backpack

Allow 8 hours

Elevation gain: 625 m (2,050 ft)
loss: 655 m (2,150 ft)

Maximum elevation: 2395 m (7,850 ft)

Maps: Barrier Mountain 82 O/12
Forbidden Creek 82 O/13

Access: Reach the south end of the trail from the junction at km 1.6 on the *Upper Red Deer River* trail. Reach the north end at the *Clearwater River* trail junction 2.4 km east of the park boundary in the Clearwater Valley.

0.0—Red Deer River Junction (1770 m).

—Steady climb above Divide Creek canyon.

6.6—Trail begins sharp descent.

8.0—Divide Creek ford (ankle-deep).

8.4—Divide Warden Cabin.

—Steady climb into alpine.

11.6—Divide Summit (2395 m).

—Descend north side of pass.

13.0—Peters Creek crossing to east side.

—Valley narrows. Numerous side scree slopes.

18.8—Peters Creek ford to west bank.

18.9—Peters Creek ford to east bank.

19.2—Peters Creek ford to west bank.

20.8—Steep climb away from creek begins.

22.4—Steep descent to Clearwater Valley.

24.0—Clearwater Valley meadows.

24.9—Old outfitter camp.

25.3—Clearwater River ford to north bank (thigh-deep and swift).

25.7—Junction (1740 m). Intersects the *Clearwater River* trail.

This horse trail branches north from the Red Deer River trail 1.6 km west of its junction with the Cascade Fire Trail. A well used warden patrol route, it crosses the lofty and scenic Divide Summit to link the Red Deer and Clearwater Valleys.

From its junction with the *Upper Red Deer River* trail, the trail climbs a steep, grassy bluff and begins a steady ascent along a mountainside west of the precipitous Divide Creek canyon. After reaching an elevation of nearly 2285 m, it plunges 150 m in less than 2 km and crosses Divide Creek just below the Divide Warden Cabin.

The trail eases its way up through open meadows from the warden cabin to the remarkably scenic Divide Summit—a 2395-m pass with fine views south across the Red Deer Valley to Mount White and the sawtooth peaks of the Bare Range. The summit is also inhabited by a large marmot colony.

Good horse trail descends north from the pass to the east of upper Peters Creek. Near the base of Mount Peters, it is forced back and forth across the creek three times in rapid succession (usually calf-deep fords). It then passes along a series of difficult scree slopes on the lower ramparts of Mount Peters before making a final climb over the northeast shoulder of the mountain and descending to an old outfitter's camp in a meadow near the Clearwater River.

The ford of the Clearwater is wide and challenging, but usually straight-forward after water levels have dropped in August. Once you've crossed the river, which serves as the park boundary, follow the trail north 0.4 km to an intersection with the Clearwater River trail. From this junction most backpackers turn west and follow the Clearwater Valley back into Banff Park (see *Clearwater River*).

87 Clearwater River

Peters Creek Junction to Clearwater Pass—30.5 km (19.0 mi)
Clearwater–Red Deer Circuit—145 km (90 mi)

Backpack

Allow 8 to 9 hours

Elevation gain: 590 m (1,950 ft)

Maximum elevation: 2330 m (7,650 ft)

Maps: Forbidden Creek 82 O/13
       Siffleur River 82 N/16
       Hector Lake 82 N/9

Access: Reach the east end of the Clearwater River trail via the *Divide Creek-Peters Creek* trail. Access the west end of the trail 3 km north of Pipestone Pass on the *North Molar-Dolomite Circuit.*

0.0—Peters Creek Junction (1740 m).

    —Follow west along old road track.

2.4—Park boundary. Road reverts to single-track.

3.4—Indianhead Lodge Warden Cabin.

3.5—Indianhead Creek ford (ankle-deep).

4.2—Junction. *Whiterabbit Pass* trail right.

7.5—Malloch Creek ford (rock-hop or calf-deep).

13.1—Trident Lake.

14.4—Junction. Martin Creek waterfalls left.

14.6—Martin Lake. Martin Creek ford at lake outlet (knee to thigh-deep).

17.1—Clearwater Lake (1905 m).

19.6—Clearwater Lakes Warden Cabin.

    —Steady climb to Clearwater Pass.

28.9—Upper Devon Lake.

30.5—Clearwater Pass (2330 m).

31.6—Junction. Intersection with *North Molar-Pipestone-Dolomite Circuit* at 27.0 km (3.0 km north of Pipestone Pass).

The Clearwater is the most remote valley in Banff Park. The valley is traversed by good trail, but getting to either end of it takes a minimum of two days. Yet this isolation preserves it as one of the last unspoiled regions in Banff Park.

The trail can be reached from the west via Pipestone Pass and the headwaters of the Siffleur River (see *North Molar-Pipestone-Dolomite Circuit*). However, the valley unfolds more dramatically when it is ascended from the park's east boundary to its scenic climax on Clearwater Pass.

The most common approach to the east end of the trail is from the Red Deer Valley via the *Divide Creek-Peters Creek* trail. This route requires a sometimes demanding ford of the Clearwater River just prior to intersecting the Clearwater trail 2.4 km east of the park boundary. This junction can also be reached by trails from Ya-Ha-Tinda Ranch or the SR940 forestry road.

From Peters Creek junction, the trail runs due west along the north side of the Clearwater into Banff Park. A kilometre beyond the boundary it passes Indianhead Lodge—one of the park's most isolated warden cabins.

The gradual ascent of the valley continues, entering mixed forest and extensive meadows near Malloch Creek. As the trail skirts north of Trident Lake, two waterfalls are heard—one across the valley on Roaring Creek and the other just below Martin Lake (a short spur trail leads to the latter).

The trail crosses Martin Creek just below Martin Lake. (The creek is best forded by hiking upstream and wade through the shallows at the lake's outlet where the current is less swift.) After this deep, soaking ford, the trail rolls along to Clearwater Lake, where there are fine views to the head of the valley.

After passing the historic Clearwater

Jim Thorsell photo

Upper Devon Lake on Clearwater Pass

Warden Cabin, the ascent to Clearwater Pass begins, gradually at first, then more steeply over the last 6 km.

Clearwater Pass is a long, curving alpine summit highlighted by the Devon Lakes. The lakes are bordered by rolling meadows and overshadowed by the cliffs of Devon Mountain. Mount Willingdon (3373 m), one of the highest mountains in the Front Ranges, rises to the north.

The trail passes beside the largest of the Devon Lakes. While the meadow near the lake is a pleasant place to camp, few will want to linger here when conditions are foul. If you are west-bound, you face a long journey before you regain forest cover and protection from the elements.

From the summit of Clearwater Pass, vague trail descends across rocky, alpine meadows to a junction with the Siffleur Valley trail 3 km north of Pipestone Pass. At this point you can descend the Siffleur Valley to the north or head south over Pipestone Pass to Fish Lakes. (See *North Molar-Pipestone-Dolomite Circuit*.)

Clearwater-Red Deer Circuit—145 km (90 mi). This is a grand but demanding wilderness tour that crosses five passes ranging in elevation from 2330 m to 2590 m. On one section, from Mosquito Creek meadows to the upper Clearwater, you are at or above treeline for 25 km. There is plenty of low elevation travel, too, along two of the most remote and scenic valleys in Banff Park—the Clearwater and Red Deer.

The circuit is not frequently hiked since it is not as well maintained or appointed as better known wilderness trips. Much of the journey travels though areas where random camping is allowed. There are numerous fords, including difficult crossings of the Clearwater and Pipestone Rivers (its best to do this trip in August or early September). The full circuit should only be considered by experienced wilderness backpackers who are comfortable in remote backcountry for 10 days or so.

The circuit can be hiked as a loop, starting and finishing at the Mosquito Creek trailhead on the Icefields Parkway. You can travel clockwise or counter-

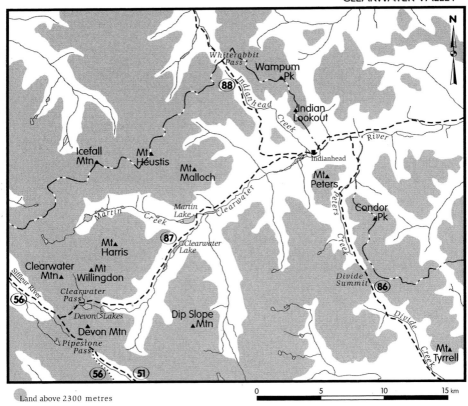

Land above 2300 metres

| 0 | 5 | 10 | 15 km |

clockwise. While the latter option saves the best scenery until the end of the trip, we prefer to hike clockwise. This allows the option of bailing out near the end of the journey at Red Deer Lakes by hiking out to Lake Louise via the Boulder Pass-Skoki Valley trail. (Many hikers plan this itinerary in advance and arrange transportation between the Mosquito Creek and Boulder Pass trailheads.)

Follow the circuit clockwise by hiking the *North Molar Pass-Fish Lakes* trail to Fish Lakes. Continue on the *North Molar-Pipestone-Dolomite Circuit* from Fish Lakes to Pipestone Pass and the Clearwater Pass junction. Traverse Clearwater Pass and descend the *Clearwater River* trail to Peters Creek

junction. Head south over Divide Summit to the Red Deer River via the *Divide Creek-Peters Creek* trail. Ascend the *Upper Red Deer River* trail to the Red Deer Lakes junction just beyond Cyclone Warden Cabin.

At this point you have two options: follow the Red Deer Lakes trail back to the *Boulder Pass-Skoki Valley* trail and out to the Fish Creek trailhead at Lake Louise; or complete the loop by descending Little Pipestone Creek to the Pipestone River crossing, fording the river, and then following the Molar Creek trail over Molar Pass and back to the Mosquito Creek trailhead. (The Boulder Pass-Skoki Valley option reduces total distance for the trip by 15 km.)

88 Whiterabbit Pass

Clearwater River to Whiterabbit Pass—12.7 km (7.9 mi)

Backpack

Allow 3 to 4 hours to pass

Elevation gain: 470 m (1,550 ft)

Maximum elevation: 2270 m (7,450 ft)

Maps: Siffleur River 82 N/16

Access: Follow the *Clearwater River* trail to the junction at 4.2 km, 700 m west of the Indianhead Creek ford. Trail angles off to north-west from *Clearwater River* trail.

0.0—Clearwater River Junction (1800 m).

—Gradual to moderate uphill to northwest.

3.4—Trail turns due north, begins steep climb.

6.1—Ridge summit (2165 m). Begin descent to Indianhead Creek.

7.9—Trail levels off above Indianhead Creek, begins ascent to pass.

10.7—Cross to east side of Indianhead Creek (rock-hop).

12.7—Whiterabbit Pass (2270 m). Park boundary.

—Trail descends to Headwaters Cabin, 6.0 km beyond pass, and Whiterabbit Creek. It eventually emerges at the North Saskatchewan suspension bridge at Kootenay Plains and David Thompson Highway (Hwy 11) 36.8 km from pass.

The Whiterabbit trail is an old outfitter's route connecting the Clearwater Valley with the Kootenay Plains to the north. It is still commonly used by horse parties, but seldom by backpackers, even though it is quite passable and scenic.

From its junction with the Clearwater River trail, 0.8 km west of the Indianhead Lodge Warden Cabin, the trail climbs over a 2165 m ridge and descends into the Indianhead drainage.

Much of the ascent of Indianhead Creek is through open meadows. The climb culminates on 2270 m Whiterabbit Pass—a broad, grassy summit with good views north into the Ram River valley.

While Whiterabbit Pass is a worthy objective for backpackers camped in the Clearwater Valley, many continue north through the Clearwater Provincial Forest to the Kootenay Plains.

North of the pass the trail makes an easy descent to the south branch of the Ram River. The river is forded to its west bank 4.7 km beyond the pass.

Just over a kilometre beyond the Ram River ford is the Headwaters Cabin—a dilapidated forest ranger cabin situated on a bluff. It commands one of the most scenic viewpoints in the Front Ranges.

The trail continues northwest from the cabin over a low divide and descends onto the headwaters of Whiterabbit Creek. The Whiterabbit is a long, straight valley marked by heavy forest and areas of deadfall (an erratic trail is maintained primarily by horse parties).

When Whiterabbit Creek runs out onto the floor of the North Saskatchewan Valley, the trail enters an area of old logging roads. Keep left at all junctions until the Siffleur River bridge is crossed. From this bridge it is a short walk to the suspension bridge across the North Saskatchewan River and the trailhead parking area on Highway 11.

National Park

10,878 sq km, Jasper is the largest of Canada's Rocky Mountain
ying along the eastern slope of the Rockies in western Alberta, the
)n the west by the continental divide and British Columbia's Mount
....u .iamber Provincial Parks and on the south by Banff National Park.

While Jasper's trail system totals more than 1200 kms, day hiking opportunities are
somewhat limited and scattered compared to other mountain parks. The largest
concentration of half-day and day trips is near Jasper townsite, but these are mostly
low elevation hikes to forest-enclosed lakes. The park's best known day trips are
Cavell Meadows beneath Mount Edith Cavell, Bald Hills and Opal Hills at Maligne
Lake, Sulphur Skyline above Miette Hot Springs, and Wilcox Pass overlooking the
Athabasca Glacier.

Jasper is best known for its backpacking trail system. Thanks to a program of trail
upgrading and bridge building started in the 1970s, it may well be the premier area
for remote wilderness hiking in North America. The North and South Boundary Trails
offer solitary rambles of over 160 km; the 80 km Jonas Pass-Brazeau Lake circuit is
the most popular loop trip; and the park's most accessible and popular backcountry
areas, the Skyline Trail and Tonquin Valley, are undeniably two of the most scenic
backpacking destinations in Canada.

Like all other mountain national parks, Jasper has a quota for all its backcountry
campgrounds. Sites on the Skyline Trail, the Jonas Pass-Brazeau Lake Loop, and in
the Tonquin Valley are the busiest, particularly in July and August. If you are planning
on camping on these trails, or any others in the park, you can reserve campsites up to
3 months prior to departure.

Information and services. Park Visitor Centres are located in downtown Jasper at
500 Connaught Drive (year around) and at the Icefield Centre (summer only). Both
centres dispense Wilderness Passes and the latest information on trail conditions, bear
sightings, weather reports, etc., but the townsite centre's trail desk is by far the most
useful for anyone setting out on overnight trips.

There are 10 road accessible campgrounds scattered throughout the park. The two
largest, Whistlers and Wapiti, are located just south of Jasper townsite. They are both
full service campgrounds and the only ones with showers.

The town of Jasper provides the full gamut of visitor services, including hotels,
banks, restaurants, gas stations, grocery stores and numerous retail outlets catering to
tourist clientele, including shops specializing in hiking gear. Food services and
accommodation are also available at the Icefield Centre, Sunwapta Falls, Miette
Junction (Pocahontas) and Miette Hot Springs during the summer months.

Access: The Yellowhead Highway (Hwy 16) is the east-west access route through the
park, and a connector to the nearest city, Edmonton, Alberta (370 km east of Jasper).
The Icefields Parkway connects Jasper with Banff National Park to the south (226 km
from Jasper to Lake Louise).

The primary means of public transportation to Jasper Park is bus. Jasper is serviced
by several east and westbound Greyhound buses that run daily between Alberta and
British Columbia on the Yellowhead Highway.

While the nearest international airport is in Edmonton, there is also a daily bus
service between Calgary International Airport and Jasper via Banff and the Icefields
Parkway in the summer.

East and westbound VIA Rail passenger trains make daily stops at the Jasper
station.

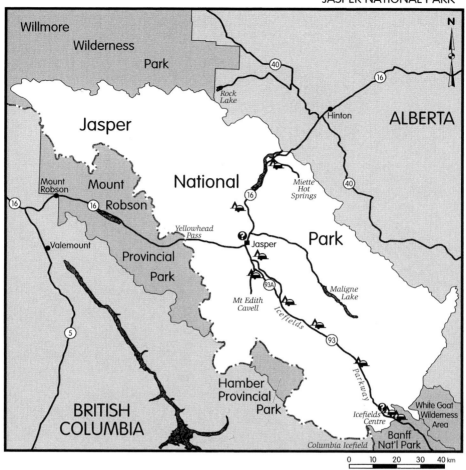

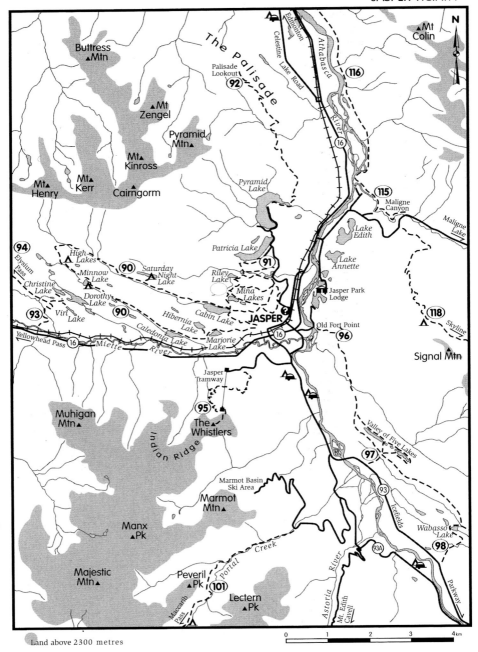

N

▲Mt
Colin

(116)

Buttress
▲Mtn

The Palisade

Palisade
Lookout
(92)

Edmonton

Celestine Lake Road

Athabasca River

▲Mt
Zengel

Pyramid
Mtn▲

16

Mt▲
Kinross

Pyramid
Lake

(115)

Mt▲
Henry

Mt▲
Kerr

Cairngorm

Maligne
Canyon

Maligne
Lake

(94)

High
Lakes

Patricia Lake

Lake
Edith

Elysium
Pass

Minnow
Lake

(90)

Saturday
Night
Lake

Riley
Lake

(91)

Lake
Annette

Christine
Lake

Dorothy
Lake

(90)

Mina
Lakes

Jasper Park
Lodge

(93)

Virl
Lake

Hibernia
Lake

Cabin Lake

JASPER

(118)

Skyline

Caledonia Lake

Yellowhead Pass

16

Miette River

Marjorie
Lake

16

Old Fort Point

(96)

Signal Mtn

Jasper
Tramway

(95)
The
Whistlers

Valley of Five Lakes

Muhigan
Mtn▲

Indian Ridge

(97)

Marmot Basin
Ski Area

93

Manx
▲Pk

Marmot
Mtn▲

Wabasso
Lake

Astoria River

93A

(98)

Majestic
Mtn▲

Peveril
▲Pk

(101)

Portal Creek

Lectern
▲Pk

Macarib Pass

Mt. Edith
Cavell

Parkway

Icefields

Land above 2300 metres

0   1   2   3   4 km

Jasper Townsite Vicinity

A number of trails extend to more than a dozen lakes in the hilly country just beyond Jasper townsite's western boundary. While none of the destinations is awe-inspiring, the wide, well-graded trails provide a variety of undemanding hikes to peaceful lakes with waterfowl, beaver and the occasional moose. And don't be surprised if you bump into one or more black bears on these trails.

The trail system itself is a veritable spiderweb that defies description. To help hikers stay on track, Parks Canada has identified the most popular routes and linking trails with yellow, numbered markers. By following these markers and referring to trail map signs, which have been erected at trailheads and important junctions, you should have little trouble finding your way around.

The 1:50,000 topographical sheet for Jasper does not show all the trails in this area, and those that are shown are sometimes represented inaccurately. To help find your way through the maze, or to create your own itinerary, we suggest you pick-up a copy of Jasper Park's *Dayhiker's Guide* at the Park Visitor Centre or purchase the 1:35,000 scale GemTrek *Jasper Up-Close* map.

The following *Mina Lakes-Riley Lake Circuit, Saturday Night Lake Circuit,* and *Cottonwood Slough Circuit* descriptions highlight three of the most popular trips.

89 Mina Lakes—Riley Lake Circuit

Pyramid Lake Drive to Upper Mina Lake—2.0 km (1.2 mi)
Mina Lakes-Riley Lake Circuit—9.0 km (5.6 mi)

Mina and Riley Lakes can be reached in less than an hour from the western edge of Jasper townsite. Though the lakes are a fairly popular destination, their setting in a mixed forest of lodgepole pine, white spruce, Douglas fir and poplar gives them a feeling of isolation and a certain charm.

From the trailhead parking area, follow trail #8 up across the slope to the left and into the forest. After a kilometre of steady uphill, the trail crosses the Cabin Lake Road (a limited access service road leading to Cabin Lake).

Grades moderate beyond the Cabin Lake Road crossing, and the trail soon comes abreast of the tiny pond known locally as Lower Mina Lake. A short distance beyond you reach the larger Upper Mina Lake and follow along its northern shore.

At 3.5 km, just beyond Upper Mina Lake, you arrive at a trail junction. Follow trail #8 to the right another 2.0 km to reach Riley Lake.

If you are doing a short walk, turn around at Riley and return the way you came. But if you are up for the complete Mina-Riley circuit, continue on trail #8 to Cottonwood Slough and its trailhead parking area on the Pyramid Lake Road. Follow trail #2 south from the parking area back to the Mina-Riley Lakes trailhead on Pyramid Lake Drive.

Access: Follow Jasper's main street (Connaught Drive) to Pine Avenue, near the town's south entrance. Continue on Pine Avenue 5 blocks to its intersection with Pyramid Lake Drive. Turn right and follow Pyramid Lake Drive along the west edge of town to a large, paved parking area opposite the Jasper Aquatic Centre and adjacent to the Jasper-Yellowhead Museum. The trail begins at the forest margin at the rear of the parking area. *Maps: Jasper 83 D/16; Jasper Up-Close (Gem Trek).*

90 Saturday Night Lake Circuit

Saturday Night Lake Circuit—24.6 km (15.3 mi)

Day trip or backpack

Allow 7 to 9 hours return

Elevation gain: 540 m (1,800 ft)

Maximum elevation: 1640 m (5,400 ft)

Maps: Jasper 83 D/16

Access: Follow Jasper's main street (Connaught Drive) to Pine Avenue, near the town's south entrance. Continue on Pine Avenue 5 blocks to its intersection with Pyramid Lake Drive. Turn left and follow Pyramid Lake Drive one block to where it joins Cabin Creek Road. Cabin Creek Road continues along the edge of town and enters a mobile home residential area. Watch for a gravel road branching steeply uphill to the right. Follow this branch 50 m to the trailhead parking area and kiosk.

0.0—Trailhead parking area (1100 m).

2.3—Marjorie Lake.

2.6—Junction. Hibernia Lake right 400 m.

4.2—Caledonia Lake.

9.2—Junction. Minnow Lake, Campground left 300 m.

12.4—Junction. High Lakes Campground right 200 m.

12.9—Cascade (1640 m). Trail turns back down-valley.

18.0—Junction. Saturday Night Lake, Campground left 500 m.

21.4—Cabin Lake (west end).

22.3—Junction. Upper Mina Lake left 0.4 km.

22.5—Cabin Lake (east end) and junction. Access road to Mina Lakes trail and Jasper ahead. Turn right across landfill dam.

23.4—Cabin Creek bridge.

24.6—Trailhead parking area (1100 m).

This trail through the hill country west of Jasper townsite is also known as the Twenty Mile Loop, though it is not nearly that long. It visits several small lakes and can be hiked as a long day or overnight trip. Or you can make a shorter trip by going only as far as Marjorie, Hibernia and Caledonia Lakes.

While most of the journey is through heavy forest with limited views, it is an excellent nature walk where you will encounter a wide variety of wildflowers, waterfowl, beaver workings and, perhaps, black bear.

Mountain bikes are also permitted on the trail, though the track is rough and steep with muddy sections west of Caledonia and Cabin Lakes.

From the trailhead on the west edge of town, the broad path immediately crosses Cabin Creek and climbs onto a low bluff with a brief view up the Athabasca Valley. Marjorie Lake appears through the forest to the left at 2.3 km, and just beyond the short side trail to Hibernia Lake branches up to the right.

A quick look at a map shows that the lakes and ridges in this rolling country tend to be elongated in an east-west direction. This landscape was partly created by a valley glacier, which once advanced down the Miette to the Athabasca Valley. Large boulders and other glacial detritus are found throughout the area.

At 4.2 km the trail skirts the north shore of Caledonia Lake, where western wood lilies and wild roses bloom in early summer. Beyond Caledonia there is a long section of forest-enclosed trail with steady uphill grades. Many forest wildflowers grow along the trail, including bunchberry, single's delight, arnica, calypso orchids and Indian paintbrush; also watch for scattered patches of red columbine—a rare flower on the east slope of the Rockies.

After passing the Minnow Lake junc-

Cabin Lake

tion (the lake and campground are 300 m to the left), the trail climbs along forested ridges to the High Lakes Campground junction. The campground is located beside a tiny lake, which is the most westerly of several small lakes contained within the Saturday Night Lake loop.

The main trail reaches the foot of a large cascade on Cabin Creek at km 12.9, where it turns back to the east and begins the return journey. The descent along the north arm of the loop is steady through a forest of spring-fed streams and beaver swamps. At 18.0 km a short, steep trail branches north to Saturday Night Lake and the last of the circuit's three campgrounds.

From Saturday Night Lake junction it is just over 3 km to the west end of Cabin Lake—the largest lake on the loop. At the east end of Cabin Lake, cross the landfill dam to the right and follow the access road leading down through the forest.

After crossing Cabin Creek 0.6 km below the lake, the trail crests an open bluff overlooking the Athabasca Valley (the best viewpoint on the circuit), then descends through forest back to the trailhead parking area.

This entire area is frequented by black bears, so backpackers should keep a clean camp and use the bear poles provided at campsites.

Cottonwood Slough

91 Cottonwood Slough

Cottonwood Slough Circuit—4.1 km (2.5 mi)

Despite its dismal name, Cottonwood Slough is quite a pleasant place. The short loop hike around this marshland, which cradles a small lake, is one of the most rewarding in the Jasper vicinity, particularly for birdwatchers. The montane slopes overlooking marsh and lake are dotted with wildflowers in spring and early summer, and there are good views across the Athabasca Valley to Signal Mountain and Mount Tekarra. Due to its low elevation, you can hike here much of the year.

The circuit starts on trail #8 and stays close to the south shoreline of the lake for 0.9 km. After passing beneath a powerline spanning the marsh, the trail climbs through forest to a junction at 1.6 km. (At this intersection, you can make a short side trip to Riley Lake by following trail #8 left for 10 minutes.)

Turn right on trail #8d to continue around the circuit. At km 1.9 you cross Cottonwood Creek and intersect trail #6, which you follow to the right.

The trail quickly climbs to grassy slopes overlooking Cottonwood Slough. This dry, south-facing slope dotted with large Douglas fir provides distant views to the southeast and is a good place to scan the lake below for waterfowl.

At 3.0 km you reach a junction where trail #6 veers left toward the riding stables; stay right and descend trail #6a into aspen groves. When you reach Pyramid Lake Road, turn right and follow it back to the trailhead parking area.

Access: Follow the Pyramid Lake Road 1.9 km (1.2 mi) from its junction with Pyramid Lake Drive on the west edge of Jasper townsite. The trailhead parking area is on the left side of the road near the bottom of a short downhill grade. *Maps: Jasper 83 D/16; Jasper Up-Close (GemTrek).*

92 Palisade Lookout

Pyramid Lake to Palisade Lookout Site—10.8 km (6.7 mi)

Day trip

Allow 3 hours one way

Elevation gain: 840 m (2,750 ft)

Maximum elevation: 2020 m (6,650 ft)

Maps: Jasper 83 D/16

Access: Follow Pyramid Lake Drive from the west edge of Jasper townsite 6.5 km (4 mi) to Pyramid Lake. Continue around the lake to the right until the road ends at a parking area near a locked access gate.

0.0—Access gate (1180 m).

—Follow gravel roadbed east along Pyramid Lake.

1.1—Pyramid Lake outlet bridge.

—Road makes a steady climb north along The Palisade ridge.

6.5—Bridged stream.

7.6—Junction. Microwave station access road left. Palisade Lookout right.

10.8—Palisade Lookout site (2020 m).

Views from the summit of The Palisade escarpment are among the most rewarding in the Jasper vicinity. From the sheer precipice where the Palisade Lookout cabin once stood, there is a broad panorama of the Athabasca Valley from Roche Miette and Jasper Lake to the snowy summit of Mount Edith Cavell. However, the hike is a long, steady uphill grind over an access road, and there are few views until you reach the top. Though it is popular with Jasper mountain bikers, few hikers are willing to face the long climb.

From the access gate at the end of Pyramid Lake Road, follow fire road skirting the shore of Pyramid Lake to the Pyramid Creek bridge. After crossing the bridge, the relentless climb of the The Palisade begins.

At km 7.6 the road forks, the right spur leading to the lookout site, the left to the Pyramid Mountain microwave station tram.

At the lookout site views suddenly open to the north and east. Across the Athabasca Valley are the sharp, sawtooth peaks of the Colin Range—named for Colin Fraser, who ran the tiny Jasper House fur trading post near the far end of Jasper Lake from 1835 to circa 1850. Roche Miette, a butte-like mountain rising to the right of Jasper Lake, presides over the valley to the northeast, and the open knoll behind the lookout site provides an excellent view of Pyramid Mountain (2766 m).

Author Don Beers reports that Jasper ski pioneer and photographer Joe Weiss often saw red foxes here when he manned the fire lookout many years ago. When we first visited the still-operating lookout in 1970, we saw the only fox we've ever encountered in the mountain parks near the cabin.

Remember to pack water on this hike, since there is only one dependable stream (km 6.5) along the way.

93 Dorothy, Christine and Virl Lakes

Yellowhead Highway to Christine Lake — 4.4 km (2.7 mi)

Half-day trip

Allow 1.5 to 2 hours one way

Elevation gain: 250 m (820 ft)

Maximum elevation: 1340 m (4,400 ft)

Maps: Jasper 83 D/16 †
  † full trail not shown

Access: Follow the Yellowhead Highway (Hwy 16) west from the Icefields Parkway (Hwy 93) junction 11 km (7 mi) to the Meadow Creek bridge. The trailhead kiosk and parking area are located just past the west end of the bridge on the north side of the highway. The hike begins on the railway service road beyond the locked access gate.

0.0—Trailhead parking area, kiosk (1220 m).

—Follow service road 150 m. Trail branches right and crosses railroad tracks.

0.2—Miette River bridge.

—Gradual climb west above river.

1.0—Trail bends right and climbs over ridge.

2.3—Minaga Creek bridge.

2.7—Junction. *Elysium Pass* left. Dorothy, Christine and Virl Lakes ahead.

3.7—Junction. Virl Lake right 0.4 km. Dorothy and Christine Lakes ahead.

4.1—Dorothy Lake (1340 m).

4.4—Christine Lake.

Of the many lakes in the rolling, heavily wooded country west of Jasper townsite, Dorothy, Christine and Virl are personal favourites. Though views from their shores are limited, these lakes provide more solitude than those nearer to town or the more popular high elevation hikes elsewhere in the park. In addition, the lakes' low elevation makes them ideal for early and late season hiking.

After clambering over the railroad right-of-way and crossing the Miette River bridge, you head upvalley above the Miette River briefly before veering right and climbing over a forested ridge. The trail descends to cross Minaga Creek at km 2.1, then makes a gradual ascent for the next 1.4 km to Virl Lake junction. A short spur trail leads to the shore of this tiny, elongated lake and views of Indian Ridge and Muhigan Mountain across the Miette Valley.

Just 400 m beyond Virl Lake junction, the main trail reaches Dorothy Lake, the largest of the three sisters. Dorothy is tightly embraced by forest and quite similar in appearance to Virl, except for a lack of distant views. Another 0.4 km brings you abreast of Christine Lake with its unique rock peninsulas and islands.

If you look at a map, you will see how these three lakes, and others west of Jasper, are all contained by low, parallel ridges running in a west-northwest to east-southeast direction. The sedimentary bedrock creating these ridges is primarily gritstone (coarse sandstone) alternating with shale. These rocks are part of the 600 million-year-old Middle Miette Formation—one of the oldest in the mountain parks—and numerous faults running through this section of the valley contributed to the formation of the ridges.

If you visit all three of the lakes, your round trip distance will be 9.6 km. But, with a map, compass and a good sense of direction, you can extend your day by

Virl Lake

exploring the forested country in the immediate vicinity of the lakes. (Iris Lake is just a short distance east of Dorothy, or you could contour around the east end of the ridge to the north of Dorothy and intersect the Saturday Night Lake Circuit near Minnow Lake.)

If nothing else, stumbling about in these woods will give you a better appreciation for the trials and tribulations of early fur traders and travellers who bushwhacked through this country during the 19th century.

94 Elysium Pass

Yellowhead Highway to Elysium Pass—15.0 km (9.3 mi) *

Day trip or backpack

Allow 7 hours one way

Elevation gain: 805 m (2,650 ft)

Maximum elevation: 2025 m (6,650 ft)

Maps: Jasper 83 D/16

Access: Follow the Yellowhead Highway (Hwy 16) west from the Icefields Parkway (Hwy 93) junction 11 km (7 mi) to the Meadow Creek bridge. The trailhead kiosk and parking area are located just past the west end of the bridge on the north side of the highway. The hike begins on the railway service road beyond the locked access gate.

0.0—Trailhead parking area, kiosk (1220 m).

— Follow service road 150 m. Trail branches right and crosses railroad tracks.

0.2—Miette River bridge.

— Gradual climb west above river.

1.0—Trail bends right and climbs over ridge.

2.3—Minaga Creek bridge.

2.7—Junction. *Dorothy, Christine and Virl Lakes* ahead. Elysium Pass left.

— Trail follows above Minaga Creek.

6.5—Stream bridge.

— Steady climb northwest toward Elysium Pass.

15.0—Elysium Pass (2025 m).

*Distances beyond 2.7 km approximate

(Trail not fully shown on maps in this book.)

When Morrison P. Bridgland conducted the first survey of the Victoria Cross Ranges west of Jasper in 1916, he was quite taken with the region's high, rolling landscape and lush alpine meadows. Because the scene brought to mind the Elysian fields of Greek mythology—the verdant paradise where heroic warriors were sent by the gods—he applied the name Elysium to the mountain overlooking this pass.

Present day hikers face a journey of near-heroic proportions to achieve their Elysium. The journey to the pass is long and follows a trail that is often muddy and sometimes vague or non-existent. While Parks Canada still lists a campground near the summit, it has no plans to maintain or improve the trail. This is simply a route for explorers.

The trail branches northwest from the *Dorothy, Christine and Virl Lakes* trail at 2.7 km and contours above Minaga Creek for just over 3 km. After crossing a side stream, it begins a more serious ascent toward the pass.

The trail climbs high onto the west slope of Emigrants Mountain, where there are fine views back across the Miette Valley to Mount Fitzwilliam and other peaks along the Great Divide. Just 1.5 km from the pass, views open out over the summit meadows and into the heart of the Victoria Cross Ranges, dominated by the glaciated twin summits of Monarch Mountain.

The trail descends from this lofty viewpoint to the stream running south from the pass (the campground lies a short distance down this stream). Though the track disappears at this point, the route north through open meadows to the summit is obvious.

Be aware that the last half of this trip traverses deluxe grizzly bear habitat, so travel alertly and follow all the rules for camping safely in bear country.

95 The Whistlers

Whistlers Road to The Whistlers Summit—7.9 km (4.9 mi)

Day trip

Allow 2.5 to 3 hours one way

Elevation gain: 1250 m (4,100 ft)

Maximum elevation: 2470 m (8,100 ft)

Maps: Jasper 83 D/16

Access: Follow the Icefields Parkway (Hwy 93) south 1.8 km (1.1 mi) from its junction with the Yellowhead Highway to the Whistlers Road. Follow Whistlers Road 2.7 km (1.7 mi) to a gravel access road branching left. Continue on this access road 300 m to the trailhead parking area.

0.0—Trailhead parking area (1220 m).

  —Steady uphill through dense forest.

3.1—Trail passes beneath tram line.

  —Trail contours southwest into large gully leading towards the summit.

5.6—Trail emerges above treeline.

  —Steady ascent up open slope west of tram terminal.

6.8—Upper tram terminal.

  —Well travelled trail rises steeply beyond the terminal.

7.9—The Whistlers Summit (2470 m).

The Whistlers is the prominent mountain immediately south of Jasper townsite, easily identified by the tramway terminal on a promontory just below the summit. Over 200,000 visitors ride the tramway each summer, and many hike the short trail from the upper terminal to the summit. However, it is also possible to hike from the base of the mountain to the top via a quite remarkable trail.

The trail up The Whistlers starts near the edge of the montane life zone, climbs through subalpine forest, and eventually ends on the mountain's 2470 m alpine summit. The vertical rise of 1250 m is one of the greatest of any trail in the mountain parks, and it is one of the few trails traversing three life zones in under 8 km. But if you are not up for such a gruelling climb, you can ride the tram up and hike down (reduced-fare tickets are available for the one-way trip).

From the trailhead parking area just off the Whistlers Road, the trail begins its long ascent in heavy bush. After passing beneath the tram line at 3.1 km, the forest becomes more open and subalpine—an area of moist meadows where a myriad of wildflowers bloom in July and early August.

The trail soon turns south and begins a steep climb of a major gully on the mountain's north slope. Shortly after emerging above treeline, it reaches the tramway's upper terminal, where you will be happy to find refreshments and a restaurant.

The final kilometre to the summit is hiked in the company of scores of tourists who have ridden the lift.

There is a 360-degree view at the top, which takes in most of the mountains and valleys in this section of the park. Only a few hardy plants survive on this wind-swept ridge, and the animal inhabitants, hoary marmots and pikas, find shelter from the elements in the rocks beneath the summit.

96 Old Fort Point

Old Fort Point Road to Old Fort Point summit — 0.8 km (0.5 mi)
Old Fort Point Circuit — 3.8 km (2.4 mi)

Half-day trip

Allow 1.5 hours for circuit

Elevation gain: 135 m (445 ft)

Maximum elevation: 1165 m (3,820 ft)

Maps: Jasper 83 D/16

Access: Follow Hazel Avenue (Hwy 93A) south from its intersection with Connaught Drive (Jasper's main street). Cross the CNR tracks to an intersection with the Yellowhead Highway (Hwy 16). Continue across the Yellowhead Highway 0.1 km to the Old Fort Point/Lac Beauvert Road junction. Turn left and follow this road 1.0 km to the Athabasca River bridge. On the opposite side of the bridge, turn right into the trailhead parking area at the foot of a rocky bluff.

0.0—Trailhead parking area (1030 m).

—Old Fort Point Circuit: follow trail #1 from information kiosk at the rear of parking area.

0.9—Junction. Trail #7a to Lac Beauvert left.

1.6—Junction. Trail #1a ahead. Old Fort Point right.

1.8—Steep climb through forest and cliffs.

2.1—Junction. Trails #1a and #9 to *Valley of the Five Lakes* left. Old Fort Point ahead.

—Steady uphill.

2.5—Junction. Unsigned side trail 200 m to Old Fort Point southeast summit.

—Gradual descent.

2.8—Trail begins climb to northwest summit.

3.1—Old Fort Point (1165 m). Short spur trail ahead through rock bluffs to summit viewpoint.

—Steady downhill with steep sections.

3.7—Junction. Trail #9c intersects from left. Heritage River monument 20 m ahead.

—Stairs to parking area.

3.8—Trailhead parking area (1030 m).

Old Fort Point rises across the Athabasca River from Jasper townsite. It is named for the first fur trade post in the Rocky Mountains, Henry House, which was constructed a short distance downstream by William Henry during the winter of 1811.

While Old Fort Point is little more than a hill, its position in the middle of the Athabasca Valley provides a 360-degree panorama that includes all the important points of interest: the townsite stretches beyond the Athabasca River to the northwest; Lac Beauvert and Jasper Park Lodge lie immediately below to the north; Mounts Hardisty and Kerkeslin, rise upvalley; and the snowy summit of Mount Edith Cavell dominates all to the south.

The shortest route to the top of Old Fort Point is only 0.8 km. This direct route begins on a staircase beside the parking area. At the top of the stairs you arrive at a monument honouring the Athabasca Heritage River and your first viewpoint—an overlook of the confluence of the Athabasca and Miette Rivers.

Stay left at the junction just beyond the monument and climb steeply up open slopes and through stands of Douglas fir until you crest the summit ridge. Just beyond a pair of stone monuments, branch left through rock outcrops to the northwest summit viewpoint.

Old Fort Point Circuit. While the trail up the northwest slope of Old Fort Point is the shortest, we prefer the longer, less direct route—sneaking up on the viewpoint from behind.

The Old Fort Point Circuit is a loop trip, which includes both the southeast and northwest summits. This hike is quite rewarding in spring and early summer when meadows are filled with wildflowers, or in late September when the numerous aspen groves turn to gold.

Jasper and the Athabasca Valley from Old Fort Point

Follow trail #1 into heavy forest from the kiosk at the rear of parking area. (Though there are a number of intersecting trails on the circuit, you stay on course by always following the yellow #1 trail markers.)

The trail is flat to gradual uphill for the first 1.5 km, passing through pleasant groves of cottonwood and aspen poplar. This section is followed by a short climb to the crest of the Old Fort Point ridge, where the trail turns back to the northwest. Here you encounter more aspen stands and montane wildflowers, including blue flax, harebells, blue-eyed grass and gaillardia.

An unsigned trail branches right onto open slopes at 2.5 km. This is Old Fort Point's southeast summit, which is virtually the same elevation as the northwest summit. While views are more limited on this promontory, it is a wonderful place for flowers.

At km 3.1 you reach the rock outcrops marking the northwest summit viewpoint. Complete the circuit by descending the steep, direct route to the staircase and parking area.

Old Fort Point to Valley of the Five Lakes. This branch trail from the Old Fort Point Circuit rolls upvalley to the Valley of the Five Lakes. It passes through numerous aspen groves and along open wetlands, which are excellent locales for birdwatching.

Though the trail is often used by mountain bikers (a demanding route with many ups-and-downs), it is also a pleasant half-day hike for those who can arrange transportation between Old Fort Point and the Valley of the Five Lakes trailhead on the Icefields Parkway.

Follow trail #9 south from its junction with the Old Fort Point Circuit at km 2.1. Continue upvalley 4 km to where trail #9a splits left from #9. Stay on #9a to the Valley of the Five Lakes. You will intersect the trail from the Icefields Parkway at the far end of the first lake.

Total distance from the Old Fort Point Circuit trailhead to the parking area on the Icefields Parkway is approximately 11.5 km. (See *Valley of the Five Lakes*.)

Wabasso Lake and Mount Kerkeslin

97 Valley of the Five Lakes

Icefields Parkway to Valley of the Five Lakes—2.0 km (1.2 mi)

These five lakes on the floor of the Athabasca Valley vary in size from just over a kilometre in length at First Lake to the tiny pond of Third Lake. While the hike to the valley and back can be completed in less than 2 hours, you can easily spend a half-day or more wandering about the lakes' circuit.

From the parking area, the first 0.5 km of trail is mainly flat through a forest of lodgepole pine. At 0.8 km the trail descends to a boardwalk across Wabasso Creek. This is followed by a brief climb to open meadow and a junction with trail #9—the valley trail running from Old Fort Point to Wabasso Lake. Continue ahead on #9a to a split, where you begin the circuit that loops around the five lakes (you can go right on #9a or left on #9b, which is our preference).

By staying on #9b you descend from the ridge and pass between First and Second Lake, where you are reunited with #9a. Turn right and follow it along the northeast shore of Second and Fourth Lakes to the northwest end of Fifth Lake. Stay right on #9a to complete the loop.

More ambitious hikers can travel southeast to Wabasso Lake or northwest to Old Fort Point via trail #9—both trips ideally completed by arranging transportation at those trailheads. (See *Old Fort Point* and *Wabasso Lake*.)

Access: Follow the Icefields Parkway (Hwy 93) south 9 km (5.5 mi) from its intersection with the Yellowhead Highway (Hwy 16). The trailhead parking area is located on the east side of the highway. *Maps: Jasper 83 D/16; Jasper Up-Close (Gem Trek).*

98 Wabasso Lake

Icefields Parkway to Wabasso Lake—3.2 km (2.0 mi)
Icefields Parkway to Skyline Trail—15.0 km (9.3 mi)

Half-day trip or backpack

Allow 1 hour to Wabasso Lake

Elevation gain: 1100 m (3,600 ft)

Maximum elevation: 2200 m (7,200 ft)

Maps: Medicine Lake 83 C/13

Access: Follow the Icefields Parkway (Hwy 93) to the Wabasso Lake parking area, located on the east side of the highway 14.5 km (9.0 mi) south of the Yellowhead Highway (Hwy 16) intersection.

0.0—Trailhead parking area (1100 m).

—Rolling forested terrain.

2.3—Ridgetop viewpoint.

3.2—Wabasso Lake.

—Trail skirts north end of lake.

4.2—Junction. Valley of the Five Lakes and Old Fort Point left (trail #9). Skyline Trail ahead.

—Steep switchbacking climb through pine forest.

13.0—Grade moderates.

14.1—Shovel Pass Lodge.

14.2—Curator Campground.

—Steep ascent.

15.0—Junction (2200 m). Intersection with the *Skyline Trail* at 19.5 km. Curator Lake left 0.9 km. Big Shovel Pass right 2.0 km.

This short trail leads to a small but very pretty lake on the floor of the Athabasca Valley. Though Wabasso is the Cree word for "rabbit," you are more likely to see muskrat along the lake's marshy shores.

The hike begins with a brief climb from the Icefields Parkway, then it rolls through lodgepole pine forest. At km 1.4 it crosses a stream and climbs onto an open ridge—a fine viewpoint for all the major peaks to the south.

From the ridgetop, it is less than a kilometre to the marsh at the southeast corner of Wabasso Lake. The trail continues around the lake's north shore, where you have the best views of the lake, its tiny island, and the impressive summits of Mounts Kerkeslin, Christie and Brussels Peak rising far to the south.

Wabasso Lake to the Skyline. The Wabasso trail continues beyond the lake and up the side of the Maligne Range for another 11 km to an intersection with the Skyline Trail. It is most often used by packtrains travelling to and from Shovel Pass Lodge.

Since the trail is steep and forest-enclosed, it has little attraction as an approach to the Skyline, but it can provide a quick exit during inclement weather. It can also be linked with the Watchtower Basin trail via Big Shovel Pass to create a 30 km traverse across the Maligne Range. (See *Watchtower Basin.*)

After passing Wabasso Lake, the trail branches into the forest to a junction at km 4.2. The Skyline option stays right and runs briefly through mixed forest before starting the long, gruelling climb.

The forest eventually thins to open views of the Athabasca Valley, and the grade moderates near the outfitter's lodge and Curator Campground. From the campground it is a short, steep climb to the Skyline Trail junction.

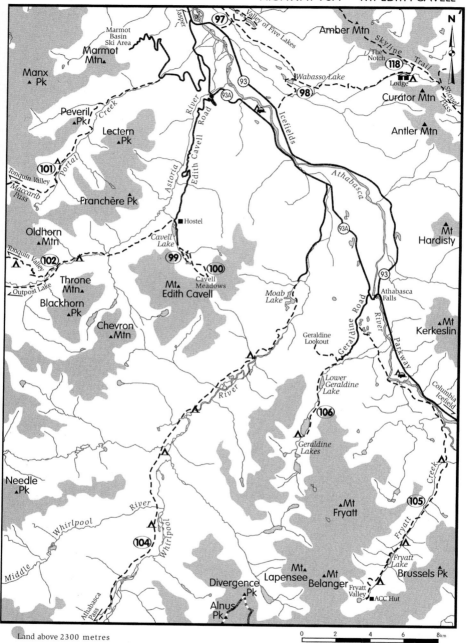

Land above 2300 metres

0   2   4   6   8km

Angel Glacier from the Path of the Glacier trail

99 Path of the Glacier

Path of the Glacier Loop—1.6 km (1.0 mi)

The Path of the Glacier trail travels through a rocky glacial basin to a tiny but exquisite lake at the toe of the rubble-covered Cavell Glacier. The lake's dark blue waters are highlighted by drifting icebergs, and its shoreline is one of the best vantage points for the Angel Glacier and the towering cliffs of Mount Edith Cavell. Signs along the trail describe the glacial events that have shaped this dramatic landscape.

While we would rank this as one of the most spectacular short trails in the Canadian Rockies, it is not a place where you're likely to find solitude. With the exception of early morning or late evening, it is a steady parade of humanity.

Begin the hike by ascending the stairwell above the parking area and then climbing steadily on paved trail along a lateral moraine for 0.5 km. From the end of pavement, the trail descends into the rockbound basin containing the lake.

From the lakeshore, the north face of Mount Edith Cavell rises an incredible 1600 m (a vertical mile) to the summit of the highest peak in this area of the park. Angel Glacier clings to the wall, though it doesn't resemble an angel quite so much these days since the once sprawling toe has receded well up onto the cliffs.

The return trail to the parking area travels beside Cavell Creek, where willows and other plants are slowly recolonizing a rocky valley bottom that was covered by ice 150 years ago.

Access: Follow the Icefields Parkway (Hwy 93) south from Jasper 7 km (4.5 mi) to Highway 93A. Continue south on 93A for 5.5 km (3.5 mi) to the Cavell Road and follow it 14.5 km (9 mi) to its terminus at the parking area beneath Mount Edith Cavell. The trail starts at the upper edge of the parking area. *Maps: Amethyst Lakes 83 D/9.*

Angel Glacier from Cavell Meadows

100 Cavell Meadows

Cavell Meadows Loop—6.1 km (3.8 mi)

Half-day trip

Allow 2 hours round trip

Elevation gain: 400 m (1,300 ft)

Maximum elevation: 2165 m (7,100 ft)

Maps: Amethyst Lake 83 D/9

Access: From its intersection with the Yellowhead Highway (Hwy 16) at Jasper townsite, follow the Icefields Parkway (Hwy 93) south 7 km (4.5 mi) to Highway 93A. Continue south on 93A for 5.5 km (3.5 mi) to the Cavell Road junction. Follow the Cavell Road 14.5 km (9 mi) to its terminus at the parking area beneath Mount Edith Cavell. The trail starts at the upper edge of the parking area.

0.0—Parking area (1765 m).

—Follows paved trail along a lateral moraine.

0.5—Junction. *Path of the Glacier* trail ahead. Cavell Meadows uphill to left.

—Trail climbs over and along the lateral moraine.

1.5—Trail begins switchbacking ascent through forest.

2.2—Junction. Trail split for Cavell Meadows loop. Keep right.

2.4—Angel Glacier viewpoint.

—Trail climbs into meadows.

3.0—Junction. South end of meadow loop. Branch trail continues ahead 100 m to a viewpoint.

—Trail turns left and continues climb across meadows.

3.2—Trail high point (2165 m).

—Steep descent to loop trail split.

3.9—Junction. Return to trail split for Cavell Meadows loop.

6.1—Parking area (1765 m).

The Cavell Meadows trail climbs to alpine meadows far above the standard tourist viewpoint for Angel Glacier. The lush, flower-filled meadows would be a worthy objective on their own, but they also provide an outstanding viewpoint for the glacier and the north wall of Mount Edith Cavell.

This is one of Jasper's most popular trails, so unless you hike it in the evening or early morning, don't expect solitude.

The hike begins on the paved Path of the Glacier trail. After 500 m it branches left and climbs over a ridge of lateral moraine. It continues along the moraine briefly (watch for hoary marmots on the rockpiles), then switchbacks up into subalpine forest—an area that is carpeted with glacier lilies, marsh marigolds and globe flowers in early summer.

At 2.2 km you reach the trail split for the loop up through the meadows. We always stay right and hike the circuit counterclockwise, which makes the ascent more gradual.

You soon climb through the last scattered trees to a viewpoint for Angel Glacier and Mount Edith Cavell. The glacier has eroded a huge amphitheatre into the uppermost cliffs of this 3363 m peak—the highest mountain in this section of the park.

The trail continues its climb above treeline until it reaches the southern end of the meadow loop. (A side trail continues ahead across a gully for another 100 m to a rocky viewpoint.) Here it bends uphill to the left and climbs across even higher terrain until finally topping-out around 2165 m. From this summit, it plunges down through lush flower-filled meadows to close the loop.

Since we first visited these meadows in 1970, a spiderweb of new trails has been created by people wandering off the main trail. These moist alpine meadows will be destroyed if this practice continues. Stay on the main trail.

Tonquin Valley

J. Monroe Thorington, an American mountaineer and historian who devoted most of his life to rambling about the Canadian Rockies, wrote eloquently of the Tonquin Valley and how its "unique combination of lake, precipice, and ice...presents itself with a singular beauty almost unequalled in alpine regions of North America."

Anyone who has visited the valley at the end of summer when the air is crisp and clear would undoubtedly support his appreciation. But in the midst of summer, when the rain is pelting down, the mosquitoes and horseflies are swarming, and the trails have been churned to mush by horses, it can resemble a backpacker's definition of hell. At such times it is better to forget the Tonquin's reputation and head elsewhere.

The Tonquin Valley is actually a 5 km-long pass whose broad crest cradles the Amethyst Lakes—a pair of beautiful connected lakes set at the base of a 1000 m wall of Precambrian quartzite called The Ramparts. The Ramparts are composed of ten spectacular castellate peaks, which are worthy of such names as Bastion, Drawbridge, Redoubt, Dungeon and Paragon. They form a glowering collection of towers and turrets that natives once believed to be inhabited by huge, supernatural beasts.

While no horrible beasts have been sighted in the valley in recent years (except for the pesky midsummer bugs), it is home to a variety of wildlife. Two celebrity species always in residence are grizzly bear and mountain caribou.

A few kilometres west of the north Amethyst Lake are Moat Lake and the twin passes of Moat and Tonquin. Chrome Lake and the heavily glaciated spires of the Eremite Valley lie just south of the Tonquin Valley. Both areas are prime day trip destinations from the valley's campsites and lodges.

Two trails of almost equal length lead into the valley—one running up the Astoria River from the Cavell Road, the other via Portal Creek and Maccarib Pass from the Marmot Basin Road. Maccarib Pass is considered the most scenic approach, while the Astoria River is the shortest route to campgrounds at the south end of the Amethyst Lakes and the Alpine Club of Canada hut at Outpost Lake. If you arrange transportation between trailheads, you can hike in on one of the trails and out on the other.

Four campgrounds are located in the valley and three others on the approach trails. Due to the area's popularity, valley campgrounds can fill up at anytime during the summer, and particularly on holiday weekends. To assure a site, you can make reservations up to 3 months in advance of your trip.

In addition to campgrounds, there are two lodges in the valley:

Tonquin-Amethyst Lake Lodge is located on the east side of Amethyst Lakes near the Narrows. The rustic Brewster Chalet, which serves as the centrepiece for the cabin camp, was built by Jasper's pioneer outfitter Fred Brewster, who first developed the site in 1939. While the lodge books horse trips throughout the summer season, it reserves 40% of its space for hikers. It is operated exclusively for hikers at reduced rates from September 15 to October 31 (weather permitting);

Tonquin Valley Backcountry Lodge is at the north end of the lakes just off the Moat Lake trail. At present it is more oriented to guided horse parties, though it does have special rates for walk-in guests. (See *Sources-Backcountry lodges.*)

Camping is not permitted in the Eremite Valley region, but the Alpine Club of Canada's Wates-Gibson Hut on the shores of Outpost Lake can accommodate up to 40 people at quite reasonable rates. (See *Sources-Huts.*)

Both the Maccarib Pass and Astoria River approaches are described on pages 198-199 and 200-201.

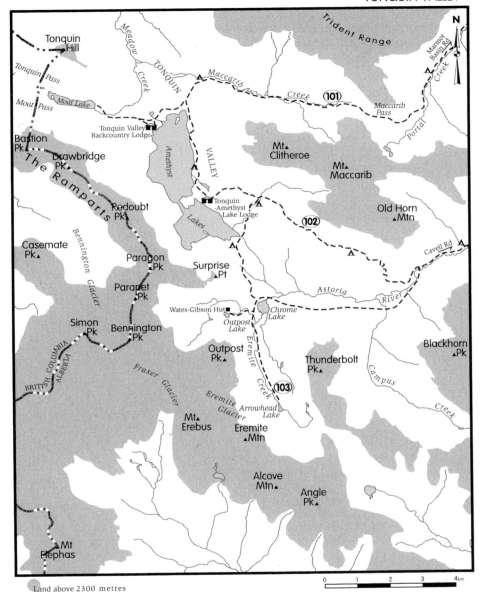

Tonquin Hill

Tonquin Pass

Moat Pass

Moat Lake

Meadow Creek

TONQUIN

Maccarib

Creek

101

Trident Range

Marmot Basin Rd

Maccarib Pass

Portal Creek

Bastion Pk

Drawbridge Pk

The Ramparts

Redoubt Pk

Tonquin Valley Backcountry Lodge

Amethyst

VALLEY

Mt Clitheroe

Mt Maccarib

Old Horn Mtn

Lakes

Tonquin -Amethyst Lake Lodge

102

Cavell Rd

Casemate Pk

Bennington Glacier

Paragon Pk

Parapet Pk

Simon Pk

Bennington Pk

Surprise Pt

Wates-Gibson Hut

Chrome Lake

Outpost Lake

Astoria River

Blackhorn Pk

Fraser Glacier

BRITISH COLUMBIA

ALBERTA

Outpost Pk

Eremite Creek

Thunderbolt Pk

Campus

Creek

Eremite Glacier

Arrowhead Lake

103

Mt Erebus

Eremite Mtn

Alcove Mtn

Angle Pk

Mt Elephas

Land above 2300 metres

0 1 2 3 4 km

101 Maccarib Pass

Marmot Basin Road to Amethyst Campground—22.9 km (14.2 mi)
Marmot Basin Road to Clitheroe Campground—26.3 km (16.3 mi)

Backpack

Allow 7 to 8 hours

Elevation gain: 730 m (2,400 ft)
           loss: 235 m (770 ft)

Maximum elevation: 2210 m (7,250 ft)

Maps: Jasper 83 D/16
       Amethyst Lakes 83 D/9

Access: From its intersection with the Yellow-head Highway (Hwy 16) at Jasper townsite, follow the Icefields Parkway (Hwy 93) south 7 km (4.5 mi) to the 93A Highway junction. Continue south on Highway 93A for 2.5 km (1.5 mi) to the Marmot Basin Road junction. Follow the Marmot Basin Road 6.5 km (4 mi) to the Portal Creek bridge and parking area.

0.0—Parking area (1480 m).

0.5—Portal Creek bridge to north side of creek.

  —Ascend Portal Creek canyon.

4.0—Circus Creek bridge.

5.0—Trail emerges into open rockslides.

8.7—Portal Creek Campground.

10.1—Trail begins steep ascent toward pass.

12.4—Maccarib Pass (2210 m).

12.9—First views into Tonquin Valley.

  —Gradual descent.

19.5—Maccarib Campground and Maccarib Creek bridge.

20.4—Junction. Tonquin Valley Backcountry Lodge (1.5 km) and Moat Lake (3.5 km) ahead. Amethyst Lakes east shore left.

  —Flat trail running south.

21.3—Amethyst Lakes-north end.

22.9—Amethyst Campground.

24.0—Tonquin-Amethyst Lake Lodge (1975 m)

  —Trail climbs east from lodge junction.

26.2—Junction. Astoria River trail ahead (see *Astoria River*). Clitheroe Campground (0.1 km), Surprise Point Campground (2.3 km) and Eremite Valley to right (see *Eremite Valley*).

Of the two main trails into the Tonquin Valley, Maccarib Pass is slightly longer and more arduous. However, it holds a definite scenic advantage over the Astoria River trail. The descent of a 6 km-long meadow west of Maccarib Pass is the scenic highlight, disclosing ever-improving views of The Ramparts and Amethyst Lakes as you approach the valley.

Starting from the Marmot Basin Road parking area, the trail climbs into the narrow canyon known as The Portal. It traverses high onto the north side of the valley and crosses rockslides below Peveril Peak, and you soon have excellent views to the head of the valley and the peaks surrounding the pass.

After descending back to the valley floor, the trail makes a 5 km climb through an open subalpine forest of Engelmann spruce and alpine fir. It finally emerges above treeline less than 2 km from the pass.

While the approach to Maccarib Pass offers some fine views, particularly to the jagged summit of Old Horn Mountain, the trail's true reward lies on the descent west from its summit. From the first glimpse of The Ramparts and Moat Pass, obtained just beyond the pass, each succeeding kilometre across alpine meadows brings better views of the Tonquin Valley and its surrounding peaks.

After passing the scenically situated Maccarib Campground at 19.5 km, the trail reaches the floor of the Tonquin Valley at a junction just north of the Amethyst Lakes. The right branch leads to Moat Lake and the Tonquin Valley Backcountry Lodge at the north end of the lakes, the left runs south along the east shore of the lakes to the Tonquin-Amethyst Lake Lodge and three of the valley's campgrounds.

Following the valley trail south from

Amethyst Lakes and The Ramparts from the Maccarib Pass trail

the junction, you come abreast of the north Amethyst Lake in less than a kilometre. The trail runs flat through scattered forest for another 1.6 km to Amethyst Campground—the most centrally located of the valley's four campgrounds.

The trail continues south for another kilometre to Tonquin-Amethyst Lake Lodge. From the lodge it climbs onto higher, drier ground along the east side of the valley to the Clitheroe Campground junction. At this intersection the Astoria River trail continues left and the trail to Surprise Point at the south end of the lakes branches down to the right (see *Astoria River* and *Eremite Valley*).

Moat Lake. The trail to Moat Lake is a popular day trip from Maccarib and Amethyst Campgrounds and the lodges. It is 3.5 kms to the lake from its intersection with the Maccarib Pass trail at km 20.4.

From Maccarib junction, the trail runs across rocky, open meadows before entering forest. A spur trail cuts left at km 1.3 and leads to the Tonquin Valley Backcountry Lodge at the north end of Amethyst Lakes—a very pretty viewpoint for the lakes and The Ramparts. (If you don't want to return to the main trail, you can continue toward Moat Lake on a trail running west from the lodge.)

From the lodge junction, the trail continues west into a vast meadow, where it becomes wet, boggy and vague (watch for markers). You cross a bridge to the north side of Moat Creek shortly before arriving at the east end of Moat Lake.

The perpendicular cliffs of The Ramparts, specifically Drawbridge and Bastion Peaks, rise above the lake's southern shoreline, while the lake stretches for more than a kilometre toward the twin passes of Moat and Tonquin on the Alberta-B.C. boundary. (A vague trail follows along the north side of the lake in that direction.)

102 Astoria River

Cavell Road to Clitheroe Campground—16.9 km (10.5 mi)
Cavell Road to Amethyst Campground—20.1 km (12.5 mi)

Backpack

Allow 6 to 7 hours

Elevation gain: 445 m (1,450 ft)
　　　　　loss: 130 m (420 ft)

Maximum elevation: 2105 m (6,900 ft)

Maps: Amethyst Lakes 83 D/9

Access: From its intersection with the Yellowhead Highway (Hwy 16) at Jasper townsite, follow the Icefields Parkway (Hwy 93) south 7 km (4.5 mi) to the 93A Highway. Continue south on 93A for 5.5 km (3.5 mi) to the Cavell Road and follow it 12.5 km (8 mi) to the roadside parking area above Cavell Lake. The trail begins from the outlet bridge at Cavell Lake.

0.0—Cavell Lake outlet bridge (1720 m).

—Descent through forest along north slope of Mt. Edith Cavell.

5.0—Astoria River bridge to north side (1660 m).

6.8—Astoria Campground.

8.2—Junction. Chrome Lake (6.5 km) and Eremite Valley left. Tonquin Valley ahead.

—Steep switchbacks up lower slopes of Oldhorn Mtn.

12.9—Maximum elevation (2105 m). Open subalpine meadows.

13.3—Junction. Switchback Campground left 0.2 km.

16.8—Junction. Left to Clitheroe Campground (0.1 km), Surprise Point Campground (2.3 km), and Eremite Valley (see *Eremite Valley*). Tonquin-Amethyst Lake Lodge and Amethyst Lakes east shore ahead.

19.0—Tonquin-Amethyst Lake Lodge (1975 m)

20.1—Amethyst Campground.

Though the hike to Amethyst Lakes via the Astoria River is not much shorter than the Maccarib Pass trail, the elevation gain is markedly less. And if you are bound for the Alpine Club of Canada hut at Outpost Lake or the campgrounds near the south end of Amethyst Lakes, the Astoria trail is by far the quickest option.

From the trailhead on the Cavell Road, the trail descends to the Cavell Lake outlet bridge and a great view of Mount Edith Cavell. Beyond Cavell Lake, it makes a long, gradual descent through forest along Mount Edith Cavell's north slope. At km 5.0, you reach the Astoria River, cross to the north side, and begin a steady ascent of the valley.

At km 8.2 the trail to Chrome Lake branches left across the Astoria on a log bridge. The main trail continues along the north side and soon begins a strenuous switchbacking climb alongside a massive rockslide on the south slope of Oldhorn Mountain. You reach the trail's maximum elevation near the 13 km mark, where the trail levels off across the west slope of Oldhorn. At this point you are greeted by the first views of The Ramparts and Amethyst Lakes.

It was from the slopes of nearby Mount Clitheroe that topographical surveyor Morrison P. Bridgland first photographed the valley in 1915 and subsequently revealed its glories to the world. The area drew a steady procession of visitors over the ensuing years, including photographers and artists: Banff photographer Byron Harmon shot the first motion picture footage of the valley from the slopes of Clitheroe in 1918; Group of Seven artists Lawren Harris and A.Y. Jackson painted in the valley in 1924; and in 1928 the famous American landscape photographer Ansel Adams visited the valley with members of California's Sierra Club.

Amethyst Lakes and The Ramparts

At km 16.8 the trail splits. The right branch descends to Tonquin-Amethyst Lake Lodge and Amethyst Campground, while the left runs downhill to the outlet for the southern lake beneath Surprise Point (Clitheroe Campground is 100 m below the junction).

Many backpackers who reach the Tonquin Valley via Astoria River stay at Clitheroe or Surprise Point Campgrounds. Both have fine views of The Ramparts and are good base camps for day trips into the Eremite Valley (see *Eremite Valley*).

Chrome Lake via Astoria Valley. This old trail serves as a direct route from the Astoria River to Chrome Lake, Eremite Valley, and the Alpine Club's Wates-Gibson Hut at Outpost Lake. It also saves 2 km and a lot of climbing for those heading to the Surprise Point Campground.

The trail branches from the Astoria River route at 8.2 km, crosses the river, and follows up the south side of the valley, reaching Chrome Lake in 6.5 km. The trail is not well maintained and tends to be narrow, rough and, with the exception of a few meadows, forest-enclosed. (You wouldn't want to run into a grizzly bear here. Stay alert and make noise when visibility is limited.)

Once you reach Chrome Lake, stay on the trail leading around its north side for 0.3 km to an intersection with the *Eremite Valley* trail. This junction is 1.9 km south of Surprise Point Campground.

Maccarib Pass-Astoria River Circuit. If you are willing to arrange transportation between trailheads, you can complete a circuit by entering the Tonquin Valley on one of the access trails and exiting via the other. (Our preference is to approach the valley via Maccarib Pass and return on the Astoria River trail.) Total distance for the circuit is 43 km.

103 Eremite Valley

Clitheroe Campground Junction to Arrowhead Lake—8.9 km (5.5 mi)

Day trip

Allow 2 to 3 hours one way

Elevation loss: 320 m (1,050 ft)
      gain: 200 m (650 ft)

Maximum elevation: 2120 m (6,950 ft)

Maps: Amethyst Lakes 83 D/9

Access: Trail begins at the Clitheroe Campground junction on the *Astoria River* trail (km 16.8). If starting from Surprise Point Campground or the Wates-Gibson Hut at Outpost Lake, subtract 2.3 km and 3.6 km respectively from the total distance to Arrowhead Lake.

0.0—Clitheroe Campground Junction (2130 m)

0.1—Clitheroe Campground.

—Steady descent.

1.8—Bridge across Amethyst Lakes outlet stream.

2.3—Surprise Point Campground.

—Trail runs south, descending steadily on rough, rocky track.

4.2—Junction (1810 m). Left to Chrome Lake north shore (0.3 km) and Astoria River shortcut trail. Outpost Lake and Eremite Valley ahead.

4.7—Junction. Outpost Lake and Wates-Gibson Hut right 1.1 km. Eremite Valley ahead.

—Trail runs through open meadows west of Chrome Lake.

5.5—Junction. Branch trail to Chrome Lake south shore left. Eremite Valley ahead.

6.8—Old Alpine Club campsite.

—Trail climbs onto rockslide. Track vague and intermittent.

8.9—Arrowhead Lake (2010 m).

While Amethyst Lakes and The Ramparts are the centrepiece of the Tonquin Valley region, the nearby Eremite Valley is another scenic highlight. Chrome Lake lies at the entrance to the valley, and the rugged, glaciated mountains surrounding tiny Arrowhead Lake at the headwaters are every bit as spectacular as the better known Ramparts. It is little wonder that these peaks have attracted alpinists ever since the first Alpine Club camps were held in the Tonquin Valley in 1926 and at Chrome Lake in 1934.

The trail into the valley from the south end of Amethyst Lakes is the most popular and worthwhile day trip from campgrounds and lodges in the Tonquin Valley. While the distance is not far, particularly from Clitheroe and Surprise Point Campgrounds, you will want to reserve a full day for the outing so you can explore the upper end of the Eremite Valley. Less energetic hikers can complete a shorter trip by only going as far as Chrome and Outpost Lakes.

The trail begins at the 16.8 km junction on the Astoria River trail, just 100 m from Clitheroe Campground. From the junction it descends to the south end of Amethyst Lakes and crosses the lakes' outlet to Surprise Point Campground.

The trail continues south from the Tonquin Valley as a rough, rocky track to a large meadow containing Chrome Lake and Penstock Creek. At the meadow's first junction, you can take a 300 m side trail left to the best shoreline viewpoint for Chrome Lake—a small but beautiful turquoise lake reflecting the mountains surrounding the head of the Eremite Valley.

The main trail continues 500 m to another junction just a short distance above Penstock Creek. The right hand branch follows Penstock Creek upstream to Outpost Lake, while the main valley trail attaches itself to Eremite Creek and follows it south for another 4 km to its

Chrome Lake

headwaters. After passing the site of the 1945 Alpine Club of Canada camp, the track is rough and vague, but the route is obvious and the destination well worth the effort.

The head of the Eremite Valley is a spectacular alpine region where glaciers crown most every peak. The most dramatic of these are Mount Erebus and Eremite Mountain, rising above Eremite Glacier to the west. The valley surrounding Arrowhead Lake is filled with rockslides and glacial moraines and offers unlimited opportunities for scrambling and exploration.

Outpost Lake—1.1 km. From the junction at km 4.7, just west of Chrome Lake, the Outpost Lake trail follows Penstock Creek upstream. It crosses to the south side of the creek at the foot of a steep forested slope, then climbs to the shores of tiny Outpost Lake. While the lake is ringed by forest, the sharp prow of Outpost Peak provides a fine backdrop.

The Wates-Gibson Hut, operated by the Alpine Club of Canada, is located on the lake's north shore. This substantial log structure was constructed in 1963. It accommodates 30 people and provides a good base for anyone who wants to spend more time in the Eremite Valley region. For information and rates, contact the Alpine Club of Canada's Canmore office (see *Sources-Huts*).

Chrome Lake–Outpost Lake via Astoria Valley. The entrance to the Eremite Valley can be reached directly without the need of detouring through the Tonquin Valley. At km 8.2 on the Astoria River route, a trail branches left and crosses to the south side of the river. It continues along that side of the valley, ascending to Chrome Lake and the junction with the Eremite Valley trail in another 7.6 km. This route is of most interest to those staying at the Alpine Club's hut on Outpost Lake. (See also *Astoria River.*)

104 Athabasca Pass

Moab Lake Parking Area to Athabasca Pass—49.1 (30.5 mi)

Backpack

Allow 2 to 3 days to Athabasca Pass

Elevation gain: 545 m (1,780 ft)

Maximum elevation: 1755 m (5,750 ft)

Maps: Athabasca Falls 83 C/12
       Amethyst Lakes 83 D/9
       Athabasca Pass 83 D/8

Access: From the junction of the Icefields Parkway and Highway 93A at Athabasca Falls, follow the 93A north 9 km (5.5 mi) to the Whirlpool Fire Road (Moab Lake) junction. Continue on the Whirlpool Road 7 km (4.5 mi) to the access gate and parking area.

0.0—Parking area (1210 m).

  —Route follows restored fire road.

0.3—Junction. Moab Lake right 0.2 km.

6.6—Whirlpool Campground.

8.6— End of roadbed.

  —Single-track trail continues along west side of Whirlpool River.

11.2—Tie Camp Campground.

15.0—Simon Creek Campground.

19.8—Middle Whirlpool River bridge.

20.3—Middle Forks Warden Cabin.

21.1—Middle Forks Campground.

25.8—Scott Gravel Flats north end.

30.9—Scott Camp Campground. Branch trail and bridge to Scott Gravel Flats.

38.8—Whirlpool River bridge to east side.

40.9—Kane Creek ford (difficult thigh-deep).

41.0—Kane Meadows Campground (1585 m).

  —Trail crosses Kane Meadows then bends south-southwest to begin ascent to pass.

48.5—Campsite (unofficial).

49.1—Athabasca Pass (1755 m). Historical marker and park boundary near north shore of Committee's Punchbowl.

During the winter of 1811, fur trader David Thompson made the first recorded crossing of Athabasca Pass. For the next forty years, the pass was the main trade route across the Canadian Rockies.

Today the long trail up the Whirlpool River to the pass is about as lonely as it was during the first half of the 19th century. It is a great place to commune with the spirits of fur traders and imagine their awe as they first wandered through this corridor of ice-clad peaks.

The first 8.5 km follows an old fire road track along the west side of the Whirlpool Valley. After the road reverts to horse trail, it continues another 3.8 km to the remains of the Otto brothers' Tie Camp. Many old artifacts lie about this site where, in the early part of the 20th century, timber was cut and floated down the Whirlpool and Athabasca Rivers to be used for railway ties.

Near km 19 a hiker's trail splits from the horse trail and leads to a bridge over the Middle Whirlpool River in another kilometre. The hiker trail rejoins the horse trail at the Middle Forks Warden Cabin 0.5 km beyond the bridge.

After a long stretch of forest hiking, you emerge onto the northern end of the extensive Scott Gravel Flats. Follow a hiker's trail that splits right from the horse trail—a detour that avoids fords of the ever-meandering channels of the Whirlpool.

Travel continues over and along the Scott Gravel Flats for 5 km to Scott Camp Campground, which is located at the southern end of the flats. This is one of the most scenic campsites on the Athabasca Pass trail, providing a dramatic view south up the Scott Creek valley to the tumbled icefalls of Scott Glacier— a tongue of the Hooker Icefield.

To this point the trail is fairly straightforward, but from here to the summit the track is less defined as it swings back and forth from gravel flats to forest.

Don Beers photo　　　*Scott Glacier and Mount Hooker from Scott Gravel Flats*

Below Kane Meadows, a footbridge crosses to the east side of the Whirlpool. Another 2 km brings you to the lower end of Kane Meadows at Kane Creek. If a bridge is not in place, you should follow cairns upstream to the best fording location. The silty creek is fed by the Kane Glacier and is the most difficult stream crossing on the trail. Kane Meadows Campground lies on the opposite side.

After fording a tributary stream a kilometre beyond Kane Meadows Campground, you begin the ascent to the pass. The track is poorly defined and usually quite boggy through this section, however the route is obvious along the east side of the Whirlpool all the way to the summit.

At the pass there is a historic marker commemorating this important fur trade route and a small pond called The Committee's Punchbowl. Here, on the crest of the continent, fur traders would stop and drink a toast to the officers of the Hudson's Bay Company.

The pass is contained by McGillivray Ridge to the east and glaciated Mount Brown to west. The latter peak was supposedly climbed by botanist David Douglas in May 1827. Douglas estimated the elevation of the mountain and nearby Mount Hooker to be 15,000 feet high, a figure which was later published on maps of the region. Many decades later mountaineers searched in vain for these two giants, not realizing that Douglas had been grossly misled concerning the base elevation of the Rockies.

Scott Glacier—3.0 km. A side-trail up Scott Creek branches south at Scott Camp Campground and crosses a bridge over the Whirlpool River. Though there is no maintained trail up the valley, you can follow snippets of trail and along open alluvial flats to a large moraine lake immediately below Scott Glacier.

105 Fryatt Valley

Geraldine Lookout Fire Road to Upper Fryatt Valley—23.2 km (14.4 mi)

Backpack

Allow 7 hours one way

Elevation gain: 820 m (2,700 ft)

Maximum elevation: 2040 m (6,700 ft)

Maps: Athabasca Falls 83 C/12†
Fortress Lake 83 C/5†
† last 3.7 km not shown

Access: From the Icefields Parkway–Highway 93A junction at Athabasca Falls 31 km (19 mi) south of Jasper townsite, follow the 93A north 1.1 km (0.7 mi) to the Geraldine Fire Road. Follow this gravel road 2.1 km (1.3 mi) to the small parking area and trail sign on the left side of the road.

0.0—Geraldine Fire Road (1220 m).

—Route follows old roadbed.

1.9—Bridges across Geraldine Creek channels.

7.2—Trail comes abreast of Athabasca River.

—Trail climbs away from river.

11.6—Lower Fryatt Campground (1280 m). Fryatt Creek bridge to east bank.

—Trail climbs east side of Fryatt Valley.

15.9—Fryatt Creek bridge to west bank.

17.7—Brussels Campground.

—Trail climbs over major rockslide.

18.7—Fryatt Lake (1715 m).

—Trail follows along west shore of lake.

19.5—Southwest end of Fryatt Lake.

—Trail winds and climbs through forest.

21.1—Headwall Campground (1780 m).

—Steep scramble up Headwall.

21.9—Top of Headwall.

22.0—Fryatt Hut (2000 m).

—Trail runs through meadows and over forested moraine.

23.2—Unnamed lake (2040 m).

The Fryatt Valley trail is a rather long, tedious grunt, and the final climb up the Headwall to the upper valley is one you will long remember. But this tiny hanging valley tucked into one of Jasper's great mountain ranges is a jewel that rewards all your efforts.

Mountain bikes are permitted on the first 11.6 km of the trail, which makes a day trip to Upper Fryatt Valley somewhat feasible. However, we suggest you leave the bikes at home and complete the hike over three days: one day to hike in and set a base camp, one day for exploring the upper valley, and one day to hike out.

The first 7 km from the Geraldine Road trailhead is flat and enclosed by forest. The trail finally comes abreast of the Athabasca River near the site of an old cable car crossing, where you will have the dubious pleasure of seeing the Icefields Parkway 200 m away on the opposite side of the river. From this point the trail veers south and begins its climb to the mouth of the Fryatt Valley.

Fryatt Creek is crossed at Lower Fryatt Campground (end of bike access), where you enter the valley proper—a narrow gorge between the towering peaks of Mounts Fryatt and Christie. The climb along the east side of the valley is steady for the next 4 km, mostly through heavy forest. At km 15.9 the track crosses to the west side of the creek and continues along open gravel flats, where the first views open out to the sharp, glaciated peaks at the head of the valley.

You climb over a major slide at km 17.7, but the summit of the rockpile provides a fine view of Fryatt Lake. After descending to the lake, the trail becomes rocky and rooty along the northwest shore.

Beyond the lake you climb through forest to the foot of the Headwall. Here, at the base of the impressive Headwall Falls, the last act in the Fryatt Valley drama unfolds—an excruciatingly steep

Fryatt Lake and the Headwall Falls below Upper Fryatt Valley

scramble that gains 200 m of elevation over the next 0.8 km.

The top of the Headwall will silence your curses. Suddenly the upper valley opens into view—ice-clad peaks and subalpine meadowland. Back to the north the lower valley stretches out beneath you and the peaks of the Maligne Range rise beyond the broad Athabasca Valley. A small waterfall dropping into a large pool near the top of the Headwall makes a fine place to rest on a warm day, and the Fryatt Hut lies less than 100 m farther along.

The hike to the lake at the head of the upper valley is short and scenic. The trail, which is wet and not always well defined, crosses wildflower meadows, and climbs a rocky, sparsely forested moraine where the creek plunges briefly into an underground passage.

The route finally descends through stands of stunted alpine fir to the shore of a small lake fed by the meltwaters of the nearby Belanger Glacier. From the lake-shore you have an unobstructed view of a crowd of rugged peaks and glaciers enclosing the head of this fine hanging valley.

From this point you can explore beyond the trail, particularly onto the slopes to the north. (Experienced scramblers can ascend to the high col between Mounts Fryatt and Belanger.)

Camping is not permitted in the Upper Fryatt Valley, but the Fryatt Hut (Sydney Vallance Hut) is operated by the Alpine Club of Canada and accommodates 12 (see *Sources-Huts*).

However, most backpackers prefer to camp at Headwall or Brussels Campgrounds and commute to the upper valley without the burden of a full pack.

106 Geraldine Lakes

Geraldine Lookout Fire Road to Second Geraldine Lake—5.0 km (3.1 mi)

Half-day trip or backpack

Allow 2 hours one way

Elevation gain: 410 m (1,340 ft)

Maximum elevation: 1890 m (6,200 ft)

Maps: Athabasca Falls 83 C/12

Access: From the junction of the Icefields Parkway and Highway 93A at Athabasca Falls (31 km south of Jasper townsite), follow the 93A north 1.1 km (0.7 mi) to the Geraldine Fire Road. Follow this gravel road 5.5 km (3.5 mi) to an access gate. The parking area and trailhead lie 50 m below the gate at the last bend in the road.

0.0—Geraldine Fire Road (1480 m).

—Moderate climb.

1.8—Lower Geraldine Lake.

—Trail skirts west shore of the lake.

2.7—Southern end of Lower Geraldine Lake.

—Steep 90 m climb. At the top, follow markers left to east side of valley.

4.2—Waterfall.

—Very steep 150 m climb.

5.0—Viewpoint overlooking Second Geraldine Lake.

—Trail contours above east shore of lake.

6.2—Second Geraldine Campground (1890 m).

Sandwiched between the steep slopes of Mount Fryatt and Whirlpool Peak, the Geraldine Lakes offer hiking options ranging from a one hour walk to a full day or more of scrambling and exploration. The first lake lies 1.8 km from the trailhead via easy trail; the trail to the second lake is boulder-strewn and often quite steep; the third and fourth lakes, and the high pass at the head of the valley, are for well-shod, off-trail explorers.

The short hike to Lower Geraldine Lake follows a moderately graded, well-travelled trail. While the serene, forest-encircled lake beneath the flanks of Mount Fryatt is pleasant enough, it only whets the appetite for what lies beyond. And what lies beyond is not for casual walkers.

The trail gets rougher as it follows the lake's west shore. Beyond the lake the track becomes very rocky and rooty as it climbs steeply beside a 90 m waterfall cascading over rock steps.

At the top of the falls you enter a short valley. Here the trail angles left (watch for markers), crosses Geraldine Creek, and skirts a small pond in the midst of a large boulderfield. At the end of this rock-choked valley there is yet another steep scramble beside a very impressive waterfall.

From a rocky ridge above the falls there are good views back down-valley and your first glimpse ahead to Second Geraldine Lake—the largest in the chain. From this vantage point you can also appreciate the staircase nature of the Geraldine Valley and how the higher lakes feed into the lower. The lakes and their basins were created as the last ice age glacier receded up the valley, creating a geological feature called *pater noster lakes*.

Although this ridgetop viewpoint will be a good turn-around for many hikers, rough trail continues along the rocky east

Waterfall below Second Geraldine Lake

shore of the second lake to its inlet and a campground. This site is a good base for further exploration upvalley.

While no formal trail exists beyond the south end of Second Geraldine Lake, experienced scramblers can follow trail snippets, cairns, and their noses for another 4 km up the valley staircase to higher lakes set beneath the 1000 m northwest wall of Mount Fryatt. You can also scramble to a 2220 m pass at the head of the valley that overlooks two un-named lakes and the Divergence Creek valley.

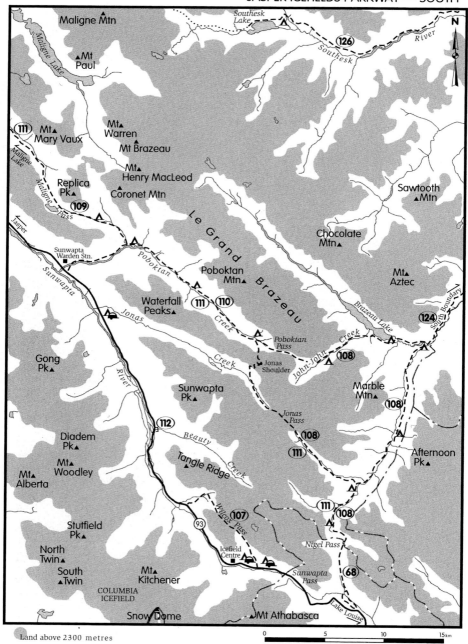

Land above 2300 metres

0   5   10   15km

Mount Athabasca from the Wilcox Pass trail

107 Wilcox Pass

Wilcox Creek Campground to Wilcox Pass—4.0 km (2.5 mi)
Wilcox Creek Campground to Tangle Falls—11.2 km (7.0 mi)

Half-day to day trip

Allow 1.5 hours to Wilcox Pass

Elevation gain: 335 m (1,100 ft)

Maximum elevation: 2375 m (7,800 ft)

Maps: Columbia Icefield 83 C/3
      Sunwapta Peak 83 C/6

Access: Follow the Icefields Parkway (Hwy 93) to the Wilcox Creek Campground, located on the east side of the highway 2.8 km (1.7 mi) south of the Icefield Centre or 1.9 km (1.2 mi) north of the Banff-Jasper boundary at Sunwapta Pass. The trailhead parking area is on the left side of the campground access road 50 m from the highway.

0.0—Wilcox Campground Road (2040 m).

—Steep climb through subalpine forest.

1.8—Trail emerges above treeline.

—Grade moderates.

2.5—Athabasca Glacier viewpoint.

—Short, steep climb to flat alpine meadows.

4.0—Wilcox Pass Summit (2375 m).

—Route continues north across pass. Track often vague.

7.2—North edge of pass (watch for markers or cairns).

—Steep descent into forest.

8.8—Trail crosses to left of creek. Track becomes more defined.

—Moderate to steep descent on slope south of Tangle Creek.

11.2—Tangle Creek trailhead (1860 m). Icefields Parkway 200 m south of Tangle Falls and 10 kms north of Wilcox Creek trailhead.

Wilcox Pass is a high alpine valley due east of the Icefield Centre and Athabasca Glacier. Beginning close to treeline, the trail quickly rises to extensive meadows and views of the Athabasca Glacier and its surrounding peaks, which are some of the highest and most dramatic in the Canadian Rockies. It is quite justifiably recognized as one of the finest day hikes in Jasper Park.

From the entrance to Wilcox Creek Campground, Canada's highest roadside campground, the trail climbs directly through a mature subalpine forest. This initial stretch is steep, gaining 120 m in less than a kilometre.

The grade moderates as you break out of the trees, and you emerge onto an open ridge overlooking the Icefields Parkway and the Athabasca Glacier. The Rockies' most famous valley glacier is the centrepiece of an exceptional panorama, which includes such ice-covered giants as Mount Athabasca (3491 m), Snow Dome (3460 m), and Mount Kitchener (3511 m).

Beyond the viewpoint, the trail climbs steeply along the edge of a gully containing a small stream. After this short, stiff ascent, it levels out across alpine tundra and heads northwest into the long U-shaped pass between Wilcox and Nigel Peaks. Here the lush, tall wildflowers of treeline are replaced by ground-hugging alpine plants, like forget-me-not, white mountain avens, and moss campion.

As soon as you reach the summit meadows, scan the nearby slopes and ridges for bighorn sheep. Mature rams hang together here each summer, leaving flocks of ewes, lambs and immature males to feed in the valley below. Wilcox Pass is one of the most reliable places to see bighorns at close range in a backcountry setting.

The official summit is reached at 4.0 km, though the pass is so long and flat it

Mount Athabasca from Wilcox Ridge

is difficult to recognize it as the highest point. (A large rock cairn beside the trail marks the spot.) Though you have left the best views of the Icefield region behind, the heavily glaciated north face of Mount Athabasca is still visible back across the meadows to the south.

Wilcox Peak and Pass are named for American mountaineer Walter Wilcox, whose horseback party first crossed the pass in 1896. The pass became the standard route north following Wilcox's trip since it avoided the rugged Sunwapta Gorge and the Athabasca Glacier, which nearly blocked the valley below.

The rising meadows and ridges to the west and east of the summit are an open invitation to wander. However, any off-trail travel should be undertaken with care and sensitivity for the environment. Avoid crossing wet, marshy areas, and always walk abreast of one another rather than single-file, since this lessens damage to fragile alpine vegetation.

One of our favourite side-trips is the climb to the crest of the ridge just south of Wilcox Peak—an amazing aerial viewpoint overlooking the Athabasca Glacier. From this lofty ridgetop, you can contemplate the pathetic lot of ant-sized tourists scurrying around snowcoaches on the glacier and at the Icefield Centre far below.

Another favourite excursion climbs around the end of Nigel Peak's northwest ridge to 2470 m Wilcox Lake—lying in a rockbound cirque beneath the mountain's west face. Follow sheep trails across the high talus slopes northeast of Wilcox Pass and continue in a northerly direction on a well defined trail around the end of the ridge. Cairns mark the route over rock ridges to a point immediately above the lake's northwest shore.

Tangle Creek. You can continue north-west through the pass and descend Tangle Creek back to the Icefields Parkway, 7 kms beyond Wilcox Pass summit. Though the trail often disappears on the tundra and rocky terrain near the northern end of the pass, a marker indicates where the descent to the Tangle Creek valley begins. As you drop into the forest a defined trail gradually takes shape. The trail emerges onto the highway at Tangle Falls, 10 kms north of the Wilcox Creek Campground trailhead.

108 Jonas Pass—Brazeau Lake Loop

Icefields Parkway to Jonas Pass—23.8 km (14.8 mi)
Jonas Pass-Brazeau Lake Loop—81.4 km (50.6 mi)

Backpack

Allow 4 to 6 days for loop

Maximum elevation: 2470 m (8,100 ft)

Minimum elevation: 1720 m (5,650 ft)

Maps: Columbia Icefield 83 C/3
    Sunwapta Peak 83 C/6

Access: Follow the Icefields Parkway (Hwy 93) to the Nigel Pass parking area, located on the northeast side of the highway 8.5 km (5.5 mi) south of the Banff-Jasper Park boundary at Sunwapta Pass. The parking area is on a gravel side road running downhill to a barrier and the trailhead.

0.0—Nigel Pass trailhead (1860 m).

7.2—Nigel Pass (2195).

7.6—Brazeau River south fork ford.

10.6—Brazeau River bridge to west side.

10.7—Boulder Creek Campground.

11.4—Boulder Creek bridge.

13.8—Four Point Campground.

14.0—Junction (1915 m). *South Boundary Trail* and Brazeau Lake ahead. Jonas Pass left.

18.4—Trail emerges above treeline.

23.8—Jonas Pass Summit (2320 m).

29.6—Jonas Shoulder Summit (2470 m).

32.8—Poboktan Creek crossing.

32.9—Junction (1810 m), Jonas Cutoff Campground. Intersection with *Poboktan Creek* trail at km 21.3. Poboktan Pass right.

35.9—Poboktan Pass (2300 m).

40.2—John-John Creek Campground.

44.4—John-John Creek bridge.

48.1—Northwest Brazeau River bridge.

48.2—Junction (1810 m). Brazeau Lake and Brazeau River Bridge Campground left 0.9 km. Brazeau River trail right.

The Jonas Pass-Brazeau Lake Loop is one of Jasper's most popular backpacking trips. Little wonder. The circuit includes one of the park's largest backcountry lakes and an extraordinary 13 km alpine traverse culminating on the park's second highest trail-accessible summit. Along the way there are glaciated peaks, lush wildflower meadows, and opportunities to view a wide variety of alpine wildlife ranging from hoary marmots to mountain caribou. It is "the grand tour" of Jasper's southern ranges.

Most backpackers take 5 days or more to complete the loop. However, if you only go as far as Jonas Pass, you can visit the circuit's scenic highlight and return in 3 days—an option which allows you to explore the pass environs with a light day pack instead of a full backpack.

Be aware that sections of the Jonas Pass trail are occasionally covered with snow into early August, particularly on the leeward side of Jonas Shoulder. Check on trail conditions at a park visitor centre before embarking on this trip.

Nigel Pass trailhead to Four Point Junction—14.0 km. The hike begins in Banff National Park and follows the 7.2 km Nigel Pass trail to the Jasper Park boundary (see *Nigel Pass,* Banff Park chapter). While Nigel Pass provides a quick scenic reward, the descent along the upper Brazeau River is very attractive as well. After hopping across the river's headwaters 400 m beyond the park boundary, you make a steep descent through rockslides to the first of several lush meadows—marshy, cottongrass flats fed by a large waterfall.

After crossing to the west side of the Brazeau at the lower end of the meadow, you pass Boulder Creek Campground and descend through 3 km of subalpine forest to another plateau with an extensive meadow. At km 13.8 you reach

Jonas Pass

50.2—Junction (1720 m). Intersection with *South Boundary Trail* at km 136.3. Nigel Pass to right across Northwest Brazeau River bridge.

50.3—Brazeau Campground.

53.5—Brazeau River bridge to east side.

58.8—Wolverine South Campground.

61.1—Brazeau River bridge to west side.

64.8—Four Point Creek Crossing.

65.6—Junction (1915 m). Close Jonas Pass-Brazeau Loop. Jonas Pass right. Nigel Pass ahead.

65.8—Four Point Campground.

68.9—Boulder Creek Campground.

72.4—Nigel Pass (2195 m).

79.6—Nigel Pass trailhead (1860 m).

Four Point Campground and, 200 m beyond, the trail split for the Jonas Pass-Brazeau Lake Loop.

Since Four Point Campground is a favourite first night destination, and the base camp for those who are day hiking to Jonas Pass, it is usually the busiest campground on the circuit. In high season, you would be advised to reserve a campsite in advance of your trip.

At Four Point you can continue down the Brazeau Valley and hike the loop counterclockwise, or strike off for Jonas Pass and complete the circuit in in a clockwise direction. Most people register to hike the loop clockwise as described here.

Four Point Junction to Jonas Cutoff Junction—18.9 km. Regardless of whether you are day hiking from Four Point Campground to Jonas Pass or backpacking over the pass, you have a long day ahead.

The journey starts with a vigorous climb along the west side of the Four

Point Valley, rising 200 m in less than 2 km to open forest. A series of small streams descending from the left herald the approach of treeline, and within a few minutes the trail levels off and leaves the last stunted alpine fir behind. (We know a number of hikers who have encountered grizzly bears here. Stay alert!)

The trail continues its gradual ascent up the southwest side of the long, narrow vale, staying just above the creek. The pass is as long as it is beautiful, and you are nearly 10 km from Four Point Junction before you reach its crest.

You maintain elevation for the next 1.5 km, bypassing a small tarn, then descending gradually to the north. After passing beneath a large rockslide the trail swings right and begins to climb towards Jonas Shoulder. The first portion of the climb is steep and the trail is sketchy in places, but the track becomes more obvious as you gain elevation.

The scenery on the Jonas Shoulder climb is spectacular, and frequent stops with map and camera are rewarding. Hoary marmots and pikas inhabit nearby rockslides, and we have seen mountain caribou on the meadows below the trail.

From the 2470 m summit of Jonas Shoulder views open out over the Poboktan Pass meadows and the forested Poboktan Valley stretching away to the northwest. Beyond the summit, the trail plunges northward to the upper Poboktan, descending a steep talus slope and spongy meadows, then angling to the east side of a major gully. Less than a kilometre after reaching treeline, you intersect the Poboktan Creek trail at Jonas Cutoff Campground.

Jonas Cutoff Campground to Brazeau Lake—16.2 km. Poboktan Pass and Brazeau Lake are the two major features on the third leg of the trip.

From Jonas Cutoff Campground, you climb southeast from the timbered Poboktan Valley onto the broad alpine meadows of Poboktan Pass in just 3 kms.

The pass and valley were named by A.P. Coleman in 1892, Poboktan being the Stoney name for the owls the party

saw in the valley. The pass is frequently visited by caribou, and grizzly bear are occasionally seen in the distance across the open tundra.

From the pass the trail drops sharply onto John-John Creek—a narrow valley composed of rockslides and open gravel flats. At the mouth of the valley you emerge onto a large slide overlooking Brazeau Lake. From this viewpoint it is just over 2 km to Brazeau Lake junction and the side trail leading to the campground at the southeast end of the lake.

Surrounded by forest, and with the ice-covered summits of Le Grande Brazeau Range rising beyond, this peaceful 5 km-long body of water is one of the largest wilderness lakes in Jasper Park.

Brazeau Lake to Four Point Junction—18.3 km. After visiting or camping at Brazeau Lake, follow the 2 km trail down the Northwest Brazeau River to an intersection with the *South Boundary Trail* in the Brazeau Valley. Here you turn for home, following the Brazeau River back to Four Point Junction and Nigel Pass.

While the ascent of the Brazeau may look a bit humdrum on the map, the valley is quite pleasant and open. Wolverine South Campground, nestled in a grove of trees on the river's east bank, is one of our favourite sites—a place where you can truly appreciate the solitude of a fine wilderness valley. (See also *South Boundary Trail*.)

Four Point Junction to Nigel Pass trailhead—14.0 km. From Four Point Junction, complete your journey back to civilization on the approach trail over Nigel Pass.

Brazeau Lake

109 Maligne Pass

Icefields Parkway to Maligne Pass—15.2 km (9.4 mi)
Icefields Parkway to Maligne Lake—47.9 km (29.8 mi)

Day trip or backpack

Allow 3 days to Maligne Lake

Elevation gain: 760 m (2,500 ft)
      loss: 610 m (2,000 ft)

Maximum elevation: 2300 m (7,550 ft)

Maps: Sunwapta Peak 83 C/6
      Southesk Lake 83 C/11
      Athabasca Falls 83 C/12

Access: Follow the Icefields Parkway (Hwy 93) to the Sunwapta Warden Station, located 31.5 km (19.5 mi) north of the Icefield Centre or 71.5 km (44.5 mi) south of Jasper townsite. Continue on the highway 200 m south of the warden station (opposite side of Poboktan Creek) to the access road branching east into the trailhead parking area.

0.0—Poboktan Creek parking area (1540 m).

0.1—Poboktan Creek bridge to north side.

6.2—Junction (1760 m). *Poboktan Creek* ahead. Maligne Pass left.

11.2—Avalanche Campground.

13.5—Maximum elevation.

   —Trail contours into pass.

15.2—Maligne Pass (2300 m).

17.8—Maligne River bridge.

18.6—Mary Vaux Campground.

19.7—Old Horse campsite.

29.0—Mary Schaffer Campground.

37.4—Maligne River suspension bridge.

43.1—Trapper Creek Campground, bridge.

46.6—Junction. Moose Lake right 100 m.

47.6—Junction. *Bald Hills* trail. Turn right.

47.9—Maligne Lake parking area (1690 m).

Maligne Pass is an outstanding alpine summit, comprised of rolling alpine meadows and numerous small lakes. It is historically significant as the pass Mary Schäffer and her party utilized in 1908 when they discovered Maligne Lake.

A surprising number of hikers travel to the pass and back in a day, albeit a very long one. Our preference is to camp at Avalanche Campground, 4 km below the pass, and day hike from there. This option allows more time to explore the extensive meadows and visit the lakes beneath the Endless Chain Ridge.

Other backpackers prefer to retrace Mary Schäffer's route over the pass and down the Maligne River to Maligne Lake, even though it is a long, soggy and somewhat tedious journey. This section also comprises the northern end of the lengthy *Glacier Trail* trek.

Like many of the higher passes in the Rockies, Maligne is often buried under snow until mid-July, and sections of trail can be churned to a quagmire after horse parties have passed this way.

Starting from the parking area on Poboktan Creek just south of the Sunwapta Warden Station, the trail immediately crosses the creek and ascends the north side of the valley. You gain 210 m of elevation over the next 6 kms to the Poboktan Creek-Maligne Pass junction. At the junction, you branch north from the Poboktan Creek trail and begin what can be a long wet climb to Maligne Pass.

The trail up the Poligne Valley crosses and recrosses the creek several times in less than 5 kms as it climbs steadily through heavy spruce-pine forest. All crossings are bridged, though these bridges are susceptible to wash-out (check at the visitor centre for a bridge update).

Beyond Avalanche Campground the trail reaches treeline and the climb moderates. Throughout this section the track

Don Beers photo

Maligne Pass

is often indistinct as it traverses boggy meadows.

At km 15.2, the trail reaches the eastern shore of a 1 km-long lake on the crest of Maligne Pass (2300 m). Vast meadows rise gradually northwest and southeast from the lake, inviting further exploration to more than half-a-dozen smaller lakes nestled against the escarpment of the Endless Chain Ridge.

Beyond the pass views open to glacier-topped Mount Mary Vaux and a long line of peaks stretching northward along the upper Maligne River valley. Backpackers continuing over the pass follow beneath this range all the way to the north end of Maligne Lake.

Maligne Pass to Maligne Lake—32.7 km. North of the pass the trail drops gradually from alpine meadows to the sparsely forested headwaters of the Maligne River. Recalling her descent from the summit on July 6, 1908, Mary Schäffer wrote: "I think I never saw a fairer valley. From our feet it swept away into an unbroken green carpet as far as the eye could see... and then the caval-

cade made a quick descent of about a thousand feet, tramping under foot thousands of blossoms of the *trollius* [globeflower] and *pulsatilla* [western anemone] which covered the way." It should also be noted that Mary and her party encountered "long patches of snow" on the pass, which "made the travelling very heavy."

With the treeline comes an easy ford of the upper Maligne River followed by another bridged crossing. After passing Mary Vaux Campground, you traverse alternate sections of forest and open willow flats, which provide scenic relief for what otherwise would be a very long stretch of forest-enclosed travel.

The long, gradual descent of the valley continues past Mary Schäffer Campground, back across the Maligne River via suspension bridge, and onwards to Trapper Creek Campground.

From Trapper Creek you complete your journey by climbing steeply for a kilometre, then rolling along through hummocky forest to an intersection with the Bald Hills trail 300 m above the parking area at the end of the Maligne Lake Road.

110 Poboktan Creek

Icefields Parkway to Jonas Cutoff Campground—21.3 km (13.2 mi)
Icefields Parkway to Poboktan Pass—24.3 km (15.1 mi)

Backpack

Allow 6 to 7 hours to Jonas Cutoff Jct.

Elevation gain: 580 m (1,900 ft)

Maximum elevation: 2120 m (6,950 ft)

Maps: Sunwapta Peak 83 C/6

Access: Follow the Icefields Parkway (Hwy 93) to the Sunwapta Warden Station, located 31.5 km (19.5 mi) north of the Icefield Centre or 71.5 km (44.5 mi) south of Jasper townsite. Continue on the highway 200 m south of the warden station, on the south side of Poboktan Creek, to the road leading to the trailhead parking area.

0.0—Poboktan Creek parking lot (1540 m).

0.1—Poboktan Creek bridge to north side.

6.2—Junction (1760 m). *Maligne Pass* left. Poboktan Pass right.

6.4—Poligne Creek bridge.

7.5—Poboktan Creek Campground.

12.0—Waterfalls Campground.

21.3—Junction (2120 m). Jonas Cutoff Campground. Intersection with *Jonas Pass-Brazeau Lake Loop* at km 32.9. Jonas Shoulder right 3.3 km; Poboktan Pass ahead 3.0 km.

The trail up Poboktan Creek and over Poboktan Pass to Brazeau Lake was constructed during the summers of 1921 and 1922 by a crew supervised by Park Warden J.M. Christie. It was the first trail to the park's remote south boundary and has served as an important warden patrol route ever since. It also serves hikers as the most direct trail to the Poboktan Pass-Jonas Shoulder environs, an optional route to Brazeau Lake, and the link between the Jonas Pass and Maligne Pass sections of the *Glacier Trail*.

The first 6.2 km of the hike follows the same route as the Maligne Pass trail. Beyond Maligne Pass junction, the trail crosses Poligne Creek and continues along the north side of Poboktan Creek. After passing Poboktan Creek Campground, it bends southeast and begins a long, steady ascent of the upper Poboktan Valley.

As you travel upvalley, you discover some of the difficulties Warden Christie faced in building the trail in the early 1920s—boggy terrain that is frequently muddy and churned-up by horse use (corduroy and alternate hiker detours help you over and around the worst spots). The cataract at Waterfalls Campground and another waterfall 2 km farther upvalley provide welcome relief from the drudgery of mud and pine-spruce forest.

At km 21.3 you descend into a pleasant little ravine containing Jonas Cutoff Campground. Since this campground is located at the Jonas Pass junction, and is only 3 km from Poboktan Pass, it is an attractive overnight destination or base camp for day trips to Poboktan Pass and Jonas Shoulder. Whether you extend your trip south over Jonas Shoulder and Pass or southeast to Brazeau Lake, you will be following the *Jonas Pass-Brazeau Lake Loop*. (See also *Glacier Trail*).

111 Glacier Trail

Maligne Lake to Nigel Creek—89.7 km (55.7 mi)

Backpack

Allow 5 to 7 days

Maximum elevation: 2470 m (8,100 ft)

Minimum elevation: 1690 m (5,550 ft)

Maps: Athabasca Falls 83 C/12
Southesk Lake 83 C/11
Sunwapta Peak 83 C/6
Columbia Icefield 83 C/3

Access: Travelling from north to south, start from the parking area on the northwest shore of Maligne Lake (see *Bald Hills*). Northbound hikers start from the Nigel Pass trailhead in Banff Park (see also *Jonas Pass-Brazeau Lake Loop*).

0.0—Maligne Lake parking area (1690 m).

4.8—Trapper Creek Campground.

18.9—Mary Schaffer Campground.

29.3—Mary Vaux Campground.

32.7—Maligne Pass (2240 m).

36.7—Avalanche Campground.

41.7—Junction (1760 m). Intersection with *Poboktan Creek* trail at km 6.2.

43.0—Poboktan Creek Campground.

47.5—Waterfalls Campground.

56.8—Junction (2120 m). Jonas Cutoff Campground. Intersection with *Jonas Pass-Brazeau Lake Loop* at km 32.9. Jonas Shoulder right.

60.1—Jonas Shoulder (2470 m).

65.9—Jonas Pass (2320 m).

75.7—Four Point Junction (1915 m). Nigel Pass right.

75.9—Four Point Campground.

79.0—Boulder Creek Campground.

82.5—Nigel Pass (2195 m).

89.7—Nigel Pass trailhead (1830 m).

In 1924, before construction of the Banff-Jasper Highway, Jasper outfitter Jack Brewster initiated one of the most scenic pack trips in the Rocky Mountains—a three week journey by horseback from Jasper to Lake Louise via the Columbia Icefield. Brewster called it "The Glacier Trail." Though most of the historic trail has been replaced by the Maligne Lake Road and Icefields Parkway, the section from Maligne Lake to the Icefield is still intact and can be hiked in a week or less.

The route runs between Maligne Lake and the Nigel Pass trailhead in Banff Park, crossing three passes—Maligne, Jonas and Nigel—along the way.

While we outline the trip in the traditional north to south direction, many hikers prefer travelling in the opposite direction, ending at Maligne Lake where there is a nearby day lodge with a restaurant and telephone.

The Skyline Trail is also a natural extension to the north end of the trip, increasing total distance from 90 to 134 kms. Since the Skyline, and the Jonas Pass section at the route's southern end, are popular routes, you would be advised to make reservations for campsites in advance of your trip.

Heading south from Maligne Lake, the trail makes a long ascent of the upper Maligne River to Maligne Pass. South of the pass you intersect the Poboktan Creek trail. Continue up the Poboktan Creek trail to Jonas Cutoff Junction, then climb over Jonas Shoulder and descend through Jonas Pass to the upper Brazeau Valley. The last leg of the trip follows up the Brazeau River to its headwaters and crosses Nigel Pass to the Icefields Parkway.

The Glacier Trail utilizes sections of three trails presented in this chapter (see *Maligne Pass, Poboktan Creek,* and *Jonas Pass-Brazeau Lake Loop* for details on each section).

112 Beauty Creek

Icefields Parkway to Stanley Falls—1.6 km (1.0 mi)

Before the old Banff-Jasper Highway was rerouted across the Sunwapta River flats, one of the popular roadside stops was Beauty Creek canyon, where a trail climbed past a series of cataracts to Stanley Falls. This trail is a bit removed from the present highway, and few visitors even know that there is something special up this unremarkable, forested gorge.

From the small roadside parking area, follow trail along the crest of a gravel, water diversion dike into an arm of forest. On the opposite side of this narrow band of trees, you emerge onto the old Banff-Jasper Highway. Turn right and follow the roadbed 0.6 km to where a bridge once spanned Beauty Creek.

The trail branches left from the road and follows along the north side of a narrow limestone canyon, climbing steadily through dense forest and passing a number of small waterfalls. The last and highest of these cataracts, Stanley Falls, is reached at 1.6 km. Beyond this fine waterfall the trail fades and the canyon opens out into a forested valley.

Access: Follow the Icefields Parkway north from the Icefields Centre 15.5 km (9.5 mi). Two kilometres south of the Beauty Creek Hostel, while crossing broad alluvial flats beside the Sunwapta River, watch for a small pull-out on the east side of the highway at the end of gravel water diversion dike. *Maps: Sunwapta Peak 83 C/6 .*

113 Lower Sunwapta Falls

Sunwapta Falls Parking Area to Lower Sunwapta Falls—1.3 km (0.8 mi)

While thousands of tourists stop along the Icefields Parkway to view Sunwapta Falls each summer, only a few make the trip to a series of cataracts 1.3 km beyond the main falls.

Lower Sunwapta Falls is composed of three major waterfalls spread over approximately 150 m of the Sunwapta River. In our opinion, the combination of solitude and open views to the surrounding mountains make this hike a far more rewarding experience than a visit to the upper falls.

From the Sunwapta Falls parking lot, follow the main viewing trail above the falls to the right. Continue past the falls viewpoint to where the paved trail ends and begin a gradual descent through lodgepole pine forest to the lower falls.

At km 0.6 the trail emerges from the

forest to open views across the Sunwapta River to the upper Athabasca Valley and the glaciated summit of Mount Quincy.

Lower Sunwapta Falls have formed where the river is cutting through a narrow canyon similar to the one containing the upper falls, but a staircase waterfall has formed instead of a single cataract.

Access: Follow the Icefields Parkway (Hwy 93) to the Sunwapta Falls junction, 54.5 km (34 mi) south of Jasper townsite and 49 km (30.5 mi) north of the Icefield Centre. The Sunwapta Falls Road leads 0.6 km to the falls parking area. *Maps: Athabasca Falls 83 C/12 (trail not shown).*

(Trail not shown on maps in this book.)

114 Fortress Lake

Sunwapta Falls to Fortress Lake—24.0 km (15.0 mi)*

Backpack

Allow 7 to 9 hours one way

Elevation loss: 60 m (200 ft)

Maximum elevation: 1400 m (4,600 ft)

Maps: Athabasca Falls 83 C/12
   Fortress Lake 83 C/5

Access: Follow the Icefields Parkway (Hwy 93) to the Sunwapta Falls junction, 54.5 km (34 mi) south of Jasper townsite and 49 km (30.5 mi) north of the Icefield Centre. The Sunwapta Falls Road leads 0.6 km to the falls parking area. The trail begins on the opposite side of the footbridge spanning the Sunwapta Falls canyon.

 0.0—Sunwapta Falls bridge (1400 m).

  —Gradual descent to Athabasca River.

 7.8—Big Bend Campground.

  —Flat to rolling along the east side of Athabasca River.

12.2—Junction. Long Lake and Chaba Warden Cabin right. Stay left.

14.2—Athabasca Crossing Campground.

15.2—Athabasca River bridge.

  —Trail runs south above Chaba River.

22.0—Chaba River ford (calf to thigh deep) to west side.

  —Sketchy trail along west side of river flats.

24.0—Fortress Pass (1340 m).

24.4—Junction. Fortress Lake and campground left 0.2 km. Rough trail continues along north lakeshore ahead.

*All distances approximate.

(Trail not shown on maps in this book.)

Fortress Lake is one of the largest lakes along the Great Divide. Though it lies in B.C.'s Hamber Provincial Park, the only trail to the lake is from Jasper Park. Because it is such a major feature, and surrounded by spectacular mountains, you would expect it to be a popular destination. However, a ford of the Chaba River near km 22 discourages all but the most dedicated.

The construction of a bridge across the Athabasca River in 1985 eliminated one of the most harrowing fords in the Rockies. However, the Chaba channels can still create difficulties, particularly from late June through mid-August (the trip is best hiked in September).

The trail runs due south from Sunwapta Falls, rolling through heavy forest along the east side of the Athabasca Valley. The first 15 kms follows old fire road, which can be easily traversed by mountain bike.

At km 15.2, the roadbed ends and single-track trail crosses the Athabasca River bridge just upstream from its confluence with the Chaba River. From the bridge, continue south along a plateau above the east side of the Chaba for approximately 6.5 kms. The trail eventually descends to the river and crosses to the west side (multi-channels, usually thigh-deep). The track is sketchy on the west side of the Chaba, but the way south to Fortress Lake is obvious.

You reach the Alberta-B.C. boundary at Fortress Pass. From the pass it is approximately 0.6 km to the east end of Fortress Lake and Hamber Park's only official campground. While rough trail continues along the north shore to other unofficial campsites, this campground offers the best views down the lake.

There is also a commercial fishing camp at the mouth of Chisel Creek on the lake's south shore, but this facility is used primarily by fly-in fishermen and is not trail-accessible.

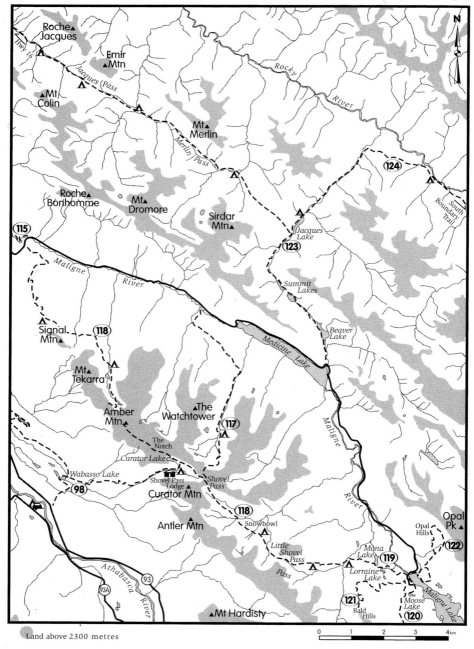

Land above 2300 metres

115 Maligne Canyon

Sixth Bridge Picnic Area to Maligne Canyon Parking Area—3.7 km (2.3 mi)

Maligne Canyon is the Rockies' most impressive limestone slit canyon. The trail along the upper canyon is usually overrun, but few ever hike its entire length. By starting below the canyon, you can enjoy peaceful sections of the Maligne River and, as the canyon gradually unfolds, gain a better appreciation of how it was formed.

Begin at Sixth Bridge Picnic Area, near the confluence of the Maligne and Athabasca Rivers, and climb gradually along the north side of the Maligne River through a forest of spruce, pine, poplar and birch. At 1.6 km you pass Fifth Bridge, which crosses the river to a parking area. Above Fifth Bridge the trail steepens and the ascent along the canyon begins.

Fourth Bridge is passed at km 2.9, and you cross Third Bridge to the south side of the canyon at km 3.1. This is the deepest (55 m) and most spectacular section, so narrow that a person could spread their arms and touch both walls.

From Third Bridge to First Bridge, and the parking lot and teahouse, you cross water-polished bedrock and overlook potholed canyon walls—a stretch better appreciated in early morning or evening with fewer people around.

Access: From its intersection with the Yellowhead Highway, follow the Maligne Lake Road 2.3 km (1.4 mi) to the Sixth Bridge access road. Turn left and follow it 1.6 km (1.0 mi) to Sixth Bridge Picnic Area. Walk across the bridge to the north side of the Maligne River to begin the hike. *Maps: Jasper 83 D/16; Jasper Up-Close (Gem Trek).*

116 Overlander Trail

Sixth Bridge Picnic Area to Cold Sulphur Spring—15.5 km (9.6 mi)

The Overlander Trail follows the east side of the Athabasca Valley from the Maligne River below Maligne Canyon to the Cold Sulphur Spring pull-out on the Yellowhead Highway. The trail receives its name from the Overlanders—adventurous emigrants who travelled upvalley in 1862 to British Columbia's Cariboo gold fields. It is a pleasant outing that passes through prime montane habitat and by an early valley homestead.

The trail is often hiked by arranging transportation between the two trailheads. It can also be cycled, though some sections are quite demanding.

Cross the Maligne River at Sixth Bridge and follow the left branch downstream past the river's confluence with the Athabasca. You continue north along the Athabasca River briefly before angling inland to rejoin the cycling trail. For the next 14 km you enjoy many open views of the valley and the Colin Range.

At km 6.5 you reach the remains of the John Moberly homestead (1898-1910) in a grassy meadow. Beyond the homestead the trail passes through a prescribed burn and above a sulphur spring (km 9.0). After traversing Morro Peak's steep, rocky slopes, it descends to the Cold Sulphur Spring on Highway 16.

Access: From its intersection with the Yellowhead Highway, follow the Maligne Lake Road 2.3 km (1.4 mi) to the Sixth Bridge access road. Turn left and follow it 1.6 km (1.0 mi) to Sixth Bridge Picnic Area. Walk across the bridge to the north side of the Maligne River to begin the hike. The Cold Sulphur Spring trailhead is located at a pull-out on the east side of the Yellowhead Highway, 18.5 km (11.5 mi) north of Jasper townsite's east exit. *Maps: Jasper 83 D/16; Snaring 83 E/1.*

117 Watchtower Basin

Maligne Lake Road to Watchtower Campground—9.8 km (6.1 mi)
Maligne Lake Road to Big Shovel Pass—13.2 km (8.2 mi)*

Day trip or backpack

Allow 3 hours to Watchtower Campground

Elevation gain: 985 m (3,250 ft)

Maximum elevation: 2375 m (7,800 ft)

Maps: Medicine Lake 83 C/13

Access: From its junction with the Yellowhead Highway (Hwy 16) 5 km (3 mi) north of Jasper townsite, follow the Maligne Lake Road 18.5 km (11.5 mi) to the Watchtower Basin trailhead. The parking area is reached via a 100 m gravel access road.

0.0—Trailhead parking area (1390 m).

—Trail crosses Maligne River via footbridge then climbs steeply.

0.5—Trail angles southeast, climbing at gradual to moderate grades.

5.6—Trail veers south and begins moderate climb along Watchtower Creek valley.

7.6—Trail opens out into Watchtower Basin.

9.6—Ford to east side of creek.

9.8—Watchtower Campground.

—Indistinct trail along east side of creek.

12.3—Obvious trail climbs talus slope beneath headwall col.

12.8—Watchtower Col (2375 m).

—Trail contours left across open slopes to Big Shovel Pass.

13.2—Big Shovel Pass Junction (2320 m). Intersection with *Skyline Trail* at km 17.6.

*Distances approximate beyond 9.8 km.

Watchtower Basin is one of our favourite long day hikes in Jasper Park since it allows access to the renowned meadows and lofty alpine ridges of the Maligne Range without having to book campsites on the popular Skyline Trail.

Many prefer a more leisurely visit and stay at Watchtower Campground. From the campground you can reach Big Shovel Pass on the Skyline Trail in a half-day and still have time to explore the vast wildflower meadows and open slopes that comprise this attractive sub-alpine valley.

From the parking area off the Maligne Lake Road, the trail heads south and immediately crosses a footbridge over the Maligne River. Beyond the river it makes a short, steep climb up the heavily forested north slope of The Watchtower. After it has gained enough elevation to leave most hikers slightly winded, it angles off to the southeast. You climb more gradually for the next 2 km but are forced to navigate a number of marshy areas.

At km 2.5 the trail gradually veers back to the south and begins a more serious climb up the Watchtower Creek valley. The grade moderates at km 7.6 as the trail enters Watchtower Basin and runs out across open meadow interspersed with scattered stands of alpine fir.

The track is boggy and indistinct for the next 4 km along the west side of Watchtower Creek. At km 9.6 you cross to the stream's east side (watch for the marker cairn) to Watchtower Campground. The campground is at the site of the old Watchtower Cabin, which served as a base for Jasper ski enthusiasts in the 1930s (the cabin was destroyed by fire in the late 1970s).

One of the easiest sidetrips from the campground is to a small lake less than a kilometre to the west, and 150 m higher

Watchtower Basin

up, on the lower slopes of The Watchtower. While there is no trail to this pretty tarn, finding your way across the meadows is no problem. The rockslides surrounding the lake are home to pikas and white-tailed ptarmigan.

Watchtower Col. The trail upvalley from the campground is sketchy to nonexistent, but the terrain is open and the route to the head of the valley (staying to the east side) is obvious. As you near the end of the valley, watch for the defined trail on the scree slope leading up to the 2375 m pass on the crest of the Maligne Range.

From this lofty col, approximately 3 km beyond the campground, views open out over the scenic heartland of the range—Big Shovel Pass, Curator Lake and The Notch.

Beyond the summit the trail angles southeast across rocky slopes for another 0.4 km to Big Shovel Pass, where it intersects with the Skyline Trail. Backpackers can continue their journey onto the Skyline by turning northwest toward Curator Lake and The Notch or southeast toward Little Shovel Pass and Maligne Lake.

You can also descend to Curator Campground and follow the Wabasso trail to the floor of the Athabasca Valley. The total distance for this traverse of the Maligne Range, from the Maligne Lake Road to the Icefields Parkway, is 30 km. (See *Wabasso Lake* trail description.)

118 Skyline Trail

Maligne Lake to Signal Mountain trailhead—44.1 km (27.4 mi)

Backpack

Allow 2 to 3 days

Elevation gain: 820 m (2,700 ft)
           loss: 1350 m (4,450 ft)

Maximum elevation: 2510 m (8,200 ft)

Maps: Athabasca Falls 83 C/12
        Medicine Lake 83 C/13

Access: Follow the Maligne Lake Road to Maligne Lake. Continue past the day lodge-boat tour complex on the main road for another 0.5 km, crossing the lake's outlet bridge to the picnic area and parking lot at road's end. The trailhead is at the upper edge of the parking area, 50 m to the right of the Bald Hills-Maligne Pass trailhead access gate.

0.0—Maligne Lake Picnic Area (1690 m).

2.1—Junction. Lorraine Lake left 0.2 km.

2.4—Junction. Mona Lake right 0.2 km.

4.8—Evelyn Creek Campground and bridge.

8.3—Little Shovel Campground.

10.3—Little Shovel Pass (2240 m).

12.2—Snowbowl Campground.

17.5—Big Shovel Pass (2320 m).

17.6—Junction. Intersection with *Watchtower Basin* trail at km 13.2. Watchtower Col right 0.4 km.

19.5—Junction. Intersection with *Wabasso Lake* trail at km 15.0. Curator Campground left 0.8 km.

20.4—Curator Lake.

22.1—The Notch (2510 m).

28.3—Centre Lakes.

30.4—Tekarra Campground (2060 m).

35.6—Junction. Signal Mtn lookout site left 0.5 km.

35.7—Signal Campground.

44.1—Maligne Lake Road (1160 m).

The Skyline Trail is one of the exceptional backpacking routes in the Rockies. Following along the rolling crest of the Maligne Range, with 25 of its 44 km at or above treeline, it is the highest trail in Jasper Park. Along the way there are vast meadows, barren windswept ridges, and expansive views that extend over much of the park. Because of its openness, larger species of wildlife can be spotted at a distance, and it is one of only a few places where we have seen mountain caribou.

There are a few considerations before you set off on the journey. Due to the trail's high, unprotected situation, you may be exposed to severe conditions if the weather turns foul; five of six campgrounds lie above 2000 m, so the temperature can drop to near freezing on clear nights, particularly in late August and September; the trail has a relatively short season, and the steep section between Curator Lake and The Notch is often snow-choked into July. It is also one of the most popular backpacking trips in the Canadian Rockies, and since Parks Canada limits the number of hikers on the trail at any given time, it is advisable to reserve campsites in advance of your trip.

Most backpackers schedule two days for the journey, and this places a lot of pressure on Curator Campground near the trail's mid-point. It is one of the Skyline's least attractive campgrounds, and the one where the site quota will most likely be filled. Consider spreading the trip over three days and overnighting at more attractive campgrounds, such as Little Shovel, Snowbowl and Tekarra.

The logical direction to hike the Skyline Trail is from Maligne Lake, starting 520 m higher than the northwest trailhead near Maligne Canyon.

From Maligne Lake Picnic Area, the trail strikes off through lodgepole pine forest and gains little elevation over the

The Snowbowl near Little Shovel Pass

first 5 km. At km 4.8 you cross Evelyn Creek and begin a switchbacking ascent to Little Shovel Pass. Views continue to improve, particularly back to the peaks surrounding Maligne Lake, as you climb through subalpine meadows with scattered stands of alpine fir to the treeless crest of the pass.

From Little Shovel Pass you drop into the lush, sprawling meadows of the Snowbowl. Even during the driest summers fresh streams tumble through the meadows, adding to the sogginess of the terrain. Ascending from the Snowbowl, the trail reaches the crest of Big Shovel Pass at km 17.5.

Shovel Pass was named in 1911 when Jasper's Otto brothers packed Mary Schäffer and a boat over the range to Maligne Lake via this improbable route. When the party encountered deep snow near the pass, the Ottos carved a pair of wooden shovels from trees below and scratched out a trail through the drifts for their horses. The shovels were erected near the summit and stood for several years as monuments to the arduous journey.

Near the pass the trail from Watchtower Basin intersects from the right. A short 0.4 km side trip to Watchtower Col provides an overview of this high, subalpine basin.

Two kilometres below Big Shovel Pass you reach the Wabasso trail junction. Less than a kilometre down this trail is Curator Campground and Shovel Pass Lodge (operated by a commercial horse outfitter). The Watchtower Basin and Wabasso trails both serve as optional routes to and from the heart of the Skyline, and the Wabasso trail is often used as an escape route during vile weather. (See *Watchtower Basin* and *Wabasso Lake*).

From Wabasso junction the trail climbs quickly to the shores of Curator Lake—a peaceful tarn in the midst of a wild, treeless landscape. Here you begin the steep ascent to The Notch—the high

Curator Lake and The Notch from near Big Shovel Pass

col leading to the summit ridge of Amber Mountain.

The Notch (2510 m) is considered the high point on the Skyline, even though the trail contours northwest for another 2 kms at virtually the same elevation. This barren divide is an extraordinary viewpoint for the Athabasca Valley and Mount Edith Cavell, and on clear days Mount Robson is visible 80 kms away to the northwest.

Just beyond the summit of Amber Mountain the trail makes a switchbacking descent to Centre Lakes, then levels off down a narrow vale to Tekarra Lake. Crossing the outlet stream below the lake, you enter scattered stands of alpine fir and begin your contour around to the northern slopes of Mount Tekarra. Views gradually open ahead to the Colin Range, Pyramid Mountain and other familiar peaks near Jasper townsite.

At km 35.6, the trail intersects the Signal Mountain fire road, just 0.5 km below the mountain's old fire lookout site (a worthwhile sidetrip for improved views over the Athabasca Valley). The

Skyline's most northerly campground lies 100 m below the junction.

From the campground, the broad road-bed runs steadily and tediously downhill through the forest for the final 8.4 km to the trailhead parking area on the Maligne Lake Road 0.8 km west of the Maligne Canyon Teahouse and parking area.

Skyline Day Hikes. You can sample some of the glories of the Skyline by day-tripping to high points from either end of the trail. The 8.3 km stretch from the Maligne Lake trailhead to Little Shovel Pass is one possibility. From the north end of the Skyline, you can reach Signal Mountain Lookout in 9 kms (this section is open to cyclists—a grim grind up, a zippy run down).

If you are a strong hiker, and willing to put in a very long day, you can also hike the 12.8 km trail to Watchtower Col. This 2375 m pass at the head of the Watchtower Basin overlooks the heart of the Skyline, stretching from Big Shovel Pass to The Notch (see *Watchtower Basin*).

119 Lorraine and Mona Lakes

Maligne Lake Picnic Area to Mona Lake—2.6 km (1.6 mi)

Escape the hubbub at the busy north end of Maligne Lake by hiking along the first 2.5 kms of the Skyline Trail to a pair of peaceful forest-encirled lakes. Mona Lake is the more substantial of the pair, and from its shore the rounded summits of the Opal Hills peek above the forest to the north.

From the picnic area parking lot, follow the Skyline Trail through thick lodgepole pine forest for 2.1 km and watch for trails branching left to Lorraine Lake. Continue on the main trail another 0.3 km to a side trail branching right to Mona Lake. Both lakes are less than 200 m from the main trail.

Mona Lake is named for Mona Harragin, a tough, self-reliant lady who worked for outfitter Fred Brewster at the

Maligne Lake Chalet during the 1920s. In 1928 Mona and her sister Agnes became the first licensed women trail guides in the mountain parks. Two years later Mona married park warden Charlie Matheson, and the couple shared a number of wilderness adventures while living at the Maligne Lake Warden Cabin.

Access: Follow the Maligne Lake Road to Maligne Lake. Continue past the day lodge-boat tour complex on the main road for another 0.5 km and cross the lake's outlet bridge to the picnic area and parking lot at road's end. The trailhead is at the upper edge of the parking area, 50 m to the right of the Bald Hills-Maligne Pass trailhead access gate. *Maps: Athabasca Falls 83 C/12.*

120 Moose Lake

Maligne Lake Picnic Area to Moose Lake—1.4 km (0.9 mi)

If you are overwhelmed by the crush of motorhomes, tour buses, and snap-shooting tourists at the north end of Maligne Lake, the Moose Lake loop offers a short walk-in-the-woods where you will find a little solitude and sanity. The trip follows a section of the Maligne Pass trail before cutting off into the forest to this quiet little tarn surrounded by pine and spruce; on the return trip you will follow along a peaceful section of the Maligne Lake shoreline.

From the access gate at the upper edge of the Maligne Lake Picnic Area, follow the broad Bald Hills trail 300 m to the Maligne Pass junction. Continue along the Maligne Pass trail for another kilometre to Moose Lake junction. Follow this branch left 100 m to the

lake—a sheltered tarn reflecting the summit of Samson Peak across Maligne Lake.

Return to the parking area by continuing along the trail running east from Moose Lake. It soon loops back to the north and descends to the Maligne Lake shoreline at km 2.4. This lakeside path leads back to the Maligne Lake Warden Cabin and the picnic area.

Access: Follow the Maligne Lake Road to Maligne Lake. Continue past the day lodge-boat tour complex on the main road for another 0.5 km and cross the lake's outlet bridge to the picnic area and parking lot at road's end. The walk begins at the trail sign beside the access gate near the parking lot entrance. *Maps: Athabasca Falls 83 C/12.*

121 Bald Hills

Maligne Lake Picnic Area to Bald Hills Lookout—5.2 km (3.2 mi)

Half-day to day trip

Allow 1.5 to 2 hours one way

Elevation gain: 480 m (1,575 ft)

Maximum elevation: 2170 m (7,120 ft)

Maps: Athabasca Falls 83 C/12

Access: Follow the Maligne Lake Road to Maligne Lake. Continue past the day lodge-boat tour complex on the main road for another 0.5 km and cross the lake's outlet bridge to the picnic area and parking lot at road's end. The hike begins at the trail sign beside the access gate near the parking lot entrance.

0.0—Maligne Lake Picnic Area (1690 m).

0.3—Junction. Moose Lake and Maligne Pass left. Continue ahead.

—Steady uphill on moderately graded roadbed.

2.5—Junction. Bald Hills footpath left.

3.2—Junction. Evelyn Creek right.

5.2—Bald Hills Lookout site (2170 m).

The Bald Hills provide an exceptional overview of Maligne Lake and its surrounding peaks. The subalpine meadows on this open ridgeline are carpeted with wildflowers in July and early August, and the gentle terrain is an open invitation to hike to even higher viewpoints beyond the old lookout site.

While the hike to Bald Hills is one of the best half-day trips in Jasper Park, it involves a rather uninspiring trudge up an old fire road that is regularly used by commercial horse parties. You should also take water along since there is no reliable source along the trail.

The trail starts its climb to Bald Hills in a fire-succession forest of lodgepole pine. Near km 2.5 the slope becomes pronouncedly subalpine with open meadows and stands of stunted alpine fir and Engelmann spruce.

The road ends near the site of the old Bald Hills fire lookout—a cabin that was removed by the park service in the early 1980s.

The old lookout site provides a panorama encompassing nearly 360 degrees. Five hundred metres below, Maligne Lake stretches southeast to The Narrows—the gateway to the upper lake. Leah Peak (2801 m) and Samson Peak (3081 m) rise on the opposite side of the valley; the prominent glaciated summits peeking above the meadows to the south are Mounts Unwin and Charlton, both well over 3000 m above sea level.

In 1908, Mary Schäffer, the Rockies' first lady of exploration, and her companions reached Maligne Lake—recording the first non-native visit since the lake's accidental discovery by a CPR surveyor in 1875. After constructing a make-shift raft, the party journeyed down the lake to The Narrows, where "there burst upon us that which, all in our little company agreed, was the finest view any of us had ever beheld in the Rockies... Yet there it lay, for the time

Maligne Lake from Bald Hills

being all ours—those miles and miles of lake, the unnamed peaks rising above us, one following the other, each more beautiful than the last." Mary returned three years later and provided most of the names for the mountains surrounding the lake, including Bald Hills.

While it is easy to hike to the lookout site and return in a half-day, we usually set aside a full day and wander the ascending ridge of the Bald Hills to the south. Follow a steep footpath leading beyond the end of the road for another kilometre to a large cairn. Continue south

through wildflower meadows and over two 2300-m promentories for another 2 km to even better views.

Bald Hills Footpath Option. While we prefer to follow the easier grades of the fire road on the ascent to Bald Hills, there is also a footpath to the site that branches left from the roadbed at km 2.5. This single-track trail is shorter and steeper than the road, so it makes a nice alternative on the way down. Watch for it branching downslope just above the lookout.

122 Opal Hills

Maligne Lake to Opal Hills Summit—3.2 km (2.0 mi)

Half-day trip

Allow 1 to 1.5 hours one way

Elevation gain: 460 m (1,500 ft)

Maximum elevation: 2160 m (7,100 ft)

Maps: Athabasca Falls 83 C/12

Access: Follow the Maligne Lake Road to Maligne Lake. Turn left into the main parking area just before the day lodge-boat rental concession and keep left to the third and uppermost parking lot. The trailhead is at the upper left corner of the parking lot.

0.0—Maligne Lake parking area (1700 m).

0.2—Junction. Maligne Lakeshore trail right.

—Very steep uphill.

1.6—Junction. Opal Hills Loop trail split. Stay right.

2.6—Trail emerges into meadow.

3.2—Trail summit (2160 m). Trail levels out into meadows behind hills.

4.7—Trail emerges from behind hills and descends into forest.

6.6—Junction. End of Opal Hills Loop. Connect back into approach trail at km 1.6.

8.2—Maligne Lake parking area (1700 m).

The Opal Hills loop is a popular half-day trip from the northwest end of Maligne Lake. Much like Bald Hills across the valley, this trip boasts excellent wildflower meadows and a good overview of Maligne Lake. However, though the trail is shorter than Bald Hills, it is a lot steeper.

There is no fooling about on the Opal Hills trail. It heads grimly upward through dense lodgepole pine forest with nary a switchback, gaining elevation at a heart-pounding rate. It can also be slippery and treacherous when wet.

The trail's upper loop begins at a junction 1.6 km into the trip. Either branch will bring you to the same point, but the right-hand option reaches the open meadows above in far less time.

Staying right at the trail split, you remain in heavy forest for another kilometre before suddenly emerging into open meadow. Soon after reaching the meadow, the trail levels off, angles left through a draw, and circles into a basin behind low hills. Climb to the top of these knolls for the best view of the valley. If it is a warm day, you will have suffered mightily on the ascent and will be happy to fall back on their grassy, south-facing slopes to relax in the sun.

Though the view isn't quite as expansive as from Bald Hills, much of lower Maligne Lake is visible, as are the twin peaks of Mounts Unwin (3268 m) and Charlton (3217 m) beyond its western shore. The rolling Bald Hills are directly across the valley, and the rounded ridges of the Maligne Range march off to the northwest. The rounded, red-hued ridges of the Opal Hills, named by Maligne Lake pioneer Mary Schäffer during her second visit to the valley in 1911, rise above the trail summit to the east.

The trail traverses the vale behind the hills then returns to the forest, where it makes a moderately steep descent back to the loop split.

Maligne Lake from Opal Hills

123 Jacques Lake

Maligne Lake Road to Jacques Lake Campground—12.2 km (7.6 mi)

Day trip or backpack

Allow 3 to 4 hours one way

Elevation gain: 90 m (300 ft)
          loss: 45 m (150 ft)

Maximum elevation: 1540 m (5,050 ft)

Maps: Medicine Lake 83 C/13

Access: From its junction with the Yellowhead Highway (Hwy 16), follow the Maligne Lake Road 28 km (17.5 mi) to the Beaver Creek Picnic Area, located on the left side of the highway opposite the southeast end of Medicine Lake.

0.0—Beaver Creek Picnic Area (1450 m).

   —Follow roadbed past access gate.

1.6—Beaver Lake.

4.8—First Summit Lake. Foot trail branches right into forest.

6.0—Second Summit Lake (1540 m). Trail follows through forest to right of lake.

7.4—Trail skirts to left of small lake.

   —Section with numerous stream crossings.

11.2—Junction. Merlin and Jacques Passes left. Jacques Lake ahead.

11.6—Jacques Lake (southwest end).

12.2—Jacques Lake Campground (1495 m).

   —Trail crosses outlet stream at north end of lake.

12.5—Jacques Lake Warden Cabin. *South Boundary Trail* continues to northeast.

The trail to Jacques Lake is unique. It travels through a narrow mountain valley, skirts four lakes, and crosses a watershed divide—all in less than 12 kms and with little gain or loss of elevation. The undemanding approach makes it a worthwhile destination for a long day hike and a good early season backpack when the high country is still choked with snow.

The trail is open to mountain bikes as far as Jacques Lake, and an old roadbed on the initial 5 km to Summit Lakes makes for easy cycling. However, the narrow, muddy single-track trail beyond Summit Lakes is rough and quite demanding.

From the access gate at Beaver Creek Picnic Area, the route follows the flat roadbed north through dense forest bordering the creek. At km 1.6 you reach the first point of interest, Beaver Lake. This pleasant, green lake, which is often inhabited by loons and other waterfowl, is a popular destination for birdwatchers, fishermen and anyone looking for a rewarding short walk.

The road continues into more open terrain beyond Beaver Lake, and views open out to the north end of the Queen Elizabeth Range—a sawtoothed series of peaks eroded from steeply tilted slabs of grey Devonian limestone.

At km 4.8 you reach the first Summit Lake—a small sink lake ringed by spruce, lodgepole pine and cottonwood poplar. Here the roadbed reverts to single-track trail, which continues northwest through forest and meadow to the second Summit Lake—yet another sink with no visible outlet.

The final stretch to Jacques Lake spends much of its time in dense forest filled with streams. The main creek, fed by numerous small tributaries, is crossed at least three times, and the rooty track is often quite muddy.

Though strong hikers can make the round trip to the lake and back in a day,

Jacques Lake

Jacques Lake's peaceful setting deserves more than a hit-and-run visit. There are nice views across the lake to the Queen Elizabeth Ranges from the small campground near the north end, though the warden cabin 300 m beyond occupies the prime real estate—overlooking the full length of the lake from a wildflower-filled meadow.

The lake is named for the mountain range to the northwest, which was named for Jacques Cardinal—a colourful Metis mountain man who tended horses in the Athabasca Valley for the Hudson Bay Company during the 1820s.

The trail continues beyond the north end of the lake to the Jacques Lake Warden Cabin, then heads northeast down Breccia Creek. This is the route followed by South Boundary Trail travellers, but there is little worthwhile scenery in that direction that can be reached on a day trip from the lake. (See *South Boundary Trail*.)

Merlin Pass–Jacques Pass. The trail to Merlin and Jacques Passes branches northwest 0.4 km south of Jacques Lake. It runs for approximately 30 kms to a trailhead parking area on the east side of the Yellowhead Highway (Hwy 16) 21 km (13 mi) north of Jasper townsite's east exit.

Though there are four campgrounds on the trail, it is an unmaintained route contained by narrow valleys and mostly forest-enclosed. The track is frequently obscure and wet, there are a number of minor fords, and no views worth mentioning from the two low-elevation passes. (In 2001, one hiker counted more than 400 downed trees across this trail.)

If you do tackle this route, purchase the Snaring 83 E/1, Miette 83 F/4, and Medicine Lake 83 C/13 topo maps at the Jasper visitor centre and mark campground locations.

124 South Boundary Trail

Maligne Lake Road to Nigel Pass trailhead—165.7 km (103.0 mi)

Backpack

Allow 7 to 10 days

Maximum elevation: 2255 m (7,400 ft)

Minimum elevation: 1360 m (4,450 ft)

Maps: Medicine Lake 83 C/13
Mountain Park 83 C/14
Southesk Lake 83 C/11
George Creek 83 C/10
Job Creek 83 C/7
Sunwapta Peak 83 C/6
Columbia Icefield 83 C/3

Access: Travelling from north to south, start from the *Jacques Lake* trailhead on the Maligne Lake Road. Northbound backpackers start at the *Nigel Pass* trailhead on the Icefields Parkway in Banff Park.

0.0—Beaver Creek Picnic Area (1450 m).

1.6—Beaver Lake.

4.8—First Summit Lake.

6.0—Second Summit Lake (1540 m).

11.2—Junction. Merlin and Jacques Passes left.

12.2—Jacques Lake Campground (1495 m).

25.0—Grizzly Campground (1360 m).

31.0—Grizzly Warden Cabin.

33.9—Rocky River suspension bridge.

37.6—Climax Campground.

39.7—Gretna Lake.

42.6—Rocky Falls.

47.9—Rocky Forks Campground (1590 m).

56.8—Medicine Tent Campground.

57.0—Rocky Pass Junction (1700 m). Rocky Pass left (see Rocky Pass).

60.9—Medicine Tent Warden Cabin.

66.1—Lagrace Campground.

70.5—Medicine Tent Lakes.

74.1—Cairn Pass (2255 m).

76.1—Cairn Pass Campground.

79.1—Cairn River Warden Cabin.

86.2—Cairn River bridge.

The South Boundary Trail is no spectacular, high country trek—there are only two alpine passes and much of the trail travels through lowland forest. But whatever the trail may lack in flashy scenery, it makes up in a feeling of total isolation. It is a long, uncompromising journey, there are unbridged stream crossings, and some days may pass without a human encounter.

Once you pass Jacques Lake at the trail's north end, or the Brazeau Lake junction near the south end, there is a sense of total commitment to the trip. The only escape route between those two points is the Rocky Pass trail, which brings you out onto one of the loneliest roads in western Canada.

Take your pick as to which way you hike the trail. Since the best scenery lies on the southern half of the route, we opt to start in the north and hike southwards toward the improving views.

Beaver Creek to Rocky Pass Junction—57.0 kms. You could not ask for an easier start to a major trek than the gentle Jacques Lake trail, and Jacques Lake Campground at km 12.2 makes a good first night destination (see *Jacques Lake*).

The trail is not so civilized beyond Jacques Lake. The track gets rougher and hikers are few and far between as you work your way northeast down the narrow Breccia Creek gorge, crossing the stream four times on footbridges. After the final crossing, the trail climbs out of the Breccia canyon, turns southeast, and descends to the Rocky River at Grizzly Campground. This 12.5 km stretch from Jacques Lake to Rocky River is mainly through forest and fairly tedious.

From the pleasant Grizzly Campground, located on a bank above the sparkling waters of the Rocky River, the trail carries on upvalley along the river's southwest side. While the track is well defined, there is an unexpected calf-deep

Mount Dalhousie from Cairn River

88.6—Southesk Lake Junction. Southesk Lake right (see *Southesk Lake*).

88.8—Cairn River ford (calf to knee-deep).

88.9—Cairn River Campground (1675 m).

93.0—Park boundary.

95.2—Southesk River suspension bridge. Park boundary.

95.9—Junction. Cardinal River left.

97.5—Southesk Campground (1610 m).

97.8—Junction. Dowling Ford left.

110.0—Isaac Creek ford (calf-deep).

110.2—Isaac Creek Campground (1585 m).

111.3—Junction. Isaac Creek Warden Cabin left.

123.1—Arete Warden Cabin.

123.7—Arete Campground.

132.4—Big Springs.

135.9—Brazeau Warden Cabin.

136.3—Junction and Northwest Brazeau River bridge (1720 m). Intersection with *Jonas Pass-Brazeau Lake Loop* at km 50.2. Brazeau Lake and Poboktan Pass right.

136.4—Brazeau Campground.

144.9—Wolverine South Campground.

151.7—Four Point Junction. Jonas Pass right.

151.9—Four Point Campground.

155.0—Boulder Creek Campground.

158.5—Nigel Pass (2195 m). Banff-Jasper Park boundary.

165.7—Nigel Pass trailhead (1830 m).

(Trail not fully shown on maps in this book)

ford of a side stream at km 33.4.

Views are limited until you cross the Rocky River suspension bridge at km 33.9 and emerge onto open willow flats on the northeast side of the river. (The bridge is 200 m upstream from where the horse trail crosses the river.)

Continuing upvalley, you are into the forest again, though there are more openings out to the steeply-tilted limestone peaks of the Front Ranges than there were back down-valley. At km 42.6, you suddenly emerge on an overlook above Rocky Falls—a waterfall staircase that creates an impressive diversion along this otherwise lacklustre section.

At km 47.9, just beneath the westward dipping limestone slabs of Mount Lindsay, you arrive at Rocky Forks Campground. Just 200 m beyond the campground, the horse trail branches right to Rocky Forks Warden Cabin, while the hiker's trail continues straight ahead. This 1.7 km hiker's cutoff is less defined than the horse trail, but it saves two fords of the Medicine Tent River. You soon rejoin the horse trail and continue your southeast course up along the Medicine Tent.

The horse trail fords the Medicine Tent at km 53.9, but again there is a hiker's trail branching left 100 m before the crossing. The path was fairly vague when last we passed that way, but the trees were well blazed. The horse trail swings back across the river to rejoin the hiker's track at the Medicine Tent Campground.

Just 200 m beyond the campground, the Rocky Pass trail intersects from the north. This is an important junction, since it is the only reasonable escape route from the South Boundary Trail along its entire length. This 11.5 km trail climbs steeply to Rocky Pass and crosses the park boundary to the Cardinal River Divide forestry road (see *Rocky Pass*).

Rocky Pass Junction to Dowling Ford Junction—40.8 km. As you continue up the Medicine Tent Valley from Rocky Pass Junction, the forest becomes more open and views improve. Beyond

Southesk River bridge

Lagrace Campground, the trail begins its climb to the summit of Cairn Pass. The Medicine Tent Lakes are passed in an open alpine meadow at km 70.5 and, after a short steep climb through the last stands of alpine fir, you reach the pass.

At 2255 m, Cairn Pass is the high point of the trip in more ways than one. The view back down the Medicine Tent to the Rocky River valley is spectacular, allowing the first good overview of the country you've been hiking through for the past couple of days. Alpine meadows stretch out on both sides of the pass. Dotted with numerous small lakes, they are about as extensive and beautiful as any in Jasper Park. The summit is also inhabited by scores of hoary marmots, who aren't that accustomed to seeing people.

Immediately above the pass to the west is the low, cone-shaped peak named Southesk Cairn. If you look closely, you can see the giant rock cairn that was erected on its summit by James Carnegie, the Earl of Southesk, when he passed this way on a hunting trip in 1859. Experi-

enced scramblers can easily ascend this peak and add a rock or two to this historical edifice.

Beyond Cairn Pass the trail continues its southeasterly course, descending through alpine and subalpine meadows for the next 5 kms. Southesk Cairn and the pass remain visible all the way to the Cairn River Warden Cabin junction. The trail bypasses the warden cabin, which lies on the opposite side of the Cairn River, and drops down into the forested Cairn Valley, staying along the river's northeast bank for the next 7 km.

At km 86.2, you cross a bridge to the south side of the Cairn. After traversing a forested rise, the trail returns to the river and crosses it (normally a calf-deep ford) just above its confluence with the Southesk River. Just 200 m before this ford, the 22.4 km trail to Southesk Lake branches right (see *Southesk River*).

Nearly 3 km beyond the Cairn River Campground, the horse trail comes abreast of the Southesk River and crosses to the south bank. In order to avoid this demanding ford, a hiker's trail continues east and climbs a forested ridge above the river. At km 93.0, the trail crosses the park boundary onto provincial forest lands and, 0.6 km farther along, intersects a broad seismic line. Turn left and follow this cut for 100 m to where the trail branches right into the forest. Another seismic line is encountered 100 m farther along. Follow this cut to the left for yet another 100 m and watch for the point where the trail exits to the right again.

Following this brief encounter with provincial forest land desecration, you switchback down steeply to a canyon containing the Southesk River. A suspension bridge spans the gorge and, on the opposite side, you return to the sanctity of the park. After taking a break on the rock slabs of this pleasant canyon, climb 0.3 km to rejoin the horse trail.

All of this wandering around in the forest takes you out of the Front Ranges and into the fringes of the Foothills. From Southesk Campground, located on a point of land overlooking a sink lake, you have your first real perspective of the surrounding countryside, comprised of great expanses of flat, forested terrain overlooked by the dramatic summits of Mount Dalhousie to the southwest.

Dowling Ford Junction to Nigel Creek—67.9 km. Just beyond Southesk Campground you reach the junction with a horse trail from Dowling Ford. This is significant since it is the point where the South Boundary Trail turns south and re-enters the mountains via the Brazeau Valley.

The trail runs through a rocky and rooty forest as it makes its ascent of the Brazeau, but the grade remains flat, as it has been ever since the Southesk suspension bridge. With the exception of some sink lakes at km 100.4, which allow open views of Tarpeian Rock, this is a long, tedious section running through a dense forest of lodgepole pine.

The scenery in the Brazeau Valley begins to improve at Isaac Creek. Here, on the rocky, dryas-covered flats near the

mouth of the Isaac Creek canyon, there is a fine view of the mountains across the valley, again dominated by the sheer 1300-m face of Tarpeian Rock.

As you follow up the Brazeau, the trail alternates between sections of forest and grassy meadows that slope down to the river. In midsummer these meadows are covered with montane wildflowers, including brown-eyed Susans, western wood lilies, harebells, and shrubby cinquefoil.

At km 132.4 there is a surprise— several large springs gushing from the base of a cliff and cascading down to the trail. Known simply as Big Springs, they create a mini-rainforest environment in the midst of a semi-arid valley and provide cool refreshment on hot summer days.

The trail runs through the grounds of the Brazeau Warden Station at km 135.9 and, 0.5 km farther along, reaches Brazeau Lake Junction. Brazeau Lake is just over 2 km northwest of this intersection, and you may want to hike to the lake—the largest along the South Boundary route. (See *Jonas Pass-Brazeau Lake Loop.*)

At Brazeau Lake Junction, you return to more travelled ways. The solitude of the past several days disappears as you enter the popular Jonas Pass-Brazeau Lake circuit, and you can expect to encounter more hikers over the final 30 km of your journey. This last leg to the Brazeau River headwaters and Nigel Pass is one of the most scenic on the entire trip, and it provides a fitting climax to your South Boundary adventure. (See also *Jonas Pass-Brazeau Loop* and *Nigel Pass.*)

125 Rocky Pass

Cardinal River Divide to South Boundary Trail—11.4 km (7.1 mi) *

Day trip or backpack

Allow 3 to 4 hours to Medicine Tent River

Elevation gain: 120 m (390 ft)
    loss: 260 m (850 ft)

Maximum elevation: 1960 m (6,430 ft)

Maps: Mountain Park 83 C/14

Access: Follow the Yellowhead Highway 22 km (13.5 mi) east from Jasper Park East Gate to its intersection with Highway 40. Continue south on Highway 40 for 48 km (30 mi) to its junction with the Cadomin road. Turn right and follow the road south (through the village of Cadomin) 23 km (14 mi) to Cardinal Divide. Continue beyond the summit for another 1.7 km to the trailhead parking area on the right side of the road.

0.0—Cardinal Divide Road parking area (1840 m).

 —Route follows seismic line southwest.

2.2—Junction. Trail branches left from seismic line.

4.4—Cardinal River fords (calf-deep).

 —Steep climb toward pass.

7.0—Rocky Pass (1960 m). Park boundary.

 —Contouring climb south from pass.

9.0—Steep switchbacking descent begins.

11.4—Junction (1700 m). Intersection with *South Boundary Trail* at km 57.0. Medicine Tent Campground right 0.2 km.

*all distances approximate.

(Trail not shown on maps in this book)

For hikers who want to access, or escape from, the heart of the South Boundary Trail quickly, the 11.5 km trail over Rocky Pass from Cardinal Divide is the only option. Rocky Pass is also a scenic and worthwhile objective as a day trip, though the long, rough drive to this remote trailhead beyond Jasper's eastern boundary will likely take as long as the hike itself.

Departing from the trailhead parking area 1.7 km east of Cardinal Divide, the trail follows a seismic line southwest. Continue until you reach a meadow around km 2.2, where the trail branches left from the arrow-straight seismic road.

Once you leave the seismic line, and beat your way through a section of willow, the horse trail to the pass is obvious running across a meadow. You skirt two small lakes then descend to the first of three quick fords of the Cardinal River.

From the last ford, you begin a steep climb to the pass. Grades moderate before the trail crosses into Jasper Park on a slope just east of the true summit.

The pass is true to its name—a rocky, windswept gap overlooking the wild Medicine Tent Valley. Day hikers can continue another 2 km or so beyond the pass to even higher views as the trail contours and climbs along open, west-facing slopes.

The final decent to the Medicine Tent Valley is quick, plunging downward along the east side of a canyon. After passing beneath a series of punchbowl waterfalls, it reaches the South Boundary Trail at a junction 200 m south of the Medicine Tent Campground. (See *South Boundary Trail*.)

If you are using the Rocky Pass trail as an exit from the South Boundary Trail, you should realize that traffic on the Cardinal River forestry road is sparse. However, those who do travel it are usually sympathetic to hitchhikers.

126 Southesk Lake

South Boundary Trail to Southesk Lake—22.4 km (13.9 mi)*

Backpack

Allow 6 to 7 hours one way

Elevation gain: 170 m (560 ft)

Maximum elevation: 1850 m (6,070 ft)

Maps: George Creek 83 C/10
      Southesk Lake 83 C/11

Access: Hike the *South Boundary Trail* to the Southesk Lake trail junction—88 km from Beaver Creek on the Maligne Lake Road; 77 km from the Icefields Parkway at Nigel Creek; or 43 km from the Cardinal Divide Road via Rocky Pass and the South Boundary Trail.

0.0—Southesk Lake Junction (1680 m).

—Rolling trail above Southesk River.

4.3—Junction. Dean Pass Horse Campground left via river ford.

—Descent to north bank of river. Muddy sections and stream fords.

21.7—Southesk Lake (1850 m).

—Trail follows north shore of lake.

22.4—Southesk Lake Campground.

*All distances approximate.

(Trail not fully shown on maps in this book.)

If Southesk Lake isn't the most remote spot in Jasper Park, it certainly feels like it. The lake is tucked away in the park's southeast wilderness and only accessible via a 22 km trek up the Southesk Valley from the South Boundary Trail.

Backpackers hiking the South Boundary Trail end-to-end seldom, if ever, visit the lake as a side trip. The handful who do visit it usually start their trip on the Cardinal River Divide and hike over Rocky Pass to the South Boundary Trail, then follow the South Boundary over Cairn Pass to Southesk Lake Junction. Total distance to the lake via this route is 65.5 kms. (See *Rocky Pass* and *South Boundary Trail*.)

The trail branches west from the South Boundary Trail at km 88.6—300 m west of Cairn River Campground. Horse parties are the most frequent trail users, so the track up the north side of the river is often muddy and cut-up.

The ascent of the valley is pleasant, open and quite gradual all the way to the lake. Beyond the Dean Pass Campground junction, there are a number of stream crossings that will cost you time as you fuss about to find the best fording point.

After passing the horse camp at the east end of Southesk Lake, the trail follows around the north shore for approximately 0.7 km to the hiker campground.

The lake is contained by unnamed peaks both north and south, which create a very wild and romantic setting. The most impressive is glaciated Maligne Mountain (3225 m), rising near the head of the valley to the west.

Horse parties often travel upvalley from the lake to Glacier Pass, then continue north down the Rocky River to Rocky Forks Campground. Though we know backpackers who have completed this loop, it is a long, rough, mostly trailless bushwhack with numerous stream crossings.

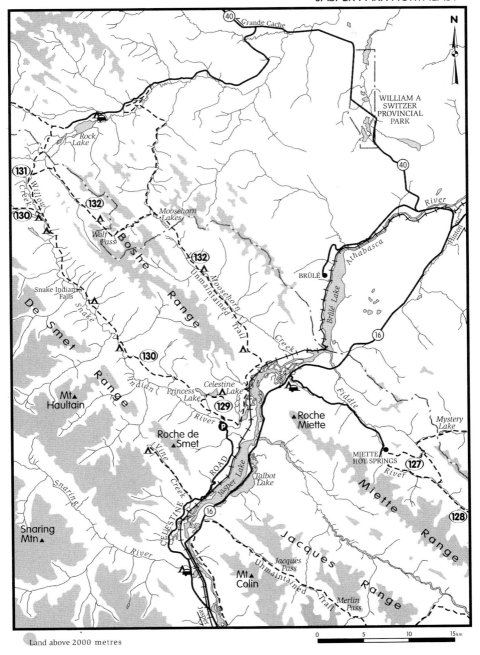

N

40 Grande Cache

WILLIAM A
SWITZER
PROVINCIAL
PARK

40

River

131

132

130

Moosehorn
Lakes

Willow Creek

Boshe Range

Wolf Pass

Snake Indian Falls

Snake

132

Moosehorn
Unmaintained Trail

Creek

BRÛLÉ

Brûlé Lake

Athabasca

Hinton

16

De Smet Range

130

Indian River

Princess Lake

Celestine Lake

129

P

Roche Miette

Fiddle

Mystery Lake

MIETTE HOT SPRINGS

127

Mt
Haultain

Roche de Smet

Vine Creek

ROAD

Jasper Lake

Talbot Lake

River

Miette Range

128

Sharing Mtn

CELESTINE

16

Snaring River

Jasper

Jacques Range

Jacques Pass

Unmaintained Trail

Merlin Pass

Mt
Colin

Jasper

Land above 2000 metres

0   5   10   15 km

127 Sulphur Skyline

Miette Hot Springs to Sulphur Skyline Summit—4.0 km (2.5 mi)

Half-day trip

Allow 1.5 hours one way

Elevation gain: 700 m (2,300 ft)

Maximum elevation: 2070 m (6,790 ft)

Maps: Miette 83 F/4

Access: From its junction with the Yellowhead Highway (Hwy 16) 7 km (4 mi) west of Jasper Park East Gate, follow the Miette Hot Springs Road south 17 km (11 mi) to its termination at the Miette Hot Springs pool parking area. Walk to the entrance of the pool complex on the right side of the building. Follow the sidewalk right 30 m to the trailhead.

0.0—Miette Hot Springs trailhead (1370 m).

—Steady uphill on paved trail and then roadbed.

0.8—Roadbed narrows to single-track trail.

—Steady ascent through old burn.

2.2—Shuey Pass Junction (1660 m). Fiddle River canyon ahead 2.3 km. Sulphur Skyline right.

—Steep switchbacking ascent.

3.4—Trail emerges above treeline.

4.0—Sulphur Skyline Summit (2070 m).

The trail to the summit of Sulphur Ridge from Miette Hot Springs is one of the best half-day trips in Jasper Park. The ridge overlooks several remote wilderness valleys—the most prominent being Fiddle River, which snakes away to the southwest for over 24 km to its headwaters on Whitehorse Pass.

This hike is particularly nice in late spring and early summer when Front Range wildflowers are in bloom, and we've often encountered bighorn sheep on the way. But be sure to pack water—this is a steep, dry hike.

The trail begins as a broad paved path, but soon reverts to roadbed and then single-track. The climb is steady for 2.2 km to a junction on the crest of Shuey Pass, where you turn right and begin an even more serious climb to the ridge.

The trail switchbacks steadily upward through scattered forest and across open, grassy slopes before reaching the ridge summit, where a wonderful 360-degree panorama unfolds.

In addition to views south to Fiddle River and the rocky pyramid of Utopia Mountain, there are impressive valleys and mountains to the north, including multi-summited Ashlar Ridge—layers of steeply-tilted limestone that have been eroded into a series of sawtooth peaks.

Mystery Lake—10.5 km. This forest-encircled lake lies just beyond the park's east boundary. It is a long, rough day trip from Miette Hot Springs, and not much fun as a backpack either.

From the junction on Shuey Pass, descend (steeply) to the Fiddle River canyon. Ford the river 0.3 km below the point of first contact (difficult during high water), then follow rough trail downstream for 2 km before climbing overgrown track to the lake.

Our recommendation: avoid the ford, and the lake, and only go as far as Fiddle River canyon (km 4.5).

Fiddle River Valley from Sulphur Skyline

128 Fiddle River—Whitehorse Pass

Miette Hot Springs to Whitehorse Pass—24.6 km (15.3 mi)

Backpack

Allow 2 days to pass

Elevation gain: 1025 m (3,350 ft)
           loss: 260 m (850 ft)

Maximum elevation: 2135 m (7,000 ft)

Maps: Miette 83 F/4
       Cadomin 83 F/3
       Mountain Park 83 C/14

Access: From its junction with the Yellowhead Highway (Hwy 16) 7 km (4 mi) west of Jasper Park East Gate, follow the Miette Hot Springs Road south 17 km (11 mi) to its termination at the Miette Hot Springs pool parking area. Start the hike from the trail kiosk at the picnic area just south of the parking lot entrance.

0.0—Miette Hot Springs (1370 m).

    —Descend paved trail.

0.4—Old hot pool site.

0.6—Source hot spring.

0.7—Junction. Horse trail intersects from right.

3.0—Fiddle Pass (1645 m).

4.6—Junction. Fiddle River horse trail left. Stay right.

4.7—Fiddle River (1400 m).

6.1*—Utopia Creek ford (ankle-to mid-calf-deep). Utopia Creek Campground.

8.8*—Junction. Fiddle Creek Warden Cabin left (across river). Continue ahead.

13.4*—Slide Creek Campground.

13.7*—Fiddle River ford to northeast bank.

20.7*—Whitehorse Pass Campground.

25.0*—Whitehorse Pass (2135 m).

*distance approximate

(Trail not fully shown on maps in this book.)

Whitehorse Pass is a beautiful alpine summit straddling Jasper Park's eastern boundary. Backpackers can reach the pass from Miette Hot Springs by following the 25 km Fiddle River trail. Though the trail is not overly long or difficult, there are a number of fords en route.

The first section from Sulphur Creek to the Fiddle River via Fiddle Pass is frequently travelled by hikers and horseback parties from Miette Hot Springs. However, the trail becomes more of a wilderness track as it proceeds upvalley along the southwest side of Fiddle River. The first of several fords occurs at Utopia Creek, just prior to reaching Utopia Creek Campground.

Just beyond Slide Creek Campground, the trail swings to the northeast side of the Fiddle—a crossing that can vary from a rock-hop to a knee-deep ford depending on the season. Farther along the horse trail crosses back to the southwest bank briefly, but hikers follow a path that stays on the northeast side. Throughout this section, the trail alternates between rockslides, forest and gravel flats.

Two more easy crossings of the Fiddle are made just prior to reaching Whitehorse Pass Campground. Here the trail angles up the river's north tributary and makes a quick ascent to the narrow notch of Whitehorse Pass on the park boundary. In addition to its fine alpine meadows, the pass provides good views back down the Fiddle Valley and to the rugged peaks of the Nikanassin Range.

You can continue on through the pass to a trailhead at the Whitehorse Creek Campground on the forestry road 6 km south of the town of Cadomin. Follow horse trail to Whitehorse Creek, then an old access road (heavily used by trail bikes and ATVs) down the north side of the creek. Distance from the pass to Whitehorse Creek Campground is approximately 17 km.

Celestine Lake Road

The Celestine Lake Road runs for 27 kms along the west side of the Athabasca Valley from the Yellowhead Highway to the Snake Indian Valley. The last 23 kms is gravel, and some spots are rough and narrow, but the road is kept open because it provides access to some wonderful montane landscape on that side of the valley and trails leading up the Snake Indian River, including *Devona Lookout* and the *North Boundary Trail*.

Two-way traffic is permitted on the 8.5 km (5.5 mi) section running from Snaring Campground to a pull-out near Corral Creek (1.3 kms beyond the Snaring Warden Station). From this point on traffic is one-way, alternating between north and south on a strict schedule, which is listed on a sign at the pull-out. As of 2000, this schedule was as follows:

Inbound (north):	Outbound (south):
8:00 am to 9:00 am	9:30 am to 10:30 am
11:00 am to 12 noon	12:30 pm to 1:30 pm
2:00 pm to 3:00 pm	3:30 pm to 4:30 pm
5:00 pm to 6:00 pm	6:30 pm to 7:30 pm
8:00 pm to 9:00 pm	9:30 pm to 10:30 pm
11:00 pm to midnight	12:30 am to 1:30 am
2:00 am to 3:00 am	3:30 am to 4:30 am
5:00 am to 6:00 am	6:30 am to 7:30 am

This information is also posted where the paved road turns to gravel 1.3 km beyond Snaring Campground. To be safe, check this sign or at the Park Visitor Centre in Jasper to make sure the times have not been altered.

While this road can be navigated by most any vehicle, it is narrow and rocky in spots. Extreme caution should be exercised. You should adhere strictly to the listed times, but be wary on blind corners—someone else might not be following the schedule. During periods of heavy rainfall, check with the Park Visitor Centre concerning conditions, since muddy sections and high water at the Corral Creek crossing could cause problems for vehicles with low clearance. No trailers are permitted on the road.

Access: Follow the Yellowhead Highway (Hwy 16) to the Snaring Campground junction, 9 km (6 mi) north of the Jasper townsite's east exit. Follow this road 6.3 km, past Snaring Campground and across the Snaring River bridge, to where the paved road ends and the gravel Celestine Lake Road branches left. The Celestine Road continues along the west side of the Athabasca Valley, past the Ewan Moberly Homestead historic site and the Snaring Warden Station, reaching the one-way limited access sign and pull-out at km 13.5.

Continuing on the one-way section beyond the pull-out, the road crosses the wooden Corral Creek sluiceway and begins to climb along the west side of the valley. Vine Creek is crossed at km 15.0 and a gated branch road to Devona Flats is passed at km 23.5. After crossing over two high points of land, the road descends to a locked access gate and parking area at km 27.0—500 m before the Snake Indian River bridge.

129 Devona Lookout

Celestine Lake Road to Celestine Lake—6.8 km (4.2 mi)
Celestine Lake Road to Devona Lookout—9.4 km (5.8 mi)

Day trip or backpack

Allow 2.5 hours to lookout

Elevation gain: 325 m (1,060 ft)

Maximum elevation: 1405 m (4,610 ft)

Maps: Snaring 83 E/1

Access: Drive the Celestine Lake Road to the locked gate at road's end—as described in the *Celestine Lake Road* introduction (see page 249). The hike begins on the road below the access gate.

0.0—Celestine Road Gate (1080 m).

— Follow road downhill.

0.5—Snake Indian River bridge.

— Moderate uphill on road.

1.9—Junction. Moosehorn trail right. Continue ahead.

5.2—Junction. *North Boundary Trail* ahead. Celestine Lake and Devona Lookout right.

6.5—Princess Lake.

6.8—Celestine Lake and Campground.

— Moderate, steady uphill on old fire road.

8.7—Road crests open ridge.

9.4—Devona Lookout site (1405 m).

The hike to Devona Lookout is a long but rewarding day trip from the end of the Celestine Lake Road. In addition to passing two pretty lakes, Princess and Celestine, the old lookout site at the end of the trail overlooks a broad swath of the Athabasca Valley stretching from near Jasper townsite to the hills beyond the park's eastern boundary. But despite its scenic rewards, you will likely find the drive to the trailhead more exciting than the hike itself.

Before the Snake Indian River bridge was decommissioned in 1993, you could drive 5 km farther on the Celestine Lake Road than you can today. That left a short walk to Princess and Celestine Lakes, and the hike to Devona Lookout could be completed in a half-day. Now the trip to the lakes and the lookout site is a full day from the end of the road.

Since mountain bikes are permitted on this section of the North Boundary Trail, time for the trip can be shortened by biking the first 5.2 kms to the Celestine Lake-Devona Lookout junction (a bit of a grunt on the way up; a nice brisk ride down). Or you can backpack to Celestine Lake Campground and hike to the lookout from there.

From the parking area at the Celestine Road gate, you descend immediately to an iron bridge across the Snake Indian River. (Erosion of the bridge foundation on the far side caused its closure to vehicles.) From the bridge there is a short, moderately steep uphill along the northeast side of the canyon. However, grades soon moderate as the road turns northwest and climbs steadily for another 4 km to the junction where the Celestine Lake-Devona Lookout fire road splits right from the North Boundary Trail track.

From the road split, it is a short, easy walk through the forest to Princess and Celestine Lakes. Both are substantial

Roche Miette and the Athabasca Valley from Devona Lookout

lakes surrounded by spruce forest and with views of the Beaver Bluffs and Bosche Range to the north. Both have long been popular with fishermen, though somewhat less so since the road closure at Snake Indian bridge.

The broad track turns southeast beyond Celestine Lake and climbs gradually along the ridge leading to the lookout. At km 8.7 it breaks out of the forest onto the crest of the ridge, where you get your first views of the Athabasca Valley.

The grassy, south-facing slopes are typical of the montane life zone—covered with the blooms of western wood lilies, Indian paintbrush, camus lilies and purple vetch from mid-June through mid-July, and brown-eyed Susans, harebells and purple asters in late July and August.

At km 9.4 you reach the site of the Devona Lookout—a fire tower that was dismantled in the mid-1980s. Continue another 150 m to the end of the ridge for your best views of the Athabasca Valley.

Jasper Lake lies directly beneath the viewpoint, and the distinctively shaped Pyramid Mountain is seen off to the south near the town of Jasper. To the northeast the Athabasca River flows through the last of the Front Ranges into the forested foothills beyond the park's eastern boundary.

By far the most impressive mountain is Roche Miette, rising across the valley beyond Jasper Lake. The mountain is composed of the massive, cliff-forming Palliser limestone—an Upper Devonian formation. As an early traveller on the Athabasca Trail recounted, Miette's Rock "derives its appellation from a French voyageur, who climbed its summit and sat smoking his pipe with his legs hanging over the fearful abyss."

130 North Boundary Trail

Celestine Lake Road to Berg Lake Parking Lot—179.4 km (111.5 mi)

Backpack

Allow 8 to 14 days

Maximum elevation: 2020 m (6,625 ft)

Minimum elevation: 855 m (2,800 ft)

Maps: Snaring 83 E/1
 Rock Lake 83 E/8
 Blue Creek 83 E/7
 Twintree Lake 83 E/6
 Mount Robson 83 E/3

Access: Drive the Celestine Lake Road to the locked gate at road's end—as described in the *Celestine Lake Road* introduction (see page 249). The hike begins on the road beyond the access gate.

0.0—Celestine Road Gate (1080 m).

0.5—Snake Indian River bridge.

5.2—Junction. Celestine Lake and *Devona Lookout* right.

17.3—Shalebanks Campground.

25.0—Seldom Inn Campground.

26.5—Snake Indian Falls (left 200 m).

27.3—Junction. Trail branches right from road.

35.6—Horseshoe Campground.

37.4—Willow Creek Junction (1355 m). *Willow Creek* trail right.

37.9—Willow Creek Campground.

39.3—Junction. Rock Creek trail right.

43.5—Mud Creek.

46.5—Deer Creek Junction (1395 m). *Glacier Pass* trail right.

46.9—Deer Creek.

49.7—Junction. Welbourne Falls left 0.4 km.

50.6—Welbourne Campground and Warden Cabin.

55.3—Milk Creek.

57.4—Nellie Lake.

61.6—Blue Creek Warden Station.

62.5—Blue Creek Campground.

62.8—Junction. McLaren Pass right.

63.0—Blue Creek suspension bridge.

In the summer of 1910, a party of European alpinists exploring the slopes of Mount Robson heard of an old Indian trail leading down the Smoky River, over a high pass and eastward along the Snake Indian River to the Athabasca Valley. Thinking the route might offer a quick and interesting exit from the mountains, they set off under the guidance of outfitter John Yates and completed the first recorded traverse of today's North Boundary Trail.

Today the North Boundary Trail is one of the best maintained wilderness trails in the Rockies, travelled by scores of backpackers every summer.

Except for Mount Robson and a brief interval on Snake Indian Pass, the trail does not offer spectacular alpine scenery. But the North Boundary country possesses its own unique and subdued brand of beauty—a wilderness of broad valleys and distant views that is inhabited by moose, caribou, bear and wolves.

The traditional eastern terminus of this long wilderness trek is the end of the Celestine Lake Road, approximately 36 km north of Jasper townsite, while the western terminus is Mount Robson's Berg Lake trail.

Though once known as the 100 Mile North Boundary Trail, we have measured the distance at 111.5 miles (179.4 km). You can shorten this by hiking the 14 km Willow Creek trail from Rock Lake on Jasper's northeast boundary to its intersection with the traditional route at km 37.4. While this option saves a day or two of rather tedious travel on the lower Snake Indian River, it misses one of the trail's highlights—Snake Indian Falls. Total distance for the North Boundary using this alternative is 156 km. (See *Willow Creek.*)

The hiking options in such a vast region are endless. Many backpackers only penetrate this wilderness for a day or two before retracing their steps.

Snake Indian Falls

63.3—Blue Creek Junction (1495 m). *Blue Creek* trail right.

74.8—Three Slides Warden Cabin.

77.5—Three Slides Campground.

85.7—Hoodoo Warden Cabin (left 200 m).

90.2—Oatmeal Camp Campground.

96.5—Snake Indian Pass (2020 m).

102.4—Byng Campground.

102.8—Byng Warden Cabin.

110.7—Twintree Lake (1558 m).

111.9—Twintree Warden Cabin.

113.6—Twintree Campground.

115.8—Twintree Creek bridge.

122.9—Donaldson Creek Campground.

125.5—Smoky River bridge.

126.0—Smoky River Junction (1385 m). Lower Smoky River right.

126.4—Lower Smoky Warden Station.

130.1—Chown Creek Campground and bridge. Bess Pass trail right.

137.2—Wolverine Warden Cabin.

138.3—Carcajou Creek.

141.2—Wolverine Campground.

151.3—Moose Pass Junction. *Moose Pass* trail left.

153.7—Adolphus Warden Station.

154.1—Adolphus Campground.

155.9—Adolphus Lake.

156.7—Robson Pass (1652 m). Jasper-Mount Robson Park boundary. Connects with *Berg Lake* trail at km 22.7.

179.4—Berg Lake trail parking area (855 m).

Strong cyclists can travel to Snake Indian Falls and back in a day (biking is permitted on the lower Snake Indian River and Willow Creek trails.) Others use the trail to reach destinations such as McLaren Pass, Glacier Pass, Blue Creek, or the Willmore Wilderness Park. But to most the attraction lies in traversing the entire trail from end to end.

While some hike the North Boundary from west-to-east, our preference is from east-to-west. Travelling in this direction provides a gradual improvement in scenery day by day, culminating at spectacular Mount Robson. Elevation gain is spread out over many kilometres on the east-to-west option and is hardly noticeable, whereas eastbound travellers face two long, gruelling climbs on the first half of their trip and an uninspiring 27 km fire road at the end.

Going east-to-west will require that you plan your trip carefully. Unless you hike from Adolphus Lake Campground (just east of Robson Pass) to the Berg Lake trailhead in a day, you will have to reserve campsites on the popular Berg Lake trail before you begin your trek. (See *Berg Lake* description, Mount Robson Park chapter.)

Celestine Lake Road Gate to Willow Creek Junction—37.4 km. Starting from the access gate on the Celestine Lake Road, you follow roadbed downhill to an iron bridge over the Snake Indian River. For the next 27 km this well-graded road follows upstream along the northeast side of the river. Travel is rather uninspiring along this section except for Snake Indian Falls—one of the most impressive and photogenic waterfalls in the Rockies.

Just beyond the falls, the road splits. Stay on the more substantial roadbed leading left and, a short distance beyond, follow the trail branching right.

At km 34 the trail runs out into broad meadows as it nears the point where the Snake Indian Valley bends to the west and Willow Creek flows in from the north. The country surrounding this junction is quite sublime, with expansive

Snake Indian Pass

views upvalley and north to Daybreak Peak.

Willow Creek Junction to Blue Creek Junction—25.9 km. At km 37.4 the Willow Creek trail intersects from the north. From this junction, the North Boundary route turns westward, passes the Willow Creek Campground, and begins its long journey toward the Great Divide. The country remains pleasant and open as the trail winds through stands of aspen and lodgepole pine and skirts meadows covered with dwarf birch, willow and shrubby cinquefoil.

Near the Deer Creek–Little Heaven trail junction, you pass through windfall created by a storm that swept this section of the valley around 1980. The tornado-like winds, which struck in the early spring, blew due east and uprooted all but the youngest and slimmest lodgepole pines. Trees were hurled into parallel piles like giant jackstraws, cutting a swath approximately 3 km long and 300 m wide.

The valley narrows as you approach the rugged peaks forming the gateway to Blue Creek and the upper Snake Indian Valley. At km 57.4 the trail passes beside Nellie Lake, and the reflection of Mount Simla in this pretty backwater provides the most inspiring view along this section. From here on there is a true sense of having entered the mountains.

Blue Creek is a significant landmark: it serves as the gateway to some very remote and scenic country on the park's northern boundary; the nearby warden station is an important base for much of the patrol activity in the northern section of the park; and, for the westbound hiker, it is the beginning of more strenuous mountain travel.

Blue Creek Junction to Snake Indian Pass—33.2 km. The trail continues west from Blue Creek Campground and, over the next kilometre, passes the McLaren Pass trail junction, crosses the Blue Creek suspension bridge and reaches the Blue Creek trail junction. (See *Blue Creek*.)

The 6 km stretch beyond Blue Creek is quite beautiful, with frequent open views across the Snake Indian River and its marshy, lake-dotted overflow plain. At Three Slides the first major glacier of the trip is seen on the slopes of Upright Mountain, rising at the head of the valley to the south. (Don't be misled into believing it is Mount Robson, as many folks are. You've got a long way to go before you reach that prize.)

At km 85.7 you pass the Hoodoo Warden Cabin and begin the climb to Snake Indian Pass. The moderate but steady uphill lifts you above the trees at km 92, where you receive your first unobstructed view ahead to the narrow gap of the pass.

Snake Indian Pass (2020 m) is set in rolling alpine meadows and contained by low, gentle ridges. Steeply tilted slabs of limestone form the most prominent peaks to the north—Snake Indian and Monte Cristo Mountains.

Since Snake Indian Pass is one of the scenic highlights of the North Boundary Trail, you might plan your itinerary so you can linger here awhile.

Snake Indian Pass to Smoky River Junction—29.5 km. West of the pass the trail descends steadily for 6 km to Byng Campground. The campground is not particularly attractive, but it is a site where many travellers end up after crossing Snake Indian Pass—a boon to local porcupines who delight in passing the night chewing on boots, pack straps and other backpacking paraphernalia.

The descent continues to the shores of Twintree Lake—the largest lake on the North Boundary. The lake received its name in 1910, when John Yates guided his party up Twintree Creek and discovered "a very beautiful lake in our side valley with two infinitesimal islands, on each of which was one fir tree." Meltwater from glaciers on Swoda Mountain and Calumet Peak flow into the lake from the south, filling its waters with glacial silt.

From the lake you continue down Twintree Creek for a short distance before crossing it and climbing over the north end of Twintree Mountain. Beyond the forested crest of this ridge, you make

a stiff 300-m descent over the next 8 km to the Smoky River bridge. It is a rocky, rooty and often boggy track—easily the toughest section on the entire trip.

Smoky River Junction to Robson Pass—30.7 km. You enter a new world once you reach the Smoky River—a region of rocky river flats and rugged, glacier-topped mountains. The valley of Chown Creek, running away to the west at km 130, is particularly scenic, dominated by the grey ramparts of 3216 m Mount Bess.

The climb up the Smoky is relatively gradual, though the track is often rough and rocky. Scenery continues to improve and, at km 144, the trail passes beneath the Mural Glacier and begins a more serious ascent toward Robson Pass.

Weather permitting, the long awaited view of Mount Robson is gained from the open meadow below Adolphus Lake. The lake lies about 1.5 km into the trees beyond this willow-covered meadow, but its western shore opens out onto the broad flats of Robson Pass, where the monarch of the Rockies towers in all its majesty.

Robson Pass to Berg Lake trailhead—22.7 km. When you reach the Mount Robson Park boundary on Robson Pass, you have returned to civilization. Within the space of a few kilometres you pass from a relatively peaceful and primitive landscape into one of the busiest backcountry areas in the mountain parks. However, when the weather cooperates, the scenery is exceptional. (For a detailed description of this final stretch, see *Berg Lake* in the Mount Robson Park chapter.)

North Boundary Options. While the North Boundary Trail as described here is the itinerary of choice for most backpackers, trails branching from the route allow for a great variety of trips. Some of these options are described over the following pages. (See *Willow Creek, Glacier Pass-McLaren Pass, Blue Creek* and *Moose Pass*.)

131 Willow Creek

Rock Lake Road to North Boundary Trail—13.9 km (8.6 mi)

Backpack

Allow 4 hours one way

Elevation loss: 140 m (450 ft)

Maximum elevation: 1495 m (4,900 ft)

Maps: Rock Lake 83 E/8

Access: Follow the Yellowhead Highway (#16) east from Jasper Park East Gate 20 km (12.5 mi) to the junction with Highway 40 (4 km west of Hinton). Follow Highway 40 north 40 km (25 mi) to the Rock Lake Road junction. Turn left and follow the Rock Lake Road 2 km (1.2 mi) to a junction beyond Moberly Creek bridge. Turn left and continue on the most defined road for 27 km (16.5 mi) to Rock Lake Campground, keeping right at major intersections. Keep right at the campground entrance and subsequent intersections, climbing around and above the north side of Rock Lake for 4.3 km (2.7 mi) to road's end at an access gate and parking area at the Wilmore Wilderness Park boundary.

0.0—Rock Lake Road access gate (1495 m).

—Follow roadbed west.

1.8—Junction. Willow Creek trail branches left from road.

—Gradual descent through lodgepole pine forest.

4.8—Willmore-Jasper Park boundary.

6.5—Rock Creek crossing (two channels, ankle-deep).

8.5—Junction. Wolf Pass left.

—Trail follows open valley and crosses boggy willow flats.

12.0—Willow Creek Warden Cabin.

13.9—Junction (1355 m). Intersection with *North Boundary Trail* at km 37.4.

The Willow Creek trail is an important access route into Jasper Park's North Boundary country. As an optional starting point for the North Boundary Trail, it saves 24 km on the trek to Mount Robson and a lot of tedious fire road walking. It is also the best access trail for loop trips north from the North Boundary Trail. The trail's only disadvantages are the lengthy drive to the Rock Lake trailhead and the Rock Creek ford.

From the access gate beyond Rock Lake, hike along the old road into Willmore Wilderness Park. Branch left from the road at km 1.8 and follow trail downhill through a fire-succession forest of lodgepole pine.

Shortly after crossing into Jasper Park, you reach Rock Creek, where there are two channels to cross. Since maintaining bridges here is difficult, expect a double ford (ankle-deep).

South of Rock Creek, the trail is mostly flat and sometimes boggy as it crosses open willow meadows. It passes through the grounds of the Willow Creek Warden Station at km 12.0 and, 2 km beyond, intersects the North Boundary Trail near the Willow Creek Campground (see *North Boundary Trail,* km 37.4).

The Willow Creek trail is open to mountain bikes, as is the lower Snake Indian River trail to the end of the Celestine Road.

Wolf Pass. This 12 km trail branches east from the Willow Creek trail 2 km south of Rock Creek crossing. It skirts the north end of the Boshe Range, then turns southeast and ascends a long forested valley to the summit of Wolf Pass.

Though there is a campground just north of the pass, this rough track is of limited interest for hikers. It is mainly used by wardens patrolling the park boundary between Willow Creek and the Moosehorn Valley. (See also *Moosehorn Lakes-Wolf Pass.*)

132 Moosehorn Lakes—Wolf Pass

Celestine Lake Road to Upper Moosehorn Lake—34.2 km (21.3 mi)

Backpack

Allow 2 days to Moosehorn Lakes

Elevation loss:155 m (500 ft)
gain: 580 m (1,900 ft)

Maximum elevation: 1585 m (5,200 ft)

Maps: Snaring 83 E/1
     Miette 83 F/4
     Entrance 83 F/5
     Rock Lake 83 E/8

Access: Drive the Celestine Lake Road to the locked gate at road's end (see *Celestine Lake Road*, page 249). The hike follows the road beyond the access gate.

0.0—Celestine Road Gate (1080 m).

0.5—Snake Indian River bridge.

1.9—Junction (1160 m). Moosehorn Lakes trail branches right.

4.2—Snake Indian River flats (1005 m).

4.8—Trail enters Snake Indian delta.

9.1—Coronach Creek.

13.5—Junction (1065 m). Moosehorn Creek uphill to left.

15.6—Ronde Creek Campground.

23.3—Moosehorn Creek fords (calf-to knee-deep) next 3.2 km.

27.3—Moosehorn Warden Cabin.

27.5—Moosehorn Campground (1310 m).

27.8—Moosehorn Meadows.

33.9—Moosehorn Pass (1585 m). Park boundary.

34.2—Upper Moosehorn Lake.

35.2—Junction. Wolf Pass left.

37.2—The Keyhole (aka The Notch).

   —Ford stream 32 times next 3 km.

40.0—Junction. Grindstone Pass right.

44.8—Wolf Pass (1935 m). Park boundary.

45.0—Wolf Pass Campground.

48.5—Wolf Pass Warden Cabin.

59.7—Junction. Intersection with *Willow Creek* trail at km 8.5.

"It required a desperate distracted ambition to make anyone go there."

This line from a novel we once read seems appropriate for Moosehorn Lakes. It was always a bit of a struggle, for minimal reward, to reach these two low elevation lakes just beyond Jasper's northeast boundary. Now the approach through the Snake Indian delta has been flooded by beaver, making the traditional access route even more of a trial.

The trail to the lakes from Willow Creek via Wolf Pass is nearly as ridiculous, requiring 32 fords through a narrow canyon called The Keyhole. Of course, you could always hike to the lakes from the Rock Lake Road on a well-pounded 16 km trail used by all-terrain vehicles.

For those who enjoy challenges, and who have spent time wading through thigh-deep swamps in mosquito-infested jungles, we present a distance outline for the circuit from the end of Celestine Lake Road to the Willow Creek trail via Moosehorn Lakes and Wolf Pass.

The first 4.2 km from the Celestine Road gate to the Snake Indian River flats follows an old roadbed and is quite straightforward. We find the flats a pleasant spot in spring when wildflowers are blooming, and there are open views across the valley to Roche Miette. It is a worthwhile half-day trip.

At km 4.8, the trail enters the Snake Indian delta, which is an incredible lush swamp, unlike anything we've seen elsewhere in the Rockies. However, you have to wade through 3 km of beaver bog to continue northeast to Roche Ronde's dry, grassy slopes.

The trail is rough and muddy in the upper Moosehorn Valley, and there are at least three knee-deep fords. Moosehorn Meadows are a valley highlight, and the lakes were nice enough when last we visited, though we hear that ATVs have beaten-up the area around Lower Moosehorn Lake quite badly.

N

20 km
0 5 10 15

Land above 2000 metres

132
130
131
Wolf Pass
Snake Indian Falls
De Smet Range
Mt Haultain
Rock Lake
Daybreak Pk
Creek
Mt Stornoway
Mt Sassenach
Mt Henday
Eagle's Nest Pass
Rock Creek
Creek
133
Deer Creek
Mt Kelsey
130
Indian
The Rajah
The Ranee
Desolation Pass
Mowitch Creek
McLaren Pass
Vega Pk
Glacier Pass
Noonday Pk
Mt Simla
Mt Perce
134
Blue
Topaz Lake
Snake
Creek
Sunset Pk
Snake Indian Mtn
130
Hardscrabble Pass
Saghali Mtn
Azure Lake
Caribou Lakes
Monte Cristo Mtn
Snake Indian Pass
Upright Mtn
Moose River
229
130
Twintree Lake
Wolverine Mtn
Calumet Pk
Moose Pass
ALBERTA
BRITISH COLUMBIA
Twintree Mtn
Swoda Mtn
Calumet Ridge
135
Adolphus Lake
Mumm Pk
Berg Lake
Smoky
Twintree Creek
130
Palu Mtn
Robson Pass
Caratou Cr.
River
Chown Cr.
Mt Phillips
Whitehorn Mtn

133 Glacier Pass—McLaren Pass

North Boundary Trail to Glacier Pass—30.3 km (18.8 mi)
North Boundary Trail to McLaren Pass—19.7 km (12.2 mi)

Backpack

Allow 2 days to Glacier Pass

Elevation gain: 705 m (2,300 ft)

Maximum elevation: 2100 m (6,900 ft)

Maps: Rock Lake 83 E/8
      Blue Creek 83 E/7

Access: Follow the *North Boundary Trail* to the junction with the Glacier Pass trail at km 46.5, just 400 m east of Deer Creek.

0.0—Deer Creek Junction (1395 m).

5.0—Ascent of Deer Creek canyon begins.

8.8—Junction. Rock Creek via lower Mowitch Creek right.

8.9—Little Heaven Campground, Junction. McLaren Pass left 10.8 km.

9.0—Little Heaven Warden Cabin(1690 m).

11.0—Mowitch Creek fords (3) next 200 m (calf to knee deep).

—Trail ascends north side of Mowitch Creek.

19.5—Spruce Tree Campground.

20.3—Junction. Desolation Pass right.

22.6—Vega Warden Cabin.

24.6—Glacier Pass Campground.

27.4—Trail bends north and begins final ascent to pass.

29.4—Glacier Pass (2100 m). Jasper-Willmore Wilderness Park boundary.

The Glacier Pass trail takes you to spectacular alpine meadows and magnificent wilderness scenery on Jasper Park's boundary with the Willmore Wilderness Park. However, the approach is long, sometimes overgrown and confusing, and there are unbridged stream crossings. Most backpackers will want to use this trail to reach McLaren Pass—a more user-friendly trail to an equally high and scenic alpine pass, and one which doesn't require nearly so much time or trouble.

Glacier Pass. The trip to Glacier Pass is for experienced wilderness travellers who don't mind sloshing across streams and beating through willow brush. Arm yourself with current 1:50,000 topo maps, but realize that these maps do not always represent trails accurately.

The trail branches northwest from the North Boundary Trail at km 46.5 and runs north of Deer Creek for nearly 5 km to the mouth of Deer Creek canyon. You climb over 150 m in the canyon before emerging into the meadows of Little Heaven (traditionally, a heavenly pasture for horses). Little Heaven Warden Cabin is on a promontory overlooking this pastoral scene, and the hiker campground and junction for the McLaren Pass trail are reached 100 m before the cabin.

The Glacier Pass trail exits the meadows 2 km north of the warden cabin and crosses to the north side of Mowitch (pronounced MAU-wick) Creek. It makes two more fords over and back across the creek in rapid succession, or you can avoid these by staying on the north side and bushwhacking upstream for 200 m. (Okay, you're boots are already wet, so why bushwhack?)

The trail remains on the north side of Mowitch Creek as it follows it upstream beneath the Starlight Range. Expect boggy, overgrown sections over the next

Glacier Pass

16 km, until you turn north and make the final ascent to Glacier Pass.

A small lake on the grassy summit is a good spot to relax and scan the open slopes for bighorn sheep and caribou. It's also a good place to contemplate your next move, which may be a circuit around the north end of the Ancient Wall to the Blue Creek valley. (See *Blue Creek.*)

McLaren Pass. This is the most attractive and least demanding excursion north from the Snake Indian Valley. A broad alpine meadow crowns McLaren Pass, and views to the southwest are exceptional—including the Snake Indian Valley, the glaciated summit of Upright Mountain, and Mount Robson, 45 km in the distance.

You can use McLaren Pass as an optional and more scenic alternative to the North Boundary Trail between Deer Creek and Blue Creek—a detour that only adds 10.6 km to your trip.

The pass is also a reasonable objective from the Willow Creek trailhead. Distance to the pass via Willow Creek, the

North Boundary Trail and Deer Creek is 43 km. From there you can complete a loop by descending to Blue Creek and returning east along the North Boundary Trail.

The trail branches west from the Glacier Pass trail at Little Heaven Campground and, after a brief descent, joins Deer Creek and follows it upstream. At last report, crossings of Deer Creek and other streams were all bridged along this 3-km section of valley.

Around km 6.5, the trail branches due west from Deer Creek and, after a short, steady ascent, turns south and climbs through open meadows to reach the 2120-m pass at km 10.8. (Vertical ascent from Deer Creek to the pass is 350 m.)

South of the pass the trail drops steeply to the lower Blue Creek valley, where it intersects the trail running up the northeast side of lower Blue Creek. While you can turn right and ascend Blue Creek from this junction, you'll likely turn left and follow the trail downstream 4 km to the North Boundary Trail near the Blue Creek Campground. (See *North Boundary Trail,* km 62.8.)

134 Blue Creek

North Boundary Trail to Azure Lake—33.0 km (20.5 mi)

Backpack

Allow 2 to 3 days to Azure Lake

Elevation gain: 470 m (1,550 ft)

Maximum elevation: 1965 m (6,450 ft)

Maps: Blue Creek 83 E/7
       Twintree Lake 83 E/6

Access: Follow the *North Boundary Trail* to the junction with the Blue Creek trail at km 63.3—300 m west of the Blue Creek suspension bridge.

0.0—Blue Creek Junction (1495 m).

   —Trail crosses dry ridge through lodge-pole pine forest.

8.3—Upper Blue Creek Campground.

8.8—Blue Creek suspension bridge and junction. Blue Creek northeast side trail and McLaren Pass right. Turn left.

   —Trail enters extensive willow meadows.

11.9—Ancient Wall horse campground.

14.7—Topaz Warden Cabin.

16.0—Topaz Campground.

21.1—Natural Arch Horse Campground.

22.7—Natural Arch viewpoint.

23.8—Caribou Inn Campground.

   —Short, steep climb to upper meadows. Trail becomes sketchy.

33.0—Azure Lake.

   —Route to Hardscrabble Pass climbs steeply along slopes north of lake.

35.0—Park boundary.*

36.0—Hardscrabble Pass (2270 m).*

*distances approximate

Blue Creek is one of the most scenic side trips from the North Boundary Trail. Starting near the Blue Creek bridge, the trail runs northwest up the 33-km valley to Azure Lake on the Jasper Park-Willmore Wilderness boundary. Along the way you can visit Topaz Lake and the Caribou Lakes—noted for their fine scenery and fishing. Azure Lake is set in open meadows astride the park boundary, and an hour or so beyond is the rocky, lake-dotted summit of Hardscrabble Pass.

While you can include Blue Creek in your North Boundary Trail itinerary, this adds 3 or 4 days to an already long journey. It is more attractive as a destination. The round trip to the Azure Lake-Hardscabble Pass environs from the Willow Creek trailhead is 146 km—substantially less than hiking the North Boundary Trail end-to-end and, some would say, more rewarding.

The first section of trail from Blue Creek Junction climbs over a dry, pine-covered ridge (there is no reliable source of water for nearly 6 km). You reach Upper Blue Creek Campground at km 8.3 and, 0.5 km beyond, cross the creek on a suspension bridge.

A trail up the northeast side of the valley connects into the main trail here. This trail, which branches from the North Boundary Trail 0.3 km west of Blue Creek Campground, is a bit more scenic than the trail up the southwest side, but rougher and muddier. It also provides access to the McLaren Pass trail, which branches north about 4 km south of this junction. (See *Glacier Pass-McLaren Pass.*)

Continuing upvalley from the bridge and junction, you immediately enter extensive meadows, which dominate the valley for the remainder of the trip.

At Topaz Campground, you can make a 1.7 km side trip to Topaz Lake—a 3-km-long lake set beneath the ramparts of

Mike McReynolds photo

Hardscrabble Pass

Monte Cristo and Snake Indian Mountains. To reach the lake, continue beyond the campground on the main trail approximately 0.4 km and ford Blue Creek. There is no defined trail on the other side, but you can backtrack downstream and pick-up occasional horse tracks and blazes leading over a rise to the lake.

As you continue up Blue Creek, the sawtoothed limestone peaks of The Ancient Wall march away to the northwest ahead of you. Just before Caribou Inn, you arrive at a viewpoint for the Natural Arch—a huge, hollowed-out upfold in the wall beneath the summit of Mount Perce.

From Caribou Inn Campground you can side-trip to Caribou Lakes, which are similar in setting to Topaz Lake. Cross the bridge over Blue Creek to Caribou Inn Warden Cabin and pick-up the rough, often vague 2.5-km track to the lower lake.

If you are planning on returning back down Blue Creek, you may want to camp at Caribou Inn and complete the journey to Azure Lake and Hardscrabble Pass as a day hike. The trail is sketchy in the upper valley, but since the meadows are dry and open, the walk to Azure Lake is quite straightforward and pleasant.

Shortly before arriving at the east end of the lake, find your own route to Hardscrabble Pass by angling up along the open grassy meadows on the north side of the valley. Then traverse a series of rock ledges around the west end of Sunset Peak to this broad alpine summit with its numerous small lakes.

Glacier Pass. By continuing into the Willmore's Sulphur Valley from Hardscrabble Pass (good trail reappears north of the pass), you can reach the South Sulphur River and return to Jasper Park by following it upstream to Glacier Pass. (Horse trails are fairly well-defined on this route, but one 8-km section on the South Sulphur River requires you to ford the river approximately 25 times.)

Though reserved for experienced wilderness backpackers, the Blue Creek-Glacier Pass-Little Heaven loop is one of the most rewarding trips along Jasper's northern boundary. (See *Glacier Pass-McLaren Pass.*)

JASPER NATIONAL PARK   263

135 Moose Pass

North Boundary Trail to Moose Pass—9.5 km (5.9 mi)

Backpack

Allow 3 hours one way

Elevation gain: 410 m (1,350 ft)

Maximum elevation: 2025 m (6,650 ft)

Maps: Mount Robson 83 E/3

Access: Follow the *North Boundary Trail* to the junction with the Moose Pass trail at km 151.3 (2.8 km north of Adolphus Campground).

0.0—Moose Pass Junction (1615 m).

0.1—Smoky River bridge.

0.4—Yates Torrent footbridge.

—Trail climbs over forested ridge.

3.5—Trail reaches Calumet Creek.

—Follow along south side of creek.

6.5—Calumet Campground.

—Steady climb to open meadows.

9.5—Moose Pass (2025 m). Intersection with *Moose River* trail at km 48.9 (see Mount Robson chapter).

Moose Pass is the most attractive side-trip from the North Boundary Trail. Its vast wildflower meadows are renowned as some of the best in the Rockies, and views of heavily glaciated mountains en route are an inspiring bonus.

While the pass can be hiked as a side-trip on the North Boundary trek, it is also an attractive extension from Berg Lake in Robson Park (from Berg Lake, you can pack to Calumet Campground and then day-trip to the pass). You can also cross the pass and descend the Moose River to the Yellowhead Highway, but this is a tough trek reserved for experienced wilderness travellers. (See *Moose River,* Robson Park.)

From the North Boundary Trail junction, the Moose Pass trail immediately crosses the creek-sized Smoky River on a log bridge. The turbulent, silt-choked Yates Torrent, fed by nearby Coleman Glacier, is just beyond (look for a hiker's bridge 300 m upstream from the horse ford, and consider abandoning the trip at this dangerous stream if the bridge is not in place).

After these crossings, the trail climbs eastward over a forested ridge to Calumet Creek. Just over 3 km beyond Yates Torrent, you emerge onto flowery alluvial flats and continue upstream beside Calumet Creek. (Expect overgrown trail with muddy stretches all the way to Calumet Campground.)

Though Calumet is designated as a horse campground, it is a good base for a day trip to the pass. As you continue upvalley from the campground, you gradually emerge into lush meadows with fine views of Calumet Peak and Glacier.

You reach the summit of the pass at km 9.5. Even if you are not backpacking on through, it is worth exploring 3 or 4 km farther along the rocky corridor to a pair of small lakes overlooking the upper Moose Valley.

136 Miette River

Decoigne Road to Miette Lake—24.2 km (15.0 mi)*

Backpack

Allow 7 to 8 hours to Miette Lake

Elevation gain: 930 m (3,050 ft)

Maximum elevation: 2050 m (6,725 ft)

Maps: Jasper 83 D/16
      Rainbow 83 D/15
      Resplendent Creek 83 E/2

Access: Follow the Yellowhead Highway (#16) to Decoigne Warden Station access road, 21 km (13 mi) west of Jasper townsite and 0.2 km east of Jasper Park West Gate. Follow the access road north across the CNR tracks and Miette River bridge 0.4 km to T-intersection. Continue left 0.5 km, past the warden station entrance, to the access gate and parking area.

0.0—Decoigne Road access gate (1120 m).

    —Trail follows roadbed due west.

4.4—Junction. Miette trail branches right.

    —Ascent along east side of Miette Valley.

14.0—Rink Warden Cabin.

19.5—Mt Bridgland tributary ford (knee-deep).

22.0—Miette Lake Campground.

    —Trail crosses Miette twice (knee-deep).

24.0—Junction. Miette Lake and campsite right 150 m. Centre Pass ahead.

    —Trail fords Miette River to west bank. Steady climb to Centre Pass. Trail disappears in meadows.

26.0—Centre Pass (2050 m).

    —Defined track re-emerges west of pass and contours high above Grant Brook.

34.0—Grant Pass (1935 m).

    —Descent to Snaring River headwaters.

36.8—Colonel Pass Campground.

37.0—Colonel Pass (1890 m).

    —Descend north side of Colonel Creek.

43.5—Moose River ford; Junction (1395 m). Intersection with *Moose River* trail at km 24.7 (see Robson Park chapter).

*all distances approximate after 4.4 km.

(Trail is not shown on maps in this book.)

The Miette River trail runs northwest along Jasper Park's west boundary from near Jasper Park West Gate to Miette Lake and Centre Pass. While the country is wild and scenic at the lake and pass, the trail is long and muddy, and there are several fords in the upper valley.

Since we have not personally hiked the trail, use the estimated distances and this description as a rough guide only.

Follow the track of an abandoned railway roadbed along the north side of the Miette River marshes for 4.4 km. The Miette River trail branches right from the roadbed 100 m before it ends where a railway bridge once spanned the river.

The trail upvalley climbs to the east, then rolls through forest. Views are limited and travel is tedious, particularly where the trail is overgrown with alder. The Rink Cabin is the only landmark of note along this section.

After fording a tributary descending from between Mounts Bridgland and Moren, the horse trail crosses and recrosses the Miette (the hikers' trail stays on the east side).

Near km 22, you reach Miette Lake Campground, approximately 2 km below the lake. You have to ford the Miette twice before you reach the short side trail to a campsite overlooking Miette Lake's southern shore.

Immediately beyond the junction, slosh across the Miette one last time, then climb westward into the Centre Pass meadows. The route crosses an open slope north of the true summit.

Though the trail disappears on the pass, a defined track reappears high on the west side (near bluffs) and leads onward to Grant Pass and Colonel Pass.

While trail descends Colonel Creek from Colonel Pass to a ford of the Moose River and an intersection with the *Moose River* trail (see Robson Park), this valley was completely consumed by fire in 1998. The trail is probably a mess.

Yoho National Park

Yoho National Park lies on the western slope of the Great Divide in British Columbia, bordered by Banff Park on the east and Kootenay Park on the south. Covering 1310 sq km of rugged mountain terrain, it is the smallest of the four contiguous national parks.

Yoho's 400-km trail system extends into nearly every corner of the park. While a few trails lead to remote areas, Yoho is best known as a day hiker's park. Most of this activity occurs in three areas—Lake O'Hara, the Yoho Valley and the Emerald Lake basin. The overwhelming popularity of these areas is the result of spectacular terrain coupled with excellent trail systems.

The Trans-Canada Highway runs through the centre of the park, sharing its main valley with the Kicking Horse River and the Canadian Pacific Railroad. The highway provides access to a number of short, scenic hikes, the most popular being Sherbrooke Lake, Paget Lookout and Wapta Falls. Longer but infrequently travelled trails ascend the Amiskwi, Otterhead, Ottertail and Ice River Valleys.

Trails to the world famous Burgess Shale and Mt. Stephen fossil beds are closed to independent hikers. These sites can only be visited on guided interpretive walks organized by the Yoho-Burgess Shale Foundation (see *Sources-Guided walks*).

Backpackers must obtain a Wilderness Pass at the Park Visitor Centre before setting out on any overnight trip. Since campgrounds have quotas, popular areas are often filled during the peak season. If you haven't reserved in advance, keep several options in mind. (There are no designated campgrounds in the Amiskwi, Otterhead and Ice River Valleys, where random camping is allowed.)

Information and services: The Park Visitor Centre is located beside the Trans-Canada Highway at the entrance to the village of Field. It provides a wide range of information on the park, including current trail reports, weather forecasts, schedules for interpretive programs and guided walks, and access information for Lake O'Hara. The visitor centre also houses a park "Friends" retail outlet, which sells books, maps and other park-oriented souvenirs. (See *Sources-Parks information* for contact addresses and numbers.)

There are four road-accessible campgrounds in the park. The most central are Monarch and Kicking Horse Campgrounds, located 5 km east of Field on the Yoho Valley Road. Hoodoo Creek and Chancellor Peak Campgrounds are located along the Trans-Canada Highway not far from the park's west boundary. Kicking Horse Campground is the only site with showers.

The village of Field is the park's only service centre. While it is one of the most scenically situated little towns in western Canada, services are limited to a post office, several cafes and restaurants, a small general store, a lodge and a dozen or so guest houses. The Yoho National Park administration office is located here, as is the office for the Yoho-Burgess Shale Foundation.

Access: The only highway access to Yoho Park is the Trans-Canada Highway. The nearest towns east of Field are Lake Louise (27 km) and Banff (84 km) in Alberta; Golden, B.C. lies 57 km to the west. The nearest international airport is in Calgary, Alberta, 210 km to the east.

While there is no formal bus depot in the park, the Field intersection beside the Park Visitor Centre is a recognized flag stop for east and westbound Greyhound buses.

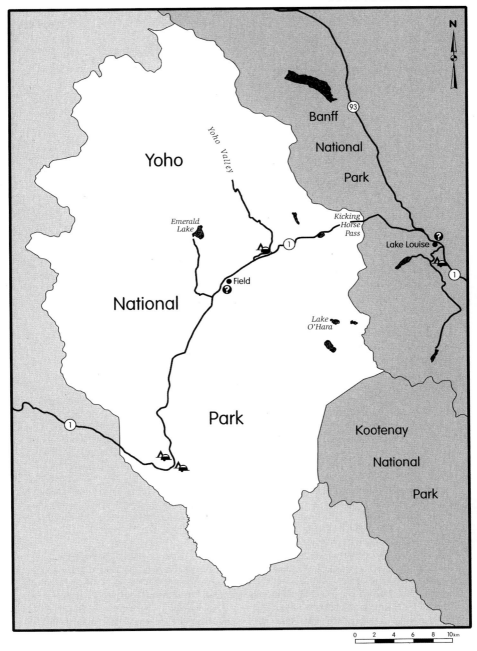

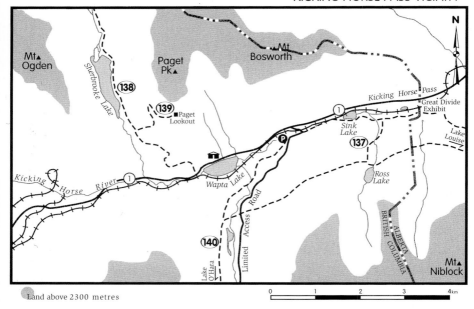

Land above 2300 metres

0   1   2   3   4 km

137 Ross Lake

Great Divide Road to Ross Lake—1.3 km (0.8 mi)

Set within a rugged amphitheatre carved from the walls of the Great Divide, this emerald tarn is a real treat for those who would escape the hiker-choked trails of nearby Lake Louise. And with the closure of the Great Divide Road in 2000, it is even less-visited than it once was. (We like to bike the 2-km paved road to the old trailhead, though you can walk this approach as well.)

The trail only rises 100 m on its brief journey from the old roadside trailhead, following a broad path through a dense, cool forest carpeted by feather mosses and bunchberry. As you near the lake, the Engelmann spruce trees become heavily draped with black *Bryoria* hair lichens, giving the forest a rather ominous, otherworldly appearance. The lake appears suddenly as an emerald flash through the trees just before you cross the horse trail running between Lake Louise and the Lake O'Hara Fire Road.

Ross Lake is a rather modest feature to commemorate the CPR's James Ross— the man in charge of building the railway across the Rockies in 1884. It is backed by the cliffs of Mount Niblock and Narao Peak and lies at an elevation of 1740 m— a few metres higher than Lake Louise.

A boardwalk skirts the marshy northern shoreline, offering a dry causeway to its outlet. Vague paths lead along the east and west shorelines to the boulderfields at its southern end.

Access: Follow the Trans-Canada Highway to the intersection with the Lake O'Hara access road, 2.9 km (1.8 mi) west of the Alberta-B.C. border. Cross the railway tracks and park at the barrier blocking the decommissioned Great Divide Road. Bike or walk along paved road 2.0 km to the Ross Lake trailhead, located on the south side of the road. (Bikes not allowed on the trail.) *Maps: Lake Louise 82 N/8; Yoho National Park; Lake Louise & Yoho (GemTrek)*

Cathedral Mountain from Sherbrooke Lake

138 Sherbrooke Lake

Wapta Lake Picnic Area to Sherbrooke Lake—3.1 km (1.9 mi)

The trip to Sherbrooke Lake is popular with families and anyone looking for an easy half-day outing to a peaceful subalpine lake. It can also be visited as a side-trip on the Paget Lookout hike (see *Paget Lookout*).

Most of the elevation gain comes over the first 1.4 km to Paget Lookout junction, where you climb 165 m through heavy forest. The trail to the lake continues straight ahead at the junction, rising more gradually over the next 0.5 km as it passes though open forest carpeted with subalpine wildflowers. When the trail levels out, the lake is just over a kilometre away.

Sherbrooke is one of the largest backcountry lakes in Yoho Park. Its waters are pale, milky blue—typical of glacier-fed lakes. However, the lake acts as a settling pond for glacial silt from the Niles Glacier, so when Sherbrooke Creek flows out of the lake, it is remarkably clear.

The trail continues along the east shore for another rough and muddy 1.4 km to the lake's north end. Mount Niles (2972 m) dominates the head of the valley, Mount Ogden (2695 m) contains the lake's western shore, and the rugged Cathedral Crags (3073 m) rise back to the south.

A rough trail continues north for 4 km to the Niles Meadows near the valley's headwall. Though this trail is infrequently maintained and sometimes covered by deadfall, the lure of open meadows and impressive cascades is hard to ignore.

Access: Follow the Trans-Canada Hwy to the Wapta Lake Picnic Area, 5.5 km (3.5 mi) west of the Alberta-B.C. border and 11 km (7 mi) east of Field, B.C. The picnic area is located on the north side of the highway 0.4 km west of West Louise Lodge. The trailhead is upslope from the shelter at the far end of the picnic area. *Maps: Lake Louise 82 N/8; Yoho National Park; Lake Louise & Yoho (GemTrek).*

139 Paget Lookout

Wapta Lake Picnic Area to Paget Lookout—3.5 km (2.2 mi)

Half-day trip

Allow 1 to 2 hours one way

Elevation gain: 520 m (1,700 ft)

Maximum elevation: 2135 m (7,000 ft)

Maps: Lake Louise 82 N/8
Yoho National Park
Lake Louise & Yoho (GemTrek)

Access: Follow the Trans-Canada Hwy to the Wapta Lake Picnic Area, 5.5 km (3.5 mi) west of the Alberta-B.C. border and 11 km (7 mi) east of Field, B.C. The picnic area is located on the north side of the highway 0.4 km west of West Louise Lodge and Service Station. The trailhead is just upslope from the shelter at the far end of the picnic area.

0.0—Wapta Lake Picnic Area (1615 m).

0.2—Junction. Trail from lodge intersects from right. Switchback to left.

—Steady uphill through forest.

1.4—Junction. Sherbrooke Lake ahead 1.7 km. Paget Lookout right.

—Steady, steep ascent.

3.5—Paget Lookout (2135 m).

The lookout cabin high on the side of Paget Peak hasn't been manned for many years, but anyone who visits the site will realize why it was considered a crucial vantage point when fire lookouts were being built throughout the mountain parks in the 1940s. Not only does the site overlook the historic Kicking Horse Pass and Valley, but it provides excellent views of the Lake O'Hara environs and the Bow Valley near Lake Louise. However, like most fire lookout trails, it is steep and dry, so be sure to carry water.

The first half-hour climbs through heavy forest along the southern flank of Paget Peak. At 1.4 km, the Sherbrooke Lake trail continues straight ahead and the Paget Lookout option branches right.

After contouring across an avalanche slope, the trail starts gaining altitude again. Though you are climbing at over 1800 m, the dry south-facing exposure displays vegetation normally found at much lower elevations, such as common juniper. A few minutes later, as the exposure becomes more westerly, you encounter subalpine species like whitebark pine. As you navigate a series of steep switchbacks, there are glimpses of the pale turquoise waters of Sherbrooke Lake far below.

The trail reaches the lookout cabin following a final 0.8 km of steep uphill. Perched near the edge of a cliff overlooking Wapta Lake, the lookout is not as high as the 2375 m shown on government topo maps, but it is still lofty enough for some pretty dramatic views. Banff Park's Bow Valley lies to the east beneath the Slate Range and Mount Richardson (3086 m); the Cataract Brook valley runs south to the glacier-mantled peaks of the Lake O'Hara region; and to the southwest the braided river flats of the Kicking Horse Valley are framed between Mounts Stephen and Field.

There is no better vantage point for one of Canada's most important moun-

Kicking Horse Valley from Paget Lookout

tain passes, the Kicking Horse, which lies 5 km east and 485 m beneath the lookout. The pass was discovered by the Palliser Expedition's Dr. James Hector on September 2, 1858, a few days after he was rendered senseless by a kick from his packhorse. In 1884, the CPR's tracks were laid through the pass.

As you overlook the rails plunging into the Kicking Horse Valley, you might wonder if the railway builders couldn't have found a better route. The "Big Hill" remained a dangerous and expensive grade until the Spiral Tunnels were completed inside Mount Ogden and the Cathedral Crags in 1909.

Unlike other mountain parks, Yoho has preserved several of its old lookout cabins as historic reminders of the days when fire suppression was a management priority. The door to the cabin is always open and provides a welcome refuge for hikers on cold, windy days. On warm, sunny days, limestone bluffs above the cabin make wonderful viewpoints where you can relax, dry out sweaty clothing and rehydrate after the stiff climb.

A rough trail leads upwards from the lookout, beckoning strong hikers to follow in the footsteps of the Reverend Dean Paget of Calgary, a founding member of the Alpine Club of Canada who climbed the mountain in 1904. The 2565-m summit lies 430 m above the lookout and can be reached in less than an hour of steady scrambling over loose rock.

Sherbrooke Lake. If you still have energy to burn on your return from the lookout, the 1.7-km side trip to Sherbrooke Lake makes a rewarding finale to the day. (See *Sherbrooke Lake* .)

Lake O'Hara

When veteran hikers get together to reminisce, the name Lake O'Hara comes up early and fondly. It is easy to understand why it is considered such a special place. Within a 5-km radius of Lake O'Hara there are 25 named lakes, numerous high, rugged mountains, and one of the most extensive and well-maintained trail systems in the mountain parks.

The trails, built over a period of nearly 50 summers by Dr. George Link, Carson Simpson and Lawrence Grassi, radiate from Lake O'Hara like spokes from a hub. Hiking options on these trails range from a simple stroll around Lake O'Hara to a challenging traverse high above the lake's basin. Hikers can follow a different trail every day and return to the campground, lodge or Alpine Club hut each evening, making the area an ideal destination for a hiking vacation.

O'Hara's scenery is dominated by the same peaks that form the impressive backdrop for Lake Louise—the continental divide summits of Mounts Lefroy (3423 m) and Victoria (3464 m). The two mountains also rise above one of the area's four distinct hiking areas—the Lake Oesa cirque. A second area is the Opabin Plateau, located between Yukness Mountain (2847 m) and Mount Schäffer (2693 m). Lake McArthur, set between Schäffer Ridge and Park Mountain makes a third. And the Duchesnay Basin, which cradles Linda, Morning Glory, Cathedral and Odaray Lakes is the fourth.

The Lake O'Hara region was first spotted from the summit of Mount Stephen by J.J. McArthur, a government surveyor working along the CPR line in 1887. Lieutenant-Colonel Robert O'Hara, an Irishman who heard about the area from McArthur, visited it shortly thereafter and was so impressed he returned repeatedly to explore its lakes, creeks and mountains.

In 1894, American mountaineer Samuel E.S. Allen completed an amazing day trip to the area from Paradise Valley near Lake Louise via Wastach, Wenkchemna and Opabin Passes. From this trip, and a subsequent visit, he provided the Stoney Indian names for many of the local peaks.

The Alpine Club of Canada held one of its earliest mountaineering camps at Lake O'Hara in 1909, and by 1911 the region was popular enough among alpinists to warrant construction of a cabin, Wiwaxy Lodge, in the Alpine Meadow just west of the lake. The CPR constructed the Elizabeth Parker Hut in the meadow in 1919 and soon after added a number of small cabins to accommodate the growing number of visitors. During the winter of 1925-26 Lake O'Hara Lodge was constructed on the lakeshore, and all of the Alpine Meadow cabins, except the Elizabeth Parker Hut, were moved to the site.

Today, a number of facilities support the many tourists, hikers and climbers who visit the area each summer:

Lake O'Hara Campground, a 30-site Parks Canada campground, is located 0.6 km north of the lake on the west side of the O'Hara access road. While few people hike to the campground, it operates the same as any backcountry campground—a Wilderness Pass is required. One small tent is allowed per site and only two sites can be occupied by a group (no more than six people in a group).

The majority of campers reserve sites for the campground up to three months prior to their visit by calling Parks Canada's Lake O'Hara reservation line (403-343-6433). A reservation fee is charged in addition to the cost of the Wilderness Pass and bus service to the campground (all fees payable by VISA or Mastercard when you make the reservation).

Three to five sites are kept open for those who have not reserved in advance. These

Lefroy Lake on the Lake Oesa trail

YOHO NATIONAL PARK   273

are available by showing up in person at the Parks Canada Visitor Centre in Field on the day prior to your trip. Sites are allocated on a first-come, first-served basis, and there is often a line-up at the door long before the centre opens.

Le Relais is located across the access road from the lakeside warden cabin at the northwest corner of the lake. This log hut sells beverages, snacks, publications and area trail maps. It also serves as a shelter and bus stop for day hikers travelling to and from the area. It is also a good place to visit for current trail conditions.

Lake O'Hara Lodge is located 200 m beyond Le Relais at road's end. It is one of the most delightful and well-appointed backcountry lodges in the Rockies. Guests are accommodated in the main lodge and in outlying cabins. For information and reservations, see *Sources-Backcountry lodges.*

Elizabeth Parker Hut is located in the Alpine Meadow, 0.7 km west of Le Relais by trail. Operated by the Alpine Club of Canada, the large cabin accommodates 24 in summer and can be booked year round. Reservations are made through the Alpine Club's Canmore Clubhouse offices (see *Sources-Huts*).

Abbot Pass Hut was constructed by the CPR in 1922 as the first high altitude climbers' hut in Canada. It is located on the crest of the Great Divide between Lake O'Hara and Lake Louise and is reached via an extremely steep 2-km scramble (see *Lake Oesa*). While it is still used primarily by climbers, strong hikers who are experienced rock scramblers often make the climb from Lake O'Hara and overnight there. The hut, which accommodates 24, is operated by the Alpine Club of Canada. Reservations are made through the Alpine Club (see *Sources-Huts*).

Access: Most O'Hara trips begin from the parking area at the bottom of the O'Hara access road. The parking lot is reached by following the Trans-Canada Highway to its junction with the Lake O'Hara access road, located 3.2 km (2 mi) west of the Alberta-B.C. boundary and 1.6 km (1 mi) east of the lodge at Wapta Lake. Follow the paved road across the CPR tracks and turn right onto the 0.8-km gravel road leading down to the parking lot.

Most visitors travel to Lake O'Hara on the shuttle bus, which makes four round trips on the access road each day during the June 19 to October 1 season (two round trips October 1 to 7). In order to protect the fragile meadows in the area and to reduce the impact on wildlife, a quota limits the number of people who can access the area by bus. Most of this quota is filled by those with reservations at the campground, the lodge, the Elizabeth Parker Hut, and the Abbot Pass Hut.

You may also hike to the lake on the 11-km access road or the unmaintained 13.5-km Cataract Brook trail, which begins at the rear of the upper parking lot (see *Cataract Brook*). Cyclists are not permitted on the access road.

A limited number of seats on the bus are available for day users, who can reserve 3 months in advance through the O'Hara line (403-343-6433). Six day-use seats can be reserved in person at the Visitor Centre the day before the trip on a first-come, first-served basis (people often line-up at the Visitor Centre door at the break of day for these prized seats).

The bus departs the lower parking lot at 8:30 a.m., 10:30 a.m., 4:30 p.m., and 7:30 p.m.; the outbound bus leaves Lake O'Hara at 7:30 a.m., 9:30 a.m., 3:30 p.m., and 6:30 p.m. (Note: Lake O'Hara is in the Mountain Time Zone, not Pacific.) While this schedule was in effect for the 2002 season, changes can occur, so always double-check the bus schedule when you reserve. (See *Sources-Park information*.)

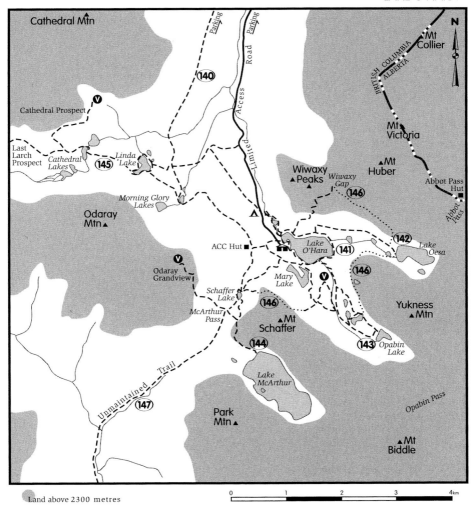

LAKE O'HARA

Cathedral Mtn

Mt Collier

N

BRITISH COLUMBIA
ALBERTA

Parking

Parking

140

Access

Road

Mt
Victoria

V

Cathedral Prospect

Limited

Abbot Pass
Hut

Last
Larch
Prospect

145

*Cathedral
Lakes*

*Linda
Lake*

Wiwaxy
Peaks

*Wiwaxy
Gap*

▲Mt
Huber

Abbot
Pass

146

*Morning Glory
Lakes*

Odaray
Mtn▲

146

ACC Hut

*Lake
O'Hara*

141

142

*Lake
Oesa*

V

Odaray
Grandview

*Mary
Lake*

146

V

*Schaffer
Lake*

Yukness
▲Mtn

*McArthur
Pass*

146

▲Mt
Schaffer

143

*Opabin
Lake*

Trail

144

*Lake
McArthur*

Opabin Pass

Unmaintained

147

Park
Mtn▲

▲Mt
Biddle

Land above 2300 metres

0   1   2   3   4km

YOHO NATIONAL PARK   275

140 Cataract Brook

Lake O'Hara Parking Area to Lake O'Hara—13.5 km (8.4 mi

Day trip or backpack

Allow 4 hours one way

Elevation gain: 435 m (1,425 ft)

Maximum elevation: 2035 m (6,650 ft)

Maps: Lake Louise 82 N/8
Yoho National Park
Lake Louise & Yoho (GemTrek)

Access: Follow the Trans-Canada Highway to its junction with the Lake O'Hara access road, 2.9 km (1.8 mi) west of the Alberta-B.C. border and 13.4 km (8.3 mi) east of Field, B.C. Follow paved road across the CPR tracks and turn right onto gravel road leading downhill 0.8 km to the Lake O'Hara parking area. The trail begins from the rear of a small, overflow parking lot above the main parking area.

0.0—O'Hara Parking Area (1600 m).

1.5—Cataract Brook bridge.

2.5—Junction. Old road from Wapta Lake intersects from right.

3.5—Narao Lakes.

—Trail climbs along lower slopes of Cathedral Mountain.

9.5—Duchesnay Creek bridge.

10.2—Junction. Linda Lake right 1.0 km. Straight ahead to Morning Glory Lakes (0.8 km) and the Alpine Meadow (2.6 km). O'Hara Campground left.

10.5—Morning Glory Creek bridge.

11.0—Junction. O'Hara Campground right.

12.9—Lake O'Hara Campground.

—Follow O'Hara access road right to Lake O'Hara and lodge.

13.5—Lake O'Hara. Le Relais hut.

13.7—Lake O'Hara Lodge (2035 m).

Prior to construction of the access road, visitors reached Lake O'Hara on foot or horseback by following the trail along the west side of the Cataract Brook valley. If you want to enter or exit the Lake O'Hara region on foot today, it is faster to do so on the access road, which provides a better walking surface and is 2 km shorter. But if you would like to take a more aesthetic and historical approach, you can still follow the old trail. You should be aware that the trail is no longer maintained (expect deadfall) and Parks Canada does not recommend the route due to possible disturbance of wildlife.

From the parking area at the foot of the O'Hara access road, the trail runs southwest through the forest and makes a short climb to Hector Gorge and a bridged crossing of Cataract Brook. At km 2.5 you cross an old access road (stay on the footpath), and in another kilometre the trail runs alongside swampy meadows cradling the Narao Lakes, where views open eastward to Narao Peak.

Beyond Narao Lakes the trail climbs through a major rockslide and then into a forest of lodgepole pine and Engelmann spruce. Avalanche slopes along these steep slopes provide views over the Cataract Valley.

At 10.2 km you come to a four-way intersection, which is just 1.0 km east of Linda Lake and 0.8 km north of Morning Glory Lakes. Take the trail to the left and, at a junction 0.8 km farther along, turn right and climb through rocky subalpine forest to the O'Hara Campground. Continue through the campground to the O'Hara access road and follow it to the right for another 10 minutes to reach the lake.

If you are not staying at the campground, you can continue straight ahead at the 10.2-km four-way junction for a slightly longer but more scenic arrival at Lake O'Hara via Morning Glory Lakes and the Alpine Meadow.

Lake O'Hara

141 Lake O'Hara Circuit

Lakeshore Circuit—2.8 km (1.7 mi)

The Adeline Link Circuit is another name for the footpath that loops around the Lake O'Hara shoreline. Dr. George Link and his wife Adeline, along with a few other Lake O'Hara regulars, began work on the trail in 1943. Adeline died of a stroke the following autumn at her home in Chicago, and the trail was completed and dedicated to her memory in 1946.

As you might expect, this walk along the shore of one of the Rockies' most beautiful lakes is a very special experience, particularly in the evening when the last rays of sun are illuminating the O'Hara basin. The trail is also the starting point for trips to Wiwaxy Gap (Alpine Circuit), Lake Oesa and the Opabin Plateau—trails branching upwards at various points along the circuit.

Starting from the Cataract Creek outlet bridge, follow the trail east along the north shoreline. Trails to Wiwaxy Gap and Lake Oesa branch left at km 0.2 and 0.8 respectively. At km 1.2, the rolling path passes beneath the beautiful Seven Sisters Falls (also known as Seven Veils Falls).

Along the lake's south shore, the Opabin Plateau East and West Circuits branch upslope at km 1.8 and 2.1. Lake O'Hara Lodge is reached at km 2.4, and from there it is a short 400 m walk along the access road to the northwest corner of the lake where you began.

Access: Travel to Lake O'Hara as described in the *Lake O'Hara* introduction. Walk to the trailhead at the Cataract Creek bridge, located at the northwest corner of Lake O'Hara, 150 m north of the Le Relais hut and the warden cabin. *Maps: Lake Louise 82 N/8; Yoho National Park; Lake Louise & Yoho (GemTrek).*

142 Lake Oesa

Lake O'Hara to Lake Oesa—3.2 km (2.0 mi)

Half-day trip

Allow 1 to 1.5 hours one way

Elevation gain: 240 m (785 ft)

Maximum elevation: 2275 m (7,460 ft)

Maps: Lake Louise 82 N/8
    Yoho National Park
    Lake Louise & Yoho (GemTrek)

Access: Travel to Lake O'Hara as described in the *Lake O'Hara* introduction. Walk to the trailhead at the Cataract Creek bridge, located at the northwest corner of Lake O'Hara 150 m north of the Le Relais hut and the warden cabin.

0.0—Lake O'Hara outlet bridge (2035 m).

—Follow lakeshore trail east.

0.2—Junction. Wiwaxy Gap left. Stay right.

0.8—Junction. Lake Oesa trail branches left, uphill from lakeshore circuit.

—Steep climb and steady uphill over rockfall and benchlands.

2.4—Lawrence Grassi memorial plaque.

2.5—Victoria Lake and Junction. Shortcut to Yukness Ledge Alpine Route right.

3.0—Junction. Intersection with *Alpine Circuit* at km 4.1. Yukness Ledge Alpine Route right, Wiwaxy Gap left.

3.2—Lake Oesa (2275 m).

Set in a high, barren cirque beneath the towering walls of the Great Divide, Lake Oesa is one of the many exquisite lakes ringing Lake O'Hara. While the trail's inspired design and the area's rugged scenery make it one of our favourites, it is also the one of the most heavily travelled trails in the O'Hara region. We usually avoid the heavy traffic by hiking it late in the day.

From the Cataract Brook bridge at the northwest corner of Lake O'Hara, follow along the lake's north shoreline. At km 0.8, the trail to Lake Oesa branches left from the lakeshore and climbs steeply to the top of a cliff, where you have a fine view back across the lake to the lodge.

Beyond the cliff viewpoint, the grade moderates as the trail rises in steps over a series of rocky terraces leading to Lake Oesa. Three small lakes are passed along the way—Yukness Lake, Lake Victoria and Lefroy Lake.

At 2.4 km you pass a plaque commemorating Lawrence Grassi. Although Grassi spent most of his life as a coal miner in Canmore, Alberta, he is best remembered for his dedication to mountaineering and trail building in the Rockies. After retiring from the mines in the late 1950s, he worked as a warden at Lake O'Hara and built many of the area's most inspired trails.

The trail reaches its maximum elevation on a rise overlooking Lake Oesa at km 3.0. The lake's name is the Stoney Indian word for "ice," so-called because it is frozen for much of the year.

Guarding the lake are Yukness Mountain (2847 m) to the south and Mount Huber (3368 m) to the north. Hidden in the towering walls beyond the lake is Abbot Pass (2922 m)—the main alpine route between Lake O'Hara and Lake Louise.

The lakeshore is composed of rockslides and talus slopes, which are home to pikas and hoary marmots.

Lake Oesa

Alpine Circuit. The high level alpine route contouring around the rocky heights of the Lake O'Hara basin crosses the Oesa trail at its highest point, 200 m west of the lake.

By hiking north on this steep route, you can reach Wiwaxy Gap in 2.0 km and then descend back to Lake O'Hara. If you follow the circuit to the south, you traverse the Yukness Ledge Alpine Route and reach the Opabin Plateau trail after 2.3 km of steep, rocky scrambling. (See *Alpine Circuit.*)

Abbot Pass. The junction of the Alpine Circuit with the Oesa trail also serves as the starting point for rock scramblers bound for Abbot Pass. After briefly following the track north toward Wiwaxy Gap, the Abbot Pass route breaks away and contours across talus slopes above Lake Oesa's north shore. Near the east end of the lake, you begin the ascent of the steep couloir leading to the pass.

There is no trail to the pass, only scramblers' tracks in the scree. The climb is steep and gruelling, and loose rocks are often dislodged, much to the distress of those below. It is also a dangerous area when snow-covered (an avalanche has claimed one life on this steep slope).

The Abbot Pass Hut is operated by the Alpine Club of Canada, and scramblers and climbers can overnight there for a nominal fee. (See *Sources-Huts.*) Only fully equipped mountaineers should consider completing the hazardous traverse beyond the pass to Lake Louise.

143 Opabin Plateau

Lake O'Hara Lodge to Opabin Lake—3.2 km (2.0 mi)
Opabin Plateau Circuit—5.9 km (3.7 mi)

Half-day trip

Allow 1 to 1.5 hours one way

Elevation gain: 250 m (820 ft)

Maximum elevation: 2285 m (7,500 ft)

Maps: Lake Louise 82 N/8
Yoho National Park
Lake Louise & Yoho (GemTrek)

Access: Travel to Lake O'Hara as described in the *Lake O'Hara* introduction. From Lake O'Hara Lodge, descend to the lakeshore and follow the trail south beyond the shoreline cabins.

0.0—Lake O'Hara Lodge (2035 m).

—Follow *Lake O'Hara Circuit* trail south.

0.3—Junction. Opabin Plateau West Circuit right.

0.4—Junction. Trail from Alpine Meadow intersects from right.

0.5—Mary Lake.

—Steep climb beneath Opabin Plateau cliffs.

1.6—Junction. All Souls Prospect right. Opabin Prospect left (50 m).

—Grade levels out.

1.9—Junction. Opabin Prospect trail rejoins from left.

—Bridged stream. Opabin Plateau Highline left.

2.6—Junction. Opabin Plateau Highline rejoins from left.

—Trail skirts Hungabee Lake west shore.

—Climb to head of valley.

3.2—Opabin Lake (2285 m). Opabin East Circuit down-valley to left.

3.5—Hungabee Lake east shore.

3.6—Junction. Yukness Ledge Alpine Route right.

4.2—Steep descent into forest begins.

5.3—Junction. Intersection with *Lake O'Hara Circuit* trail at km 1.8. Lake O'Hara Lodge left.

5.9—Lake O'Hara Lodge (2035 m).

The Opabin Plateau Circuit is one of the classic hikes of the Rockies. The plateau is a short hike from Lake O'Hara Lodge and the Elizabeth Parker Hut, but you can easily spend a full day exploring and photographing its larch-fringed meadows and numerous small lakes. It is little wonder Opabin was a favourite locale for a number of Canadian landscape artists.

The circuit makes an elongated loop, which runs up one side of the plateau and down the other. The west and east side trails are known as the Opabin Plateau West Circuit and the Opabin Plateau East Circuit. Because it is the shortest route, the West Circuit is usually used on the approach from Lake O'Hara. Along the way a network of criss-crossing trails leads to scenic points within the loop. One of the Lake O'Hara area trail maps, sold at the Le Relais hut and the lodge, is essential to understanding all the options.

Starting from Lake O'Hara Lodge, follow the O'Hara lakeshore circuit in a counterclockwise direction, heading south along the lake's west shore. Just 300 m beyond the lodge complex, the West Circuit trail branches right. After passing Mary Lake, it climbs steeply through cliffs forming the northern escarpment of the plateau.

The trail reaches the top of the cliff at km 1.6, where a short trail branches left to Opabin Prospect—an outstanding cliff-top viewpoint overlooking Lake O'Hara, the Cataract Valley and the distant summit of Cathedral Mountain.

Beyond the Opabin Prospect junction, the trail enters the plateau meadows, passes along the west shore of Hungabee Lake and ascends a rocky benchland to the head of the valley and Opabin Lake. (A highline trail branches left from the trail at km 1.9, traverses the crest of a rocky ridge leading upvalley, and rejoins the main trail at km 2.6.) Until you reach the benchland at the valley's head, you

Odaray and Cathedral Mountains from Opabin Plateau

are continually passing through stands of alpine larch—a photographer's dream in mid-September when their needles have turned to gold.

From the alpine shores of Opabin Lake you have fine views in all directions. Great, glowering walls rise above the head of the valley, the most impressive being Hungabee Mountain (3492 m) and Mount Biddle (3319 m), which guard Opabin Pass and Glacier to the south. Hungabee means "the chieftain" in Stoney, while Opabin means "rocky"; both were named by the American mountaineer Samuel E.S. Allen following his solo journey into the area via Opabin Pass in August, 1894.

From Opabin Lake, you complete the circuit by returning to Lake O'Hara on the East Circuit trail. The trail descends through alpine meadow and a scattering of stunted larch trees as it skirts great rockslides beneath Yukness Mountain. (Watch for hoary marmots and pikas.)

After passing the east shore of Hungabee Lake a kilometre below Opabin Lake, the trail drops into forest and descends steeply to Lake O'Hara.

You reach the lakeshore trail just 300 m east of the West Circuit junction. You can complete the Opabin Circuit by turning left and walking back to the lodge, or go right and continue around the lake to the O'Hara access road near the Le Relais hut.

Yukness Ledge Alpine Route. This section of the Alpine Circuit branches from the Opabin East Circuit at km 3.6 beside the east shore of Hungabee Lake. By following this route across the rockslides and ledges of Yukness Mountain, you can complete a highline traverse to Lake Oesa. An Opabin Plateau-Lake Oesa loop trip makes a good full day outing.

All Souls Prospect Alpine Route. The All Souls trail, which branches from the Opabin West Circuit at km 1.6, is the western end of the Alpine Circuit. This rugged, 1.8 km alpine route crosses All Souls Prospect to Schäffer Lake on the Lake McArthur trail. (See *Alpine Circuit* for descriptions of both alpine routes.)

144 Lake McArthur

Lake O'Hara to Lake McArthur—3.5 km (2.2 mi)

Half-day trip

Allow 1 to 1.5 hours one way

Elevation gain: 310 m (1,025 ft)

Maximum elevation: 2345 m (7,700 ft)

Maps: Lake Louise 82 N/8
    Yoho National Park
    Lake Louise & Yoho (GemTrek)

Access: Travel to Lake O'Hara as described in the *Lake O'Hara* introduction. The hike begins from the trailhead beside Le Relais hut on the O'Hara access road, 0.6 km south of the campground and 0.2 km north of the lodge.

0.0—Lake O'Hara access road (2035 m).

—Trail climbs to Alpine Meadow.

0.3—Junction. Big Larches Route to Schäffer Lake left. Keep right.

—Trail crosses Alpine Meadow.

0.6—Elizabeth Parker Hut and Junction. Linda Lake right. Keep left.

—Moderate to steep uphill.

1.5—Junction. Big Larches Route rejoins from left.

1.6—Schäffer Lake and Junction. McArthur Pass right. Stay left for Lake McArthur high route.

—Trail climbs shoulder of Mt. Schäffer and skirts rockslide.

2.4—Junction (2210 m). McArthur Pass-Odaray Highline right. Lake McArthur left.

—Moderate to steep uphill along cliffs and boulderfields.

3.0—Trail summit (2345 m).

—Gradual descent to lake.

3.5—Lake McArthur (2250 m).

Lake McArthur is the largest and deepest lake in the O'Hara area. The 85 m depth of the lake contributes to its deep blue colour, which contrasts with the brilliant white of the Biddle Glacier beyond its far shore. The pyramid-shaped summit of Mount Biddle rises above the glacier, lending a symmetry to the scene that has attracted artists and photographers for decades.

The trail leads to the Alpine Meadow from the trailhead beside the Le Relais hut. At a junction beside the Elizabeth Parker Hut, keep left and climb southwest through dense subalpine forest to Schäffer Lake.

Just 50 m beyond the Schäffer Lake outlet bridge, the high trail to Lake McArthur branches left from the McArthur Pass trail. This high option skirts around the lake's south shore and then climbs steeply through alpine larch to the shoulder of Mount Schäffer. It then follows the edge of a rock band for a short distance, where there are good views north to Cathedral Mountain.

At km 2.4 you pass the junction for the short connector trail leading down to McArthur Pass and the Odaray Grandview trail (see below). Stay left and continue on the high trail as it bends around the west ridge of Mount Schäffer and climbs along cliffs and boulderfields to the trail summit and the first view of Lake McArthur. The final 0.5 km descends through beautiful alpine meadows and rocky ridges to the lake.

Big Larches Route. This alternate trail branches south from the Lake McArthur trail at km 0.3, on the eastern edge of the Alpine Meadow. It runs 0.3 km toward Mary Lake, then branches right and climbs steeply along a rockslide beneath Mount Schäffer's cliffs. You pass through stands of giant alpine larch on the ascent, then rejoin the main trail at km 1.5 on the shores of Schäffer Lake.

Lake McArthur and Mount Biddle

This option is only 300 m longer than the main trail, but since it is very steep and rocky in places, it is usually hiked on the return from Lake McArthur.

Odaray Grandview. This optional side-trip from the Lake McArthur trail follows the Odaray Highline and Grandview trails north from McArthur Pass to a high viewpoint on the east slope of Odaray Mountain. Odaray Grandview overlooks much of the O'Hara basin, including Lake O'Hara and nearly all of its outlying lakes. Along the way you also have a "grand view" of the Goodsirs, Yoho's highest peaks, across the Ottertail Valley to the south.

While you can reach the Odaray Highline by hiking directly to McArthur Pass from Schäffer Lake, we prefer the Lake McArthur high route approach (it's a bit longer but more open and scenic).

From the high route junction at km 2.4, descend to McArthur Pass and pick-up the Odaray Highline running north. At a junction 1.1 km beyond McArthur Pass, the Grandview trail branches uphill to the left. The last 1.0 km is more alpine route than trail, mostly following paint marks and cairns up a very steep slope. A large cairn atop a moraine marks the Grandview summit viewpoint.

Restrictions: Since Parks Canada has identified McArthur Pass and the Odaray Plateau to be part of a narrow wildlife corridor occasionally used by grizzly bears and other species travelling between McArthur Creek and the Cataract Valley, it has imposed travel restrictions on the Odaray Highline route and closed all other trails on the plateau.

During summer 2000, Parks will allow hikers unsupervised access to the Odaray Highline trail with certain voluntary restrictions. This is considered a pilot project, so check at the park visitor centre, the parks website, the Le Relais hut or the lodge for a policy update before hiking this trail.

145 Linda Lake—Cathedral Basin

Lake O'Hara Campground to Linda Lake—3.7 km (2.3 mi)
Lake O'Hara Campground to Cathedral Basin—7.4 km (4.6 mi)

Day trip

Allow 2 to 3 hours to Cathedral Basin

Elevation gain: 305 m (1,000 ft)

Maximum elevation: 2315 m (7,600 ft)

Maps: Lake Louise 82 N/8
Yoho National Park
Lake Louise & Yoho (GemTrek)

Access: Travel to Lake O'Hara as described in the *Lake O'Hara* introduction. From near the last campsite on the north edge of the O'Hara Campground, follow the trail leading into the forest.

0.0—Lake O'Hara Campground (2010 m).

—Gradual descent through forest.

1.9—Junction. O'Hara access road right. Linda Lake left.

2.4—Morning Glory Creek bridge.

2.7—Junction. Cataract Brook trail right. Morning Glory Lakes and Alpine Meadow left. Linda Lake ahead.

3.7—Linda Lake and Junction (2090 m). Keep right.

—Trail circles north side of Linda Lake.

4.5—Junction. Linda Lake south shore left. Cathedral Basin right.

—Gradual uphill.

5.6—Cathedral Lakes.

—Gradual to moderate uphill.

6.1—Junction. Duchesnay Pass and Last Larch Prospect left. Cathedral Basin right.

—Steep uphill via forest and rockslide.

6.6—Uphill ends.

—Trail contours right toward Cathedral Basin.

7.1—Cathedral Platform Prospect (2315 m).

7.4—Cathedral Basin and Monica Lake.

The trail to Linda Lake and the Cathedral Basin is the longest hike from Lake O'Hara. It is also the least crowded. Pleasant subalpine lakes along the way, coupled with a spectacular overview of the O'Hara basin from Cathedral Platform Prospect, make it a very rewarding trip.

Starting from the north end of O'Hara Campground, the trail descends through forest for 1.9 km to a broad trail running west from the O'Hara access road. Turn left and continue 1.8 km to Linda Lake. Stay right on the lake's north shoreline trail and follow it to fine views back across the lake to distant Hungabee Mountain, Mount Biddle, and other peaks beyond Lake O'Hara.

If you are looking for a short, easy hike, Linda Lake is sufficient reward. But the real glory of this area is the Cathedral Basin, 3.7 km farther along and 225 m higher up.

To reach the Cathedral Basin, continue around Linda Lake and follow the trail branching west at the far end of the lake. This trail climbs gradually through subalpine forest interspersed with meadows. At km 5.6, it crosses a bridge between the first and second Cathedral Lakes. The lower lake, also known as Vera Lake, is situated in a meadowy area overlooked by the north wall of Odaray Mountain. Just 0.4 km beyond, the Last Larch Prospect junction is passed, and the steep ascent to Cathedral Basin begins.

The last 1.3 km follows rough, rocky trail, which is frequently more route than track. After climbing through a major rockslide, the trail contours east to the mouth of the Cathedral Basin.

Views on the ascent are outstanding, but they reach their pinnacle at the lip of the cirque—the Cathedral Platform Prospect. No other viewpoint gives quite so complete an overview of the Lake O'Hara region. High on the side of

Lake O'Hara basin from Cathedral Prospect

Cathedral Mountain, you are viewing the area much as surveyor J.J. McArthur did when he first saw it from the summit of nearby Mount Stephen in 1887. The upper Cataract Valley stretches southeast to Lake O'Hara and its surrounding peaks. The meadows and lakes of the Duchesnay Valley lie immediately below, backed by the north face of Odaray Mountain.

A short stroll down through alpine meadow from the Prospect brings you to tiny Monica Lake in the heart of the Cathedral Basin cirque.

Linda Lake via Alpine Meadow—4.7 km. If you are staying at Lake O'Hara Lodge or the Elizabeth Parker Hut, we suggest you follow the trail running north from the Alpine Meadow to Linda Lake. While this alternate route to the lake is slightly longer, it passes by the second Morning Glory Lake and is a bit more interesting than the trail from the campground.

If you are starting from Lake O'Hara, hike the Alpine Meadow trail from the access road to the junction in front of the Elizabeth Parker Hut. Keep right and continue on the trail leading north, skirting a small pond at the far end of the meadow and entering the forest beyond.

From the Alpine Meadow, the trail contours through dense subalpine forest for 1.8 km and then descends to cross Morning Glory Creek at the inlet to the second Morning Glory Lake. The shortcut to Linda Lake branches left just beyond the stream crossing.

The shortcut from Morning Glory Lakes is very rocky and rooty. It makes a moderately steep ascent through forest, then descends to the south shore of Linda Lake. Turn left to reach the junction with the standard route (km 4.5) at the west end of the lake. Stay left to continue on to Cathedral Basin, or turn right to skirt back along the lake's north shore.

146 Alpine Circuit

Lake O'Hara Alpine Circuit—11.8 km (7.3 mi)

Day trip

Allow 4 to 5 hours round trip

Minimum elevation: 2035 m (6,675 ft)

Maximum elevation: 2530 m (8,300 ft)

Maps: Lake Louise 82 N/8
Yoho National Park
Lake Louise & Yoho (GemTrek)

Access: Travel to Lake O'Hara as described in the *Lake O'Hara* introduction. Walk to the trailhead at the Cataract Creek bridge, located at the northwest corner of Lake O'Hara 150 m north of the Le Relais hut and the warden cabin.

0.0—Lake O'Hara outlet bridge (2035 m).

— Follow lakeshore trail.

0.2—Junction. Wiwaxy Gap left.

— Very steep, steady uphill.

2.1—Wiwaxy Gap (2530 m).

— Steep descent to southeast.

4.1—Junction (2275 m). Cross *Lake Oesa* trail at km 3.0. Lake Oesa left 0.2 km.

— Cross Oesa outlet and traverse Yukness Ledge Route.

6.4—Junction. Intersection with *Opabin Plateau* trail at km 3.6. Follow Opabin East Circuit left.

6.8—Opabin Lake (2285 m). Follow Opabin West Circuit right.

8.4—Junction. Opabin Prospect right. Follow All Souls' Route to left at junction 50 m ahead.

— Meadows followed by steep, rocky ascent.

9.3—All Souls' Prospect (2475 m).

— Extremely steep descent (loose rock and ledges).

10.2—Junction. Big Larches trail right. Schäffer Lake left.

10.3—Schäffer Lake Junction. Intersection with *Lake McArthur* trail at km 1.5.

11.8—Lake O'Hara (2035 m).

The Alpine Circuit traverses high above the Lake O'Hara basin and allows you to survey much of the region's best scenery on a single outing. However, most of this circuit is not over traditional trail, but instead follows rough paths, paint marks and cairns across steep slopes, through rockslides, and along exposed ledges. The circuit was once called the "Alpinist's Traverse", an appropriate name when stormy weather or lingering snow transforms the hike into a hazardous expedition.

Yet, when the weather is fine, and the route is bare and dry, the scramble around this inspired route is surprisingly straightforward. But even under the best conditions, it should only be undertaken by fit hikers who are not bothered by exposed heights.

Starting the circuit by climbing to Wiwaxy Gap is more strenuous than by heading to Schäffer Lake and All Souls' Prospect first and then moving around the basin counterclockwise. But by labouring up Wiwaxy first, you put the toughest climb behind you early in the day, and if you can scamper to this lofty col without undue fear or suffering, you'll know you're tough enough for the trip.

Start at O'Hara's outlet bridge and follow the lakeshore trail 0.2 km to where the Wiwaxy trail branches uphill to the left. The distance to the gap is just under 2 km, but it will seem twice as far. In addition to wiggling straight up through forest and across scree, the narrow path skirts exposed ledges—wide enough to walk comfortably but just a step away from lots of air.

Wiwaxy Gap is a grand viewpoint for the O'Hara basin. In addition to views back across the lake, the col looks north to the lower Cataract Valley and the mountains near Kicking Horse Pass.

From the gap the route makes a descending traverse along the south slope

Lake O'Hara from All Souls' Prospect

of Mount Huber to Lake Oesa, which is frequently visible ahead. Its all ledges and steep rockslides, but paint marks and cairns keep you on-route.

The Alpine Circuit crosses the Oesa trail on a rocky knoll 200 m west of the lake, and if you made an early start, it is a fine place to stop for lunch.

Beyond this bluff a new traverse begins (watch for paint marks), descending to cross the Oesa outlet stream and then climbing west to the tumbled cliffs of the Yukness Ledge Alpine Route. This traverse, which skirts around Yukness Mountain and drops you onto the Opabin Plateau, is very steep, rocky and demanding (watch carefully for paint marks and cairns).

After intersecting the Opabin East Circuit, walk the well-graded Opabin Plateau trail to the head of the valley. From Opabin Lake descend the opposite side of the plateau on the Opabin West Circuit. The short detour to Opabin Prospect on the northern lip of the plateau is

a worthwhile diversion, and when you return to the Opabin West Circuit, you are just 50 m from the next important junction—the trail to All Souls' Prospect.

The All Souls' Alpine Route is the last traverse and, in some respects, the most demanding. After ascending through meadows, it climbs steeply across rockslides beneath Mount Schäffer via a narrow track to All Souls' Prospect—a natural platform on the mountain's north ridge. The view across Lake O'Hara from this marvellous viewpoint allows you to retrace the entire Alpine Circuit—an appropriate finale to the day.

From All Souls' Prospect there is one last very steep descent (paint marks and cairns again) to the Big Larches trail near Schäffer Lake. If you are still feeling your oats, return to Lake O'Hara via the steep but scenic Big Larches trail (see *Lake McArthur*). Otherwise, continue left 100 m to Schäffer Lake and shuffle down the Lake McArthur trail to the Alpine Meadow and Lake O'Hara.

147 McArthur Creek

Lake O'Hara to Ottertail River—12.4 km (7.7 mi)

Backpack

Allow 4 hours to Ottertail River

Elevation gain: 175 m (570 ft)
    loss: 730 m (2,400 ft)

Maximum elevation: 2210 m (7,250 ft)

Maps: Lake Louise 82 N/8
    Yoho National Park
    Lake Louise & Yoho (GemTrek)

Access: Travel to Lake O'Hara as described in the *Lake O'Hara* introduction. The hike begins from the trailhead beside Le Relais hut on the O'Hara access road, 0.6 km south of the campground and 0.2 km north of the lodge.

0.0—Lake O'Hara access road (2035 m).

    —Trail climbs to Alpine Meadow.

0.3—Junction. Big Larches Route to Schäffer Lake left. Keep right.

0.6—Elizabeth Parker Hut and Junction. Linda Lake right. Keep left.

    —Moderate to steep uphill.

1.5—Junction. Big Larches Route rejoins trail from left.

1.6—Schäffer Lake and Junction. Lake McArthur high route left. McArthur Pass right.

    —Steady climb through forest.

2.1—McArthur Pass (2210 m).

2.4—Junction. Lake McArthur low route left. Keep right.

    —Moderate to steep descent.

6.4—McArthur Creek bridge.

    —Downhill grades moderate through avalanche slopes.

12.4—Junction (1480 m). Intersection with *Ottertail River* trail at km 14.5. McArthur Creek Campground left 0.4 km.

(Trail not fully shown on maps in this book.)

The McArthur Creek trail connects the Lake O'Hara area to the head of the Ottertail Valley. Most hikers use the trail at the beginning or end of an extended backpacking trip, usually via Kootenay Park's Goodsir Pass to the south.

The only scenery of note is on the section from Lake O'Hara to McArthur Pass. As the trail descends McArthur Creek, the route runs through forest and, lower down, avalanche slopes. While these slide areas do provide open views, particularly south toward the Goodsirs, they also create a rich habitat for grizzly bears (see restrictions below).

Starting from the Le Relais trailhead at Lake O'Hara, you follow a straightforward 2.1-km trail running through the Alpine Meadow and up to McArthur Pass. The trail is not maintained south of the pass, but a rough track descends steeply for the next 3 km into the McArthur Creek valley.

The trail crosses McArthur Creek at km 6.4, and grades moderate as it descends the lower half of the valley through dense forest broken by avalanche slopes and then meadows. At km 12.4 it intersects the Ottertail River trail 0.4 km west of the McArthur Creek Campground (see *Ottertail River*).

Stay vigilant for bears throughout the McArthur Creek valley and make noise when visibility is limited.

Restrictions: Because it runs through prime grizzly habitat and an important wildlife corridor, travel in the McArthur Creek valley is currently restricted—only 2 parties per week after August 15. Hikers must obtain a permit from a Parks Canada Visitor Centre, either by reserving up to 3 months in advance or registering at the Yoho Visitor Centre in person 24 hours before your trip (first-come, first-served). Contact the visitor centre or Yoho's website for current policy (see *Sources-Parks information*).

148 Ottertail River

Trans-Canada Highway to McArthur Creek Campground—14.9 km (9.3 mi)

Backpack

Allow 4 to 5 hours one way

Elevation gain: 285 m (935 ft)

Maximum elevation: 1480 m (4,850 ft)

Maps: Lake Louise 82 N/8
Golden 82 N/8
Yoho National Park
Lake Louise & Yoho (GemTrek)

Access: Follow the Trans-Canada Highway to the Ottertail River bridge, 8.5 km (5.5 mi) west of Field. The trailhead parking area is located on the south side of the highway 0.2 km east of the bridge.

0.0—Trailhead access gate (1195 m).

— Follow old fire road, gradual to moderate uphill.

2.8—Hoodoos viewpoint.

—Gradual uphill above river.

3.5—Giddie Creek bridge.

5.2—Moderately steep downhill next 1.0 km.

6.2—Float Creek bridge.

—Road climbs away from river and continues gradual ascent of valley.

14.5—Junction. *McArthur Creek* trail left.

14.6—McArthur Creek bridge.

14.9—McArthur Creek Campground (1480 m).

15.1—McArthur Creek Warden Cabin.

15.5—Ottertail River bridge.

16.2—Junction. *Goodsir Pass* ahead (see Kootenay Park chapter). Ottertail Falls left 1.5 km.

(Trail not shown on maps in this book.)

While old fire roads usually make for rather tedious hiking, the one up the Ottertail River is reasonably pleasant. It climbs gradually along semi-open slopes overlooking the river, passes above a small group of hoodoos, and provides frequent views of the Ottertail Range.

The road is mainly used by backpackers as an optional access-exit route for Goodsir Pass and the northern end of Kootenay Park's Rockwall Trail. It is also open to cyclists as far as the McArthur Creek Warden Cabin.

From the access gate beside the Trans-Canada Highway, the old roadbed climbs into a mixed forest of lodgepole pine, white spruce and aspen. At 1.4 km it emerges onto a bench above the Ottertail River, where views open out across the Kicking Horse Valley to the Van Horne Range and up the Ottertail to Mounts Hurd and Ennis.

At km 2.8 you pass above a steep cutbank where a number of hoodoos have been created by the erosion of calcareous soils and gravels along the river. The exposed soils are also utilized as a mineral lick by local mountain goats.

Beyond Float Creek, the road swings away from the river and gradually climbs through a subalpine forest of Engelmann spruce and alpine fir. The McArthur Creek trail intersects from the left at 14.5 km (see *McArthur Creek*), and a well-sheltered campground is passed on the right 400 m further along.

Just 200 m beyond the campground, the road ends at the McArthur Creek Warden Cabin, which sits on a pleasant, open bench with a fine view of the twin summits of Mount Goodsir.

Trail continues beyond the end of the road, running south from the warden cabin and crossing the Ottertail River. A 1.5-km trail to Ottertail Falls branches left at km 16.2, while the main trail continues south to Goodsir Pass (see *Helmet Creek*, Kootenay Park chapter).

Yoho Valley—Emerald Lake

Emerald Lake was discovered by pioneer outfitter Tom Wilson in 1882 while he was packing for the CPR survey. Having lost some horses, he followed their tracks up the Emerald Valley from the Kicking Horse River to this hidden gem.

Despite the early discovery of Emerald Lake, the nearby Yoho Valley wasn't explored until 1897 when the German alpinist Jean Habel reached the valley from Emerald Lake via Yoho Pass. Habel reported on the valley's exceptional features, which included an impressive array of glaciated peaks, extensive icefields, and what was for many years considered Canada's highest waterfall—the stunning 254 m Takakkaw Falls. Though Takakkaw is now ranked as the country's second highest waterfall, the valley's reputation has not diminished over time.

Edward Whymper, conqueror of Switzerland's Matterhorn, explored the region for the Canadian Pacific Railway in 1901. Though he was 61 years old, he climbed and hiked throughout the Yoho Valley area, photographing all the major mountains and valleys. From his long experience in Europe, he saw the recreational potential of the Yoho and recommended the construction of several trails.

In 1903, the CPR opened its first backcountry chalet at Emerald Lake—the forerunner of today's Emerald Lake Lodge. Three years later the area gained further notoriety when the Alpine Club of Canada based its first annual mountaineering camp at Yoho Lake.

Today Emerald Lake, Yoho Valley, and the adjacent Little Yoho Valley constitutes one of the Canadian Rockies' major backcountry recreation areas. Many of the trails in the region interconnect, creating hiking options that can be tailored to the strength and available time of almost any hiking party.

Emerald Lake is connected to the Yoho Valley by the Yoho Pass trail, yet most people hike it as a separate area. The circuit around Emerald Lake is a favourite with families and lodge guests both summer and winter. The Yoho-Burgess Pass Circuit, which makes a high traverse along Wapta Mountain, is the most popular day trip from the lake. Emerald Basin and Hamilton Lake are both rewarding half-day hikes.

The Yoho Valley's most popular day hike is the Iceline Trail, which is one of the few trails constructed in the mountain parks in the past 30 years. The Iceline and the valley-bottom Yoho River trail are approaches to the valley's best features—Twin Falls, Little Yoho Valley, and Whaleback. All of these areas can be reached in a day by strong hikers, though many prefer to overnight in the valley and make shorter hikes to these points of interest.

A number of facilities in the Yoho Valley serve as good base camps. In addition to a walk-in campground just beyond the Takakkaw Falls parking area, there are four backcountry campgrounds in the valley environs. These are popular sites, so you should reserve ahead or keep your itinerary flexible.

Whiskey Jack Hostel, 1.0 km south of Takakkaw Falls, offers reasonably priced accommodation to both members and non-members of the International Hostelling Association. The Iceline Trail and Yoho Lake hikes both start from the hostel's parking area, but those not staying at the hostel should park at the Takakkaw Falls parking area and hike the 1.0-km connector trail back to the trailhead.

Twin Falls Chalet is located at the head of the Yoho Valley. The chalet, which is a National Historic Site, provides accommodation and meals for a limited number of overnight guests throughout the summer. Hikers can also drop in for afternoon tea.

The Alpine Club of Canada's Stanley Mitchell Hut is another historic log shelter near the head of the Little Yoho Valley. It can accommodate 28 self-sufficient guests during the summer.

See *Sources-Backcountry lodges*, *Hostels* and *Huts* for contact details.

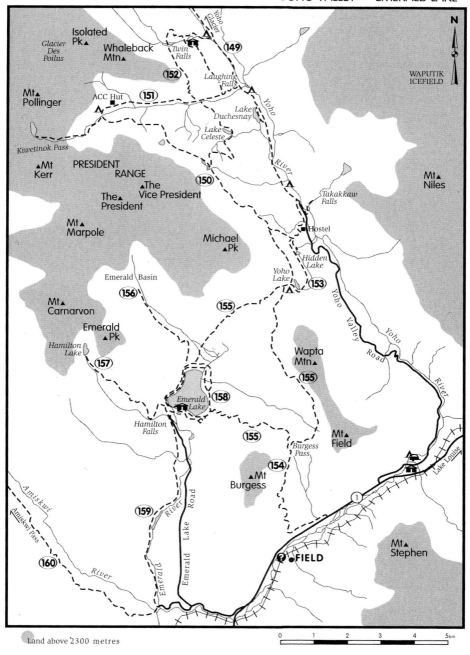

N

Isolated
Pk▲

*Glacier
Des
Poilus*

Whaleback
Mtn▲

*Twin
Falls*

(149)

*Yoho
Glacier*

WAPUTIK
ICEFIELD

(152)

*Laughing
Falls*

ACC Hut

(151)

Yoho

Mt▲
Pollinger

Kiwetinok Pass

*Lake
Duchesnay*

*Lake
Celeste*

River

Mt▲
Niles

PRESIDENT
RANGE

▲Mt
Kerr

(150)

*Takakkaw
Falls*

The▲
Vice President

The▲
President

Michael
▲Pk

*Hidden
Lake*

Mt▲
Marpole

■Hostel

*Yoho
Lake*

(153)

Emerald Basin

(156)

(155)

Mt▲
Carnarvon

Emerald
▲Pk

Wapta
Mtn▲

Yoho

*Hamilton
Lake*

(157)

(155)

*Emerald
Lake*

(158)

Yoho Valley Road

River

*Hamilton
Falls*

(155)

Mt▲
Field

*Burgess
Pass*

(154)

▲Mt
Burgess

Amiskwi

Emerald Lake Road

(159)

River

1

Mt▲
Stephen

Amiskwi Pass

(160)

River

❓ ●FIELD

Emerald

● Land above 2300 metres

0   1   2   3   4   5km

149 Twin Falls

Takakkaw Falls Parking Area to Twin Falls—8.2 km (5.1 mi)

Day trip or backpack

Allow 2 to 3 hours one way

Elevation gain: 290 m (950 ft)

Maximum elevation: 1800 m (5,900 ft)

Maps: Lake Louise 82 N/8
      Hector Lake 82 N/9
      Blaeberry River 82 N/10
      Yoho National Park
      Lake Louise & Yoho (GemTrek)

Access: Follow the Trans-Canada Highway to the Yoho Valley Road junction 3.7 km (2.3 mi) east of Field. Follow the Yoho Valley Road north 13 km (8 mi) to its termination at the Takakkaw Falls parking area. Continue around the main parking area 0.4 km to the trailhead parking area.

0.0— Yoho Valley Road trailhead (1510 m).

    —Follow old roadbed north.

0.3— Takakkaw Falls Campground.

0.5— Trail sign on north edge of campground.

    —Trail runs across alluvial plain and into scattered forest.

2.2— Junction. Angel's Staircase viewpoint right. Point Lace Falls left 0.2 km.

3.6— Junction. Duchesnay Lake left 0.2 km.

4.2— Laughing Falls and Campground.

4.3— Junction. *Little Yoho Valley* trail left.

4.7— Twin Falls Creek bridge.

6.4— Junction. Yoho Glacier right.

6.6— Twin Falls Campground.

    —Steady switchbacking climb.

8.1— Junction. *Whaleback* right. Twin Falls Chalet left.

8.2— Twin Falls Chalet (1800 m). Twin Falls Creek and base of Twin Falls 100 m ahead.

The trail along the Yoho River from Takakkaw Falls to Twin Falls was originally cut by a CPR trail crew in 1901. Today it is one of the most frequently hiked trails in the Yoho Valley. While it is not particularly inspiring, it does pass a number of fine waterfalls and is the most direct route to Twin Falls. Its is also popular because it provides access to two very scenic trails—Whaleback and Little Yoho Valley.

The trail is flat and straightforward nearly all the way to Twin Falls. The first 2.2 km follows a road-width track which, after skirting the Takakkaw Falls walk-in campground and crossing a rocky alluvial wash, enters a forest of pine and spruce. Three waterfalls are passed on the way upvalley—Angel's Staircase Falls and Point Lace Falls at km 2.2, and the impressive Laughing Falls at km 4.2. Beyond Point Lace Falls junction, the road reverts to a single-file path.

At km 3.6, a 200-m trail branches left to Lake Duchesnay—a shallow green lake that slowly dries up to the size of a pond by early autumn. Just beyond Duchesnay junction another short trail branches right to the edge of the Yoho River, where you can observe the explosive action of this glacial torrent cutting its channel. Across the river are the ice-covered Waputik Mountains, dominated by the sharp peak of Trolltinder Mountain (2917 m).

After passing Little Yoho Valley junction and the Laughing Falls Campground, the trail crosses Twin Falls Creek and continues its northerly course through heavy forest with occasional glimpses of Twin Falls through the trees. At the Yoho Glacier trail junction, the main trail stays left and begins its final ascent to Twin Falls.

The Yoho Valley trail ends at Twin Falls Chalet, where you can view the double falls leaping 180 m off a massive cliff of Cathedral limestone.

Twin Falls is formed by a stream from Glacier des Poilus, which splits into two branches just above the precipice. Before Twin Falls Chalet was constructed by the CPR, the left falls occasionally dwindled to a trickle or shut off altogether when an obstruction blocked the channel. When this happened, CPR employees were dispatched to the lip of the falls to correct this scenic problem—with dynamite! (The name "Canadian Pacific Rockies" on some early maps may not have been all that inappropriate.)

Twin Falls Chalet was constructed by the CPR in 1923 and first opened for business the following year. The rustic Swiss-style log building has been operated by Fran Drummond of Calgary since 1962. It provides accommodation and meals for a limited number of guests throughout the summer, as well as afternoon tea for both guests and hikers. (See *Sources-Backcountry lodges*.)

Twin Falls Options. From Twin Falls, you have several excellent hiking option.

The trail over Whaleback strikes off from the junction 100 m north of the chalet and climbs to some of the best views of the upper Yoho Valley.

By following the Marpole Lake and Celeste Lake trails south from the chalet for 7.5 km, you can intersect the Iceline Trail near its summit, which is by far the most scenic route back to Takakkaw Falls. (See *Whaleback, Little Yoho Valley*, and *Iceline Trail* descriptions.)

Yoho Glacier—2.3 km. This short trail branches north from the Twin Falls trail at km 6.4. It travels through dense forest and across relatively level terrain to the edge of a cutbank overlooking the Yoho River and the snout of the Yoho Glacier. It is often hiked as a half-day trip from Twin Falls Campground or the chalet.

Twin Falls

150 Iceline Trail

Yoho Valley Road to Iceline Summit—6.4 km (4.0 mi)
Yoho Valley Road to Little Yoho Campground—10.4 km (6.5 mi)

Day trip or backpack

Allow 2 hours to Iceline Summit

Elevation gain: 685 m (2,250 ft)

Maximum elevation: 2210 m (7,250 ft)

Maps: Lake Louise 82 N/8
Blaeberry River 82 N/10
Yoho National Park
Lake Louise & Yoho (GemTrek)

Access: Follow the Trans-Canada Highway to the Yoho Valley Road junction 3.7 km (2.3 mi) east of Field. Follow the Yoho Valley Road north 13 km (8 mi) to its termination at the Takakkaw Falls parking area. Follow the trail leading to the base of the falls and, just before the Yoho River bridge, turn right and hike the 1.0-km connector trail leading back to the Whiskey Jack Hostel parking area. The trailhead sign is located at the north end of the hostel parking area.

0.0—Whiskey Jack trailhead (1520 m).

—Steady uphill.

1.1—Junction. Hidden Lakes left 0.3 km.

1.3—Junction. Yoho Pass and Lake ahead. Iceline right.

—Steady uphill across avalanche slopes.

2.5—Junction. Yoho Lake left 2.4 km. Iceline right.

—Steady climb into rocky terrain.

4.6—Lake outlet stream (rock-hop).

5.6—Lake outlet stream (rock-hop).

5.7—Junction. Celeste Lake and Twin Falls right.

6.4—Iceline Summit (2210 m).

7.4—Lake outlet (rock-hop).

—Trail descends into subalpine forest.

10.2—Junction (2075 m). Kiwetinok Pass ahead 2.5 km. *Little Yoho Valley* trail right across Little Yoho River bridge.

10.4—Little Yoho Campground.

10.7—Stanley Mitchell Hut.

One of Yoho Park's newest trails is one of its most scenic and popular. Designed as a replacement for the old Highline and Skyline Trails, the Iceline takes you much higher than the old route to expansive views of the Yoho Valley and the edge of the Emerald Glacier.

Some hikers approach the Iceline from the north after trekking to the head of the Little Yoho Valley, but most attack it in a more direct fashion from the trailhead at the Whiskey Jack Hostel. You can hike to Yoho Lake and begin the Iceline traverse from there (see *Yoho Lake*), or, as most people do, take the direct route and save 4 km.

By either route, you will arrive at a junction high on the open avalanche slopes of the President Range. This is where the real glories of the Iceline begin as it climbs over the terminal and ground moraines of the Emerald Glacier. The glacier is a constant companion above the trail from km 3.5 to 8.0, and the first of three small rockbound lakes is passed at km 4.6.

While the trail appears to be contouring northwestward, rolling up and down over glacial debris, it is actually climbing relentlessly. But the continually improving views of the Yoho Valley help to conceal the effort of the ascent. Finally, at km 6.4, the trail reaches its highest point on the crest of a moraine.

While some turn for home on this summit, many are tempted to continue on to the Little Yoho Valley. The trail descends to one last lake and crosses the last ridge of glacial debris to the open subalpine forest of the Little Yoho. The twin pyramids of The Vice President and The President rise above the trail to the south, and Isolated Peak and the long ridge of the Whaleback are across the valley to the north.

Once you reach the forest, you descend gradually for 2.2 km along the

Emerald Glacier from Iceline Trail summit

route of the old Skyline Trail to a bridged crossing of the Little Yoho River. At this point the Iceline intersects with the Little Yoho Valley trail.

Strong day hikers can continue down along the north side of the valley to the Yoho Valley trail, the Marpole Lake connector to Twin Falls, or climb to the crest of the Whaleback. Backpackers will likely wash ashore for the night at the Little Yoho Campground or the Stanley Mitchell Hut. (See *Little Yoho Valley.*)

Twin Falls Option. If you are doing a day trip loop of the upper Yoho Valley, you won't likely want to add kilometres by continuing to the head of the Little Yoho Valley. The most direct route to Twin Falls branches downhill from the Iceline Trail at km 5.7, just 0.7 before the Iceline Summit.

This branch, known as the Celeste Lake trail, descends into the forest, skirts the shores of tiny Celeste Lake, and contours north to an intersection with the Little Yoho Valley trail. At this juncture

you turn right and follow the Little Yoho trail 0.7 km to the Marpole Lake trail junction. Continue north on the Marpole trail, which crosses a rockslide at the foot of the Whaleback to Marpole Lake and Twin Falls Chalet. Total distance from the Iceline junction to Twin Falls is 7.5 km—mostly downhill or flat walking through dense subalpine forest.

You can also take the scenic route to Twin Falls from the Little Yoho trail by crossing over the Whaleback, but this adds kilometres and a very stiff climb to your day.

From Twin Falls, you complete your Yoho Valley loop by returning to the Takakkaw Falls parking area on the *Twin Falls* trail. Total distance for this valley circuit is 22.5 km.

151 Little Yoho Valley

Laughing Falls Junction to Little Yoho Campground—5.5 km (3.4 mi)

Day trip or backpack

Allow 1.5 hours to Little Yoho Campground

Elevation gain: 520 m (1,700 ft)

Maximum elevation: 2135 m (7,000 ft)

Maps: Blaeberry River 82 N/10
    Yoho National Park
    Lake Louise & Yoho (GemTrek)

Access: From the trailhead at the Takakkaw Falls parking lot, follow the *Twin Falls* trail to the 4.3 km junction at Laughing Falls. The Little Yoho Valley trail branches uphill to left.

0.0—Laughing Falls Junction (1615 m).

  —Steep uphill switchbacks.

1.6—Junction. Twin Falls ahead. Little Yoho Valley left.

  —Steady uphill, moderate grades.

2.2—Junction (1905 m). *Whaleback* trail right.

2.3—Junction. Celeste Lake and Iceline Trail left.

5.2—Stanley Mitchell Hut.

5.5—Little Yoho Campground.

5.7—Little Yoho River bridge (2075 m). Cross bridge to junction. *Iceline Trail* left. Kiwetinok Pass right 2.5 km.

The Little Yoho Valley is one of the prime destinations for backpackers in the Yoho Valley region. The campground at the head of the valley and the Stanley Mitchell Hut are ideally situated as base camps for short excursions to such worthy objectives as Whaleback and Kiwetinok Pass. And the Iceline Trail, which contours high along the President Range, connects nicely with the Little Yoho Valley trail to create a scenic loop trip that includes this beautiful hanging valley.

Many visitors to the Little Yoho Valley are backpackers looking for the most direct route to the campground or the Stanley Mitchell Hut. That route follows the Twin Falls trail up the Yoho Valley 4.3 km from Takakkaw Falls to its junction with the Little Yoho Valley trail at Laughing Falls (see *Twin Falls*). From this intersection, the trail climbs due west along the north side of the Little Yoho River.

Over the first 2 km, the trail climbs steeply through the forest via a series of switchbacks. On one of these switchbacks, at km 1.6, the Marpole Lake trail from Twin Falls intersects (keep left at this confusing junction or you will find yourself at Twin Falls in a half-hour or so). The Whaleback trail branches right at the 2.2-km mark, and just 100 m farther along, the Celeste Lake trail branches left across the river.

The forest becomes progressively more subalpine and open as you continue up-valley to the Stanley Mitchell Hut, located on the edge of a large meadow at km 5.2. The Little Yoho Campground lies 300 m farther along.

While the head of the valley is enclosed by impressive mountains, the most dramatic and dominating are the glaciated peaks of the President Range, which rise above the meadow to the south.

The log Stanley Mitchell Hut was

The President Range from the summit of Kiwetinok Pass

constructed by the Alpine Club of Canada in 1939. It accommodates 28 and is one of only a few Alpine Club huts accessible by trail. (For booking information, see Alpine Club of Canada, *Sources-Huts*).

Iceline Trail Option. Just beyond the campground, the Little Yoho Valley trail crosses the river to a junction with the Kiwetinok Pass trail and the north end of the Iceline Trail.

The Iceline runs from a trailhead at the Whiskey Jack Hostel parking area, and since the distance to the Little Yoho Campground is virtually the same as the Yoho Valley approach from Takakkaw Falls, it serves as an optional access route to the campground and the Stanley Mitchell Hut. It is a lot more strenuous, however, particularly if you are shouldering a full backpack.

When the weather is reasonable, the Iceline is the most scenic return route down-valley. You come out at the Whiskey Jack parking area, 1 km from the Yoho Valley trailhead parking area at Takakkaw Falls. (A trail parallels the

road back to the Takakkaw parking area.) In fact, strong hikers often complete this 21 km circuit in a single day. (See *Iceline Trail*.)

Kiwetinok Pass—2.5 km. This short, steep trail climbs to the headwaters of the Little Yoho Valley on the 2450-m summit of Kiwetinok Pass—a rocky, windswept col that cradles a small lake. The pass provides fine views of both the Little Yoho Valley to the east and the Kiwetinok Valley to the west. It is usually hiked as a half-day trip from the Little Yoho Campground or the Stanley Mitchell Hut.

The trail starts at the junction across the river from the Little Yoho Campground, where it immediately begins its westerly ascent to the pass. The last half of the trip is very steep and the track is often vague (watch for cairns).

The pass is sandwiched tightly between the slopes of Mounts Pollinger and Kerr, and mostly filled by the waters of Kiwetinok Lake. It can be a cold bleak spot when the weather is foul, and the lake often remains ice-covered into July.

152 Whaleback

Twin Falls Chalet to Little Yoho Junction—6.6 km (4.1 mi)

Day trip or backpack

Allow 1.5 hours to Whaleback Summit

Elevation gain: 410 m (1,350 ft)

loss: 305 m (1,000 ft)

Maximum elevation: 2210 m (7,250 ft)

Maps: Blaeberry River 82 N/10
     Yoho National Park
     Lake Louise & Yoho (GemTrek)

Access: From the trailhead at the Takakkaw Falls parking lot, follow the *Twin Falls* trail 8.1 km to the Whaleback trail junction, 100 m north of Twin Falls Chalet. The south end of the Whaleback traverse is accessible from the 2.2-km junction on the *Little Yoho Valley* trail.

0.0—Twin Falls Junction (1800 m).

  —Trail climbs steeply via long switchbacks.

2.7—Twin Falls Creek near top of falls.

2.8—Unmarked junction. Waterfall Valley right.

2.9—Twin Falls Creek suspension bridge.

  —Steady climb.

4.5—Whaleback ridge summit (2210 m).

  —Steep switchbacking descent.

6.6—Junction (1905 m). Intersection with *Little Yoho Valley* trail at km 2.2.

One of the highest and most scenic trails in the Yoho Valley runs across the Whaleback ridge between Twin Falls Chalet and the Little Yoho Valley. The trail summit provides an exceptional view of the entire headwaters of the Yoho Valley and, most particularly, the vast expanse of the Wapta Icefield.

Though we have hiked the Whaleback as part of a full day loop trip via the Iceline Trail, upper Little Yoho and Yoho River trails, the 26 km distance makes for a rather strenuous outing. Most hikers prefer to visit the Whaleback as a day trip from Twin Falls Chalet, the Stanley Mitchell Hut, or campgrounds in the Yoho and Little Yoho Valleys. This option allows more time for exploration, including a side trip up the beautiful Waterfall Valley.

The north end of the Whaleback traverse intersects the Yoho Valley trail 100 m north of Twin Falls Chalet (see *Twin Falls*). From this junction, the trail switchbacks up through the rock bands that create the 180-m precipice for Twin Falls. After reaching the top of the cliff, the trail descends to Twin Falls Creek at the very brink of the falls—a viewpoint that is not for the faint of heart. (Stay clear of Twin Falls Creek near the lip of the falls! This dangerous area has claimed one life.)

From the top of the falls, the trail climbs to a suspension bridge spanning Twin Falls Creek. (The bridge is removed in winter, so early season hikers should check at the visitor centre to make sure it has been replaced.) Across the bridge it begins a steady climb across the flank of the Whaleback. The trail runs close to treeline where there are excellent views back to the north to the Yoho Glacier, the upper Waterfall Valley, and the white expanse of the Glacier des Poilus.

The high point of the trip, both in elevation and scenery, comes at km 4.5,

Mont des Poilus from the Whaleback

where the trail turns the corner of the Whaleback ridge. Marked by a stone cairn and brass plaque commemorating an avalanche fatality, the viewpoint provides one of the most commanding overviews of the upper Yoho Valley of any trail accessible point in the region. Many nearby peaks were named by British mountaineer Edward Whymper when he visited the valley in 1901, including The President, The Vice President, Mount Kerr, Mount Pollinger, Isolated Peak, and the Whaleback itself.

From the viewpoint, the trail descends 300 m in 2.1 km to join the Little Yoho Valley trail. At this junction you can follow either the Celeste Lake shortcut or the Little Yoho Valley trail to the Iceline Trail. By turning left, you descend the Little Yoho trail to the Yoho River, or use the Marpole Lake connector trail to contour back around the end of the Whaleback to Twin Falls.

Waterfall Valley—2.0 km. This sublime side trip from the Whaleback trail follows tributaries of Twin Falls Creek through alpine meadows to an excellent viewpoint for Mont des Poilus and the vast Glacier des Poilus.

The unmarked track up the vale branches right from the Whaleback trail just below the Twin Falls Creek suspension bridge. After passing an old campsite, the trail climbs steadily through meadows and beside small streams to an old morainal ridge near the head of the valley. (The trail is indistinct in its upper reaches, so watch for cairns.) From the top of this moraine you have the best views of the Glacier des Poilus region.

153 Yoho Lake

Yoho Valley Road to Yoho Lake—3.7 km (2.3 mi)

Half-day trip

Allow 1 to 1.5 hours to Yoho Lake

Elevation gain: 290 m (950 ft)

Maximum elevation: 1815 m (5,950 ft)

Maps: Lake Louise 82 N/8
Yoho National Park
Lake Louise & Yoho (GemTrek)

Access: Follow the Trans-Canada Highway to the Yoho Valley Road junction 3.7 km (2.3 mi) east of Field. Follow the Yoho Valley Road north 13 km (8 mi) to its termination at the Takakkaw Falls parking area. Follow the trail leading to the base of the falls and, just before the Yoho River bridge, turn right and hike the 1.0-km connector trail leading back to the Whiskey Jack Hostel parking area. The trailhead sign is located at the north end of the hostel parking area.

0.0—Whiskey Jack trailhead (1520 m).

—Steady uphill.

1.1—Junction. Hidden Lakes left 0.3 km.

1.3—Junction. Iceline Trail right. Yoho Lake left.

3.7—Yoho Lake (1815 m).

—Trail skirts south end of lake.

4.0—Junction. Iceline Trail right. Yoho Pass left.

4.6—Yoho Pass (1815 m). Intersection with *Yoho Pass-Burgess Pass Circuit* at km 6.3. Burgess Pass left. Emerald Lake ahead.

This is one of the shortest hikes in the Yoho Valley. Though the lake is historically interesting as the site of the Alpine Club of Canada's first annual camp in 1906, it is forest-enclosed and rather unremarkable. However, the lake and nearby Yoho Pass can be linked with other trails to create a number of rewarding day trips.

Starting from the Whiskey Jack parking area, the trail immediately switchbacks up a major avalanche path and into dense subalpine forest. At km 1.1, a short side trail branches left to Hidden Lakes—two tiny ponds appropriately hidden in the forest.

Just 200 m beyond Hidden Lakes junction, the Iceline Trail branches right (you will return down this trail if you make the loop trip north from Yoho Lake). Stay left and continue your steady climb through the trees for another 2.4 km to the lake.

Though this small, green lake is surrounded on three sides by forest, its western shoreline is bordered by a lush meadow that is filled with wildflowers for much of the summer.

From a junction on the west side of the lake, you can branch left and continue through meadow and trees for another 0.6 km to Yoho Pass—a trail junction in the midst of forest. From this point you can turn left and follow a high trail south along Wapta Peak to Burgess Pass, or stay right and descend to Emerald Lake (see *Yoho Pass-Burgess Pass Circuit*).

Yoho Lake Loop. The most scenic route back to the Whiskey Jack parking area follows the trail running north from the lake. After climbing through forest, you emerge on high open slopes overlooking the Yoho Valley and Takakkaw Falls. Intersect the Iceline Trail 2.4 km from the lake and follow it downhill to the 1.3 km junction on the Yoho Lake trail. Total round trip distance for the loop is 8.9 km.

154 Burgess Pass

Burgess Pass trail parking area to Burgess Pass—7.3 km (4.5 mi)

Day trip

Allow 2.5 hours one way

Elevation gain: 930 m (3,060 ft)

Maximum elevation: 2180 m (7,160 ft)

Maps: Lake Louise 82 N/8
     Yoho National Park
     Lake Louise & Yoho (GemTrek)

Access: Follow the Trans-Canada Highway to the access road for the Burgess Pass trail, located on the north side of the highway 1.2 km east of the Field townsite intersection. Follow the access road (keep left at split) 0.4 km to the parking area.

0.0—Trailhead parking area (1250 m).

  —Trail climbs gradually to west above highway.

0.7—Trail begins steep climb toward pass.

3.0—Forest begins to thin.

3.8—Open rockslide.

  —Steady uphill via switchbacks.

7.0—Trail crosses steep, open slope.

7.3—Burgess Pass (2180 m).

  —Trail contours east along summit ridge.

7.6—Junction. Intersection with *Yoho Pass-Burgess Pass Circuit* at km 12.4. Emerald Lake left. Yoho Pass right.

We used this trail on our first ev
Burgess Pass many years ago. W
pleased with the views from the to
it was a hot day and the steady climb
the south-facing slope was gruelling.

We've since visited the pass severa
times by less strenuous routes—the *Yoho Pass-Burgess Pass Circuit* from Emerald Lake, and as a through hike from Yoho Valley via Yoho Pass and then down the Burgess Pass trail to the Kicking Horse Valley trailhead. But if you'd like the workout, you can still approach it from the Kicking Horse by starting from the relocated trailhead just off the Trans-Canada Highway east of Field.

The trail runs west through the forest above the Trans-Canada for nearly a kilometre before it turns north and begins the relentless climb to the pass. Views are limited by forest for the first 3 km, but beyond that point the trees begin to thin, and you catch occasional glimpses of Mount Stephen. An open rockslide at km 3.8 provides an unfettered view of Stephen, the Cathedral Crags, and the Kicking Horse Valley running away to the southwest.

There is a giddy view over a sharp cliff into the Emerald Lake basin when you reach the pass at km 7.3. However, the best views back over the Kicking Horse Valley are achieved by leaving the trail and traversing eastward through stands of alpine fir and larch to the highest point on the summit ridge.

The trail reaches a junction 300 m beyond the crest of the pass. Here the trail to Emerald Lake branches down to the left, or you can stay right and traverse the open slopes of Wapta Mountain to Yoho Pass. (See *Yoho Pass-Burgess Pass Circuit.*)

And remember what we said at the outset: this is a steep, dry hike, so make sure you have a good supply of water along.

ss—Burgess Pass Circuit

Loop from Emerald Lake—19.7 km (12.2 mi)

```
                    .ɔu m (7,160 ft)
        ₋ouise 82 N/8
    ɢolden 82 N/8
    Yoho National Park
    Lake Louise & Yoho (GemTrek)
```

Access: Follow the Trans-Canada Highway to its intersection with the Emerald Lake Road, 2 km (1.2 mi) west of the Field townsite intersection. Follow the Emerald Lake Road north 8.5 km (5.3 mi) to its termination at the Emerald Lake parking area. The trailhead kiosk is located at the north end of the parking area beside the bridge to Emerald Lake Lodge.

0.0—Emerald Lake parking area (1300 m).

—Trail follows *Emerald Lake Circuit* around west shore of lake.

1.6—Junction. Emerald Basin left. Keep right.

1.7—Junction. Emerald Lake Circuit ahead. Yoho Pass left.

3.5—Major stream. Trail begins to climb.

4.4—Falls viewpoint.

6.4—Yoho Pass and Junction (1815 m). Yoho Lake ahead 0.6 km. Burgess Pass right.

—Trail climbs south along Wapta Peak.

12.5—Junction (2180 m). Burgess Pass summit left 0.3 km. Emerald Lake right.

—Trail switchbacks down through forest.

18.3—Junction. Intersection with *Emerald Lake Circuit* at km 3.8. Keep left.

18.8—Junction. Peaceful Pond and Emerald Lake parking area left. Lodge ahead.

19.1—Emerald Lake Lodge chalets and Junction. Turn left for Emerald Lake parking area.

19.7—Emerald Lake parking area (1300 m).

There aren't many good loop trips for day hikers in the Canadian Rockies, but the Yoho Pass-Burgess Pass Circuit is one of the best. You travel beside the shores of Emerald Lake, visit two passes, and make a high traverse across Wapta Mountain, where you overlook the lake and all its surrounding peaks. All of this in the space of 20 km and without having to backtrack. If you can only do one hike at Emerald Lake, and you are up to a fairly long day, this is the one to consider.

We always hike this circuit in a clockwise direction since it provides a gradual approach to the circuit's highest point on Burgess Pass. The hike departs from the north end of the Emerald Lake parking area and follows the Emerald Lake shoreline circuit around the west side of the lake for the first 1.7 km. At 0.3 km it crosses a major avalanche path, where you look back across the lake to the lodge and Mount Burgess—the scene that graced the back of the $10 bill for many years.

At the north end of the lake the Yoho Pass route breaks away from the lakeshore trail and crosses a sparsely forested alluvial fan—an extensive outwash of silt and gravel from the President Range's Emerald Basin. Beyond the flats you begin the steep climb to Yoho Pass. Views back to Emerald Lake improve as you gain elevation, and there is a fine waterfall to the north below Michael Peak.

There is little to indicate your arrival at Yoho Pass other than a moderation of the uphill grade and a trail junction in the forest. This is the first corner on the triangular circuit, where you stay to the right and head south to Burgess Pass. However, a short walk of 0.6 km on the left-hand branch leads to Yoho Lake—a pretty tarn fringed by a lush wildflower meadow. This is the approach to the Yoho Valley taken by the German alpinist Jean Habel on his journey of discovery in

The President Range from the slopes of Wapta Mountain

1897, and the route followed by members of the Alpine Club of Canada to their first annual camp at Yoho Lake in 1906. (See also *Yoho Lake.*)

The trail to Burgess Pass climbs 300 m along the slopes of Wapta Mountain over the next 6 km. Despite the steady ascent, the beauty of this section dispels any sense of drudgery. Open wildflower meadows are scattered along the way, and there are impressive views down to Emerald Lake and back to the heavily glaciated President Range.

As you near Burgess Pass, you may see people labouring away on a ledge far above the trail. This is the site of the world famous Burgess Shale Beds, where paleontologists work each summer unearthing many new and wonderful Middle Cambrian fossils. Though a steep, rough trail leads to the site, hikers are not permitted to go there except on guided tours led by the Yoho-Burgess Shale Foundation. (See *Sources-Guided walks.*)

The second corner of the circuit triangle is reached at Burgess Pass junction. By hiking a short distance on the left-hand branch, and then up to the highest point on Burgess Pass, you can look down to the Kicking Horse Valley and across to Mount Stephen—the highest and most impressive peak near Field. This trail also serves as an optional route to Burgess Pass from the Kicking Horse Valley. (See *Burgess Pass.*)

The trail back to Emerald Lake cuts downhill to the right from Burgess Pass junction. There are a few more good views before the trail plunges into the trees. The trail switchbacks down into a cool, moist forest quite unlike what you'd normally encounter in the Rockies—a micro-environment dominated by western red cedar.

The steady, steep downhill ends at an intersection with the *Emerald Lake Circuit* 5.5 km below Burgess Pass. The route back to the lodge and parking area stays left and follows the lake's southern shore.

156 Emerald Basin

Emerald Lake to Emerald Basin—4.6 km (2.9 mi)

Half-day trip

Allow 1.5 hours one way

Elevation gain: 225 m (740 ft)

Maximum elevation: 1525 m (5,000 ft)

Maps: Golden 82 N/8
      Yoho National Park
      Lake Louise & Yoho (GemTrek)

Access: Follow the Trans-Canada Highway to its intersection with the Emerald Lake Road, 2 km (1.2 mi) west of the Field townsite intersection. Follow the Emerald Lake Road north 8.5 km (5.3 mi) to its termination at the Emerald Lake parking area. The trailhead kiosk is located at the north end of the parking area beside the bridge to Emerald Lake Lodge.

0.0—Emerald Lake parking area (1300 m).

—Trail follows *Emerald Lake Circuit* around west shore of lake.

1.6—Junction. Lake circuit right. Emerald Basin left.

2.3—Junction. Yoho Pass ahead. Emerald Basin left.

—Steep ascent on rocky, rooty trail.

2.8—Trail flattens out above gorge.

3.8—Avalanche path.

4.1—Trail drops to floor of Emerald Basin.

—Trail follows up valley bottom.

4.6—Emerald Basin cairn (1525 m). End of official trail.

Emerald Basin is a rocky, avalanche-swept amphitheatre carved from the imposing cliffs of The President Range. The short trail branching up to the basin from the north end of Emerald Lake is a bit rough, but it does escape the bustle of more popular Emerald Lake trails.

The trail follows the Emerald Lake shoreline circuit around the west side of the lake for 1.6 km to the first of two junctions just beyond the lake's north shore. Turn left and continue north through scattered lodgepole pine for 0.7 km to another junction, where the trail to Emerald Basin branches uphill to the left.

There is a short, steep climb as the rocky and rooty trail begins its ascent of Emerald Basin drainage. The grade moderates once you reach the edge of a deep gorge, where views open across the chasm to Michael Peak.

Another kilometre through a cool, moist forest of western hemlock and red cedar brings you to a major avalanche path, where the trail descends to the stream on the valley floor. A rough, rocky trail continues up-valley to a large rock cairn—the end of official trail in the midst of the Emerald Basin.

Though the basin is well below treeline, avalanches have cleared much of the forest cover from the surrounding slopes (snow from these slides often lingers in the basin through mid-summer). Views are totally open to the steep slopes and massive cliffs that tightly embrace the basin, including an impressive limestone wall at the head of the valley, which forms the end of The President's south ridge. Views back down-valley include Wapta Mountain, Mount Burgess and the lofty summit of Mount Stephen beyond Burgess Pass.

You can follow snippets of trail upstream for another kilometre or so to the head of the valley, where a pair of waterfalls plunge from the cliffs. This is also a good area for spying mountain goats.

Emerald Basin

157 Hamilton Lake

Emerald Lake to Hamilton Lake—5.5 km (3.4 mi)

Day trip

Allow 1.5 to 2 hours one way

Elevation gain: 850 m (2,800 ft)

Maximum elevation: 2150 m (7,050 ft)

Maps: Golden 82 N/8
       Yoho National Park
       Lake Louise & Yoho (GemTrek)

Access: Follow the Trans-Canada Highway to its intersection with the Emerald Lake Road, 2 km (1.2 mi) west of the Field townsite intersection. Follow the Emerald Lake Road north 8.5 km (5.3 mi) to its termination at the Emerald Lake parking area. The trailhead is located at the entrance to the parking area on the west side of the road.

0.0—Emerald Lake parking area (1300 m).

0.2—Junction. Emerald River trail left. Stay ahead.

—Moderate uphill through forest.

0.8—Hamilton Falls.

—Steady switchbacking ascent.

3.9—Emerald Lake viewpoint.

—Grade moderates.

5.5—Hamilton Lake (2150 m).

This steep trail climbs densely forested slopes to a small tarn tucked into a hanging valley between Mount Carnarvon and Emerald Peak. While Hamilton Lake is blessed by a remarkable setting and far-reaching views, many hikers seem to avoid it, probably because of the rather grim, relentless approach.

The trail escapes the busy Emerald Lake parking area with little fanfare, slipping quickly into the forest from a simple trail sign at the parking lot entrance.

A short distance into this mature subalpine forest you encounter Hamilton Falls—a more popular destination than the lake above. This cascade drops down a steep limestone staircase, where the action of the water has smoothed and dissolved bedrock to form numerous pothole depressions. At a switchback a short distance up the trail, there is a fine view of the upper falls as well.

The route is closed-in and arduous beyond the falls, and there are no open views until the 4-km mark, where a short side trail leads through the trees to a viewpoint overlooking Emerald Lake. Beyond the viewpoint the grade moderates somewhat, and the trail soon emerges onto open slopes overlooking the Kicking Horse Valley.

Just as you are relegating yourself to another half-hour or so of steep slogging, the trail suddenly cuts upward and pops into the Hamilton Lake cirque.

Beautiful as it is unexpected, the lake extends to the very lip of its amphitheatre, its water riffled by the occasional down-slope breeze. By stepping across the outlet, you can continue along the west shore to a pleasant knoll and look back through the cirque's entrance to the Kicking Horse Valley. In the far distance, and framed perfectly through the opening, is glacier-capped Mount Vaux and the twin towers of Mount Goodsir—the highest summits in Yoho Park.

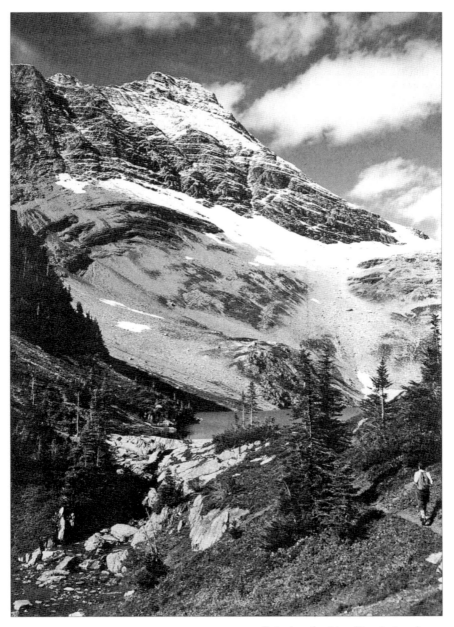

Entering the Hamilton Lake cirque

YOHO NATIONAL PARK   307

158 Emerald Lake Circuit

Emerald Lakeshore Circuit—5.2 km (3.2 mi)

Half-day trip

Allow 1.5 hours

Elevation gain: nil

Maximum elevation: 1300 m (4,250 ft)

Maps: Golden 82 N/8
  Yoho National Park
  Lake Louise & Yoho (GemTrek)

Access: Follow the Trans-Canada Highway to its intersection with the Emerald Lake Road, 2 km (1.2 mi) west of the Field townsite intersection. Follow the Emerald Lake Road north 8.5 km (5.3 mi) to its termination at the Emerald Lake parking area. The trailhead kiosk is located at the north end of the parking area beside the bridge to Emerald Lake Lodge.

0.0—Emerald Lake parking area (1300 m).

—Follow paved trail through picnic area and around southwest corner of lake.

0.3—Avalanche path. End of paved trail.

—Trail runs north along lake's west shoreline.

1.5—Junction. Intersection with horse trail.

1.6—Junction. Emerald Basin left.

1.7—Junction. Yoho Pass left.

—Cross open alluvial plain along lake's north shore.

2.2—Inlet bridge.

—Follow through dense forest along east shore.

3.8—Junction. Burgess Pass left. Lakeshore trail bends right.

4.3—Junction. Peaceful Pond cutoff to parking area left.

4.6—Junction. Emerald Lake Lodge complex. Turn left for parking area.

—Cutoff trail runs behind lodge complex.

5.2—Emerald River footbridge and parking area (1300 m).

The trip around Emerald Lake's shoreline requires no more than a couple of hours of easy walking. It is surprisingly scenic, with many open views to Mount Burgess and the President Range, and an excellent place to experience the vegetation of this mild and moist western slope forest. Trails to Emerald Basin, Yoho Pass and Burgess Pass also branch from the circuit.

You can hike the circuit clockwise or counterclockwise, but for some reason we always go clockwise. Following the paved trail leading from the north end of the Emerald Lake parking area, you soon turn the northwest corner of the lake and enter a large avalanche path. Here you get your first good view across the lake—the much-photographed scene of Emerald Lake and Mount Burgess. The pavement ends beyond avalanche path but the trail remains wide, and there are a number of log benches at lakeside.

After joining the horse trail, you bend right and pass two junctions in rapid succession—trails continuing north to Emerald Basin and Yoho Pass. The circuit continues across an alluvial plain, where there are views south across the lake to the lodge and the distant Ottertail Range. At the far side of the alluvial flats, you cross the inlet bridge and turn south along the eastern shoreline.

The east shore is quite different from the west. It is heavily forested, moist and cool, and dominated by lush vegetation, including thimbleberry, bunchberry, alder, western red cedar, and fallen spruce trees covered with feather moss. (We always find moose droppings on this section of trail.)

The trail bends right at the lake's southeast corner and climbs into forest above the lake's south shore back to the lodge. At km 4.3 you can take the Peaceful Pond cutoff back to the parking area or continue ahead to the lodge.

159 Emerald River

Kicking Horse Fire Road to Emerald Lake—7.7 km (4.8 mi)

Half-day trip

Allow 2 hours one way

Elevation gain: 140 m (450 ft)

Maximum elevation: 1300 m (4,250 ft)

Maps: Golden 82 N/8
Yoho National Park
Lake Louise & Yoho (GemTrek)

Access: Follow the Trans-Canada Highway to its intersection with the Emerald Lake Road, 2 km (1.2 mi) west of the Field townsite intersection. Follow the Emerald Lake Road north 2 km (1.2 mi) to the Natural Bridge parking area. Continue west from the parking area on the gravel Kicking Horse Fire Road 1.6 km (1.0 mi) to a barricade just east of the Emerald River bridge. The trailhead is located just across the bridge.

From the north end of the trail, begin the hike at the *Hamilton Lake* trailhead near the entrance to the Emerald Lake parking area.

0.0—Kicking Horse Fire Road at Emerald River bridge (1160 m).

—Trail climbs above Emerald River gorge.

1.5—Trail comes abreast of Emerald River.

2.2—Amiskwi trail bridge foundations (1200 m).

—Trail continues along river.

3.8—Trail breaks away from river.

—Dense forest with occasional small stream crossings (bridged or rock-hop).

5.8—Trail summit (1340 m).

—Gradual descent.

7.4—Junction. Horse corrals and Emerald Lake Road right 150 m. Stay ahead.

7.5—Junction. *Hamilton Lake* left. Emerald Lake parking area right.

7.7—Emerald Lake parking area (1300 m).

You can pretend you are Tom Wilson searching for your lost horses during the summer of 1882 by hiking the Emerald River trail north from the Kicking Horse River and "discovering" Emerald Lake. The 7.7-km trail is straight-forward and undemanding as it makes a gradual ascent through dense forest. Distant views are limited except for the occasional glimpse of Mounts Carnarvon and Burgess ahead, but the first 4 kms stays near the Emerald River, which makes for a pleasant forest walk.

Starting from the lower trailhead near the confluence of the Emerald and Kicking Horse Rivers, the trail climbs through pine forest to a viewpoint overlooking a narrow gorge cut by the Emerald River. It then descends to the river's west bank and stays close to this broad, shallow stream for the next 2 km.

At km 2.2 you arrive at old, wooden bridge foundations where a fire road to the Amiskwi Valley once crossed the river. A clearing at the crossing makes a pleasant spot for a rest or snack, and a good turnaround point if you are just doing a short walk.

Continuing north toward Emerald Lake, the trail finally breaks away from the river at 3.8 km and climbs gradually through rooty spruce forest and along dry, pine-covered slopes. Two or three small streams are crossed. Eventually, it reaches its high-point at 5.8 km, in the midst of a lush fir forest carpeted with ferns and feather moss.

After a brief, gradual descent, you pass a branch trail to the Emerald Lake horse corrals. Continue ahead on often-muddy horse trail for a few metres to where it crosses the Hamilton Lake trail. Turn right and follow this trail 200 m to the Emerald Lake parking area.

Many who hike the entire trail arrange transportation between trailheads and start at the slightly higher Emerald Lake parking area.

160 Amiskwi River

Amiskwi Picnic Area to Amiskwi Pass—35.5 km (22 mi)*

Backpack

Allow 2 days to Amiskwi Pass

Elevation gain: 820 m (2,700 ft)

Maximum elevation: 1980 m (6,500 ft)

Maps: Golden 82 N/8
Blaeberry River 82 N/10
Yoho National Park

Access: Access: Follow the Trans-Canada Highway to its intersection with the Emerald Lake Road, 2 km (1.2 mi) west of the Field townsite intersection. Follow the Emerald Lake Road north 2 km (1.2 mi) to the Natural Bridge parking area. Continue west from the parking area on the gravel Kicking Horse Fire Road 1.6 km (1.0 mi) to a barricade just east of the Emerald River bridge. Walk west on the fire road 200 m, crossing the Emerald and Amiskwi River bridges, to the Amiskwi River trailhead.

0.0—Amiskwi River trailhead (1160 m). Road split. Kicking Horse Fire Road left. Stay right on Amiskwi Fire Road.

—Steady climb on well-graded roadbed for 2 km.

15.0—Fire Creek bridge.

17.0—Junction. Otto Creek Warden Cabin left. Stay right and cross Otto Creek bridge. (End of bike access).

24.0—Amiskwi River ford (calf-deep).

29.0—End of fire road.

31.5—Amiskwi Falls.

35.5—Amiskwi Pass (1980 m).

36.8—Ensign Creek logging road (1960 m).

*all distances approximate

(Trail not fully shown on maps in this book.)

The meadows above Amiskwi Pass provide wonderful views of the heavily-glaciated peaks of the Mummery Group. However, the hike up the Amiskwi Valley to the pass is one of the longest and most remote wilderness trips in Yoho Park. Of course, if you want to cheat, you can reach Amiskwi Pass in less than a half hour from the Ensign Creek logging road (see below).

Despite following an old access road for 29 km and passing through extensive sections of fire-scarred landscape, the trek up-valley provides many peaceful and scenic moments. The road is also open to cyclists as far as the Otto Creek bridge at km 17, and random camping is permitted throughout the valley.

The Amiskwi road begins 200 m west of the Amiskwi River's confluence with the Kicking Horse River. After passing the access gate, it climbs steadily for 2 km before levelling off well above the river. This road was created by the last commercial logging operation in the mountain parks (operations ceased in 1968), and old mill sites and log storage areas are still in evidence at several points in the valley.

The road traverses high along the west side of the valley until Fire Creek, where it begins to descend to the river. Between Fire Creek and Otto Creek you traverse the open slopes of the appropriately named Burnt Hill, which provide good views across the valley to the President Range.

After reaching the valley floor, the road rolls through burned and unburned sections of forest. It crosses the un-bridged Amiskwi at km 24 (knee-deep ford) and continues up the east side of the river for another 5 km to its termination at an old mill site. Single-track trail continues to the pass.

You pass beneath Amiskwi Falls near km 31, ford the Amiskwi (calf-deep), and enter unburned forest for the final stretch

Don Beers photo

The Mummery Group from the Amiskwi Lodge meadows

to the pass. Views from Amiskwi Pass are limited, but an ascent of the slope to the northeast reveals the Mummery Group in all its splendour.

North of the summit, and the Yoho Park boundary, you descend 1.3 km to the end of the Ensign Creek logging road on B.C. forest lands.

Amiskwi Pass via Ensign Creek. This may be the easiest way to reach Amiskwi Pass, but it is undoubtedly the longest and toughest drive to a short hike in the Rockies. Much of the approach is over unsurfaced forestry and logging roads, so a vehicle with higher clearance is desirable, though under most conditions not necessary.

Follow the Trans-Canada Highway west 11 km from the Highway 95 intersection at Golden, B.C., and turn right onto the Moberly Branch Road. Continue 2.2 km to the Golden-Donald Road and turn left. Follow 1 km to the Oberg-Johnson Road and turn right. Continue 1.7 km to the Moberly School Road and

turn left. The Moberly School Road becomes the Blaeberry Road in less than 1 km and leads up the Blaeberry Valley.

You reach the Mummery Creek Recreation Site 44 km from the Trans-Canada Highway. Continue another 3 km to where the Ensign Creek logging road branches right from the Blaeberry Road, crossing a bridge to the east side of the river. Follow this narrow road as it switchbacks steeply upwards to a road split at 7.5 km. Stay right and climb steadily south along the Ensign Creek valley for another 8 km to road's end in an old clearcut below Amiskwi Pass. (Watch for logging trucks and other vehicles on the upper Blaeberry and Ensign Creek roads.)

Once you reach the parking area, you have a 1.3-km hike to Amiskwi Pass. The best views lie up the steep slope to the northeast, as does Amiskwi Lodge, which provides hut style, self-serve accommodation. There is no defined trail to the lodge at this time, but directions are provided for those who reserve space there. (See *Sources-Backcountry lodges.*)

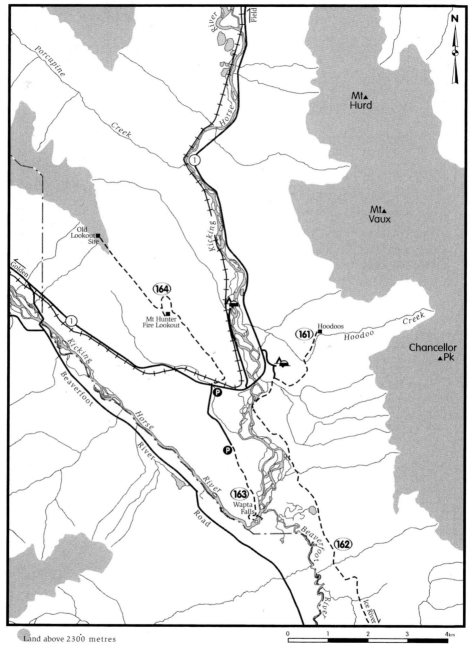

N

Porcupine Creek

Mt Hurd

Mt Vaux

Old Lookout Site

Kicking Horse River

Field

(164)

Mt Hunter Fire Lookout

(161) Hoodoos

Hoodoo Creek

Chancellor Pk

Golden

(1)

Kicking Horse River

Beaverfoot

P

P

River Road

(163) Wapta Falls

Beaverfoot River

(162)

Ice River

Land above 2300 metres

0   1   2   3   4km

Leanchoil Hoodoos

161 Leanchoil Hoodoos

Hoodoo Parking Area to Hoodoos—3.1 km (1.9 mi)

This short steep trail climbs into a narrow valley where you will discover some of the most extraordinary hoodoo formations in the mountain parks. These sentinel-like pillars of silt, gravel and stone have been formed by erosion, which has eaten away at a bank of partly consolidated, calcareous glacial debris. Unlike most other hoodoos in the Canadian Rockies, cap rocks sit like flat hats on top of the pillars, protecting the material beneath from erosion.

The trail circles around the Hoodoo Creek Campground to the Hoodoo Creek bridge at 1.5 km. (Campers can reach this point from the rear of the campground.) After this flat forest prelude, the last 1.6 km climbs nearly 250 m along the north slope of the Hoodoo Creek valley.

When you reach the Hoodoos, the trail splits: the right-hand path runs to the base of the formations, the left climbs to a good viewpoint above. Chancellor Peak is the dramatic mountain rising above the valley to the southeast.

The Scottish name Leanchoil prefixed to these hoodoos takes its name from the nearby CPR railway siding.

Access: Follow the Trans-Canada Highway to the Hoodoo Creek Campground, located 22.5 km (14 mi) west of Field or 7 km (4.5 mi) east of Yoho Park's west boundary. Follow the paved access road 0.6 km to the campground entrance. Branch right just before the entrance kiosk and follow the gravel road leading south 0.4 km to the Hoodoos trail parking area. *Maps: McMurdo 82 N/2; Yoho National Park.*

162 Ice River

Hoodoos Parking Area to Upper Ice River Cabin—25.2 km (15.7 mi)

Backpack

Allow 2 days to Upper Ice River

Elevation gain: 375 m (1,200 ft)

Maximum elevation: 1495 m (4,900 ft)

Maps: McMurdo 82 N/2
  Mount Goodsir 82 N/1
  Yoho National Park

Access: Follow the Trans-Canada Highway to the Hoodoo Creek Campground, located 22.5 km (14 mi) west of Field or 7 km (4.5 mi) east of Yoho Park's west boundary. Follow the paved access road 0.6 km to the campground entrance. Branch right just before the entrance and follow the gravel road leading south 0.4 km to the Hoodoos trail parking area. The Ice River trail begins at the access gate to the right of the parking area entrance.

0.0—Trailhead access gate (1120 m).

—Gently rolling roadbed along swampy meadows and through heavy forest.

6.0—Steep Creek.

10.0—Tallon Creek.

18.8—Lower Ice River Warden Cabin (1280 m).

—Trail crosses bridge and park boundary to east side of Ice River.

19.0—Junction. Kootenay River trail ahead. Upper Ice River left.

21.2—Mollison Creek.

24.4—Sodalite Creek.

25.2—Upper Ice River Warden Cabin.

Situated on the southern boundary of Yoho Park, the Ice River trail is yet another low elevation valley that is short on scenery but well endowed with peace and solitude. The upper valley is of interest to amateur geologists since it lies in the centre of the most important intrusive igneous complex in the Rockies—an area with significant deposits of zinc and blue sodalite.

The old road to the Lower Ice River Warden Cabin is open to cyclists, which is the most popular way to visit the valley. Random camping is permitted along the Beaverfoot Valley to the Lower Ice River Warden Cabin, but camping is not permitted on the upper Ice River. Hikers and cyclists should be aware that the entire route runs through prime grizzly country.

The first kilometre of trail follows the roadbed down through the forest to the site of the old Leanchoil Warden Cabin beside the Kicking Horse River. From these open flats, the road turns southwest and, after a short stretch along the Kicking Horse, enters forest and rolls along the east side of the Beaverfoot Valley for nearly 18 km to the Lower Ice River Warden Cabin.

The road ends at the warden cabin and, just beyond, crosses a bridge and the park boundary to a junction on the southeast side of the Ice River. The trail ahead runs to clearcuts and a logging road and leads out to the Beaverfoot Road in another 10 km; the trail up the Ice River branches left.

The Ice River trail makes a gradual ascent along the east side of the river, re-entering Yoho Park approximately 1.5 km beyond the junction. It stays on this side of the river all the way to the Upper Ice River Warden Cabin. This dubious route is mostly enveloped by forest, which is a rather dense mix of Douglas fir, white spruce, poplar and alder, and there are few views worth mentioning.

Wapta Falls

163 Wapta Falls

Wapta Falls Parking Area to Wapta Falls—2.3 km (1.4 mi)

The Wapta Falls trail makes an excellent afternoon outing—it is short, wide and well-defined and, with the exception of a short, steep descent to the lower viewpoint, flat and undemanding. The objective of the hike is a 30-m-high waterfall on the Kicking Horse River—Yoho's largest waterfall by water-volume.

The hike follows the flat bed of an old access road for 1.0 km before narrowing to a traditional single-track. You travel through a cool, mossy forest for the last half of the journey—a rich mixture of alder, birch, western red cedar and cottonwood poplar.

You arrive at the fenced upper viewpoint overlooking the falls at 1.9 km. While the view is impressive, we always continue down to the riverside beach below the falls—a steep, switchbacking descent.

The view of the falls from the riverside is partially obscured by a ridge of erosion resistant rock jutting across the river, but at low water you can continue upstream to better vantage points. There is also a nice mountain backdrop created by the Chancellor Range from this angle.

A slightly longer alternate trail climbs back to the upper viewpoint from the riverside. It is a more moderately-graded route that passes through some incredibly lush vegetation, which includes the insidious devil's club.

Access: Follow the Trans-Canada Highway to the Wapta Falls access road, which branches south from the highway 5 km (3 mi) east of Yoho Park's west boundary, or 25 km (15.5 mi) west of Field. The gravel road continues south 1.8 km (1.1 mi) to the trailhead parking area. *Maps: McMurdo 82 N/2; Yoho National Park.*

164 Mount Hunter Lookout

Trans Canada Highway to Lower Lookout — 3.6 km (2.2 mi)
Trans Canada Highway to Upper Lookout Site—6.0 km (3.7 mi)

Day trip

Allow 2 to 2.5 hours to upper lookout

Elevation gain: 950 m (3,100 ft)

Maximum elevation: 2050 m (6,730 ft)

Maps: McMurdo 82 N/2
        Yoho National Park

Access: Follow the Trans-Canada Highway to the Wapta Falls access road, 5 km (3 mi) east of Yoho Park's west boundary or 25 km (15.5 mi) west of Field townsite. Park just inside the entrance to the Wapta Falls road and cross the Trans-Canada Highway to the Mount Hunter Lookout trailhead.

0.0—Trans-Canada Highway trailhead (1115 m).

0.3—Trail crosses railroad tracks.

   —Steady uphill through forest.

0.7—Ridgetop viewpoint.

   —Open views continue for 2 km.

3.4—Junction (1600 m). Mt Hunter Lookout left 0.2 km. Upper Lookout ahead.

   —Moderate to steep uphill.

6.0—Upper Lookout site (2065 m).

Most fire lookout sites have two things in common: they have far-reaching views, usually down one or more major valleys; and the trails leading to the lookouts are excruciatingly steep. The two lookout sites on Mount Hunter's southeast ridge certainly fit this profile.

If you are looking for a good workout, this is the trail for you. Views from both lookout sites—one situated at 1600 m, the other at 2065 m—are certainly rewarding, though they are mostly aimed at the broad open valley to the south where the Kicking Horse and Beaverfoot Rivers meet. Make sure to pack water because there isn't any along the trail and this is a very hot, dry climb on a sunny midsummer's day.

After crossing the CPR tracks and climbing a short distance through forest, the trail breaks out onto the crest of the ridge leading to the lookouts. There is a dramatic change in forest cover and vegetation on this south-facing ridge, as spruce forest is replaced by a more open, montane environment of Douglas fir, Rocky Mountain juniper and ground-hugging common juniper.

Views of the Beaverfoot Range and Valley continue to improve as the trail climbs along this lightly forested ridge for nearly 2 km. Then it angles off into heavy forest again for the final climb to the lower lookout.

Though the lookout hasn't been manned in many years, the tower and the lookout keeper's cabin were still standing in 1998. (The cabin is open and serves as a shelter on inclement days, but stay off the tower.)

Views toward the Ottertail Range are partially blocked by large microwave communications panels, but the vista south down the Beaverfoot Valley is unfettered. The Beaverfoot River is the boundary between Yoho Park and provincial forest lands. When we first hiked

Beaverfoot and Kicking Horse Valleys from Mount Hunter's upper lookout site

here in 1970, the west side of the Beaverfoot was totally denuded by clearcuts, but they have since been replanted and are hardly noticeable today.

Unfortunately, the Trans-Canada Highway is still visible and audible, even though it lies nearly 500 vertical metres below. Of more interest is the broad swath of downed timber above the highway. No, its not a B.C. clearcut, but rather the aftermath of the "Yoho Blow"—a severe windstorm that swept through the valley November 21, 1993. More than 200 hectares of forest on both sides of the highway were flattened by winds exceeding 100 km per hour.

If you still have energy to spare, you can climb along the ridge for another 2.6 km to the upper lookout site, which is twice as high above the valley as the lower lookout. Views are more limited on the upper trail, but the forest becomes quite noticeably subalpine as you near trail's end. A well-constructed piece of trail with shale reinforcement announces the final 500 m to the lookout keeper's log cabin.

From the cabin you walk out onto the open ridge where the wooden-legged lookout tower once stood. Like most of the fire lookouts in the mountain parks, Mount Hunter was erected in the early 1940s. Though it was later replaced by the lower tower, it stood until the early 1990s when Parks Canada removed it.

Views are similar to those from the lower lookout site, though more expansive and impressive due to the higher elevation.

Kootenay National Park

Kootenay National Park is a 1406-sq-km reserve on the British Columbia side of the continental divide—the last national park to be created in the Canadian Rockies in 1920. It is bounded on the north by Yoho National Park and on the east by Banff National Park and Mount Assiniboine Provincial Park.

Of the four adjoining mountain national parks, Kootenay is possibly the least known by the average visitor. However, its 200-km trail system runs to some of the most rugged scenery and interesting natural features in the range.

All Kootenay hikes start from Highway 93. Many are short and ideally suited for families or those looking for undemanding walks. Marble Canyon and the Paint Pots, near the north end of the park, are both popular self-guiding nature trails; Stanley Glacier, Dog Lake, and Cobb Lake are rewarding half-day outings; Floe Lake and Kindersley Pass are two of the park's most popular full-day trips.

Though no section of the park seems to be very far from Highway 93, there are several excellent backpacking routes. Trails up Tumbling, Helmet, Numa and Floe Creeks lead to the spectacular Rockwall escarpment, which forms part of the park's western boundary. These trails can be linked in a variety of ways to make shorter, overnight loop trips, or you can complete a classic multi-day trip along the Rockwall Trail.

Kaufmann Lake is another attractive backpack at the north end of the park, and several other routes link with trails in Banff, Yoho and Mount Assiniboine Parks.

Campgrounds are conveniently spaced along all these routes, and there is a tent quota for each. Reservations for sites can be made through the Kootenay National Park Information Centre from June to September, or the park administration office from October to May. (See *Sources-Parks information.*)

Information and services. Two park visitor centres operate during the summer season. The Kootenay National Park Information Centre (June to mid-September) is located in Radium village near the road to Redstreak Campground. The Vermilion Crossing Visitor Centre is located at Kootenay Park Lodge on Highway 93, 63 km (39 mi) north of the park's west entrance and 31 km (19 mi) south of the Banff-Kootenay Park boundary. Off-season information is available at the park administration office at Radium, B.C. (See *Sources-Parks information.*)

McLeod Meadows and Marble Canyon Campgrounds operate along Highway 93 during the summer season. The park's largest and only full service campground is Redstreak, which is accessed by a road running from the village of Radium.

Radium, B.C., is located just beyond the park's west gate at the intersection of Highways 93 and 95. It is the main service centre for the park and the site of the park administration offices. Services include restaurants, accommodations, grocery stores, service stations, souvenir shops, a post office and a RCMP detachment. Accommodation inside the park is limited to a lodge and bungalow camp opposite the Radium Hot Springs pool, and Kootenay Park Lodge at Vermilion Crossing (seasonal).

Access: Highway 93 is the only road through the park. The highway intersects the Trans-Canada Highway at Castle Junction in Banff Park and Highway 95 at Radium, B.C. The nearest international airport is at Calgary, Alberta, 264 km east of Radium; commercial flights also operate out of Cranbrook, B.C., 145 km south of Radium on Highway 93/95.

Radium is a stop for Greyhound buses running between Calgary and southeastern B.C., and between Cranbook and Golden, B.C.

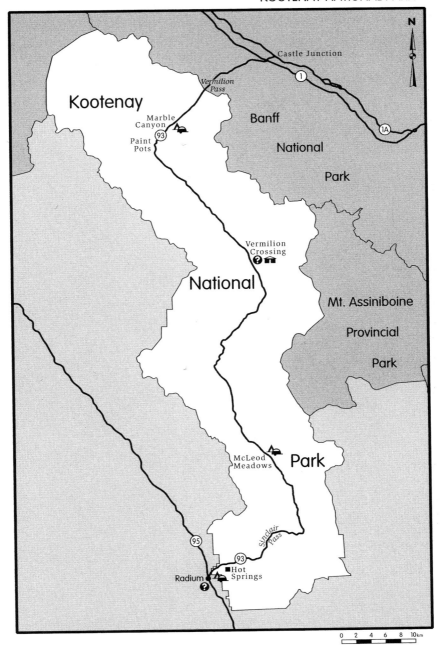

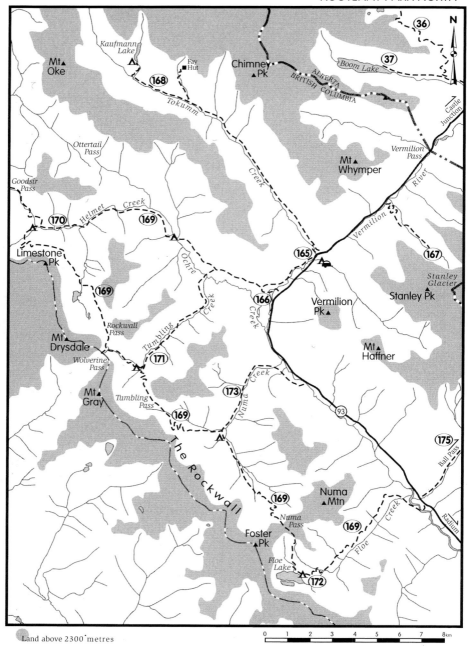

Land above 2300 metres

0 1 2 3 4 5 6 7 8km

165 Marble Canyon

Marble Canyon Circuit—1.4 km (0.9 mi)

Marble Canyon is one of the most popular self-guiding nature walks in Kootenay Park. Broad, well-graded trails follow along both sides of the canyon to its head, where the waters of Tokumm Creek fall into the chasm from Prospector's Valley. A number of bridges span the canyon, allowing you to hike up one side and back the other, or switch back and forth from one side to the other at will.

The canyon was created by the action of water flowing through narrow joints in the limestone bedrock. Over many centuries the stream dissolved limestone and widened the cracks to form the canyon. In several sections evidence of the abrasive action of rocks and gravel being swirled in the current is seen as smoothed, concave indentations and rounded potholes in the canyon walls.

While the space between its walls varies from only 3 m to 18 m, the canyon reaches a depth of nearly 60 m (200 ft). In addition to allowing access from one side of the canyon to another, the bridges provide giddy views into the dark abyss.

Access: Follow Highway 93 to the Marble Canyon parking area, located on the northwest side of the highway 7.0 km (4.3 mi) west of the Banff-Kootenay (Alberta-B.C.) boundary at Vermilion Pass. The trail begins at the trail kiosk sign at the rear of the parking area. *Maps: Mount Goodsir 82.*

166 Paint Pots

Paint Pots Parking Area to Upper Paint Pots—1.0 km (0.6 mi)

The short trail leading to the Paint Pots is another very popular nature walk in the northern region of Kootenay Park. Interpretive signs along the way describe the geology and history of the Ochre Beds—one of the park's unique features.

After descending through the forest and crossing a suspension bridge over the Vermilion River, you enter a meadow where iron-rich mineral waters have stained clay deposits brilliant hues of yellow and red. The trail crosses this colourful meadow and then climbs briefly through the forest to an opening containing the Paint Pots, which have been formed by iron oxide deposits building up around three cold mineral springs.

Before the arrival of the white man, native tribes from both sides of the mountains came here to collect the coloured clays for body paint. These early peoples believed the springs to be sacred places inhabited by animal spirits.

Early white settlers also mined the ochre for a brief period and shipped it to Calgary for use as a base for paint. You will understand why if you get the colourful mud on your boots—it takes some dedicated rinsing to get it off.

Access: Follow Highway 93 to the Paint Pots parking area, located on the northwest side of the highway 9.5 km (6.0 mi) west of the Banff-Kootenay boundary at Vermilion Pass. The trail begins at the trailhead kiosk at the rear of the parking area. *Maps: Mount Goodsir 82 N.*

167 Stanley Glacier

Highway 93 to Stanley Glacier Basin—4.2 km (2.6 mi)

Half-day trip

Allow 1.5 hours one way

Elevation gain: 365 m (1,200 ft)

Maximum elevation: 1950 m (6,400 ft)

Maps: Mount Goodsir 82 N/1

Access: Follow Highway 93 to the Stanley Glacier parking area, located on the southeast side of the road 3.2 km (2.0 mi) west of the Banff-Kootenay Park boundary at Vermilion Pass. The trail begins at the Vermilion River footbridge immediately below the parking area.

0.0—Vermilion River footbridge (1585 m).

—Trail switchbacks up through old burn.

2.4—Stanley Creek bridge.

—Steady climb above Stanley Creek.

4.2—Stanley Glacier basin (1950 m).

This easy half-day outing runs from the Vermilion River to a rockbound hanging valley containing Stanley Glacier. The trail is often snowfree in early June, and the hike is very rewarding in the spring and early summer when wildflowers blanket the trailside and numerous waterfalls and avalanches tumble off of Stanley Peak's northeast face.

After crossing the Vermilion River, the trail climbs steadily for over 2 km along the valley's southwest slope. When we first hiked here in 1970, two years after the Vermilion Pass burn swept the valley, this was a scorched landscape of charred logs and naked spars rising against the sky. Today the slope has totally revegetated with dense stands of lodgepole pine. However, the forest remains open enough to support an interesting variety of wildflowers, including fireweed, yellow columbine, heart-leaved arnica and Labrador tea.

Shortly after levelling out at the top of the slope, the trail angles northeast and crosses Stanley Creek. It continues up-valley for more than a kilometre from the bridge, following the edge of the creek and along cool, green stands of Engelmann spruce and alpine fir that escaped the flames of '68.

The last section of defined trail crosses avalanche paths and climbs a rocky, sparsely forested slope before ending atop an old moraine in the midst of the basin's boulder fields. From this vantage point you can survey the entire basin, including the tumbled icefall of Stanley Glacier at the head of the valley.

Particularly impressive are the massive Cambrian limestone cliffs beneath Stanley Peak. This wall rises over 450 m, and dozens of waterfalls cascade down its face in late spring. (A few years ago we witnessed a massive avalanche that poured over this precipice and covered much of the wall in a cloud of snow.)

Stanley Glacier basin

Though the moraine is a fine viewpoint and a pleasant lunch-stop, you can continue on for another kilometre or so following snippets of trail and cairns to the larch and fir-topped plateau at the head of the valley. Though it is a stiff climb over broken rock, and sometimes snowfields, the stream-fed meadow atop the cliff provides an outstanding viewpoint for the toe of the Stanley Glacier. Along the way, watch for the hoary marmots, pikas and ptarmigan who make their home in this rocky amphitheatre.

Also look for a pair of small caves at the base of the Stanley Peak cliff about halfway between the end of trail and the upper plateau (approximately 100 m beyond a major waterfall). These shallow caverns were dissolved from the wall at a time when the Stanley Glacier filled this basin. You can reach the caves by making a short climb up a talus slope. Inside you will find the abundant droppings of the cave inhabitants—little brown bats.

168 Kaufmann Lake

Marble Canyon Parking Area to Kaufmann Lake—15.0 km (9.3 mi)

Backpack

Allow 4.5 to 6 hours one way

Elevation gain: 570 m (1,870 ft)

Maximum elevation: 2060 m (6,750 ft)

Maps: Mount Goodsir 82 N/1
　　　 Lake Louise 82 N/8

Access: Follow Highway 93 to the Marble Canyon parking area, located on the northwest side of the highway 7.0 km (4.3 mi) west of the Banff-Kootenay Park boundary at Vermilion Pass. The hike begins from the trail kiosk sign at the rear of the parking area.

0.0—Marble Canyon parking area (1490 m).

　—Trail branches right from Marble Canyon trail in 30 m.

0.7—Junction. Upper Marble Canyon left. Continue ahead.

1.6—Trail narrows to single track.

3.2—Trail emerges onto open flats beside creek.

　—Gradual to moderate uphill along creek.

8.5—Tributary stream bridge.

10.3—Tributary stream bridge.

10.4—Junction. Fay Hut right 2.4 km.

12.2—Landslide area.

13.2—Tributary stream bridges.

13.5—Trail begins steep switchbacking climb.

14.7—Grade moderates.

15.0—Kaufmann Lake and Campground (2060 m).

The trail up Prospector's Valley leads to the remote northwest corner of Kootenay Park and a hanging valley containing Kaufmann Lake. Kaufmann is a classic Canadian Rockies lake, beautifully coloured and cradled by the towering Wenkchemna Peaks—the same mountains that form the dramatic backdrop for Banff's Moraine Lake.

After branching right from the Marble Canyon nature trail just 30 m beyond the parking area, the trail climbs briefly and then runs northwest above the canyon as a broad gravel track. After passing the canyon, it follows an old roadbed for another kilometre before narrowing to a single-file path through a forest of lodgepole pine, Engelmann spruce and alpine fir.

Just beyond the 3-km mark, the trail emerges into open meadows beside Tokumm Creek. For the remainder of the journey upvalley, you follow rough, rooty trail that is seldom far from the creek's rushing waters.

Prospector's Valley was named by tourist-explorer Walter Wilcox in 1899 after he discovered an old prospector's camp near its mouth. The name Tokumm is Stoney Indian for "red fox"—something we've seldom seen in the Rockies.

You cross a second major tributary stream at km 10.3 (where the trail to Fay Hut branches right). Another 3 km of rocky trail brings you to the multi-channeled outlet stream from Kaufmann Lake. Once you've crossed these bridged streamlets, the final ascent to Kaufmann Lake begins—a steep, rough 1.5-km climb. The grim uphill slog finally relents just before your arrival at the south end of the lake.

Deltaform Mountain (3424 m), Mount Tuzo (3249 m) and Mount Allen (3301 m) provide the lake's backdrop, and the combination of cliffs, glacier ice and blue-green water creates one of the loveliest views in Kootenay Park. It is a

Kaufmann Lake

very peaceful spot, where we have seen mule deer quietly browsing along the margins of the alpine fir-larch forest and counted a rich assortment of wildflowers in the lush shoreline meadows.

Fay Hut—2.4 km. The hut is located on the south slope of the Wenkchemna Peaks high above the Prospector's Valley. This tiny log cabin was constructed in 1927 by the Alpine Club of Canada as the club's first climber's hut.

This historic log cabin's primary function is to serve climbers bound for nearby summits or the lofty Neil Colgan Hut; however, it is a pleasantly high and remote place for strong hikers to overnight. To reserve space, contact the Alpine Club's Canmore clubhouse (see *Sources-Huts*).

Immediately after crossing the second major Tokumm Creek tributary at km 10.3, the trail to the hut branches up to the right. It climbs steeply along the west side of the stream and then, near the 1830-m level, crosses to the east side and angles up and away from the tributary. It becomes less defined as it climbs and, after working up through cliff bands and a steep couloir, it suddenly arrives at the well-hidden, one room cabin.

The Rockwall

Following his epic trek from the U.S.-Canada border to the Yukon in 1988, British author Chris Townsend wrote us to say that the Rockwall Trail was "the best trail I walked in the mountain parks!" How can we disagree? Of four different cover photos used on *The Canadian Rockies Trail Guide* since 1971, three have been from The Rockwall region.

The Rockwall is the eastern escarpment of Kootenay Park's Vermilion Range. As you drive Highway 93 between the Paint Pots and Vermilion Crossing, there are numerous tantalizing glimpses west to this sheer limestone wall. But The Rockwall is even more impressive close-up—a remarkable combination of high passes, larch forests, wildflower meadows, towering waterfalls, and glaciers. It is quite understandable why it is Kootenay's best known hiking area.

The Rockwall's recreational history began in 1923 when outfitter Walter Nixon guided a group of visiting dignitaries to Tumbling Pass and the Wolverine Plateau. Included in his party were H.B. Clow, president of the Rand McNally map company, and John Murray Gibbon, publicist for the Canadian Pacific Railway. Before the journey ended, the group concurred that it was the most scenic alpine route they had ever ridden. They also agreed that recreational horseback riders should have the opportunity to do wonderful trips like this annually. With the support of Gibbon and the CPR, the Trail Riders of the Canadian Rockies was formed the following year.

Walter Nixon returned to The Rockwall in the autumn of 1924 to cut the first trail along the escarpment in preparation for the Trail Riders' annual ride the following summer. Over the next four decades, the Trail Riders returned several times to this exceptional area. As trails were established up the short valleys leading to the range, the region became increasingly popular with other horseback parties and, to a lesser extent, hikers and backpackers.

In 1969, Jim Thorsell included the Rockwall Trail in his proposed route for the Great Divide Trail. Though the Great Divide Trail was never formally established, Jim's proposal did draw the attention of a growing number of hikers, and the area soon secured a reputation as one of the finest backcountry destinations in the Rockies.

Four side valleys lead to The Rockwall—Helmet Creek, Tumbling Creek, Numa Creek and Floe Creek, and well-maintained trails along these streams are the primary access routes to the range. Between the headwaters of these four valleys, there are three high alpine passes—Rockwall, Tumbling and Numa—which are connected by trails to allow travel along the length of the escarpment.

Options. With such a comprehensive trail system, there are numerous ways to visit The Rockwall and sample its spectacular scenery.

Floe Lake is by far the most popular destination, both for day hikers and backpackers.

The classic backpack is the *Rockwall Trail* circuit, which runs between the *Floe Lake* and *Helmet Falls* trailheads. This four-to-five-day trek crosses all three passes and travels for 30 km beneath The Rockwall's escarpment. The trip can also be extended into Yoho Park utilizing Goodsir Pass, or to Banff Park via the *Hawk Creek-Ball Pass* trail.

Shorter backpacks can be completed over only one or two passes. (All of the single pass loop trips have also been done in a long day by strong hikers.)

Or you can hike to a campground at the headwaters of one of the four valleys and day trip to nearby passes.

Descriptions for the *Rockwall Trail, Helmet Falls, Tumbling Creek, Floe Lake,* and *Numa Creek* are found on pages 328 to 336.

Floe Lake and The Rockwall from the Numa Pass trail

KOOTENAY NATIONAL PARK 327

169 Rockwall Trail

Paint Pots Parking Area to Floe Lake Parking Area—54.4 km (33.8 mi)

Backpack

Allow 4 days

Maximum elevation: 2355 m (7,720 ft)

Minimum elevation: 1325 m (4,350 ft)

Maps: Mount Goodsir 82 N/1

Access: To reach the south end of the trail, follow Highway 93 to the *Floe Lake* parking area. The north end of the route starts at the Paint Pots parking area and follows the *Helmet Creek* trail.

0.0—Paint Pots parking area (1450 m).

3.7—Junction. *Tumbling Creek* trail left.

6.0—Ochre-Helmet Junction Campground.

14.3—Junction. Goodsir Pass right.

14.9—Helmet Falls Campground (1760 m).

18.1—Limestone Summit (2170 m).

19.1—Helmet Creek south fork bridge (1920 m).

23.0—Rockwall Pass (2240 m).

23.4—Junction. Wolverine Pass right 0.5 km.

26.5—Tumbling Creek Campground.

26.8—Tumbling Creek Junction (1890 m). Intersection with *Tumbling Creek* trail at km 10.3.

29.1—Tumbling Pass (2210 m).

33.9—Numa Creek Junction (1525 m). Intersection with *Numa Creek* trail at km 6.4.

34.4—Numa Creek Campground.

41.2—Numa Pass (2355 m).

43.9—Floe Lake and Campground (2040 m).

54.4—Floe Lake Parking Area (1325 m).

The 30-km trail running beneath The Rockwall between Helmet Falls and Floe Lake is extraordinary for its variety and beauty. It travels beneath massive limestone walls and hanging glaciers and traverses three alpine passes and numerous wildflower meadows. In early summer, waterfalls tumble from the cliffs, including one of Canada's highest—Helmet Falls. In autumn, the passes are bathed in the golden glow of alpine larch.

The only negative aspect of this journey, at least for the overburdened backpacker, is the way the trail rises and falls like a roller coaster as it ascends passes and plunges into intervening valleys. However, each of these valleys has trail connections to Highway 93, allowing entry or exit at a number of points. (See *Tumbling Creek* and *Numa Creek*.)

The Rockwall circuit, running from the Paint Pots to the Floe Lake trailhead (or visa versa), is the most popular multiday trip along the range. Some backpackers hike The Rockwall as part of an even longer trip connecting to Banff Park via Ball Pass or Yoho Park via Goodsir Pass, but these options require time-consuming transportation arrangements between distant trailheads. The beauty of the Rockwall circuit is that, after 4 or 5 days on the trail, you emerge only 13 km from where you started on Highway 93.

It's six-of-one, half-a-dozen of the other whether you start at the north end of the circuit and hike south or visa versa. While there is a small elevation advantage north to south, our main reason for describing the trail in that direction is to save Floe Lake until the end of the journey. (There are few sights more inspiring than your first view of Floe Lake from Numa Pass.)

However, if the weather forecast is good, and sites are available at Floe Lake Campground, you may wish to start at the south end and work north.

Tumbling Pass and Glacier from Rockwall Pass

Starting from the Paint Pots, you have a long, gradual climb as you travel up Ochre and Helmet Creeks to Helmet Falls (see *Helmet Creek* for detailed description). If you plan a layover day at Helmet Falls Campground, you can day-trip to nearby Goodsir Pass.

From Helmet Falls you turn south and make a strenuous up-and-down ascent to Rockwall Pass. You gain 410 m of elevation in 3.2 km to Limestone Summit—a ridge extending eastward from Limestone Peak. (There are nice views of Helmet Falls as you struggle upwards.) From the summit, you plunge to the south fork of Helmet Creek, then climb steeply again to Rockwall Pass.

Rockwall Pass, with its vast wild-flower meadows and far-reaching views, is a wonderful place to linger. Just 0.4 km beyond the summit, a short trail branches off to Wolverine Pass, where views stretch west across the Columbia Valley to the Purcell Range and The Bugaboos.

Descending north from Rockwall Pass, you can see the trail far ahead rising alongside the Tumbling Glacier to the summit of Tumbling Pass—one of The Rockwall's classic views.

You reach Tumbling Creek Campground 300 m before the junction with the Tumbling Creek trail (see *Tumbling Creek* for area details). From this point, the trail climbs beside Tumbling Glacier's terminal moraine to Tumbling Pass. From the 2210-m summit, there is another wonderful view south to your next objective—Numa Pass.

Yet another dramatic loss of elevation across avalanche paths brings you to an intersection with the *Numa Creek* trail and, 500 m beyond, Numa Creek Campground.

The ascent to Numa Pass is one of the most gruelling of the entire trip, but the sudden appearance of Floe Lake with its Rockwall backdrop makes it all worthwhile. From the 2355-m pass, the trail's high point, you have a pleasant 2.7-km saunter down through meadows and larch groves to the lake and its deluxe campground.

The trip's final 10.5 km descends Floe Creek to Highway 93, which can be hiked in 3 hours or less. (See *Floe Lake* for details.)

170 Helmet Creek

Paint Pots Parking Area to Helmet Falls Campground—14.9 km (9.3 mi)

Backpack

Allow 5 hours to Helmet Falls

Elevation gain: 310 m (1,000 ft)

Maximum elevation: 1760 m (5,775 ft)

Maps: Mount Goodsir 82 N/1

Access: Follow Highway 93 to the Paint Pots parking area, located on the northwest side of the highway 9.5 km (5.9 mi) west of the Banff-Kootenay boundary at Vermilion Pass.

0.0—Paint Pots parking area (1450 m).

—Follow Paint Pots nature trail.

0.3—Vermilion River suspension bridge.

1.0—Paint Pots.

—Pick-up trail into forest beyond Paint Pots.

1.3—Junction. Marble Canyon right 3.2 km. Stay left.

3.7—Junction. *Tumbling Creek* trail left.

6.0—Junction. Ottertail Pass ahead. Turn left.

6.3—Ochre Creek crossing. Helmet-Ochre Junction Campground.

6.5—Helmet Creek suspension bridge.

—Switchbacks followed by gradual uphill on south side of creek.

12.0—Helmet Creek suspension bridge.

14.3—Junction. Goodsir Pass right 4.0 km. Helmet Falls ahead.

14.9—Helmet Falls Campground and Warden Cabin.

The Helmet Creek trail is the north end of the popular Rockwall Trail circuit. But even if you aren't following this route along the length of the range, the trail accesses some exceptional features at the north end of The Rockwall. These include 300-m Helmet Falls, one of Canada's highest, and the meadows and larch forests of Goodsir Pass, Limestone Summit and Rockwall Pass.

Follow the Paint Pots nature trail for the first 1.0 km. At the end of the nature trail, skirt around the edge of the clay mudflats surrounding the ochre springs and pick-up the track running into the forest on the opposite side.

After joining the trail from Marble Canyon at km 1.3, you follow nearly level terrain along the east side of Ochre Creek for nearly 5 km. At km 3.7, the Tumbling Creek trail branches left (the trail you will return on if you complete the loop over Rockwall Pass from Helmet Falls).

At km 6.0, you turn left to Helmet-Ochre Junction Campground and cross to the west side of Ochre Creek. Just 200 m beyond the crossing, a suspension bridge takes you to the true right bank of Helmet Creek and the ascent of Helmet Valley begins.

The trail quickly gains elevation via a series of switchbacks, then climbs steadily along the south side of Helmet Creek. A second suspension bridge takes you back to the north side of the creek at km 12.0, and you soon glimpse Helmet Falls ahead through the trees.

The trail to Goodsir Pass branches north at km 14.3. Stay on the left branch for 600 m to reach the Helmet Falls Campground near the warden cabin.

The highlight of any visit to the Helmet Creek headwaters is undoubtedly Helmet Falls, spewing from the escarpment enclosing the head of the valley. Limestone Peak (2878 m), Helmet Mountain (3138 m) and Sharp Mountain

The Goodsirs from Goodsir Pass

(3049 m) are the three summits that create the massive amphitheatre, and Sharp Glacier feeds the falls.

Rockwall Pass—8.1 km. One of the best day trips from Helmet Falls Campground follows the *Rockwall Trail* south to Rockwall Pass. From that 2240-m summit you have a classic view south along The Rockwall that includes Tumbling Pass and Glacier. It is a rather steep up-and-down hike that gains a total of 730 m by the time you reach the pass.

You can complete a loop back to the Paint Pots trailhead by continuing over the pass and descending Tumbling Creek to the Ochre Valley junction. We consider this the most scenic of The Rockwall single-pass loop trips, and the only one that brings you back where you started. Total round trip is 37 km. (See *Rockwall Trail* and *Tumbling Creek*.)

Goodsir Pass—4.0 km. Goodsir Pass is a high, long, glorious alpine meadow near the boundary between Kootenay and

Yoho Parks. It can be hiked either as a day trip from Helmet Creek Campground or by backpackers bound for Yoho Park.

The trail begins at the junction 0.6 km below the campground and climbs 450 vertical metres to the pass. Despite the rise, the trail is well routed and maintained, and a steady pace will soon take you into a scattered larch forest near treeline.

Once you crest the pass meadows, your attention is immediately drawn to the looming, glaciated spires of Sentry Peak (3267 m) and the twin towers of Mount Goodsir (3561 m)—the highest mountain in Yoho Park.

You cross the park boundary into Yoho Park 1.6 km beyond the summit. The trail makes a steep, steady descent, mainly through heavy forest, to Goodsir Creek and the Ottertail River. The Ottertail bridge and the intersection with the Ottertail River trail lies 8.3 km beyond Goodsir Pass. (See *Ottertail River*, Yoho Park chapter.)

171 Tumbling Creek

Paint Pots Parking Area to Tumbling Creek Campground—10.6 km (6.6 mi)

Day trip or backpack

Allow 4 hours to Tumbling Pass

Elevation gain: 760 m (2,500 ft)

Maximum elevation: 2210 m (7,250 ft)

Maps: Mount Goodsir 82 N/1

Access: Follow Highway 93 to the Paint Pots parking area, located on the northwest side of the highway 9.5 km (5.9 mi) west of the Banff-Kootenay boundary at Vermilion Pass.

0.0—Paint Pots parking area (1450 m).

　—Follow Paint Pots nature trail.

0.3—Vermilion River suspension bridge.

1.0—Paint Pots.

　—Pick-up trail into forest beyond Paint Pots.

1.3—Junction. Marble Canyon right 3.2 km. Stay left.

3.7—Junction. *Helmet Falls* trail ahead. Turn left.

4.1—Ochre Creek suspension bridge.

　—Steady climb along north side of Tumbling Creek.

6.6—Tumbling Creek bridge.

9.4—Tumbling Falls viewpoint.

10.3—Junction (1890 m). Intersection with *Rockwall Trail* at km 27.6. Right to Tumbling Creek Campground (0.3 km) and Rockwall Pass (3.8 km). Tumbling Pass ahead 2.3 km.

The Tumbling Creek trail is yet another access route to The Rockwall. While the trail makes a relatively long approach to the head of the Tumbling Valley, it is the most direct route to two of the range's finest alpine meadows on Tumbling and Rockwall Passes. The Tumbling Creek Campground at the head of the valley is a good base for half-day hikes to either of these summits. Or you can continue your backpack south to Numa Pass or north to Helmet Falls as part of an extended circuit along the Rockwall Trail.

The trail follows the Paint Pots nature trail for 1.0 km, then enters heavy forest on the opposite side of the mudflats surrounding these ochre springs. After joining a trail from Marble Canyon at km 1.3, it runs northwest along the east side of Ochre Creek valley.

At km 3.7, the Tumbling Creek trail parts ways with the Ochre Creek route, forking down to the left and crossing the creek to begin the long ascent of the Tumbling Valley. (If you complete a loop over Rockwall Pass to Helmet Falls, you will return to this junction on the way home.)

Throughout the remainder of the journey, the turbulent waters of Tumbling Creek are a constant companion. A fine waterfall is passed at km 9.4, and, just a kilometre beyond, you reach the intersection with the Rockwall highline route (see *Rockwall Trail*). Tumbling Creek Campground lies 300 m to the right on the opposite side of the creek.

Tumbling Pass—2.3 km. From the campground junction, it is a short hike to Tumbling Pass. The final 2 kms to the pass follows a series of steep switchbacks, which climb alongside a high terminal moraine deposited by the Tumbling Glacier. As the trail grinds its way upwards, views improve on all sides. Tumbling Glacier and The Rockwall rise above the trail to the west, while

Mount Gray and Tumbling Glacier from the Rockwall Pass meadows

back to the north are the open meadows leading to the Wolverine Plateau and Rockwall Pass.

From the pass, you can see the grey, eastern escarpment of The Rockwall snaking away to the south. The high saddle of Numa Pass lies between the sharp pyramid of Foster Peak and the rounded summit of Numa Mountain. In the foreground, the trail drops away toward the Numa Creek valley, threading its way across a meadow that is filled with wildflowers in summer and bordered by golden larch in late September.

South of the pass, the trail descends to a junction with the Numa Creek trail. By descending that trail you return to Highway 93 at the Numa Falls Picnic Area, or you can continue south along the Rockwall Trail to Numa Pass and Floe Lake. (See *Numa Creek* and *Rockwall Trail*.)

The Tumbling Creek-Tumbling Pass-Numa Creek trip is 24 km long, and is often completed as a day trip by hikers who have arranged transportation at the Paint Pots and Numa Falls trailheads.

Rockwall Pass—3.8 km. By following the Rockwall Trail north from Tumbling Creek Campground, you can reach the open meadows of the Wolverine Plateau and Rockwall Pass after 3 km of steady climbing. This summit is every bit as scenic as Tumbling Pass, and the meadows are far more extensive.

The term "Rockwall" takes on new meaning here. In fact, not until you are directly beneath the gap of Wolverine Pass do you realize there is a cleft in the 500-m-high wall. A short side trail leads to this gap, where views stretch west to the Purcell Range beyond the Columbia Valley.

From Wolverine Pass junction, the Rockwall Trail continues through alpine meadows to the summit of Rockwall Pass and points north. By following this route, you can make a loop trip back to the Paint Pots via Helmet Creek or continue over Goodsir Pass to Yoho Park. (See *Rockwall Trail* and *Helmet Creek*.)

172 Floe Lake

Highway 93 to Floe Lake—10.5 km (6.5 mi)
Highway 93 to Numa Pass—13.2 km (8.2 mi)

Day trip or backpack

Allow 3 to 4 hours to Floe Lake

Elevation gain: 715 m (2,350 ft)

Maximum elevation: 2040 m (6,700 ft)

Maps: Mount Goodsir 82 N/1

Access: Follow Highway 93 to the Floe Lake-Hawk Creek parking area, located on the west side of the highway 22.5 km (14 mi) south of the Banff-Kootenay boundary at Vermilion Pass and 8.3 km (5.2 mi) north of the Vermilion Crossing Visitor Centre.

0.0—Floe Lake parking area (1325 m).

—Trail descends to Vermilion River.

0.4—Vermilion River bridge.

—Trail contours northwest to Floe Valley.

1.7—Floe Creek bridge.

—Moderate to steep climb along north side of Floe Valley.

5.7—Steep switchbacks next 0.3 km.

8.0—Steep switchbacks next 2 km.

10.1—Trail levels off.

10.5—Floe Lake and Campground (2040 m). Numa Pass north 2.7 km. (See also *Rockwall Trail* and *Numa Creek*.)

Set beneath a 1000-m limestone escarpment and a sprawling necklace of glacial ice, Floe Lake is easily a match for any beauty spot in the Rockies. Beyond its north shore a subalpine forest of alpine fir and larch grades upward to the treeless meadows of Numa Pass—a summit that provides a wonderful high-level view of the entire Floe Lake cirque.

The trail to this hanging valley begins near the Vermilion River. It crosses the river and, just over 1 km beyond, joins the Floe Creek drainage, following that narrow valley upwards for the remainder of the hike. Though travel is mainly through a forest of lodgepole pine, spruce and alpine fir, many areas have been swept by avalanches, which provide open views.

Occasionally, you catch a glimpse of the imposing Rockwall ahead. At km 7.2, near the top of a short, steep grade, views open back down the Floe Valley to the Ball Range on the eastern horizon.

Just 300 m beyond the viewpoint, you enter a mature spruce-fir forest. Here the switchbacks begin that carry you up the last 2 km to Floe Lake. Water bottles should be filled at this point, since the trail is steep and there is no water until the lake.

Floe Lake is situated at 2040 m, well into the upper subalpine life zone. Trees along its northern shore are scattered and somewhat stunted, and, in midsummer, many varieties of wildflowers carpet the surrounding meadows. In autumn, the golden needles of alpine larch provide a brilliant foreground for the lake, glacier and The Rockwall.

The Rockwall is composed of a dark grey Cambrian limestone (Ottertail Formation)—the east-facing escarpment forming the backbone of the Vermilion Range for 40 km. A small glacier clings to the base of the wall and plunges to the southern edge of the lake, and the

Floe Lake from Numa Pass

resulting ice floes give the lake its name. There is also a lagoon created by the ridgetop of a terminal moraine, which loops out into the lake and partitions off a section of its waters.

The campground in the forest above the shore is a bit deluxe for some tastes, but it is a wonderful place to relax close to one of the best views in the Rockies. However, it is a busy campground in midsummer, so consider reservations if you want to be assured of a site.

Numa Pass—2.7 km. For strong day hikers, or those camped at Floe Lake, the trail continuing to Numa Pass is a must. Branching away from the lakeshore just before the warden cabin, the trail rises nearly 300 m en route to the pass.

Views from Numa Pass are some of the most expansive of any trail in the park. Set between Foster Peak (3204 m) on the west and Numa Mountain (2725 m) to the east, it is by far the best viewpoint for Floe Lake. To the north, set off by sheer walls, limestone pinnacles and hanging glaciers, the long face of

The Rockwall runs off toward Yoho Park. The sharp snowy mountains to the far north are the Wenkchemna Peaks, which rise above the Valley of the Ten Peaks in Banff Park.

Strong day hikers and backpackers can complete a circuit back to Highway 93 by descending the Numa Creek trail north of Numa Pass—an option that emerges at the Numa Falls Picnic Area 8 km north of the Floe Lake trailhead. Total distance for the Floe Lake-Numa Pass-Numa Creek trip is 27 km. (See *Numa Creek.*)

Rockwall Trail. The Floe Lake trail is the southern terminus for the Rockwall Trail—a 55 km route that runs northwest along the face of the Vermilion Range to Helmet Falls and then back to Highway 93 at the Paint Pots trailhead. In addition to crossing three high and very scenic passes, the route intersects three trails running up Numa, Tumbling and Helmet Creeks, which allows for a variety of itineraries. (See *Rockwall Trail.*)

173 Numa Creek

Numa Falls Picnic Area to Rockwall Trail Junction—6.4 km (4.0 mi)

The first 3 kms of this trail make for a pleasant nature walk from the Numa Falls Picnic Area. The trail also serves as the shortest access route to the Rockwall Trail, but there is little reason to use it except as an optional exit. Views along the trail are limited, and the climb to worthwhile viewpoints, like Tumbling and Numa Passes, is excruciatingly steep and long.

The trail starts at Numa Falls Picnic Area and immediately crosses a bridge over the Vermilion River at a small canyon 100 m beyond the picnic site. It then contours northwest above the river to the mouth of the Numa Creek valley.

After entering the Numa Creek drainage, it crosses a bridge at km 3.0 to the true left bank of the creek and makes a steady, uneventful ascent of this narrow, forested valley.

The trail intersects the Rockwall Trail 500 m north of Numa Creek Campground (see *Rockwall Trail,* km 33.9). From this junction, you can continue right 4.8 km to Tumbling Pass or left 7.3 km to Numa Pass. Both of these switchbacking trails are steep and gruelling.

Access: Follow Highway 93 to the Numa Falls Picnic Area, located beside the Vermilion River 14 km (8.5 mi) south of the Banff-Kootenay boundary and 16.5 km (10.3 mi) north of the Vermilion Crossing Visitor Centre. From the far end of the picnic area, walk 100 m to the Vermilion River footbridge. *Maps: Mount Goodsir 82 N/1.*

174 Verendrye Creek

Vermilion Crossing Picnic Area to Upper Verendrye Creek—4.3 km (2.7 mi)

The Verendrye Creek trail is a forest-enclosed path extending up a tight side-valley to the base of Mount Verendrye. It fizzles out near the head of the valley in an area swept by avalanches, where there are limited views of Mount Verendrye and the sheer eastern escarpment of the Vermilion Range. Unfortunately, this is one view that is better from the highway.

Though the trail is no longer maintained, it remains a pleasant walk, particularly for guests at nearby Kootenay Park Lodge or picnickers who want to stretch their legs for an hour or so.

Starting from the rear of the picnic area, the trail climbs gradually through a cool, well-shaded forest of lodgepole pine and spruce. It reaches Verendrye Creek at km 2.1, where it crosses to the creek's north bank. Many hikers accept the limited view of Mount Verendrye from this point and turn for home. However, more dedicated souls can cross the creek and continue up-valley.

Beyond the crossing, a rough track continues along the north side of the creek. At km 3.5, you enter an area of avalanche paths and, 800 m farther along, the trail finally disappears on a large gravel outwash beside the creek.

Access: Follow Highway 93 to the Vermilion Crossing Picnic Area, located on west side of the highway 29.5 km (18.5 mi) south of the Banff-Kootenay boundary and across the highway from Kootenay Park Lodge and the Vermilion Crossing Visitor Centre. The trail begins at the rear of the picnic area. *Maps: Banff 82 O/4, Mount Goodsir 82 N/1 (trail not shown).*

175 Hawk Creek—Ball Pass

Highway 93 to Ball Pass—10.1 km (6.3 mi)

Day trip or backpack

Allow 3 to 4 hours one way

Elevation gain: 885 m (2,900 ft)

Maximum elevation: 2210 m (7,250 ft)

Maps: Mount Goodsir 82 N/1
      Banff 82 O/4

Access: Follow Highway 93 to the Floe Lake-Hawk Creek parking area, located on the west side of the highway 22.5 km (14 mi) south of the Banff-Kootenay boundary at Vermilion Pass and 8.3 km (5.2 mi) north of the Vermilion Crossing Visitor Centre. The trail begins on the east side of the highway opposite the parking area entrance.

0.0—Trail sign (1325 m).

  —Trail follows north along highway.

0.4—Hawk Creek highway bridge.

  —Trail runs northeast on old roadbed.

1.1—Trail begins climb along northwest side of canyon.

  —Steady moderate to steep ascent.

4.6—Tributary stream bridge.

7.4—Steep switchbacks begin.

8.8—Trail enters subalpine meadow.

  —Steep ascent to pass.

10.1—Ball Pass (2040 m). Banff-Kootenay Park boundary. Trail connects with *Bow Valley Highline Trail* 2.7 km beyond pass. (See also *Shadow Lake Area Hikes*.)

While Ball Pass is a scenic summit fringed by alpine larch, the climb up Hawk Creek is relentless, rocky and dry. It is better to visit the pass from the Banff Park side, either as a day trip from Shadow Lake or as part of an extended backpack over the Great Divide from the Bow Valley Highline Trail.

From the trail sign opposite the parking area, the trail follows along Highway 93 for 400 m to the Hawk Creek highway bridge. Cross the bridge to the north side and follow the path up into the forest, where you pick-up an old roadbed running northeast.

The road climbs gradually through a pleasant forest, and its margins are carpeted with wild strawberries in late July and early August. (A great temptation so early in the hike.)

Fill your water bottle when you cross the tributary stream at km 4.6 in preparation for the climb ahead—a long, steep, waterless traverse across open, south-facing avalanche paths and massive rockslides. This is an arid desert on warm, sunny days, and there is no relief until the stream-fed meadows just below the pass.

The pass is a narrow notch in the middle of the Ball Range. Rockslides have turned the northern lip of the pass into a rather tumbled, desolate place, but a scattered forest of larch and alpine fir interspersed with patches of meadow soften the rest of the summit. Glacier-capped Mount Ball (3311 m) rises above the pass to the north, while the Haiduk Valley runs away to the northeast toward Shadow Lake.

Banff-bound backpackers will find the first campground of the journey 2.7 km to the east, where the trail intersects with the Bow Valley Highline Trail (see *Bow Valley Highline Trail* km 21.0 and *Shadow Lake Area Hikes*, Banff Park chapter).

176 Honeymoon Pass—Verdant Creek

Highway 93 to Honeymoon Pass—5.6 km (3.5 mi)
Highway 93 to Egypt Lake Campground via Verdant Creek—21.5 km (13.4 mi)

Day trip or backpack

Allow 2 hours to Honeymoon Pass

Elevation gain: 730 m (2,400 ft)

Maximum elevation: 1995 m (6,550 ft)

Maps: Banff 82 O/4

Access: Follow Highway 93 to the Honeymoon Pass-Verdant Creek parking area, located on the east side of the highway 30.5 km (19 mi) south of the Banff-Kootenay boundary and 300 m north of the Vermilion Crossing Visitor Centre and Kootenay Park Lodge.

0.0—Trail kiosk (1325 m).

—Narrow, rooty trail through forest followed by steep switchbacks.

3.7—Uphill grade moderates.

3.9—Open avalanche slope.

5.6—Honeymoon Pass (1995 m).

—Steady descent to Verdant Creek.

7.7—Verdant Creek ford.

8.4—Verdant Creek Campground.

9.1—Verdant Creek ford.

11.6—Verdant Creek Warden Cabin and Junction (1675 m).

—Trail crosses Verdant Creek, ascends East Verdant Creek (wet, brushy and indistinct).

18.2—Redearth Pass (2090 m). Banff-Kootenay boundary.

18.8—Junction. Natalko Lake left 1.9 km.

21.3—Junction. Intersection with *Healy Pass-Egypt Lake* trail at km 12.2. Egypt Lake Campground left 200 m.

Except for its questionable role as a route from Kootenay Park to Egypt Lake in Banff Park, the Honeymoon Pass-Verdant Creek trail has little to recommend it. The grades are steep, the track is frequently poor, and there are few open views. It is strictly for wilderness travellers who enjoy solitude and the challenge of rough trail.

The ascent to the pass is no honeymoon. The climb is steady and steep, gaining 670 m of elevation over 5.6 km. Except for an avalanche slope part way up, which provides a glimpse of Mount Verendrye back across the valley, views are non-existent. The pass is not much better—a few tiny meadows surrounded by trees.

Beyond the pass, the trail makes a quick descent to Verdant Creek. Continuing down-valley, you ford Verdant Creek, pass the valley's only campground, then cross back to the west side of the creek. This section is wetter and less defined than the stretch up to Honeymoon Pass.

From Verdant Creek Warden Cabin, the trail to Redearth Pass branches northeast, crosses Verdant Creek, and begins a rather gruelling ascent of the East Verdant Creek valley. The track is often indistinct, and blazes are frequently the only indication that you are still on-route. In the upper portion of the valley, the vague trail crosses and recrosses East Verdant Creek a number of times.

Redearth Pass is rather long and undistinguished. At the northern edge of the pass a steep 1.9 km trail branches left to Natalko Lake at a poorly-defined junction (watch for a sign or cairn to the left). Though the lake lies in Kootenay Park, it is usually visited as a day trip from the Egypt Lake Campground, which is only 2.5 km beyond the Natalko Lake junction. (See *Egypt Lakes Area Hikes,* Banff Park chapter.)

177 Simpson River—Ferro Pass

Highway 93 to Ferro Pass—22.9 km (3.5 mi)
Highway 93 to Lake Magog Campground—32.2 km (20.0 mi)

Backpack

Allow 2 days to Lake Magog

Elevation gain: 1020 m (3,350 ft)

Maximum elevation: 2270 m (7,450 ft)

Maps: Mount Assiniboine 82 J/13

Access: Follow Highway 93 to the Simpson River trail parking area, located on east side of the highway 5.9 km (3.7 mi) south of the Vermilion Crossing Visitor Centre and 57 km (35.5 mi) north of Kootenay Park West Gate at Radium. The parking area is beside a footbridge crossing the Vermilion River.

0.0—Vermilion River footbridge (1250 m).

—Follows old roadbed.

0.2—Junction. Mt Shanks Lookout ahead. Turn right.

0.9—Trail reaches Simpson River.

—Trail follows north side of Simpson Valley.

8.8—Kootenay-Mt Assiniboine Park boundary.

10.9—Junction (1400 m). Upper Simpson Valley ahead. Ferro Pass right across suspension bridge.

11.0—Surprise Creek Cabin and Campground.

—Steep climb along Surprise Creek for 2.5 km.

18.4—Rock Lake.

19.2—Campground.

22.9—Ferro Pass (2270 m).

26.5—Nestor Creek bridge (1995 m). Mitchell Meadows Campground.

29.6—Junction. Cerulean Lake west end.

31.3—Sunburst Lake Cabin.

31.8—Junction. Assiniboine Lodge ahead. Magog Campground right.

32.2—Lake Magog Campground (2165 m). (See also Ferro Pass, *Mount Assiniboine Area Hikes*.)

The first section of this trail along the Simpson River is a pleasant nature walk in spring and early summer. However, the primary purpose of the trail is to get you out of Kootenay Park and into the remote wilderness of northern Mount Assiniboine Provincial Park. When connected to the Ferro Pass trail, it is also an alternate, though not particularly popular, access route to Lake Magog at the foot of Mount Assiniboine.

From the trailhead footbridge across the Vermilion River, you follow a roadbed to open flats near the confluence of the Vermilion and Simpson Rivers. Here the trail swings east and follows the Simpson River for 10 km to the mouth of Surprise Creek. Though trail continues up the Simpson, most backpackers turn right for Ferro Pass and Mount Assiniboine.

The Ferro Pass trail immediately crosses the Simpson via a suspension bridge to Surprise Creek Campground and shelter cabin, then begins a long, steep climb up the Surprise Creek valley. The climb to Rock Lake is scenically humdrum (dense forest), but above the lake the scenery improves, featuring the massive rock wall of Simpson Ridge and Indian Mountain. At Ferro Pass views suddenly open out to Mount Assiniboine, The Marshall, Mount Watson, and Wedgwood Lake.

Beyond the pass you descend along the slopes of Nestor Peak to Mitchell Meadows Campground at Nestor Creek. Then the trail makes a contouring climb to Cerulean Lake and Sunburst Valley.

When you arrive at Cerulean Lake, you are entering Assiniboine's core trail network. If you are bound for Magog Campground, continue on past Cerulean and Sunburst Lakes to the branch trail angling right to the campground. (See also Ferro Pass, *Lake Magog Area Hikes* in Assiniboine Park chapter.)

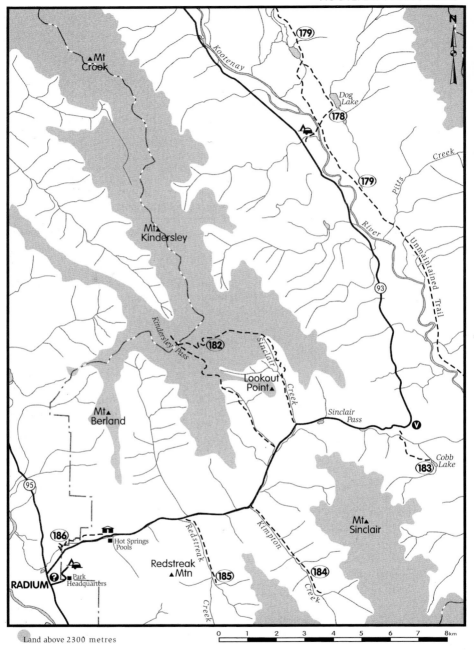

Land above 2300 metres

0 1 2 3 4 5 6 7 8km

Dog Lake and the Mitchell Range

178 Dog Lake

McLeod Meadows Picnic Area to Dog Lake—2.6 km (1.6 mi)

Dog Lake is a shallow, marsh-fringed lake with fine open views of the Kootenay Valley. The lake's location, in one of the most temperate valleys in the Canadian Rockies, makes it an excellent area for experiencing the montane forest ecosystem. And because of its low elevation, the short trail to the lake can be hiked earlier and later in the season than most.

From the picnic area, the trail runs across a meadow and through the middle of the campground, exiting at a trail sign beyond the last campsite access road. Just 200 m beyond the campground, you cross two channels of the Kootenay River via suspension bridges.

Climbing beyond the river, the trail crosses the East Kootenay Trail and continues up into a dry forest of Douglas fir, white spruce and lodgepole pine—a slope covered with the brilliant orange blooms of western wood lilies in July.

The wide, well-graded trail reaches its high point at km 1.9, then descends through a cooler forest carpeted with feather moss and bunchberry.

At km 2.6, a side trail branches right 100 m to the lake's marshy west shore, where you have views across the lake to two prominent peaks of the Mitchell Range—Mounts Daer and Harkin.

Follow the trail leading around to open dryas flats at the lake's north end (stay right at a signed junction). Here there are more open views south and a large lakeside wetland filled with equisetum.

Access: Follow Highway 93 to the McLeod Meadows Picnic Area, located on the east side of the highway 26.5 km (16.5 mi) north of Kootenay Park West Gate at Radium and 0.5 km (0.3 mi) south of McLeod Meadows Campground. The trail begins near the picnic shelter. (Campers start from the rear of the campground.) *Maps: Mount Assiniboine 82 J/13 (trail not shown).*

Kootenay Valley Fire Roads

After a major forest fire swept the Kootenay Valley in 1926, a network of fire roads was constructed to allow wardens and firefighters rapid access to all parts of the valley. Today the roads are no longer used by park service vehicles and they are slowly revegetating along their margins.

While these abandoned roads make for pretty humdrum hiking, their low elevation does permit access in early spring and late autumn when other trails are still snow-covered, and easy grades make for comfortable walking. They are also popular with cyclists and cross-country skiers.

Two of these roads, the West Kootenay Trail and East Kootenay Trail, extend beyond park boundaries to B.C. forest lands. Cyclists should refer to Doug Eastcott's *Backcountry Biking in the Canadian Rockies* for further details on these extensions.

179 East Kootenay Trail

McLeod Meadows Picnic Area to Daer Creek—7.3 km (4.5 mi)
McLeod Meadows Picnic Area to Pitts Creek—5.7 km (3.5 mi)

The East Kootenay Fire Road was built to access the east side of the Kootenay Valley during fire emergencies. From a point near the confluence of the Vermilion and Kootenay Rivers, the road runs south for 36 km to the park's southern boundary near the Cross River. Today part of the road's northern section is inaccessible due to bridge removal, but the southern half remains intact and is a popular route for cyclists.

Hikers most often sample the central section of the old fire road on short trips from McLeod Meadows Picnic Area or Campground. The gently graded roadbed makes for undemanding walking, and despite unremarkable scenery, these outings are rewarding in spring when the valley's first flowers are coming into bloom.

Follow the Dog Lake trail from either the McLeod Meadows Picnic Area or the rear of the campground (see *Dog Lake*). After crossing the Kootenay River suspension bridges just beyond the campground, you continue on the Dog Lake trail for another 250 m to its intersection with the fire road. At this point you can turn left and follow the road north 6.4 km to Daer Creek, or turn right and go south 4.8 km to Pitts Creek.

The washout of the Daer Creek bridge limits travel to the north. However, the bridge over Pitts Creek was still intact the last we heard, allowing cyclists to continue south for another 20 km to the Cross River forestry road beyond the park's southern boundary. (This section is not being maintained by the park's trail crew.)

There is usually a fair amount of bear activity along the floor of the Kootenay Valley in the spring and early summer, so hikers and cyclists should always travel cautiously along this route.

Access: Follow Highway 93 to the McLeod Meadows Picnic Area, located on the east side of the highway 26.5 km (16.5 mi) north of Kootenay Park West Gate at Radium and 0.5 km (0.3 mi) south of McLeod Meadows Campground. The trail begins near the picnic shelter. (Campers start from the rear of the campground.) *Maps: Mount Assiniboine 82 J/13, Tangle Peak 82 J/12.*

180 West Kootenay Trail

Kootenay Crossing Warden Station to Park Boundary—9.8 km (6.1 mi)

The West Kootenay Trail is a fairly boring 10-km road walk that is of more interest to cyclists and cross-country skiers than hikers. The trail is well removed from the Kootenay River most of the way, so there is little relief from the tedium of pine and spruce forest. However, a short branch road near the park boundary does lead to the river and, perhaps, some fine fly fishing.

Start from the access gate at the south edge of the Kootenay Crossing Warden Station and follow the well-graded road 0.9 km to the Dolly Varden Trail split. Stay right and continue northwest onto a benchland above the river.

There are few ups-and-downs as the broad track runs through the forest west of the river. Just before crossing a bridge over a major tributary at km 6.2, the roadbed descends to an interesting marsh environment near the Kootenay River.

At km 9.7, just 100 m before the park boundary, a 0.9-km branch road cuts right and crosses a low hill to the river. The main road continues across the park boundary, where it turns into a rough, wet, brushy track that eventually reaches the Beaverfoot Road approximately 12 km beyond the park.

Access: Follow Highway 93 to the Kootenay Crossing Warden Station, situated on west side of the highway 42.5 km (26.5 mi) north of the Kootenay Park West Gate at Radium and 20.5 km (12.5 mi) south of the Vermilion Crossing Visitor Centre. Turn into the warden station and keep left on the road leading to an access gate. *Maps: Spillimacheen 82 K/16.*
(Trail not shown on maps in this book.)

181 Dolly Varden Trail

Kootenay Crossing Warden Station to Crook's Meadow—11.2 km (7.0 mi)

This fire road begins at the Kootenay Crossing Warden Station and loops south along the west side of valley before returning to Highway 93 at Crook's Meadow group campground. Though forest-enclosed, it does offer a bit more interest with its ups-and-downs than most of the valley's fire roads. It also accesses the Luxor Pass trail.

From the access gate at the south edge of the warden station, follow the fire road 0.9 km to the Dolly Varden-West Kootenay road split. Stay left and climb over a low, forested ridge before plunging down to the meadows of Dolly Varden Creek. These meadows provide the only open views, and the bridge over the creek (km 3.6) makes a pleasant rest stop.

Beyond the creek, the road climbs past the Luxor Pass junction (km 4.1), then rolls through a stream-filled forest of white spruce, Douglas fir and aspen. You finally descend to Highway 93 at Crook's Meadow. (Cyclists can complete a 20-km loop by riding back to the warden station on the highway.)

Luxor Pass—4.3 km. This little used trail branches southwest from the Dolly Varden Trail at km 4.1. It climbs a steep, densely forested slope and exits the park via Luxor Pass (1905 m). It soon reaches logging roads on the west slope of the Brisco Range.

Access: Follow Highway 93 to the Kootenay Crossing Warden Station, situated on west side of the highway 42.5 km (26.5 mi) north of the Kootenay Park West Gate at Radium and 20.5 km (12.5 mi) south of the Vermilion Crossing Visitor Centre. Turn into the warden station and keep left on the road leading to an access gate. *Maps: Spillimacheen 82 K/16.*
(Trail not shown on maps in this book.)

182 Kindersley Pass—Sinclair Creek Circuit

Highway 93 to Kindersley Summit—9.8 km (6.1 mi)
Kindersley Pass-Sinclair Creek Circuit—16.2 km (10.1 mi)

Day trip

Allow 5 hours for circuit

Elevation gain: 1055 m (3,450 ft)

Maximum elevation: 2395 m (7,850 ft)

Maps: Tangle Peak 82 J/12

Access: Follow Highway 93 to the Kindersley Pass trailhead parking area, located on the south side of the highway 9.5 km (6 mi) east of Kootenay Park West Gate at Radium (trailhead on opposite side of road). The Sinclair Creek trail parking area is on the north side of the highway 1.2 km east of the Kindersley Pass trailhead.

0.0—Kindersley Pass trailhead (1340 m).

—Moderate uphill through forest.

2.7—Avalanche slope.

—Steady climb along avalanche path.

6.1—Lookout Point ridge.

—Trail crosses avalanche paths.

8.4—Kindersley Pass (2210). Park boundary.

—Trail cuts up to right. Steep ascent across open slopes.

9.8—Kindersley Summit (2395 m).

—Follow markers down to Sinclair Creek headwaters.

11.2—Good trail reappears east side of valley.

11.7—Trail enters forest.

—Steep switchbacking descent.

14.5—Sinclair Creek bridge to west side.

16.2—Sinclair Creek trailhead (1435 m).

—Descend Highway 93.

17.4—Kindersley Pass trailhead (1340 m).

The hike to Kindersley Pass and the high, alpine ridges beyond is one of the most scenic day trips in Kootenay Park—and one of the most strenuous. After nearly 10 km of steady climbing, you will be more than happy to relax on the 2395-m crest of Kindersley Summit and enjoy the view. Or perhaps stroll along the high traverse to nearby Nixon Creek Summit and scan the slopes for the flocks of bighorn sheep that summer in this range.

While you can always return from the summit the way you came, the traditional and quickest way is to complete a loop by descending to the Sinclair Creek headwaters and picking up the 5-km trail leading down-valley to the highway. This route brings you back to the highway just east of the Kindersley Pass trail parking area, leaving a quick 1.2-km downhill road walk back to your vehicle.

Though it is 100 m lower than Sinclair Creek, we always start at the Kindersley Pass trailhead and make a longer but more gradual ascent to the summit. This trail climbs steadily up a narrow, densely forested valley, which opens suddenly at km 2.7 into a series of avalanche paths. As you ascend above the first slide area and cross a small divide just west of Lookout Point, you enter cool subalpine forest of Engelmann spruce and alpine fir.

More avalanche paths are crossed near Kindersley Pass, and piles of snow from these slides often linger into late summer. Along the margins of the retreating snowbanks, glacier lilies and western anemones can often be found in bloom, even in August.

Kindersley Pass is a bit of an anti-climax after the stiff 8.4-km climb to its summit, yet a small meadow at the pass makes a pleasant rest stop. It also provides the first good views northward to the long procession of peaks comprising the Brisco Range.

Climbing to Kindersley Summit

The true glory of the hike begins above the pass. By following the trail ascending the ridge to the north, you soon emerge through the last stands of larch onto open slopes dotted with stunted islands of alpine fir. At km 9.8, you reach the highest point on the trip where the trail crests a ridge between two rocky peaks. From this lofty saddle, views open to the headwaters of Sinclair Creek and an endless sea of peaks stretching away to the northeast.

From Kindersley Summit, you can side-trip along a high path contouring around the head of the Sinclair Creek basin for 2 km to Nixon Creek Summit. This is alpine walking at its best, and though the trail is indistinct at times, there is no problem sighting its trace on the open slope ahead.

At Nixon Creek Summit, new views open along the crest of the Brisco Range and down to the forested headwaters of Nixon Creek. Rock scramblers can ascend the 2530-m peak immediately above this col for an even better view.

Sinclair Creek Option. To complete the Kindersley Pass-Sinclair Creek Circuit, descend due east from the Kindersley Summit saddle across steep avalanche slopes to the head of the Sinclair Valley. (Watch for markers and cairns.) Once the valley floor is reached near a series of small cascades, a faint trail materializes. This rough track follows the west side of the creek for 100 m, then crosses to the east side. Not far beyond it turns into good trail and descends from the avalanche-swept basin back into a cool, closed forest.

This steep downhill track brings you back to Highway 93 at the Sinclair Creek trailhead parking area. From there it is an easy stroll down along highway to the Kindersley Pass trailhead.

183 Cobb Lake

Highway 93 to Cobb Lake—2.7 km (1.7 mi)

This forest-encircled lake on the lower slopes of Mount Sinclair is noted for its mirror reflections and peaceful setting. The trail makes a nice escape from the busyness of Highway 93, but be aware that you lose more elevation than you gain on the way to the lake; be prepared for a bit of climbing on the way out.

While the trail is usually snowfree from early May to late October, it is most rewarding in spring (late May-early June) when many forest wildflowers bloom, including heart-leaved arnica, blue clematis and false solomon seal.

From the roadside pull-out just east of Sinclair Pass, the trail switchbacks down through a heavy forest dominated by lodgepole pine, white spruce and the occasional aspen poplar.

There are also a few old Douglas fir giants. Thanks to their thick, protective bark, these patriarchs survived a forest fire through this section of the Kootenay Valley in 1918. (Look for charred bark around the base of these trees.)

After a steady descent over 1.6 km, you cross Swede Creek and climb for the final kilometre to the lake.

Some folks like to wet their fishing lines in the lake in hopes of hooking the elusive brook trout that are frequently seen leaping from its waters. (A park fishing license is required.)

Access: Follow Highway 93 to a roadside pull-out on the south side of the highway 14.5 km (9 mi) from Kootenay Park West Gate and 0.6 km (0.4 mi) west of the Kootenay Valley Viewpoint. *Maps: Tangle Peak 82 J/12.*

184 Kimpton Creek

Highway 93 to Trail's End—4.8 km (3.0 mi)

When midsummer heat is beating down on nearby Radium and the Columbia Valley, folks escape to Sinclair Canyon and walk along the cool, heavily forested Kimpton Creek trail.

From the bridge over Sinclair Creek 150 m below the parking area, the trail joins Kimpton Creek and stays along its rushing waters for the next 1.7 km. Along the first 300 m a large limestone cliff rises above the west side of the creek, creating a bit of a canyon and helping to trap the cool air generated by the creek.

Douglas fir and white spruce dominate the forest canopy, though deciduous trees, like Douglas maple, white birch and aspen, do grow in areas where sunlight breaks through.

If you are hiking here to escape the heat, don't bother climbing the switch-backs at km 1.6. The trail climbs above the creek at this point and begins a steady ascent above the gorge on a semi-open southwest-facing slope—not a cool place on a warm day.

Views are limited throughout the journey, though above the switchbacks you can look across the gorge to a lime-stone hogback and avalanche paths.

The trail's official end is marked by a sign about halfway to Kimpton Pass.

Access: Follow Highway 93 to a small road-side parking area on the Sinclair Creek side of the highway 7.0 km (4.3 mi) east of Kootenay Park West Gate. Walk back down the highway 150 m to the trailhead footbridge across Sinclair Creek. *Maps: Tangle Peak 82 J/12.*

185 Redstreak Creek

Highway 93 to Trail's End—2.3 km (1.4 mi)

The Redstreak Creek trail probes the narrow confines of a side-valley intersecting Sinclair Canyon from the south. While there are no open views, the gorge is a unique environment dominated by deciduous trees—a wonderful place in spring when new leaves are unfolding and wildflowers like false solomon seal, arnica and fairybells are blooming on the forest floor.

From the trailhead bridge over Sinclair Creek, you immediately climb above the creek via a series of switchbacks and stay well east of the stream for the remainder of the hike.

The forest floor is well shaded initially and covered with feather moss and bunchberry; where sun filters through, there are wild roses and junipers.

Grades become gradual at 0.5 km and you enter an unusual woodland dominated by Douglas maple along with a scattering of white birch and aspen. At km 1.0 a windstorm has felled hundreds of less flexible lodgepole pine trees, which are piled like kindling beneath the hardwoods.

The trail becomes narrow and rooty before reaching the "end of trail" sign at a small spring-fed streamlet (the only water on the trail).

Access: Follow Highway 93 to the trailhead parking area on the south side of the highway 4.5 km (2.8 mi) east of Kootenay Park West Gate. The trail begins at the footbridge across Sinclair Creek. *Maps: Tangle Peak 82 J/12 (trail not shown).*

186 Juniper Trail

Highway 93 to Juniper Trail Summit—2.1 km (1.3 mi)
Juniper Trail Circuit—4.6 km (2.9 mi)

In just over 2 km, the Juniper Trail visits a damp canyon filled with western red cedar, switchbacks up an arid slope dotted with Rocky Mountain juniper and Douglas fir, and climbs along the rim of Sinclair Canyon to an excellent viewpoint for Radium and the Columbia Valley. Though the hike is short, the climb is a real cooker on warm, sunny days, so pack water.

From the trailhead parking area, the trail loses 45 m of elevation in 0.4 km to the bridge over Sinclair Creek. Just before the bridge, a 100 m trail branches right to a view of the creek pouring down from Sinclair Canyon.

Beyond the cool, cedar-shaded bridge, the trail climbs dry, semi-open slopes via a series of well-graded switchbacks to

the canyon rim at km 1.3. By continuing another 0.8 km, you will reach a bench near the trail summit and fine views of the Columbia Valley and Purcell Range. Elevation gain from the bridge to the summit is 200 m.

You can turn around at the top or continue on and descend through dense forest to the parking area opposite the Radium Hot Springs pool. From there, follow sidewalks back along the highway and through the canyon 1.4 km to the trailhead.

Access: Follow Highway 93 to a parking area on the north side of the highway 300 m east of Kootenay Park West Gate and just below the entry to Sinclair Canyon. *Maps: Radium Hot Springs 82 K/9 (trail not shown).*

Waterton Lakes National Park

At 518 sq km, Waterton Lakes National Park is the smallest of the five national parks in the Canadian Rockies. Tucked into the southwest corner of Alberta, it is bounded on the west by British Columbia's Akamina-Kishinena Provincial Park, on the south by the U.S. border and Glacier National Park, and on the north and east by the rolling prairies of southern Alberta.

There are over 170 kms of trail in Waterton Lakes National Park. The park's trails are the best constructed in the Canadian Rockies—moderately graded, well-marked, scenically routed and, as might be expected, heavily travelled. Most trails in the park can be hiked in a day, and nearly all lead to small subalpine lakes nestled in hanging valleys.

The most popular day trips branch from the park's main roads. Rowe Lakes-Lineham Ridge and the Carthew-Alderson hikes start from the Akamina Parkway, as do two popular day trips to Forum Lake and Wall Lake in British Columbia's Akamina-Kishinena Park (see *Akamina-Kishinena Provincial Park*). The Twin Lakes area and Goat Lake are reached via the Snowshoe Trail from the end of the Red Rock Parkway. The Bertha Lake trail, which is the park's most popular day hike, strikes off from the edge of Waterton townsite, and the unique Crypt Lake trip is usually initiated from the village marina with a 3 km boat ride.

While there are campgrounds on many of the shorter trails, serious backpacking opportunities are limited in such a small park. The Tamarack Trail, which runs along the Great Divide for 36 km from the Akamina Parkway to Red Rock Canyon, is the park's best known route. Though the Snowshoe-Blakiston Circuit can be completed in a long day, it too is often backpacked. And the Waterton Lakeshore trail can be utilized to access wilderness trails in the northern region of Glacier National Park, Montana.

As in other Rocky Mountain national parks, you must obtain a Wilderness Pass for any overnight outing in Waterton's backcountry. Quotas are observed in all campgrounds, and since many of these sites are very popular, particularly on weekends, you should consider reserving space during the 3 month period prior to your trip.

If you plan on backpacking into Glacier National Park from Waterton, you can obtain a U.S. Park Service Backcountry Use Permit either at the Waterton Visitor Reception Centre or at Glacier's Park Backcountry Permit Centres prior to your trip.

Information and services. The Waterton Visitor Reception Centre is located at the entrance to Waterton townsite (at the top of the hill opposite the Prince of Wales Hotel). It provides the usual range of park information services, including trail reports, weather forecasts, a variety of free pamphlets concerning park activities and issues, and schedules for interpretive programs and guided walks. It also dispenses Wilderness Passes for backcountry camping, park fishing licenses, and books relating to the park and region.

There are two main roadside campgrounds in the park: Waterton Townsite, located just south of the townsite's business district; and Crandell Mountain on the Red Rock Parkway. The smaller Belly River Campground is located on the Chief Mountain Highway (Hwy 6) near the U.S. border. The townsite campground is the only full service facility (hook-ups and showers).

Waterton townsite is the park's only service centre. Composed of summer cottages and a small business district, it provides basic services that include grocery stores, restaurants, gas stations, a laundromat, an outdoor sport-hiking shop, a hostel, and a number of lodges and motels. There are no banks, but ATM machines are available.

Though Waterton is slowly developing a year round economy, it is still primarily a

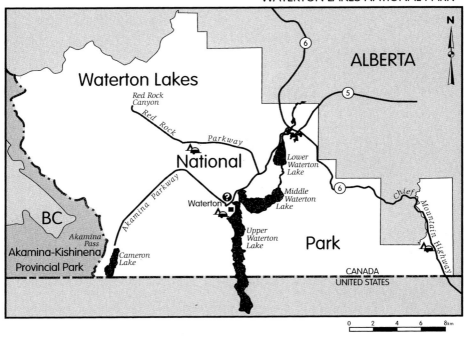

seasonal village. Many businesses are closed from early October to mid-May. Pincher Creek (48 km) and Cardston, Alberta (45 km), are the nearest full service towns to the park.

Access. Two provincial highways provide access to the park entrance: Highway #6 from Pincher Creek; and Highway #5 from Cardston. The Chief Mountain International Highway is the most direct route from Glacier National Park, Montana, but is only open in summer.

The nearest Alberta cities serviced by commercial airlines are Lethbridge (130 km) and Calgary (264 km). There is Greyhound bus service between the park and Calgary during the summer.

Commercial shuttle services transport hikers to Cameron Lake, Red Rock Canyon and other trailhead locations. Sightseeing cruise boats on Upper Waterton Lake also provide hiker drop-offs at Crypt Landing for the Crypt Lake trail and the Goat Haunt dock for trails into northern Glacier National Park. (See *Sources-Transportation*.)

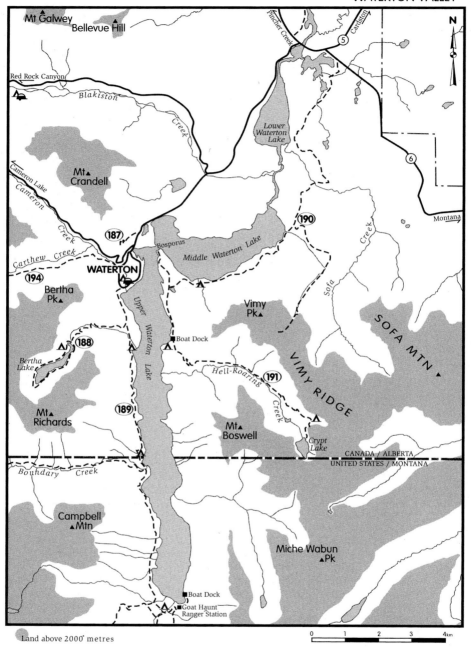

N

Mt Galwey
Bellevue Hill

Pincher Creek

Cardston

5

Red Rock Canyon

Blakiston Creek

Lower Waterton Lake

6

Montana

Cameron Lake

Cameron Creek

Mt Crandell

187

190

Carthew Creek

Bosporus

Middle Waterton Lake

Sofa Creek

SOFA MTN

194

WATERTON

Upper Waterton Lake

Vimy Pk

Bertha Pk

Boat Dock

Bertha Lake

188

Hell-Roaring Creek

191

VIMY RIDGE

Mt Richards

189

Mt Boswell

Crypt Lake

CANADA / ALBERTA
UNITED STATES / MONTANA

Boundary Creek

Campbell Mtn

Miche Wabun Pk

Boat Dock
Goat Haunt Ranger Station

Land above 2000' metres

0   1   2   3   4km

Upper Waterton Lake from Bear's Hump

187 Bear's Hump

Waterton Park Visitor Centre to Bear's Hump—1.2 km (0.7 mi)

The Bear's Hump is the most popular short hike in Waterton Park. This popularity stems from its proximity to Waterton townsite and the wonderful overview it provides of the Waterton Valley, the town, and the prairies to the northeast. However, it is one of the steepest short trails in the Rockies, climbing a heart-pounding 240 m in just over a kilometre.

The hike starts from the Waterton Visitor Centre parking area at the entrance to the townsite. From there it is all trees and steady, steep uphill until you emerge onto the lofty limestone bluff overlooking Upper Waterton Lake.

There are no trees to block the view from this promontory (rock and wind leave only a few stunted bonsai), which is part of Crandell Mountain's south ridge. Your gaze is immediately drawn down the lake to the mountains of Montana's Glacier National Park. The most prominent and massive peak beyond the end of the lake is 3190 m Mount Cleveland—the highest mountain in the Waterton-Glacier International Peace Park.

The townsite sprawls at your feet, spread across an alluvial fan created by Cameron Creek. The stately Prince of Wales Hotel also lies immediately below, perched on a promontory above the Bosporous narrows connecting Upper and Middle Waterton Lakes.

The wind is nearly always blowing on Bear's Hump, so take a windbreaker, even if its sunny and warm. And if the weather is stormy and vile, avoid the hike all together.

Access: Start from the rear of the Waterton Park Visitor Centre, located at the entrance to Waterton Townsite. *Maps: Waterton Lakes 82 H/4; Waterton Lakes National Park.*

188 Bertha Lake

Waterton Townsite to Bertha Lake—5.8 km (3.6 mi)

Day trip or backpack

Allow 1.5 hours one way

Elevation gain: 460 m (1,500 ft)

Maximum elevation: 1755 m (5,750 ft)

Maps: Waterton Lakes 82 H/4
        Waterton Lakes National Park

Access: Follow Evergreen Avenue south along the west side of Waterton townsite to the trailhead parking area road, which branches right 400 m south of Cameron Falls and opposite the townsite campground. The road leads uphill between cottages to the parking area.

0.0—Trailhead parking area (1295 m).

  —Trail climbs south through forest.

1.5—Junction. Waterton Lakeshore trail left. Stay right.

  —Trail climbs along north side of Bertha Creek.

2.6—Lower Bertha Falls.

  —Trail crosses Bertha Creek and makes switchbacking ascent along south side of valley.

5.1—Bertha Lake viewpoint. Trail summit.

5.8—Bertha Lake Campground (1755 m).

  —Trail continues along north shore.

7.4—West end of Bertha Lake.

The 6 km trail leading from Waterton townsite to Bertha Lake is one of the most popular day hikes in Waterton Park. Though it is hardly a remote backcountry location, the lake is appointed with a campground, so it attracts a mixed bag of day hikers and campers. Although the number of people detracts somewhat from the scene, it is still one of the prettiest backcountry lakes in the park.

The trail is fairly steep, but well graded. From the southwest corner of the townsite, it climbs gradually for 2 km through a forest rich with undergrowth and wildflowers.

At the lakeshore trail junction, it breaks out of the trees briefly onto an open slope with excellent views of Upper Waterton Lake. The rather stunted, brushy looking trees on this sunny promontory are limber pine—a species that thrives in dry, rocky locales.

At km 2.6, you cross the creek beneath Lower Bertha Falls and begin the steep climb to the hanging valley containing Bertha Lake. After a steady ascent through the forest, you pass Upper Bertha Falls—a cascade spilling over a staircase of brick-red argillite.

At km 5.1 the trail reaches its highest point, where you receive your first view of the lake. In another 0.7 km you arrive at water's edge near the campground.

The trail continues along the lake's north shore to its far end, lying beneath a vertical wall connecting Mounts Alderson and Richards. The thin, dark band stretching across this headwall is a diabase sill, created by molten rock intruded between the layers of grey limestone and dolomite long before the uplift of the Rockies.

The lake was named for Bertha Ekelund, once a resident of the Waterton area. Bertha is reputed to have tried to pass counterfeit currency. They say she was sent to jail and never seen in Waterton again.

Bertha Lake

189 Waterton Lakeshore

Waterton Townsite to Goat Haunt Boat Dock—13.0 km (8.1 mi)

Day trip or backpack

Allow 4 hours one way

Elevation gain: 100 m (350 ft)
    loss: 115 m (375 ft)

Maximum elevation: 1395 m (4,580 ft)

Maps: Waterton Lakes 82 H/4
   Waterton Lakes National Park

Access: Follow Evergreen Avenue south along the west side of Waterton townsite to the trail-head parking area road, which branches right 400 m south of Cameron Falls and opposite the townsite campground. The road leads uphill between cottages to the parking area.

0.0—Trailhead parking area (1295 m).

 —Trail climbs south through forest.

1.4—Junction. Lake viewpoint left. Keep right.

1.5—Junction. Bertha Lake right. Keep left.

 —Trail descends toward lakeshore.

2.4—Bertha Bay Campground and boat dock.

 —Trail rolls along lakeshore.

5.8—International boundary monument. Boundary Bay Campground and boat dock.

6.3—Boundary Creek bridge.

6.4—Junction. Boundary Creek trail right.

 —Trail rolls through forest above lakeshore.

11.5—Junction. Boulder Pass right. Keep left.

12.1—Junction. Rainbow Falls right 0.8 km. Keep left.

12.6—Goat Haunt Ranger Station.

 —Continue around end of lake to boat dock.

13.0—Goat Haunt boat dock (1280 m).

The 13 km trail running south along the west shore of Upper Waterton Lake from Waterton townsite to the Goat Haunt boat dock in Montana offers several options: a short walk to Bertha Bay; a day hike to the international boundary and back; a one-way day trip to the south end of the lake, returning by tour boat; or an extended backpack into the northern wilderness of Glacier National Park.

The lakeshore trail strikes off from the townsite on the same trail as Bertha Lake and climbs through lush, flower-filled forest for 1.5 km to Bertha Lake junction. At this split, you branch left and immediately descend to Bertha Bay—a stony beach that is one of the prettiest spots along Upper Waterton's shoreline.

Beyond Bertha Bay, the trail rolls along the rocky lower slopes of Mount Richards to the international boundary and Boundary Bay. Sitting in the quiet lakeside picnic area at Boundary Bay is a unique experience. Across the lake you can see the slash line marking the Canada-U.S. border on the slopes of Mount Boswell. This cut-line and the large boundary cairn nearby are the only signs that you are passing from one nation to another.

After crossing Boundary Creek, the trail rolls south through enclosed forest above the shoreline. There are no open views worth mentioning until you cross the Waterton River and branch left to Goat Haunt Ranger Station at the south end of the lake. From the ranger station, paved trail leads east around the shore to the tour boat landing.

If you plan on riding the tour boat back to town, check the schedule before you depart and leave plenty of time to catch the last boat at the Goat Haunt dock. If you are backpacking into Glacier National Park, you must have a Glacier backcountry permit and report to the Goat Haunt ranger for immigration clearance.

190 Wishbone Trail—Vimy Peak

Chief Mountain Highway to Bosporous—13.2 km (8.2 mi)*
Chief Mountain Highway to Vimy Basin—11.8 km (7.3 mi)*

Day trip or backpack

Allow 4 hours to Bosporous

Elevation gain: 70 m (230 ft)
loss: 90 m (295 ft)

Maximum elevation: 1370 m (4,500 ft)

Maps: Waterton Lakes 82 H/4
Waterton Lakes National Park

Access: Follow Highway 5 east from the park entrance junction for 0.9 km to the Chief Mountain Highway (Hwy 6) intersection. Turn right and continue on Chief Mountain Highway 0.5 km to a gated access road on the right. Park in the pullout on the north side of the highway.

0.0—Access gate (1300 m).

—Follows Y Camp access road.

2.6—Y Camp site.

—Road ends. Single-track angles southeast.

5.5—Sofa Creek crossing.

7.0—Junction (1295 m). Vimy Basin left 4.8 km. Wishbone Trail ahead.

—Trail climbs above Middle Waterton Lake.

10.8—Wishbone Campground. End of bike access.

12.0—Loon Lake Junction. Bosporous straits right 1.2 km. Crypt Landing left.

—Trail follows above Upper Waterton Lake.

14.0—Crypt Landing and Crypt Landing Campground (1280 m).

* All distances approximate

This relatively flat trail through aspen-cottonwood woodland does not rise to breathtaking views, but it does offer access along the east side of the Waterton Valley and to the Vimy Peak trail. The trail is open to cyclists to Wishbone Campground, but overgrown sections make for difficult biking.

The Wishbone follows roadbed for 2.6 km to the Y Camp site on Lower Waterton Lake. Beyond this pleasant shore it reverts to a single-track through more poplars and across open grassy sections, where it is often vague and overgrown.

After passing Vimy junction, the trail reaches Middle Waterton Lake and rolls along its shore to Wishbone Campground. Bike access ends here, so cyclists must continue on foot.

The junction at tiny Loon Lake is where most turn right and follow the 1.2 km Bosporous trail over the ridge between Middle and Upper Waterton Lakes. The shallow Bosporous strait connects the two lakes and separates you from the Prince of Wales Hotel on its lofty promontory.

The main trail continues south along Upper Waterton Lake for another 2 km to Crypt Landing Campground and the Crypt Lake trail.

Vimy Peak. Views from the 2347 m summit of Vimy Peak extend over the Waterton Valley and out to the prairie. However, the trail to Vimy Basin is very steep, it passes through dense bush where grizzlies are wont to roam, and from trail's end you still have an hour of rock scrambling to reach the top.

The trail begins its steep climb from the 6.0 km junction on the Wishbone Trail. Once you reach the basin on the east side of the mountain 4.8 km from the junction, the trail fizzles and you follow the line of least resistance up steep scree and broken rock to the summit.

191 Crypt Lake

Crypt Landing to Crypt Lake—8.7 km (5.4 mi)

Day trip or backpack

Allow 2.5 to 3.5 hours one way

Elevation gain: 675 m (2,220 ft)

Maximum elevation: 1955 m (6,420 ft)

Maps: Waterton Lakes 82 H/4
    Waterton Lakes National Park

Access: Book passage on the tour boat crossing Upper Waterton Lake to Crypt Landing dock. Or follow the Wishbone Trail 14.0 km from the Chief Mountain Highway to Crypt Landing.

0.0—Crypt Landing (1280 m).

0.4—Junction. Hell-Roaring Falls right 1.0 km.

—Switchbacking ascent through forest.

2.4—Last switchback.

3.0—Junction. Upper cutoff to Hell-Roaring Falls.

3.5—Twin Falls viewpoint.

5.6—Burnt Rock Falls.

—Switchbacking climb.

7.9—Crypt Lake Campground.

8.1—Tunnel.

8.5—Entrance to Crypt Lake cirque. Top of Crypt Falls.

8.7—Crypt Lake (1945 m).

Crypt Lake has more tricks and amusements than any trail in the Rockies. You cross the Rockies' windiest lake by tour boat, ascend a narrow valley past a staircase of waterfalls, climb an iron ladder, crawl through a tunnel, tippytoe along a cliff whilst clinging to a cable, and skirt above a precipice where a stream suddenly bursts from underground and plunges 175 m. And if that doesn't satisfy your taste for the bizarre, you can stroll along the shore of the most perfect cirque lake in the Rockies and visit another country.

If you are day hiking to the lake, book the early morning tour boat to Crypt Landing on the eastern shore of Upper Waterton Lake, and check with the captain concerning pick-up time in the late afternoon.

While this is the most popular way of reaching the trail, you can also hike to Crypt Landing Campground via the 14 km *Wishbone Trail.* Either way, you may consider camping at Crypt Landing to allow a full day for the hike.

Just 0.4 km into the hike you pass a side trail to Hell-Roaring Falls, which loops south to Hell-Roaring Canyon and its impressive waterfall, then climbs rough track to reconnect with the Crypt trail at km 3.0. (Save the falls for the return trip, and only if you have time to spare before catching your boat.)

The trail quickly gains elevation through spruce and fir forest via a series of switchbacks, then heads upvalley through more open country and passes a viewpoint for Twin Falls.

Beyond Burnt Rock Falls, a beautiful 15 m waterfall dropping over limestone and red argillite, the trail climbs across open talus slopes and up another series of steep switchbacks to Crypt Lake Campground (one of the park's most heavily used sites).

The last 0.8 km to the lake is not well-suited for the claustrophobic, acrophobic

Crypt Lake

or obese. A short jaunt across talus brings you to a sheer wall—an apparent cul de sac but for a ladder leading up to a dark hole in the rock. At the top of the ladder a 20 m tunnel cuts through the mountain spur—a cramped shaft that nearly brings you to your hands-and-knees. At the end of the tunnel, you emerge onto a ledge across an exposed precipice, where a cable offers support for the faint-of-heart.

At the entrance to Crypt cirque, the lake's outlet stream suddenly surfaces from beneath a pile of boulders and leaps over a cliff to form Crypt Falls.

Crypt Lake is certainly no anticlimax to its multi-faceted approach. Its waters are of the deepest green and seldom free of ice, even in mid-summer when ice-floes drift on its surface. Surrounded by 600 m cliffs, it is a textbook example of a glacially-carved cirque.

By keeping to the east shore, you can walk to the far end of the lake, which rests precisely on the Canada-U.S. boundary. No immigration officer to greet you here, only the occasional mountain goat patrolling the slopes above. However, the Wilson Range forms one of the most effective barriers anywhere along the 6500 km border.

Allow enough time to catch the last boat back to Waterton, and please spare this beautiful valley by not shortcutting switchbacks on the way down.

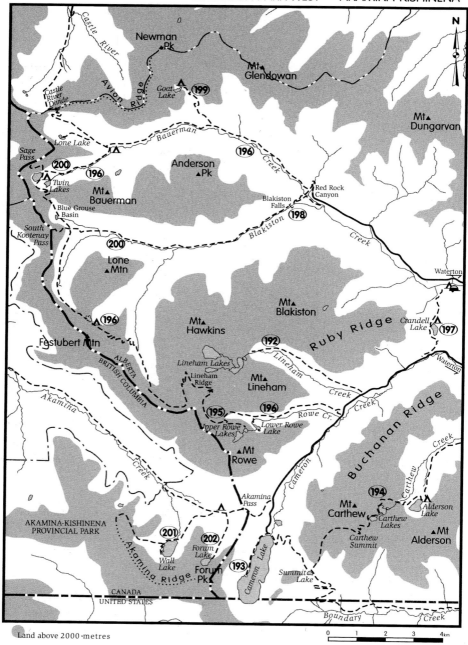

N

Newman
Pk

Mt
Glendowan

Castle
River

Avion
Ridge

Goat
Lake

199

Mt
Dungarvan

Castle
River
Divide

Lone Lake

Bauerman

196

Creek

Sage
Pass

200

Anderson
Pk

Red Rock
Canyon

196

Twin
Lakes

Mt
Bauerman

Blakiston
Falls

198

Blue Grouse
Basin

South
Kootenay
Pass

200

Blakiston

Creek

Lone
Mtn

Waterton

Mt
Blakiston

Mt
Hawkins

Ruby Ridge

Crandell
Lake

197

196

Festubert Mtn

192

Lineham

Creek

Waterton

ALBERTA
BRITISH COLUMBIA

Lineham Lakes

Lineham
Ridge

Mt
Lineham

Akamina

195

196

Rowe Cr.

Creek

Upper Rowe
Lakes

Lower Rowe
Lake

Mt
Rowe

Buchanan Ridge

Creek

Carthew

Akamina
Pass

194

Mt
Carthew

Alderson
Lake

Carthew
Lakes

AKAMINA-KISHINENA
PROVINCIAL PARK

201

202

Cameron

Cameron Lake

Mt
Alderson

Carthew
Summit

Wall
Lake

Forum
Lake

Forum
Pk

193

Summit
Lake

Akamina Ridge

CANADA
UNITED STATES

Boundary

Creek

Land above 2000 metres

0   1   2   3   4km

192 Lineham Falls

Akamina Parkway to Lineham Falls—4.2 km (2.6 mi)

The Lineham Creek trail ascends the valley between Mounts Blakiston and Lineham to a view of a 100 m waterfall tumbling from a massive cliff below the Lineham Lakes basin. Despite some nice open views back down-valley and fine early summer wildflower displays, few hikers bother with the trail. Frustration, we suppose, since the real beauties of the valley—a cluster of lakes in a tiny larch-laced basin—are well guarded by the Lineham Falls cliff.

The trail is quite straightforward as it ascends the north side of the Lineham Creek valley. After a relatively steep climb along open, south-facing slopes, the grade moderates through mixed forest in the upper valley.

You emerge from the trees at trail's end to views of the falls and its imposing cliffs 500 m beyond. If you wish, you can walk climber's paths across this broad, subalpine meadow toward the cliff and then angle over to the base of the falls. (Scan the cliff and upper valley slopes for mountain goats.)

Only experienced climbers who have registered for a hazardous activity with the warden service should attempt to reach Lineham Basin. If you don't qualify, hike the trail to Lineham Ridge, which provides an outstanding overview of this unique, lake-filled hanging valley (see *Rowe Lakes—Lineham Ridge*).

Access: From Waterton townsite, follow the Akamina Parkway 9.5 km (6.0 mi) to the trailhead parking area, located on the right side of the road just east of Lineham Creek bridge. *Maps: Sage Creek 82 G/1; Waterton Lakes National Park.*

193 Cameron Lakeshore

Cameron Lake Parking Area to Avalanche Slope—1.5 km (0.9 mi)

The short trail along Cameron Lake's west shore is a pleasant outing through cool subalpine forest—a welcome escape from the crowds at the lake's parking area and boat dock. There are a number of fine gravel beaches for lounging and picnicking along the way, and the avalanche slope at trail's end always offers a chance of seeing a grizzly bear.

The Cameron Lakeshore trail is broad and flat as it passes from the open gravel beach at the north end of the lake into a forest of Engelmann spruce and alpine fir. The forest is typical of Waterton's subalpine—lush and green, filled with cow parsnip, thimbleberry, menziesia and red monkey-flower. Mount Custer, with the Herbst Glacier clinging to its north face, rises beyond the far end of the lake.

The southern end of Cameron Lake lies in Montana's Glacier National Park, but you should turn back once you reach the huge avalanche path below Forum Peak. (The alder-covered slope is often occupied by one or more grizzlies, and park wardens don't want hikers bumping into them at close range in the bush.) But if you have binoculars, take them along and scan the slopes before you turn for home.

Access: From Waterton townsite, follow the Akamina Parkway 16 km (10 mi) to the parking area at Cameron Lake. From the lakeshore interpretive sign, follow the shoreline trail to the right. *Maps: Sage Creek 82 G/1; Waterton Lakes National Park.*

194 Carthew—Alderson Trail

Cameron Lake to Carthew Summit—7.9 km (4.9 mi)
Cameron Lake to Waterton townsite—20.1 km (12.5 mi)

Day trip or backpack

Allow 6 to 7 hours

Elevation gain: 650 m (2,135 ft)
        loss: 1015 m (3,330 ft)

Maximum elevation: 2311 m (7,582 ft)

Maps: Sage Creek 82 G/1
      Waterton Lakes 82 H/4
      Waterton Lakes National Park

Access: From Waterton townsite, follow the Akamina Parkway 16 km (10 mi) to its terminus at the Cameron Lake parking area. From the lakeshore interpretive sign, follow the shoreline trail left to the Cameron Creek bridge.

0.0—Cameron Creek bridge (1660 m).

—Steady switchbacking climb through dense forest.

3.0—Trail emerges into subalpine forest.

4.2—Summit Lake (1935 m).

4.3—Junction. Boundary Creek right. Carthew Summit left.

—Steep climb through dwindling forest.

7.9—Carthew Summit (2311 m).

—Steep descent across scree slopes.

9.3—Upper Carthew Lake.

9.8—Lower Carthew Lake.

—Trail descends steeply into forest.

13.1—Alderson Lake and Campground (1875 m).

—Steady descent along slopes of Bertha Peak.

20.1—Waterton townsite (1295 m). Cameron Falls.

The 20 km Carthew–Alderson Trail between Cameron Lake and Waterton is the most popular one-way hike in the Canadian Rockies. It is a classic Waterton trail that takes you through subalpine forest and meadows, along the shores of four high lakes, and across vast scree slopes of red and green argillite. And at Carthew Summit, you stand atop one of the highest trail-accessible viewpoints in the Waterton-Glacier International Peace Park.

Since Cameron Lake is 365 m higher than Waterton, most everyone hikes the trail from west to east. If you have two vehicles at your disposal, you can set-up transportation between trailheads. However, many hikers either bum a ride to Cameron or book space on one of the commercial hiker shuttles that service this trail (the Park Visitor Centre can direct you to these services). Or, if you don't want to play the transportation game, you can still experience the best the trail has to offer by hiking round-trip to Carthew Summit from Cameron Lake.

From Cameron Lake, the trail switchbacks up through a lush forest, climbing 275 m in just over 3 km. There are brief glimpses down to Cameron Lake and out to the surrounding mountains, primarily Forum Peak (2415 m) to the west and Mount Custer (2708 m) to the south.

Near the 3 km mark the trail levels off and runs southeast through open forest to tiny Summit Lake. The meadows surrounding the lake are filled with wildflowers throughout mid-summer, including stands of tall, showy beargrass, and often visited by curious mule deer. It is an excellent spot to take a lengthy break before facing the climb ahead.

The downhill trail to Glacier Park's Boundary Creek branches right at Summit Lake, but you stay left and begin the ascent to Carthew Summit—375 m over the next 3.6 km via a series of steep

The peaks of Glacier National Park from Carthew Summit

switchbacks. Views improve rapidly to the south as the trail climbs above treeline and crosses slopes stained red by the broken argillites of the Kintla Formation. (Make sure to pack water—this is a hot, dry climb on a sunny day.)

Though views from Carthew Summit's barren ridge are exceptional, they are even better from the lower summit of Mount Carthew—a 15 minute scramble to the north. A sea of peaks rises from Glacier National Park to the south, including nearby Chapman Peak (2867 m), with the Hudson Glacier and Lakes Nooney and Wurdeman on its northern flank. It is all quite wonderful on a clear day, but not a spot to linger when a storm is moving in.

From Carthew Summit the trail descends across steep scree slopes into the basin containing the Carthew Lakes. The lakes are visible ahead throughout the descent, cradled in the rocky barrens between Mounts Carthew and Alderson. You reach Upper Carthew Lake 1.4 km below the summit, and skirt the north shore of Lower Carthew 500 m farther along.

Beyond Lower Carthew Lake the trail drops rapidly across two rock formations to Alderson Lake, lying at the foot of the impressive 700 m north face of Mount Alderson. A campground at the lake, the only one on the route, is most frequently used by backpackers who have hiked in from Waterton townsite.

From Alderson Lake the trail scurries down along the Carthew Valley between Buchanan Ridge and Bertha Peak, descending steadily through a forest of pine, spruce and Douglas fir. Just before reaching Waterton, it joins Cameron Creek, passes the town's hydro station, and soon emerges at the edge of town 50 m south of Cameron Falls.

195 Rowe Lakes—Lineham Ridge

Akamina Parkway to Upper Rowe Lakes—6.4 km (4.0 mi)
Akamina Parkway to Lineham Ridge—8.6 km (5.3 mi)

Day trip

Allow 2.5 to 3 hours to Lineham Ridge

Elevation gain: 950 m (3,115 ft)

Maximum elevation: 2560 m (8,400 ft)

Maps: Sage Creek 82 G/1
Waterton Lakes National Park

Access: Follow the Akamina Parkway from Waterton townsite to the Rowe Lakes trailhead parking area, located on the right side of the road 10 km (6 mi) from the townsite.

0.0—Akamina Parkway (1610 m).

0.3—Rowe Creek cascades.

—Steady uphill.

2.3—Avalanche slope.

3.9—Junction. Lower Rowe Lake left 0.2 km. Upper Rowe Lakes ahead.

5.2—Rowe Meadow Junction. Lineham Ridge right 3.4 km. Upper Rowe Lakes left.

—Steep grade with switchbacks.

6.4—Upper Rowe Lakes (2165 m).

The Rowe Lakes trail transports you to three small lakes at the upper limits of the subalpine and one of the park's best wildflower meadows. While you can easily spend the day relaxing beside the lakes and photographing flowers in the Rowe Basin meadow, strong hikers will want to continue onward and upward to the incredible panoramic view from Lineham Ridge—the highest trail-accessible point in Waterton Park.

The trail has a very pretty beginning. The first 300 m follows along the north side of Rowe Creek, where a series of cascades slides over one of the most colourful stream beds imaginable—a long chute of brilliant red argillite. While you may not have worked up a thirst so early in the hike, you should bottle some of Rowe Creek's sparkling water for the dry 3 km ahead.

Beyond the creek you climb across a semi-open slope scattered with lodgepole pine, but as you continue up the valley, the pine grades into a mature forest of spruce and alpine fir.

At km 3.9, a 200 m spur trail branches left to Lower Rowe Lake. Despite the lake's diminutive size, the steep walls of the surrounding amphitheatre enhance its setting, and the subalpine forest along its shore is a pleasant place to stop and relax for awhile.

From the junction, the trail continues its climb to the upper lakes, eventually emerging into the Rowe Meadow at the head of the valley. This lush meadow is where many end their hike, pulling out their cameras in preparation for a hard day of wildflower photography.

A bridge at the far edge of the meadow spans a tributary stream to a junction. At this split the Tamarack Trail branches right and begins its ascent to Lineham Ridge, while the trail to Upper Rowe Lakes cuts left and climbs a steep slope into a stand of alpine larch.

The Rowe Lakes basin from Lineham Ridge

The larger of the two Upper Rowe Lakes is backed against the cliffs of the Great Divide and surrounded by stunted stands of alpine fir and larch. (When we were last there, we saw bighorn sheep on the slopes above.) By continuing down to its tiny sister lake, you can peek over the lip of this hanging valley to the waters of Lower Rowe Lake, 150 vertical metres below.

Lineham Ridge. If you get back to the Rowe Meadow junction with time and energy to spare, a hike to the top of Lineham Ridge would most certainly be the high point of your day. Follow the Tamarack Trail option from the meadow to reach the crest of the ridge in another 3.4 km of steady climbing.

Since the ridge is nearly as high as most of the surrounding mountaintops, the views are magnificent. A sea of mountains stretches out in all directions (we've identified peaks as far away as 50 km), while on the opposite side of the ridge, the beautiful, deep blue Lineham Lakes lie in their verdant basin.

196 Tamarack Trail

Akamina Parkway to Red Rock Canyon—36.4 km (22.6 mi)

Backpack

Allow 2 to 3 days

Maximum elevation: 2560 m (8,400 ft)

Minimum elevation: 1495 m (4,900 ft)

Maps: Sage Creek 82 G/1
      Waterton Lakes National Park

Access: Northbound travellers start from the Akamina Parkway on the *Rowe Lakes-Lineham Ridge* trail. Southbound hikers start from the Red Rock Canyon parking area and follow the *Snowshoe Trail.*

0.0—Akamina Parkway (1610 m).

3.9—Lower Rowe Lake Junction (1965 m).

5.2—Rowe Meadow Junction. Upper Rowe Lakes left 1.2 km. Tamarack Trail right.

8.6—Lineham Ridge (2560 m)

13.8—Blakiston Creek south fork (1890 m).

15.7—Festubert Saddle (2225 m).

17.7—Lone Lake and Campground (2025 m).

21.5—Junction. South Kootenay Pass left 1.0 km. Continue ahead.

21.6—Junction (1920 m). Intersection with *Snowshoe-Blakiston Creek Loop* at km 14.8. Red Rock Canyon right 10.1 km. Continue ahead.

22.2—Blue Grouse Basin.

22.9—Bauerman Divide (2070 m).

24.1—Junction. Lower Twin Lake right 0.3 km. Stay left.

24.7—Upper Twin Lake and Campground (1950 m).

24.8—Junction. Sage Pass left 1.5 km.

27.9—Junction (1720 m). Snowshoe Campground and Warden Cabin. Trail to Lost Lake (1.9 km) and Castle River Divide (3.1 km) to left. Follow *Snowshoe Trail* right.

31.8—Junction. *Goat Lake* left 2.4 km.

36.4—Red Rock Canyon (1495 m).

The Tamarack Trail is the longest backpack in Waterton Park. For nearly 23 of its 36 kms, the trail is less than a kilometre from the crest of the Great Divide as it passes over high ridges, through stands of alpine larch and lush meadows, and near several small lakes.

The trail runs between the Akamina Parkway on the south to Red Rock Canyon in the park's northwest corner. While the journey is very rewarding, some of the route's best scenery can be visited on long day trips or shorter backpacks from either end of the trail. (See *Rowe Lakes–Lineham Ridge* and *Snowshoe Trail–Blakiston Creek Loop.*)

There is an elevation advantage to starting the trip from the south end, though you may question the benefit after travelling 17.7 kms and climbing nearly 1300 vertical metres on the up-and-down route to the first campground at Lone Lake. The initial 8.6 km of the trip follows the *Rowe Lakes–Lineham Ridge* trail—a steady ascent to 2560-m Lineham Ridge, the highest trail-accessible point in the park.

From Lineham Ridge, the trail makes a long, switchbacking descent to Blakiston Creek's south fork, followed by another tough climb to a 2225-m saddle on Festubert Mountain's east ridge. From this summit, it drops rapidly to Lone Lake Campground near the trip's midpoint.

Beyond Lone Lake, the trail levels out through larch forest and subalpine meadows. At km 21.6 it intersects the *Snowshoe-Blakiston Creek Loop* at the Blakiston Valley junction. Continue northwest through Blue Grouse Basin and over Bauerman Divide to Twin Lakes and Upper Twin Lake Campground.

The final 12 kms is somewhat anticlimactic, as the route descends to the Snowshoe Trail and follows its broad track down the Bauerman Valley to Red Rock Canyon.

197 Crandell Lake

Akamina Parkway to Crandell Lake—0.8 km (0.5 mi)
Crandell Campground to Crandell Lake—2.5 km (1.6 mi)

Crandell is a forest-encircled lake set in a narrow gap between Mount Crandell and Ruby Ridge. While the scenery surrounding the lake is unexceptional, either of two short trails leading to the lake make a pleasant nature walk, particularly for families.

The lake is a very short walk from the Akamina Parkway to the south, and only a bit longer on the northern approach from Crandell Campground and the Red Rock Parkway. With so much accessibility, it is little wonder the trail is well trodden and the lakeshore usually quite busy.

The approach from Akamina Parkway climbs along an old wagon road and crosses a low ridge to the lake. The trail from the north leaves from the southwest corner of Crandell Campground, or alternately from the Canyon Church Camp road just west of the campground, and climbs gradually to the north end of the lake.

Access: From the south, follow the Akamina Parkway to a parking area on the right side of the road 7 km (4.5 mi) beyond Waterton townsite. Access from the north is via the Crandell Campground trailhead, located at the campground's southwest corner. (Another trailhead, located just west of the campground on the Canyon Church Camp access road, provides access for hikers not staying at the campground.) *Maps: Waterton Lakes 82 H/4; Waterton Lakes National Park.*

198 Blakiston Falls

Red Rock Canyon to Blakiston Falls—1.0 km (0.6 mi)

You don't have to hike very far up Blakiston Creek from Red Rock Canyon to reach one the valley's best features—Blakiston Falls. While quite a few people walk to the falls, the trail is a peaceful contrast to the traffic jams at Red Rock Canyon.

As you walk along the trail from Red Rock Canyon to the falls, you are following in the footsteps of one of Waterton's earliest European visitors, Lieutenant Thomas Blakiston. Blakiston was a member of John Palliser's British North American Exploring Expedition when he descended the valley from South Kootenay Pass in September, 1858. He subsequently provided the first detailed description of the region, and named the Waterton Lakes for the noted British naturalist Charles Waterton.

After a short climb through a forest dominated by lodgepole pine, you emerge above a gorge and look down upon Blakiston Falls. Viewing platforms extend out over the canyon and allow views from below and immediately above the waterfall.

Access: From its junction with Highway 5 just north of Waterton townsite, follow the Red Rock Parkway 15 km (9 mi) to its terminus at Red Rock Canyon parking area. Cross the footbridge over the canyon, turn left and follow the Red Rock Canyon trail downhill to the Bauerman Creek footbridge, where the trail to Blakiston Falls begins. *Maps: Sage Creek 82 G/1; Waterton Lakes National Park.*

199 Goat Lake

Red Rock Canyon to Goat Lake—7.0 km (4.3 mi)

Day trip or backpack

Allow 2 to 3 hours one way

Elevation gain: 530 m (1,750 ft)

Maximum elevation: 2025 m (6,650 ft)

Maps: Sage Creek 82 G/1
      Waterton Lakes National Park

Access: From its junction with the Park Entrance Road 2 km (1.2 mi) north of Waterton townsite, follow Red Rock Parkway 15 km (9 mi) to its terminus at Red Rock Canyon. The trail begins at the canyon footbridge at the west edge of the parking area.

0.0—Red Rock Canyon (1495 m).

—Gentle grades on roadbed.

2.4—Side stream crossing.

3.4—Side stream crossing.

4.1—Enter mature forest and begin gradual climb.

4.6—Junction (1570 m). *Snowshoe Trail* ahead. Goat Lake right.

—Steady moderate to steep climb.

5.0—Trail emerges on open slopes.

5.7—First switchbacks.

—Steep climb along open slopes.

6.5—Trail enters Goat Lake cirque. Grades moderate.

6.7—Waterfall.

—Trail follows Goat Lake outlet stream.

7.0—Goat Lake (2025 m).

—Trail continues around north shore.

7.2—Goat Lake Campground.

Goat Lake is a shallow, emerald-hued lake surrounded by subalpine forest, lush wildflower meadows, and high ridges of crimson argillite. The small cirque containing the lake, perched high above the Bauerman Valley, is a textbook example of a hanging valley, and, as the name suggests, one of the best places in the park to see mountain goats.

The lake is a good objective for day hikers, even though the last 2.4 km climbs 455 m (1,500 ft). Or you can backpack to the pleasant campground in the open forest along its northern shore. Either way, the ascent up the south-facing slope from the Bauerman Valley will wilt even the most enthusiastic on a warm day.

The first hour from Red Rock Canyon follows the Snowshoe Trail along the north side of Bauerman Creek (see *Snowshoe Trail-Blakiston Creek Loop*). The wide track is a restored fire road, which rolls gently through a pleasant open forest of aspen, cottonwood and pine. Creekside meadows along the way provide fine views of the 700-m north face of Anderson Peak and its distinctive dark band of diabase rock. (Since the Snowshoe Trail is open to mountain bikes, you can save 30 minutes in, and even more time on the way out, by cycling the 4.6 km stretch to the Goat Lake trail junction.)

If you are feeling a little parched by the time you reach the Goat Lake trail junction, you should fill your water bottle from Bauerman Creek. The climb ahead is steep and dry, and there is no water until you reach a waterfall at the entrance to the cirque.

Climbing from the dense forest of pine and spruce along Bauerman Creek, the trail gains elevation rapidly and emerges onto open slopes above the valley in less than 0.5 km. Views extend back across the valley to Anderson Peak and west to the Great Divide near Twin Lakes.

Goat Lake and Avion Ridge

As the trail nears the entrance to the Goat Lake cirque, the steep grade moderates. Limestone outcrops along this section of trail contain fossilized remains of stromatolites, visible as a series of swirls in the rock. These cyanobacterial colonies were one of the earth's earliest life forms, part of a reef that thrived in Precambrian seas over one billion years ago!

Goat Lake is a quiet body of water reflecting forest on three sides and a headwall formed by Avion Ridge. The trail continues around the north shore to a pretty little campground sheltered by scattered stands of alpine fir.

Beyond the campground there is an extensive meadowland where yellow glacier lilies bloom along the edges of receding snowbanks in early summer. Later in the season the meadows fill with a wide variety of subalpine flowers, dominated by tall, white-topped beargrass.

The steep scree slope descending to the water's edge on the west shore is etched by the trails of mountain goats, which are commonly seen on the cliffs above. The long crest of Avion Ridge is capped by the brilliant red argillite common throughout Waterton Park. Named for a town in France where Canadians fought in 1917, Avion forms part of the northwest boundary of the park.

Avion Ridge. This high ridge is a popular objective for strong hikers and rock scramblers since it provides exceptional views out over much of Waterton Park. Though it is often hiked as a circuit (starting at Castle River Divide and ending at Goat Lake), anyone camping at Goat Lake can day trip to the ridge.

The route to the ridge climbs steep scree slopes beneath Newman Peak (watch for scramblers' trails worn into the loose rock), then traverses to the col west of Newman Peak. Once you've attained Avion Ridge, you can wander south and west along its crest for another 3 km. (See *Snowshoe-Blakiston Creek Loop Hikes:* Castle River Divide-Avion Ridge.)

200 Snowshoe Trail—Blakiston Creek Loop

Red Rock Canyon to Twin Lakes Campground—11.7 km (7.3 mi)
Snowshoe-Blakiston Creek Loop—24.9 km (15.5 mi)

Day trip or backpack

Allow 3 to 4 hours to Twin Lakes

Elevation gain: 575 m (1,900 ft)

Maximum elevation: 2070 m (6,800 ft)

Maps: Sage Creek 82 G/1
      Waterton Lakes National Park

Access: From its junction with the Park Entrance Road 2 km (1.2 mi) north of Waterton townsite, follow the Red Rock Parkway 15 km (9 mi) to its terminus at Red Rock Canyon. The trail begins at the canyon footbridge at the west edge of the parking area.

0.0—Red Rock Canyon (1495 m).

—Gentle grades on roadbed.

2.4—Side stream crossing.

3.4—Side stream crossing.

4.0—Gradual climb into mature forest.

4.6—Junction. *Goat Lake* right 2.4 km.

8.5—Junction (1720 m). Snowshoe Campground and Warden Cabin. Trail to Lost Lake (1.9 km) and Castle River Divide (3.1 km) to right. Twin Lakes left.

—Steady climb with sections of switchbacks.

11.6—Junction. Sage Pass right 1.5 km.

11.7—Upper Twin Lake and Campground (1950 m).

12.3—Junction. Lower Twin Lake left 0.3 km.

13.5—Bauerman Divide (2070 m).

14.2—Blue Grouse Basin.

14.8—Junction (1920 m). *Tamarack Trail* ahead. Blakiston Creek left.

—Moderate to steep downhill.

18.4—Blakiston Creek-Lone Creek confluence.

—Gradual descent through forest and avalanche paths.

23.9—Blakiston Falls.

24.9—Red Rock Canyon (1495 m).

The Snowshoe Trail and Blakiston Creek trail both begin at Red Rock Canyon. While neither of these valley-bottom routes is terribly exciting, they do provide access to some fine subalpine meadows and lakes beneath the Great Divide in the park's northwest corner. Since the two trails are linked together at their far end by a trail paralleling the divide, you can hike out on one and back on the other to complete a 25 km loop trip.

The Snowshoe Trail is an old fire road that is open to cyclists, so it is quite popular to peddle to road's end at Snowshoe Campground and then hike to scenic points of interest like Twin Lakes or Lost Lake. We have also hiked the entire circuit in a long day, though this only allowed time for one short side-trip. And since there are several rewarding side-trips along the route, it is worthwhile to backpack to Snowshoe or Upper Twin Lake Campgrounds and spend a day or two exploring.

We prefer to hike the circuit counter-clockwise by starting on the Snowshoe Trail. This broad track runs through open montane forest near Bauerman Creek with little gain or loss of elevation for the first 4 km. As you roll through grassy meadows and scattered stands of poplar and pine, there are continuous views south to the massive cliffs of Anderson Peak.

Two unbridged tributaries flow across the trail at km 2.4 and 3.4. While these streams are easy rock-hops in late summer, you may experience some difficulties early in the season or during periods of heavy rainfall.

At the 4 km mark, the roadbed climbs gradually into coniferous forest, which limits your views for the remainder of the journey to road's end at Snowshoe Campground and Warden Cabin.

The trail to Lost Lake and Castle River

Blue Grouse Basin

Divide branches northwest from the end of the Snowshoe Trail, but you will want to cross the nearby bridge and follow the Twin Lakes trail to the southwest if you are completing the circuit. The trail climbs steadily through heavy forest and across avalanche slopes at the foot of Mount Bauerman to reach Upper Twin Lake in just over 3 km.

Upper Twin Lake is a pretty tarn backed against the Great Divide immediately beneath Sage Pass. Along with the smaller Lower Twin Lake, it serves as the headwaters for Bauerman Creek. Meadows near the lakes are filled with wildflowers in midsummer, including tall, spiky stands of beargrass—a member of the lily family that is unique to this section of the Canadian Rockies.

Continuing south from Twin Lakes, the trail makes a short climb along steep scree and rock ledges to a beautiful stand of alpine larch on the crest of the ridge connecting Mount Bauerman to the Great Divide. On the ascent you have a fine view back down the Bauerman Valley to the mountains above Red Rock Canyon.

Beyond the summit, you descend into Blue Grouse Basin (aka Peck's Basin) and skirt a small pond surrounded by moist meadows and more beargrass.

At km 14.8, you arrive at the Blakiston Creek trail junction. The *Tamarack Trail* continues south from this split, however, this is the point where circuit hikers will turn east and return down the Blakiston Valley to the Red Rock Canyon trailhead.

Other than avalanche paths, which provide views to two of the park's highest peaks, Mount Blakiston (2940 m) to the south and Anderson Peak (2683 m) to the north, the descent of the Blakiston Valley is mostly forest-enclosed and uneventful. When you reach the canyon containing the valley's best natural feature, Blakiston Falls, you'll know you only have 1.0 km remaining to reach the Red Rock Canyon parking area.

Side-trips from the circuit to South Kootenay Pass, Sage Pass, Lost Lake and Castle River Divide–Avion Ridge are described on the following page.

Snowshoe—Blakiston Creek Hikes

There are a number of hikes that can be added to the *Snowshoe-Blakiston Creek Loop*. With the exception of Avion Ridge, all are short half-day trips from either Snowshoe or Upper Twin Lakes Campgrounds. Distances are listed from junctions on the circuit (*indicates distance approximate).

Castle River Divide–Avion Ridge—8 km*. The trail to Castle River Divide has little to recommend it except as an approach to the Avion Ridge route, which is one the finest ridge hikes in the Rockies. Once you've scrambled to the 2420-m crest of the ridge, views stretch southeast over much of Waterton Park and the Castle River headwaters to the north.

There is no defined trail from Castle River Divide to Avion Ridge, so take a 1:50,000 scale topo map as a guide. And reserve this lofty traverse for sunny, blue sky days; the ridge would be a grim and dangerous place to get caught in a storm.

Follow the Castle River Divide trail northwest from the junction at the end of the Snowshoe Trail. The forested climb is gradual to moderate, but becomes steeper as you near the pass. At km 3.1 you crest the forest-enclosed pass on the park boundary. Here you turn east and climb toward Avion Ridge.

Don't expect to find more than snippets of path as you climb through scattered larch and meadows. Stay on the high ground that leads upward along the line of the park boundary (use your map). Eventually, this becomes a more defined ridge, which you continue along to steep red argillite scree slopes and the crest of Avion Ridge.

At the top of the ridge, you follow its crest east and then north, staying near the 2400 m level for nearly 3 km. Eventually you arrive on a col southwest of Newman Peak overlooking Goat Lake.

At this point it is probably easiest to return the way you came. However, some hikers traverse the steep scree on the south slopes of Newman Peak and pick their way down to Goat Lake. (Watch for hiker's tracks in the scree and avoid rock bluffs.) At Goat Lake, you can return to the Snowshoe Trail in the Bauerman Valley via the *Goat Lake* trail.

Lost Lake—1.9 km. Lost Lake sits quite nicely beneath the Great Divide as the smallest lake in the park's northwest corner. Cyclists can work the kinks out of their legs by hiking the short trail to the lake from the end of the Snowshoe Trail, and backpackers can visit it as an easy, after-dinner walk from Snowshoe Campground.

Starting from the junction at the end of the Snowshoe Trail, follow the Castle River Divide trail northwest. The trail to Lost Lake branches left from the Castle River trail at km 0.8 and follows near the lake's outlet stream to its source.

Sage Pass—1.5 km. From a junction near the shore of Upper Twin Lake, a short steep trail climbs to the 2160-m summit of Sage Pass atop the Great Divide. The sparsely-treed summit provides grand views of Twin Lakes and the Bauerman Creek valley to the east, and not-so-great views to the west of logging roads on the headwaters of British Columbia's Sage Creek.

South Kootenay Pass—1.8 km. South Kootenay Pass was used by the Kootenay Indians as a route to the buffalo plains of southwestern Alberta, and their trail was followed by the Palliser Expedition's Thomas Blakiston when he discovered Waterton Lakes in 1858. Views from the 2260 m pass are limited to the Blakiston Valley, which runs away to the east, and the logging-scarred upper Kishinena Valley to the west.

The trail to the pass begins 100 m south of the Blakiston Creek junction (km 14.8). It switchbacks up the lower slopes of Kishinena Peak, then traverses south onto the lightly forested summit.

Akamina-Kishinena Provincial Park

At 109 sq km, Akamina-Kishinena Provincial Park is one of the smallest parks in the Canadian Rockies. It is snuggled into the southeast corner of British Columbia, sharing a common boundary with Waterton Park along the Great Divide. The international boundary and Montana's Glacier National Park borders it to the south, while B.C. forest lands, with active logging operations, contain the park to the west and north.

Throughout most of its past, the park area was remote wilderness. Before the arrival of Europeans, the Kootenay Indians travelled up Kishinena Creek and over the Great Divide to hunt buffalo on the plains of southwest Alberta. Thomas Blakiston, magnetic observer with the Palliser Expedition, traversed the Kishinena Valley en route to South Kootenay Pass and Waterton Lakes in 1858. In 1860 and 1861 members of the American and British Boundary Commissions camped near Akamina Pass while completing the survey of the international boundary from the Pacific coast to the crest of the Great Divide.

Soon after oil was discovered on Cameron Creek in 1901, a tote road was constructed over Akamina Pass to allow for further drilling on Akamina Creek. Following the completion of the "Akamina Highway" to Waterton Park's Cameron Lake in 1927, Waterton boosters lobbied to have the old tote road improved and extended down the Akamina and Kishinena Valleys to connect to the Flathead North Fork road along the west side of Glacier National Park. However, nothing came of the proposal, and the Akamina-Kishinena remained the domain of a handful of trappers, commercial outfitters, and grizzly bears.

As logging operations began moving up the Kishinena Valley in the 1970s and 80s, the B.C. government moved to protect this special wilderness. In 1986 it was designated a Provincial Recreation Area and, on July 12, 1995, it received full protection as a Class A Provincial Park.

While there are a number of primitive trails in the park's more remote valleys, the only maintained trails run to Forum and Wall Lakes beneath Akamina Ridge in the park's southwest corner. Both are accessed by hiking into the park on the old roadbed over Akamina Pass and have become popular day hikes from the Akamina Parkway in Waterton Lakes Park.

Information and services. An information kiosk at Akamina Pass greets hikers who ascend the 1.5 km trail from Waterton Park. The board displays maps of the park and current bulletins concerning park use and conditions. Park brochures are often available at this kiosk.

During the summer, park rangers are stationed 0.8 km beyond the Akamina Pass park entrance. However, the rangers have many tasks and are not always at their cabin.

The park's main campground, Akamina Creek, is located 0.9 km from Akamina Pass on the Wall Lake trail. (A campground at Wall Lake was closed in 1997.) As of summer 2000, camping fees were $5 per person per night.

Access: From Waterton townsite, follow the Akamina Parkway 15 km (9.5 miles) to the Akamina Pass trailhead parking area, located on the east side of the road 1.0 km from its termination at Cameron Lake. The trail to Akamina Pass is located on the west side of the road.

201 Wall Lake

Akamina Parkway to Wall Lake—5.2 km (3.2 mi)

Day trip

Allow 1.5 hours one way

Elevation gain: 110 m (350 ft)

Maximum elevation: 1780 m (5,850 ft)

Maps: Sage Creek 82 G/1
      Waterton Lakes National Park†
      † trail not shown

Access: Follow the Akamina Parkway 15 km (9.5 mi) from Waterton townsite to the Akamina Pass trailhead parking area, located on the east side of the road 1.0 km north of Cameron Lake. The trail begins on the opposite side of the road.

0.0—Akamina Pass trailhead (1670 m).

—Steady uphill on old roadbed.

0.9—Grades level off.

1.5—Akamina Pass (1780 m). Park information kiosk. Alberta-B.C. boundary markers.

—Gradual to moderate descent.

2.2—Junction (1770 m). Ranger station (0.2 km), Forum Falls (0.3 km) and *Forum Lake* (2.2 km) left. Wall Lake ahead.

2.4—Akamina Creek Campground.

2.5—Junction. Wall Lake left across Akamina Creek bridges.

—Single-track trail contours through forest.

3.2—Junction. Horse trail branches right. Hiker trail stays left.

4.8—Major avalanche path.

5.2—Wall Lake (1770 m). Outlet bridge.

—Trail follows lakeshore west.

5.6—Junction. Bennett Pass right.

5.8—Wall Lake west shore.

Wall Lake was a favourite destination for horseback tours led by Waterton's pioneer outfitter Bert Riggall during the 1920s. Today it is the most popular hike in Akamina-Kishinena Park.

The pretty, emerald lake is quite scenically situated beneath the north face of Akamina Ridge. Large snowfields extend out into its waters from the base of this wall into midsummer, adding a brilliant contrast to the shadowed cliffs and deep green of lake and forest.

The hike begins on the moderately graded tote road that leads from Waterton's Akamina Parkway to the Alberta-B.C. boundary on Akamina Pass. After passing the park's information kiosk on the pass, the roadbed descends through spruce-pine forest to Forum Lake junction and Akamina Creek Campground.

Just 50 m beyond the campground, the Wall Lake trail branches left from the road and crosses log bridges over Akamina Creek. Single-track trail follows around the end of a heavily forested ridge, staying close to the 1750 m level as it contours into the Wall Lake cirque. (This contouring trail saves distance and elevation loss over the old route up Wall Creek, which is still displayed on topo maps.)

At km 4.7 you enter a stand of old Engelmann spruce trees, some snapped by avalanches descending from Akamina Ridge. Just beyond, the trail crosses a verdant slide path filled with fireweed, sticky geranium and ragwort.

The trail crosses Wall Creek to the northeast end of Wall Lake at km 5.2. While the best overview of the lake is from this point, you will want to follow around the north end of the lake to the site of the old campground at a small lagoon on the west shore.

The forest along on the west side of the lake is quite lush, filled with red elderberry, gooseberry, heart-leaved arnica,

Wall Lake and Akamina Ridge

red monkey flower and black twinberry, and it is sometimes visited by mule deer. It is a pleasant spot to relax, eat your lunch, and scan the bluffs of Akamina Ridge for mountain goats.

Trail continues beyond the old campsite for another 300 m to open flats at the south end of the lake, near the headwall snowfield. Be wary of venturing onto this steep snowpatch, particularly early in the season when it extends into the lake. Kay Riggall, the young daughter of outfitter Bert Riggall, got stranded on its icy surface during a trip to the lake in the 1920s and barely escaped a slide into the lake's frigid waters.

Bennett Pass—Akamina Ridge. The 3 km trail to Bennett Pass runs from Wall Lake to a 2180 m summit at the northwest end of Akamina Ridge. The steep trip to the pass includes flower-filled meadows and a high, windswept viewpoint for the rugged twin-pyramids of Kintla and Kinnerly Peaks in Glacier National Park.

The trail, which isn't shown on topo maps, branches up into the forest 200 m before the old campsite on Wall Lake's west shore. The first kilometre is quite steep as it climbs through heavy forest and avalanche paths, but grades moderate somewhat as it makes its way northwest to the gap near the end of Akamina Ridge.

Most who hike to the pass continue the journey by following the crest of Akamina Ridge back to the east. While there is no defined trail, you can easily follow the ridgeline all the way to Forum Peak on the Great Divide—a distance of 5 km from Bennett Pass. Along the way you overlook Wall, Forum and Cameron Lakes on the Canadian side of the border, and Upper Kintla Lake in Glacier National Park.

This is definitely one of the most spectacular ridge walks in this section of the Rockies. Since the closure of Wall Lake Campground, the hike is a long, strenuous day from the Akamina Parkway trailhead or Akamina Creek Campground. It is strictly for strong hikers and should only be attempted when the weather is good.

202 Forum Lake

Akamina Parkway to Forum Lake—4.4 km (2.7 mi)

Day trip

Allow 1.5 hours one way

Elevation gain: 350 m (1,150 ft)

Maximum elevation: 2020 m (6,650 ft)

Maps: Sage Creek 82 G/1
     Waterton Lakes National Park†
     † trail not shown

Access: Follow the Akamina Parkway 15 km (9.5 mi) from Waterton townsite to the Akamina Pass trailhead parking area, located on the east side of the road 1.0 km north of Cameron Lake. The trail begins on the opposite side of the road.

0.0—Akamina Pass trailhead (1670 m).

—Steady uphill on old roadbed.

0.9—Grades level off.

1.5—Akamina Pass (1779 m). Park information kiosk. Alberta-B.C. boundary markers.

—Gradual to moderate descent.

2.2—Junction (1770 m). Akamina Creek Campground (0.3 km) and *Wall Lake* (3.0 km) ahead. Forum Lake left.

2.4—Ranger station.

2.5—Junction. Forum Falls right 50 m.

—Steady climb through forest.

3.6—Forum Creek bridge to west side.

3.8—Grades level off into Forum cirque.

4.4—Forum Lake (2020 m).

Forum Lake lies in a high cirque beneath Akamina Ridge and Forum Peak in the southeast corner of Akamina-Kishinena Park. Unlike the lushly forested shores of nearby Wall Lake, this small sink lake is cradled in a rocky basin with only a scattering of stunted fir and larch trees nearby. While the distance to Forum is nearly a kilometre shorter than to Wall, you have to climb 250 m over the final 2 km, so the approach takes nearly as long.

The first 2.2 km of the hike runs over the same route as Wall Lake, following an old roadbed to Akamina Pass from the Akamina Parkway in Waterton Park. The Forum Lake trail branches left from the broad track 0.7 km west of the pass and, after passing the park headquarters cabin, arrives at Forum Falls junction—a one minute side-trip to a forest-enclosed waterfall on Forum Creek.

The climb to the lake begins just beyond the falls—steep and steady through alpine fir. Grades moderate after 0.3 km and the trees thin as you pass through a series of small meadows. The trail crosses Forum Creek at km 3.6, where you obtain your first views ahead to Forum Peak and Akamina Ridge. The final stretch climbs gradually through beargrass meadows and across lush avalanche paths filled with false hellebore, ragwort and meadow rue.

Though the lake's headwall is formed by grey limestone cliffs, its rocky shoreline is coloured with shards of red and green argillite. All of these sedimentary formations have their origin in warm Precambrian seas, and some pieces of red argillite preserve the ripple marks of ancient shorelines. Today the ancient rocks near the lake provide sanctuary for pikas.

Strong scramblers can ascend the ridge northeast of the lake and follow it south to its intersection with Akamina Ridge—one of the finest viewpoints in the park. (See also *Wall Lake*.)

Forum Lake

Peter Lougheed Provincial Park

Lying on the eastern slopes of the Great Divide in Alberta, Peter Lougheed Provincial Park is part of the 4,000 sq km Kananaskis Country multi-use recreation area, created in 1977 to "alleviate congestion in National Parks, and to provide greater recreation opportunities for Albertans." The park is 509 sq km in area and shares boundaries with Banff National Park to the northwest, British Columbia's Height of the Rockies and Elk Lakes Provincial Parks to the west and south, and Alberta's Elbow Sheep Wildland Park to the east.

Three major roads provide access to the trails profiled in this guide (all roads are referred to as "Trails," so don't get confused): Kananaskis Trail (Hwy 40) traverses the park from north to south; Kananaskis Lakes Trail branches from Kananaskis Trail in the heart of the park and provides access to Upper and Lower Kananaskis Lakes; and the Smith-Dorrien/Spray Trail (Hwy 742) provides access to the Smith-Dorrien Pass region in the park's northwest corner.

There are more than 100 km of official hiking trails in the park, ranging from short interpretive walks to multi-day backpacks. All trails were redeveloped when the park was established in 1977, so they are among the best designed in the mountain parks.

Most of these hikes are concentrated near Lower and Upper Kananaskis Lakes, including the park's two premier backpacking routes to North and South Kananaskis Passes. Smith-Dorrien Pass is the starting point for two very popular hikes to Chester Lake and Burstall Pass. Highwood Pass (2206 m) is the starting point for the Ptarmigan Cirque hike—one of the finest short trips in the park.

Random camping is not permitted in the park's backcountry, and backpackers must obtain a permit to overnight in any of the park's five backcountry campgrounds. Permits cost $3.00 per person per night, and can be purchased at any Kananaskis Country visitor centre or by phone (see *Sources–Parks information*).

Aside from hiking, mountain biking and fishing are popular activities in Peter Lougheed Park, but both are strictly regulated. Visitors planning to bike or fish in the park should check with park staff for current restrictions.

Information and services. The park's main visitor information centre is located on Kananaskis Lakes Trail 3.5 km south of its junction with Kananaskis Trail (Hwy 40). The Barrier Lake Visitor Information Centre is north of the park on the Kananaskis Trail (Hwy 40) approach, 6.5 km south of the Trans-Canada Highway. Both centres are open year round to provide full information services, dispense brochures, maps, books, and issue backcountry permits.

All of the park's roadside campgrounds are located near the Kananaskis Lakes and are accessed via the Kananaskis Lakes Trail. (Elkwood is the largest and the only one with showers.) Other vehicle-accessible campgrounds are located along the Kananaskis Trail (Hwy 40) just north of the park.

Boulton Creek Trading Post, located at km 9.7 on Kananaskis Lakes Trail, is a general store-restaurant and the only commercial outlet for basic camping supplies and groceries within the park. A general store-gas station is located at Fortress Mountain junction 2.6 km north of the park boundary on Kananaskis Trail (Hwy 40). The nearest commercial accommodation is at Kananaskis Village, 21 km north of the park boundary on Highway 40. The closest full service town is Canmore.

Access: Primary access to Peter Lougheed Provincial Park is via Kananaskis Trail (Hwy 40), which intersects the Trans-Canada Highway 80 km west of Calgary and 30 km east of Canmore. The park can be reached more directly from Canmore via the Smith-Dorrien/Spray Trail (Hwy 742)—a well-maintained, all-season gravel road.

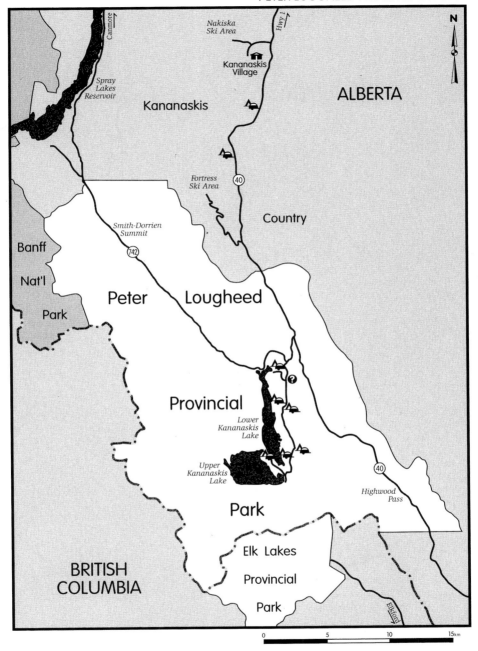

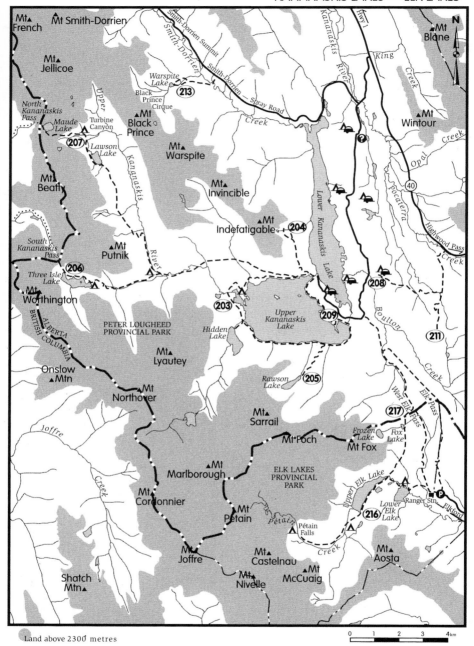

Land above 2300 metres

203 Upper Kananaskis Lake

Upper Kananaskis Lake Circuit—16.2 kms (10.2 mi)

Day hike

Allow 4 to 5 hours

Elevation gain: 45 m (150 ft)

Maximum elevation: 1770 m (5,800 ft)

Maps: Kananaskis Lakes 82 J/11†
Kananaskis Lakes (Gem Trek)
† trail not shown

Access: From the Trans-Canada Highway, follow Kananaskis Trail (Hwy 40) for 50 km (31 mi) and turn right on Kananaskis Lakes Trail. Drive another 15 km (9.5 mi) to the North Interlakes Day Use Area. The trailhead kiosk is at the north end of the parking lot.

0.0—Trailhead kiosk (1725 m).

—Trail crosses Kananaskis Lakes intake dam and spillway.

0.3—Junction. *Mount Indefatigable* right. Upper Lake Circuit ahead.

—Trail proceeds on old fire road.

0.5—Junction. Fire road splits. Stay right.

0.9—Junction. *South Kananaskis Pass* and *North Kananaskis Pass* ahead. Upper Lake Circuit left.

—Trail descends to lake and follows shoreline.

2.2—Palliser rockslide.

2.4—Junction. Stay left.

3.7—Point Campground.

4.4—Lower Kananaskis Falls.

4.5—Kananaskis River bridge.

—Trail ascends above shoreline to hike's high point (1770 m).

6.7—Trail rejoins lakeshore.

10.6—Junction. *Rawson Lake* right.

10.7—Sarrail Creek Falls and bridge.

11.8—Junction. Stay left

—Trail runs between lake and parking area to boat launch and dam. Proceed across dam.

12.7—North end of dam.

14.7—Junction. Old roadbed to right. Stay left.

16.2—Trailhead kiosk (1725 m). North Interlakes Day Use Area.

Despite its length, the Upper Kananaskis Lake Circuit is an easy trip that offers an ever-changing panorama of the lake and the mountains that ring it. Because it provides access to several other trails, sections of the route can be very busy. The ideal time to hike it is mid-week in mid-September: take a lunch, map, field guides, a reflective turn of mind, and plan to spend a leisurely day with curiosity as your guide.

Moving counterclockwise from the North Interlakes trailhead kiosk, the first leg of the trail traces the north shore of the lake, with views of the glacier-carved mountains to the west and south: Mt. Putnik (2940m); Mt. Lyautey (3082 m); Mt. Sarrail (3174); Mt. Foch (3180 m) and Mt. Fox (2973 m). Just shy of the 1 km mark, the trail veers left, descends to the lake, then climbs over a massive rockslide that in some earlier era spilled down from Mt. Indefatigable and pushed well out into the lake. The resultant spit is now the site of the Point Campground.

Past the campground, the trail skirts a small bay and crosses the Lower Kananaskis Falls via a sturdy wooden bridge. Beyond the bridge it angles southeast and climbs to its high point 42 metres above the lake. Views are limited, but the forest is green and lush, providing great opportunities to sink down in a carpet of feather moss and contemplate the flora at hand.

Trail traffic picks up near Rawson Lake junction, and increases to include cars, dogs and Frisbees as you pass through the Upper Lakes Day Use Area. Pick your way between the parking lots and picnic tables, and head across Upper Kananaskis Lake's main dam, taking advantage of the fine views ahead to Mt. Indefatigable and the Opal Range. Beyond the dam, the Upper Lake Circuit wends its way through pleasant open forest back to the starting point.

204 Mount Indefatigable

North Interlakes Parking Area to Mount Indefatigable Viewpoint—2.7 kms (1.8 mi)

Half-day trip

Allow 1.5 to 2 hours one way

Elevation gain: 500 m (1,650 ft)

Maximum elevation: 2230 m (7,320 ft)

Maps: Kananaskis Lakes 82J/11†
      Kananaskis Lakes (Gem Trek)
      † trail not shown

Access: From the Trans-Canada Highway, follow Kananaskis Trail (Hwy 40) for 50 km (31 mi) and turn right on Kananaskis Lakes Trail. Drive another 15 km (9.5 mi) to the North Interlakes Day Use Area. The trailhead kiosk is at the north end of the parking lot.

0.0—Trailhead kiosk (1725 m).

   —Follow across Kananaskis Lakes intake dam and spillway.

0.3—Junction. Mt. Indefatigable trail right.

   —Steady ascent through subalpine forest.

1.0—Steep rock bands with loose rock.

   —Very steep ascent with loose rock. First views of Upper Kananaskis Lake.

1.5—Wendy Elekes Viewpoint (1999 m).

   —Steady climb along ridge.

2.4—Junction. Unofficial path to Mt. Indefatigable northeast ridge left. Stay ahead.

2.7—"End of Trail" sign and bench (2230 m).

The Mount Indefatigable trail is worthy of its namesake: a rocky sweat-monger of a route that angles unrelentingly up the peak's eastern ridge. Fortunately, the Indefatigable trail is not interminable, and hikers in relatively decent shape soon reach one of the finest viewpoints overlooking the Kananaskis Lakes.

The trail begins modestly enough, running west along the lakeshore circuit briefly before abruptly veering right at a signed junction. After undulating through fir and spruce for another 0.6 km, it climbs through rock bands (keep your head up and choose your route from several available options).

The trail climbs wickedly for the next 0.5 km before topping out on a rocky promontory known as the Wendy Elekes Viewpoint. A wooden bench offers an invitation to catch your breath and look down on Upper and Lower Kananaskis Lakes. It is a stunning view, especially late in the day when the lakes are burnished by the low-angle sun.

From Elekes Viewpoint, the incline of the trail moderates a bit as it moves north along the lip of an impressive limestone escarpment. Alpine larch begin to intrude into the subalpine forest, making the hike a special treat in mid-September when their needles turn an incandescent gold.

The trail flattens out near the 2.4 km mark and continues for another 300 m to a sign and bench marking the end of official trail.

Indefatigable Ridge. You can reach an even higher viewpoint for this section of the Kananaskis Valley by extending your hike for another 40 minutes or so to the summit of Mount Indefatigable's northeast ridge. From an unsigned junction at km 2.4, follow a narrow path that climbs through subalpine forest then bends right and fizzles out in a meadowed basin. Scramble up the rocky slope north of the basin to the ridge's 2460-m crest.

Upper Kananaskis Lake from Mount Indefatigable trail

205 Rawson Lake

Upper Lake Parking Area to Rawson Lake—3.5 km (2.2 mi)

Half-day trip

Allow 1.5 hours one way

Elevation gain: 300 m (1,000 ft)

Maximum elevation: 2025 m (6,650 ft)

Maps: Kananaskis Lakes 82 J/11†
Kananaskis Lakes (Gem Trek)
† trail not shown

Access: From the Trans-Canada Highway, follow the Kananaskis Trail 50 km (31 mi) and turn right on Kananaskis Lakes Trail. Follow the Kananaskis Lakes Trail 12.5 km (7.8 mi) to the Upper Lake Day Use Area and park in the southernmost of the three parking lots. The trail begins at the southern corner of the parking lot as part of the *Upper Kananaskis Lake* circuit.

0.0—Upper Lake parking lot (1725 m).

—Trail contours just above Upper Kananaskis Lake.

1.1—Sarrail Creek Falls bridge.

1.2—Junction. *Upper Kananaskis Lake Circuit* ahead. Rawson Lake left.

—Trail begins moderate-to-steep climb through forest.

2.7—Trail levels off into cirque.

3.2—First of several sections of log corduroy.

3.3—Trail split (stay left).

3.5—Rawson Lake (2025 m).

3.6—Elevated outhouse.

—Minor trail fork (stay left). Trail runs below cliff bands.

3.9—Park interpretive sign. End of official trail.

The trail to Rawson Lake offers a relaxed half-day trek to a small, forest-shaded lake set in a spectacular glacier-carved cirque. Because of the lake's easy access and spectacular setting, the trail can be a busy one in mid-summer, but the lake's perimeter is big enough to offer all visitors a quiet spot of their own. For hikers seeking more of a challenge, some stout vertical scrambling beyond the end of the trail provides both solitude and an inspiring high mountain vista.

The trail begins on the *Upper Kananaskis Lake* circuit, following a wide, pleasant path through a mature subalpine forest of Englemann spruce and subalpine fir. Small creeks tumble down from the left, and the Upper Kananaskis Lake is a constant companion on the right.

A bridge crosses Sarrail Creek at km 1.1, and the mists rising from a boisterous 10-metre cataract will delight small children and cool overheated parents on hot summer afternoons. The falls herald the Rawson Lake turn-off just 100 m beyond.

The middle section of the trail consists of 1.5 km of switchbacks up through the forest to the Rawson Lake cirque. Hikers who find they are breathing harder than they would like should consider that the trail, as a relatively recent addition to the area, offers a vast improvement over the old access, which involved a vegetation-gripping ascent directly up the outlet stream. Such was certainly the experience of Dr. Donald Rawson, a limnologist who did pioneering fisheries research in the Kananaskis in the late 1930s, and for whom the lake is named.

The end of the steepest part of the climb is signaled by sections of split log that span a boggy section of forest floor. At this point you have reached the lip of the Rawson Lake cirque, and it is only a couple of hundred more metres to the lake's outlet.

Rawson Lake

The sudden appearance of the lake, accompanied by signs prohibiting fire and camping, may suggest the hike is over. In fact, the best lies ahead: following the trail along the southeast shore for a few hundred metres, you'll encounter small meadows and some cliff bands. It is there you'll begin to feel physically the presence of the curved, soaring headwall that wraps around the western end of the lake.

An intimidating face of 350-million year-old Carboniferous limestones, the headwall drops from the summit of Mount Sarrail (3174 m) over 1200 m to the lake below. Rawson Lake is typical of many of the cirque lakes in the Rockies, but by virtue of the symmetry and height of the headwall, it is a particularly impressive example. Even in late July, remnants of last year's snow hug the bottom of the cliffs, and the lakeshore blooms profusely with alpine buttercup, fringed grass-of-Parnassus, and twinberry.

Just shy of the 4-km mark, a park interpretive sign spells out the end of the official trail, warning that the shoreline and surrounding slopes are fragile, and that grizzly bear sightings are common in the area beyond.

If you have ascertained that there have not been recent grizzly sightings in the area (check with park staff before the hike), you can proceed around the end of the lake on a rough-hewn trail and scramble upslope to the obvious saddle to the northwest. It is a solid 350 vertical metres to the saddle, but the view down the other side to the Kananaskis Lakes is a worthy reward.

206 South Kananaskis Pass

North Interlakes Parking Area to Three Isle Lake Campground—11.7 km (7.3 mi)
North Interlakes Parking Area to South Kananaskis Pass—14.2 km (8.8 mi)

Day hike or backpack

Allow 4.5 hours to Three Isle Lake

Elevation gain: 565 m (1,850 ft)

Maximum elevation: 2290 m (7,515 ft)

Maps: Kananaskis Lakes 82 J/11
Kananaskis Lakes (Gem Trek)

Access: From the Trans-Canada Highway, follow the Kananaskis Trail (Hwy 40) for 50 km (31 mi) and turn right on the Kananaskis Lakes Trail. Drive another 15 kms (9.5 mi) to the North Interlakes Day Use Area. The trailhead kiosk is at the north end of the parking lot.

0.0—Trailhead kiosk (1725 m).
 —Trail crosses Kananaskis Lakes intake dam and spillway.
0.3—Junction. *Mount Indefatigable* right.
0.9—Junction. *Upper Kananaskis Lake* trail left.
2.1—Trail crosses Palliser rockslide.
4.0—Invincible Creek bridge.
5.8—Kananaskis River bridge.
7.3—Spring.
 —Gravel outwash flats and small streams (bridged).
8.0—Junction (1790 m) and Forks Campground. *North Kananaskis Pass* ahead. Three Isle Lake-S. Kananaskis Pass left.
9.4—Trail enters large avalanche chute.
 —Stone steps.
10.1—Tributary stream bridge.
 —Steep scree, 250-m ascent up valley headwall.
11.5—Top of headwall (2190 m).
 —Gentle descent to Three Isle Lake.
11.7—Three Isle Lake Campground.
 —Trail skirts north shore of Three Isle Lake.
12.8—Trail sign for South Kananaskis Pass.
13.3—North end of Three Isle Lake.
 —Trail climbs moderately through forest.
14.2—South Kananaskis Pass (2290 m).

The trail to Three Isle Lake and South Kananaskis Pass is one of the most popular hikes in Peter Lougheed Provincial Park. While some brave souls attempt it as a day trip, most choose to backpack, with Three Isle Lake Campground as the overnight destination. Others pack in only as far as the Forks, and then day hike from there. The latter approach means a longer second day, but with less weight to carry up a high, steep headwall.

The first leg of the trip traces the north shore of Upper Kananaskis Lake via a narrow dirt fire road, bypassing the trail junctions to *Mount Indefatigable* and the *Upper Kananaskis Lake Circuit.* Aside from some wonderful views across the lake up to the hanging valley between Mounts Lyautey and Sarrail, the trail's most interesting offering is the Palliser talus field—a tremendous rockslide that several centuries ago roared down from the upper reaches of Mount Indefatigable and out into the lake.

The fire road—as well as the mountain bike traffic permitted on it—ends at Invincible Creek. Beyond, the trail becomes an exceptionally pleasant, essentially level, single-width path that runs through some spectacular old growth forest carpeted with moss and horsetails and dappled with sunlight. The forest's stand of 400-year-old lodgepole pine is Alberta's oldest.

Just before the 6 km mark, the trail crosses the cascading Kananaskis River and proceeds along its southern bank between Mount Lyautey and the southern end of the Spray Mountains. The trail twists more, and has more rocks and roots than the previous section, but remains comfortable underfoot. Views ahead, however, reveal a looming headwall that promises travel of a very different nature.

A spring of gin-clear water at km 7.3

Three Isle Lake

heralds a reach of avens-laced gravels and several small streams braiding their way to the Kananaskis River. The Forks Campground, at km 8.0, is perched just above the Kananaskis River in dense forest at the foot of Mount Putnik.

The South Kananaskis Pass trail veers left (west) at the campground, and begins climbing along the north bank of Three Isle Creek. Eventually, the forest is left behind for the willow and alder of some high avalanche chutes (a good place to make some noise to alert any bears in the area). The willow-alder bush then gives way to the high, steep scree slopes and rock bands of the headwall. It is at this point backpackers usually second-guess their decision to hike beyond the Forks with a full pack.

Not far above the rock bands, the trail loses some of its incline, traverses to the top of the headwall, and then wanders down to the Three Isle Lake Campground. In mid-summer, with the water levels up, the lake is the picture of gentle wilderness, framed by forest and the heights of Mount Worthington (2838 m).

From Three Isle Lake it is an easy 2.5-km jaunt to South Kananaskis Pass. The trail snakes along the sinuous northeast shore of the lake, affording views to Mount Worthington and time to contemplate the enduring mystery of Three Isle Lake: Why are there only two Isles?

Beyond the end of the lake, the trail climbs gradually through an open subalpine forest peppered with old man's beard, heart-leaved arnica, fleabane, paintbrush, and valerian. Scattered larches signal the approach of treeline, but the trail doesn't actually break free of the forest until it reaches the pass itself, marked by a large cairn and a sign reading: "Height of the Rockies Wilderness Area. Welcome to B.C." Beyond, open meadows stretch away to the pyramid of Mount Beatty (2999 m). For those with the time and energy, a walk down-valley to Beatty Lake is a great addition to an already great hike.

PETER LOUGHEED PROVINCIAL PARK   385

207 North Kananaskis Pass

North Interlakes Parking Area to Turbine Canyon Campground—16.2 km (10.1 mi)
North Interlakes Parking Area to North Kananaskis Pass—18.3 km (11.4 mi)

Backpack

Allow 5 hours to Turbine Canyon Campground

Elevation gain: 645 m (2,100 ft)

Maximum elevation: 2370 m (7,775 ft)

Maps: Kananaskis Lakes 82 J/11
Kananaskis Lakes (Gem Trek)

Access: From the Trans-Canada Highway, follow the Kananaskis Trail (Hwy 40) for 50 km (31 mi) and turn right on the Kananaskis Lakes Trail. Drive another 15 km (9.5 mi) to the North Interlakes Day Use Area. The trailhead kiosk is at the north end of the parking lot.

0.0—Trailhead kiosk (1725 m).

—Trail crosses Kananaskis Lakes intake dam and spillway.

0.3—Junction. *Mount Indefatigable* right.

0.9—Junction. Upper *Kananaskis Lake Circuit* left.

2.1—Trail crosses Palliser rockslide.

4.0—Invincible Creek bridge.

5.8—Kananaskis River bridge.

7.3—Spring.

8.0—Junction (1790 m) and Forks Campground. *South Kananaskis Pass* left. North Kananaskis Pass ahead.

—Trail parallels Kananaskis River then makes switchbacking climb up avalanche slopes.

12.4—Trail tops ridge above Putnik's Pond.

—Trail crosses old moraine, rock gardens, open larch forest.

14.3—Lawson Lake (2220 m).

—Trail skirts west shore of the lake.

16.0—Junction. Park Ranger cabin left.

16.1—Maude Brook bridge.

16.2—Turbine Canyon Campground.

—Trail turns west along north bank of Maude Brook.

17.0—Trail summit (2370 m).

—Maude Lake.

18.3—North Kananaskis Pass (2360 m).

North Kananaskis Pass is a rolling alpine ridge perched on the Great Divide at the boundary of Peter Lougheed Provincial Park and B.C.'s Height of the Rockies Provincial Park. The hike to the pass is notable for the variety of terrain it traverses, and memorable for the scenery along the way. It can be approached as either a trip of two full days with an overnight stay at the Turbine Canyon Campground, or as a trip involving three days, with a short hike to the Forks Campground on day one, a long day hike to the pass and back on the second, and a short trip out on the third.

The first section of the trip duplicates that to Three Isle Lake and South Kananaskis Pass as far as the Forks Campground at km 8.0 (see *South Kananaskis Pass*). From the Forks, however, the North Kananaskis Pass trail swings away to the north. Pick your way through the campground and follow the trail as it traces the pools and riffles of the Kananaskis River along its west bank. Unfortunately, the delightful riverside stretch is soon replaced with a long, sustained climb up an avalanche slope whose only virtue is some impressive views back to Mount Lyautey.

After turning the corner on a number of switchbacks, the trail traverses north into the forest, where the appearance of some treeline-favouring larch trees attest to its altitude. Mount Putnik and Mount Beatty now dominate to the west, and the long, ragged ridge of the Spray Mountains to the east.

At 12 km, the trail suddenly pops out of the forest on the crest of a rock ridge and descends toward a small tarn known as Putnik's Pond. The open meadows beyond and glacier-draped Mount Beatty (2999m) offer a sense of what lies ahead—a long, glorious traverse of a high (2200 m) bench running beneath Beatty.

Maude Lake

The bench walk opens with some spectacular rock gardens and moves on to an open larch forest featuring trees 60 cm or more in diameter, views ahead to Mount Maude (3042 m), the Haig Glacier and Mount Jellicoe (3246), and finally the shores of Lawson Lake. (If there aren't a lot of other hikers around, shout hello to the sheer wall of Mount Black Prince across the lake and listen to the double echo bounce back to you—one of the best in the Rockies!)

At the far end of Lawson Lake, you'll pass a sign indicating a ranger cabin (off to the left) and, just beyond, the bridge over Maude Brook and the Turbine Canyon Campground. The campground's namesake, a narrow defile that drops abruptly away toward the Kananaskis River, lies just to the east, downstream, and is well worth investigating.

The trail to North Kananaskis Pass, involving another 2.1 km of hiking and an additional 152 m elevation gain, swings west at the campground and rises through the last dwarfed trees, crossing a high rocky ridge (the high point of the hike at 2370 m) and descending to Maude Lake, a lovely alpine catchment that reflects both the colour of the sky and the austere flanks of Mount Maude that rise directly above it.

A short distance beyond Maude Lake you'll find a sign indicating that you have, indeed, reached North Kananaskis Pass. The trail continues beyond the pass, dropping so precipitously into Leroy Creek and the Height of the Rockies Provincial Park that most hikers won't be tempted to stray beyond the pass. Looking down Leroy Creek, the spectacular Royal Group, featuring Mounts Prince Edward and Prince Henry, dominate the skyline.

208 Boulton Creek Loop

Boulton Creek Circuit—3.0 km (1.9 mi)

This short loop walk near the Boulton Creek Trading Post and Campground introduces you to the forest environment of the Kananaskis Lakes valley. In midsummer you will encounter a wonderful variety of woodland plants and flowers, but be prepared for the not-so-wonderful mosquitoes.

Immediately after crossing the trailhead footbridge, the trail passes the historic Boulton Cabin, which was used by forest rangers in the 1930s. For the next 0.5 km it runs flat through lodgepole pine forest sheltering an understorey of buffaloberry and a scattering of forest wildflowers, including bunchberry, heart-leaved arnica, ragwort and occasional stands of fireweed.

At km 0.7 the trail skirts the edge of the Boulton Campground and follows along an open bluff above Boulton Creek. It soon veers back into the forest, composed of a dense "doghair" stand of lodgepole pine. (The pine reseeded so thickly following a forest fire that the light-starved trees have stagnated. Shade tolerant white spruce are struggling upwards through the tumbled mass.)

At the end of the loop the trail descends to Boulton Creek and crosses a footbridge to the creek's true left bank. It follows the creek back to the trailhead, passing through dense forest and along horsetail bogs (mosquito heaven).

Access: Follow the Kananaskis Lakes Road 10 km (6 mi) from the Highway 40 intersection to Boulton Bridge Picnic Area. The parking area is 50 m off the highway to the left. The trail starts at a footbridge over Boulton Creek. *Maps: Kananaskis Lakes 82 J/11 (trail not shown); Kananaskis Lakes (Gem Trek).*

209 Interlakes Trail

Canadian Mount Everest Expedition Loop—2.2 km (1.4 mi)

The official name for this trail is the Canadian Mount Everest Expedition Trail. A rather intimidating moniker for a short woodland loop trail to a promontory overlooking Upper and Lower Kananaskis Lakes. Though we are happy to honour those who made the first Canadian ascent of Everest in 1982, we prefer the original descriptive name for this easy trail with its numerous interpretive signs and benches.

The well-graded trail climbs through a typical valley-bottom forest of spruce and pine to the loop split at km 0.2. Stay right and continue through dense forest carpeted with feather moss and lichen.

A staircase assists the climb to the summit viewpoint at km 1.2, where you have a 360-degree panorama of the valley. Though Lower Kananaskis Lake is visible to the north, the best view is west to Upper Kananaskis Lake.

This rocky point is quite open and dry, and harebells, vetches and asters bloom amidst a ground cover of low-growing junipers and kinnikinnick in midsummer.

From the summit, the trail makes a steep descent across open slopes, with continual good views of Upper Kananaskis Lake, then re-enters the forest and completes the loop back to the parking area.

Access: From its junction with Highway 40, follow the Kananaskis Lakes Road 13 km (8 mi) to the Interlakes Trail (Canadian Mount Everest Expedition Trail) access road, which branches left opposite the entrance to Mount Sarrail Campground. The access road reaches the trailhead parking area within 100 m. *Maps: Kananaskis Lakes 82 J/11 (trail not shown); Kananaskis Lakes (Gem Trek).*

Elbow Lake

210 Elbow Lake

Kananaskis Trail (Hwy 40) to Elbow Lake—1.3 km (0.8 mi)

Elbow Lake is a small, serene body of water nestled between subalpine forest and talus fields beneath Mt. Rae. The lake's only problem is that it involves a hike of just 1.3 km and an elevation gain of only 125 metres. Add to that a 15-site backcountry campground, plus mountain bike and equestrian access, and you have all the makings of a backcountry social on summer weekends.

The trail begins as an old access road that leaves the parking lot with a short, sharp ascent up and around the southern flank of Mount Elpoca. A trailside bench at 0.5 km allows you to catch your breath and enjoy an expansive view back down the Kananaskis Valley to the Spray Mountains and Kananaskis Range.

The trail moderates its climb across a large avalanche runout, and bumps up and over the forested summit of Elbow Pass (2100m) to arrive at the lake. Most hikers pick their way through the camp-

ground and follow the trail around the lake.

The outlet at the far end of the lake is a source of the Elbow River, and marks the boundary between Peter Lougheed Provincial Park and the Elbow Sheep Wildland Park.

Day hikers usually turn left after crossing the Elbow and finish the loop by traversing a series of talus slopes, which offer numerous views across the lake to Mount Rae.

Access: From the Trans-Canada Highway, follow the Kananaskis Trail (Hwy 40) for 62 km (38.5 mi) to the Elbow Pass Day Use Area. The trail begins from the parking lot trail kiosk. (Hwy 40 is closed beyond the Kananaskis Trail–Kananaskis Lakes Trail junction from December 1 to June 15.) *Maps: Kananaskis Lakes 82 J/11; Kananaskis Lakes (Gem Trek).*

(Trail not shown on maps in this book.)

211 Kananaskis Lookout

Boulton Creek Trading Post to Kananaskis Fire Lookout—6.2 km (3.9 mi)

Day hike

Allow 2 hours one way

Elevation gain: 418 m (1,371 ft)

Maximum elevation: 2118 m (6,949 ft)

Maps: Kananaskis Lakes 82 J/11
    Kananaskis Lakes (Gem Trek)

Access: From its junction with the Kananaskis Trail (Hwy 40), follow the Kananaskis Lakes Trail 9.7 km (6 mi) to the Boulton Creek Trading Post. Turn left and find your way to the upper parking lot. The trail begins on the asphalt bicycle path at the southeast corner of the parking lot.

0.0—Boulton Creek Trading Post parking lot (1700 m)

—Trail starts south along bicycle path.

0.2—Junction. Amphitheatre ahead (outhouses on the left). Turn left.

—Follow Whiskey Jack Trail uphill on wide gravel path, crossing campground loop roads twice.

1.3—Junction. Reclaimed access road veers right. Stay left.

2.5—Small creek and picnic table.

3.8—Junction. Intersection with Pocaterra Trail. Turn right.

4.4—Junction. Tyrwhitt Trail left. Stay right.

—Trail climbs steeply toward lookout.

6.2—Kananaskis Fire Lookout (2118m)

The trip to the Kananaskis Fire Lookout should be mandatory for anyone planning to spend much time exploring the Kananaskis Lakes region. The lookout provides an impressive overview of the lakes—the heart of Peter Lougheed Provincial Park—which in turn offers an excellent opportunity to understand the way the tangled topography around the lakes fits together.

There are several approaches to the lookout, but by far the most popular is the leisurely climb through the forest from Boulton Creek Trading Post and Campground. Although the hike begins amidst the development associated with the campground, and the trail receives heavy use from mountain bikers, the trip is a pleasant and rewarding experience.

The first leg of the trip, starting at the Trading Post parking lot, follows the Whiskey Jack Trail, which takes about a kilometre to shake its campground trappings and establish itself as a gentle climb through pine-spruce forest featuring gurgling creeks and a lush variety of forest flowers. The trail is actually an old access road, complete with remnant road signs advising hikers of steep grades and stops.

Just shy of the 4-km mark, the Whiskey Jack Trail intersects with the Pocaterra Trail. Turn right at the "T" and follow Pocaterra for 0.6 km to its junction with the Tyrwhitt Trail, where you should again stay to the right.

Beyond the junction, the Pocaterra Trail becomes the Lookout trail proper, a name change that heralds the last leg of the climb. The Pocaterra Trail, combined with the Whiskey Jack, Packers, and Tyrwhitt Trails, provides a network of Nordic skiing trails during the winter. (Fortunately, the trail nomenclature is considerably more confusing than the trail system itself!)

Beyond Tyrwhitt junction, the lookout trail begins a sustained climb, and most

Kananaskis Lakes from Kananaskis Fire Lookout

hikers will find themselves shifting from second gear to compound low. Nearing the lookout, the road's incline eases and the forest thins to preview the scenery ahead. A sign just below the lookout reminds hikers of their manners: respect the lookout person's work and privacy, and don't ask for water and food.

The lookout sits atop a small, cleared knoll and provides an unimpeded view across the valley to the Kananaskis Lakes. With a map spread out on one of the hilltop picnic tables, you can sort out the peaks, passes and drainages that provide much of the best hiking and scrambling in the park. From the west, the array of mountains that wraps around the lakes includes Mounts Fox (2973 m), Foch (3180m), Sarrail (3174 m), Lyautey (3082 m), Putnik (2940 m), and Indefatigable (2670 m).

Highway 40 to Kananaskis Lookout— 4.5 kms. Despite being a shorter approach with less elevation gain, the fire road leading from Kananaskis Trail (Hwy 40) to the lookout is not a good choice for hikers due to a lack of parking at the trailhead. This option is better suited to mountain bikers who cycle to the trail or, perhaps, hikers who can arrange a drop-off.

The gated fire road is at an unmarked turn-off on the right side the Kananaskis Trail 59 km (37 mi) south of the Trans-Canada Highway. Follow the roadbed south on a gradual ascent along the west slope of the Elk Range.

The Pocaterra trail joins the road from the right at km 0.5 and you intersect the Whiskey Jack Trail from Boulton Creek at km 2.2. Complete the final 2.4 kms to the lookout as described above.

Elk Pass Power Line Option. For hikers with the luxury of two vehicles and a willingness to work a short shuttle, it is possible to add variety to the trip by descending south from the lookout to the Elk Pass power line trail. When you reach the power line road, follow it northwest to the Elk Pass trailhead.

The option is not an official trail, but it is well-marked and frequently travelled. It is approximately 6.5 kms from the fire lookout to the Elk Pass trailhead.

212 Ptarmigan Cirque

Highwood Pass (Hwy 40) to Ptarmigan Cirque summit—1.8 km (1.1 mi)

Half-day trip

Allow 45 minutes one way

Elevation gain: 210 m (700 ft)

Maximum elevation: 2415 m (7,920 ft)

Maps: Mount Rae 82 J/10†
      Kananaskis Lakes (Gem Trek)
      † trail not shown

Access: From its junction with Kananaskis Lakes Trail, follow Kananaskis Trail (Hwy 40) south 35 km (21.5 mi) to Highwood Pass. The trailhead parking area on west side of road just south of the summit. (Note: Highway 40 is closed south of the Kananaskis Trail—Kananaskis Lakes Trail junction from December 1 to June 15.)

0.0—Highwood Pass parking area (2205 m).

   —Trail runs across meadows on west side of highway.

0.4—Junction. Stay right and cross to east side of highway.

   —Steady, steep climb through forest.

1.0—Meadow margin viewpoint.

1.1—Junction. Ptarmigan Cirque loop split. Stay left.

1.2—Trail climbs above trees into alpine meadows.

1.5—Grades moderate through rolling meadow.

1.8—Ptarmigan Cirque trail summit (2415 m).

   —Trail turns right, crosses stream and descends southeast side of meadows.

2.4—Waterfalls viewpoint.

   —Trail descends steeply into forest.

2.5—Junction. Return to Ptarmigan Cirque loop split.

3.6—Highwood Pass parking area (2205 m).

(Trail not shown on maps in this book.)

Ptarmigan Cirque is one of the shortest routes to the alpine in the mountain parks, which is what you'd expect when you start the trip from Highwood Pass—the highest point in Canada accessible by public road. The amphitheatre is contained by rockslides and the limestone cliffs of Mounts Arethusa and Rae, but alpine meadows and wildflowers are the area's prize. And don't be surprised if you run into a flock of mountain sheep.

Despite its short length, the trail is no casual stroll. You must do a bit of climbing to reach the meadows. The hike begins at the Highwood Meadows parking area just south of Highwood Pass and follows the meadows nature trail back toward the 2206-m summit. The trail splits after 400 m, and the Ptarmigan Cirque trail crosses the road and begins a steady climb to the cirque.

The ascent through the upper reaches of subalpine forest is a bit demanding, but there are many excuses to stop in early summer when the woods are filled with the blooms of glacier lilies, larkspur, heart-leafed arnica, fleabane, and light pink Indian paintbrush.

At km 1.1 the trail splits to create a loop through the meadows above. The left branch immediately climbs above the treeline and then levels out into the rolling meadows of Ptarmigan Cirque, where you are greeted by forget-me-nots, white and red mountain heather, and vast fields of western anemone.

At the upper end of the loop, the trail reaches a steep, rocky terminal moraine, where it swings right, crosses a small stream, and begins a gradual descent along the east side of the meadows. On this return leg, views open to Pocaterra Cirque and the twin summits of Mount Tyrwhitt on the west side of Highwood Pass. Just before re-entering the forest and returning to the loop split, you receive one last reward—a deeply eroded gorge containing a series of waterfalls.

Ptarmigan Cirque

Warspite Lake

213 Black Prince Cirque

Black Prince Day Use Area to Warspite Lake—2.1 kms (1.3 mi)

This short interpretive trail transports you to the emerald waters of Warspite Lake beneath the encircling walls of Black Prince Cirque. Indeed, the trail's ratio of reward to effort must be one of the best in the Rockies, just as its name must be one of the most romantic. (Mount Black Prince was named by surveyor Arthur O. Wheeler to honour a British cruiser of the same name that was sunk during WWI's Battle of Jutland.)

After picking up interpretive pamphlets at the parking lot trailhead (1735 m), cross the Smith-Dorrien Creek bridge and begin a gradual climb into the forest via an old logging road. A number of interpretive trail markers punctuate the route, providing frequent opportunities to stop and ponder the trail's changing subalpine environs.

At the 1 km mark, the trail veers right from the road and, 0.4 km beyond, passes the loop split (stay right). The rocky

east shore of Warspite Lake (1830m) is reached at km 2.1.

The lake is a placid tarn, handsomely offset by the dark forest beyond, the glacier-carved amphitheatre of Mount Black Prince, and the incised ridge of Mount Warspite. Numerous large boulders provide comfortable platforms for soaking up sun and solitude.

Loop back down-valley to the approach trail by skirting the southeast corner of the lake and traversing a rockslide that in early summer blooms profusely with penstemon, columbine and androsace.

Access: From its junction with Kananaskis Trail (Hwy 40), follow Kananaskis Lakes Trail 2.2 km (1.4 mi) to the Smith-Dorrien/Spray Trail junction. Follow the Smith-Dorrien/Spray Trail 8.3 km (5.2 mi) to the Mount Black Prince Day Use Area. *Maps: Kananaskis Lakes 82 J/11 (trail not fully shown);* Kananaskis Lakes (Gem Trek).

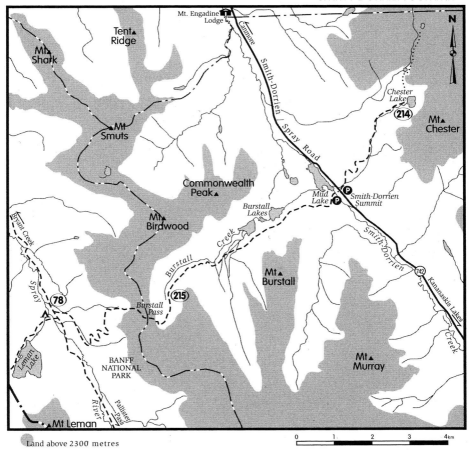

Land above 2300 metres

214 Chester Lake

Smith-Dorrien/Spray Lakes Road (Hwy 742) to Chester Lake—4.5 km (2.8 mi)

Half-day trip

Allow 1.5 hours one way

Elevation gain: 315 m (1,030 ft)

Maximum elevation: 2220 m (7,280 ft)

Maps: Spray Lakes Reservoir 82 J/14†
     Kananaskis Lakes (Gem Trek)
     † trail not shown

Access: Follow the Smith-Dorrien—Spray Lakes Road (Hwy 742) 45 km (28 mi) from downtown Canmore to Smith-Dorrien Summit, or 20 km (12.5 mi) northwest from the road's junction with Kananaskis Lakes Trail. The Chester Lake trailhead parking area is located on the east side of the road, opposite the south end of Mud Lake.

0.0—Trailhead parking area (1905 m).

    —Gradual to moderate uphill over old logging track.

0.5—Junction. Keep right.

    —Steady climb through spruce-fir on logging roadbeds.

2.2—Junction. Single-track trail branches left from logging road.

    —Climb through subalpine forest.

2.7—Trail flattens out across meadow.

3.9—Enter extensive meadow below lake.

4.5—Chester Lake (2220 m).

If you hike to Chester Lake on a summer weekend, you will not be alone. It often feels like half of Calgary has descended on this tiny lake beneath the limestone walls of The Fortress and Mount Chester. But if go during the week, you will find its less-crowded shores and flower-filled meadows well worth the short hike.

The initial 2 kms are not overly inspiring as the trail weaves its way up through a spiderweb of old logging roads. But once you escape this pre-park era clearcut, you enter a mature forest of Engelmann spruce and alpine fir.

After less than a kilometre of steady ascent through the forest, the trail runs out across an open meadow, which is filled with alpine buttercups in late June and early July. The meadow also provides your first view ahead to the rugged summits of Mount Galatea (3185 m), The Fortress (3000 m) and Mount Chester (3054 m)—the peaks containing the Chester Lake cirque. The remainder of the trip is mainly flat, alternating between meadow and forest, and then one final long meadow leading to the lake.

The cliffs of Mount Chester create a dramatic setting for the lake, while the nearby rockslides are home to a healthy pika population. However, the meadows near the lake's outlet provide most of the colour. Shortly after the last snow has disappeared, usually in late June, the meadow at the west end of the lake turns into a vast field of golden glacier lilies.

Three Lakes Valley. A trail follows along the lake's west shore and then climbs over the a larch-covered rise to the narrow Three Lakes Valley beneath Mount Galatea. Scramble up this tight, rocky vale for another 1.5 km, passing three tiny lakelets and enjoying good views back across Smith-Dorrien Summit to the heavily glaciated peaks of the Great Divide.

Chester Lake and Mount Chester

215 Burstall Pass

Smith-Dorrien/Spray Lakes Road (Hwy 742) to Burstall Pass—7.5 km (4.7 mi)

Day trip

Allow 2 to 2.5 hours one way

Elevation gain: 475 m (1,550 ft)

Maximum elevation: 2375 m (7,800 ft)

Maps: Spray Lakes Reservoir 82 J/14
Kananaskis Lakes (Gem Trek)

Access: Follow the Smith-Dorrien/Spray Lakes Road (Hwy 742) 45 km (28 mi) from downtown Canmore to Smith-Dorrien Summit, or 20 km (12.5 mi) northwest from the road's junction with Kananaskis Lakes Trail. The Burstall Pass trailhead parking area is located on the west side of the road at the south end of Mud Lake.

0.0—Trailhead parking area (1900 m).

—Follows old logging road.

2.5—Trail passes above Burstall Lakes.

3.3—Road reverts to single-track trail.

3.9—Trail crosses Burstall Creek flats (ankle deep channel fords).

4.5—Climb from flats into forest.

5.5—Trail enters open meadow.

6.4—Steady climb to pass begins.

7.5—Burstall Pass (2375 m). Park boundary.

—Trail descends draw to northwest (vague track) then contours south to avalanche slopes and descends steeply.

10.6—Trail levels off and travels north through scattered forest.*

12.2—Junction (1905 m).* Intersection with *Upper Spray River-Palliser Pass* trail at km 19.8 (see Banff Park chapter).

*distance approximate

Burstall Pass is one of the finest trail-accessible summits in this section of the Rockies—a high, open region of rocky outcrops and alpine meadows on the Peter Lougheed-Banff Park boundary. Views from the 2375 m pass are quite extensive and encompass some of the highest peaks in Peter Lougheed, Banff, Height of the Rockies and Mount Assiniboine Parks—including Mount Assiniboine.

Understandably, the pass is one of the park's most popular day hikes and is particularly busy on weekends. It can also be quite messy early in the season when the braided flats beyond Burstall Lakes flood (we usually hike this trail late July through September to avoid several calf-deep fords). Backpackers also use the trail as an "express route" to the upper Spray Valley at the southern end of Banff Park.

The trail begins its journey from a parking area at the south end of Mud Lake on Smith-Dorrien Summit and follows an old logging road for 3 km to a point above the Burstall Lakes. Few hikers bother to linger at these lakes, which lie just off the trail to the right (their shores are marshy and usually well guarded by armies of mosquitoes).

The willow flats beyond the lakes provide a good view south to Mount Robertson (3194 m) and the Robertson Glacier. But that inspiring glacier is responsible for the silty runoff that inundates this section of trail early in the summer. (Later in the season you can tiptoe across the braided channels on rocks or logs.)

From the Burstall Creek flats, you begin the climb to the pass, rising steadily through subalpine forest and across avalanche paths. The trail levels briefly in a long meadow beneath Mount Birdwood before bending south and resuming the heart-pounding ascent to the summit.

Mount Birdwood from Burstall Pass

The rolling summit ridge of the pass is an open invitation to wander and explore, particularly towards South Burstall Pass. The meadows cradled between the summit's rocky bluffs fill with the blooms of wildflowers from early July to mid-August, including western anemone, white mountain avens, golden fleabane, alpine cinquefoil, pearly everlasting and white Indian paintbrush.

Mount Birdwood (3097 m) rises quite dramatically to the north above the Burstall Creek headwaters, but it is rather puny compared to glacier-draped Mount Sir Douglas (3406 m), which forms the crest of the Great Divide 5 km to the south. And both these peaks pale in comparison to the pyramid of Mount Assiniboine (3610 m), the highest mountain in the southern Canadian Rockies, which is visible on clear days just over 20 km away to the northwest.

Upper Spray Valley. By continuing due west through the pass on obvious trail, passing a large sinkhole, you arrive at a fine viewpoint for Leman Lake and Banff Park's upper Spray Valley. But if you are bound for that remote valley, retreat to the sinkhole, skirt its west side, and look for cairns leading down a large gully to the northwest. Persevere down this vale for 0.5 km or so until good trail re-emerges.

After passing through larch groves and small meadows, the trail turns south along the Spray Valley's western slope and contours onto a major avalanche path. Then it plunges downward, losing more than 200 m of elevation in the space of 2 km.

When you reach the valley bottom at the toe of the avalanche path, the trail turns back to the north and parallels the Spray River trail for nearly 2 km. It eventually breaks through the scattered forest to join that route in open meadow beside the Spray River 0.2 km north of the Leman Lake trail junction (see *Upper Spray River-Palliser Pass,* Banff Park chapter).

Elk Lakes Provincial Park

Elk Lakes is a 173 sq km provincial park at the headwaters of British Columbia's Elk River. The park is bordered on the north by the Great Divide and Alberta's Peter Lougheed Provincial Park, to the west and south by B.C.'s Height of the Rockies Provincial Park, and on the east by B.C. forest lands.

Lower and Upper Elk Lake form the park's core. The lakes, which are only a kilometre apart, are blessed with a spectacular backdrop of high, heavily glaciated peaks to the west, including Mounts McCuaig, Nivelle and Castelneau.

The lakes were quite remote and relatively inaccessible until a power line was constructed over Elk Pass in 1951. Soon adventurous motorists and four-wheel drive enthusiasts began accessing the lakes and Elk Pass via the rough, power line service road connecting Kananaskis Lakes and the Elk Valley.

With increased visitation, the B.C. parks department established a small recreational reserve around the lakes in 1955. In 1973 it was enlarged to 56 sq km to create Elk Lakes Recreation Area to the south was annexed and the park expanded to its present size.

While there are wilderness routes up the Cadorna Creek valley in the southern section of the park, the only regularly maintained trails are in the core area surrounding the Elk Lakes. The lakes can be visited on a long day hike or backpack from Alberta's Peter Lougheed Park via West Elk Pass, or they can be reached in less than an hour from the parking area at the end of B.C.'s Elk Valley forestry road. The core trail from the forestry road also extends beyond Upper Elk Lake to Pétain Falls and Basin—the only full day trip from the Elk River trailhead or Lower Elk Lake Campground.

Mountain bikes are not permitted on any park trails (see *Access* below).

Information and services. The park headquarters-ranger cabin, located on the Elk Lakes trail just beyond the Elk River road parking area, is only staffed during the summer. (Since rangers are often out in the park tending to other duties, check the trailhead kiosk for general information and trail condition reports.) Information can also be obtained through the B.C. Parks regional office in Wasa, B.C. or the park website (see *Sources-Park information*).

There are only two developed backcountry campgrounds in the park—Lower Elk Lake and Pétain Creek (0.9 km beyond Upper Elk Lake). These sites have tent pads, toilets, food caches and fire pits or rings for open campfires. A fee of $5.00 per person per night is charged at both sites (self registration).

Access: If you drive to the park entrance at the headwaters of B.C.'s Elk River, the lakes are little more than a short stroll from the trailhead. However, unless you live or are travelling in the Crowsnest Pass region, it is an epic journey to get there.

The first leg of the trip requires reaching Sparwood, B.C. via Highway 3. From Sparwood follow paved Highway 43 north 33 km (21 mi) to the village of Elkford. Beyond Elkford a gravel forestry road continues along the west side of the Elk River for another 44 km (27 mi), then crosses to the east side of the river to join the Kananaskis Power Line road. From this crossing it is another 23 km (14 mi) to the Elk Lakes trailhead parking area at the park's east boundary. (Several forest service campgrounds are located on the road between Elkford and the park, including two within 5 kms of the park boundary.)

You can also reach Elk Lakes from Alberta's Peter Lougheed Provincial Park by hiking the *Elk Lakes via West Elk Pass* trail or cycling the limited access Kananaskis Power Line service road over Elk Pass to the park entrance parking lot.

Mount Aosta and Lower Elk Lake

216 Elk Lakes via Elk Valley

Elk Valley Road to Upper Elk Lake—4.5 km (2.8 mi)
Elk Valley Road to Pétain Falls—7.5 km (4.7 mi) *

Half-day to day trip

Allow 1.5 hours one way

Elevation gain: 315 m (1,030 ft)

Maximum elevation: 2220 m (7,280 ft)

Maps: Kananaskis Lakes 82 J/11†
Kananaskis Lakes (Gem Trek)
† trail not shown

Access: From Sparwood, B. C., follow Highway 43 and the Elk River forestry road 100 km (62 mi) north to the trailhead parking area for Elk Lakes Provincial Park at road's end. (See also Access, *Elk Lakes Provincial Park*, page 400.)

0.0—Elk Lakes parking area (1740 m). Trailhead kiosk.

0.1—Park headquarters-ranger station.

0.2—Elkan Creek bridge and Junction. West Elk Pass via Elkan Creek right 4.0 km. Stay ahead.

—Pass along meadows and through forest on mainly flat trail.

1.2—Lower Elk Lake (1730 m). Lower Elk Lake Campground.

1.7—Elk River bridges.

1.8—Junction. Viewpoint left 1.2 km. Upper Elk Lake ahead.

—Trail climbs gradual to moderate through lush forest.

2.5—Upper Elk Lake and Junction (1740 m). West Elk Pass right across outlet bridge (see *Elk Lakes via West Elk Pass*). Pétain Creek and Falls left.

—Rough trail follows along east shore of Upper Elk Lake.

4.5—South end of Upper Elk Lake. Trail crosses alluvial flats beyond lake.

5.4—Pétain Creek Campground (1755 m).

—Trail crosses bridge and follows west side of Pétain Creek

7.5—Pétain Waterfalls Viewpoint.*

* distance approximate

If British Columbia's Elk Valley had been connected to Alberta by a good, paved road over Elk Pass, as many valley residents desired, Elk Lakes would rival nearby Kananaskis Lakes in popularity. As it is, these scenic gems with their spectacular backdrop of peaks and glaciers are reserved for those who are willing to make the long, rough drive north from Elkford, B.C., or who hike or bike to it from Alberta's Peter Lougheed Park.

Regardless of how you get there, the park's core trail to Lower and Upper Elk Lakes is one of the easiest short hikes in the Rockies. You can also continue past the upper lake to Pétain Falls—a series of waterfalls beneath Mount Castelneau.

The trail begins at the parking lot at the end of the Elk Valley road and a trailhead kiosk with park map, general info and current trail condition reports. It passes the park headquarters-ranger station 100 m beyond the parking area and immediately descends to the Elkan Creek bridge and a junction for the low trail to West Elk Pass.

Beyond the bridge you follow good gravel-fill trail along the edge of some fine willow-dwarf birch meadows, containing the meandering Elk River, and into mossy subalpine forest where glacier lilies, globeflowers, fairybells and heart-leaved arnica bloom in profusion in early summer. Though the trail rolls up and down a bit, there is no significant gain or loss of elevation.

Shortly after coming abreast of the Elk River, you reach Lower Elk Lake and its pleasant campground. Views across the lake are quite stunning, particularly on still mornings when its waters mirror distant pyramid-shaped peaks to the southwest and Mount Aosta (2944 m) near its southern shore.

After skirting the lake's northeast shore, the trail re-enters forest and

crosses the bridged channels of the Elk River to the Viewpoint trail junction (see below). Stay right and climb gravel track through lush forest to the upper lake.

You reach Upper Elk Lake where the Fox Lake trail intersects via a bridge over the lake's outlet (see *Elk Lakes via West Elk Pass*). The scene is similar to the lower lake, but you get a better overview of the lake and distant peaks by crossing the bridge and following the Fox Lake trail up a scree slope for 100 m or so.

The south-facing cliffs of Mount Fox rise above the northeast end of the lake, and in early summer numerous waterfalls gush down the escarpment to create a "weeping wall."

The gravel-fill trail ends at this point and a rocky and rooty track continues along the lake's east shore for 2 km to its far end. However, it's not worth hiking unless you are bound for Pétain Falls.

Pétain Waterfalls. This impressive waterfall cascades down from the Pétain Glacier at the head of the Upper Elk Lake valley. A viewpoint near the base of the falls can be reached in 1.5 hours or so from the north end of Upper Elk Lake.

Follow the rough trail along the lake's east shore (flooded in spots in early summer) and, at the far end, emerge onto alluvial flats covered by willows and scattered islands of spruce. Continue along the flats for another 0.9 km to Pétain Creek Campground (tent pads at this site can be inundated by the over-flowing creek in early summer).

Cross a bridge to the west side of the creek just beyond the campground and continue upvalley for approximately 2 km until you emerge from spruce forest into a meadow with the best view of the the waterfalls and the Castelneau Glacier. If you wish, you can continue through meadows to a point near the base of the main waterfall.

Viewpoint Trail. This 1.2 km trail branches from the main trail at km 1.8 and, after skirting the west shore of Lower Elk Lake, climbs to the top of a 1860 m promontory overlooking the lower lake and the Elk Valley.

You gain 130 m of elevation on this short side-trip and pass above some hazardous cliffs (travel with care).

217 Elk Lakes via West Elk Pass

Kananaskis Trail Parking Area to Lower Elk Lake Campground—10.2 km (6.3 mi)

Day trip or backpack

Allow 2.5 to 3 hours one way

Elevation gain: 225 m (750 ft)
loss: 215 m (700 ft)

Maximum elevation: 1945 m (6,380 ft)

Maps: Kananaskis Lakes 82 J/11†
Kananaskis Lakes (Gem Trek)
† trail not shown

Access: Follow Kananaskis Trail (Hwy 40) to its intersection with Kananaskis Lakes Trail. Continue south on the Kananaskis Lakes Trail 12.0 km (7.5 mi) to the Elk Pass trailhead parking area, located on the left side of the road 0.5 km before Upper Lake Day Use Area.

0.0—Elk Pass parking area (1720 m).

1.0—Road reaches powerline.

1.3—Road branches right from powerline.

2.0—Fox Creek crossing (culvert). Junction. West Elk Pass trail branches right from powerline access road.

3.7—Enter marshy, willow-covered meadow.

4.1—Junction. Branch road to powerline left. Continue ahead.

4.6—Junction. Follow trail branching right from roadbed.

5.1—West Elk Pass (1905 m). Junction. Elk Lakes Park headquarters via Elkan Creek ahead (4.0 km). Fox Lake right.

5.2—Junction. Frozen Lake route right. Fox Lake left.

6.0—Fox Lake (1945 m).

7.0—Steady downhill begins.

7.5—First views of Lower Elk Lake and Elk Valley.

8.9—Upper Elk Lake and Junction (1740 m). Intersection with *Elk Lakes via Elk River* trail. Upper Elk shoreline trail and Pétain Falls right. Lower Elk Lake left.

9.8—Lower Elk Lake.

10.2—Lower Elk Lake Campground (1730 m).

While the Elk Lakes can be reached on a short hike from the trailhead at the end of B.C.'s Elk River road, not many people are willing to make the long drive to get there. A longer but more popular hike to the lakes is from Alberta's Peter Lougheed Park. By following old roadbeds and trail over West Elk Pass, you can reach the lakes on an easy backpack or long day hike.

There are a number of routes over Elk Pass that can be used to reach the lakes. The road beneath the power line between B.C.'s Elk Valley and Kananaskis Lakes is a popular route for mountain bikes, but not an attractive option for hikers. The most direct and scenic hiking route goes by way of West Elk Pass and Fox Lake, an approach that provides fine views of Elk Lakes as it descends along the east slope of Mount Fox.

You have a number of intersecting roads to contend with as you climb from the parking area in Lougheed Park to Elk Pass. The first kilometre follows a service road upwards through a dense forest of lodgepole pine and Engelmann spruce to the powerline. After walking the broad cut beneath the hydro towers for 300 m, you follow roadbed branching right into the forest and descend to Fox Creek at km 2.0.

After crossing Fox Creek, the road climbs gradually along the true right (east) side of the creek for the next 2.5 kms to willow and dwarf birch-covered meadows on Elk Pass. The cool subalpine forest and meadows beside the revegetating road margins offer a lush display of wildflowers in midsummer, including fireweed, asters, arnica, harebells, and Indian paintbrush.

At km 4.6, you turn right onto single-track trail, which crosses a narrow meadow and runs through forest for 0.5 km to a junction on West Elk Pass. Standing atop the Great Divide and the Alberta-B.C. boundary, you have two

Upper Elk Lake

options for approaching Elk Lakes: the trail ahead descends Elkan Creek for 4.0 kms to the park headquarters near the Elk River trailhead; the right branch, our preference, climbs to Fox Lake and makes a more direct and scenic approach to Upper Elk Lake via the slopes of Mount Fox.

You follow narrow rooty trail southwest along the Alberta-B.C. boundary for a short stretch before angling south to Fox Lake—a small sink lake beneath the east face of Mount Fox and the highest point on the hike.

The trail continues south along the slopes of Mount Fox and, a kilometre beyond Fox Lake, begins a steady descent to Elk Lakes. There is a good viewpoint for Lower Elk Lake and the Elk Valley on an avalanche path at km 7.8 and, while crossing a talus slope less than a kilometre beyond, you get your first view of Upper Elk Lake.

The trail completes its descent at Upper Elk Lake's outlet bridge, where you intersect the park's core trail (see *Elk Lakes via Elk River*). Day hikers usually linger for awhile at Upper Elk Lake, then continue to Lower Elk Lake. Backpackers have a choice of camping at Lower Elk Lake Campground or following the trail along Upper Elk Lake's southeast shore to Pétain Creek Campground (0.9 km beyond the far end of the lake).

Elkan Creek Option. While the Elkan Creek trail is mainly through forest and a bit longer than the Fox Lake approach, it does provide a different return route to West Elk Pass. Pick-up the trail at its junction with the trail from the Elk River road 1.0 km below Lower Elk Lake (100 m west of the ranger cabin). After a steady climb of 4.0 km near the course of Elkan Creek, you arrive back at the Fox Lake junction on West Elk Pass.

Mount Assiniboine Provincial Park

Created in 1922, British Columbia's Mount Assiniboine Provincial Park is a 386 sq km reserve bounded on the east by the continental divide and Banff National Park, on the west by Kootenay National Park, and on the south by B.C. Provincial Forest lands.

The focal point of the park is Mount Assiniboine (3618 m)—the highest peak south of the Columbia Icefield. The mountain soars well above nearby peaks and is visible for many kilometres in all directions. It is distinctive not only for its height but for its pyramid shape, which bears a resemblance to Switzerland's Matterhorn (throughout much of its early history it was known as "the Matterhorn of the Rockies").

While wilderness trails traverse remote valleys in the northern two-thirds of the park, most visitation is centred on Lake Magog at the base of Mount Assiniboine. Lake Magog lies in a basin at 2165 m directly beneath the mountain's north face, and a vast meadowland scattered with stands of alpine fir and larch extends north and east from its shores. Most people overnighting in the park stay at Mount Assiniboine Lodge or B.C. Parks' Naiset Cabins and Lake Magog Campground.

There are many excellent hikes from Lake Magog, ranging from half-day jaunts to Wonder Pass, Nub Peak and Sunburst Valley to full day outings to locations like Og Pass, Windy Ridge, Og Lake, and Ferro Pass (see pages 411-419). You need to spend at least two or three days in the area to begin to appreciate this amazing region centred on one of North America's most beautiful mountains.

Lake Magog Campground. Most backpackers stay at the Lake Magog Campground near the lake's west shore. Open fires are prohibited, so campers are limited to gas or propane camp stoves for cooking. Small spring-fed streams near the campground are the only source of water. A fee of $5.00 per person per night is charged. (No fee is charged at campgrounds beyond the park's core area.)

Group camping (up to 25 persons) is permitted at O'Brien Meadows, located just off the Assiniboine Pass trail 0.5 km west of the park boundary. Use of this site is permitted by advance reservation through the Kootenay District office in Wasa, B.C. (See *Sources-Park information.*)

Naiset Cabins. These five rustic cabins above the east shore of Lake Magog were built by Alpine Club of Canada founder A.O. Wheeler in 1925 as overnight accommodation for patrons of his Banff-Assiniboine walking tour. Today they are operated by B.C. Parks as overnight shelter cabins. The nightly fee is $15 per person, or $30 for a family. In summer the cabins are available on a first-come, first served basis only, so be prepared to camp if all beds are occupied.

Mount Assiniboine Lodge. The original Mount Assiniboine Lodge was constructed above the east shore of Lake Magog during the summer of 1928. It was built by the CPR at the behest of the Marquis degli Albizzi and Erling Strom, who operated it as the first ski lodge in the Canadian Rockies. The small lodge and its six outlying guest cabins soon became a popular summer destination as well, and Strom took sole ownership of the lease in 1936.

The lodge was enlarged to its present configuration between 1958 and 1963, and the Strom family continued to operate it until 1983 when B.C. Parks recovered the lease. Since that time the lodge and cabins have been operated by concessionaires Sepp and Barb Renner of Canmore, Alberta.

Assiniboine Lodge is one of the finest backcountry lodges in the Rockies, and the view from the lodge and cabins is beyond compare. (See *Sources-Backcountry lodges.*) The lodge also offers afternoon tea to campers from 4 to 5 p.m.

Mount Assiniboine and Lake Magog

Park headquarters. Headquarters for the park is a chalet-style cabin located 200 m east of the Naiset Cabins. Park rangers are stationed here throughout the summer months.

Access: You have two access options for the Lake Magog area of Assiniboine Park—backpack or helicopter.

The shortest and most popular hiking route to Lake Magog is via the *Bryant Creek-Assiniboine Pass* trail (see Banff Park chapter, pages 152-153). Total distance from the Mount Shark trailhead in Kananaskis Country to Assiniboine Lodge via this route is 25.3 km (26.7 km to Magog Campground).

If you book the bus to Sunshine Village, the access route via Citadel Pass and the Valley of the Rocks is not much farther and more scenic. Since you begin the trip at 2200 m, there is also less elevation gain than via Bryant Creek and Assiniboine Pass. Distance from Sunshine Village to Assiniboine Lodge is 27.5 km. (See *Assiniboine via Citadel Pass,* page 409.)

Two other trails are considerably longer and not nearly as popular. The trail from Kootenay Park via Simpson River and Ferro Pass to Lake Magog Campground is 32.2 km (see *Simpson River-Ferro Pass,* page 339). You can also follow the historic route used by Albizzi and Strom, which runs from Banff to Assinboine via Brewster Creek, Allenby Pass and Og Pass—a total distance of 42.7 km to the campground (see *Brewster Creek-Allenby Pass,* pages 150-151).

Many lodge guests, campers and climbers fly to Lake Magog by helicopter. Flights originate from the Mount Shark heli-pad in Alberta's Kananaskis Country and land at the Assiniboine Park heli-pad near Assiniboine Lodge. Anyone overnighting in the park can book a flight, one-way or round trip, through Mount Assiniboine Lodge reservations. These flights operate throughout the summer on Wednesdays, Fridays and Sundays (Monday replaces Sunday on holiday weekends). The cost of a one-way flight is $100 per person (summer 2000), and there is a per person baggage weight limit of 50 lbs. (See *Sources-Backcountry access.*)

218 Mount Assiniboine via Citadel Pass

Sunshine Village to Assiniboine Lodge—27.5 km (17.1 mi)

Backpack

Allow 1 to 2 days

Maximum elevation: 2395 m (7,850 ft)

Minimum elevation: 1980 m (6,500 ft)

Maps: Banff 82 O/4
     Mount Assiniboine 82 J/13

Access: Travel to Sunshine Village as described in the *Sunshine Meadows* area introduction (page 52). From the log building at the core of the lodge complex, follow the gravel road leading uphill to the southeast. (See *Citadel Pass*, Banff Park chapter.)

0.0—Sunshine Village (2200 m).

1.3—Junction. *Rock Isle Lake* ahead 0.5 km. Citadel Pass left.

5.2—Quartz Ridge (2395 m).

5.8—Howard Douglas Lake and Campground (Su8).

9.3—Citadel Pass (2360 m). Banff-Assiniboine Park boundary.

—Steady descent into the Golden Valley.

12.5—Junction. Porcupine Campground downhill to right. Stay left on high route above the valley.

—Trail enters rocky, forest terrain at head of Golden Valley.

16.5—Junction. Simpson River trail intersects from right. Continue ahead.

—Trail winds and rolls through Valley of the Rocks.

22.2—Og Lake and Campground (2060 m).

—Gradual ascent through Og Meadows.

26.3—Junction. Og Pass and old Assiniboine Pass horse trail left. Continue ahead.

26.5—Junction. Horse trail to Sunburst Lake right. Continue ahead.

27.0—Junction. Intersection with *Assiniboine Pass* trail at km 24.8. Assiniboine Pass left. Assiniboine Lodge and Lake Magog right.

27.3—Junction. Magog Campground ahead 1.6 km. Assiniboine Lodge left.

27.5—Mount Assiniboine Lodge (2180 m). Naiset Cabins and park headquarters ahead 0.5 km.

The trail from Sunshine Village via Citadel Pass and Valley of the Rocks is undoubtedly the most scenic and varied approach to Mount Assiniboine. While the more popular *Bryant Creek-Assiniboine Pass* trail is shorter, the Citadel approach is only 3 km longer and there is actually a slight net loss of elevation over the course of the journey. The only disadvantage is the lack of water, so make sure you carry an adequate supply.

To enjoy the advantages of the Citadel approach, you must book the shuttle bus to Sunshine Village (see *Sunshine Meadows,* page 52), which costs a bit of money and requires that you arrange your departure to coincide with the bus schedule. If you don't take the bus, add 6.5 km to the trip by starting at the bottom of the Sunshine Village access road.

The first 9.3 km from Sunshine Village follows the very scenic *Citadel Pass* trail (see page 56). After this wonderful, rolling meadow walk, with occasional views of Mount Assiniboine in the distance, you cross into Assiniboine Park at Citadel Pass and descend steeply into the Golden Valley at the headwaters of the Simpson River.

If you want to spend the night at Porcupine Campground, continue to the bottom of Golden Valley. However, through-hikers should follow the trail branching left on the steep, open slope well above the valley floor and contour southwest into the Valley of the Rocks.

The Valley of the Rocks is a long, dry, forest-enclosed vale that features a wild array of giant boulders—the remains of a gigantic rockslide. Og Lake marks the end of the valley, and where the trail enters a series of open meadows. Views ahead to Mount Assiniboine are continuous over the final 5 km to Assiniboine Lodge and Lake Magog. (See also Og Lake, *Lake Magog Area Hikes.*)

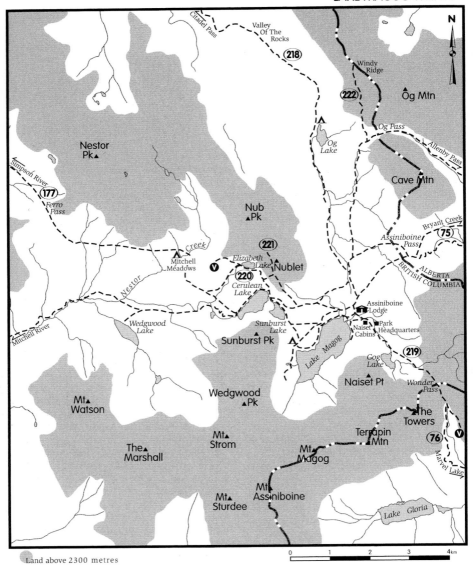

Land above 2300 metres

N

Citadel Pass
Valley
Of The
Rocks
(218)
Windy
Ridge
(222)
Og Mtn
Og Pass
Allenby Pass
Og
Lake
Cave Mtn
Nestor
Pk
Simpson River
(177)
Ferro
Pass
Bryant Creek
(75)
Assiniboine
Pass
Nub
Pk
BRITISH COLUMBIA
ALBERTA
Creek
(221)
Elizabeth
Lake
Nublet
Mitchell
Meadows
V
(220)
Cerulean
Lake
Assiniboine
Lodge
Nestor
Park
Headquarters
Naiset
Cabins
Wedgwood
Lake
Sunburst
Lake
Mitchell River
Sunburst Pk
Lake Magog
(219)
Gog
Lake
Naiset Pt
Wonder
Pass
Mt
Watson
Wedgwood
Pk
The
Towers
Terrapin
Mtn
(76)
V
Mt
Strom
The
Marshall
Mt
Magog
Marvel
Lake
Mt
Sturdee
Mt
Assiniboine
Lake Gloria

0   1   2   3   4km

Lake Magog Area Hikes

Mount Assiniboine's core area is one of the best hiking locales in the Rockies. On the following pages, we describe four of our favourite trips from Lake Magog—*Wonder Pass, Sunburst Valley, Nub Peak,* and *Og Pass-Windy Ridge.*

Other rewarding hikes follow the area's main access trails. If you're not travelling into or out of the park on one of these routes, consider them as alternate day hikes from Lake Magog. (All distances are from the Assiniboine Pass trail junction 0.2 km north of Assiniboine Lodge.)

Assiniboine Pass—2.1 km. If you are flying to and from the park and staying at Assiniboine Lodge or Naiset Cabins, you might like to hike to Assiniboine Pass and peer down the upper Bryant Creek valley to see how most backpackers reach the park.

From the lodge junction, follow the trail climbing gradually to the northeast. The well-beaten track rolls through scattered subalpine forest and across O'Brien Meadows before reaching the summit. (See also *Bryant Creek-Assiniboine Pass,* pages 152-155.)

Og Lake—5.1 km. The hike to Og Lake retraces the southern end of the access trail from Sunshine Village via Citadel Pass. It is an undemanding trail that descends gradually through a series of meadows to the shores of this rockbound sink lake at the base of Og Mountain. On your return, you have continuous views of Mount Assiniboine.

Follow the Assiniboine Pass trail northwest from the lodge junction for 0.3 km to the Og Lake junction. Turn left and follow the Og trail due north along the valley floor to the vast Og Meadows and the lake. (See also *Assiniboine via Citadel Pass,* page 409.)

Ferro Pass—10.7 km. The longest day trip from Lake Magog provides a different perspective of the area. Escaping the confines of the lake and Mount Assiniboine, you travel due west via Sunburst Valley to a 2270 m pass overlooking Wedgwood Lake and a massive, glacier-capped wall formed by Wedgewood Peak, The Marshall and Mount Watson.

Follow the *Sunburst Valley* trail to the Elizabeth Lake junction at the north end of Cerulean Lake. Continue on the main trail along Cerulean's northwest shore and pass the junction for Wedgwood Lake at the west end of the lake (stay right). The trail to Ferro Pass continues west from the Sunburst Valley, making a long, steady descent through subalpine forest to the Nestor Creek bridge on the edge of Mitchell Meadows at km 7.1.

The remainder of the hike is a long, steady ascent. As the trail approaches the pass, it swings across a major avalanche path and makes a series of steep switchbacks to gain the last 135 m of elevation to the summit.

Though the pass provides acceptable views, a short scramble to higher ground west or east of the summit allows a more unfettered vista. (See also *Simpson River-Ferro Pass,* page 339.)

Wedgwood Lake—7.4 km. Hardly anyone backpacks into the park via the Mitchell River, but the trail does access this forest-enclosed lake beneath the massive cliffs of Wedgwood Peak, The Marshall, and Mount Watson.

The trail branches left from the Ferro Pass route at the west end of Cerulean Lake (4.0 km from Assiniboine Lodge) and loses 900 m over the next 3 km, which will have to be regained on the return journey. This section is usually muddy, sometimes overgrown, and there are a couple of minor stream crossings.

Branch left from the Mitchell River trail at km 6.6 and follow boggy track for 0.9 km to Wedgwood's north shore. The views across the lake to the glaciated cliffs of the Assiniboine group are quite fine, and you will certainly find more solitude here than on any other area trail.

219 Wonder Pass

Mount Assiniboine Lodge to Wonder Pass—3.1 km (1.9 mi)

Half-day trip

Allow 1 hour one way

Elevation gain: 215 m (700 ft)

Maximum elevation: 2395 m (7,850 ft)

Maps: Mount Assiniboine 82 J/13

Access: Begin hike from Mount Assiniboine Lodge or the Naiset Cabins. (Magog Campground campers reach the lodge via the 1.5 km trail skirting around the north end of Lake Magog.)

0.0—Mount Assiniboine Lodge (2180 m).

0.5—Naiset Cabins. Park headquarters-ranger cabin.

—Trail climbs along Gog Creek.

1.1—Gog Creek bridge.

1.4—Junction. Gog Lake right 100 m.

—Steep pitch followed by steady uphill through larch stands.

2.2—Trail emerges into open meadows.

3.1—Wonder Pass (2395 m). Trail intersects with *Wonder Pass* trail from Bryant Creek in Banff Park (see page 155).

The hike to Wonder Pass from Lake Magog features Gog Lake, pure stands of alpine larch, vast wildflower meadows, and views that extend over much of the park's core area. And by extending the hike to a viewpoint on the slopes of Wonder Peak, you will discover marvellous views of Marvel Lake.

For backpackers travelling to and from Assiniboine via Bryant Creek, Wonder Pass is an obvious choice on the return journey. For those utilizing other routes, or who flew to the park by helicopter, the pass should rank high on a list of priority hikes from Lake Magog.

The trail begins its ascent to the pass from the park headquarters-ranger cabin and Naiset Cabins (500 m south of Assiniboine Lodge) and follows a shallow vale southeast along Gog Creek. After crossing the creek at km 1.1, it comes abreast of Gog Lake. The lake lies beyond a marshy meadow beneath Naiset Point and is quite a wonderful place to relax on a sunny day. It is also a fine destination for evening walks from the lodge or the Naiset Cabins.

Above the lake, the trail climbs in stages through alpine larch stands interspersed with open meadows. This is a particularly beautiful section during the third week of September when the autumn gold of larch needles is most brilliant.

After climbing through the last stunted larch trees, the trail emerges into a vast, rolling alpine meadowland leading to the summit of the pass. In the midst of this open landscape, you have your first good views back over the core area of the park—vistas that stretch northward along the course of Og Valley to Citadel Pass and beyond. (You can even see the ski lifts on Brewster Rock above Sunshine Village.)

Views into Banff Park from the pass are limited by the slopes of Wonder Peak and The Towers, which create a narrow

View into Banff Park from Wonder Pass

window south to mountains across the Marvel Lake valley. Backpackers leaving Assiniboine Park on this route descend Banff Park's *Wonder Pass* trail to ever-improving views of the valley and, eventually, Marvel Lake itself.

Wonder Viewpoint. While the views from Wonder Pass are wonderful, the pass takes its name from Wonder Peak, which was christened by interprovincial boundary surveyors who established a station on its summit in 1913. The wondrous view they had from the mountaintop was of Marvel Lake and Lake Gloria in Banff Park—lakes that cannot be seen from Wonder Pass.

While you may not want to climb the peak to confirm the surveyors' wonder, you can continue beyond the pass for another 2 km to an open slope on the mountain and approximate their view.

Descend into Banff Park through rocky meadows for 0.7 km to where the trail to the viewpoint angles off to the left (marked by cairns). This narrow track climbs gradually along the southwest slope of Wonder Peak then makes a steep descent to the viewpoint.

This is a grand vantage point for Marvel Lake and Lake Gloria, lying between your toes over 500 vertical metres below. The extensive icefield stretching between Aye and Eon Mountains feeds these two lakes, but since Gloria filters out most of the silt from this glacier before it reaches Marvel, its colour is a milky turquoise compared to the darker blue of Marvel.

The ice-clad summits of the Assiniboine group create an impressive amphitheatre at the head of the Marvel Valley, while the lightly forested summit of Marvel Pass can be seen southwest of Marvel Lake and Peak.

220 Sunburst Valley

Mount Assiniboine Lodge to Elizabeth Lake—3.9 km (2.4 mi)

Half-day trip

Allow 1 to 1.5 hours one way

Elevation gain: 120 m (400 ft)

Minimum elevation: 2300 m (7,550 ft)

Maps: Mount Assiniboine 82 J/13

Access: The hike begins from Mount Assiniboine Lodge junction, 0.2 km north of the lodge. Starting from Magog Campground, follow the Sunburst Lake shortcut trail that branches left at the north edge of the campground for 0.4 km to intersect the hike at km 1.8 (subtract 1.4 km from all distances below).

0.0—Mount Assiniboine Lodge junction (2180 m).

0.1—Junction. Nub Peak right. Continue ahead.

—Flat trail through meadows above Lake Magog.

1.4—Junction. Magog Campground left (0.2 km). Continue ahead.

1.8—Junction. Magog Campground left (0.4 km). Continue ahead.

2.2—Sunburst Lake.

—Trail follows northeast shoreline.

2.3—Sunburst Cabin.

2.8—Cerulean Lake.

3.0—Junction (2210 m). Ferro Pass and Wedgwood Lake left. Elizabeth Lake right.

—Steady uphill along shallow valley.

3.5—Junction (2300 m). Nub Ridge uphill to right 0.9 km (see *Nub Peak*). Continue ahead.

—Trail descends to Elizabeth Lake.

3.9—Elizabeth Lake outlet (2270 m). Junction. Chuck's Ridge ahead 0.8 km. Ferro Pass trail left 1.4 km.

Sunburst Valley lies a short distance west of Lake Magog. The valley contains Sunburst and Cerulean Lakes and is reached on flat, undemanding trail from either Assiniboine Lodge or Magog Campground. Most hikers include nearby Elizabeth Lake in their itinerary, and those looking for a longer outing continue up Nub Ridge.

From Assiniboine Lodge, follow the area's core trail southwest along a plateau above Lake Magog. At km 1.4 the campground trail splits left, but you continue to the right through the forested vale leading to Sunburst Lake.

Sunburst Lake is a sparkling little gem set beneath the cliffs of Sunburst Peak. The trail follows its shoreline and immediately passes Sunburst Cabin, which was built by Banff outfitter Pat Brewster in the mid-1930s. It was operated as a guest camp from 1951 to 1970 by Elizabeth "Lizzie" Rummel, and though it has been used as a residence for B.C. Parks staff in recent years, for those who knew this warm-hearted hostess, it will always belong to Lizzie.

Only a narrow band of forest separates Sunburst from its larger neighbour Cerulean Lake. The trail stays near Cerulean's northeast shore to a junction at its north end. While you can continue to the west end of the lake from this intersection, most hikers turn right and complete a short climb over a forested divide to tiny Elizabeth Lake—a pretty lake surrounded by alpine fir and larch that is named for Lizzie Rummel.

From Elizabeth Lake's outlet, you can continue in a westerly direction for 1.4 km to a junction with the Ferro Pass trail west of Cerulean Lake, then return to Cerulean to complete a circuit of the Sunburst Valley. However, there isn't much to see, so we suggest a side trip to Chuck's Ridge or extending your hike to Nub Ridge.

Sunburst and Cerulean Lakes

Chuck's Ridge. This 0.8 km trail branches right from the main trail on the opposite side of the Elizabeth Lake outlet bridge and climbs steeply to a ridge extending southwest from Nub Peak. The ridge, which overlooks the headwaters of the Mitchell River and Wedgwood Lake, was named for Charles "Chuck" Millar, an early guide employed by Erling Strom at Assiniboine Lodge.

Nub Ridge. Without adding a lot of distance to your day, you can climb to the crest of Nub Ridge and the Nublet for the classic high-angle view of Lake Magog and Mount Assiniboine. The connector trail to the ridge branches northeast from the Elizabeth Lake trail at km 3.5. After 0.9 km of steady uphill, it intersects the ridge trail at km 2.4 (see *Nub Peak*).

221 Nub Peak

Mount Assiniboine Lodge to Nublet—2.9 km (1.8 mi)

Half-day trip

Allow 1.5 hours one way

Elevation gain: 350 m (1,150 ft)

Maximum elevation: 2530 m (8,300 ft)

Maps: Mount Assiniboine 82 J/13

Access: Begin hike from the junction 0.2 km north of Mount Assiniboine Lodge.

0.0—Assiniboine Lodge junction (2180 m).

0.1—Junction. Nub Peak right.

0.5—Junction. Horse trail to Og Meadows right. Continue ahead.

1.0—Junction. Horse trail to Sunburst Lake left. Nub Peak right.

—Steady uphill through subalpine forest.

2.1—Trail crests Nub Ridge.

—Trail ascends crest of Nub Ridge.

2.3—Nub Ridge Summit (2390 m).

—Gradual descent along ridgetop.

2.4—Junction. Elizabeth Lake trail downhill to left 0.9 km. Nublet and Nub Peak ahead.

—Steep narrow trail climbs through rocky bluffs.

2.9—Nublet Summit (2530 m).

One of the finest views of Mount Assiniboine is from the crest of Nub Ridge. The promontory is strategically situated just north of the Assiniboine group to provide a perfect panorama of all the peaks surrounding this magnificent pyramid and the lakes scattered near its base.

While the short hike to the ridge will reveal the classic, much-photographed view of Mount Assiniboine with Magog, Sunburst and Cerulean lakes, you can get an even higher perspective by continuing another 0.6 km to the Nublet—a 2530-m alpine platform immediately above the ridge to the north. And if you are really looking for a workout, scramble up the last step to the summit of Nub Peak (2743 m) for the full 360-degree overview of the park's core area.

If you are staying at Assiniboine Lodge or the Naiset Cabins, start the hike from the Assiniboine Pass trail junction 0.2 km north of the lodge. Follow the trail west 100 m and branch right onto the trail angling across the meadows toward Nub Ridge. You soon leave the meadows and begin a gradual climb through a forest of Engelmann spruce, alpine fir and scattered alpine larch.

At km 1.0, the horse trail to Sunburst Lake branches left. Stay right and begin the climb to the ridge via a shallow draw. This vale is bordered by lots of small larch trees, which form a golden corridor in mid-September. As you near the upper end of the draw, views begin to open ahead to the rocky slopes of the Nublet.

The trail reaches the crest of the ridge at km 2.1 and follows up along its backbone for another 0.2 km to its highest point. From this viewpoint the Assiniboine environs are spread like a map at your feet: a great wall formed by Wedgwood Peak, The Marshall and Mount Watson looms above the heavily forested shores of Wedgwood Lake to the southwest; Sunburst and Cerulean Lakes are wrapped around the rocky promonto-

Mount Assiniboine basin from Nub Ridge

ry of Sunburst Peak directly beneath the ridge to the south; and the sparkling waters of Lake Magog, the park's largest lake, stretch beneath the incomparable "horn" of Mount Assiniboine.

Continuing north, the trail makes a slight descent to the junction for the connector trail down to Elizabeth Lake. A less defined track continues ahead to the top of the Nublet, ascending through rocky bluffs and eventually enters a large alpine meadow. The Nublet isn't really a peak but more of an extensive platform that allows a loftier view of Mount Assiniboine and the Lake Magog basin.

While defined trail ends on the Nublet plateau, strong hikers can extend the journey upwards for another 1.5 km to the summit of Nub Peak—a steep but obvious scramble. While the foreground for Mount Assiniboine is not nearly as balanced and interesting from the peak as the ridge, views are more expansive, particularly to the Og Meadows–Og Lake environs immediately below the summit to the east.

Elizabeth Lake–Sunburst Valley. If you haven't already hiked to Sunburst Valley and Elizabeth Lake, this is a logical way to return from Nub Ridge. The option only adds 2.0 km to the return trip and allows you to visit all the lakes on the Sunburst Valley route.

From the 2.4-km junction on Nub Ridge, follow the 0.9-km connector trail that switchbacks down to the summit of the Sunburst Valley trail (km 3.5). Elizabeth Lake is just 0.4 km downhill to the right from this junction. After paying this tiny lake among the larches a visit, return to the junction and descend to Cerulean and Sunburst Lakes. (See *Sunburst Valley.*)

If you are staying at Lake Magog Campground, the Sunburst Valley trail is a shorter, more direct approach to Nub Ridge, saving the 1.5-km detour back to the Nub Peak trailhead near the lodge.

222 Og Pass—Windy Ridge

Mount Assiniboine Lodge to Windy Ridge—7.2 km (4.5 mi)

Day trip

Allow 2.5 to 3 hours to Windy Ridge

Elevation gain: 470 m (1,550 ft)

Maximum elevation: 2650 m (8,700 ft)

Maps: Mount Assiniboine 82 J/13

Access: Begin the hike from the Mount Assiniboine Lodge junction, 0.2 km north of the lodge and 1.6 km east of Magog Campground on the Assiniboine Pass trail.

0.0— Assiniboine Lodge junction (2180 m).

—Follow Assiniboine Pass trail northeast.

0.3—Junction. Assiniboine Pass ahead. Og Pass left.

0.8—Junction. Horse trail to Sunburst Lake left. Continue ahead.

1.1—Junction. Og Lake ahead. Og Pass right.

—Trail angles north across Og Meadows.

1.4—Junction. Assiniboine Pass horse trail right. Og Pass left.

3.2—Trail climbs from meadows into forest.

—Steady climb through forest.

4.7—Trail levels out into Og Pass.

5.0—Junction (2300 m). Ahead to Og Pass summit (0.3 km) and Allenby Pass trail (5.8 km). Windy Ridge left.

5.3—Trail passes above treeline.

—Moderately steep climb across rocky meadows.

6.4—Trail levels out briefly on alpine meadow.

—Steep ascent of scree slope.

7.2—Windy Ridge (2650 m).

The trail to Windy Ridge via Og Pass is one of the most rewarding day trips in Assiniboine Park. No other trail provides such an expansive panorama of Mount Assiniboine and the Lake Magog basin, and the wildflower meadow on the slopes below Windy Ridge is one of the finest in the Rockies. And once you reach the trail's 2650-m summit, you will have attained one of the highest points in the mountain parks accessible by defined trail.

Begin the hike on the Assiniboine Pass trail 0.2 km north of Assiniboine Lodge. (You will have to hike 0.7 km to reach this junction if you are staying at Naiset Cabins or 1.6 km from Magog Campground.) Follow the trail northeast toward the pass 0.3 km before branching left on the Og Lake-Citadel Pass trail. After descending a shallow vale and passing through a draw, you emerge onto the vast, open expanse of Og Meadows, where the trail to Og Pass and Windy Ridge splits right and continues north toward Og Mountain.

After leaving the meadows, the trail ascends steadily for 1.5 km through a subalpine forest of Engelmann spruce, alpine fir and, eventually, larch. At km 4.7, it levels off into the 1-km-long vale comprising Og Pass. In another 300 m you arrive at the Assiniboine-Banff Park boundary and the unmarked junction for the Windy Ridge trail.

While you may be eager to continue your climb to Windy Ridge, a short side-trip to the east will bring you to the true summit of Og Pass and, not far beyond, a pretty lake backed against the rocky north slope of Cave Mountain. The moist meadows surrounding the lake support a luxuriant growth of wildflowers in midsummer, including ragwort, purple fleabane, valerian, fringed grass-of-Parnassus, red-stemmed saxifrage and white paintbrush.

If the weather is reasonable, you will

Mount Assiniboine from the Windy Ridge trail

most certainly want to continue your journey to Windy Pass from the junction near the park boundary. While the trip becomes more strenuous beyond the Og Pass junction, the views are increasingly rewarding as you ascend the west slope of Og Mountain.

Just 2.4 km above the junction, the climb moderates briefly as the trail traverses a grassy ridge. At a lofty 2515 m, this open slope provides a fantastic panorama that stretches from the peaks of the Assiniboine group on the south to Kootenay Park's Rockwall and Yoho Park's twin-towered Goodsir Peak on the northwestern horizon.

If you have any doubts about how much higher Mount Assiniboine is than its neighbouring peaks, they will be dispelled from this viewpoint. Every other summit in the vicinity lies at least 300 m beneath this towering 3618-m pyramid.

This slope is one of the finest alpine wildflower meadows in the Rockies. In late July and early August it is covered with the colourful blooms of forget-me-nots, arnica, contorted lousewort, golden fleabane, alpine speedwell, red-stemmed saxifrage and moss campion.

After one last uphill grunt over a steep scree slope, the trail crests a high saddle just below Og Mountain's summit. From this crest, you have a mountaineer's-eye view of the ranges to the east and the upper Brewster Creek valley (you can see Halfway Lodge on the edge of a meadow near the head of the valley). A dizzy precipice drops away from the eastern lip of Windy Ridge, where you can peer warily down between your toes for 400 vertical metres to a beautiful hanging valley cradling a tiny azure lake.

Mount Robson Provincial Park

With an area of 2170 sq km, British Columbia's Mount Robson is the largest provincial park in the Canadian Rockies. The park's eastern boundary is formed by a 200 km stretch of the continental divide, a border it shares with Jasper National Park. With the exception of tiny Mount Terry Fox Provincial Park on its western border, the park is bounded on all other sides by B.C. forest lands.

Despite the park's relatively large size, most visitation is centred around Mount Robson—the highest mountain in the Canadian Rockies at 3954 m (12,972 ft). This giant remained unclimbed until an Alpine Club of Canada party led by the Austrian-born guide Conrad Kain reached its summit in 1913—the same year that the B.C. Legislature created Mount Robson Provincial Park. Even today it is considered a difficult and dangerous ascent, mostly due to the heavy weather created by its lofty summit. (Of 58 parties registered to climb it in 1995, only seven reached the top.)

The park's first recreational trail was built along the Robson River to Berg Lake in the spring of 1913 by Jasper outfitter Donald "Curly" Phillips in preparation for the Alpine Club of Canada camp. Sections of the trail have been relocated and upgraded over the years, but it remains the most heavily travelled trail in the park. The initial 4.2 km of the trail leading to Kinney Lake is the park's most popular day hike.

Shorter walks near Mount Robson Viewpoint lead to Overlander Falls and Viewpoint Lookout (a higher vantage point for Mount Robson). The short hike to Yellowhead Mountain Viewpoint and a longer, more demanding trip to Mount Fitzwilliam basin are the two most frequently hiked routes in the east section of the park. The only multi-day backpack is Moose River—a remote wilderness track that is only completed by a handful of experienced backpackers each season.

Berg Lake is the only trail requiring a camping permit (see *Berg Lake,* page 429).

Information and services. Headquarters for the park are at the Mount Robson Visitor Information Centre at Mount Robson Viewpoint, 60 km west of the B.C.-Alberta border on Highway 16. The visitor centre operates from May to September 30, dispensing a full range of information on the park and B.C. Tourism opportunities as well as registering hikers and collecting overnight fees for the Berg Lake trail. Off season information is available through the park headquarters office (see *Sources-Park information*).

Three of the park's four road accessible campgrounds are at Mount Robson Viewpoint: Robson Meadows (125 sites) and Robson River (19 sites) are operated by B.C. Parks; Emperor Ridge Campground (37 sites) is operated privately. Lucerne Campground (32 sites) is 10 km west of the B.C.–Alberta boundary on Highway 16.

A cafe-camp store adjacent to the Visitor Information Centre provides meals, gasoline, basic groceries, refreshments, and souvenirs. Mount Robson Guest Ranch, the only commercial accommodation in the park, is 3 km from the visitor centre on the south side of the Fraser River. Another lodge is located outside the park, 6 km west of the visitor centre on Highway 16.

The nearest towns to Mount Robson Viewpoint are Valemount, B.C. (45 km) and Jasper, Alberta (82 km).

Access: The only highway access through the park is the Yellowhead Highway (Hwy 16). Though VIA Rail passenger trains traverse the park daily on the CNR line, the nearest stations are beyond the park at Jasper, Alberta, and Valemount, B.C. (a flag stop). Greyhound buses make daily runs east and west on the Yellowhead Highway with scheduled stops at Valemount and flag stops (arranged in advance) at Mount Robson Viewpoint.

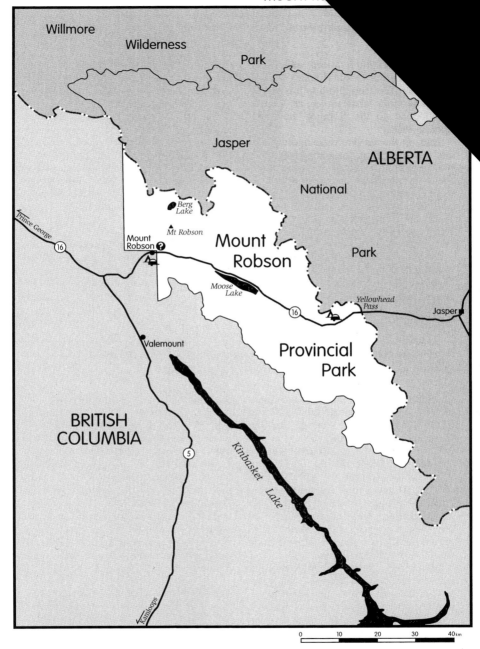

l peace-
highest
forest-
a good
upper

ng east

_... ___ cnd_ of the visitor
centre parking lot. At km 0.4 you pass a
water storage tank and follow an old
roadbed uphill, climbing at a moderate
grade through a mixed forest of western
red cedar, Douglas fir, white spruce,
aspen, Douglas maple, alder, thimbleberry and occasional devil's club.

At km 1.2 the Viewpoint Lookout trail
branches left from the roadbed and, 200
m beyond, begins a steep, switchbacking

ascent. A viewpoint with a bench at km
2.7 allows you to catch your breath and
look down upon the Yellowhead Highway and Fraser Valley.

The trail crests the Viewpoint Lookout
summit at 3.3 km—425 m above your
starting point. To the northeast the forest
opens to a fine view of the south face of
Mount Robson. On the south side of the
promontory, there are views down to the
Fraser River and Overlander Falls and to
the distant Cariboo Mountains.

Access: Hike begins on a gated service road
running from east end of Mount Robson
Viewpoint parking area. *Maps: Mount Robson
83 E/3 (trail not shown); Mount Robson Park.*

224 Overlander Falls

Overlander Falls Parking Area to Overlander Falls—0.5 km (0.3 mi)
Overlander Falls-Fraser River Circuit—6.0 km (3.7 mi)

A short trail descends to a viewpoint
for this broad waterfall on the Fraser
River. The falls are named for the
"Overlanders"—fortune-seekers who
bushwhacked down-valley en route to the
Cariboo gold fields in 1862.

You can also extend the trip to the falls
into a half-day outing by completing a
circuit that begins and ends at the visitor
centre parking area. In addition to the
falls, you will experience the area's rich
and varied forest environment and a 2 km
stretch of the Fraser River.

The circuit follows the Viewpoint
Lookout trail for 1.2 km to where the
trail to the lookout branches left. You can
side-trip to the lookout at this junction
(add 4.2 km to the trip), or simply continue on the circuit by following the
roadbed east. In another kilometre you
cross the Yellowhead Highway to the
Overlander Falls parking area and

descend the 0.5-km trail to the falls.

After visiting the falls, return to a junction 100 m above the viewpoint and follow the trail branching left. It descends
above the Fraser River for approximately
2 km, passing an old cabin built by
Dennis Hogan, a contractor involved in
the construction of the original rail lines
down the valley between 1912 and 1914.

You emerge on the Hargreaves Road
where it crosses the Fraser River. After
peering into the river's gorge from the
bridge, follow the road north back to the
visitor centre parking area.

Access: The direct trail to the falls begins from
a parking area on the south side of the
Yellowhead Highway (Hwy 16) 1.4 km (0.9 mi)
east of Mount Robson Viewpoint. The circuit
trip begins at the east end of Mount Robson
Viewpoint parking area. *Maps: Mount Robson
83 E/3 (trail not shown); Mount Robson Park.*

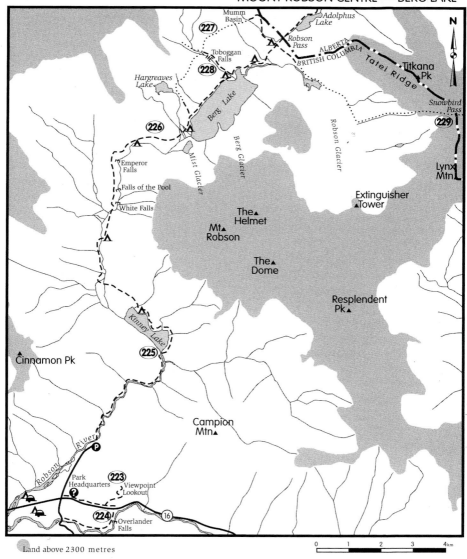

N

Adolphus
Lake

Mumm
Basin

227

Robson
Pass

Toboggan
Falls

228

ALBERTA
BRITISH COLUMBIA

Tatei Ridge

Titkana
Pk

Hargreaves
Lake

Berg Lake

Robson Glacier

Snowbird
Pass

226

229

Lynx
Mtn

Emperor
Falls

Mist Glacier

Berg Glacier

Extinguisher
Tower

Falls of the Pool

White Falls

The
Helmet

Mt
Robson

The
Dome

Resplendent
Pk

Kinney Lake

225

Cinnamon Pk

Campion
Mtn

Robson River

P

223

Park
Headquarters

Viewpoint
Lookout

224

16

Overlander
Falls

Land above 2300 metres

0   1   2   3   4 km

225 Kinney Lake

Berg Lake Trail Parking Area to Kinney Lake—4.5 km (2.8 mi)
Berg Lake Trail Parking Area to Kinney Lake Campground—6.8 km (4.2 mi)

Day hike or backpack

Allow 1.5 hours one way

Elevation gain: 130 m (425 ft)

Maximum elevation: 985 m (3,230 ft)

Maps: Mount Robson 83 E/3
      Mount Robson Park

Access: From Mount Robson Viewpoint junction, follow the road running north beyond the service station-general store for 2 km to the Berg Lake trail parking area. Hike begins at the Robson River bridge at the far end of the parking area.

0.0—Robson River bridge (855 m).

—Flat travel on roadbed near Robson River.

0.8—Cinnamon Rockslide.

—Trail climbs over open rockslide.

1.4—Trail enters cedar-hemlock forest.

2.7—Trail emerges from cedar-hemlock forest.

—Steady, moderate ascent.

3.3—Robson River cataracts.

4.3—Robson River bridge (985 m). Kinney Lake outlet.

4.4—Junction. Kinney Lake Picnic Area left 150 m.

—Trail climbs around southeast end of lake.

4.9—Boardwalk to Kinney Lake viewpoint.

5.7—Trail crosses alluvial outwash along east shore.

—Trail follows eastern shoreline.

6.8—Kinney Lake Campground (985 m).

7.2—Mountain bike access limit (bike rack). Berg Lake trail continues up into forest (see *Berg Lake*).

Berg Lake is the most popular backpack in the Rockies, and the initial 4.5 km of that route to Kinney Lake is the park's most popular day hike. While this large, glacier-fed lake beneath Mount Robson is an attractive destination, the forest you travel through to get there is of equal interest.

The hike follows an old roadbed all the way to the lake, but the track is quite natural and enjoyable to walk. Most of the first kilometre is flat and easy, travelling through lush forest and seldom far from the Robson River.

At 0.8 km you emerge from the forest and climb over a rockslide. This large slide sloughed down from a gully on the east slope of Cinnamon Peak in May, 1986. It has been slowly revegetating ever since and is covered with a colourful display of wildflowers in early summer, including red-stemmed saxifrage, harebells and red columbine.

On the opposite side of the slide, the trail runs into a wonderful forest of western red cedar and western hemlock. The cool, well-shaded understorey is carpeted with feather moss, bunchberry, ferns, thimbleberry and some humongous devil's club. You feel like you've suddenly entered B.C.'s coastal rainforest, and, indeed, this is the farthest east in the province that this forest type appears. This unique forest results from a microclimate created by the mass of nearby Mount Robson, which "catches" weather systems and deposits moisture in this valley.

Near the 3-km mark you climb from the cedar-hemlock forest and come abreast of the Robson River again at a series of cascades. The trail continues its ascent to a bridge across the river, where you have your first view of Kinney Lake and the glaciated pyramid of Whitehorn Mountain beyond. (Before you cross the bridge, scan the nearby rocks for pikas,

Kinney Lake and Mount Whitehorn

this being one of the lowest locales where these tiny members of the hare family are seen in the Rockies.)

As soon as you cross the Robson River, a side-trail branches left to Kinney Lake Picnic Area. The small gravel beaches at this site are pleasant spots to relax and eat your lunch in late summer, but they are often flooded by high lake levels earlier in the season.

The lake is named for the Reverend George Kinney, who made several desperate attempts to climb Mount Robson between 1907 and 1909. On the final expedition, Kinney and his inexperienced companion, Donald "Curly" Phillips, reached a point very near the summit.

Though most hikers end their trip at the picnic area, it is tempting to follow the main trail around to the lake's eastern shoreline. There is a bit of a climb before you descend to the east shore, and in the midst of this forested traverse, there is an elevated boardwalk leading out through

the trees to a view over the lake.

Once the trail returns to the lakeshore, you cross an alluvial wash that fingers down through the cottonwoods to form a broad gravel beach. Continue along the lake, passing a number of rocky beaches, until you reach Kinney Lake Campground.

The campground is situated on the shoreline not far from the north end of the lake. It is a pleasant site with a substantial, log picnic shelter, and a fine destination for families or anyone who doesn't want to work too hard to enjoy a backcountry camp-out.

While the campground is a busy place in midsummer, we will always remember stopping there on a warm evening at the end of September while hiking out from Berg Lake. There was nary a soul around as we rested and watched the last rays of sun illuminate the golden cottonwoods and aspen along the shore, and the lake was a shimmering layer of glass beneath the shadowed slope of Cinnamon Peak.

226 Berg Lake

Robson River Parking Area to Berg Lake Campground—20.2 km (12.6 mi)

Backpack

Allow 7 to 10 hours one way

Elevation gain: 790 m (2,600 ft)

Maximum elevation: 1640 m (5,380 ft)

Maps: Mount Robson 83 E/3
Mount Robson Park

Access: From Mount Robson Viewpoint, follow road branching north beside service station-store 2 km to the Berg Lake trail parking area. Trail begins at the Robson River bridge.

0.0—Berg Lake trailhead (850 m).

4.3—Kinney Lake outlet bridge.

6.8—Kinney Lake Campground (985 m).

7.2—Mountain bike access limit (bike rack).

8.7—Robson River bridge to alluvial flats.

9.0—Bottom of Whitehorn Hill.

—Steady climb next 1.0 km.

10.8—Robson River suspension bridge. Whitehorn Ranger Station left 150 m.

10.9—Whitehorn Campground (1115 m).

11.8—Robson River bridge.

—Steady steep climb next 3.5 km.

12.3—White Falls Viewpoint.

13.4—Falls of the Pool Viewpoint.

14.8—Junction. Emperor Falls right 0.2 km.

15.4—Emperor Falls Campground (1630 m).

17.8—Hargreaves Creek bridges.

18.1—Marmot Campground. Southwest end of Berg Lake.

18.4—Junction. *Hargreaves Glacier* left.

20.2—Berg Lake Campground (1640 m).

20.3—Toboggan Creek bridge and junction. *Toboggan Falls* trail left.

21.3—Rearguard Campground.

21.7—Junction. *Snowbird Pass* right. Berg Lake Ranger Station left. Robson Pass ahead.

22.3—Junction. Left to Robson Pass Campground (0.1 km) and *Mumm Basin*.

22.7—Robson Pass (1652 m). Robson-Jasper Park boundary. Connects to Jasper's *North Boundary Trail* at km 156.7.

The Berg Lake trail is one of the most popular backpacking trips in the mountain parks (13,000 visitor nights in 1998.) Little wonder. This turquoise lake, dotted with icebergs and backdropped by the ice-bound north wall of the Canadian Rockies' highest peak is one of the wonders of the mountain world.

Hikers attack the 790-m ascent to Berg Lake with a variety of strategies: traditionalists backpack to one of four campgrounds at the lake in a day; the realists stage the trip over two days by camping at Kinney Lake or Whitehorn before assaulting the steep Valley of a Thousand Falls; the masochists hike to Berg and back in a day, often using mountain bikes over the first 7.2 kms to facilitate their marathon; and the "sissies" helicopter to Robson Pass on one of two days each week when landings are allowed. Whichever strategy you use, read the information at the end of this description concerning fees and quotas.

From the Robson River bridge at the trailhead parking area, a broad, road-width track climbs gradually along the Robson River through a micro-rainforest to Kinney Lake (see *Kinney Lake*). After crossing the Kinney Lake outlet bridge, single-track trail continues around the lake's eastern shoreline to Kinney Lake Campground with its fine lakeside views.

At km 7.2 the trail branches up into the forest to avoid the ever-changing channels of the Robson River on the alluvial plain north of Kinney Lake. This rooty and rocky section rolls up and down sharply for 1.5 km until it descends to a bridge over the river and crosses the broad alluvial plain. At the far side of the outwash flats, the trail begins a steady climb of Whitehorn Hill—a moderate to steep grade that mounts the first major step on the journey to Berg Lake.

After gaining nearly 150 m, you descend to the Robson River beneath

Berg Lake and Mount Robson

Whitehorn Mountain where a suspension bridge spans the river to Whitehorn Campground.

Enjoy the short, flat walk beyond Whitehorn Campground to a second bridge back across the river, because the real work is about to begin—a steady, steep 450-m climb along the Valley of a Thousand Falls. Three major waterfalls are passed on the ascent—White Falls, Falls-of-the-Pool and the magnificent Emperor Falls—and each viewpoint provides a welcome respite from the gruelling climb.

The trail finally levels off at Emperor Falls Campground then rolls along the open, braided channels of the Robson River, where you get your first glimpse of the majestic north wall of Mount Robson. Views of the mountain and its glaciers become increasingly spectacular as you near Berg Lake.

After passing Marmot Campground at the southwest end of the lake, the trail rolls along above the northwest shoreline to Berg Lake, Rearguard and Robson Pass Campgrounds. Views across the lake's powder-blue waters to Mount Robson are exceptional. Two rivers of ice, Mist and Berg Glacier, tumble down from the mountain's uppermost reaches, the latter terminating at the edge of the lake. The groan and rumble of these two overburdened bodies of ice is constant, and chunks of ice calving from Berg Glacier often drift into the lake.

The 3954 m summit of Mount Robson lies more than two vertical kilometres above the lake. First climbed in 1913 by Albert MacCarthy, William Foster and their guide Conrad Kain, it has been the object of many subsequent expeditions. It is still considered one of the most difficult ascents in Canada, mainly due to the mountain's unpredictable weather. The mountain also displays the greatest section of Cambrian rock known in Canada—some 4000 metres thick.

Berg Lake Campground is the most popular of four campgrounds near the lake, thanks in part to the old Berg Lake Chalet situated in its midst. The chalet was constructed in 1927 by outfitter Roy

Hargreaves and was used by commercial horse parties until the late 1970s. B.C. Parks has restored the heritage cabin for day use and renamed it the Hargreaves Shelter. While you cannot overnight there, it is a cozy and welcome refuge during inclement weather.

Rearguard, Robson Pass and Marmot Campgrounds can also be quite busy during high season, so be flexible about where you camp or make a reservation in advance of your trip.

Robson Pass lies just over 2 km beyond the northeast end of the lake and at virtually the same elevation. The pass is a gateway to the remote northwest corner of Jasper National Park and a good approach to Robson's Moose Pass region. Adolphus Lake lies less than a kilometre beyond the pass—a short and easy trip from any of Berg's northeast campgrounds. (See *North Boundary Trail and Moose Pass* in the Jasper Park chapter and *Moose River* in this chapter.)

There are a number of fine day trips within easy reach of any of the Berg Lake campgrounds, including *Toboggan Falls, Mumm Basin-Hargreaves Glacier,* and *Snowbird Pass* (see pages 430-433).

Emperor Falls

Berg Lake and Glacier

Berg Lake trail information

The Berg Lake trail is renowned as the best managed trail in the Rockies. With the exception of a short section of rough terrain beyond Kinney Lake, and the grunt up the Valley of a Thousand Falls, the trail is broad, easily graded and well maintained. Mountain bikes are allowed to km 7.2 (0.4 km beyond Kinney Lake Campground).

As of this writing, and despite cutbacks in funding, B.C. Park Rangers are still stationed at Whitehorn and Berg Lake (near Robson Pass) throughout the hiking season. If a health or safety emergency occurs while rangers are absent, visitors can use two-way radios mounted outside ranger cabins to call for assistance.

There are seven campgrounds along the trail with large tent pads and cable-rigged bear poles for storing food. Large open-air shelters at Kinney Lake and Whitehorn and the enclosed Hargreaves Shelter at Berg Lake are available for day use. Robson Pass is the only campground where open fires are permitted.

There is a camping fee of $5 per person per night to overnight at any of the campgrounds on the trail. Campground quotas were introduced in 1997 to help preserve the vegetation around the sites and insure that campgrounds do not turn into small cities. As of this writing, there are usually vacant sites somewhere at Berg Lake on most days, but you should be flexible about where you camp. You can also reserve sites up to two months in advance of your trip by calling the B.C. Parks campground reservation line (1-800-689-9025).

There is also helicopter access to Robson Pass for anyone overnighting at Berg Lake. The service is available on Fridays and Mondays (Tuesday replaces Monday on holiday weekends) throughout the summer. During summer 2000, the cost of the flight from the heli-pad near Mount Robson Viewpoint to Robson Pass was $155 per person (minimum 4 passengers). See *Sources–Backcountry access,* Robson Heli-Magic.

227 Mumm Basin—Hargreaves Glacier

Mumm Basin–Toboggan Falls Circuit—8.1 km (5.0 mi)
Mumm Basin–Hargreaves Glacier Circuit—11.6 km (7.2 mi)

Day trip

Allow 5 hours for Mumm-Hargreaves circuit

Elevation gain: 500 m (1,650 ft)

Maximum elevation: 2150 m (7,050 ft)

Maps: Mount Robson 83 E/3†
 Mount Robson Park†
 †trail not shown

Access: Follow the *Berg Lake* trail to Robson Pass Campground Junction at km 22.

0.0—Robson Pass Campground Junction (1650 m).

0.1—Robson Pass Campground.

—Steep ascent on defined track.

0.6—Stream bridge.

—Steep to very steep uphill.

1.0—First views of Berg Lake-Robson Pass.

1.7—Alberta-B.C. boundary marker.

—Steep ascent over rocky terrain.

2.0—Rock cairn viewpoint.

—Faint track climbs across rock slabs and heather meadows. Cairns and markers.

2.5—Stream crossing.

3.0—Mumm Basin Summit (2150 m).

3.4—Stream crossing in rocky gorge.

—Steep descent across scree slope.

4.4—Defined track re-enters forest.

4.9—Junction (1920 m). Intersection with *Toboggan Falls* trail at km 1.2: Toboggan Falls and Berg Lake Campground left; Toboggan Creek Cave right 1.0 km; Hargreaves Glacier ahead.

5.1—Toboggan Creek bridge.

—Climb over ridge.

6.3—Hargreaves Glacier lateral moraine.

6.6—Junction. Hargreaves Lake viewpoint right 0.3 km. Berg Lake left.

—Steep descent.

7.7—Junction (1640 m). Intersection with *Berg Lake* trail at km 18.4.

Mumm Basin provides the classic, much-photographed overview of Berg Lake and Mount Robson. It is one of the most popular day trips from campgrounds in the Berg Lake vicinity and a must for anyone who has a day to spare at the lake. And if the weather is good, you should consider extending the high traverse to Hargreaves Lake at the toe of the Hargreaves Glacier. Otherwise, shorten the loop and return to Berg Lake on the Toboggan Falls trail.

Rough trails to Mumm Basin and Hargreaves Glacier evolved over several decades as campers and guests at Berg Lake Chalet scrambled to these viewpoints. However, it wasn't until the late 1980s that park rangers tied the snippets of trail together with cairns, markers and a bit of trail work to define the routes. But make no mistake, the Mumm Basin–Hargreaves Glacier traverse is steep and demanding, and in many sections you must watch carefully for cairns and markers to stay on route.

We like to begin the Mumm Basin-Hargreaves Glacier circuit from the Robson Pass Campground junction. This approach travels across the basin's high slopes from northeast to southwest, keeping the best views ahead rather than back over your shoulder.

You pick-up the Mumm Basin trail at the rear of Robson Pass Campground. The trail leads into a forest of lodgepole pine and spruce and soon begins a steep ascent. You cross a small stream at km 1.2, then angle east and continue gaining elevation across steep side slopes and rocky terrain at a heart-throbbing rate. As the forest thins, you get your first views of Mount Robson, Berg Lake, Robson Pass and Glacier.

After passing an Alberta-B.C. boundary marker at km 2.3, the trail climbs to a rocky promontory with a large rock cairn. This 2100 m platform is a good

Robson Glacier, Berg Lake and Mt. Robson from Mumm Basin trail

place to stop for a breather since it provides an exceptional 180 degree panorama stretching from Adolphus Lake in Jasper Park to the mountains west of Mount Robson.

Beyond the cairn viewpoint, the trail angles left and climbs directly toward Mumm Basin. Grades moderate as you follow snippets of trail, cairns and yellow markers along the lip of the basin, traversing slab rocks, heather meadows and crossing a small stream. The highest point on the traverse (2150 m) is reached on a high meadow at km 3.0. Berg Lake and Mount Robson dominate the scene.

From the summit, you begin a steady 2 km descent to Toboggan Creek. There are several steep plunges as you step your way down along open scree slopes and cross the largest of the basin's outlet streams in a boulder-filled gully. Views ahead to Robson and Berg Lake are exceptional, but you must watch carefully for cairns and markers on this trackless descent.

Defined trail re-emerges just before you re-enter forest, and not long after

you reach the Toboggan Falls trail at a four-way junction above Toboggan Creek. At this point you can descend the Toboggan Falls trail to the Berg Lake trail in 1.2 km (see *Toboggan Falls),* or continue southwest to Hargreaves Glacier to complete the full circuit.

If you continue to Hargreaves Glacier, stay straight ahead at the four-way junction and descend 0.2 km to a bridge over Toboggan Creek. Beyond the creek, the trail climbs over a ridge and approaches a large lateral moraine deposited by the Hargreaves Glacier. Not long after the trail begins its descent toward Berg Lake, you reach a junction where a 0.3 km side-trail leads right to a viewpoint for Hargreaves Lake and Glacier.

After returning to the main trail, continue downslope through scattered forest to an intersection with the Berg Lake trail near the southwest end of Berg Lake (0.3 km east of Marmot Campground). Regardless of which campground you started from, by the time you return to your site you will have completed a 11.6 km circuit.

Rick McDonald photo — *Mount Robson from Toboggan Falls trail*

228 Toboggan Falls

Toboggan Creek Junction to Toboggan Falls—1.0 km (0.6 mi)
Toboggan Creek Junction to Toboggan Creek Cave—2.0 km (1.2 mi)

This short, steep trail leads to a series of cataracts sluicing over limestone slabs to create a remarkable natural waterslide. You can continue up along Toboggan Creek for another kilometre to a small cave near the creek's headwaters, or use the trail as an access or exit route for the *Mumm Basin–Hargreaves Glacier* traverse.

The hike up Toboggan Creek begins from a junction 100 m beyond Berg Lake Campground on the Berg Lake trail. After a short steep climb to the lower end of the Toboggan Creek canyon, the trail detours east into the forest briefly before returning to the creek where it slides merrily down over the limestone bedrock. Climb along this waterslide for the next 0.5 km, but stay back from its edge: if you slipped, you would not enjoy the ride.

The trail reaches the lower end of Toboggan Falls at km 0.9. Another 100 m of steep climbing brings you to a wooden bench and a viewpoint for the upper section of the falls and Mount Robson's north face.

If you continue up along Toboggan Creek for another 0.2 km, you reach a four-way intersection with the *Mumm Basin–Hargreaves Glacier* trail. While some hikers branch off to one of these high viewpoints, you can also continue the climb along the east side of the creek for another kilometre to reach a 30 m cave beneath the south ridge of Mount Anne-Alice (take a headlamp if you plan on entering the cavern).

Access: Hike the *Berg Lake* trail to the Toboggan Falls trail junction 0.1 km east of Berg Lake Campground (east side of Toboggan Creek bridge). *Maps: Mount Robson 83 E/3 (trail not shown); Mount Robson Park.*

Rick McDonald photo

Mount Robson from Snowbird Pass

229 Snowbird Pass

Snowbird Pass Junction to Snowbird Pass—9.2 km (5.7 mi)*

Snowbird Pass is an exceptional viewpoint for the ice-covered east slopes of Mount Robson, Resplendent Mountain and the vast Reef Icefield to the east. The extensive, marmot-infested meadows on the approach to this 2425 m summit only enhance its reputation as one of the finest day trips from Berg Lake.

Defined trail is scarce on this long, demanding hike, and a traverse along Robson Glacier's lateral moraine requires sturdy footwear. Take a map and be prepared to do a fair amount of route-finding (with the assistance of cairns and markers) and to gain 780 m of elevation, much of it over the last half of the trip.

From its junction with the Berg Lake trail near the Berg Lake Ranger Station, the trail runs southeast across alluvial flats near Robson Glacier's outlet stream to the moraines east of a small lake at the glacier's toe.

Follow snippets of trail and cairns along the lateral moraine bordering the east side of the glacier (you come abreast of this great river of ice at km 2.4). The moraine is in a continual state of collapse due to melting of its ice core, and park rangers have been forced to do some re-routing in recent years (watch for cairns).

When you near the main stream draining Snowbird Meadows (km 5.6), a trail branches east and switchbacks steeply upwards to the vast, rocky meadows. Stay north of the outlet stream as you climb steadily over the meadows toward the gap between Titkana Peak and Lynx Mountain. The final ascent to the pass is through boulders and quite steep.

Access: Hike the *Berg Lake* trail to Snowbird Pass Junction at km 21.7 (1.0 km west of Robson Pass). *Maps: Mount Robson 83 E/3 (trail not shown); Mount Robson Park.*

*distances approximate

230 Moose River

Yellowhead Highway to Moose Pass—48.9 km (30.4 mi)

Backpack

Allow 3 to 5 days to Smoky River

Elevation gain: 945 m (3,100 ft)

Maximum elevation: 2025 m (6,650 ft)

Maps: Rainbow 83 D/15
　　　Resplendent Creek 83 E/2
　　　Mount Robson 83 E/3

Access: Follow the Yellowhead Hwy (#16) to the trailhead access road on the north side of the highway 3 km (2 mi) east of the Moose Lake Boat Launch and 0.5 west of the Moose River highway bridge. Follow access road to the trailhead kiosk.

0.0—Moose River trail kiosk (1080 m).

　　—Cross CNR tracks. Trail branches left from road.

3.6—Trail reaches Moose River.

4.2—Campsite.

11.1—Resplendent Creek cascades.

15.3—Resplendent Campground. Ford Resplendent Creek to east bank.

17.8—Trail branches northeast from Resplendent Creek.

20.1—Trail reaches Moose River.

26.0—Trio Mountain Campground.

30.8—Moose River fords (four crossings next 2.5 km).

34.7—Moose River ford to east side.

36.4—Moose River ford to west side.

　　—Two crossings of Steppe Creek.

38.3—Steppe Creek Campground. Steppe Creek ford.

40.6—Moose River ford to east side.

43.8—Slide Lake Campground.

48.9—Moose Pass (2025 m). Mt Robson-Jasper Park boundary. Intersection with *Moose Pass* trail (see page 264).

(Trail not shown on maps in this book.)

Moose River is major tributary for the upper Fraser River. A 49 km trail runs up the valley from near the river's confluence with the Fraser to the summit of Moose Pass. After crossing the pass into Jasper Park, it descends through extensive meadows and along Calumet Creek to intersect Jasper's *North Boundary Trail* 5.4 km north of Robson Pass.

Moose River is one of the most demanding trips in the mountain parks, mainly due to numerous fords. Yet, it is still a fairly popular trip, probably because it can be linked with the Berg Lake trail to create a partial circuit around the Mount Robson massif. (Some backpackers descend the valley after visiting Berg Lake.) It is a route reserved for experienced wilderness travellers and usually hiked late in the season when river levels are down.

From the trailhead, you cross the CNR tracks on a gravel road then branch left onto well-defined trail. After crossing a forested ridge at the end of the Rainbow Range, the trail descends to the Moose River at km 3.6.

The 7 km stretch along the Moose to Resplendent Creek is rather flat and uneventful except for sections of trail that are muddy and overgrown. Views along the river flats stretch northwest to Lynx Mountain and the Reef Icefield near the head of the Resplendent Valley.

The trail passes the confluence of the Moose River and Resplendent Creek near the 10 km mark and starts ascending the latter valley above a series of cascades. The Resplendent Creek detour may appear unreasonable on the map, but not when you encounter this stream. Fed by the Reef Icefield, Resplendent is a major tributary that contributes much of the water volume of the lower Moose. You must travel upstream nearly 5 km to reach a reasonable ford.

At km 15.3 you reach Resplendent Campground, where you should ford this

Mike McReynolds photo

Wildflower meadows below Moose Pass

silty stream to its east bank. The hiker trail continues up along the east side of the creek for 2.5 km before reuniting with the horse trail. At that point, you turn northeast and cross a forested ridge to return to the Moose River at km 20.1.

The trail continues up a forested stretch of the Moose Valley and, shortly before coming abreast of the mouth of Colonel Creek, enters a burn. During the summer of 1998, a lightning-ignited fire burned much of the valley from here to Upright Creek and most of the Colonel Creek drainage to the east. While the fire didn't create major problems on the Moose River trail, connecting to Jasper Park via the Colonel Creek trail would likely be difficult now (see *Miette River,* Jasper Park chapter).

At a point nearly 5 km beyond Trio Mountain Campground, the wet work begins in earnest with the first of four fords of the Moose over the next 2.5 km. There are two more fords of the river at kms 34.7 and 36.4, followed by two crossings of Steppe Creek before you arrive at Steppe Creek Campground.

Slosh across Steppe Creek again as you depart the campground and, just over 2 kms beyond, ford the Moose River one last time. From this crossing the trail climbs steadily to higher and drier ground on its final ascent through gradually thinning forest to Moose Pass.

Slide Lake Campground is beautifully situated near a small lake amidst islands of stunted alpine fir. It is the last campground before the pass, which can be seen beyond the treeless meadows and a large rockslide to the northwest. (This is prime grizzly territory, so take extra care if you camp here.)

While the final approach to the 2025 m summit is rocky and barren, the true reward comes on the Jasper Park side—a descent through one of the finest wildflower meadows in the Rockies. (See *Moose Pass,* Jasper Park chapter, for details on the 9.5 km section connecting to the North Boundary Trail.)

Note: check at the park visitor centre for the latest info on trail conditions and pick-up a copy of the park's trail brochure-sketch map, which will help you find your way on this difficult trail.

231 Mount Fitzwilliam

Yellowhead Highway to Mount Fitzwilliam Basin—13.0 km (8.1 mi)

Day trip or backpack

Allow 4 to 5 hours one way

Elevation gain: 945 m (3,100 ft)

Maximum elevation: 2060 m (6,750 ft)

Maps: Rainbow 83 D/15
       Jasper 83 D/16

Access: Follow the Yellowhead Highway (Hwy 16) to the Yellowhead Lake Picnic Area and boat launch, located on the north side of the highway 7 km (4.5 mi) west of the Alberta-B.C. boundary and 3 km (2 mi) east of Lucerne Campground. The trailhead is on the south side of the highway opposite the entrance to the picnic area.

0.0—Trail sign (1115 m).

—Trail follows pipeline right-of-way west above highway.

0.7—Junction. Trail branches left from roadbed.

—Steady switchbacking ascent.

2.7—Trail crests forested ridge.

—Steep switchbacking ascent.

3.3—Underground stream. Trail begins to climb again.

6.3—Rockingham Creek bridge and Campground (1605).

—Rocky, rooty trail.

10.1—Rockslide area. Trail bends due south toward Fitzwilliam Basin.

—Faint trail through forest above marshy meadow and lake.

11.7—Fitzwilliam Basin headwall.

—Route follows tributary stream to left. Steep ascent along east side of headwall.

13.0—Fitzwilliam Basin (2060 m). Campsite.

(Trail not shown on maps in this book.)

This alpine basin containing a number of small lakes on the east slope of Mount Fitzwilliam is the most rewarding hike near Yellowhead Pass. However, the last 7 kms are unmaintained and quite rough, so only strong hikers should attempt to reach the basin and return in a day. The trip is ideal as a light overnight backpack, which allows time to explore the entire basin.

The trip begins somewhat inauspiciously on a pipeline right-of-way above the Yellowhead Highway. While it might not seem so, this cutline through the forest is an important piece of history for the people of the Robson Valley. When the Trans Mountain Oil Pipeline was constructed through Yellowhead Pass in 1952—the first pipeline across the Rockies—it heralded the coming of the Yellowhead Highway nearly 20 years later.

Once you break free from this broad reminder of the park's industrial past, you start to gain elevation along wide, well-graded trail. The trail switchbacks steadily upward through a mixed forest of lodgepole pine, white birch, aspen and a few old Douglas fir, which limits views to a few brief glimpses of the Yellowhead Pass environs.

The uphill grades relent once you top a 1370 m ridge at km 2.7, but dense "doghair" stands of lodgepole pine totally enclose the track. The climb soon resumes and continues through forest to Rockingham Creek Campground.

The campground is set at the north end of an extensive meadow beneath the western wall of Mount Fitzwilliam. On the east side of Rockingham Creek, the superhighway trail suddenly turns into a rocky, rooty wilderness track that contours above Fitzwilliam Creek through scattered forest and willow meadows. (Watch for markers on trees when the trail becomes faint.) Frequent muddy sections reveal the tracks of the

Kataka Mountain from the Mount Fitzwilliam trail

mountain's inhabitants, including deer, moose and, occasionally, bear.

When the valley bends south around the slopes of Fitzwilliam, defined trail all but disappears. As you near the base of the headwall guarding the lakes, you turn left and follow the stream flowing from the largest of the basin's lakes above. This stream descends along the eastern side of the headwall, and the hike is completed by scrambling up along its course to the basin.

At the top of the headwall you suddenly emerge near the north end of the basin's largest lake, which is a scenic highlight along the eastern edge of this wonderful little plateau contained by Mount Fitzwilliam, Bucephalus Peak, Mount Clairvaux and Kataka Mountain. The Jasper topo map (83 D/16) is handy for orienting yourself to the basin, which can be explored rather thoroughly in a half-day from the largest lake on the east side to a small tarn 2 kms to the west beneath Mount Fitzwilliam.

There is a small primitive campsite with a bear pole and privy near the point where you emerge into the basin. While it is a scenic spot to overnight, some backpackers prefer to camp at Rockingham Creek and attack the final 7 kms of rough trail, and the very steep scramble along the basin headwall, with a light day pack.

Viscount Milton of Fitzwilliam named Mount Fitzwilliam for himself at the suggestion of his Stoney guide when he crossed Yellowhead Pass in 1863 with his travelling companion Dr. Walter B. Cheadle. Reputed to be the first trans-Canadian tourists, Milton and Cheadle later published a book about their difficult journey, which celebrated the heroics of Cheadle's ungainly steed Bucephalus during the crossing of the Rockies. In 1917, boundary surveyors bestowed the horse's name on the peak near Fitzwilliam.

232 Yellowhead Mountain Viewpoint

Yellowhead Lake Parking Area to Yellowhead Mountain Viewpoint—1.5 km (0.9 mi)

Yellowhead Pass has been one of the important routes across the Rockies for more than 150 years, and one of the best places to view this historic pass is from the slopes of Yellowhead Mountain. The short hike to a viewpoint on the mountain is particularly rewarding in autumn when aspen and birch leaves turn to gold and the first snows dust the ramparts of Mount Fitzwilliam across the valley.

The hike begins from a parking area beneath the Canadian National Railway tracks on the north side of Yellowhead Lake. Cross the tracks and follow the trail as it climbs steadily through stands of aspen mixed with pine and birch.

The grade is initially steep, but moderates as the trail contours to the right across the slope to the viewpoint—an opening in the trees with a bench that overlooks Yellowhead Lake, Mount Fitzwilliam and the peaks of the Selwyn Range to the west.

The trail continues beyond the viewpoint, climbing through the forest to an avalanche slope around the 5 km mark. Though the track becomes vague, it is possible to continue even farther up the mountain. Views are limited, however, and since the route climbs through prime bear habitat, it is seldom hiked.

Access: Follow the Yellowhead Highway (Hwy 16) to the junction with a gravel access road on the north side of the highway 1.7 km (1.1 mi) east of Lucerne Campground and 8.5 km (5.5 mi) west of the Alberta-B.C. boundary. Follow gravel road for 1.0 km to the trailhead parking area below the CNR tracks. *Maps: Rainbow 83 D/15 (trail not shown); Mount Robson Park.*

(Trail not shown on maps in this book.)

233 Portal Lake

Portal Lake Circuit—1.0 km (0.6 mi)

Portal Lake is a tiny tarn just a few metres west of the Alberta-British Columbia boundary. The circuit trail along its shores and through the forest to the east allows you an opportunity to stretch your legs for 20 minutes or so and walk on the backbone of the continent.

From the parking area, follow the trail running along the east shore of this glassy lake for 300 m to a point near its north end. The dark, precipitous bluffs containing the lake are composed of some of the oldest rock in this section of the Rockies—Precambrian shales of the Middle Miette Group.

As you near the end of the lake, the trail branches right and climbs steeply through a dense, stunted forest of lodgepole pine. After a vertical ascent of 30 m, it reaches the interprovincial boundary cutline and the continental divide. Descend steeply along this broad cut for 150 m before following trail back into British Columbia. The forest floor is quite lush in early summer, when it is carpeted with the blooms of bunchberry and heart-leaved arnica.

The trail runs flat for the final 0.2 km, completing the circuit back to the parking area through a boggy spruce forest filled with equisetum (horsetails).

Access: Follow the Yellowhead Highway (Hwy 16) to the Yellowhead Pass Picnic Area, located on the north side of the highway at the Alberta-British Columbia boundary (3.2 km west of Jasper Park West Gate). *Maps: Jasper 83 D/16 (trail not shown); Mount Robson Park.*

(Trail not shown on maps in this book.)

Sources

PARKS INFORMATION

Following is a list of parks with mailing addresses, phone and fax numbers, e-mail addresses and websites. With the exception of B.C. Parks, phone and fax numbers are for park visitor centres. Websites provide the latest information on fees and trail conditions, restrictions and closures.

Banff National Park
Box 900, Banff, Alberta T1L 1K2
Banff info phone: 403-762-1550
fax: 403-762-1551
Lake Louise info phone: 403-522-3833
e-mail: banff.info@pc.gc.ca
website: www.parkscanada.gc.ca/banff

Jasper National Park
Box 10, Jasper, Alberta T0E 1E0
phone: 780-852-6176
fax: 780-852-5601
e-mail: jnp.info@pc.gc.ca
website: www.parkscanada.gc.ca/jasper

Yoho National Park
Box 99, Field, B.C. V0A 1G0
phone: 250-343-6783
fax: 250-343-6012
O'Hara phone: 250-343-6433
e-mail: yoho.info@pc.gc.ca
website: www.parkscanada.gc.ca/yoho

Kootenay National Park
Box 220, Radium, B.C. V0A 1M0
phone: 250-347-9505 (June-Sept.)
fax: 250-347-6307 (June-Sept.)
phone: 250-347-9615 (off-season)
fax: 250-347-9980 (off-season)
e-mail: kootenay.reception@pc.gc.ca
website: www.parkscanada.gc.ca/
    kootenay

Waterton Lakes National Park
Waterton Park, Alberta T0K 2M0
phone: 403-859-5133
fax: 403-859-5147
e-mail: waterton.info@pc.gc.ca
web: www.parkscanada.gc.ca/waterton

Mount Robson Provincial Park
Box 579, Valemount, B.C. V0E 1Z0
phone: 250-566-4325
fax: 250-566-9777
Berg Lake camping reservations:
phone:1-800-689-9025
website: wlapwww.gov.bc.ca/bcparks/
    explore/parkpgs/mtrobson.htm

Mount Assiniboine,
Elk Lakes,
Akamina-Kishinena Provincial Parks
B.C. Parks Kootenay District
Box 118, Wasa, B.C. V0B 2K0
phone: 250-422-4200
fax: 250-422-3326
Mount Assiniboine website:
wlapwww.gov.bc.ca/bcparks/explore/
    parkpgs/mtassini.htm
Elk Lakes website:
wlapwww.gov.bc.ca/bcparks/explore/
    parkpgs/elklakes.htm
Akamina-Kishinena website:
wlapwww.gov.bc.ca/bcparks/explore/
    parkpgs/akamina.htm

Peter Lougheed Provincial Park
Suite 201,
800 Railway Avenue
Canmore, Alberta T1W 1P1
Barrier Lake Info phone: 403-673-3985
Barrier Lake Info fax: 403-673-3684
backcountry permits: 403-591-7075
e-mail: barriervisitor.infocenter@gov.ab.ca
website: www.gov.ab.ca/env/parks/
    prov_parks/kananaskis

WEATHER

Environment Canada
Atmospheric Environment Service
website: www.weatheroffice.ec.gc.ca
Banff weather phone: 403-762-2088
Jasper weather phone: 780-852-3185
Website displays weather maps and forecasts for Alberta, B.C., and specific mountain communities (Banff, Jasper and Waterton). Weather phones provide current conditions and long-range forecasts. Website and phone forecasts are updated throughout the day.

BOOKS AND MAPS

Friends of Banff National Park
P.O. Box 1695
Banff, Alberta T0L0C0
phone: 403-762-8918
fax: 403-762-2933
website: www.friendsofbanff.com
Non-profit organization selling books and maps specific to the mountain national parks, emphasizing Banff National Park. Mail order catalogue available. Website catalogue for on-line orders.

Friends of Jasper National Park
P.O. Box 992
Jasper, Alberta T0E 1E0
phone: 780-852-4767
fax: 780-852-4799
website: www.visit-jasper.com/
　　　　friendsofjasper
Non-profit organization selling books and maps specific to the mountain national parks, emphasizing Jasper National Park. Main shop located in the Jasper Visitor Centre. Mail order catalogue available and website catalogue for on-line orders.

The Friends of Kananaskis Country
Suite 201, 800 Railway Avenue
Canmore, Alberta T1W 1P1
phone: 403-678-5508
fax: 403-678-5505
website: www.gov.ab.ca/env/parks/
　　　　prov_parks/kananaskis/friends
Non-profit organization selling books, trail brochures and maps specific to Peter Lougheed Provincial Park and Kananaskis Country. Mail order catalogue available. Website catalogue for on-line orders.

Banff Book and Art Den
Box 1420, 94 Banff Avenue
Banff, Alberta T1L 1B3
phone: 403-762-3919
fax: 403-762-4126
e-mail: information@banffbooks.com
website: www.banffbooks.com
The largest and most complete bookstore in the Canadian Rockies. Stocks all books pertaining to the region plus Gem Trek recreational maps and a selection of government topographic maps.

Map Town
#100, 400 5th Avenue S.W.
Calgary, Alberta T2P 0L6
phone: 403-266-2241
fax: 403-266-2356
website: www.maptown.com
Best single source for all government topographical maps. Also carries most guidebooks and the full line of Gem Trek maps. Website catalogue for online orders.

Gem Trek Publishing Ltd.
Box 1618
#6, 245 2nd Avenue E.
Cochrane, Alberta T0L 0W0
phone: 403-932-4208
toll-free phone: 1-877-688-6277
fax: 403-932-4893
e-mail: maps@gemtrek.com
website: www.gemtrek.com
Produces the best series of recreation maps for the mountain parks. Website displays map coverage and individual samples of each map. Sold in a wide variety of outlets throughout the mountain parks and nearby communities, or ordered by mail or through website.

BACKCOUNTRY LODGES

Brewster's Shadow Lake Lodge
Box 2606
Banff, Alberta T0L0C0
phone: 403-762-0116
fax: 403-760-2866
e-mail: shadow@telusplanet.net
website: www.brewsteradventures.com/
　　　　shadowlake
Located near Shadow Lake, Banff National Park. Summer season: late June to early October.

Skoki Lodge
Box 5
Lake Louise, Alberta T0L 1E0
phone: 403-522-3555
fax: 403-522-2095
e-mail: skoki@skilouise.com
website: www.skokilodge.com
Located in the Skoki Valley east of Lake Louise, Banff National Park. Summer season: mid-June to mid-September.

Sundance Lodge
Warner Guiding and Outfitting Ltd.
Box 2280
Banff, Alberta T0L 0C0
phone: 403-762-4551
fax: 403-762-8130
e-mail: warner@horseback.com
website: www.horseback.com
Operates Sundance and Halfway Lodges in the Brewster Creek valley, Banff National Park. Summer season: early May to late October.

Tonquin-Amethyst Lake Lodge
Tonquin Valley Adventures
Box 1795
Jasper, Alberta T0E 1E0
phone: 780-852-1188
fax: 780-852-1155
e-mail: info@tonquinadventures.com
website: www.tonquinadventures.com
Located along the east side of Amethyst Lakes near the Narrows. Summer season: late June to October 31 (weather permitting).

Tonquin Valley Backcountry Lodge
Box 550
Jasper, Alberta T0E 1E0
phone: 780-852-3909
fax: 780-852-3763
e-mail: info@tonquinvalley.com
website: www.tonquinvalley.com
Located at the north end of Amethyst Lakes in the Tonquin Valley, Jasper National Park. Summer season: July 1 to September 20.

Lake O'Hara Lodge
Box 55
Lake Louise, Alberta T0L 1E0
phone: 250-343-6418 (in-season)
phone: 403-678-4110 (off-season)
website: www.lakeohara.com
Located at Lake O'Hara, Yoho National Park. Summer season: mid-June to September 30.

Twin Falls Chalet
P.O. Box 23009
Connaught P.O.
Calgary, Alberta T25 3B1
phone/fax; 403-228-7079
Located at the base of Twin Falls in the Yoho Valley, Yoho National Park. Season: late June to early autumn.

Amiskwi Lodge
phone: 403-678-1800
e-mail: info@amiskwi.com
website: www.amiskwi.com
Located above Amiskwi Pass just beyond the northwest boundary of Yoho Park. Hut style accommodation for 12 to 16 people. Summer season: late June to early October.

Mount Assiniboine Lodge
Box 8128, Canmore, Alberta T1W 2T8
phone: 403-678-2883
fax: 403-678-4877
email: assinilo@telusplanet.net
website: www.canadianrockies.net/
        Assiniboine
Located at Lake Magog, Mount Assiniboine Provincial Park. Summer season: mid-June to early October.

HUTS

The Alpine Club of Canada
Box 8040, Canmore, Alberta T1W 2T8
phone: 403-678-3200
fax: 403-678-3224
e-mail: alpclub@telusplanet.net
website: www.alpineclubofcanada.ca
Operates a network of alpine huts throughout the Rockies. Stanley Mitchell Hut in the Little Yoho Valley, Elizabeth Parker Hut at Lake O'Hara, and Wates-Gibson Hut in the Eremite Valley are accessible by hiking trails. Reservations are recommended and accepted up to 6 months in advance for members, 30 days in advance for non-members.

HOSTELS

Hostelling International—Canada
Southern Alberta Region
#203, 1414 Kensington Road N.W.
Calgary, Alberta T2N 3P9
phone: 403-283-5551
fax: 403-283-6503
e-mail: sab@hostellingintl.ca
website: www.hostellingintl.ca/Alberta
Operates roadside hostels throughout the mountain parks, many located near hiking trails. Reservations are recommended during high season.

BACKCOUNTRY ACCESS

White Mountain Adventures
#7, 107 Boulder Crescent
Canmore, Alberta T1W 1K9
phone: 403-678-4099
toll-free phone: 1-800-408-0005
fax: 403-678-5187
e-mail: info@canadiannatureguides.com
website: www.canadiannatureguides.
            com
Provides shuttle bus service to Sunshine
Meadows, Banff National Park. Operating daily
June 20 (conditions permitting) to September 30.

Mount Assiniboine Lodge
Box 8128
Canmore, Alberta T1W 2T8
phone: 403-678-2883
fax: 403-678-4877
email: assinilo@telusplanet.net
website: www.canadianrockies.net/
            Assiniboine
Books charter flights from Mt. Shark Heliport in
the Spray Lakes valley to the Lake Magog area
of Mt. Assiniboine Provincial Park for campers
as well as lodge guests. Helicopter access on
Wednesdays, Fridays and Sundays (Monday
replaces Sunday on long weekends), early
June to early October.

Robson Helimagic Inc.
Box 18
Valemount, B.C. V0E 2Z0
phone: 250-566-4700
fax: 250-566-4333
e-mail: brigitta@robsonhelimagic.com
website: www.robsonhelimagic.com
Books charter flights for campers and climbers
to Robson Pass near Berg Lake on Fridays and
Mondays (Tuesday replaces Monday on long
weekends).

Waterton Inter-Nation Shoreline Cruise
Box 126
Waterton, Alberta T0K 2M0
phone: 403-859-2362
fax: 403-938-5019
e-mail: wscruise@cadvision.com
website: watertoninfo.ab.ca/m/cruise
Operates sightseeing tours on Upper Waterton
Lake, Waterton Lakes National Park as well as
hiker drop-off and pick-up to Crypt Landing and
the Crypt Lake trail. Daily operation from early
May through early October.

GUIDED WALKS

Interpreters in the five national parks
offer a variety of guided walks from late
June to Labour Day (check with park visitor centres for locations and schedules).
A number of private operators based at
mountain communities in and near the
parks offer guided walking tours.

One tour of specific interest to Yoho
Park visitors is the guided hike to the
Burgess Shale Beds near Field organized
by the Yoho-Burgess Shale Foundation.
For schedules and rates contact:

Yoho-Burgess Shale Foundation
Box 148
Field, British Columbia V0A 1G0
phone: 250-343-6006
fax: 250-343-6426
e-mail: burgshal@rockies.net
website: www.burgess-shale.bc.ca

Recommended reading

Following are books we endorse for anyone spending time in the Rockies and who wants to explore the trails and natural history of the region more completely. All of these titles are available in regional bookstores, outdoor sports shops, and through parks' "Friends" shops and websites.

The Wonder of Yoho
The World of Lake Louise
Banff-Assiniboine: A Beautiful World
Jasper-Robson: A Taste of Heaven
by Don Beers (Calgary: Highline Publishing). All of the above hiking guides deal with specific areas within the mountain parks and are written and illustrated by veteran hiker-photographer Don Beers. They cover these areas in much more detail than is possible in our guidebook—including main trails and many side routes. Filled with excellent colour photography and entertaining historical anecdotes. A true labour of love.

Kananaskis Country Trail Guide: Volume 1, Third Edition
by Gillean Daffern (Calgary: Rocky Mountain Books, 1996). The most complete coverage of trails in Alberta's Peter Lougheed Provincial Park and the adjacent Kananaskis Country recreation area. Also describes many popular off-trail routes. Companion edition *Kananaskis Country Trail Guide: Volume 2* covers the eastern Front Ranges and Foothills of the recreation area.

Hiking Canada's Great Divide Trail
by Dustin Lynx (Calgary: Rocky Mountain Books, 2000).The Great Divide Trail is the most popular long-distance backpacking route in the Rockies. It is an unofficial trail that runs north along the continental divide for approximately 1200 kms from Waterton Lakes National Park to British Columbia's Kakwa Lake Provincial Park. This guidebook provides the most detailed description of the route.

Backcountry Biking in the Canadian Rockies, Second Edition
by Doug Eastcott (Calgary: Rocky Mountain Books, 1999). Written by a park warden, this is the most comprehensive guide to mountain biking trails in and around the mountain parks.

Mountain Footsteps: Hikes in the East Kootenay of Southeastern British Columbia
by Janice Strong (Calgary: Rocky Mountain Books, 1998). A guide covering hiking trails in the southern Rockies and British Columbia's Purcell Range. Most trails are not in national and provincial parks, though the book does include the B.C. Parks of Elk Lakes, Top of the World, Height of the Rockies in the southern Rockies, and parks in the Purcell Range.

Handbook of the Canadian Rockies, Second Edition
by Ben Gadd (Jasper: Corax Press, 1995). And last, but not least, one of the most comprehensive natural history guides ever published in North America. Covers everything—geology, weather and climate, plants, insects, fish, amphibians, reptiles, birds, mammals, etc. Also a condensed historical chronology and brief introduction to recreational activities. "The bible" for Canadian Rockies' naturalists.

Index

Names and pages in bold type refer to main trail headings used in this book.

446